320 ITALIAN RECIPES

ACETO
BALSAMICO
di Modena
Mazzetti
6%
0586

320 ITALIAN RECIPES

Delicious dishes from all over Italy, with a full guide to ingredients and techniques, and every recipe shown step by step in 1600 photographs

Kate Whiteman, Jeni Wright, Angela Boggiano and Carla Capalbo

southwater

This edition is published by Southwater, an imprint of Anness Publishing Ltd, Hermes House,
88–89 Blackfriars Road, London SE1 8HA; tel. 020 7401 2077; fax 020 7633 9499
www.southwaterbooks.com; www.annesspublishing.com

UK agent: The Manning Partnership Ltd; tel. 01225 478444; fax 01225 478440; sales@manning-partnership.co.uk
UK distributor: Book Trade Services; tel. 0116 2759086; fax 0116 2759090; uksales@booktradeservices.com; exportsales@booktradeservices.com
North American agent/distributor: National Book Network; tel. 301 459 3366; fax 301 429 5746; www.nbnbooks.com
Australian agent/distributor: Pan Macmillan Australia; tel. 1300 135 113; fax 1300 135 103; customer.service@macmillan.com.au
New Zealand agent/distributor: David Bateman Ltd; tel. (09) 415 7664; fax (09) 415 8892

Publisher: Joanna Lorenz
Senior Editor: Linda Fraser
Designers: Siân Keogh, Patrick McLeavey and Ian Sandom
Photographers: William Adams-Lingwood, Amanda Heywood and Janine Hosegood (cut-outs)
Home Economists: Carla Capalbo and Lucy McKelvie
Stylists: Carla Capalbo, Amanda Heywood and Marian Price

NOTES
For all recipes, quantities are given in both metric and imperial measures and, where appropriate, in standard cups and spoons.
Follow one set of measures, but not a mixture, because they are not interchangeable. Standard spoon and cup measures are level. 1 tsp = 5ml,
1 tbsp = 15ml, 1 cup = 250ml/8fl oz.Australian standard tablespoons are 20ml. Australian readers should use 3 tsp in place of 1 tbsp
for measuring small quantities.American pints are 16fl oz/2 cups. American readers should use 20fl oz/2.5 cups in place of 1 pint when measuring
liquids. Electric oven temperatures in this book are for conventional ovens. When using a fan oven, the temperature will probably need to be reduced
by about 10–20°C/20–40°F. Since ovens vary, you should check with your manufacturer's instruction book for guidance.
Medium (US large) eggs are used unless otherwise stated.

Front cover shows Pasta with Tomato and Chilli Sauce – for recipe, see page 253.

Contents

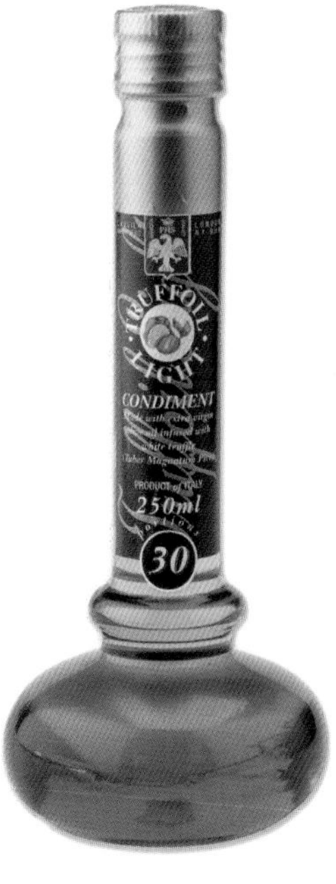

Introduction

Italian cookery reflects the fact that the country was unified only in 1861. Until then, each region produced its own characteristic cuisine, relying exclusively on ingredients that could be gathered, cultivated or reared locally. Nowadays, of course, regional produce can be easily transported all over the country, but Italians still prefer to base their cooking on local ingredients, because they regard quality and freshness as more important than diversity and innovation. So the most flavoursome sun–ripened tomatoes, aubergines and peppers are still found in the south, the freshest seafood is on offer along the coast, the finest hams come from the area where the pigs are raised, and so on. *La cucina italiana* remains distinctly regional; northern Italian cooking, for example, incorporates ingredients that are simply never found in the recipes of Sicily and Naples, and vice-versa. In the dairy-farming north, butter is used in place of the olive oil so prevalent in the south; bread and polenta are eaten instead of pasta. The only unifying feature is the insistence on high quality ingredients. Good food has always been essential to the Italian way of life. *La cucina italiana* is one of the oldest cooking cultures in the world, dating back to the ancient Greeks and perhaps even earlier. The Romans adored food and

This Italian butcher's shop (below) not only sells the local *cinghiale* (wild boar), but also cured meats, cheeses and other essential cooking ingredients.

often ate and drank to excess; it was they who really laid the foundations of Italian and European cuisine. The early Romans were peasant farmers who ate only the simple, rustic foods they could produce, like grain, cheeses and olives. For them, meat was an unheard-of luxury; animals were bred to work in the fields and were too precious to eat. Trading links with other parts of the world, however, encouraged Roman farmers to cultivate new vegetables and fruits and, of course, vines, while their trade in salt and exotic spices enabled them to preserve and pickle all kinds of meat, game and fish. Food became a near-obsession and ever more elaborate dishes were devised to be served at the decadent and orgiastic banquets for which the Romans were famed. The decline and fall of the Roman Empire led inevitably to a deterioration in the quality of cooking and a return to simple, basic foods. For centuries, regional cuisine reverted to its original uncomplicated style. With the Renaissance, however, came great wealth and a new interest in elaborate food. Once again, rich families strove to outdo each other with lavish banquets where courses of rich, extravagant foods were served – truffles, song–birds, game, desserts dripping with honey and spices – all washed down with quantities of wine. The poor, of course, continued to subsist on the simple foods they had

Olives, top, growing in groves alongside grape vines on an Umbrian hillside, and a selection of cured sausages and air-dried *prosciutto* hanging in store (above) are just two of the vast array of traditional Italian ingredients that are now exported around the world.

Italian cooks insist on high quality cooking ingredients and even local delicatessens such as this (right) are packed full of fresh and preserved ingredients and other foods – fruity cakes and crisp biscuits, such as *panforte* and *cantucci*, dried *fagioli* (*beans*), flavourful olive oils and vinegars, *prosciutto crudo* (cured hams), traditional cheeses, such as Parmigiano Reggiano, pickles and preserves, marinated olives, canned tomatoes and bottled sauces.

The sun-drenched southern regions of Italy provide essential store cupboard ingredients, such as full-flavoured green and black olives and delicious sun-dried tomatoes.

always eaten, but the wealthier middle classes developed a taste for fine foods and created their own bourgeois dishes. The finer features of Italian cooking even reached the French, when Catherine de' Medici went to Paris to marry the future Henri II, taking fifty of her own cooks with her. They introduced new ingredients and cooking techniques to France and in return learnt the art of French cuisine. In those regions of Italy which border France, you can still find reciprocal influences of French cooking, but, generally speaking, Italians do not like elaborately sauced dishes, preferring to let the natural flavours of their raw ingredients speak for themselves.

The essence of Italian cooking today is simplicity. The Italian way of cooking fish is a good example of this. In coastal areas, freshly caught fish is most often simply chargrilled over hot coals, then served with nothing more than a splash of extra virgin olive oil, a wedge of lemon and freshly ground black pepper. Recipes like *carpaccio di tonno*, in which the fish is so delicious raw that cooking seems unnecessary, and *branzino al forno*, where the delicate flavour of fennel is used to compliment rather than obscure the fresh taste of the fish, are typically simple, as is *grigliati di calamari*, squid chargrilled with chillies to reflect its robust character.

Italians learn to appreciate good food when they are young children, and eating is one of the major pleasures of the day, no matter what the day of the week or time of the year. Witness an Italian family gathered around the Sunday lunch table in a local restaurant, and consider how the Italian menu of *antipasti* followed by pasta, rice or gnocchi, then fish, meat and vegetables served in sequence is devised so that each can be savoured separately – both the food and the occasion are to be enjoyed as long as possible. The first course, or *antipasti*, is a unique feature. In restaurants, this can be a vast array of different dishes, both hot and cold, from which diners can choose as few or as many as they wish. At home with the family, it is more likely to be a slice or two of *salami* or *prosciutto crudo* with fresh figs or melon if these are in season. But no matter how humble or grand the setting or the occasion, the *antipasti* is always visually tempting. Dishes like *bruschetta casalinga* and *peperoni arrostiti con pesto*, which look so attractive, are typical in this way.

The variety and diversity of the Italian ingredients available in supermarkets and delicatessens will surely inspire you to concoct any number of delicious meals, from a simple dish of pasta to a full-blown four-course dinner. A plate of *antipasti* followed by pasta or risotto flavoured with seasonal ingredients, then simply-cooked meat or fish and finally a local cheese and fruit make a veritable feast. You could prepare a different meal along these lines every day of the year and almost never repeat the same combination. If you visit Italy, avail yourself of the wonderful local ingredients to prepare a menu full of the flavours of the region. Every area has its own special delights that make cooking a real pleasure.

Fresh ingredients are highly prized by Italian cooks and are often sold from the local outdoor markets: Dozens of *carciofi* (globe artichokes) are tied ready for transport to a local market (below), and an outdoor stall is piled high with a typically wide selection of high-quality fresh herbs and salad leaves, vegetables and fruits (bottom).

The Ingredients

Italian cooks have traditionally relied on local ingredients – whatever could be gathered, cultivated or reared locally. Today, our supermarkets and delicatessens are full of these flavourful, good-quality ingredients. This comprehensive guide provides essential information on the huge range of Italian foods and shows you how to prepare and cook them.

Pasta

If there is one ingredient that sums up the essence of Italian cooking, it must surely be pasta, that wonderfully simple and nutritious staple that can be formed into an almost infinite variety of shapes and sizes. In Italy, pasta is an essential part of every full meal and does not constitute a meal on its own. Il primo, *as the pasta course is known, is eaten between the* antipasto *(appetizer) and* il secondo *(the main course). Sometimes small pasta shapes are served in soup as* pasta in brodo. *There are two basic types of pasta,* pastasciutta *(dried) and* pasta fresca *(fresh).*

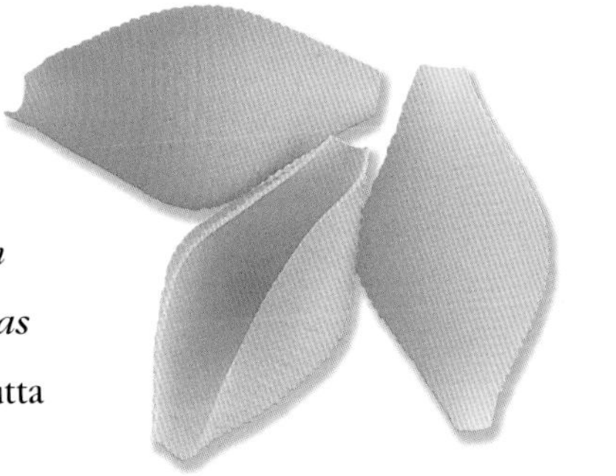

Dried pasta is nowadays factory-made. The dough is made from hard durum wheat, which produces an elastic dough, ideal for shaping into literally hundreds of different forms, from long, thin spaghetti to elaborate spirals and frilly, bow-shaped *farfalle*. Basic pasta dough is made only from durum wheat and water, although it is sometimes enriched with eggs (*pasta all'uovo*), which add an attractive yellow tinge, or coloured and flavoured with ingredients like spinach (*pasta verde*) or squid ink (*pasta nera*). These traditional flavourings are more successful than modern gimmicky creations such as chocolate-flavoured pasta. (Most Italians would throw up their hands in horror at this inauthentic folly.) Dried pasta has a nutty flavour and should always retain a firm texture when cooked. It is generally used for thinner-textured, more robust sauces.

Fresh pasta is usually made by hand, using superfine plain white flour enriched with eggs. Unlike dried pasta dough, it can be easily kneaded and is very malleable. Fresh pasta is often wrapped round a stuffing of meat, fish, vegetables or cheese to make ravioli, tortelli or cappelletti, or layered with sauce and meat or vegetables, as in lasagne.

Commercially made fresh pasta is made with durum wheat, water and eggs. The dough is harder than that used for hand-made pasta, but it can be easily kneaded by machine. The flavour and texture of all fresh pasta is very delicate, so it is best suited to more creamy sauces.

History

The argument about the origins of pasta will probably rage on forever; the Chinese claim that they were the first to discover the art of noodle-making and that pasta was brought to Italy by Marco Polo. The Italians, of course, claim it as their own invention. Historians tell us that the Romans and probably even the ancient Greeks used to eat pasta. Certainly the climate of southern Italy was ideally suited to growing durum wheat, so this theory is quite likely, but the popularity of pasta really spread in the 14th century, when bakeries in southern Italy started to sell pasta as an alternative to bread.

Then, as now, pasta became the traditional *primo* of the south, although in the poorest areas it constituted a complete meal. Its popularity filtered up to the north of Italy and by the 19th century huge factories had been set up to mass-produce vast quantities of pasta, which became an integral part of all Italian cooking.

Buying and Storing

Always buy dried pasta made from Italian durum wheat. Even after the packet has been opened, dried pasta will keep for weeks in an airtight container. Hand-made fresh pasta will only keep for a couple of days, but it can be successfully frozen. Machine-made fresh pasta is pasteurized and vacuum-packed, so it will keep in the fridge for up to two weeks and can be frozen for up to six months. When buying coloured and flavoured pasta, make sure that it has been made with natural ingredients.

Cooking Pasta

Allow about 75 g/3 oz pasta per serving as a first course. All pasta must be cooked in a large saucepan filled with plenty of salted, fast-boiling water.

For long shapes like spaghetti, drop one end of the pasta into the water and, as it softens, push it down gently until it bends in the middle and is completely immersed.

Cooking times vary according to the type, size and shape of the pasta, but, as a general rule, filled pasta takes about 12 minutes, dried pasta needs 8–10 minutes and fresh pasta only 2–3 minutes. All pasta should be cooked al dente*, so that it is still resistant to the bite. Always test pasta for doneness just before you think it should be ready; it can easily overcook. To stop the cooking, take the pan off the heat and run a little cold water into it, then drain the pasta.*

Preparing Fresh Pasta

1 Allow 1 egg to 100 g/3½ oz superfine plain flour (Italian *tipo 00* is best). Sift the flour and a pinch of salt into a mound on a clean work surface and make a well. Break the eggs into the well and gradually work in the flour until completely amalgamated.

2 Knead the dough with floured hands for at least 15 minutes, until it is very smooth, firm and elastic. (If you are short of time or energy, you can do this in a food processor.)

3 Chill the dough for 20 minutes, then roll it to the required thickness and cut it into your desired shape. (You can buy a specially shaped rolling-pin to make the squares for filled pasta.) A pasta machine will make this process much easier. Leave the pasta to dry for at least 1 hour before cooking it.

Pasta Varieties

Pasta shapes can be divided roughly into four categories: long strands and ribbons, flat, short and filled.

The best-known long variety is spaghetti, which comes in a thinner version, spaghettini, and the flatter *linguine*, which means "little tongues". *Bucatini* are thicker and hollow – perfect for trapping sauces in the cavity. Ribbon pasta is wider than the strands: fettuccine, *trenette* and tagliatelle all fall into this category. Dried tagliatelle is usually sold folded into nests, which unravel during cooking. A mixture of white and green noodles is known as *paglia e fieno* (straw and hay). Pappardelle are the widest ribbon pasta; they are often served with s*ugo alla lepre* (hare sauce). The thinnest pasta strands are vermicelli (little worms) and ultra-fine *capelli d'angelo* (angel's hair).

In Italy, flat fresh pasta is often called *maccheroni*, not to be confused with the short tubes with which we are familiar. Lasagne and cannelloni are larger flat rectangles, used for layering or rolling round a filling; dried cannelloni are already formed into wide tubes. Layered pasta dishes like this are cooked *al forno* (baked in the oven). Fillings for fresh pasta squares include meat, pumpkin, artichokes, ricotta and spinach, seafood, chicken and rabbit. There are dozens of names for filled pasta, but the only difference lies in the shape and size. Ravioli are square, tortelli are usually round, while tortellini and *anolini* are ring-shaped.

As for pasta shapes, the list is almost endless and the names wonderfully descriptive. There are *maltagliati* (badly cut), *orecchiette* (little ears) and *cappellacci* (little hats), while from the natural world come penne (quills), *conchiglie* (little shells), *farfalle* (butterflies) and *lumache* (snails).

When choosing the appropriate pasta shape for the sauce, there are no hard and fast rules, but long, thin pasta is best for olive-oil-based and delicate seafood sauces. Short pasta shapes with wide openings (like *conchiglie* and penne) will trap meaty or spicy sauces, as will spirals and curls. Almost any pasta is suitable for tomato sauce.

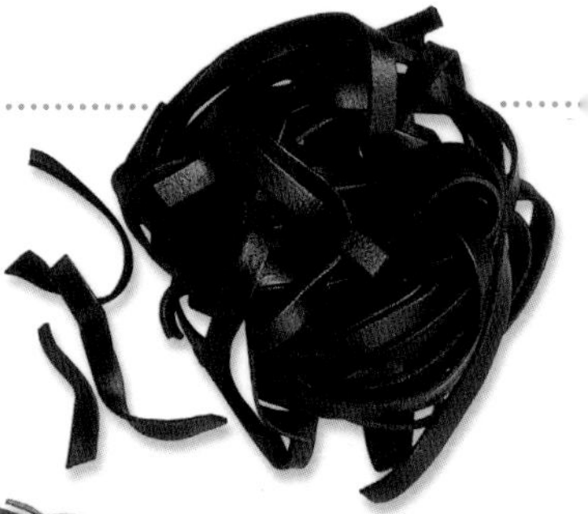

Tonnarelli al nero
Flavoured and coloured with squid ink

Spinach fettuccine

Plain fettuccine

Bavette
Flavoured with porcini *(ceps)*

Paglia e fieno

Long Pasta

Fresh tagliatelle
Flavoured with squid ink

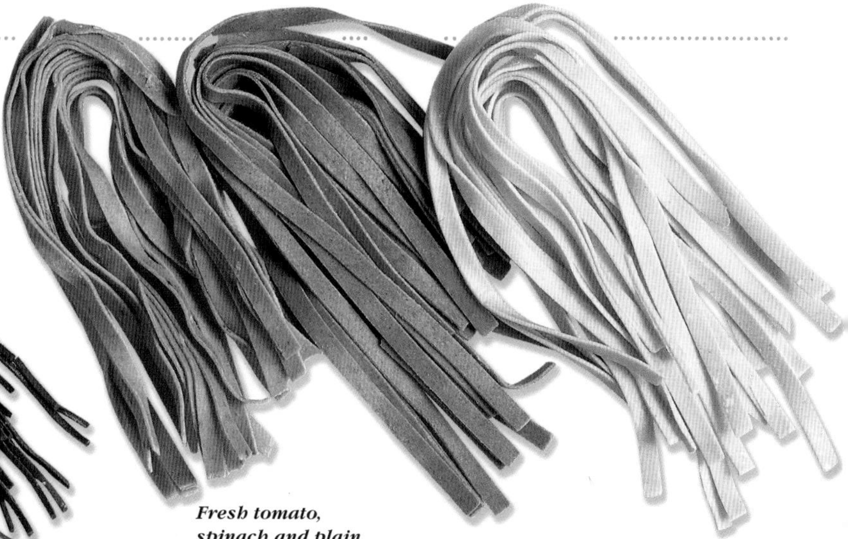

Fresh tomato, spinach and plain tagliatelle

Fresh spaghetti

Fresh paglia e fieno

Fresh tagliolini

Long Pasta

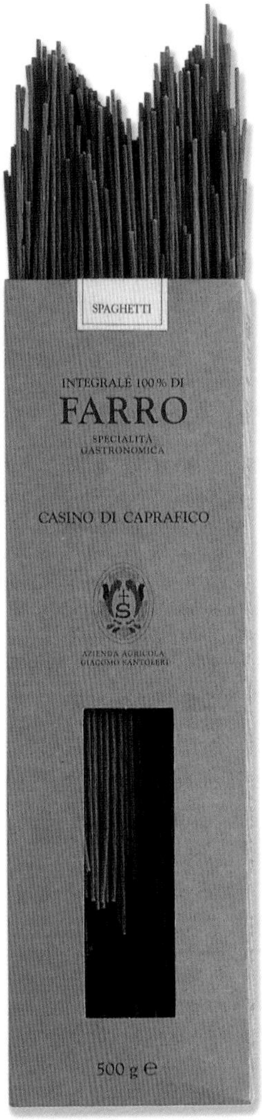

Wholemeal farro

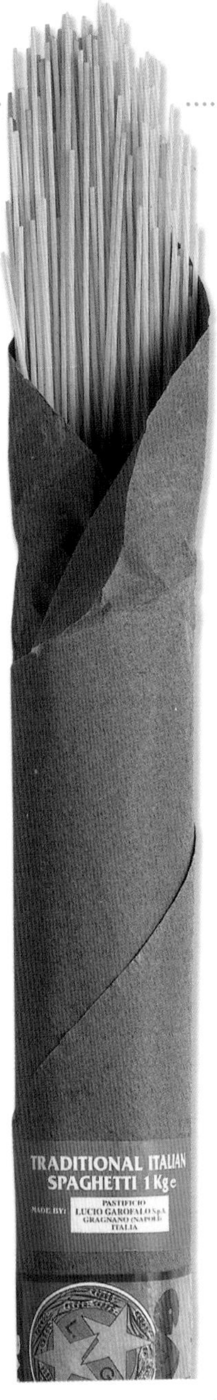

Long, plain spaghetti
Still sometimes sold in the traditional blue paper roll

Spaghetti tricolore
Mixed plain, spinach and tomato spaghetti

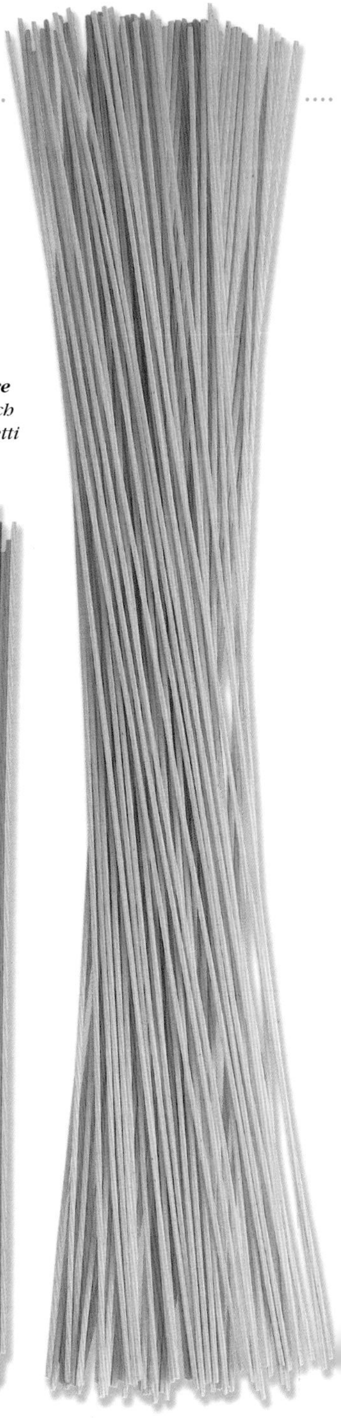

Long, plain spaghetti

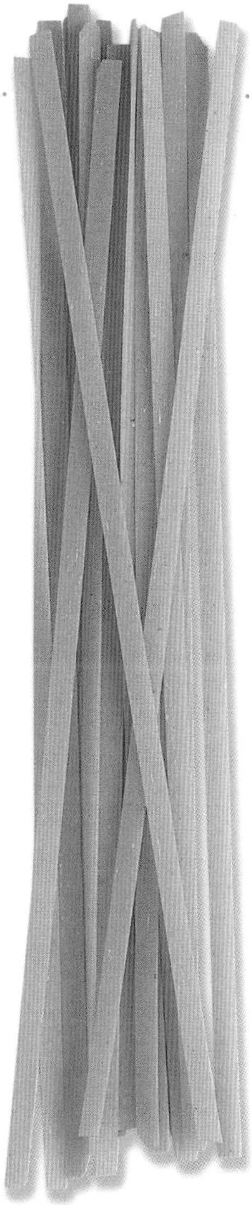

Fettuccelle

Linguine

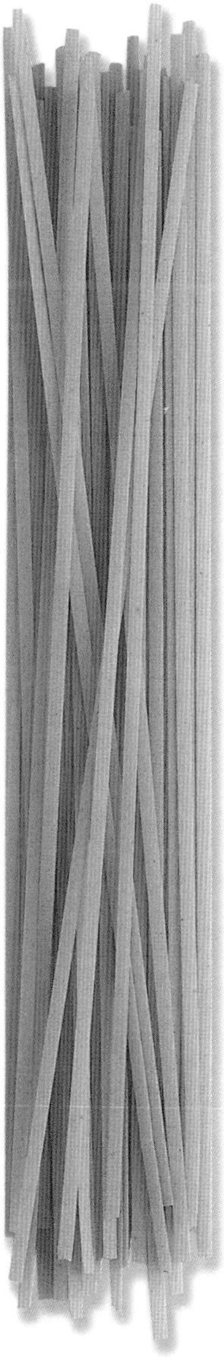

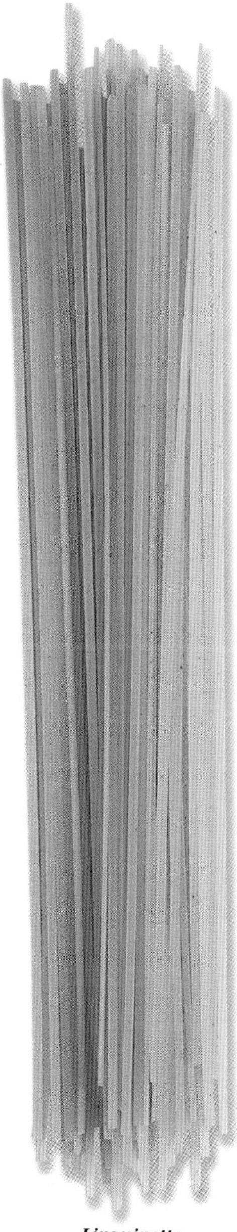

Linguinette

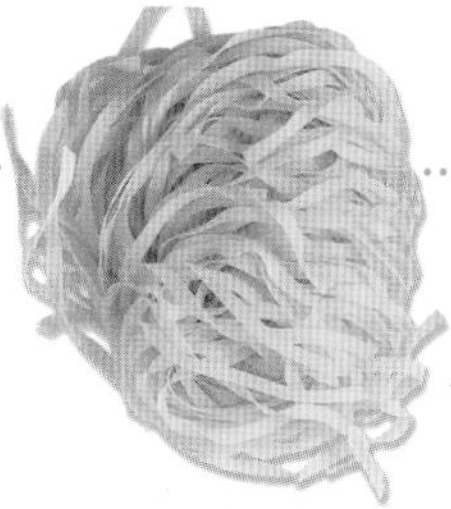

Plain tagliatelle

Tagliatelle
Flavoured with squid ink

Mushroom-flavoured tagliatelle

Spinach tagliatelle

Long Pasta

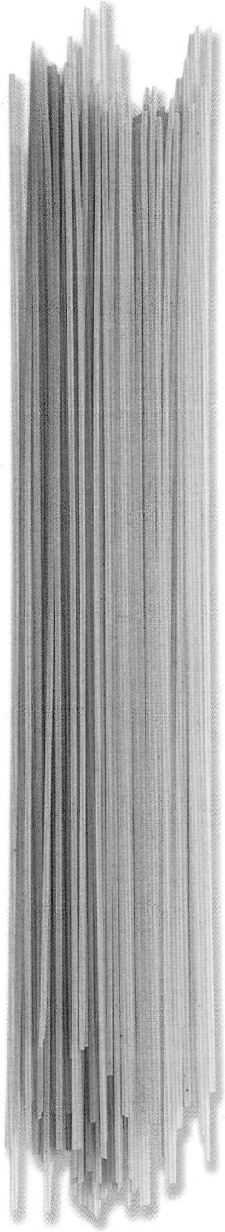

Vermicelli

Bucatini

Ziti

Lasagnette

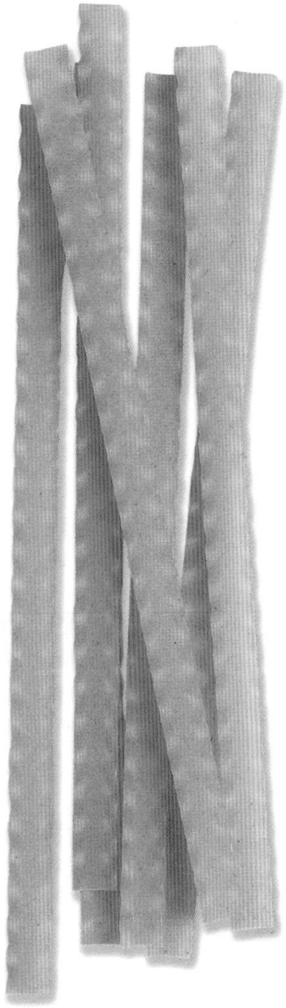

Angel's hair pasta

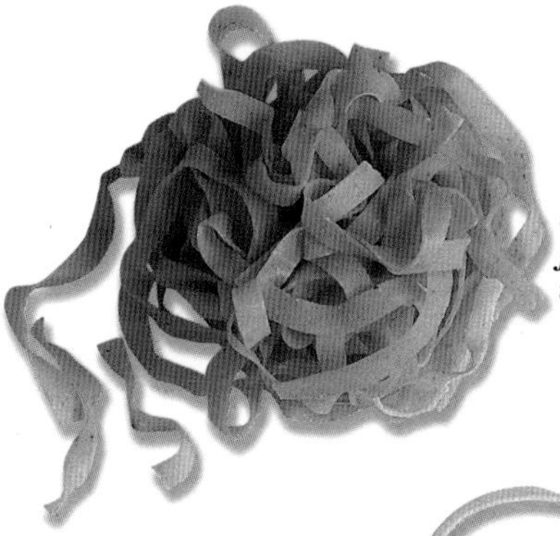

Chilli-flavoured tagliatelle

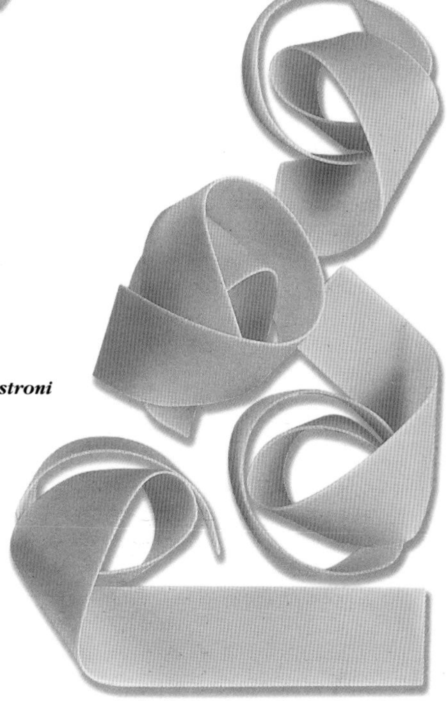

Nastroni

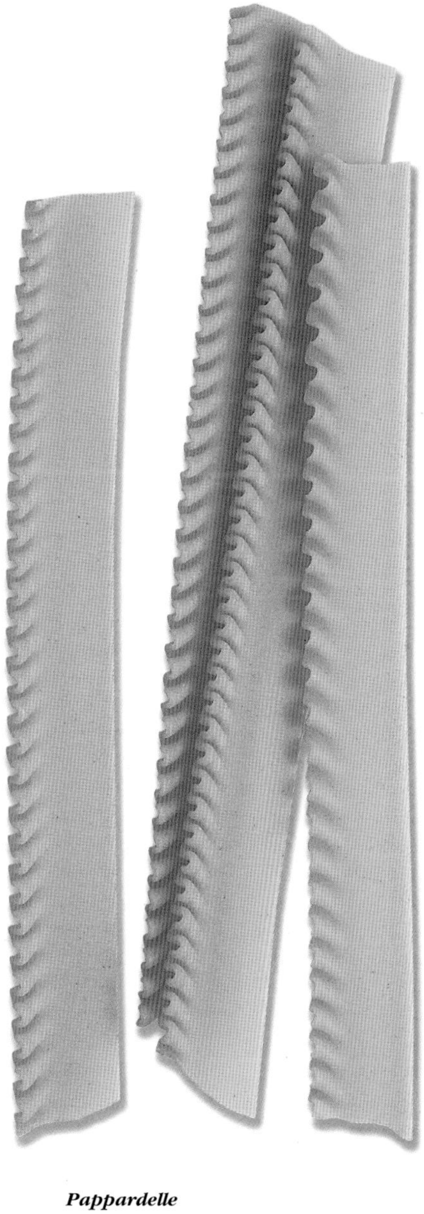

Pappardelle

Short Pasta

Orrecchiette pomodoro

Farfalle

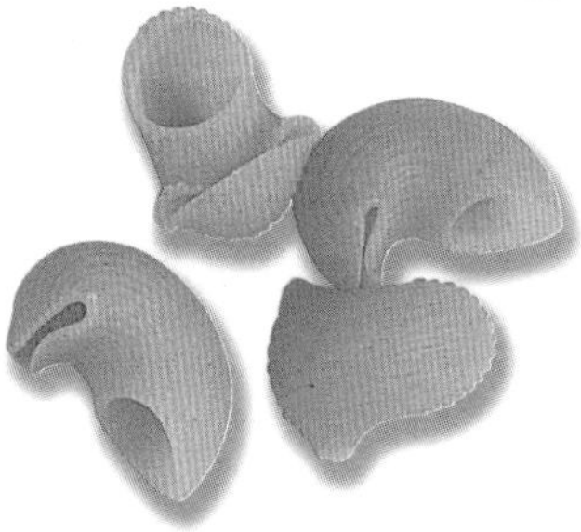

Pipe rigate

Chilli-flavoured fusilli

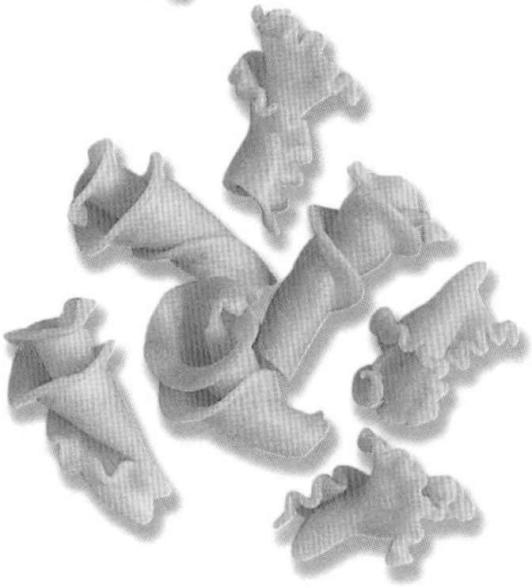

Gigli del gargano

Plain and spinach farfalle

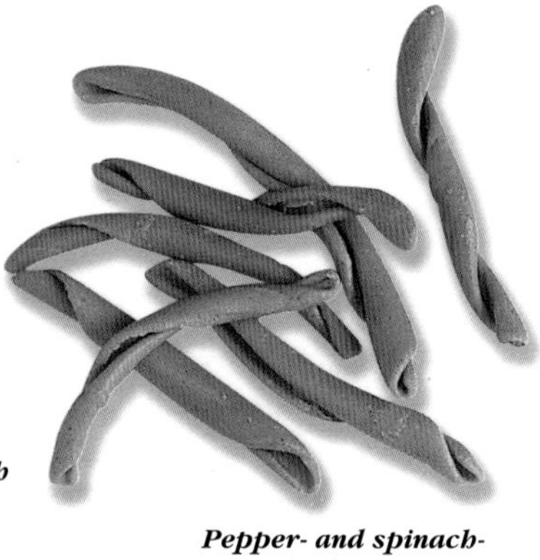

Pepper- and spinach-flavoured fusilli

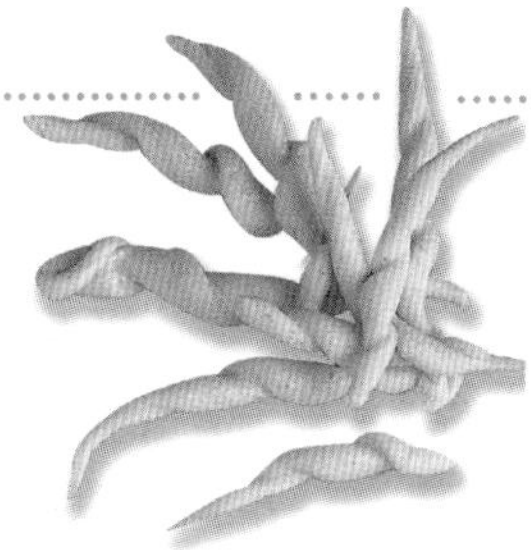

Trofie

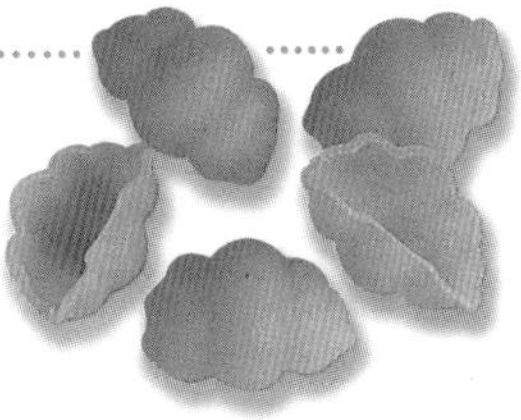

Plain pasta shells

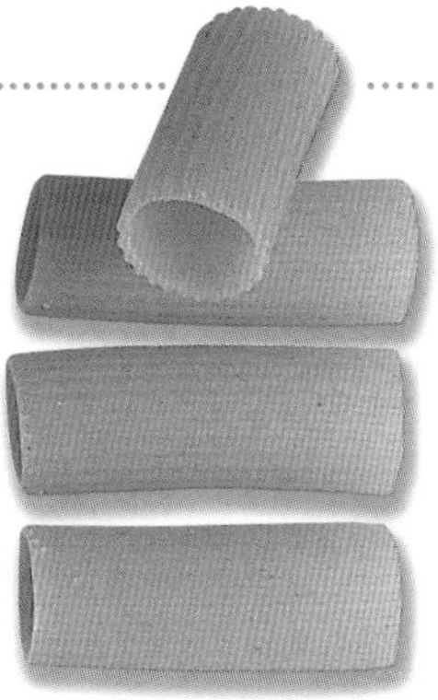

Rigatoni

Conchiglie rigate paglia e fieno

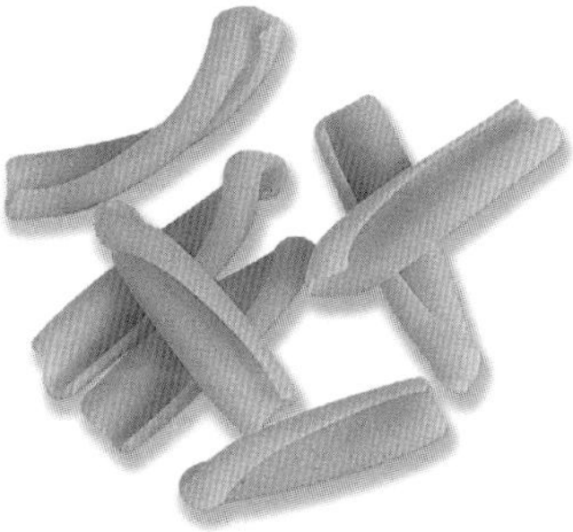

Fusillata caserreccia

Lumachoni rigati

Conchiglie rigate

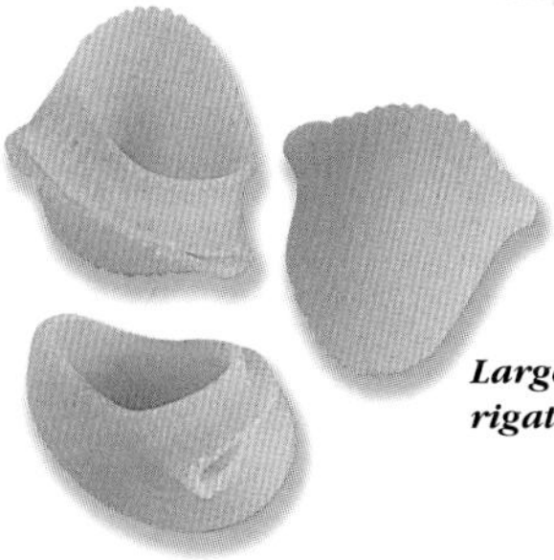

Large lumache rigate

Multi-coloured fusilli
Plain, flavoured with tomato, spinach and fish – and simply coloured blue

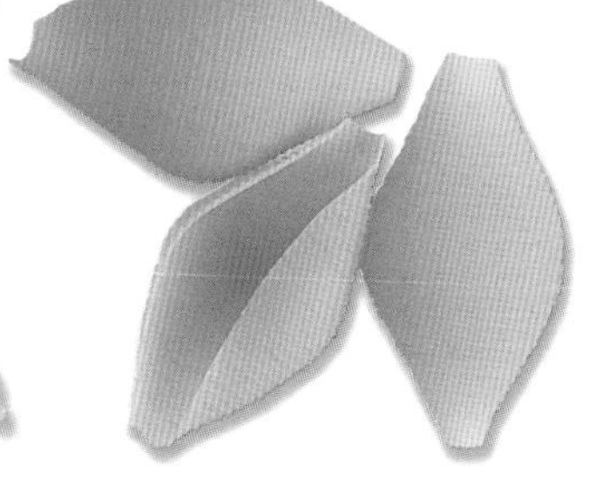

Large conchiglie

Short Pasta

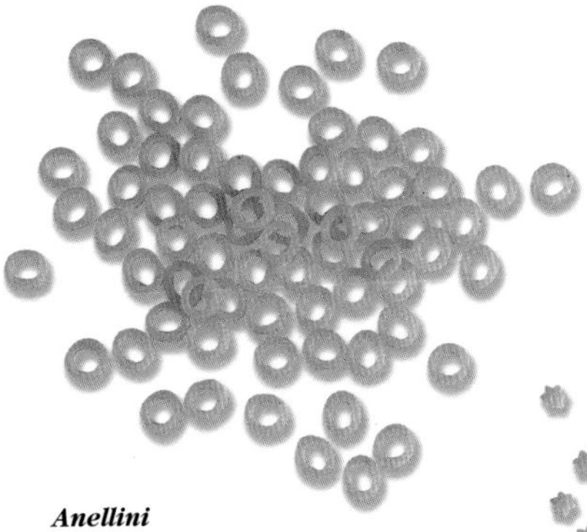

Anellini

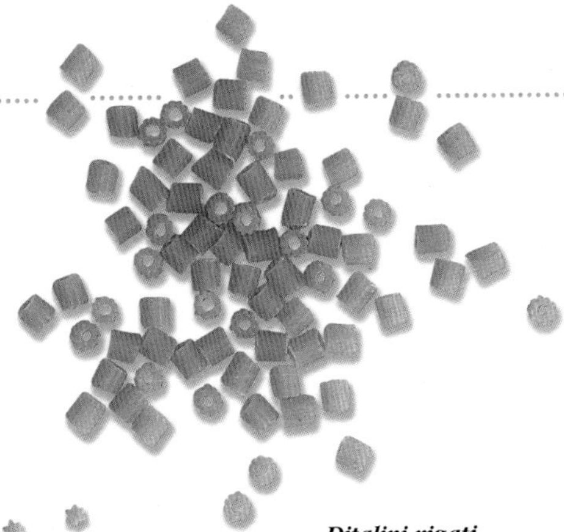

Ditalini rigati

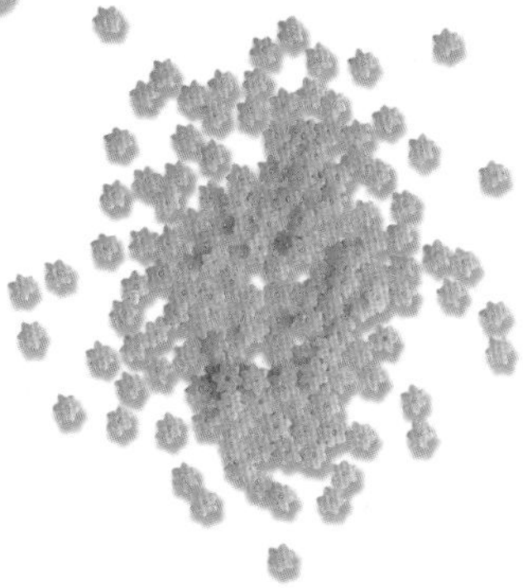

Stellette

Pennette rigati

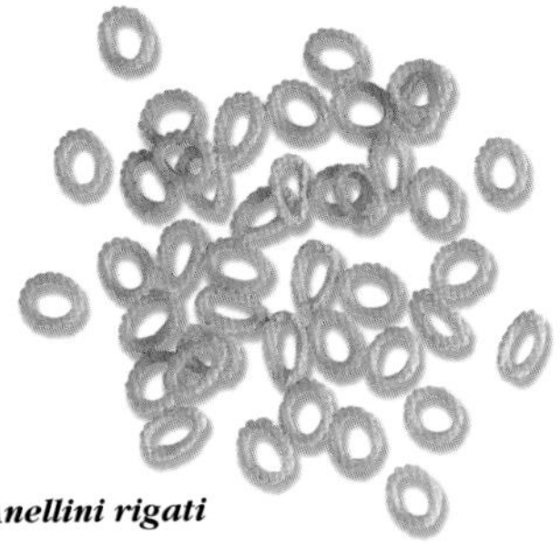

Anellini rigati

Fresh macaroni rigati

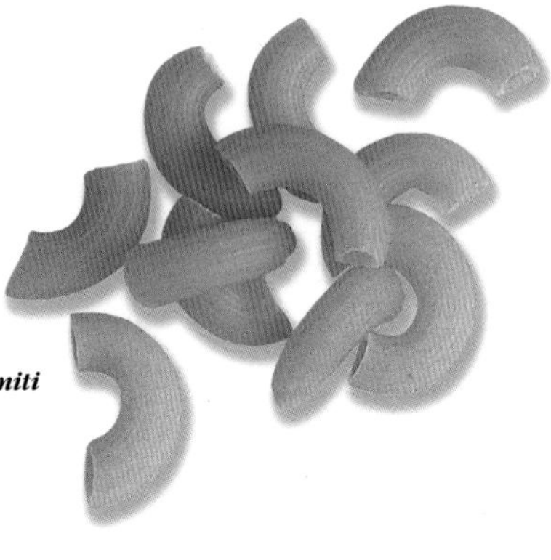

Gremiti

Penne

Penne rigate
Flavoured with chilli

Penne rigate
Flavoured with squid ink

Penne rigate

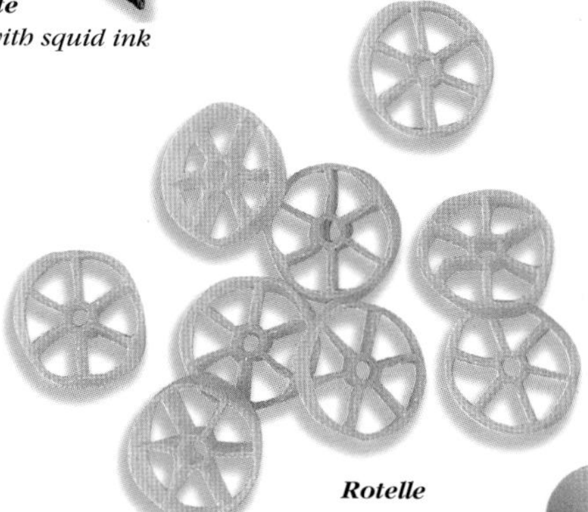

Rotelle

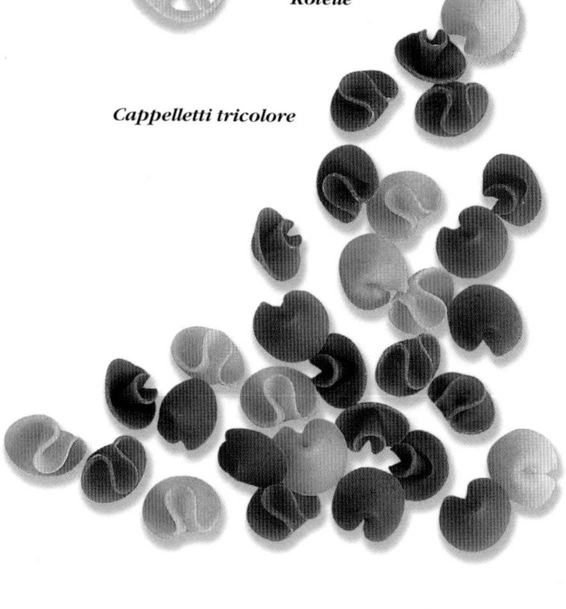

Cappelletti tricolore

Penne rigate
Flavoured with spinach

Flat Pasta

Lasagne

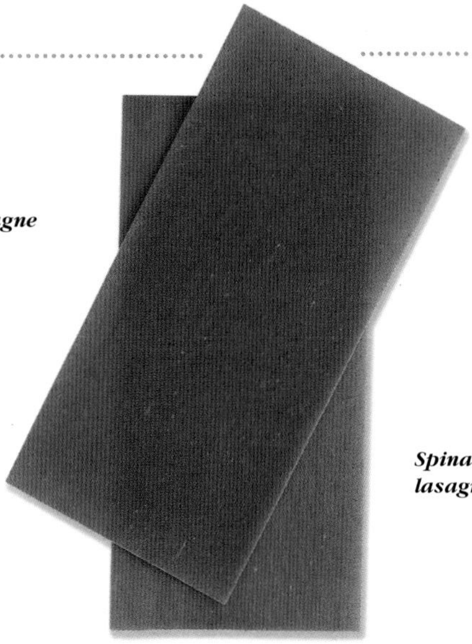

Spinach lasagne

Fresh lasagne

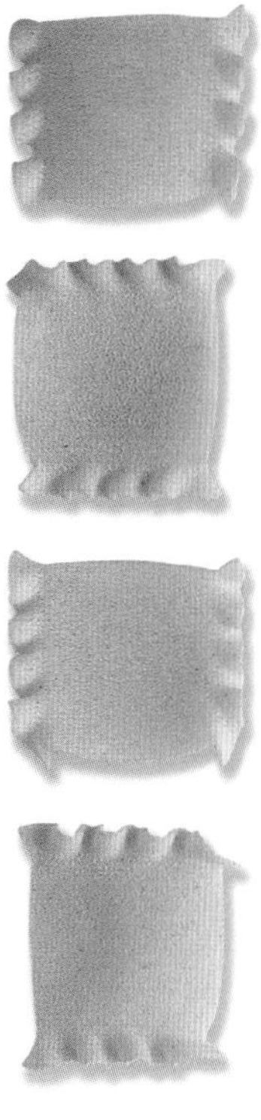

Tacconi

Filled Pasta

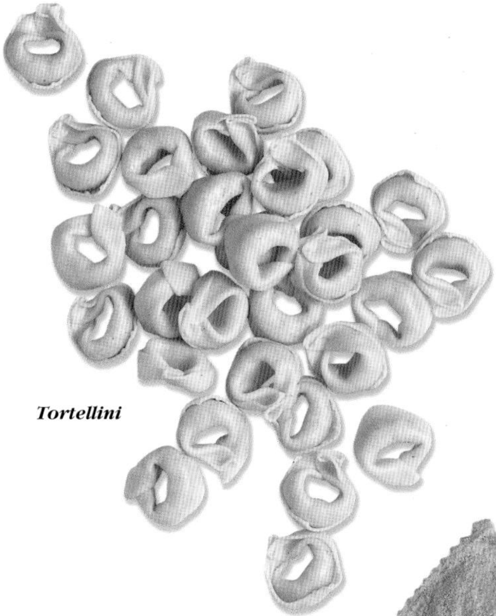

Tortellini

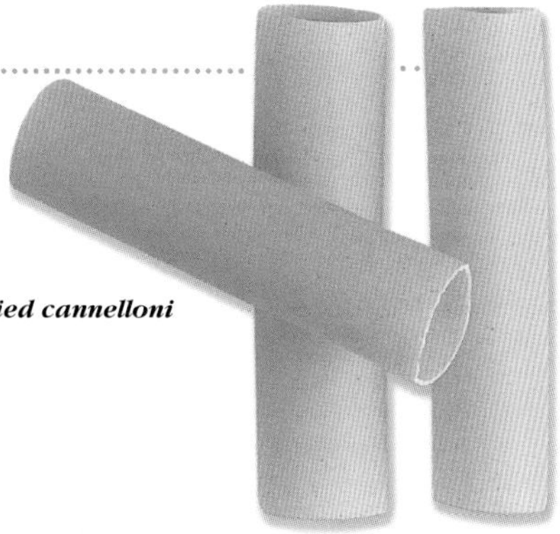

Dried cannelloni

Fresh ravioli

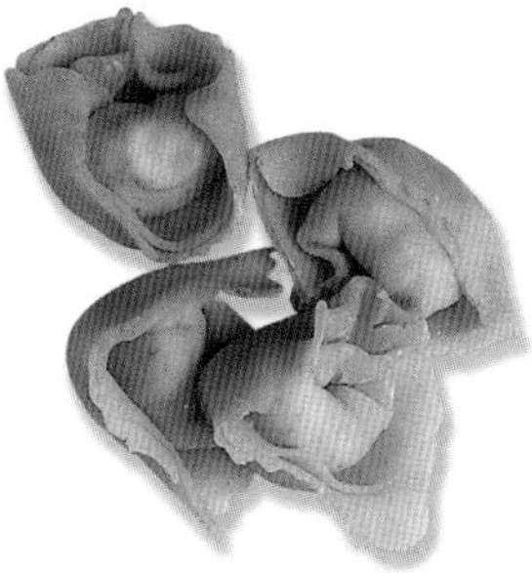

Fresh tortelli

Cappelletti
Filled with sun-dried tomatoes

Cappelletti fantasia
These multi-coloured cappelletti are bought ready for filling and cooking

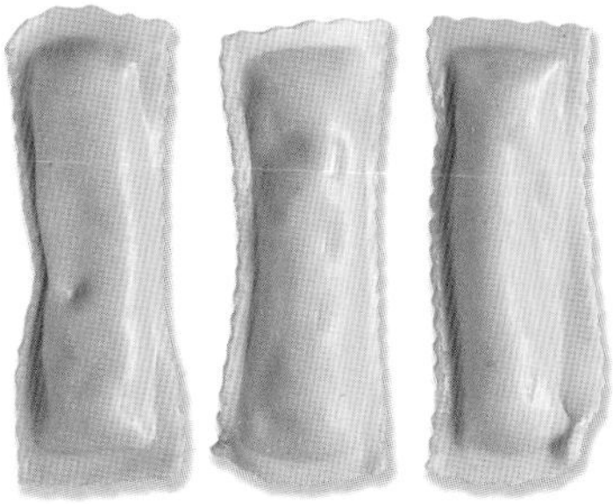

Fresh filled cannelloni

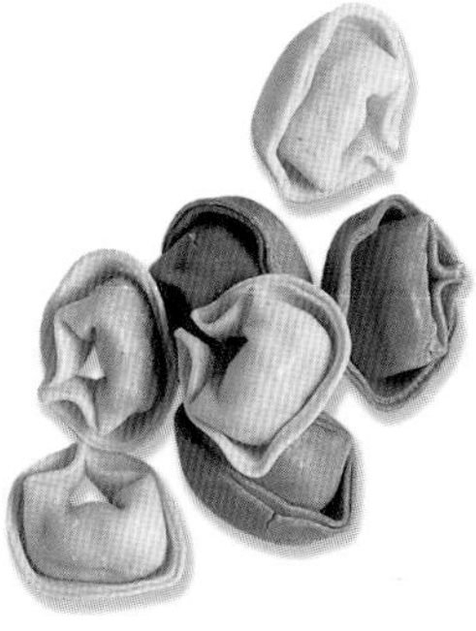

Tortelli
Plain and flavoured with spinach

Gnocchi

Gnocchi fall into a different category from other pasta, being more like small dumplings. They can be made with semolina (milled durum wheat), flour, potatoes or ricotta and spinach and may be shaped like elongated shells, ovals, cylinders or flat discs, or roughly shredded into *strozzapreti* (priest-stranglers); at their worst, shop-bought gnocchi resemble large greyish maggots. However they are made, gnocchi should be extremely light and almost melt in the mouth.

Culinary Uses

Gnocchi can be served like any pasta, as a first course, in clear soup or occasionally as an accompaniment to the main course. Almost any pasta sauce is suitable for serving with gnocchi; they are particularly good with a creamy Gorgonzola sauce or they can be served simply, drizzled with olive oil and dredged with freshly grated Parmesan.

Buying and Storing

Gnocchi are usually sold loose on delicatessen counters. They are quite filling, so a small portion is enough for a first course; allow 115 g/4 oz per serving. They will keep in a polythene bag in the fridge for two or three days. Home-made gnocchi dough will also keep for a couple of days before cooking.

Cooking Gnocchi

With the exception of oven-baked gnocchi alla romana, *all other types of gnocchi should be poached in a saucepan of lightly salted, barely simmering water.*

Drop the gnocchi into the water in batches and cook for about 5 minutes; they will rise to the surface when they are done. Scoop out the cooked gnocchi with a draining spoon and transfer to a plate: keep them warm while you cook the rest.

Fresh plain gnocchi

Fresh potato gnocchi

Gnocchi di patate

The best-known type of gnocchi are those from northern Italy made with potatoes and a little flour. To make 4 servings, peel 500 g/ 1¼ lb floury potatoes and boil until very tender. Drain and mash until smooth, then mix in 1 large egg and season with salt and pepper. Add 100–115 g/3½–4 oz plain flour, a little at a time, stirring well with a wooden spoon until you have a smooth, sticky dough that forms a ball on the spoon (you may not need all the flour). Turn out the dough on to a floured surface and knead for about 3 minutes, until soft and smooth. Cut the dough into 6 equal pieces and, with floured hands, roll these into sausage shapes about 2 cm/¾ in in diameter. Slice the dough into 2 cm/¾ in discs. Hold a fork in your left hand and press the discs against the tines just hard enough to make ridges, then flip them downwards off the fork so that they curl up into elongated shell shapes. Poach them as above.

Fresh spinach and ricotta gnocchi

Fresh gnocchi made with semolina

Spinach and Parmesan gnocchi

Spinach and ricotta gnocchi

These attractive green gnocchi originated in Tuscany where, confusingly, they were known as ravioli. For 4 servings, you need:
350 g/12 oz cooked spinach, well drained and finely chopped
225 g/8 oz ricotta, mashed until smooth
2 eggs
100 g/3½ oz/1 cup freshly grated Parmesan
40 g/1½ oz/3 tbsp plain flour
65 g/2½ oz/5 tbsp butter, melted
salt, pepper and nutmeg

1 Put the spinach, ricotta and seasoning in a saucepan and cook gently, stirring continuously, for 5 minutes. Off the heat, beat in the eggs, 40 g/1½ oz/3 tbsp of the Parmesan and the flour. Chill the mixture for at least 4 hours. Lightly shape into small cylinders and roll them in a very little flour. Poach them as described, left.

2 Preheat the oven to 180°C/350°F/Gas 4. Pour a little melted butter into a serving dish and put in the cooked gnocchi. Sprinkle with some of the remaining Parmesan and place in the oven.

3 Add the rest of the gnocchi as they are cooked and anoint them with melted butter and Parmesan. Replace the dish in the oven for another 5 minutes before serving.

Gnocchi alla romana

These substantial gnocchi from Lazio are made with semolina milled from durum wheat.
For 4-6 servings, you need:
1 litre/1¾ pints/4 cups milk
225 g/8 oz semolina
75 g/3 oz freshly grated Parmesan
2 eggs, plus an extra yolk, lightly beaten
60 g/2½ oz/5 tbsp butter
salt, pepper and nutmeg

1 Bring the milk to the boil, season with salt, pepper and nutmeg, then add the semolina in a steady stream, whisking for about 15 minutes, until the mixture is very thick. Off the heat, stir in half the Parmesan and the beaten eggs.

2 Pour the mixture into a greased baking tray to a thickness of about 1 cm/½ in, or spread it over a dampened work surface. Leave to cool completely, then cut out 3 cm/1¼ in discs with a plain or fluted pastry cutter.

3 Preheat the oven to 230°C/350°F/Gas 8. Layer the semolina discs in a buttered baking dish, dotting each layer with flakes of butter and a sprinkling of grated Parmesan, finishing with the cheese. Bake the gnocchi in the hot oven for about 15 minutes, until browned on top.

Rice, Grains & Pulses

Almost as important as pasta in Italian cooking are rice, polenta and pulses, which all appear as primi piatti *(first courses) in various guises. Like all basically agricultural countries, Italy relied heavily on these protein-rich ingredients when luxuries like meat were in short supply, and a host of wholesome and delicious recipes were developed using these modest ingredients.*

Riso (Rice)

Italy produces more rice and a greater variety of rice than anywhere else in Europe. Most of it is grown in the Po Valley in Piedmont, where conditions are perfect for cultivating the short-grain Carnaroli, Arborio and *Vialone Nano* rice, which make the best risotto. Italian rice is classified by size, ranging from the shortest, roundest *ordinario* (used for puddings) to *semifino* (for soups and salads), then *fino* and finally the longer grains of the finest risotto rice, *superfino*. *Superfino* rice swells to at least three times its original size during cooking, enabling it to absorb all the cooking liquid while still retaining its shape and firm *al dente* texture combined with a creamy smoothness.

History

The Saracens first introduced rice to Italy as long ago as the 11th century (some believe even earlier), but it only became popular in the 16th century, when it began to be cultivated on a large scale in the Po Valley. Traditionally, rice has played a much greater part in the cooking of northern Italy than in the south, particularly in the Veneto, where the famous dish of *risi e bisi* (Venetian dialect for "rice and peas") opened the banquet served every year by the Doges to honour their patron Saint Mark.

Superfino Carnaroli rice **(left and above)**
This short-grained variety is one of the finest Italian rices. Its ability to absorb liquid and cook to a creamy smoothness while still retaining its shape makes it perfect for risotto

Arborio rice

Superfino Arborio rice

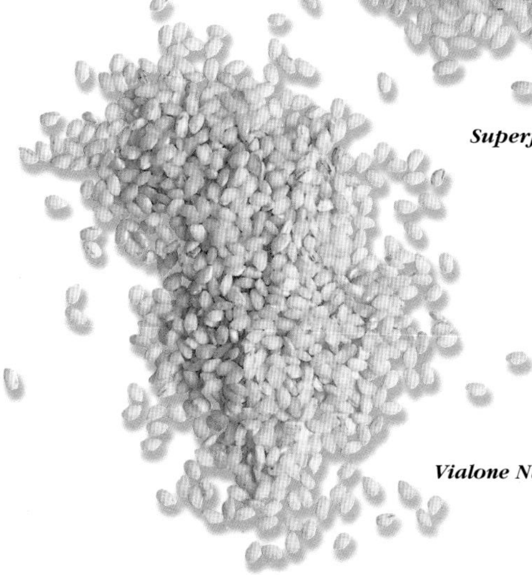

Vialone Nano rice

Preparing Risotto

The most famous of all Italian rice dishes is risotto, which was invented in Milan in the 16th century. A good risotto can be made only with superfine rice. All risotti are basically prepared in the same way, although they can be flavoured with an almost endless variety of ingredients. The rice is coated in butter or oil, then simmering stock is added, one ladleful at a time, and the rice is stirred over a low heat until all the liquid has been completely absorbed.

Only then is more stock added and the risotto is cooked in this way for about 20 minutes until the rice is tender and creamy. The final touch is called mantecatura*; off the heat, a knob of butter or a couple of spoons of olive oil and some freshly grated Parmesan are stirred into the risotto to make it very creamy.*

Leftover cold risotto can be rolled into balls enclosing a piece of mozzarella, coated in fine breadcrumbs and deep-fried to make supplì al telefono *or the Sicilian equivalent,* arancini.

Riso (Rice)

Rice is often used in Italian soups; it combines well with almost all vegetables and makes a substantial addition to minestrone. Baked rice dishes are also popular. Cooked rice is layered in a buttered ovenproof dish with meatballs, vegetables or poultry and cheese, then topped with breadcrumbs and baked in the oven until the top is crispy and brown. The Italians never serve main dishes on a bed of rice, but prefer to serve plain boiled rice on its own with plenty of butter and cheese stirred in.

Buying and Storing

Buy only special superfine risotto rice for use in Italian cooking. Shorter grain *semifino* is best for soups, and *ordinario* for puddings (try *riso nero*, a rice pudding topped with melted chocolate). Once you have opened the packet, reseal it tightly; you can then keep the rice in a dry place for several months.

Semifino rice

Brown semifino rice

Supplì al telefono

These rice croquettes contain mozzarella, which, when cooked, melts into strings that resemble "telephone wires". For 4 servings, you will need:

2 eggs, lightly beaten
225 g/8 oz cold, cooked risotto
50 g/2 oz Parma ham, cut into 1 cm/½ in dice
115 g/4 oz Mozzarella, cut into 1 cm/½ in dice
fine dried breadcrumbs, for coating
oil, for deep-frying
salt and freshly ground black pepper

1 Mix the eggs into the cold risotto and season to taste with plenty of salt and pepper.

2 Form the rice mixture into balls about the size of a small orange and make a hollow in each one. Fill this with a cube of ham and one of cheese, then roll each ball in your hand to enclose the ham and cheese completely, adding a little more rice if necessary.

3 Spread out the breadcrumbs in a shallow tray or plate and roll the rice balls in the breadcrumbs to coat them lightly.

4 Heat the oil in a deep, heavy-based pan and deep-fry the rice balls in batches for 3–5 minutes until golden brown. Drain on kitchen paper and keep warm while you cook the remainder. Serve piping hot.

COOK'S TIP

When cooking rice, a good rule of thumb is: the better the rice, the longer the cooking time required, so ordinario *will need only 10-12 minutes' cooking compared with up to 20 minutes for* superfino.

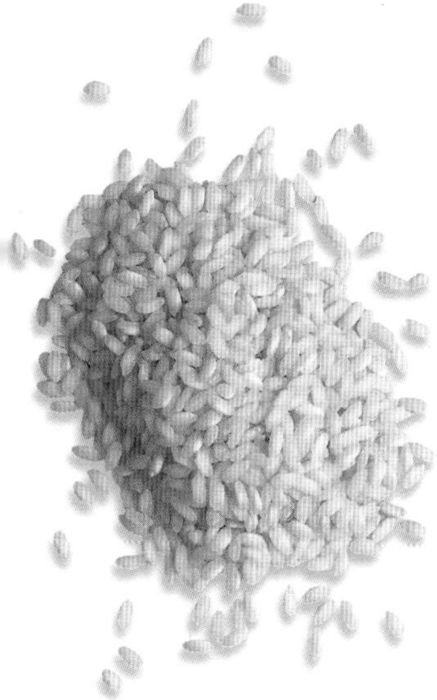

Ordinario rice

Farro

This is the Tuscan name for spelt, a hard brown wheat with pointed grains, which is very little used in other parts of Italy. Farro is much harder than other wheat and therefore takes longer to process and cook, but it will grow even in poor soil. In Tuscany it is used to make *gran farro*, a delicious and nourishing soup, which is served as a first course instead of pasta.

CULINARY USES

Farro is used mainly as an ingredient for soups, but in remoter country areas of Italy it is sometimes used to make bread.

Farro

COOK'S TIP

Farro is a very hard grain and must be boiled for up to 3 hours to make it digestible before adding to other recipes. It can also be simply cooked and served with olive oil and freshly ground black pepper.

Gran farro

This Tuscan soup is often served as a first course instead of pasta.

For 4 servings, you will need:

250 g/8 oz dried borlotti or cannellini beans, soaked overnight, then drained
1 onion, chopped
2 garlic cloves, chopped
100 g/3½ oz finely chopped pancetta
4 sage leaves
a pinch of chopped fresh oregano
45 ml/3 tbsp olive oil
225 g/8 oz chopped fresh tomatoes
150 g/5 oz prepared farro
salt, freshly ground black pepper and grated nutmeg

1 Cook the beans in fresh water until tender (reserve the cooking water). Rub the beans through a vegetable mill. Gently cook the onion, garlic, pancetta and herbs in the olive oil until pale golden brown. Add the tomatoes, season with salt, pepper and nutmeg, then simmer for 10 minutes.

2 Add the bean purée and enough of the cooking water to make a thick soup. Stir in the farro and simmer for 45 minutes, adding more water if the soup becomes too thick. Serve with some extra virgin olive oil to trickle into it.

Polenta

For centuries, polenta has been a staple food of the north of Italy, particularly around Friuli and the Veneto. This grainy yellow flour is a type of cornmeal made from ground maize, which is cooked into a kind of porridge with a wide variety of uses. Polenta is sometimes branded according to the type of maize from which it is made. *Granturco* and *Fioretto* are the two most common types.

In Italy, polenta is available ground to various degrees of coarseness to suit different dishes, but there are two main types – coarse and fine. Coarse polenta has a more interesting texture but takes longer to cook.

Grilled or Fried Polenta

Pour the cooked polenta on to a wooden board and spread it to a thickness of about 2.5 cm/1 in. Leave it to cool and harden, then cut into squares.

Fry in hot vegetable oil until crunchy and golden, then drain on kitchen paper or grill until golden brown on both sides.

To make a pasticciata *(layered baked dish) of polenta, cut the cold polenta horizontally into 1 cm/½ in slices and layer it in a buttered baking dish with your chosen sauce, mushrooms, cheeses etc. Bake in a hot oven for about 15 minutes, until the top is lightly browned.*

History

The Romans made a savoury porridge they called *puls* using *farro*, a kind of spelt, and the tradition continued in northern Italy, where gruels were prepared from local cereals like buckwheat, barley and oats. Maize or corn was only introduced into Italy from the New World in the 17th century; soon it was being grown in all the north-eastern regions, where cornmeal overtook all other types of grain in popularity, because it combined so well with the local dairy products. Traditionally, polenta was cooked in a *polaio*, a special copper pot which hung in the fireplace; here, it was stirred for at least an hour, to be served for breakfast, lunch or dinner (sometimes all three).

Culinary Uses

Polenta is extraordinarily versatile and can be used for any number of recipes, ranging from rustic to highly sophisticated. Although it is most often served as a first course, it can also be used as a vegetable dish or main course and even made into biscuits and cakes. Plain boiled polenta can be served on its own, or enriched with butter and cheese to make a very satisfying dish. It goes wonderfully well with all meats, sausages and game, helping to cut the richness and mop up the sauce. It can be cooled and cut into squares, then fried, grilled or baked and served with a topping or filling of mushrooms, meat, vegetables or cheese. Fried or grilled squares of polenta form the basis of *crostini,* which are served as an *antipasto*.

Fine polenta

BUYING AND STORING

It is possible to buy quick-cooking polenta, which can be prepared in only 5 minutes. However, if you can spare the 20 minutes or so that it takes to cook traditional polenta, it is best to buy this for its superior texture and flavour. Whether you choose coarse or fine meal is a matter of personal preference; for soft polenta or sweet dishes, fine-ground is better, while course-ground meal is better for frying. Once you have opened the bag, put the remaining polenta in an airtight container; it will keep for at least a month.

Coarse polenta

COOK'S TIP

Polenta can be cooked in water, stock or a mixture of water and milk. Whichever liquid you use, cook the polenta very slowly and steadily so that it does not go lumpy. Allow 50–75 g/2–3 oz/½ cup polenta meal per person.

SWEET POLENTA FRITTERS

Polenta can be used to make sweet as well as savoury dishes. To make enough fritters to serve four, combine 750 ml/1¼ pints/3 cups milk, 75 g/3 oz/6 tbsp caster sugar and a pinch of salt in a saucepan and bring to the boil. Add 150 g/5 oz polenta in a steady stream, stirring constantly for 20 minutes. Off the heat, stir in 25 g/1 oz/2 tbsp butter, 3 egg yolks and the grated rind of 1 lemon and continue to stir for 1 minute. Spread out the polenta on a dampened baking sheet to a thickness of 1 cm/½ in. When cold, cut into rectangles or diamonds. Coat lightly with fine dry breadcrumbs, then deep-fry in hot oil until golden. Drain on kitchen paper and dust with icing sugar before serving.

Recipe for Basic Polenta

To make a basic polenta for 4–6 people, bring to the boil 1.5 litres/2½ pints/6 cups salted water or stock.

Gradually add 300 g/11 oz/2 cups polenta in a steady stream, stirring continuously with a wooden spoon.

Continue cooking, stirring all the time, until the polenta comes away from the sides of the saucepan. This will take 20–30 minutes (5 minutes for quick-cooking polenta).

One alternative, foolproof (though unauthentic) method is to put the polenta meal into a saucepan, add salt, then stir in the cold water, bring the mixture slowly to the boil and simmer gently for about 20 minutes, stirring occasionally.

Another is to cook the polenta for 5 minutes, then finish cooking it in the oven for about an hour.

Pour the cooked polenta into a serving dish, season with pepper and stir in abundant quantities of butter and a strong-flavoured cheese – Parmesan, Fontina, Bel Paese and Gorgonzola are all delicious with piping hot polenta.

Pulses

Fagioli (haricot beans)

Haricot beans are another staple of Tuscan cooking; indeed, the Tuscans are sometimes nicknamed "the bean-eaters", although haricot beans are eaten all over Italy. The most popular varieties include the pretty red-and-cream speckled borlotti, the small white cannellini (a kind of kidney bean), the larger *toscanelli* and *fagioli coll'occhio* (black-eyed beans). All these are eaten as hearty stews, with pasta and in soups, and cannellini are often served as a side dish simply anointed with extra virgin olive oil. *Ceci* (chick-peas) and *fave* (broad beans) are also popular.

History

Beans were a staple of the Roman and Greek diet, and several recipes for bean stews survive from that period. Many of the beans were brought to Italy from the Middle East, but some, like *fave*, were indigenous and were used as ritual offerings to the dead at Roman funerals. Haricot beans have always been a popular peasant food, but, during the Renaissance, Catherine de Medici attempted to refine Italian cuisine, and beans fell out of favour with the nobility and sophisticated urban dwellers. Thanks to their highly nutritious and economical qualities, however, beans and pulses have once again become an important element in Italian cooking.

Culinary Uses

Haricot beans can be made into any number of nutritious soups and stews, or served as the basis of a substantial salad like *tonno e fagioli* (tuna and beans). A popular Tuscan dish is *fagioli all'uccelletto* (beans cooked like little birds). Cooked cannellini beans are combined with chopped garlic, fresh sage leaves and tomatoes and simmered for about 15 minutes until tender and fragrant. This dish is delicious served with coarse country sausages.

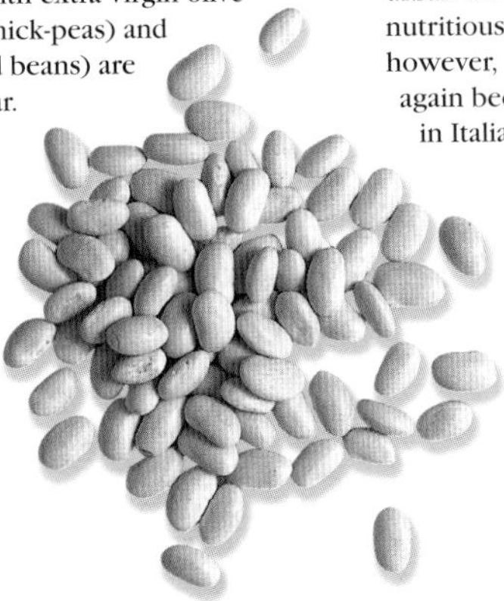

Dried cannellini beans

Dried red borlotti beans

Dried borlotti beans

Dried cannellini beans

BUYING AND STORING

During the summer and early autumn in Italy, you may find fresh haricot beans, sometimes still in the pod. Borlotti beans come in an attractive speckled pod, cannellini in a slim yellowish pod. The pods represent a high proportion of the weight, so allow at least 300 g/11 oz per serving. Most haricot beans, however, are sold dried. Try to buy these from a shop with a quick turnover, or they may become wizened and very hard. Prepacked beans will have a "best before" date on the packet. Loose beans will keep for several weeks in a cool dry place, but are at their best soon after purchase.

If you haven't the time to prepare dried beans, canned varieties make an acceptable substitute, but you cannot control the texture and they are sometimes too mushy. They are, however, fine for recipes that call for puréed beans. Bear in mind, though, that they are an expensive alternative to dried beans.

Canned borlotti beans

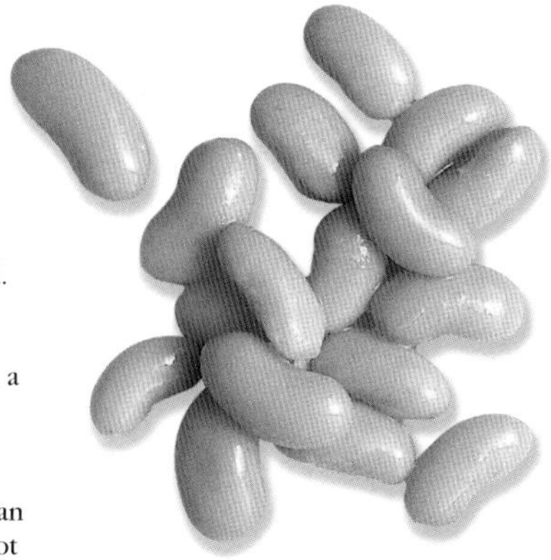

Canned haricot beans

Canned cannellini beans

Canned black-eyed beans

COOKING BEANS

All dried beans should be soaked for about 8 hours in cold water or 4 hours in boiling water before cooking (this is not necessary for fresh beans). Discard the soaking water before cooking the beans.

Cook the beans in plenty of unsalted boiling water. Boil briskly for 10 minutes (this is essential to kill off the toxins, which may cause severe stomach upsets), then simmer for 1–2 hours, depending on the size and freshness of the beans.

You can add whatever flavourings you wish to the cooking liquid, but never add salt or any acidic ingredients, such as tomatoes or vinegar, until the beans are cooked, or they will never become tender however long you cook them. To make a hearty stew, after the initial boiling, the beans can be mixed with pancetta, *garlic and herbs and cooked very slowly in the oven.*

Pulses

Fave (broad beans)

Broad beans are nicest eaten fresh from the fat green pod in late spring and early summer when they are very small and tender with a bittersweet flavour. They are particularly popular in the area around Rome, where they are eaten raw with *prosciutto crudo*, salami or Pecorino. Later in the season, they should be cooked and skinned (hold the hot beans under cold running water; the skin will slip off quite easily). Cooked *fave* have a milder flavour than raw and are excellent with ham and *pancetta*. When buying fresh *fave* in the pod, allow about 350 g/12 oz per person; it may seem a lot, but the pods themselves are comparatively heavy, so a lot goes only a little way. Dried *fave* should be soaked, and the skins removed before cooking. They are used for soups and stews and need about 45 minutes' cooking.

Chick-peas
These round golden pulses can be bought dried (above), or canned and ready to use (left)

Broad beans
Dried fave *need to be soaked overnight before cooking*

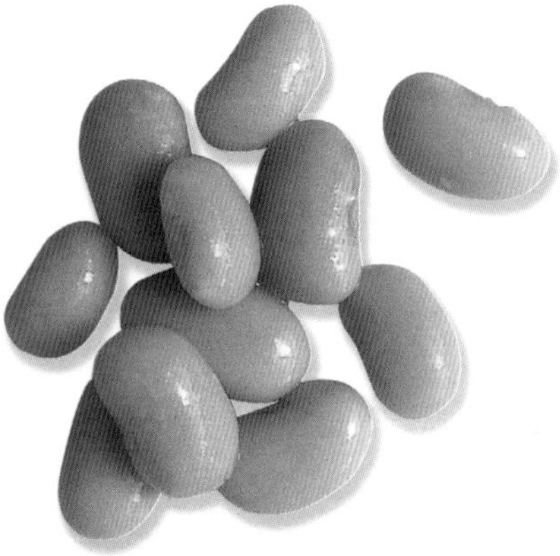

Broad beans
The canned beans (right) are ready to use

Ceci (chick-peas)

These round golden pulses are shaped rather like hazelnuts and have a distinctive, nutty flavour. They are the oldest of all known pulses and, though not indigenous to Italy, have become very popular in Italian country cooking.

CULINARY USES

Chick-peas are cooked and used in the same way as haricot beans and are an essential ingredient of *tuoni e lampo* (thunder and lightning), a sustaining dish of pasta and chick-peas served with tomato sauce and Parmesan. They can also be served cold, dressed with lemon juice, chopped fresh herbs and olive oil, to make a substantial salad.

> **COOK'S TIP**
> *Chick-peas can be very hard, so it is best to soak them for at least 12 hours, then cook them in plenty of boiling water for up to 2 hours.*

Lenticchie *(lentils)*

Although lentils grow in pods, they are always sold podded and dried. Italian lentils are the small brown variety, which are grown in the area around Umbria; they do not break up during cooking and are often mixed with small pasta shapes or rice for a contrast of flavours and textures. They make the perfect bed for cooked sausage, such as zampone or cotechino, and are delicious served cold dressed with olive oil. The ultimate Italian pulse feast must surely be *imbrecciata*, a nutritious and sustaining soup from Umbria made with chick-peas, haricot beans and lentils.

Brown lentils
These are available in different sizes, large (below) and small (above)

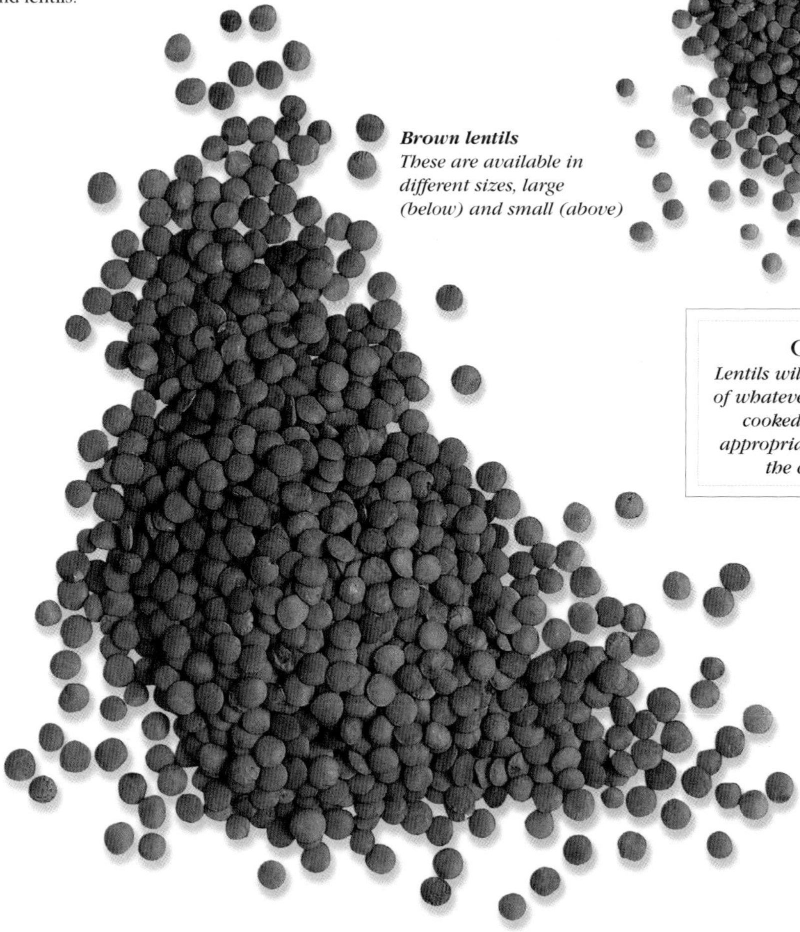

COOK'S TIP
Lentils will absorb the flavours of whatever aromatics they are cooked with, so add any appropriate herbs or spices to the cooking liquid.

Cheeses

Italy has an even greater variety of cheeses than France, ranging from fresh, mild creations like mozzarella to aged, hard cheeses with a very mature flavour, such as Parmesan. All types of milk are used, including ewe's, goat's and buffalo's, which produces the best mozzarella, and some cheeses are made from a mixture of milks. As in France, the Italians eat their cheese after the main course, either accompanied or followed by fresh fruit. You will not, however, find the large selection of cheeses offered on a French menu; Italian restaurants serve only one or two types of cheese and rarely have a cheeseboard.

Many of the cheeses made in Italy are suitable for cooking. What would a pizza be without its delicious, stringy topping of melted mozzarella, or a pasta dish without a grating of fresh Parmesan?

History

Fresh, rindless cheeses were first introduced to Italy by the ancient Greeks, who taught the Etruscans their cheese-making skills. They in turn refined the craft, developing the first long-matured cheeses with hard rinds, which could last for many months and would travel. Today's Parmesan and Pecorino cheeses are probably very similar to those produced 2,500 years ago.

In ancient days, the milk was left to curdle naturally before being made into cheese. The Romans discovered that rennet would speed up this process. Originally, they probably used rennet made from wild artichokes (this is still used in remoter parts of Italy), but later they began to use animal rennet. The process used to make farmhouse cheeses today has changed very little since Roman times.

Italian cheeses can be divided into four categories: hard, semi-soft, soft and fresh. Some cheeses have an enormously high fat content; others are low in fat and suitable for dieters. Many Italian cheeses are eaten at different stages of maturity; a cheese which has been matured for about a year is known as *vecchio*; after 18 months, it becomes *stravecchio* and tends to have a very powerful flavour. Almost all Italian cheeses can be eaten on their own and used for cooking.

Hard Cheeses

Asiago

This cheese from the Veneto region develops different characteristics as it ages. The large round cheeses with reddish-brown rinds each weigh 10–12 kg/22–55 lb. They are made from partially skimmed cow's milk and have a fat content of only 30 per cent. Asiago starts life as a pale straw-coloured dessert cheese, pitted with tiny holes, with a mild, almost bland flavour. After six months, the semi-matured cheese (*Asiago da taglio*) develops a more piquant, saltier flavour, but can still be eaten on its own. Once it has matured for 12 to 18 months, the *stravecchio* cheese becomes grainy and sharp-tasting, resembling an inferior Grana Padano, and is really only suitable for grating and cooking.

Asiago

Parmesan

Parmesan is by far the best-known and most important of the Italian hard cheeses. There are two basic types - Parmigiano Reggiano and Grana Padano - but the former is infinitely superior.

Parmigiano Reggiano

Parmigiano Reggiano can be made only in a strictly defined zone, which lies between Parma, Modena, Reggio-Emilia, Bologna and Mantua. The farmers of this area claim that the cheese has been made there for over 2,000 years; certainly it appears to be almost identical to that produced by the Etruscans and the methods of production have scarcely changed. The milk comes only from local cows, which graze on the area's rich pastureland.

It takes about 600 litres/132 gallons of milk to make one 30-35 kg/ 70-80 lb wheel of Parmigiano Reggiano. The milk is partially skimmed and some of the whey from the previous day's cheese-making is added, then the mixture is carefully heated before rennet is added to encourage curdling. (The rest of the whey is fed to local pigs destined to become Parma hams.) The curds are poured into wheel-shaped forms and the cheese is then aged for a minimum of two years; a really fine Parmesan may be aged for up to seven years. During this time, it is nurtured like fine wine, until it becomes pale golden with a slightly granular flaky texture and a nutty, mildly salty flavour. Authentic Parmigiano Reggiano has the word "Reggiano" stamped on the rind.

Grana Padano

This cheese is similar to Parmigiano Reggiano, but is inferior in flavour and texture. Although it is made in the same way, the milk used comes from other regions and the cheese is matured for no more than 18 months, so it does not have the crumbly texture of Reggiano and its flavour is sharper and saltier. Its grainy texture (hence the name "grana") makes it fine for grating and it can be used for cooking in the same way as Reggiano.

Culinary Uses

A really good Parmigiano Reggiano can be eaten on its own, cut into chunks or slivers; it is delicious served with ripe pears and a good red wine. But Parmesan, both Reggiano and grana, really comes into its own when used for cooking. Unlike other cheeses, it does not become stringy or rubbery when exposed to heat, so it can be grated over any number of hot dishes, from pasta, polenta and risotto to minestrone, or layered with aubergines or truffles and baked in the oven. Slivers of fresh Parmesan are also excellent with asparagus or in a crisp salad. Don't throw away the rind from Parmesan; use it to add extra flavour to soups and vegetable stocks.

Parmigiano Reggiano

Grana Padano

Buying and Storing

If possible, buy Parmigiano Reggiano, which is easily recognizable by the imprint "Reggiano" in pinpricks on the rind. Whether you buy Reggiano or grana, always buy it in a piece cut from a whole wheel and grate it freshly when you need it; if possible, avoid pre-packed pieces and never buy ready-gratedParmesan, which is tasteless. Tightly wrapped in foil, a hunk of Parmesan will keep in the fridge for at least a month.

Hard Cheeses

Pecorino

All Italian cheeses made from ewe's milk are known as Pecorino, but they vary enormously in texture and flavour, from soft and mild to dry and strong. The best-known hard Pecorino cheeses are *romano* from Lazio and *sardo* from Sardinia; both are medium-fat, salty-tasting cheeses with a sharp flavour, which becomes sharper the longer the cheeses are matured. The milder *sardo* is usually aged for only a few weeks; the *romano* for up to 18 months. Hard Pecorino is a pale, creamy colour with a firm granular texture with tiny holes like Parmesan. Sicilian *Pecorino pepato* is studded with whole black peppercorns, which add a very piquant note.

Fresh Pecorino comes from Tuscany and is sometimes known as *caciotta.* This semi-hard cheese has a delicious mild, creamy flavour, but is not easy to find outside Italy, as it keeps for a very short time.

History

Pecorino romano is probably the oldest Italian cheese, dating back to Roman times. Then, as now, the cheeses were shaped and laid on *canestri* (rush mats, rather like hammocks) to be air-dried. Sicilian Pecorino is still called *canestro* after these rush mats.

Culinary Uses

Hard Pecorino can be grated and used exactly like Parmesan. It has a more pungent flavour, which is well suited to spicy pasta dishes, such as *penne all'arrabiata*, but it is too strong for more delicate dishes like risotto or creamy chicken dishes. *Caciotta* can be cubed and marinated in olive oil for about 2 hours, then served with a grinding of black pepper to make a delicious and unusual *antipasto*.

Buying and Storing

Fresh or semi-hard Pecorino should be eaten the day you buy it, but well-matured Pecorino will keep in the fridge for several weeks wrapped tightly in foil.

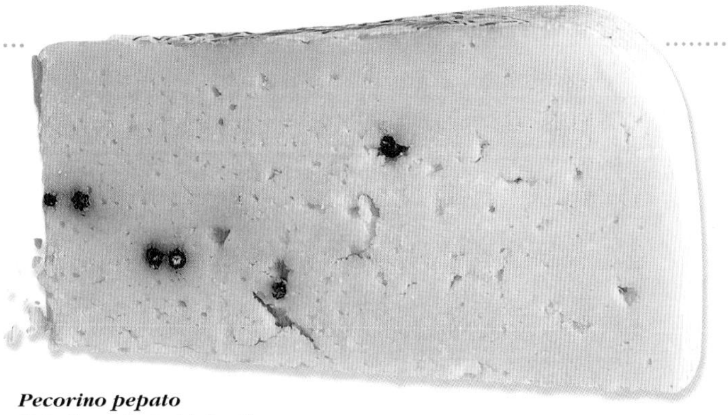

Pecorino pepato
This cheese is studded with whole black peppercorns

Pecorino sardo
A milder version that is aged for only a few weeks

Caciotta
A semi-hard cheese with a mild, creamy flavour

Provolone

A southern Italian cheese, straw-white in colour with a smooth, supple texture and an oval or cylindrical shape, Provolone comes in many different sizes (some enormous) and can often be found hanging from the ceiling in Italian delicatessens. Provolone can be made from different types of milk and rennet; the strongest versions use goat rennet, which gives them a distinctively spicy flavour. In the south of Italy, buffalo milk is often used, and the cheeses are sometimes smoked to make *provolone affumicato*. The cheese is made by the *pasta filata* (layering) process, which gives it a smooth, silky texture; the curds are left to solidify, then they are cut into strips before being pressed together into a sausage shape. This is salted in brine for 6 to 12 hours, then the cheese is shaped and left to mature.

Variations on Provolone include *caciocavallo*, a smooth smoky cheese made from a mixture of cow's and goat's or ewe's milk, which develops a sharp flavour that becomes sharper as it matures. It takes its name from the way the oval cheeses are tied up in pairs and hung up to dry over a wooden pole, as though on horseback. (One fallacious theory is that the cheese was originally made from mare's milk; another is that the cheeses were stamped with a horse, which is the symbol of Naples.) In Calabria, a version called *burrino* is made enclosing a lump of unsalted butter in the centre of the cheese, so that when it is sliced, it resembles a hard-boiled egg.

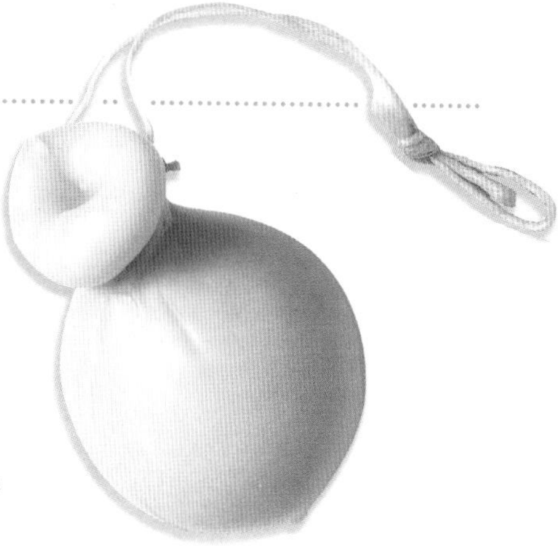

Provolone burrino
There is a lump of butter buried in the centre of this cheese, so that when cut it resembles a hard-boiled egg yolk

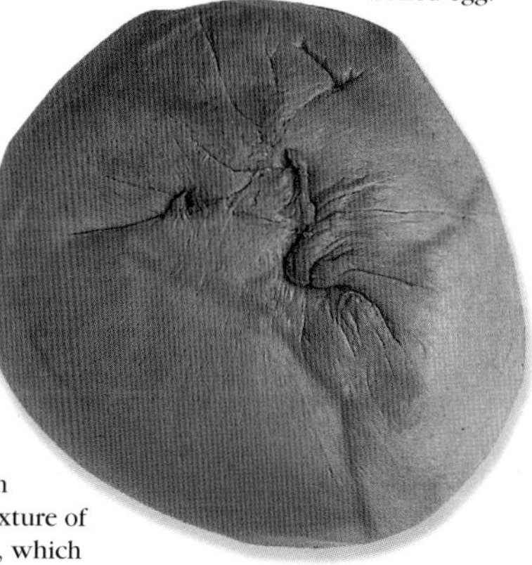

Provolone affumicato

Culinary Uses

Milder fresh Provolone can be eaten on its own or in a sandwich with mortadella or ham. Once it becomes strong, it should only be used for cooking; its stringy texture when melted makes it ideal for pizzas and pasta dishes.

Buying and Storing

Enclosed in their wax rinds, Provolone and similar cheeses will keep for months. Once they have been opened, they should be eaten within a week. Provolone can be used for cooking in the same way as Parmigiano Reggiano.

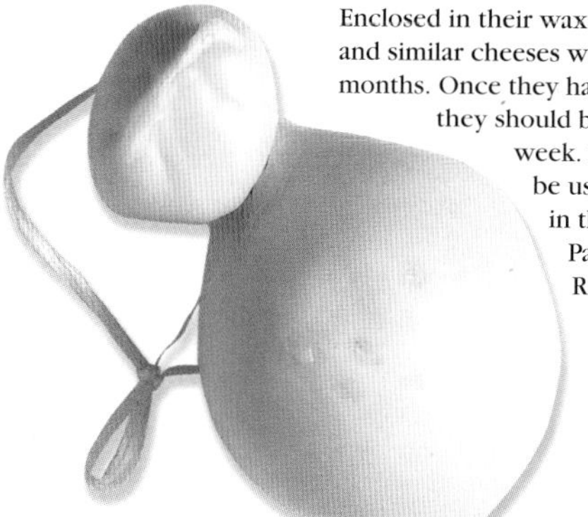

Provolone
The stringy texture when melted makes this cheese particularly good for pizzas

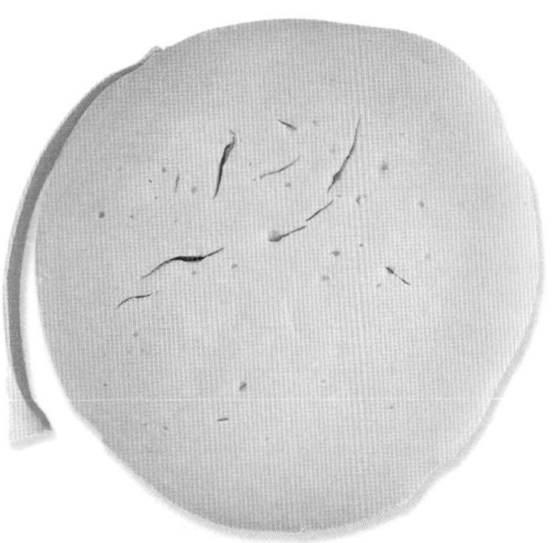

Provolone

Semi-hard Cheeses

Bel Paese

This cheese, poetically named "beautiful country", is a baby among Italian cheeses, having been created by the Galbani family from Lombardy early this century. Made from cow's milk, it contains over 50 per cent fat, which makes it very creamy. It is the colour of buttermilk, with a very mild flavour, and is wrapped in pale yellow wax to preserve its freshness. A whole Bel Paese weighs about 2 kg/$4^{1}/_{4}$ lb, but it is often sold ready-packed in wedges.

Culinary Uses

Bel Paese can be eaten on its own; its mild creaminess makes it popular with almost everyone. It is also excellent for cooking, with a good melting quality, and can be used as a substitute for mozzarella, but because it is rather bland it will not add much flavour to a dish.

Buying and Storing

Like most cheeses, it is best to buy a wedge of Bel Paese cut from a whole cheese; pre-packed pieces tend to be soggy and tasteless, although they are fine to use in cooking. Use freshly cut cheese as soon as possible after purchase, although wrapped in foil or clear film it will keep in the fridge for two or three days.

Fontina

The only genuine Fontina comes from the Val d'Aosta in the Italian Alps, although there are plenty of poor imitations. True Fontina is made from the rich unpasteurized milk of Valdostana cows and has a fat content of 45 per cent. Although Fontina is nowadays produced on a large scale, the methods are strictly controlled and the cows are grazed only on alpine grass and herbs. Because it is matured for only about four months, the cheese has a mild, almost sweet, nutty flavour and a creamy texture, with tiny holes. Longer-matured Fontina develops a much fuller flavour and is best used for cooking. A whole Fontina weighs about 15–20 kg/33–44 lb; the cheese is pale golden and the soft rind is orangey-brown. The rind of authentic Fontina has the words "Fontina dal Val d'Aosta" inscribed in white writing.

History

Fontina has been made for at least 500 years; it is mentioned in the "dairy bible"' *La Summa Lacticiniorum* of 1477. Its name probably comes from the mountain peak Fontin.

Culinary Uses

Fontina is delicious eaten on its own, and because it melts beautifully and does not become stringy, it can be used instead of mozzarella in a wide variety of dishes. It is also perfect for making a *fonduta*, the Italian equivalent of a Swiss cheese fondue.

Fontina
The sweet nutty flavour and creamy texture of this cheese makes it delicious to eat on its own

Bel Paese
This creamy, mild-flavoured cheese can also be eaten on its own, and it is excellent for cooking, too

Soft Cheeses

Taleggio

A square creamy cheese from Lombardy with a fat content of almost 50 per cent, Taleggio has a mild, salty-sweet flavour, which can become pungent if it is left to age for too long (it reaches maturity after only six weeks). The cheeses are dipped in brine for about 14 hours before maturing, which gives them a slightly salty tang. Each cheese with its soft edible rind weighs about 2 kg/$4^1/_4$ lb. If you intend to eat the rind, remove the paper from the top!

Culinary Uses

Taleggio is perfect eaten on its own as a cheese course. Like Fontina, it melts into a velvety smoothness when cooked and does not become stringy, so it can be used in any cooked dish that requires a good melting consistency.

Buying and Storing

Both Fontina and Taleggio should be eaten as soon as possible after purchase. If necessary, they can be tightly wrapped in waxed paper or clear film and kept in the fridge for a day or two.

Taleggio
Perfect to eat on its own, taleggio has a mild, sweet flavour

Stracchino

Stracchino is made from very creamy milk and matured for only about ten days, and never longer than two months. The smooth rindless cheese with a fat content of about 50 per cent is reminiscent of Taleggio, but softer-textured and with a sweeter flavour. Robiola is a small, square stracchino weighing about 100 g/$3^1/_2$ oz. Because these cheeses are so delicate, they are wrapped in plasticized paper to preserve their freshness.

Stracchino
A soft-textured cheese with a sweet flavour

History

The name Stracchino comes from the Lombardian dialect word meaning "tired". It does not reflect on the quality of the cheeses, but merely indicates that they were traditionally made in the winter months when the cows were tired from their long trek down from the mountains to their winter quarters on the plain of Lombardy. Some farmhouse-produced Stracchini are still made only in winter, but most are now produced all year round.

Culinary Uses

Stracchino should only be eaten as a dessert cheese; it is not suitable for cooking. On Christmas Eve in Lombardy, Robiola is served as a special delicacy with the spicy candied fruit relish, *mostarda di Cremona*.

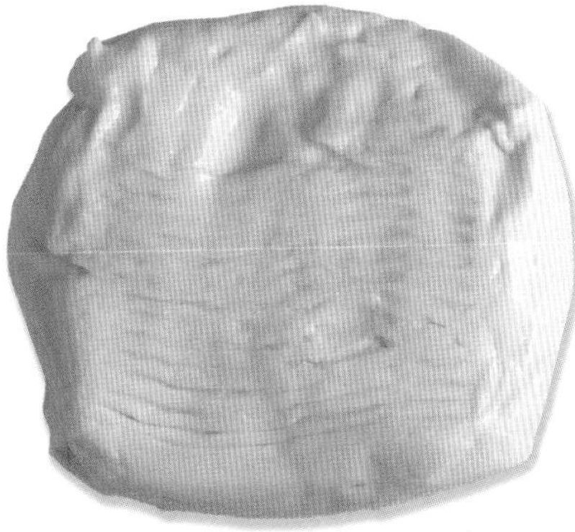

Robiola
This is a small square stracchino and is always wrapped in paper to preserve its freshness

Soft Cheeses

Gorgonzola

The proper name for this famous blue-veined cheese is Stracchino Gorgonzola, because it is made from the curds of stracchino. Originally made only in the town of Gorgonzola, the cheese is now produced all over Lombardy. Gorgonzola is prepared by making alternate layers of hot and cold curds. The difference in temperature causes the layers to separate, leaving air pockets in which the mould (*penicillium glaucum*) will grow. The best Gorgonzola cheeses are left until the mould forms naturally, but more commonly copper wires are inserted into the cheese to encourage the growth. The cheeses are matured from three to five months; the longer the ageing, the stronger the flavour.

Gorgonzola is a very creamy cheese, the colour of buttermilk, with greenish-blue veining and a fat content of 48 per cent. Its flavour can range from very mild (*dolce*) to extremely powerful (*piccante*). The best-known mild version outside Italy is Dolcelatte (sweet milk), which is exceptionally creamy and delicately flavoured. Another version, *torta*, consists of Gorgonzola and mascarpone arranged in alternate layers like a cake.

History

Gorgonzola has been made in the village of the same name since the 1st century AD, when the cheeses were matured in the chilly caves of the Valsassina.

Culinary Uses

Although it is usually eaten as a cheese course, Gorgonzola is also used in cooking, particularly in creamy sauces for vegetables or pasta or as a filling for pancakes and ravioli. It is delicious stirred into soft polenta, or spread on deep-fried polenta *crostini*. Surprisingly, cooking diminishes the flavour of Gorgonzola, so that it does not dominate a delicate dish.

Buying and Storing

Supermarkets sell vacuum-packed portions of Gorgonzola, which are acceptable but not nearly as good as a wedge cut from a whole, foil-wrapped cheese. If you don't like a very strong flavour, be sure to buy Gorgonzola *dolce* or Dolcelatte. Wrapped in clear film, the cheese will keep for several days in the fridge.

Torta
This striped cheese consists of layers of Gorgonzola and mascarpone

Dolcelatte
An exceptionally creamy, delicately flavoured Gorgonzola

Gorgonzola
The greenish-blue veining is typical of this classic cheese

Fresh Cheeses

Caprini

These little disc-shaped goat's cheeses come from southern Italy. They have a pungent flavour, which becomes even stronger as the cheeses mature. Fresh Caprini do not travel well, so you will rarely find them outside Italy, but they are available bottled in olive oil flavoured with herbs and chillies.

Culinary Uses

Fresh goat's cheeses can be fried and served warm with salad leaves as an appetizer, or crumbled over pizzas to make an unusual topping. Bottled Caprini should be drained and eaten as a cheese course. If you like a spicy kick, trickle over some of the oil from the jar, but beware – it will be very piquant.

Caprini
Rarely found fresh outside Italy, these cheeses are usually found bottled in flavoured olive oil

Mascarpone

This delicately flavoured triple cream cheese from Lombardy is too rich to be eaten on its own (it contains 90 per cent fat), but can be used in much the same way as whipped or clotted cream and has a similar texture. Mascarpone is made from the cream of curdled cow's milk. It is mildly acidulated and adds a distinctive richness to risottos and creamy pasta sauces. It takes only 24 hours to produce, so it tastes very fresh, with a unique sweetness that makes it ideal for making desserts. A new lighter version called *fiorello light* is now being produced for the health-conscious. While it is useful for those on a diet, it is nothing like as good as the real thing.

Culinary Uses

In Italy, mascarpone is used for savoury dishes as well as desserts. It makes wonderfully creamy sauces for pasta and combines well with walnuts and artichokes. Mascarpone can also enhance the texture and flavour of risottos or a white bean soup. It is most commonly used in desserts, either served with fresh berries, or as a filling for pastries. It is an essential ingredient of tiramisu and can be churned into a rich, velvety ice cream.

Buying and Storing

Delicatessens in Italy serve fresh mascarpone by the *etto* (about 100 g/ 3½ oz) from large earthenware bowls, but outside Italy it is sold in 250 g/ 9 oz or 500 g/1¼ lb plastic tubs. Although the flavour is not as good, pre-packed cheese will keep for a week in the fridge; fresh mascarpone should be eaten immediately.

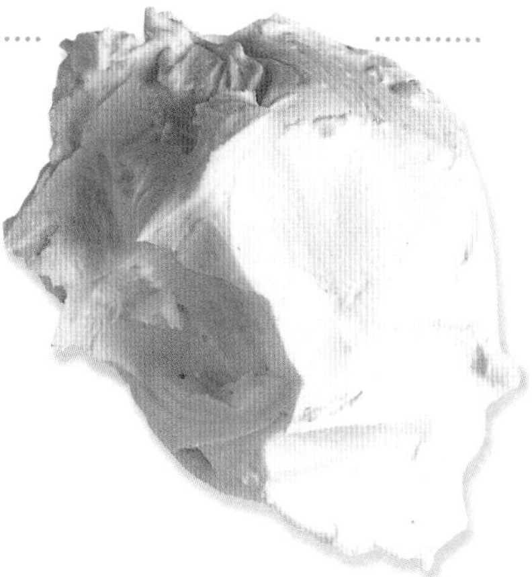

Cook's Tip

To lighten the texture of mascarpone and make it less rich, fold in some beaten egg white.

***Mascarpone* (above and below)**
A triple cream cheese that is too rich to eat on its own, but is ideal for desserts. It is an essential ingredient in tiramisu

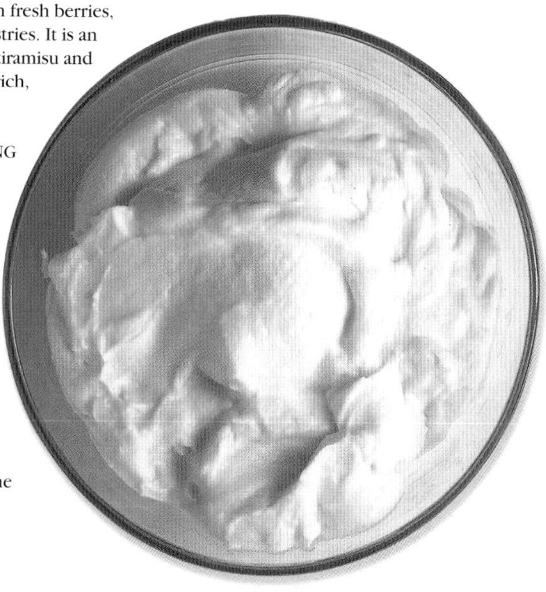

Fresh Cheeses

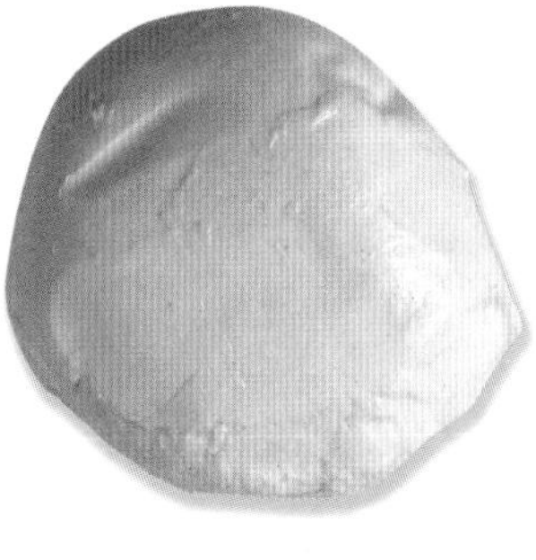

Cow's milk mozzarella
Known as fior di latte *- "flower of the milk"*

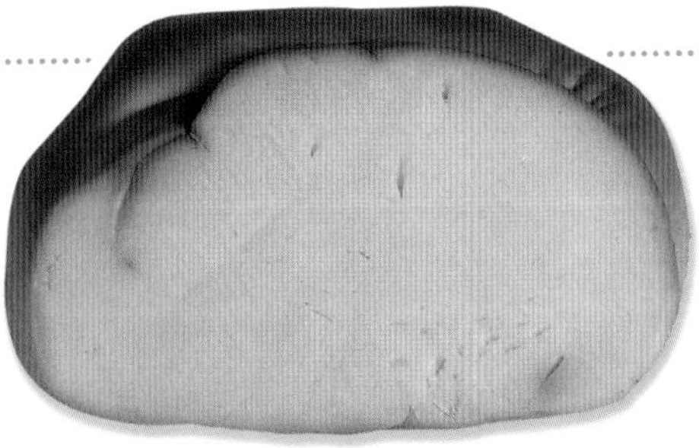

Smoked mozzarella
This cheese has a very smooth texture, a rich golden colour and an interesting smoky flavour

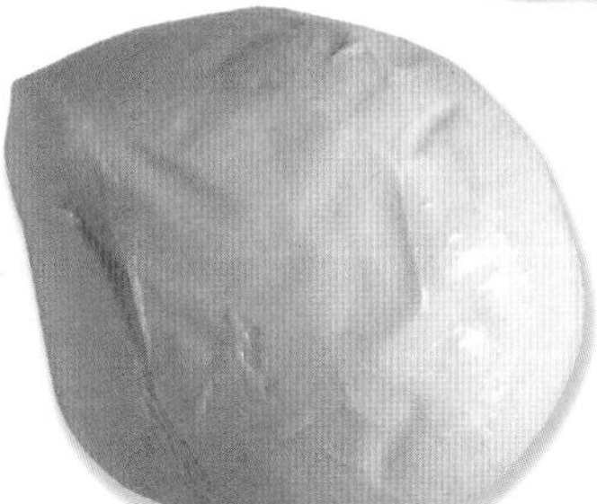

Mozzarella
The best is made from buffalo milk

Mozzarella

Italian cooking could hardly exist without mozzarella, the pure white, egg-shaped fresh cheese, whose melting quality makes it perfect for so many dishes. The best mozzarella is made in the area around Naples, using water buffalo's milk. It has a moist, springy texture and a deliciously milky flavour. The cheeses are made by the *pasta filata* (layering) method, where the curds are cut into strips, then covered with boiling water. As they rise to the surface, they are torn into shreds and scrunched into egg-shaped balls each weighing about 200 g/ 7 oz. These are placed in light brine for 12 hours, then packed in their own whey inside a paper or polythene wrapping to keep them fresh.

Other types of mozzarella include a cow's milk version called *fior di latte* (flower of the milk) and tiny balls of cheese called *bocconcini* (little mouthfuls). Sometimes, the cheese is wound into plaits called *treccie*. All these are fresh cheeses, but mozzarella can also be smoked, which gives it a golden-brown colour and an interesting flavour. You will also find in supermarkets a pale yellow semi-hard mozzarella, which is sometimes sold ready-grated. This is the type used in cheap pizzas; it resembles mozzarella only in name and should be avoided.

History

No one is quite sure when water buffaloes were brought to Italy from India. They may have been introduced by the Greeks or the early Christians; certainly by the 16th century they had become a feature of southern Italian agricultural life. At this time, farmers began to use the buffalo milk to make mozzarella. Its popularity soon spread to the northern regions, where cheese-makers started to produce inferior versions made from cow's milk.

Culinary Uses

Fresh mozzarella is delicious served in an *insalata tricolore*, a salad in the colours of Italy, with white mozzarella, red tomatoes and fresh green basil. Smoked mozzarella is good in sandwiches or as part of an *antipasto*. When cooked, mozzarella becomes uniquely stringy, so it is perfect for topping pizzas or filling *mozzarella in carrozza* (mozzarella in a carriage), sandwiches dipped in beaten egg and deep-fried. A favourite Roman dish is *supplì al telefono*: mozzarella wrapped inside balls of cooked rice and fried until it melts to resemble telephone wires.

Buying and Storing

Cow's milk mozzarella is perfectly adequate for cooking, but for a really fine cheese try to buy *mozzarella di bufala*. Unopened, mozzarella will keep in the fridge for several days, but once the wrapping has been pierced it should be eaten as soon as possible. Opened mozzarella can be kept for a brief time in a covered bowl containing the whey from the bag or, failing that, skimmed milk or lightly salted water.

Mozzarella bocconcini
The name means "little mouthfuls"

Ricotta
Widely used in Italian cooking, ricotta can be combined with spinach for a ravioli filling, or used in desserts, such as cheesecake

Ricotta salata
This hard, salted version of the cheese has a compact, flaky texture and can be used as a substitute for Parmesan or Pecorino

Ricotta

Ricotta derives its name (literally "recooked") from the process of reheating the leftover whey from hard cheeses and adding a little fresh milk to make a soft white curd cheese with a rather solid yet granular consistency and a fat content of only about 20 per cent. The freshly made cheeses are traditionally put into baskets to drain and take their hemispherical shape and markings from these *cestelli* (little baskets).

Commercially produced ricotta is made from cow's milk, but in rural areas ewe's or goat's milk is sometimes used.

Ricotta salata is a hard, salted version of the cheese, made from the whey of Pecorino. It has a compact, flaky texture and looks rather like a hard Pecorino.

Culinary Uses

Ricotta is widely used in Italian cooking for both savoury and sweet dishes. It has an excellent texture but very little intrinsic flavour, so it makes a perfect vehicle for seasonings like black pepper and nutmeg or chopped fresh herbs. In its best-known form, it is puréed with cooked spinach to make a classic filling for ravioli, cannelloni or lasagne, or delicious light gnocchi.

It is often used in desserts, such as baked cheesecakes, or it can be sweetened and served with fruit.

Hard *ricotta salata* can be grated and used as a lower-fat substitute for Parmesan or Pecorino.

Buying and Storing

Fresh ricotta should always be eaten the day it is bought, as it quickly develops a sour taste. Most supermarkets sell a pre-packed version of the cheese, which has a much longer keeping time.

Ricotta salata is sometimes sold in pre-packed wedges, but for a good flavour and texture you should buy it freshly cut from a whole cheese. Tightly wrapped in foil, it will keep in the fridge for up to a month.

Cured Meats & Sausages

Every region of Italy has its own special cured meats and sausages, each differing as widely as the regions themselves. Prosciutto crudo *and* salami *appear in every guise and often constitute an* antipasto *(appetizer) on their own.*

HISTORY

Italy was traditionally an agricultural country, so almost every rural family kept a pig and cured every part of it, from snout to tail, to provide food for the family throughout the year. In any Italian larder, a range of home-cured hams, sausages and bacon would be found hanging from the ceiling. Nowadays hundreds of different types of hams, cured meats and sausages are commercially produced, many still using the old artisanal methods. Wherever you travel in Italy, you will find regional variations on the same theme.

Most of these cured meats are served as an *antipasto* before a meal. A Tuscan *antipasto* will consist of a selection of thinly sliced *affettati* (sliced ham and *salami*), and it is sometimes served with pickled vegetables, which are designed to whet the appetite.

Prosciutto crudo

Italy is famous for its *prosciutto crudo*, salted and air-dried ham that requires no cooking. The most famous of these hams, *prosciutto di Parma*, comes from the area around Parma, where Parmesan cheese is also made. The pigs in this region are fed partly on the whey from the cheese-making process, which makes their flesh very mild and sweet. Because they are always reared and kept in sheds and never allowed to roam outdoors, they tend to be rather fatty. Parma hams are made from the pig's hindquarters, which are lightly salted and air-dried for at least one year (and sometimes up to two). The zone of production of Parma ham is restricted by law to the area between the Taro and Baganza rivers, where the air and humidity levels are ideal for drying and curing the hams. In fact, every year thousands of ready-salted hams are sent here from neighbouring regions to be dried and cured in the unique air around Parma.

Prosciutto di Parma
The most famous Italian ham comes from the area around Parma, where Parmesan is also made

Prosciutto cotto

Italy also produces a range of cooked hams, usually boiled. They can be flavoured with all sorts of herbs and spices. Cooked ham is sometimes served as an *antipasto* together with raw ham, but it is more often eaten in sandwiches and snacks.

San Daniele

Some people regard these hams from the Friuli region as superior even to Parma ham. San Daniele pigs are kept outside, so their flesh is leaner, and their diet of acorns gives it a distinctive flavour. San Daniele is produced in much smaller quantities than Parma ham, which makes it even more expensive.

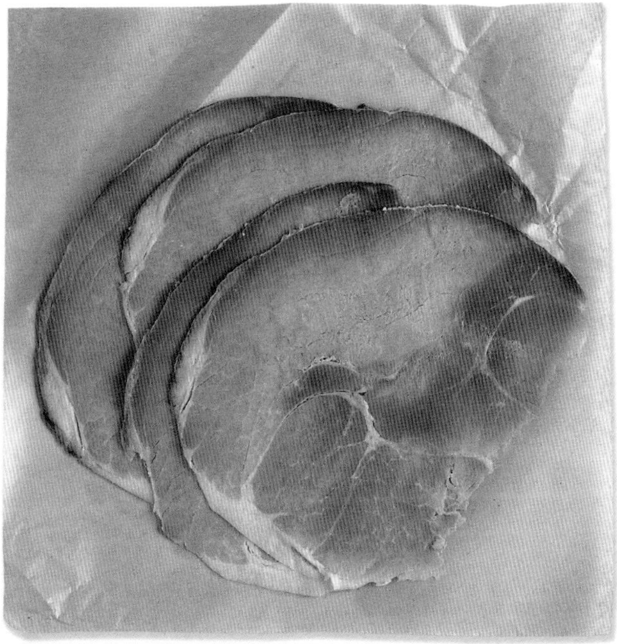

Prosciutto cotto
This cooked ham is sometimes served with sliced cured hams as an antipasto

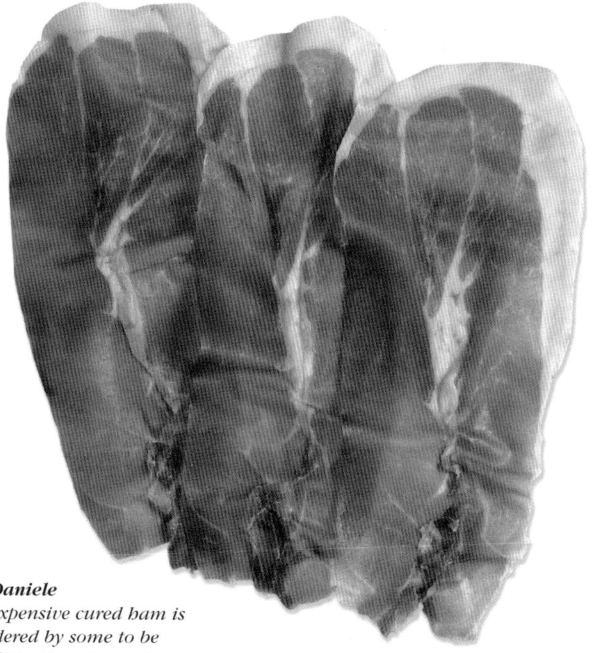

San Daniele
This expensive cured ham is considered by some to be even finer than Parma ham

Culinary Uses

Wafer-thin slices of *prosciutto crudo* are delicious served with melon or fresh figs or, when these are out of season, with little cubes of unsalted butter. If you serve bread with this ham, that too should be unsalted to counterbalance the salty-sweetness of the ham. *Prosciutto crudo* can be rolled up with thin slices of veal and sage leaves and pan-fried in butter and white wine or Marsala to make *saltimbocca alla romana*, finely chopped and added to risotti and pasta sauces, or used as a filling for ravioli.

Buying and Storing

The best part of the ham comes from the centre. Avoid buying the end pieces, which are very salty and rather chewy. Because *prosciutto crudo* should be very thinly sliced, buy only what you need at any one time or it may dry out. Ideally you should eat it on the day it is bought, although it will keep in the fridge for up to three days.

Cured Meats

Pancetta and Lardo

Pancetta resembles unsmoked bacon, except that it is not sold sliced, but rolled up into a sausage shape. It is made from pork belly, which is cured in salt and spices, to give it a mild flavour. *Lardo* is very similar (but flat) and less readily available.

CULINARY USES

Pancetta can be eaten raw as an *antipasto* (although it is very fatty), but it is usually cut into strips and cooked like bacon. It is an essential ingredient for *spaghetti alla carbonara.*

Pancetta
These round rolled slices of cured pork belly are the Italian equivalent of unsmoked bacon

Smoked pancetta
The smoked version of pancetta *is sold in thin strips rather than being rolled*

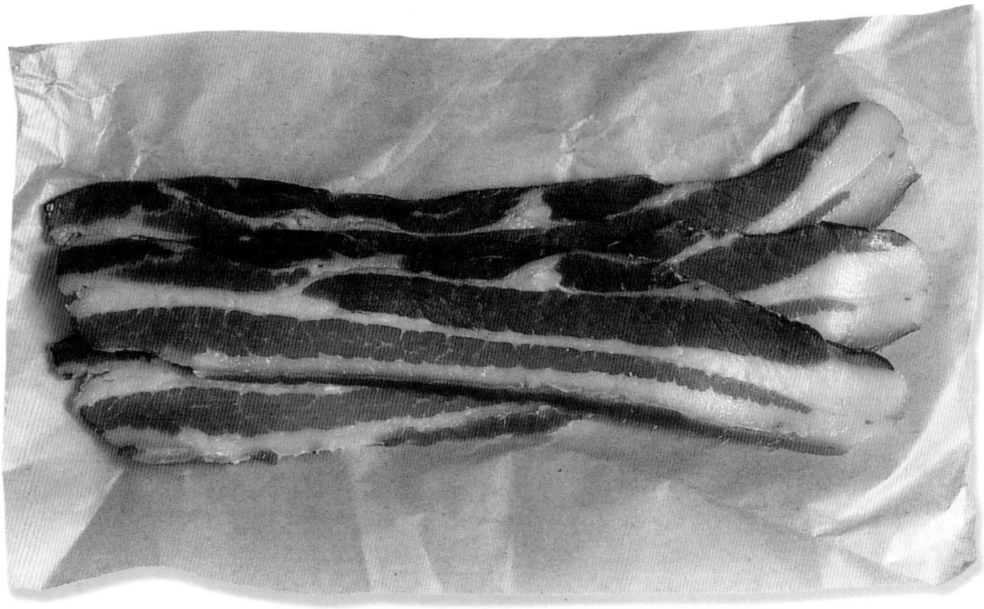

Speck

This fatty bacon is made from pork belly, which is smoke-cured over beechwood with herbs and spices, then air-dried. Sometimes it is covered with peppercorns or dried herbs, which add a distinctive flavour. It comes from the Tyrol, near the Swiss border, which explains its German-sounding name.

Culinary Uses

Speck is too fatty to be eaten raw, but it is used to add flavour to soups, stews and sauces. It is excellent cooked with fresh peas or lentils.

Buying and Storing

Italian bacon is sold in the piece, not sliced. Wrapped in clear film, *pancetta*, *lardo* and *speck* will keep in the fridge for up to one month.

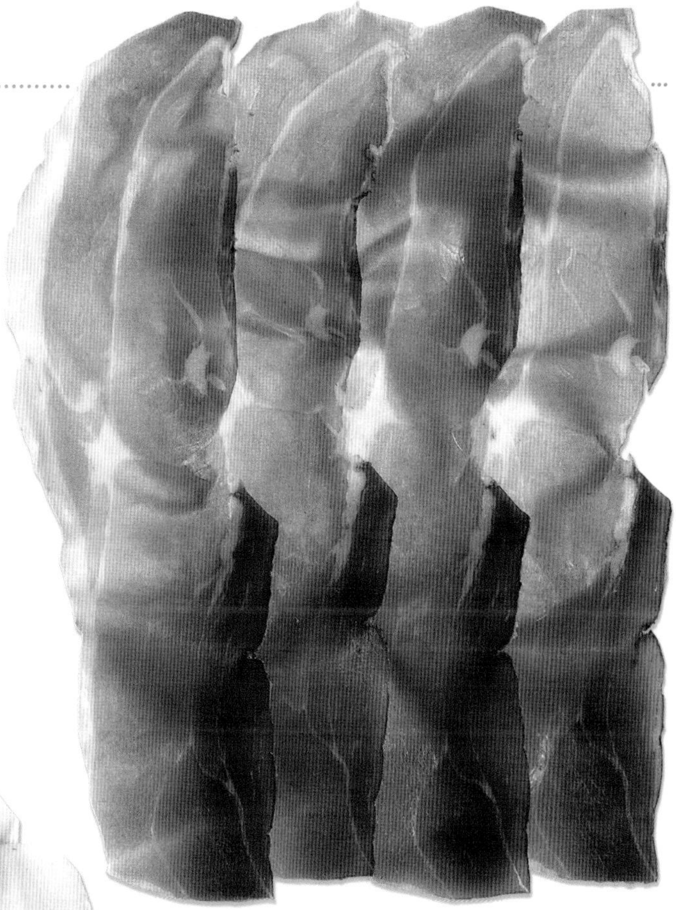

Speck
A fatty ham, smoke-cured over beechwood with herbs and spices, then air-dried

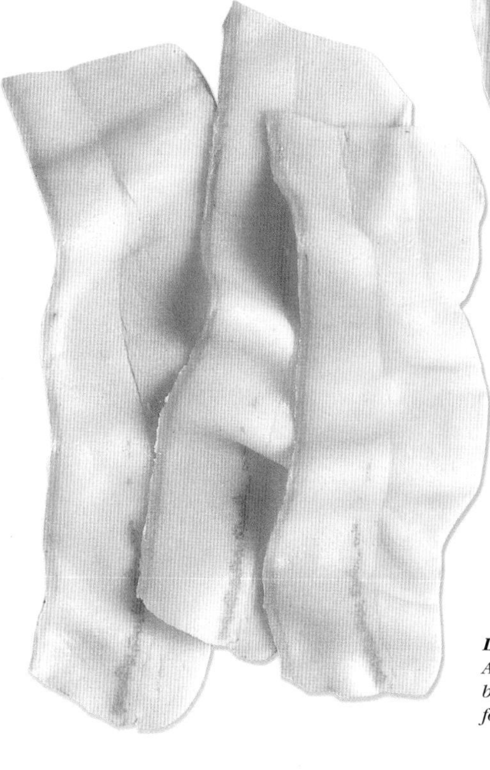

Lardo
An extremely fatty Italian bacon that is always used for cooking

Cured Meats

Bresaola

This cured raw beef is a speciality of Valtellina in Lombardy, but it is eaten and enjoyed all over Italy. It can be made from any cut of beef, but prime fillet produces the best bresaola. It is first cured in salt, then air-dried for many months before being pressed to produce an intensely dark red meat, which resembles *prosciutto crudo* in flavour, but is more delicate and less salty. Like *prosciutto crudo*, it is always sliced wafer-thin and served in small quantities, so you don't need to buy very much. Each bresaola weighs 2-3 kg/4¼-6¼ lb, depending on the size of the original cut of beef.

Culinary Uses

Bresaola is often served as an *antipasto*, sliced very thinly and simply dressed with a drizzle of extra virgin olive oil and a sprinkling of fresh lemon juice. In Lombardy, bresaola is sometimes wrapped around a filling of soft goat's cheese and then rolled up like cannelloni.

Buying and Storing

Only buy bresaola made from beef fillet. You can tell the type from the shape; that made from fillet is long with rounded edges, like the original cut of beef, while the cheaper bresaola made from other leg cuts is pressed into an oblong shape. Use it as soon as possible after slicing, preferably the same day, or it will dry out and develop an unpleasantly sharp flavour.

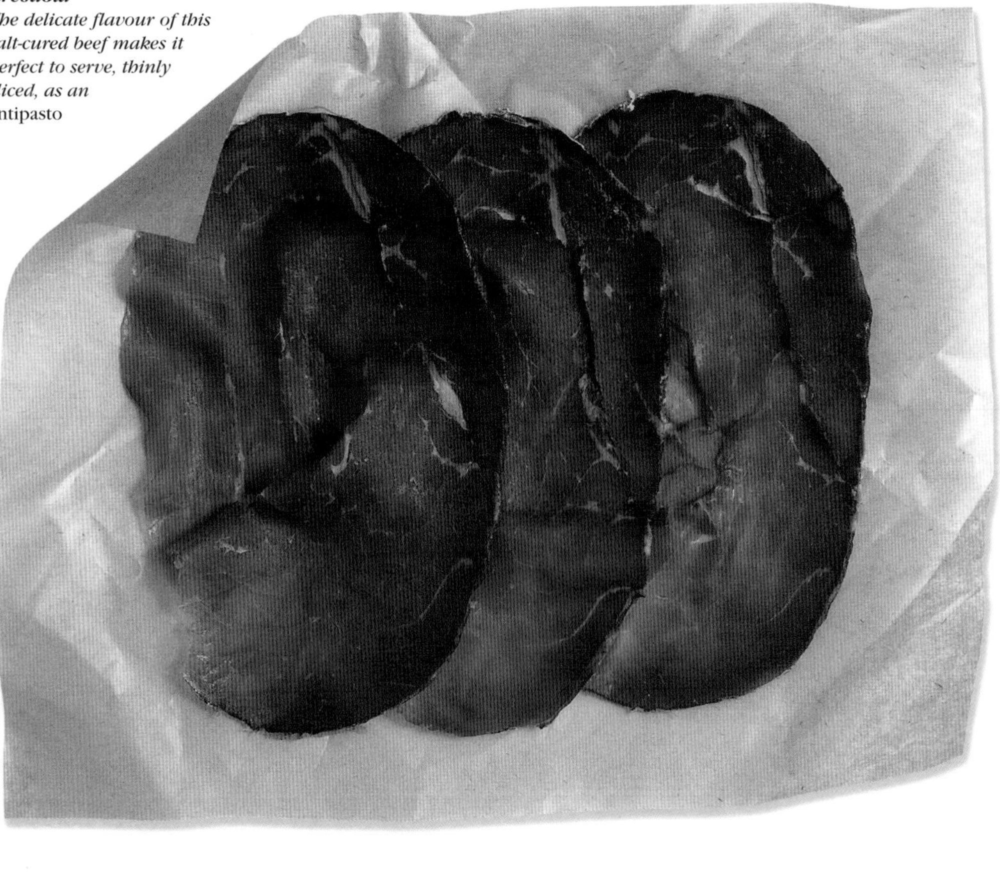

Bresaola
The delicate flavour of this salt-cured beef makes it perfect to serve, thinly sliced, as an antipasto

Sausages

Italy boasts almost as many different sausages as there are towns. Practically all are made with pork, although venison and wild boar sausages are popular in country areas. Most sausages and *salami* are factory-produced nowadays, but many towns in Italy still have *salumerie* (sausage shops) selling home-made sausages flavoured with local produce, such as wild mushrooms or herbs and spices. The most famous sausage-producing town is Bologna. Fresh sausages are made from coarsely chopped pork and contain a high proportion of fat for extra flavour. They are usually sold in links, tied together with string. Most Italian sausages, however, are cured and ready to eat.

Luganega

A speciality of northern Italy, luganega is a mild spiced country sausage made from pork, which often contains Parmesan cheese. Sometimes known as *salsiccia a metro*, because it is sold in a long continuous rope, which is coiled up like a snake, and is sold by the metre or whatever length you require. It can be grilled or pan-fried with white wine and is often served on a bed of lentils or mashed potatoes. Luganega can also be cut into short lengths and stirred into a hearty risotto.

Cotechino

A large fresh pork sausage weighing about 1 kg/2¼ lb, which has been lightly spiced and salted for only a few days. Cotechino is a speciality of Emilia Romagna, Lombardy and the Veneto. It takes its name from *coteca* meaning "skin".

Cooking Cotechino

Cotechino is boiled and served hot, often as part of a bollito misto *(mixed boiled meats). Pierce the skin in several places and place the sausage in a large saucepan. Cover with cold water and bring slowly to the boil, then simmer slowly for 2–3 hours.*

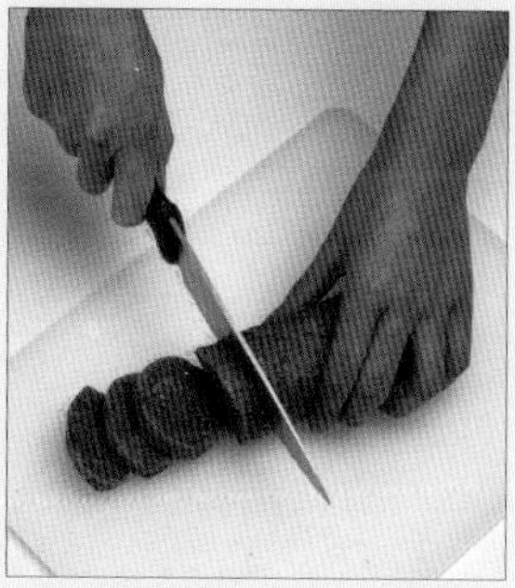

Slice the cotechino thickly and serve on a bed of cooked lentils, mashed potatoes or cannellini beans.

Luganega
This mildly spiced sausage, which is coiled up like a snake, is sold by the metre, or whatever length you require

Sausages

Coppa

This salted and dried sausage is made from neck or shoulder of pork, and the casing is made from natural skin. *Coppa* has a roughly rectangular shape and a rich deep red colour. It comes from Lombardy and Emilia Romagna, although, confusingly, in Rome you will find a *coppa* that is a sort of pig's head brawn (this variety is never exported).

Zampone

This speciality sausage from Modena is a pig's trotter stuffed with minced pork shoulder and other cuts, including some skin. The stuffing has a creamy texture and the skin of the trotter encloses it to retain its original shape, complete with feet. Each zampone weighs up to 2 kg/4¼ lb.

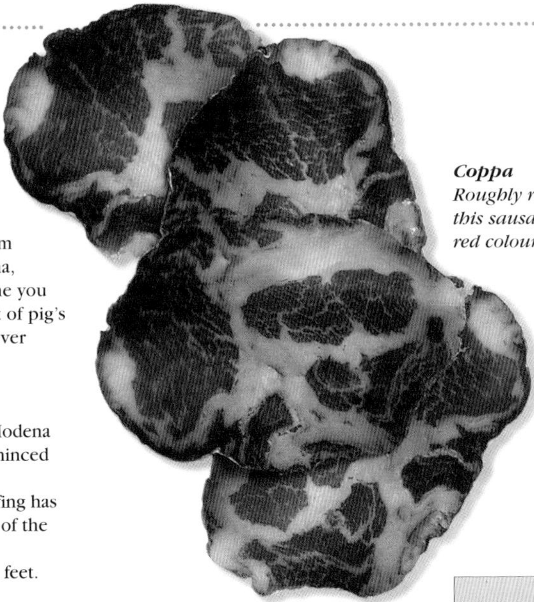

Coppa
Roughly rectangular in shape, this sausage has a rich, deep red colour

Cooking Zampone

A raw zampone needs to be boiled for 2–3 hours, depending on the size, although some vacuum-packed varieties are already part-cooked and need only to be heated through. For a fresh zampone, make a couple of incisions in the skin and cook in the same way as cotechino. Zampone is traditionally sliced into rings and served with lentils or mashed potatoes. A bollito misto *often contains a zampone.*

Zampone
A part-cooked zampone needs only to be heated through

Mortadella

The most famous of all the sausages from Bologna, mortadella is also the largest, often having a diameter of up to 45 cm/18 in. Nowadays it is cooked in hot-air ovens to a core temperature of 72°C/140°F, which means that it will keep for several weeks. It is considered to be the finest Italian pork sausage, with its wonderfully smooth texture, although it has a rather bland flavour. Apart from its huge size, mortadella is distinctive for its delicate, pale pink colour studded with cubes of creamy white fat and sometimes pale green pistachios. It is the original *bologna* or "boloney" so beloved in America.

Buying

Authentic Bolognese mortadella is made only from pure pork, but cheaper varieties may contain all sorts of other ingredients, such as beef, tripe, pig's head, soya flour and artificial colourings.

Beware of mortadella that looks too violently pink and, if you are buying it sliced and pre-packed, check the ingredients on the packet before you buy.

Culinary Uses

Mortadella is usually thinly sliced and eaten cold, either in a sandwich or as part of a plate of assorted cold meats as an *antipasto*. It can also be cubed and stirred into risotti or pasta sauces just before the end of cooking, or finely chopped to make an excellent stuffing for poultry or filled pasta.

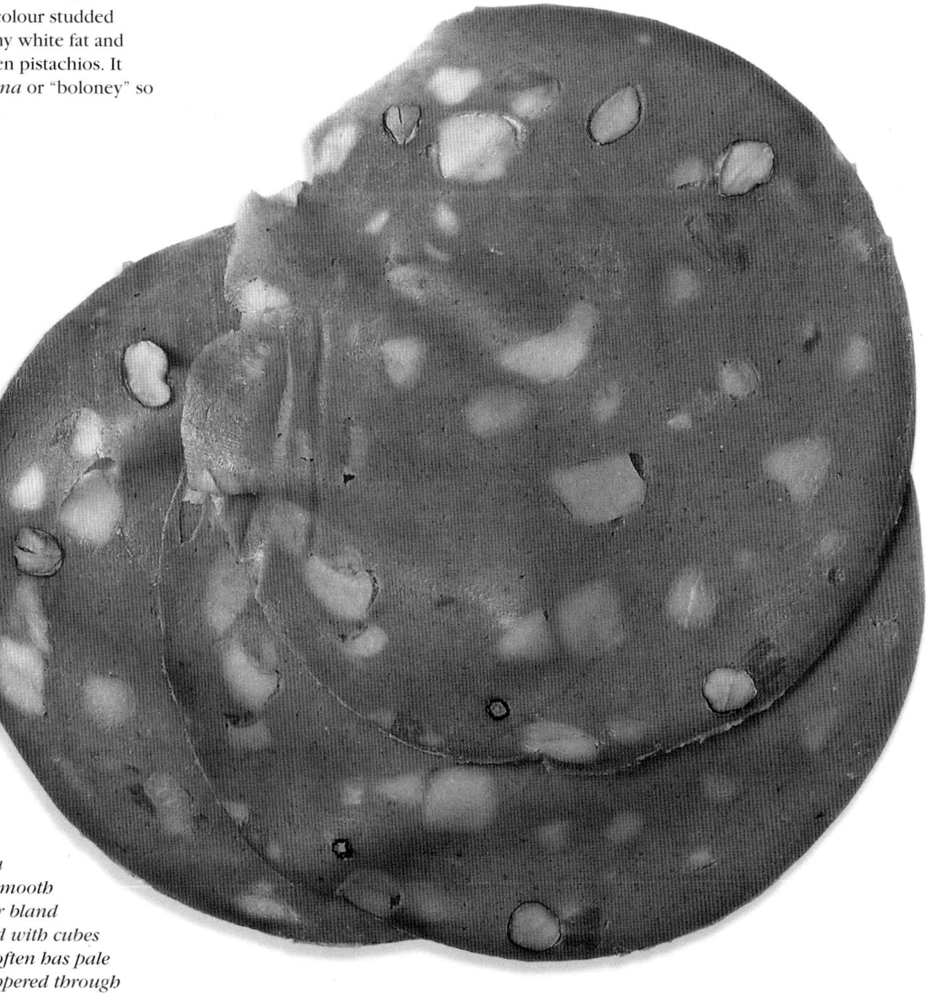

Mortadella
Considered to be the finest Italian cooked sausage, mortadella has a wonderfully smooth texture, but a rather bland flavour. It is studded with cubes of creamy fat, and often has pale green pistachios peppered through the meat

Salami

Salami

There are dozens of types of *salami*, whose texture and flavour reflect the character and traditions of the different regions of Italy. Essentially, all *salami* are made from pure pork, but the finished product varies according to the kind of meat used, the proportion of lean meat to fat, how finely it is minced, the seasonings and the period of drying and seasoning.

Salame di Felino

This soft, coarse-cut sausage comes from Felino near Parma and is regarded as one of the finest Italian *salami*. It has a very high proportion of lean pork to fat and is flavoured with peppercorns, a small amount of garlic and the local white wine. Because it is only very lightly cured, it has a very delicate flavour but does not keep well. You may find it in good Italian delicatessens, where it is easily recognizable by its uneven truncheon shape, which makes it look hand-made. Like its neighbour, Parma ham, *salame di Felino* is very expensive, but well worth the cost.

Salame fiorentina

This large coarse-cut pork sausage from Tuscany is often flavoured with fennel seeds and pepper, when it is known as *finocchiona*. The fennel gives it a very distinctive flavour.

Salame di Felino
One of the finest Italian salame *– this lightly cured sausage is flavoured with peppercorns, garlic and white wine*

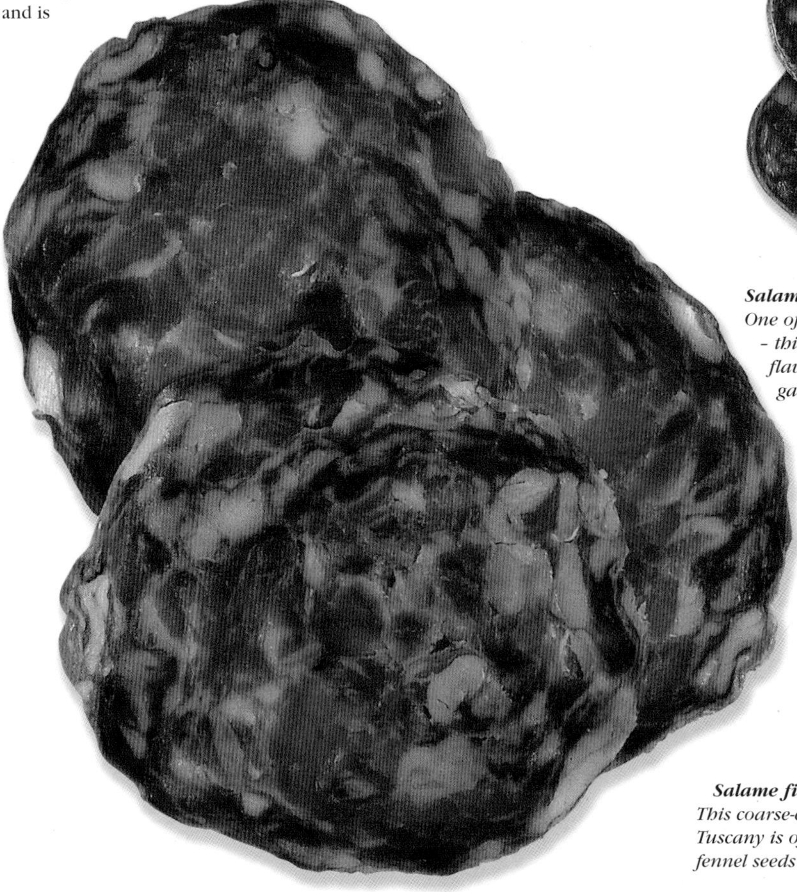

Salame fiorentina
This coarse-cut pork sausage from Tuscany is often flavoured with fennel seeds and pepper

Salame milano

Probably the most commonly found of all *salami*, this Milanese sausage is made from equal quantities of finely minced pork, fat and beef, seasoned with pepper, garlic and white wine. It is deep red in colour and speckled with grains of fat resembling rice. Also known as *crespone*, it is mass-produced and regarded as inferior to most other *salami*. There is also a small whole *salame milanese*, weighing about 500 g/1¼ lb, called *cacciatoro*, which is cured and matured for a much shorter time and has a more delicate flavour and softer texture.

Salame sardo

This fiery red *salame* from Sardinia is a rustic sausage flavoured with red pepper. A similar sausage is *salame napoletano* from Naples, which uses a mixture of black and red pepper for a powerful kick.

Salame ungharese

Despite its name, this *salame* is manufactured in Italy, using a Hungarian recipe. It is made from very finely minced pure pork or pork and beef, and flavoured with paprika, pepper, garlic and white wine. The fat is evenly spread throughout the sausage, giving it a mottled appearance.

Buying and Storing

With the exception of *salame di Felino*, almost all *salami* can be bought ready-sliced and vacuum-packed, but taste much better if they are freshly cut from a whole *salame*. A good delicatessen will slice the *salami* to the thickness you require. Ideally, it should be eaten the same day, but it will keep for three or four days in the fridge.

Salame ungharese
Made in Italy to a Hungarian recipe

Salame sardo
A fiery salame *flavoured with red pepper*

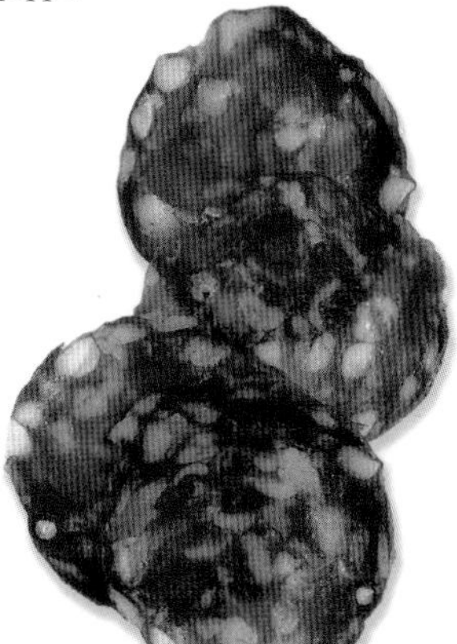

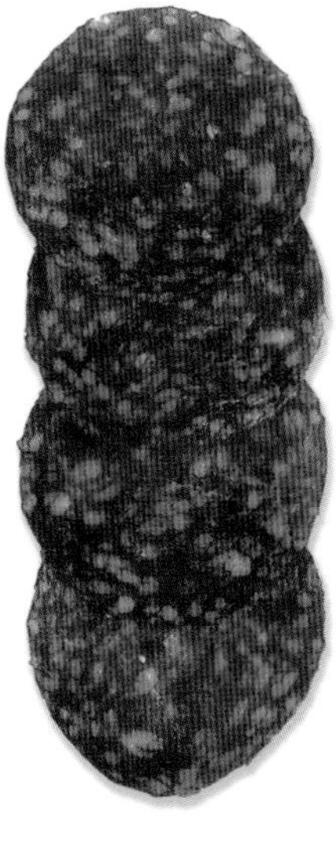

Salame milano

Salame napoletano
Similar to salame sardo, *this* salame *uses a mix of black and red pepper*

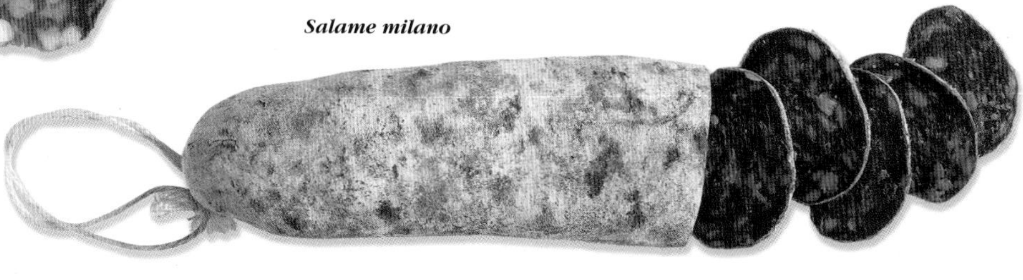

Cacciatoro
This small whole salame milanese *is cured and matured for only a short time*

Meat & Poultry

Until recently, meat did not figure largely in Italian cooking, which relied much more heavily on the peasant staples of pasta, bread, vegetables and, in coastal areas, fish. As the country became more prosperous, however, more people added meat to their daily diet and now animals are farmed all over Italy to provide veal, pork, beef, lamb and kid.

Veal is a favourite meat in Italy and appears in innumerable recipes from every region. The best comes from milk-fed calves that are reared in Piedmont. The area around Rome is famous for its lamb, and spit-roasted suckling lamb and kid are popular specialities of the region. Superb beef cattle are bred in Tuscany, but the beef from other regions comes from working cattle that have reached the end of their useful lives, and is best used for stews and dishes that require long, slow cooking.

Many peasant families in Italy still own a pig, which provides pork as well as a huge variety of hams, sausages and other cured meats. Every part of the pig is eaten in one form or another, from snout to tail. Indeed, Italians never waste any edible part of their meat, so offal of all kinds is used in many dishes. A Tuscan *fritto misto* is composed of a variety of offal ranging from brains to sweetbreads and lungs, while the Milanese version also includes cockscombs - so, unless you are an offal lover, be warned if you see these dishes on a menu!

Poultry is another popular food. Factory farming does exist in Italy, but many flavoursome free-range birds are still available. Chicken, guinea fowl and turkey appear in a huge variety of simple and delicious dishes, usually filleted for quick cooking. Duck and goose make their appearance, too, often cooked with sharp fruits to counteract the richness of the meat. Many recipes use wild duck, shot by the enth-usiastic (some say over-enthusiastic) hunters who abound in every region. Mercifully, the Italian habit of shooting every type of wild bird, whether edible or not, is less prevalent than it was; but hunters are lax about observing a close season for shooting, so game, both feathered and furred, seems to be available almost all year round.

Abbacchio and agnello (lamb)

Lambs are bred mainly in southern Italy, particularly in the area around Rome. They are slaughtered at different ages, resulting in distinctive flavours and texture. The youngest lamb is *abbacchio*, month-old milk-fed lamb from Lazio, whose pale pinkish flesh is meltingly tender. *Abbachio* is usually spit-roasted whole. Spring lamb, aged about four months, is often sold as *abbacchio*. It has darker flesh, which is also very tender and can be used for roasting or grilling. A leg of spring lamb weighs about 1-1.5 kg/ 2¼-3½ lb. Older lamb (*agnello*) has a slightly stronger flavour and is suitable for roasting or stewing.

Lamb cutlets
Allow at least three small, succulent lamb cutlets like these per serving

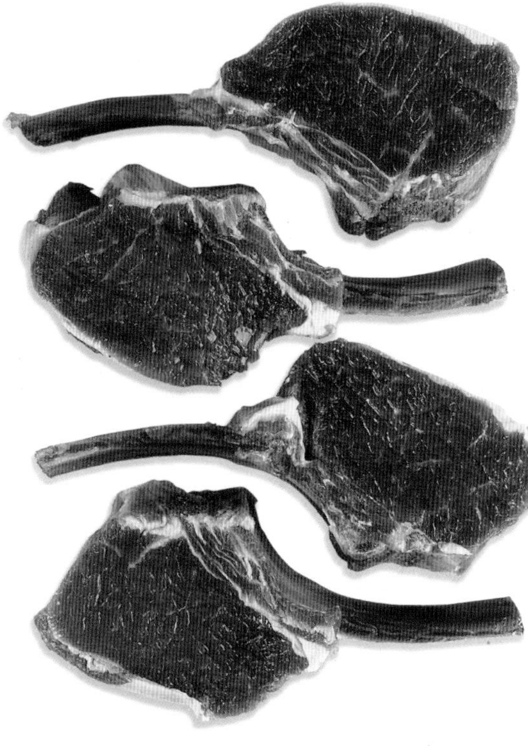

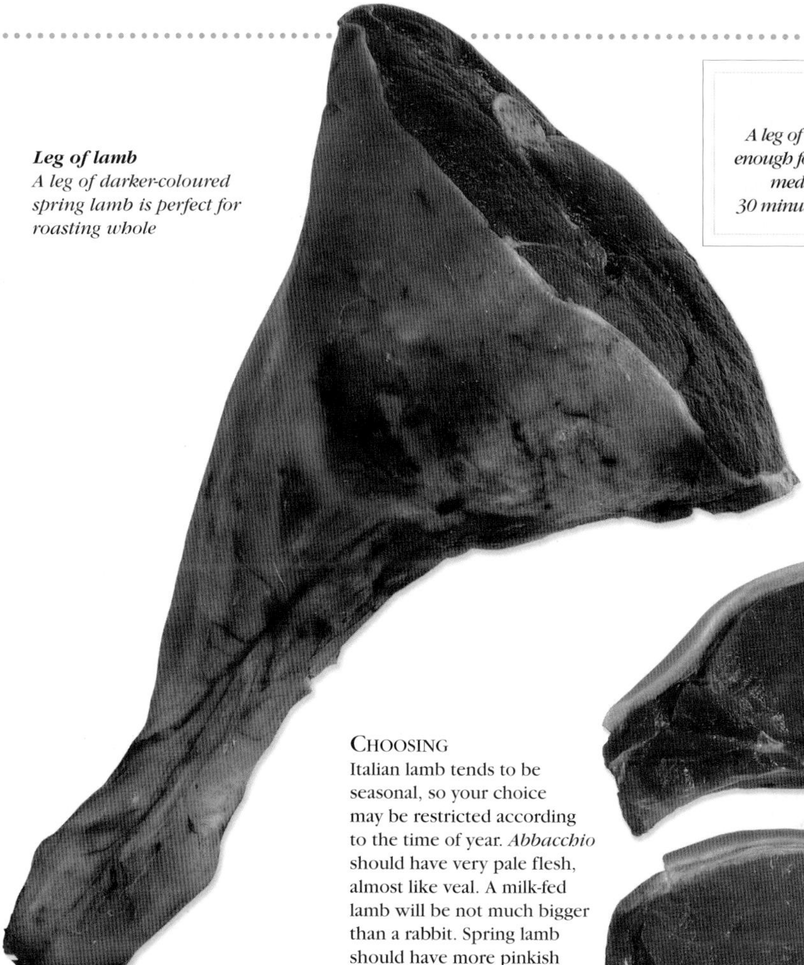

Leg of lamb
A leg of darker-coloured spring lamb is perfect for roasting whole

> **COOK'S TIP**
> *A leg of baby* abbacchio *is only enough for two people. Roast in a medium oven for about 30 minutes, basting occasionally.*

CHOOSING

Italian lamb tends to be seasonal, so your choice may be restricted according to the time of year. *Abbacchio* should have very pale flesh, almost like veal. A milk-fed lamb will be not much bigger than a rabbit. Spring lamb should have more pinkish flesh and very little fat. Mature lamb should have dark red flesh with a layer of creamy fat on the outside.

CULINARY USES

Lamb is cooked in a variety of ways, from *al forno* (roast) to *costolette alla milanese* (fried breaded cutlets). Roast lamb is the traditional Easter dish. It is not cut into thin slices, but served in large chunks, which should be so tender that they fall off the bone. A favourite recipe for spring lamb is *agnello alla giudea* (Jewish-style lamb), braised in a delicate egg and lemon sauce.

Maiale (pork)

Most Italian pork is transformed into sausages, *salami* and hams, but fresh meat is enjoyed all over Italy, often combined with local herbs like rosemary, fennel or sage. Different regions eat different parts of the pig; Tuscany is famous for its *arista di maiale alla fiorentina*, (loin of pork roasted with rosemary), while in Naples *il musso* (the snout) is considered a great delicacy.

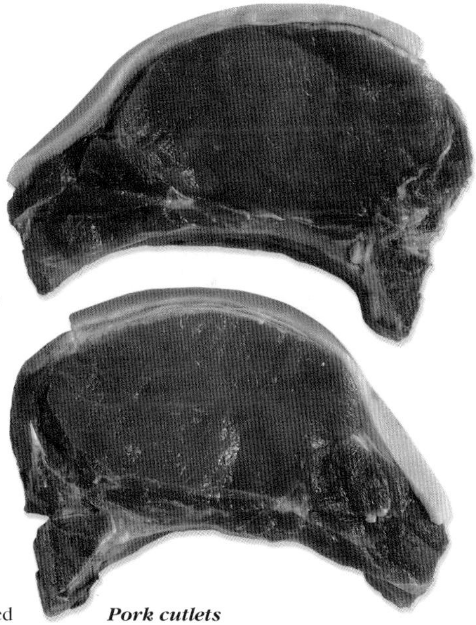

Pork cutlets
Tender chops or cutlets can be grilled or braised with herbs

CULINARY USES

Pork chops or cutlets can be grilled or braised with herbs or artichokes. Loin of pork is deliciously tender braised in milk (*arrosto di maiale al latte*), or it can be roasted with rosemary or sage.

Meat & Poultry

Manzo (beef)

The quality of Italian beef has an unjustifiably poor reputation. It is true that in agricultural areas, particularly the south, beef can be stringy and tough. This is because the cattle are working animals, not bred for the table, and are only eaten towards the end of their hard-working life. This type of beef is only suitable for long, slow-cooked country stews. In Tuscany, however, superb beef cattle from Val di Chiana produce meat that can rival any other world-renowned beef and which provide the magnificent *bistecche alla fiorentina* (T-bone steaks).

CULINARY USES

Thick-cut T-bone steaks (*bistecche alla fiorentina*) from Val di Chiana cattle are grilled over wood fires until well-browned on the outside and very rare inside. Rump or fillet steaks are also cooked very rare and sliced on the bias as a *tagliata*. A modern creation is *carpaccio*, wafer-thin slices of raw beef marinated in olive oil and aromatics and served as an *antipasto*. Thinly sliced topside is rolled around a stuffing to make *involtini* (beef olives). A favourite Italian family dish is *bollito misto*, a mixture of boiled meats and offal including beef. Leftover boiled beef can be sliced and made into a salad.

Less tender cuts of meat are usually braised, stewed or minced to be used in *ragù* (meat sauce) or *polpettone* (meat balls).

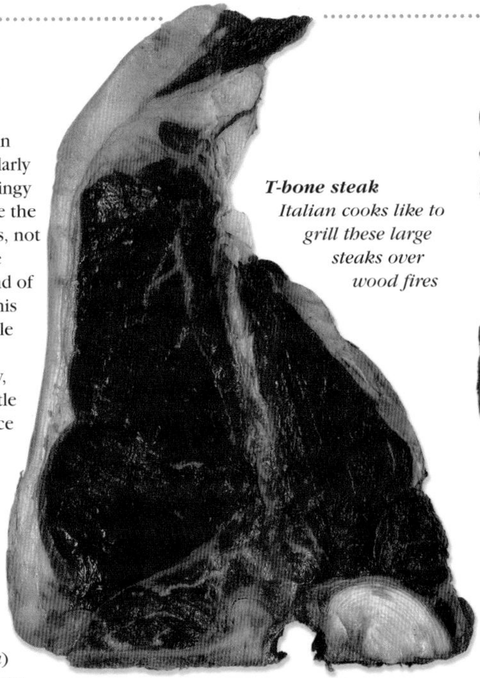

T-bone steak
Italian cooks like to grill these large steaks over wood fires

Beef olives
Thinly sliced topside rolled around a flavourful stuffing

Minced beef
Less tender cuts of beef are minced and used for ragù *(meat sauce) or* polpettone *(meatballs)*

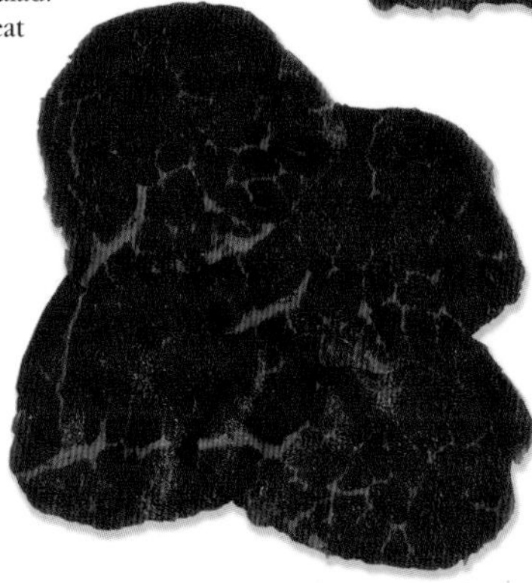

Carpaccio
These wafer-thin slices of raw beef are simply marinated in olive oil and served as an antipasto

Frattaglie (offal)

Nothing is wasted in Italian butchery, so a huge variety of offal is available. Liver is a great favourite; the finest is *fegato di vitello*, tender calf's liver, which is regarded as a luxury. Chicken livers are popular for topping *crostini* or for pasta sauces and pork liver is a speciality of Tuscany. Butchers often sell pig's liver ready-wrapped in natural caul (*rete*), which keeps the liver tender as it cooks. Lamb's and calf's kidneys (*rognoni or rognoncini*), brains (*cervello*) and sweetbreads (*animelle*) are specialities of northern Italy. They are similar in texture and flavour, but sweetbreads are creamier and more delicate. Every region has its own recipes for tripe (*trippa*); this almost always comes from veal calves rather than other cattle, whose tripe has a coarser texture and flavour. All parts of a veal calf are considered great delicacies. The head is used in *bollito misto* (mixed boiled meats), and the trotters give substance to soups and stews. Oxtail (*coda di bue*) comes from older beef cattle.

COOKING OFFAL

Most offal will benefit from being soaked in milk before cooking to remove any coarseness of flavour. Some types, like liver and brains, require very little cooking in order to preserve their delicate texture. In Venice, thinly sliced calf's liver is cooked with onions to make *fegato alla veneziana*; this is often served with grilled polenta. The Milanese version is coated in egg and breadcrumbs and fried in butter. The simplest and one of the most delicious ways with liver is to sauté it quickly in butter with fresh sage. Brains and sweetbreads can be blanched, then quickly fried in butter, or pounded to a paste and made into croquettes (*crocchette*). Kidneys should be sautéed in butter, or braised with wine and onions or Marsala (*trifolati*). Pre-prepared (dressed) tripe will have been scrubbed, soaked and boiled by the butcher, but it should still be blanched for 30 minutes before cooking. Tripe can be prepared *alla fiorentina* in tomato sauce flavoured with oregano or marjoram; the version from Parma (*alla parmigiana*) is fried in butter and topped with Parmesan cheese, while in Bologna, eggs are added to the mixture.

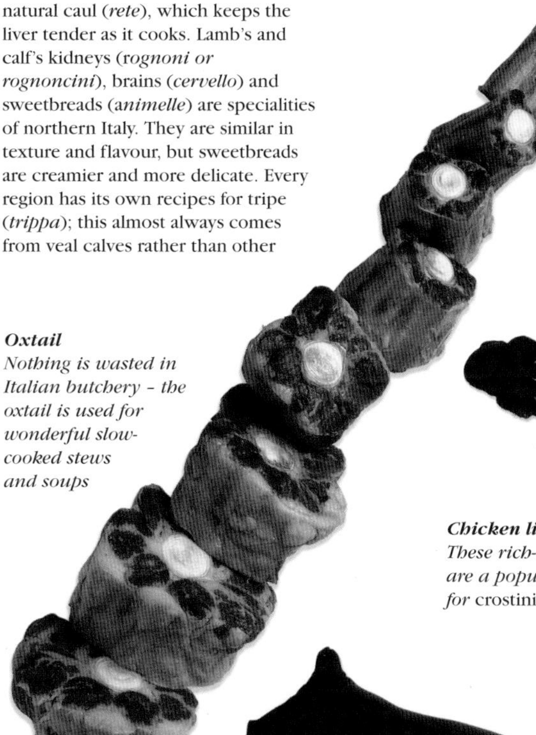

Oxtail
Nothing is wasted in Italian butchery – the oxtail is used for wonderful slow-cooked stews and soups

Chicken livers
These rich-tasting livers are a popular topping for crostini

Pig's liver
This is a speciality of Tuscany

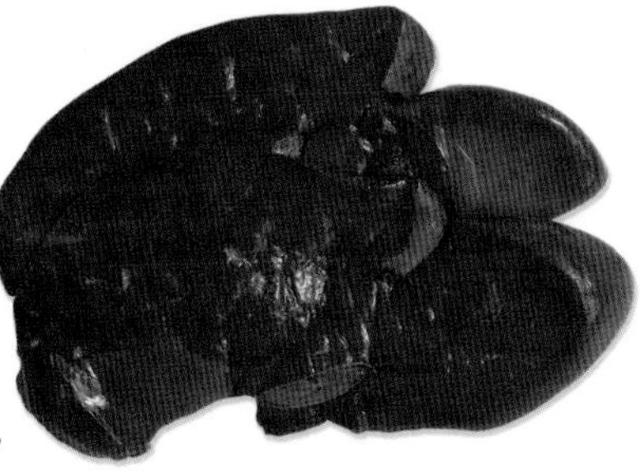

Calf's liver
Thinly sliced, this is often simply pan-fried with onions

Meat & Poultry

Vitello (veal)

Veal is the most popular meat in Italy and appears in hundreds of different recipes. Like lamb, calves are slaughtered at different ages to produce different qualities of meat. The best and most expensive veal is *vitello di latte* from Piedmont and Lombardy. The calves are fed only on milk and are slaughtered at just a few weeks old, producing extremely tender, very pale meat with no fat. Older calves, up to nine months old, are known as *vitello*. Their flesh is still tender, but darker in colour than milk-fed veal. *Vitellone* is somewhere between veal and beef. It comes from bullocks aged between one and three years, which have never worked in the fields and whose flesh is therefore still quite tender and lighter in colour than beef.

Culinary Uses

Young, milk-fed veal is ideal for *scaloppine* (escalopes) and *piccate* (thin escalopes), which need very little cooking. *Vitello* can be served as chops, cutlets or a rolled roast. The shin is cut into *osso buco* (literally "bone with a hole"), complete with bone marrow, or *schinco* (the whole shin), and braised until meltingly tender. An unusual combination which works wonderfully well is *vitello tonnato*, cold roast veal thinly sliced and coated in a rich tuna sauce. *Vitellone* should be treated like tender beef. It can be grilled, roasted or casseroled, but it is not suitable for escalopes or similar cuts.

Choosing

Young veal should have very pale, slightly rosy fine-grained flesh with no trace of fat. *Vitellone* should be pinker and paler than beef, with only a faint marbling of fat, and should feel firm, not flabby. Escalopes and *piccate* must be cut only from very young veal. They should be sliced across the grain so that they keep their shape and do not shrivel during cooking. If you are buying boned veal, ask the butcher to give you the bones, which make wonderful stock.

Veal escalopes
These are always sliced very thinly across the grain

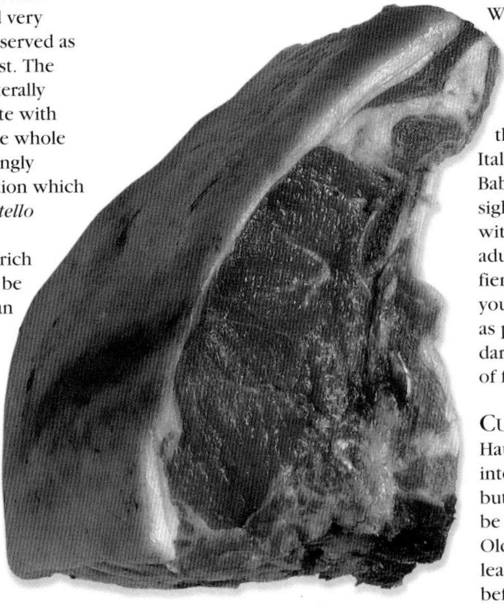

Loin of veal
Usually boned, then roasted with herbs - the bones make the most wonderful stock

Cooking Veal

Escalopes should be pounded lightly, dusted with flour and fried for just a few moments on each side. The pan juices can be mixed with lemon, white wine or Marsala to make a sauce. Very thin escalopes can be rolled around a stuffing and braised in tomato sauce. Cutlets can be coated with egg and breadcrumbs alla milanese *and fried until golden, or seasoned with herbs and gently cooked with white wine.* Costolette alla valdostana *are stuffed with Fontina cheese and fried in butter.*
Loin of veal is usually boned and roasted with herbs, or braised in milk. Less tender cuts like shoulder and breast are casseroled or braised.

Cinghiale (wild boar)

Wild boar are the ancestors of the domestic pig, which used to roam in large numbers in the forests of Tuscany and Sardinia, but which are becoming increasingly rare thanks to the predisposition of some Italians to shoot anything that moves. Baby wild boar are an enchanting sight, with light brown fur striped with horizontal black bands. The adults have coarse, brown coats and fierce-looking tusks. The flesh of a young *cinghiale* is as pale and tender as pork; older animals have very dark flesh, which is tougher but full of flavour.

Culinary Uses

Haunches of wild boar are made into hams, which are displayed in butchers' shops. Young animals can be cooked in the same way as pork. Older boar must be marinated for at least 24 hours to tenderize the meat before roasting or casseroling. The classic sweet and sour sauce, (*agrodolce*), sharpened with red wine vinegar, complements the gamey flavour of the meat.

Coniglio (rabbit) and lepre (hare)

Farmed and wild rabbits often replace chicken or veal in Italian cooking. The meat is very pale and lean and the taste is somewhere between that of good-quality farmhouse chicken and veal. Wild rabbit has a stronger flavour, which combines well with robust flavours; farmed rabbit is very tender and much more delicate.

Hare cannot be farmed, so the only animals available come from the wild. Given the Italian obsession with hunting, it is a miracle that the hare population has not been totally decimated. These wily creatures, however, must sometimes escape the gun, as they continue to breed. A hare weighs about twice as much as a rabbit (2 kg/4¼ lb is about average). The flesh is a rich, dark brown and has a strong gamey flavour similar to that of wild rabbit.

Hare
This is always wild - the rich brown flesh has a strong gamey flavour

Rabbit
This can be bought either farmed or wild - wild rabbit has a stronger flavour

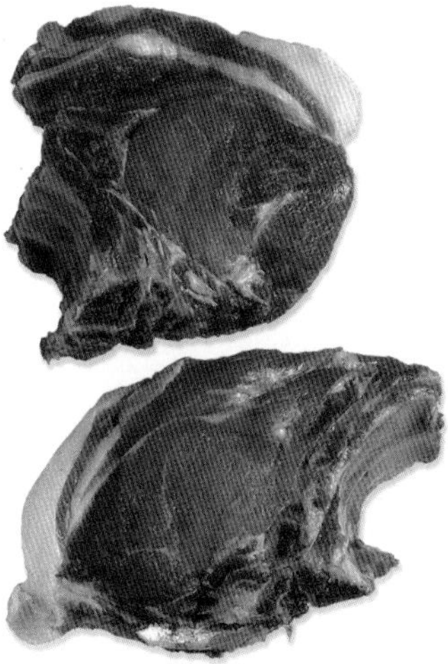

Wild boar
Chops like these can be cooked in the same way as pork

Culinary Uses

Farmed rabbit can replace chicken or turkey in almost any recipe. Wild rabbit can be stewed or braised in white wine or Marsala, or with aubergines, bacon and tomatoes. It can be roasted with root vegetables or fresh herbs. In Sicily, rabbit is often cooked with sultanas and pine nuts in an *agrodolce* (sweet and sour) sauce.

Hare is generally casseroled in red wine or Marsala, cooked *in agrodolce* or made into a rich sauce for pappardelle or other wide noodles. Both rabbit and hare are often served with polenta or fried bread.

Cooking Rabbit and Hare

Wild rabbit and hare must be cut into six or eight pieces and marinated in red wine and aromatics for 24 hours before cooking. If you like a sweet and sour flavour (game in agrodolce *is very popular in Italy), add plenty of red wine vinegar to the marinade. A rabbit weighing about 1 kg/2¼ lb when cleaned will need about 1½ hour's braising or stewing; a hare needs about 2 hours.*

Meat & Poultry

Fagiano (pheasant)

Occasionally in the Italian countryside, you may still catch a glimpse of a pheasant with its beautiful plumage and long tail feathers. Cock pheasants have bright, iridescent blue and green feathers, while hens are browner and less dramatic-looking. Pheasant farming is still unknown in Italy, and wild pheasants are something of a rarity, so they are regarded as a luxury. They are not hung, but are eaten almost as soon as they are shot, so their flavour is less gamey than in some other countries. Although pheasants are expensive, they are meaty birds for their size, so a cock pheasant will feed three to four people and a hen pheasant two to three.

Culinary Uses

Hen pheasants are smaller than cocks, but their meat is juicier and the flavour is finer. Young hen pheasants can be roasted with or without a stuffing, but cock birds are more suitable for casseroling. Pheasant breast can tend to be dry, so they should be well barded with bacon or thickly smeared with butter before roasting. A good knob of butter placed inside the cavity will help to keep the flesh moist. For special occasions, pheasants can be stuffed with candied fruits or pomegranate seeds and nuts. Pheasant breasts can be sautéed and served with a wine or balsamic vinegar sauce, but they can sometimes be rather dry.

Pheasant
Usually eaten as soon as they are shot, Italian pheasants are less gamey than in some other countries. Remember that pheasants contain lead shot pellets, so take care not to bite on these!

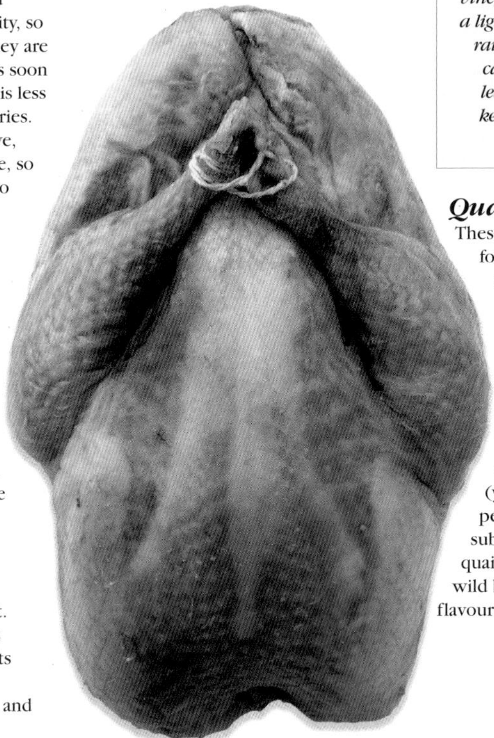

Cooking Quail

Quail should be browned in butter until golden all over, then roasted in a hot oven for about 15 minutes. Their flavour is well complemented by the fruit of the vine, so they are often served with a light sauce containing grapes or raisins soaked in grappa. They can also be wrapped in vine leaves before roasting, which keeps them moist and adds a delicious flavour.

Quaglie (quail)

These small migratory birds are found in Italy throughout the summer months. Wild quails have the reputation of being so stupid that they never run away from hunters, but stay rooted to the spot as sitting targets. As a result, they have become very rare, and most of the birds now available are farmed. They are very small (you need two to serve one person) and have a delicate, subtly gamey flavour. Farmed quails have less flavour than the wild birds and benefit from added flavourings, such as grapes.

Quail
These birds have a very delicate, gamey flavour. They are very small, and so you will need to serve two per person.

Cooking Pheasants

Unless you know for sure that a pheasant is very young, it is best to wrap the breast in streaky bacon before roasting to prevent dryness. To roast a pheasant, put a knob of butter inside the cavity, or make a stuffing, drape bacon rashers over the breast and roast at 200 °C/400 °F/Gas 6 for about 40 minutes, until tender. Plain roast pheasant is often served with a risotto. Pheasant can also be pot-roasted or casseroled with wine and herbs. If you are serving cock birds, it is worth removing the lower part of the legs after cooking, as they contain hard sinews that are not pleasant to eat.

Faraona (guinea fowl)

Guinea fowl are extremely decorative birds with luxuriant grey-and-white spotted plumage. They originated in West Africa, but are now farmed all over Europe, so that, although they are technically game, they are classified as poultry. They taste similar to chicken, but have a firmer texture and a more robust flavour.

Cooking Guinea Fowl

Although their abundant plumage makes them seem larger, guinea fowl are only about the size of a small spring chicken, so one bird will not feed more than three people. To roast guinea fowl, bard the breasts with bacon rashers and roast like chicken, basting frequently. A vegetable stuffing will keep the flesh moist. Guinea fowl can be substituted for chicken or turkey in any recipe.

Culinary Uses

Guinea fowl are hugely popular in Italy, where they are served in much the same ways as chicken. The flesh of an adult guinea fowl is firmer than that of a chicken, so it is best to bard it or cover the breasts with bacon rashers before roasting. The breasts are sometimes sautéed and served with the pan juices mixed with balsamic vinegar, or with a sauce of cream and Marsala. The birds can be roasted or pot-roasted whole, or cut into serving pieces and casseroled with mushrooms (wild mushrooms are especially delicious) or herbs. A favourite autumn dish in Tuscany is guinea fowl braised with chestnuts.

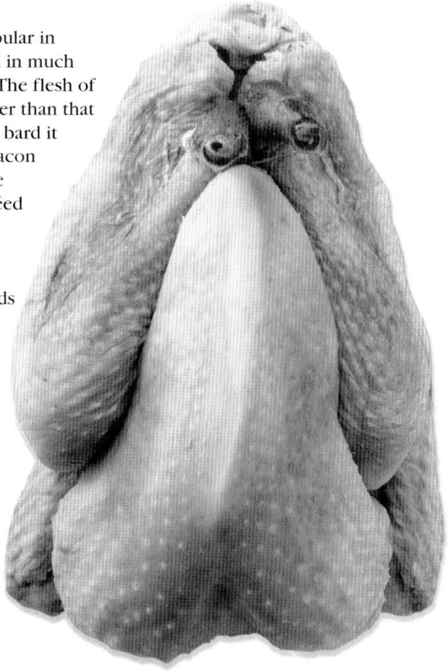

Guinea fowl
These popular birds can be pot-roasted, roasted or casseroled with wild mushrooms

Piccione (pigeon)

Wood pigeons have dark, gamey flesh and a robust flavour, which the Italians love. They are generally too tough to roast, but they make the most delicious casseroles. Domestic pigeons are also reared for food and you will often see large dovecotes in farmyards. Domestic birds are less likely to be tough than wild ones, but their flavour is less robust.

Wild pigeon
Italians love the rich, robust flavour of these small birds; however, they can be very tough, so cook them very slowly, either by braising or casseroling

Cooking Pigeons

Wild pigeons can be tough, so, unless you are sure that they are young, it is best to casserole them. In Tuscany, they are braised with tomatoes and olives; the classic Venetian way is to stew them with pancetta, *ox tongue and fresh green peas. If you desperately want to roast wild pigeons, marinate them in a red wine marinade for three days before cooking, then stuff them with a moist vegetable stuffing. Cover the breasts with streaky bacon and roast in a hot oven for about 20 minutes, basting with the marinade every few minutes.*

Fish & Shellfish

Italy's extensive coastal waters once teemed with a huge variety of fish and shellfish, many unique to that part of the Adriatic and Mediterranean. Sadly, pollution and over-fishing have taken their toll, and there is no longer the abundance of seafood there once was, but what remains is of excellent quality. A visit to an Italian fish market will reveal fish and shellfish of every description, some beautiful, some hideous, many unknown outside Italy. Italians like their seafood very fresh and tend to cook it simply, without elaborate sauces. Large fish are usually plainly grilled or baked and dressed with olive oil, or baked in cartoccio *(enclosed in a paper bag). Small fry are deep-fried for a crisp* fritto misto di mare. *Every coastal area has its own version of fish soup, which uses a mixture of local fish and constitutes a meal in itself -* cacciucco *from Livorno, cold* burrida *from Sardinia,* brodetto *from the Adriatic coast - each region claims that its version is the best.*

It is impossible to give a complete list of all the fish that you will find in Italy. Popular favourites include *coda di rospo* (monkfish), *dentice* (dentex - a white-fleshed fish found only in Italy), *sogliola* (sole) and even non-indigenous fish such as salmon.

Freshwater fish - trout, perch, carp and eels - abound in the lakes and rivers and are eaten with gusto. Eels are regarded as a particular delicacy and are cooked in many different ways, from grilling to baking, stewing and frying.

Some fish are dried, salted or preserved in oil. The most popular is tuna, which is packed in olive oil and sold by weight from huge cans. *Baccalà* is salted dried cod, which is creamed to a rich paste or made into soups and stews. Anchovies are salted, or packed in olive oil, or preserved in a sweet and sour marinade. Sardines are also very popular and are used to make a Sicilian pasta sauce.

Anchovies
Canned in olive oil (above) or salted (left) - these tiny, strong-tasting fish are used to add flavour to pasta sauces and salads

Salt cod *(baccalà)*
This dried fish is creamed to a paste or made into soups and stews

Choosing Fresh Fish

You can almost guarantee that any fish you buy in an Italian early morning market will be ultra-fresh, but in fishmongers and restaurants you should look for pointers. Fish should have bright, slightly bulging eyes and shiny, faintly slimy skin. Open up the gills to check that they are clear red or dark pink and prod the fish lightly to check that the flesh is springy. All fish should have only a faint, pleasant smell; you can tell a stale fish a mile off by its disagreeable odour.

Orata (gilt-head sea bream)

This Mediterranean fish takes its name from the crescent-shaped golden mark on its domed head and the gold spots on each cheek. It has beautiful silvery scales and slightly coarse but delicious flaky white flesh. Orate usually weigh between 600 g/1 lb 6 oz and 1 kg/2¼ lb; a larger fish will serve two greedy people. Orata is best simply grilled, baked *in cartoccio* or barbecued.

Pesce spada (swordfish)

In Italy, you will occasionally find a whole swordfish on the fishmonger's slab. These huge Mediterranean fish, up to 5 metres/15 feet long and weighing 100–500 kg/220–1200 lb, are immediately recognizable by their long sword-like upper jaw. Because of their size, they are more usually sold cut into steaks. Their firm, close-grained, almost meaty flesh has given them a nickname of "steak of the sea".

Cooking Swordfish

Swordfish tends to be dry, so it should be marinated in oil and lemon juice or wine and herbs before cooking. It is excellent grilled or barbecued, or part-cooked in butter or olive oil, then baked in a sauce. Its firm texture makes it ideal for kebabs. It is plentiful in the waters around Sicily, where it is cooked with traditional Mediterranean ingredients like tomatoes, olives, capers, sultanas and pine nuts. Another popular Sicilian dish is bracciole di pesce spada, *thin slices of swordfish rolled around a stuffing of breadcrumbs, mozzarella and herbs and grilled. It is also delicious sliced wafer-thin, marinated in olive oil, lemon juice and herbs and served raw.*

Swordfish
Often either baked or grilled, this firm-fleshed fish needs to be marinated to keep it moist during cooking

Tuna
Immensely popular throughout Italy, canned tuna in oil is either sold by weight from huge cans or bought in small cans like these

Fish

Sarde or sardelle (sardines)

Fresh sardines probably take their name from Sardinia, where they were once abundant. These small, silvery fish are still found in Mediterranean waters, where they grow to about 13 cm/5 in. They are at their best in spring. Allow about four larger sardines or six smaller fish per serving. Sardines have very oily flesh and should only be eaten when extremely fresh. They can also be bought preserved in oil or salt.

Sardines
These fresh fish are at their best in the spring

Preparing and Cooking Sardines

Sardines should be gutted before cooking. If the fishmonger has not already done this, cut the head almost through to the backbone and pull it off; the gut will come away with the head.

Sardines can be barbecued, grilled or baked alla genovese *with potatoes, garlic and parsley. Their oily flesh combines well with spices and tart ingredients like capers and olives. In Sicily they are stuffed with breadcrumbs, pine nuts, sultanas and anchovies and fried, then finished in the oven (a* beccaficcu*). Sardines can also be deep-fried, either plain or stuffed with mushrooms, herbs and cheese (*alla ligure*) or with chopped spinach and cream (*alla romana*).*

Spigola or branzino (sea bass)

The silvery sea bass, which come from Mediterranean waters, are as beautiful to look at as to eat, although their rapacious nature has earned them the nickname of "sea wolf". These slim, elegant fish are almost always sold whole and rarely weigh much more than 1 kg/2¼ lb, so one fish will feed no more than two or three people. Sea bass is prized for its delicate white flesh and lack of irritating small bones. As a result, it is never cheap.

One way of bringing the price down is to farm sea bass, but the flavour of the farmed fish is not so fine as that of wild sea bass, whose predatory habits ensure that their flesh develops a full flavour. So far, farming of these wonderful fish does not seem to have caught on in Italy, where flavour is rarely compromised for cost.

Preparing and Cooking Sea Bass

Sea bass should be gutted before cooking. They have quite hard scales, which should be removed before grilling or pan-frying. Scale the fish with a de-scaler or blunt knife, working from the tail towards the head. If you are going to poach or bake sea bass, leave the scales on, as they will hold the fragile flesh together.

Sea bass has rather soft flesh, so it is best grilled, barbecued or pan-fried and dressed with a trickle of olive oil. It can be stuffed with sprigs of fresh herbs (fennel is particularly good) and baked in the oven for 20–30 minutes, depending on the size of the fish. For spigola alla livornese*, lay the fish in an ovenproof dish on a layer of rich tomato sauce, sprinkle with seasoned breadcrumbs and olive oil and bake.*

Triglia (red mullet)

These small Mediterranean fish rarely weigh more than 1 kg/2¼ lb. They have bright rose-coloured skin and a faint golden streak along their sides. Their flesh is succulent with a distinctive, almost prawn-like flavour, quite unlike any other fish. The liver of red mullet is regarded as a great delicacy and is not removed during cooking, which gives the mullet its nickname of "sea woodcock". Red mullet are extremely perishable and should be eaten the day they are bought. The skin should always look very bright; dullness is a sure indication that the fish is not fresh.

Preparing and Cooking Red Mullet

Larger fish should be scaled before cooking, but be warned - this is a delicate operation, as the skin is very fragile. Scaling is worth the effort, however, as it reveals the wonderful red skin in all its glory. Red mullet combines well with traditional Mediterranean flavours of olive oil, black olives, herbs, garlic, saffron and tomatoes. It can be baked, grilled or cooked in cartoccio *with powerful herbs like rosemary or fennel. For* triglia all'italiana, *place whole red mullet on a bed of finely chopped mushrooms and onions that have been sweated until soft and mixed with fresh breadcrumbs, and bake for 20 -30 minutes.*

Red mullet
The flesh of these pretty fish has a distinctive almost prawn-like flavour

Sea bass
Prized for their delicate white flesh, these slim, elegant fish are almost always sold whole

Shellfish

Italian coastal waters are host to a huge variety of shellfish and crustaceans, many with wonderfully exotic names like *datteri di mare* (sea dates; a kind of mussel), *tartufi di mare* (sea truffles; a type of clam) and *fragolino di mare* (sea strawberry; a tiny octopus that turns bright pink when cooked). Almost all seafood is considered edible, from clams to *cannolichi* (razor-shells), *lumache di mare* (sea snails) and *canestrelli* (small scallops). Shrimps and prawns come in all sizes and colours, from vibrant red to pale grey, while crustaceans range from bright orange crawfish to blue-black lobsters.

Cooking Squid and Cuttlefish

Small squid and cuttlefish should be cooked only briefly – just until they turn opaque – or they will become rubbery and tough. Larger specimens need long, slow cooking to make them tender. They can be stuffed with minced fish or meat, anchovies and seasoned breadcrumbs or rice, and baked with tomatoes and wine sauce until tender, or cut into rings and fried in a light batter, or simply dusted with seasoned plain flour and deep-fried. Squid and cuttlefish are also delicious stewed in their own ink; seal the molluscs in hot oil with some chopped onions and garlic, add finely chopped fresh parsley and seasoning, then cover with dry white wine and a little water and simmer gently for 15 minutes. Crush the ink sacs, mix the inky liquid with a little cold water and 30 – 45 ml/ 2–3 tbsp plain flour and work to a smooth paste. Add the flour mixture to the pan and cook for another 5–10 minutes.

Squid
Large specimens like this one need long, slow cooking to make them tender – conversely small baby squid should be cooked very quickly or they will become tough

Calamari or totani (squid) and seppie (cuttlefish)

Despite their appearance, squid and cuttlefish are actually molluscs, whose shell is located inside the body. They are indistinguishable in taste, but cuttlefish have a larger head and a wider body with stubbier tentacles. The cuttlebone much beloved of budgerigars and parrots is the bone of the cuttlefish inside the body. Once this has been removed, cuttlefish are very tender. The "shell" of a squid is nothing more than a long, thin, transparent quill. Both *seppie* and *calamari* have ten tentacles.

Squid and cuttlefish are immensely popular in Italy, cut into rings and served as part of either an *insalata di mare* (seafood salad) or *fritto misto* (mixed fried fish). Their black ink is used to flavour and colour risotto and fresh pasta.

Preparing and Cooking Mussels

Scrub the shells under cold running water. Pull away the "beard" protruding from the shell. Give any open mussels a sharp tap; they should close immediately. Discard any which do not, as they are probably dead. The simplest way to cook mussels is alla marinara. *For 4 people, finely chop 1 large onion, 2 garlic cloves and 15 ml/1 tbsp chopped parsley, put in a large pan with 300 ml/10 fl oz/2¼ cups white wine and simmer for 5 minutes. Add the scrubbed mussels, cover and steam, shaking the pan from time to time, for 5 minutes, or until the shells have opened. Discard any unopened mussels, sprinkle the rest with extra parsley and serve. For a richer sauce, transfer the mussels to a bowl and reduce the sauce over a high heat. Pour over the shellfish and serve.*

Preparing Squid

You can usually buy squid ready cleaned, but failing that, it is easy to prepare it yourself. Hold the body in one hand and the head in the other, and pull away the head gently but firmly. The soft entrails will come away cleanly. Cut off the tentacles and remove the dark ink sac from the head.

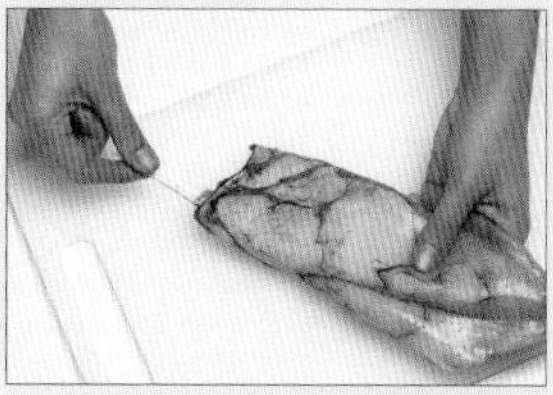

Pull out the transparent quill and rinse the body inside and out. Peel off the purplish membrane. Unless the squid are tiny enough to serve whole, cut the body into 5 mm/ ¼ in rings and the tentacles into manageable pieces.

Polipi *(octopus)*

These are much larger than squid and have only eight tentacles. Their ink sac is not located in the head but in their liver, and the ink has a strong, pungent taste. Octopuses look and taste similar to squid, but need a good deal of preparation. They must be pounded (99 times, some say) to tenderize them before they are subjected to very long, slow cooking.

If you can find very small octopuses, they can be cooked in the same way as squid, but otherwise it is less trouble to substitute squid or cuttlefish.

Octopus
When small, these can be cooked like squid

Cozze *(mussels)*

Mussels, with their smooth texture and sweet flavour, make an attractive addition to many pasta and fish dishes. Pollution in the Mediterranean had threatened the indigenous mussel population, but nowadays most Italian mussels are farmed by the *bouchot* method, on ropes attached to long stakes set in pure seawater, which keeps the molluscs clean and healthy and free from grit and sand. In Italian fish markets on the Adriatic coast, you may find small sweet local mussels with different names like *peoci* or *datteri di mare*. These can be prepared in the same way as other mussels.

Choosing

Mussels, are sold by the litre in Italy, and are very inexpensive. Because the shells constitute so much of the weight, allow at least 500 ml/ generous 1 pint/2½ cups mussels per serving. Choose those which feel heavy for their size and discard any with broken shells. Use mussels the day they are gathered or bought.

Mussels
Steamed mussels combine well with black fettuccine or tagliatelle

Culinary Uses

Once mussels have been steamed open, they can be served with a garlicky tomato sauce, or baked on the half shell with garlic butter or a breadcrumb topping. For *cozze gratinate al forno*, lay the mussels on the bottom shells in an ovenproof dish, sprinkle lavishly with breadcrumbs seasoned with garlic and parsley and drizzle with olive oil. Bake in a hot oven for 10 minutes.

Shelled cooked mussels are combined with prawns and squid for an *insalata di mare* (seafood salad), or used as a pizza topping, while mussels in the shell are often mixed with other seafood and pasta for dishes like *spaghetti allo scoglio* ("spaghetti of the rock").

Shellfish

Gamberetti, gamberelli and gamberoni *(shrimps, prawns and scampi)*

There are so many different varieties of shrimps and prawns in Italian coastal waters that it is almost impossible to recognize them all. The smallest are the *gamberetti*, small pink or brown shrimps which are usually boiled and served simply dressed with olive oil and lemon juice as part of an *antipasto*. Next in size come the *gamberelli*, pink prawns with a delicate flavour. These are the prawns that are most commonly used in a *fritto misto di mare* (mixed fried seafood). *Gamberi rossi* are the larger variety of prawn, which turn bright red when they are cooked. They are highly prized for their fine, strong flavour, and are eaten plainly cooked and dipped into a bowl of *maionese* (mayonnaise). Best (and most expensive) of all are *gamberoni*, large succulent prawns from the Adriatic, which have a superb flavour and texture. Similar to these is the *cicala*, which resembles a small flattish lobster.

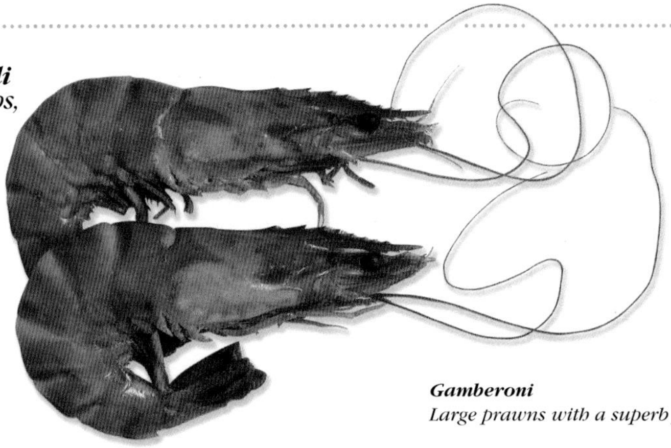

Gamberoni
Large prawns with a superb flavour

Cooking Shrimps, Prawns and Scampi

Whatever the size, all types of shrimps and prawns can be cooked briefly in boiling salted water (sea water, if possible) until they turn pink. Shrimps will take only 1-2 minutes, large prawns and scampi up to 5 minutes. The robust flavour of prawns makes them ideal for serving in a rich tomato or cream sauce or with rice. Shell them after cooking.
To grill gamberoni, *rub the shells with olive oil and coarse salt and grill over charcoal or on a grilling pan, turning them frequently. When they turn opaque, slit them through the underside and open them out flat like a butterfly. Brush the underside with oil and grill until just cooked.*
Peeled prawns and scampi can be pan-fried in olive oil flavoured with garlic and/or chilli, parsley and capers; or coated in batter or egg and breadcrumbs and deep-fried.

Gamberi rossi
These large prawns turn bright red when cooked

Preparing Shrimps, Prawns and Scampi

Shrimps, prawns and scampi should be de-veined before or after cooking. Pull off the heads, shell the tails and pick out the black thread-like intestine with a knife tip.

Choosing

Almost all the shrimps and prawns you buy in Italy are sold uncooked. They should have bright shells that feel firm; if they look limp or smell of ammonia, do not buy them.

Culinary Uses

Shrimps and prawns are extremely versatile and can be used in a wide variety of dishes. Small shrimps are served as *antipasti*, either on their own, or as a stuffing for tomatoes. They can be added to risotto and pasta dishes or seafood sauces.

Prawns combine well with almost any other seafood. They are usually included in an *insalata di mare* (seafood salad) or *fritto misto di mare* (mixed fried seafood). They make a fine *antipasto* added to an *insalata russa* (Russian salad) or served with haricot beans dressed with extra virgin olive oil. They combine well with a spicy tomato sauce or mushrooms, and can be used for seafood casseroles. Large prawns and scampi can be skewered or split and grilled, or boiled and served with mayonnaise or lemon.

Gamberetti
These small pink shrimps are delicious simply dressed with olive oil and lemon juice

Vongole (clams)

There are almost as many different types of clam as there are regions in Italy, ranging from tiny smooth-shelled *arselle* or *vongole* to long thin razor shells and the large Venus clams with beautiful ridged shells called *tartufi di mare* ("sea truffles"). All have a sweet flavour and a slightly chewy texture. Because they vary so much in size, it is best to ask the fishmonger how many clams you will need for a particular dish.

Clams
These smooth-shelled vongole *are often steamed and served as part of a seafood salad*

Preparing and Cooking Clams

Their habit of burying themselves in the sand makes clams rather gritty, so they should be left in fresh water for an hour or so to open up and disgorge the sand inside the shells. To open large clams, either use an oyster knife, or put them in a medium oven for a few minutes until they gape open.

Clams can be served raw like oysters, or cooked in exactly the same way as mussels (see page 70). The cooking time depends on the size of the clams; tiny specimens take only a minute or two. Steamed shelled clams are often served as part of an insalata di mare *or in a risotto. Miniature clams in their shells are stewed with olive oil, garlic and parsley and served with their juices (*in bianco*) or in a tomato sauce (*in rosso*) for* spaghetti alle vongole, *or served on fried bread as* crostini. *Large varieties can be pan-fried with lemon and parsley, or stuffed with seasoned breadcrumbs and grilled or baked.*

Vegetables

Vegetables have always played a very important role in Italian cooking, particularly in the south of the country, where meat was a luxury that few could afford. They are most often served as dishes in their own right, rather than accompaniments, and the range of imaginative vegetable recipes from all over Italy seems infinite.

One of the great joys of Italy is shopping at the markets, where an astonishing range of seasonal vegetables is on offer, from asparagus, beans and *cavolo nero* from the north to aubergines, peppers and courgettes from Calabria and Sicily. In spring and summer, you will find at least ten different varieties of salad leaves, and you will be overwhelmed by the aroma of freshly picked local tomatoes still on the vine. Italians almost never buy imported or out-of-season vegetables, but prefer to purchase fresh seasonal produce bursting with flavour.

Asparagi (asparagus)

Asparagus has been grown commercially in north-eastern Italy for over 300 years and is still highly prized as a luxury vegetable. It has a short growing season from April to early June and is really only worth eating during this period. Both green and white asparagus are cultivated in Italy; the green variety is grown above ground so that the entire spear is bright green. They are harvested when they are about 15 cm/6 in high. The fat white spears with their pale yellow tips are grown under mounds of soil to protect them from the light, and harvested almost as soon as the tips appear above the soil to retain their pale colour. Both varieties have a delicious fresh grassy flavour.

White asparagus
This variety is grown under mounds of earth to retain the pale colour

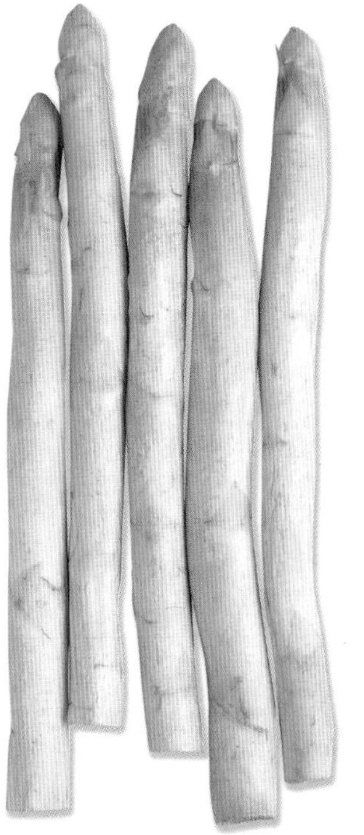

Green asparagus
Enjoyed by Italians, simply boiled or roasted in olive oil

Culinary Uses

In spring, Italians enjoy young asparagus spears simply boiled, steamed or roasted in olive oil and served as a *primo* (first course) with butter and freshly grated Parmesan. For an extra treat, they add a fried egg and dip the asparagus tips into the creamy yolk. When served as a vegetable accompaniment, asparagus can be crisply fried in egg and breadcrumbs. The tips also make a luxury addition to risotto.

Buying and Storing

Asparagus starts to lose its flavour as soon as it has been cut, so be sure to buy only the freshest spears. The best guide is the tips, which should be firm and tight. If they are drooping and open, the asparagus is past its best. The stalks should be straight and fresh-looking, not yellowed and wizened or very woody at the base. Allow about eight medium spears per serving as a first course and always buy spears of uniform thickness so that they cook evenly. Asparagus will keep in the vegetable drawer of the fridge for two or three days.

Preparing and Cooking Asparagus

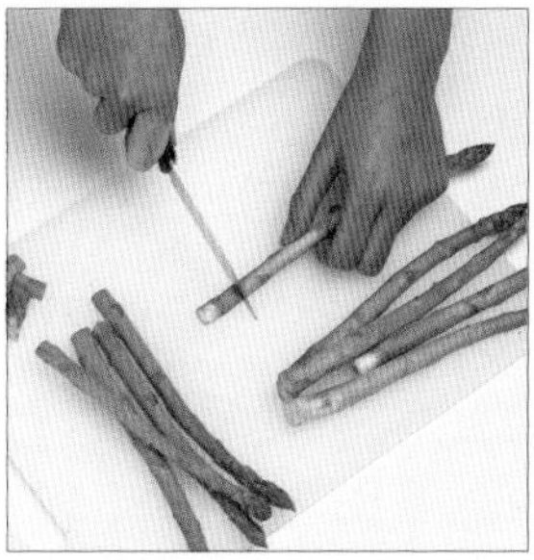

Freshly cut garden asparagus needs no trimming, but cut off at least 2 cm/¾ in from the bottom of the stalks of bought spears until the exposed end looks fresh and moist. Peel the lower half with a potato peeler. (You need not do this for very thin stalks.)

Boiling asparagus can be problematical, since the stalks take longer to cook than the tips. The ideal solution is to use a special asparagus kettle, so as to immerse the stalks in boiling water whilst steaming the tips.

Asparagus can equally well be stood upright in a deep pan of boiling water, tented with foil and cooked for 5 - 8 minutes, until tender but still al dente. *Alternatively, steam the spears in a vegetable steamer. Serve with a drizzle of extra virgin olive oil or melted butter.*

Asparagus can also be successfully microwaved. Wash the spears and lay them in an oval dish in a single layer with the tips all pointing the same way. You do not need added water. Cover tightly with microwave cling film and cook on full power for 5 minutes per 500 g/1¼ lb. If the spears are not quite done, turn them over and cook for a little longer.

To roast asparagus, heat some olive oil in a roasting pan, turn the spears in the oil, then roast in a hot oven for 5–10 minutes.

To fry, roll the spears in beaten egg and fine dried breadcrumbs, then fry them a few at a time in very hot olive oil until crusty and golden. Drain on absorbent paper and sprinkle with sea salt.

Cardi (cardoons)

Cardoons are related to artichokes, but only the leaf-stalks are eaten. They are commercially grown in mounds of soil to keep them creamy white, but in the wild, the stalks are pale green and hairy and can grow to an enormous size. The tough outer stalks are always discarded, and only the inner stalks and hearts are eaten. Cardoons are a popular winter vegetable in Italy and can be found in the markets ready-trimmed.

Culinary Uses

Cardoons can be eaten raw as a salad, or cooked in a variety of ways - fried, puréed or boiled and served with melted butter or a rich cream and Parmesan sauce. They are traditionally used as a vegetable to dip into the hot anchovy and garlic fondue known as *bagna cauda*.

Buying and Storing

Cardoons bought in the market will have been trimmed of their outer stalks and are sold with a crown of leaves, rather like large heads of celery. The stalks should be plump and creamy-white and not too hairy. Wrapped in a plastic bag, they will keep in the vegetable drawer of the fridge for two or three days.

Preparing and Cooking Cardoons

Cut off the roots and peel the stalks with a potato peeler to remove the stringy fibres. Cut the stalks into 5 cm/2½ in lengths and the hearts into wedges, and drop into acidulated water to prevent discoloration. Blanch in boiling salted water, then simmer or fry gently in butter until tender. To serve in a sauce, put the blanched cardoons in an ovenproof dish, cover with sauce, sprinkle with grated Parmesan and bake in a very hot oven until browned.

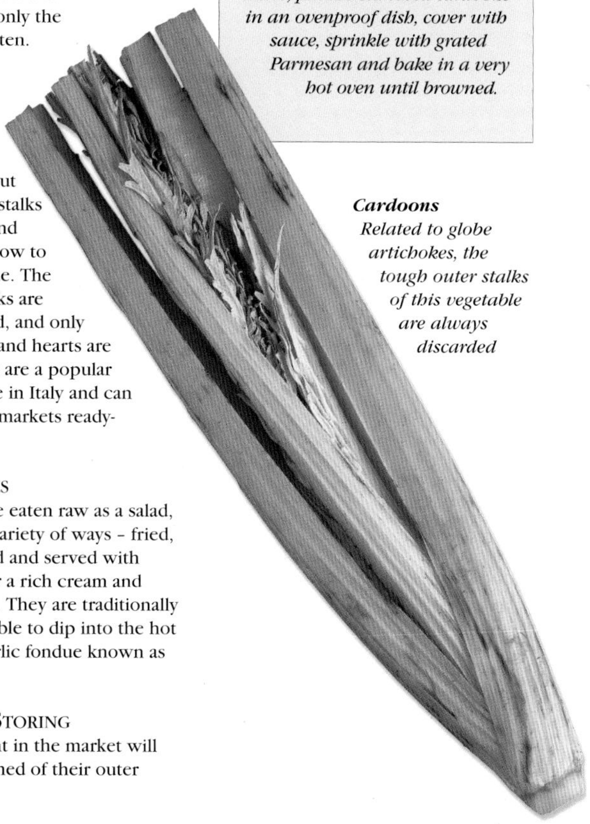

Cardoons
Related to globe artichokes, the tough outer stalks of this vegetable are always discarded

Vegetables

Carciofi (globe artichokes)

As their appearance suggests, artichokes are a type of thistle. Originating from Sicily, where they grow almost wild, they are cultivated throughout Italy and are a particular speciality of Roman cooking. The artichoke itself is actually the flower bud of the large, silvery-leaved plant. There are many different varieties, from tiny purple plants with tapered leaves, which are so tender that they can be eaten raw, to large bright or pale green globes, whose leaves are pulled off one by one and the succulent flesh at the base stripped off with your teeth.

History

Although artichokes have always grown like weeds in Sicily, they were first cultivated near Naples in the 15th century. Their popularity spread to Florence, where they became a favourite dish of the Medici family. They were believed to have powerful aphrodisiac properties and women were often forbidden to eat them!

Culinary Uses

Tiny tender artichokes can be quartered and eaten raw or braised *alla romana* with olive oil, parsley and garlic. Large specimens can be served boiled with a dressing to dip the leaves into, or stuffed with savoury fillings. They can be cut into wedges, dipped in batter and deep-fried. A favourite Italian dish is the ancient Jewish recipe *carciofi alla giudea*, where the artichokes are flattened out and deep-fried twice, so that the outside is very crisp while the inside remains meltingly moist.

Buying and Storing

Artichokes are available almost all year round, but they are at their best in summer. Whichever variety you are buying, look for tightly packed leaves (open leaves indicate that they are too mature) and a very fresh colour. When an artichoke is old, the tips of the leaves will turn brown. If possible, buy artichokes still attached to their stems; they will keep fresher and the peeled, cooked stems are often as delicious as the artichoke itself.

Artichokes will keep fresh for several days if you place the stalks in water like a bunch of flowers. If they have no stalks, wrap them in clear film and keep in the vegetable drawer of the fridge for a day or two.

Preparing and Cooking Globe Artichokes

Tiny tender artichokes can be quartered and eaten raw.

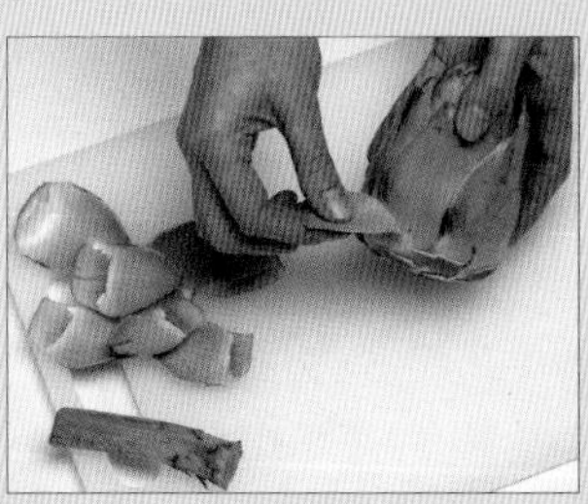

For large artichokes, snap off the stalk and pull off the tough outer leaves. Rub the cut surfaces with lemon juice to prevent discoloration and keep the prepared artichokes in a bowl of acidulated water until ready to cook.

Boil large whole artichokes for about 30 minutes, until the outer leaves can be pulled off easily.

Drain them upside-down, then pull out the centre leaves and scoop out the inedible hairy choke with a spoon before serving. For stuffed artichokes, remove the choke before cooking and fill the cavity with your chosen stuffing. Braise them in olive oil and water, or invert them on to an ovenproof dish, pour over a mixture of olive oil and water, cover with foil and bake in the oven at 190°C/375°F/ Gas 5 for about 1 hour.

Very small artichokes should be quartered and boiled, braised or stewed until tender. The chokes are so soft that the artichokes can be eaten in their entirety.

Globe artichokes
These popular vegetables are actually the flower bud of a type of large thistle

Cavolo (cabbage)

Cabbage is an essential ingredient of many Italian hearty winter soups. Three main types are used; *cavolo verza* (curly-leaved savoy cabbage), which is used in Milanese dishes, *cavolo cappuccio* (round white or red cabbage) and the speciality of Tuscany, *cavolo nero*, a tall leafy cabbage whose name means "black cabbage", but which is actually dark purplish green.

Culinary Uses

Italians rarely eat cabbage as a vegetable accompaniment, but prefer to include it in hearty soups, such as *ribollita* or minestrone, or to stuff and braise the outer leaves and serve them as a main course.

Buying and Storing

Cabbage heads should be solid and firm, with fresh, unyellowed leaves. It is best to buy them complete with their outer leaves; not only are these tasty for cooking, but they protect the hearts and give a good indication of the freshness of the cabbages. A cabbage will keep in the vegetable drawer of the fridge for up to a week.

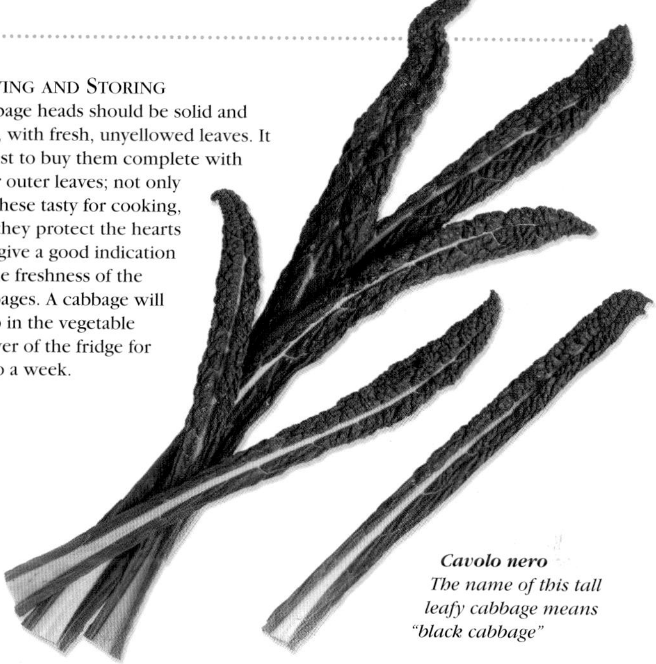

Cavolo nero
The name of this tall leafy cabbage means "black cabbage"

Red and white cabbage
The red variety is often cooked gently with apples and spices to serve with rich meats, while the white variety is added to soups and stews

Savoy cabbage
This curly-leaved cabbage is used in Milanese dishes

Preparing and Cooking Cabbage

Cut off the outer leaves and stalk, cutting out a cone-shaped section of the stalk from the inside of the cabbage. To use the leaves for stuffing, blanch them in boiling water for about 3 minutes, until malleable. For soups and braised dishes, coarsely shred the cabbage and wash it well.

Cabbage can be cooked in a variety of ways. The simplest cooking method is to toss shredded cabbage in butter or olive oil until just tender. Never overcook cabbage; it should still retain some crunch. Winter cabbages are good shredded and braised with pancetta *and garlic, while* cavolo rosso *(red cabbage) can be spiced with apples, cinnamon and cloves and stewed in a little white wine to cut the richness of pork, duck or roast goose.*

Vegetables

Cipolle (onions)

Onions are an essential part of Italian cooking. Many varieties are grown, including mild yellow onions, the stronger-flavoured white onions and their baby version, which is used for pickling and sweet-and-sour onions. The best-known Italian onions are the vibrant deep red variety, which are delicious raw (in a tuna and bean salad, for example, or cooked).

CULINARY USES

The best Italian onions are grown in Piedmont, so many classic Piedmontese recipes include these versatile bulbs. Large onions can be stuffed with Fontina or minced meat and herbs, and baked. Baby white onions are traditionally cooked *in agrodolce*, a sweet-and-sour sauce of sugar and wine vinegar, and served cold as an *antipasto* or hot as a vegetable accompaniment.

BUYING AND STORING

You will often find young fresh onions in Italian markets. These are sold in bunches like large, bulbous spring onions, complete with their leaves. They have a mild flavour and can be used for pickling or in salads. They will keep in the fridge for three or four days; wrap them tightly to stop their smell pervading everything else in the fridge. Older onions have thin, almost papery skins that should be unblemished. The onions should feel firm and not be sprouting green leaves. They quickly deteriorate once cut, so it is best to buy assorted sizes, then you can use a small onion when the recipe calls for only a small amount. Stored in a dry, airy place, onions will keep for many weeks.

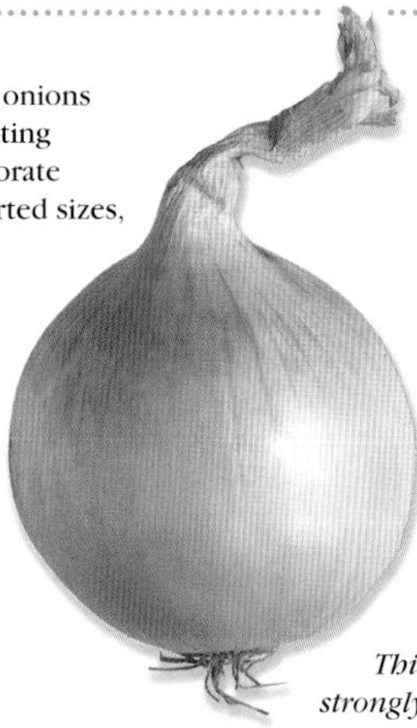

White onion
This variety is very strongly flavoured

Red onion
This vibrant red variety is now widely available – they are delicious raw

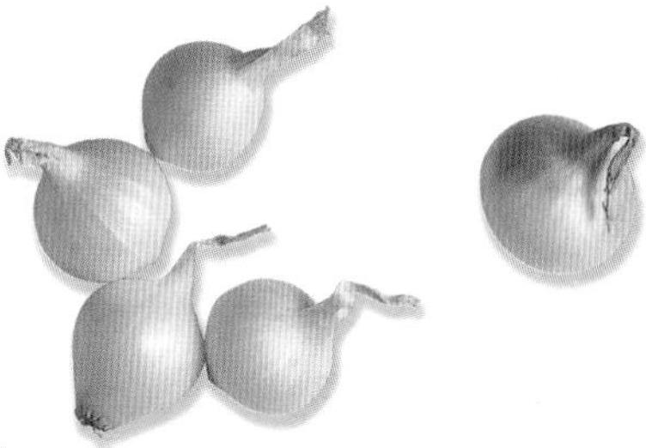

Baby white onions
Traditionally cooked in agrodolce, *a classic Italian sweet-and-sour sauce, and served cold as an* antipasto

Yellow onions
These mild onions are best cooked gently in olive oil

PREPARING AND COOKING ONIONS

Some onions are easier to peel than others. The skins of red and yellow onions can be removed without much difficulty, but white onions may need to be plunged into boiling water for about 30 seconds to make peeling easier.

There are all sorts of old wives' remedies to stop your eyes watering when peeling onions. The most effective method is to hold them as far away from you as possible while you peel! For most cooked dishes, onions should be sliced or chopped, but for salads they are sliced into very thin rings.

The flavour of onions will develop in different ways, according to how you cook them. In Italian cooking, they are rarely browned, which gives them a bitter taste, but are generally sweated gently in olive oil to add a mellow flavour to a multitude of dishes.

Finocchio (fennel)

Originally a medicinal remedy for such disagreeable conditions as flatulence, fennel has become one of the most important of all Italian vegetables. Bulb or Florence fennel (so-called to distinguish it from the feathery green herb) resembles a fat white celery root and has a delicate but distinctive flavour of aniseed and a very crisp, refreshing texture.

Culinary Uses

Fennel is delicious eaten raw, dressed with a vinaigrette or as part of a mixed salad. In southern Italy, raw fennel is served with cheese as a dessert instead of fruit - an excellent aid to digesting a meal.

When cooked, the aniseed flavour becomes more subtle and the texture resembles cooked celery. Braised fennel is particularly good with white fish. Fennel can be cooked in all the same ways as celery or cardoons.

Fennel
The distinctive aniseed flavour makes this vegetable a perfect partner for white fish

Buying and Storing

Fennel is available all year round. If possible, buy it with its topknot of feathery green fronds, which you can chop and use as a herb or garnish in any dish where you would use dill. The bulbs should feel firm and the outer layers should be crisp and white, not wizened and yellowish. It should have a delicate, very fresh scent of aniseed and the crisp texture of green celery. Whole fennel bulbs will keep in the fridge for up to a week. Once cut, however, use them immediately, or the cut surfaces will discolour and the texture will soften. Allow a whole bulb per serving.

Preparing and Cooking Fennel

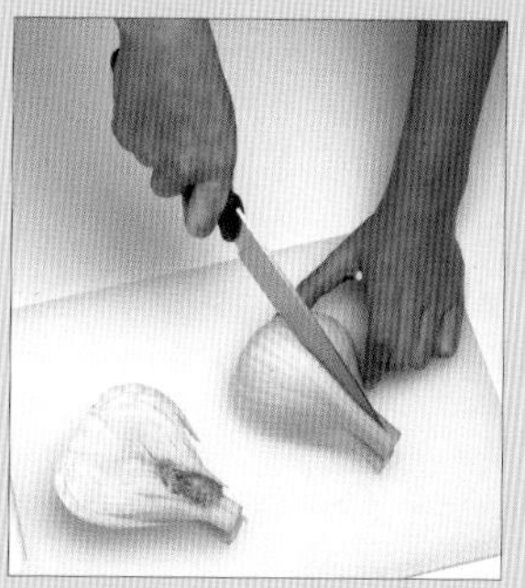

If the outer layer of the fennel bulb seems stringy, peel it with a sharp knife. Cut off the round greenish stalks protruding from the top. For salads, cut the bulb vertically into thin slices. For cooked dishes, quarter the bulb. Any trimmings can be chopped and used for soups or sauces for fish.

Fennel can be sautéed, baked or braised. For all cooked fennel recipes, blanch the quartered bulbs in a large saucepan of salted boiling water until it is just tender.

To sauté, heat about 25 g/1 oz butter per bulb with some chopped garlic, drain the fennel and fry it gently in the butter until very tender. To enhance the flavour, add a teaspoon of Pernod or other aniseed-flavoured alcohol.

Braised fennel should be cooked in a little olive oil using a covered frying pan.

To bake fennel, lay the blanched bulbs in a buttered ovenproof dish, season, dot with butter and sprinkle a generous quantity of freshly grated Parmesan over the top. Bake in the oven at 200°C/400°F/Gas 6 for 20-30 minutes, or until the top is bubbling and golden brown.

Vegetables

Melanzane (aubergines)

The versatile aubergine plays an important role in the cooking of southern Italy and Sicily, possibly because its dense, satisfying texture makes a good substitute for meat. You will find many different aubergines in Italian markets, the two main types being the familiar deep purple elongated variety and the rotund paler mauve type, which has a thinner skin. Some are small, some huge, but they all taste similar and can be used in the same way for any recipe.

Preparing Aubergines

Some people believe that aubergines should always be sliced and salted for about 30 minutes before cooking to draw out the bitter juices; others deem this unnecessary. Salting does stop the aubergine soaking up large quantities of oil during cooking, so on balance it seems worth doing.

Slice or dice the aubergines, place them in a colander, sprinkle with 15 ml/1 tbsp salt per 1 kg/2¼ lb. Place a dish on the aubergines and weight it down. Leave for 30 minutes. Rinse the aubergines and dry with kitchen paper.

If aubergines have a very tough skin, it is best to peel them (unless you are stuffing them and need the skin as a container). Otherwise, leave the skin on, as its colour will enhance the appearance of the finished dish.

Buying and Storing

Shape and size are not important when choosing aubergines; the essentials are tight, glossy skins and a fairly firm texture. Do not buy aubergines with wrinkled or damaged skins. They should feel heavy for their size; a light aubergine will probably be spongy inside and contain a lot of seeds. They will keep in the fridge for up to a week.

Aubergines
The familiar deep purple variety plays an important role in the cooking of southern Italy

History

Aubergines originated in Asia. They were cultivated in Europe in the Middle Ages, but only very rarely featured in Italian cooking at the time, since they were regarded with suspicion; indeed, the name *melanzane* comes from the Latin *melum insanum* (unhealthy apple). This mistrust had been overcome by the Renaissance, and aubergines began to be grown and used extensively in the south of Italy.

Culinary Uses

Aubergines are extremely versatile vegetables and add a wonderful depth of flavour to any dish in which they appear. They can be grilled, baked, stuffed, stewed and sautéed, on their own or with other ingredients, and the rich colour of their skins enhances the appearance of many different Italian dishes.

Cooking Aubergines

The simplest way of cooking aubergines is to slice and fry them in a generous quantity of very hot olive oil.
For a more substantial dish, coat them in light batter, then fine breadcrumbs, and fry until golden brown.
To bake them, halve the aubergines lengthways, removing the calyx and stalk. Make slashes in the flesh and rub it with a cut garlic clove. Drizzle some olive oil over the top, cover with foil and bake in a hot oven for about 1 hour, until very soft. Season with salt and pepper and add lemon juice to taste.
Probably the most famous Italian aubergine dish is melanzane alla parmigiana, *where the aubergines are layered with rich tomato sauce and Parmesan and baked in the oven. A favourite Sicilian dish,* caponata, *combines them with celery and a piquant sweet-and-sour sauce enlivened with olives and sometimes capers.*

Peperoni (sweet peppers)

Generically known as capsicums, the shape of these sweet peppers gives them the alternative name of "bell peppers". Although they come in a range of colours - green (these are unripe red peppers), red, yellow, orange and even purplish-black - all peppers have much the same sweetish flavour and crunchy texture, and are interchangeable in recipes. They are a very healthy food, being rich in vitamin C. The locally grown peppers you will see in the markets in Italy are much larger and more misshapen than the uniformly perfect, hydroponically grown specimens that are usually found in Britain, but their flavour is sweet and delicious.

Culinary Uses

Each region of Italy has its own specialities using peppers. They can be used raw or lightly roasted in salads or as an *antipasto* and can be cooked in a variety of ways - roasted and dressed with olive oil or vinaigrette dressing and capers, stewed (as in *peperonata*), or stuffed and baked. Peppers have a great affinity with other Mediterranean ingredients, such as olives, capers, aubergines, tomatoes and anchovies.

Buying and Storing

Choose firm peppers with unwrinkled, shiny skins. Size does not matter unless you plan to stuff the peppers, in which case choose roundish shapes of uniform size. The skin of green peppers may be mottled with patches of orange or red; this indicates that the pepper is ripening, and as long as the pepper is unblemished, there is no reason not to buy it. Peppers can be stored in the fridge for up to two weeks.

Cooking Peppers

To make a classic Italian peperonata, *sweat sliced onions and garlic in olive oil, add sliced peppers, cover the pan and cook gently until just tender. Add an equal quantity of peeled, deseeded and chopped tomatoes, a splash of wine vinegar and seasoning and cook, uncovered, until meltingly tender. For* peperonata alla romana, *stir in some capers at the end.*

Peppers
Locally grown Italian peppers are often larger and more misshapen than the uniformly perfect varieties grown in hot-houses

Vegetables

Preparing and Cooking Peppers

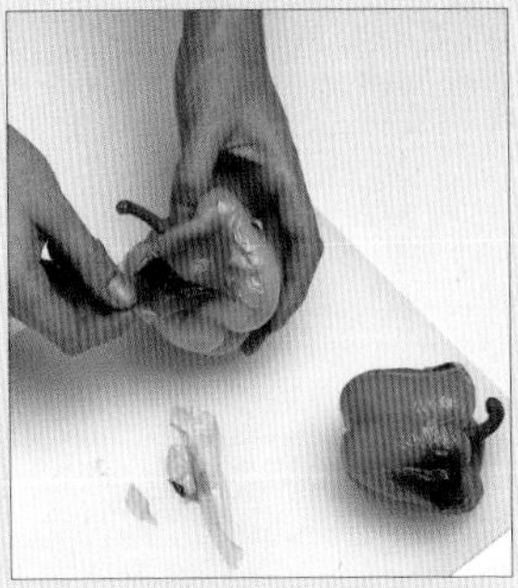

Place the peppers under a very hot grill or hold them over a gas flame and turn them until the skin blackens and blisters. Put them in a plastic bag, seal and leave until the peppers are cool enough to handle. The thin skin will peel off easily.

To slice peppers, halve them lengthways, cut away the calyx and stem and pull out the core, seeds and white membranes. Cut the flesh into strips.

To stuff peppers, cut off the stalk end and remove the seeds and membranes. Fill the pepper with your chosen stuffing (rice, vegetables, meat – what you will) and replace the stalk end. Arrange the peppers in a shallow ovenproof dish, drizzle over some olive oil and pour in enough water to come about 2 cm/¾ in up the sides of the peppers. Bake at 200°C/400°F/Gas 6 for about 1 hour.

For baked peppers alla piemontese, *halve the peppers lengthways and fill each with a chopped tomato, a chopped anchovy fillet and a little chopped garlic. Arrange the peppers on a baking tray, rounded side down. Drizzle over some olive oil and bake at 200°C/400°F/Gas 6 for about 30 minutes.*

Pomodori (tomatoes)

It is impossible to imagine Italian cooking without tomatoes, which seem to be a vital ingredient in almost every recipe. But these "golden apples" were unknown in Italy until the 16th century, when they were brought from Mexico. At first they were grown only in the south, but as their popularity spread, tomatoes were cultivated all over Italy and were incorporated into the cooking of every region. Italians grow an enormous variety of tomatoes, from plum tomatoes (San Marzano are the best) to ridged, pumpkin-shaped, green-tinged salad tomatoes, bright red fruits bursting with aroma and flavour, and tiny *pomodorini* (cherry tomatoes).

Culinary Uses

Tomatoes are used in so many different ways that it is hard to know where to begin. They can be eaten raw, sliced and served with a trickle of extra virgin olive oil and some torn basil leaves (basil and tomatoes have an extraordinary affinity). They are the red component of an *insalata tricolore*, partnering white mozzarella and green basil to make up the colours of the Italian flag. Raw ripe tomatoes

Cherry tomatoes
Bright red and bursting with flavour, these tiny tomatoes can be used to add colour and flavour to any dish

Plum tomatoes
San Marzano are the best variety of these smooth-skinned tomatoes

can be chopped with herbs and garlic to make a fresh-tasting pasta sauce, or made into a topping for *bruschetta*.

Tomatoes can be grilled, fried, baked, stuffed, stewed and made into sauces and soups. They add colour and flavour to almost any savoury dish.

Buying and Storing

Tomatoes are at their best in summer, when they have ripened naturally in the sun. Choose your tomatoes according to how you wish to prepare them. Salad tomatoes should be very firm and easy to slice. The best tomatoes for cooking are the plum tomatoes which hold their shape well and should have a fine flavour. Tomatoes will only ripen properly if left for long enough on the vine, so try to buy "vine-ripened" varieties. If you can find only unripe tomatoes, you can ripen them by putting them in a brown paper bag with a ripe tomato or leaving them in a fruit bowl with a banana; the gases the ripe fruits give off will ripen the tomatoes, but, alas, they cannot improve the flavour.

Try to buy tomatoes loose so that you can smell them. They should have a wonderful aroma. If the flavour is not all it should be, add a good pinch of sugar to enhance it. For cooked recipes, if you cannot find really flavourful tomatoes, use canned instead. The best are San Marzano plum tomatoes which are grown near Salerno. In Italy, you will often find large knobbly green tomatoes, which are sold as *pomodori insalata.* Although you can allow them to ripen in the usual way, Italians prefer to slice these tomatoes thinly and eat them in their unripe state as a crunchy and refreshing salad.

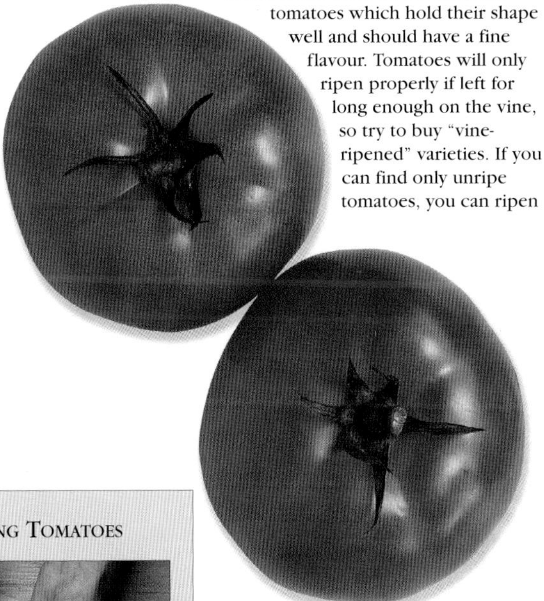

Large tomatoes
Not always as smooth as these, locally grown Italian tomatoes bought from a market can be very ridged and almost pumpkin-shaped

Vine-ripened tomatoes
Tomatoes sold on the vine are likely to have a far better flavour than those sold loose

Peeling Tomatoes

It is easy to remove the skin from tomatoes. Prick the tomatoes with the point of a sharp knife, plunge them into a bowl of boiling water for about 30 seconds, then refresh in cold water. Peel away the skins, cut the tomatoes into quarters or halves and remove the seeds using a teaspoon.

Vegetables

Spinaci (spinach)

Spinach and its close relatives, *bietola* (Swiss chard) and *biete* (spinach beet), are dark green leafy vegetables, rich in minerals (especially iron) and vitamins. Unlike many other vegetables, they are often served in Italy as an accompaniment to a main course, although they appear in numerous composite dishes as well. All spinach, whether flat-leafed or curly-leafed, has a distinctive metallic flavour, which people either love or loathe. The latter should avoid dishes *alla fiorentina*, which use spinach in large quantities.

Curly-leaf spinach is a summer variety with very dark green leaves. Winter spinach has flat, smooth leaves, but tastes very similar. Usually, only the leaves are eaten and the stalks are discarded. Spinach has a delicate, melting quality and should be cooked only very briefly.

The coarser *bietola* contains less iron and has a less pronounced flavour than spinach. The leaves have broad, tender creamy or pale green midribs, and both the leaves and stalks are eaten, but are cooked in different ways. *Bietola* is available all year round, but is particularly popular in autumn and winter, when more delicate spinach is not available. No one is quite sure why it is called Swiss chard; the Swiss certainly eat it, but in much smaller quantities than the French or Italians.

Biete (spinach beet) has a much smaller stalk and more closely resembles spinach. The stalks are usually left attached to the leaves for cooking. The coarser texture of *biete* makes it more suitable than spinach for recipes that require more than the briefest cooking. Balls of ready-cooked *biete* are often sold in Italian delicatessens.

History

Spinach was originally cultivated in Persia in the 6th century and was brought to Europe by Arab traders some thousand years later. It had become very popular in France, Spain and England by the 16th century, when it was used for both sweet and savoury dishes, but it did not reach Italy until the 18th century.

Culinary Uses

Tender young spinach leaves can be eaten raw in salads or cooked and served cold with a dressing of olive oil and lemon. Cooked spinach is used to make gnocchi and is often combined with ricotta to make fillings for pasta and *crespoline* (pancakes). Florentine-style recipes usually contain spinach, and it is a classic partner for eggs, fish, poultry and white meats. Spinach, *biete* and *bietola* are all used in savoury tarts, such as *torta alla pasqualina*, an Easter speciality. They make excellent soups and soufflés. *Bietola* stalks are delicious sautéed in butter and baked in a white sauce sprinkled with Parmesan.

Spinach
The tender young leaves can be eaten raw; larger leaves need to be cooked

Spinach beet
The coarse texture of biete *makes it more suitable than spinach for slower-cooked recipes*

Buying and Storing

All types of spinach should look very fresh and green, with no signs of wilting. The leaves should be unblemished and the stalks crisp. Spinach and spinach beets contain a very high proportion of water and wilt down to about half their weight during cooking, so always buy far more than you think you will need – at least 250 g/9 oz per serving. Loose spinach should be used as soon as possible after buying. Packed loosely into a plastic bag, it will keep in the fridge for a couple of days. Unopened bags of pre-packed spinach will keep for up to a week.

Bietola (Swiss chard)

Pull off the green leaves from the stems. Snap the veins and leaf stalks and remove the stringy parts (do not cut with a knife, or the strings will not come away). Wash as for spinach and cut the stalks into 6–8 cm/ 2½–3½ in lengths.

Swiss chard
Available all year round, this vegetable is particularly popular in winter when the more tender spinach is not available

Preparing and Cooking Spinach and Swiss Chard

Spinach and spinach beet: Carefully pick over the spinach, discarding any withered or damaged leaves and tough stalks. Wash thoroughly in several changes of water until no signs of earth or grit remain.

Spinach should be cooked with only the water which clings to the leaves after washing. Sauté it in butter with a clove of chopped garlic for about 5 minutes; overcooked spinach will be unpleasantly watery. To stew spinach, put it in a large saucepan, cover and cook gently until wilted, turning it over halfway through cooking. Drain and gently squeeze out the excess moisture with your hands. Toss in butter or olive oil, season with freshly grated nutmeg or chop finely and use for gnocchi and pasta fillings.

Swiss chard leaves can be cooked exactly like spinach. The prepared stalks should be blanched until tender in salted water or vegetable stock, then baked in a sauce or tart, sautéed in butter or used as a stuffing. A popular bietola *dish is a* sformato*, a savoury, moulded, baked custard.*

Vegetables

Zucca (squash) and zucchini (courgettes)

Squashes and courgettes are widely used in northern Italian cooking. Both have large, open, deep-yellow flowers, which are considered a great delicacy. Squashes come in a variety of shapes and sizes, from huge orange pumpkins to small, pale butternut squashes and green acorn squashes. They all have dense, sweet-tasting flesh. Courgettes are like small marrows, with shiny green skin and a sweet, delicate flavour. In Italy, tiny specimens are often sold with their flowers attached.

Culinary Uses

The pumpkin is the symbol of Mantua and recipes *alla mantovana* use the flesh a multitude of ways, from *tortelli alla zucca* (pumpkin-filled tortelli) to risotti, soups and sweet dessert tarts. Pumpkin flowers can be coated in batter and deep-fried, stuffed with a filling of ricotta, or chopped and added to risotti for extra colour and flavour.

Courgettes combine well with other Mediterranean vegetables, like tomatoes and aubergines. They can be dipped in batter and deep-fried, made into fritters or served with a white sauce seasoned with Parmesan or nutmeg. Served cold with a mint-flavoured vinaigrette (*zucchini a scapece*) or tomato sauce, they can be part of an *antipasto*. They can be halved and stuffed with a meat or vegetable filling. Young courgettes can also be thinly sliced or grated and eaten raw in a salad.

Buying and Storing

Courgettes are available almost all year round, but are at their best in spring and summer. The smaller and skinnier courgettes are, the better they taste. They should have very glossy green skins and feel very firm. Do not buy flabby courgettes or those with blemished skins. Larger specimens are useful for stuffing. If you can find them in markets, go for tiny courgettes with their flowers attached. Allow 250 g/9 oz courgettes per serving.

Courgettes
These familiar vegetables combine well with other Mediterranean vegetables

Pumpkins
Italians use the flesh of these large vegetables in a multitude of ways

Small pumpkins
Like their larger cousins, these small pumpkins have dense, sweet-tasting flesh

They will keep in the vegetable drawer of the fridge for up to a week.

Squashes should feel firm and heavy for their size. It is not worth buying enormous pumpkins (other than for decorative purposes), as their flesh tends to be stringy and flavourless. All whole squashes keep well, but once they are opened, they should be wrapped in clingfilm and kept in the fridge for no more than three days.

If you are lucky enough to find squash or courgette flowers (the best way is to grow your own), they must be cooked straight away, as they are extremely perishable.

Preparing Courgettes, Squashes and Pumpkins

Courgettes should be topped and tailed, then sliced, diced, cut into batons or grated as appropriate. They do not need peeling.

Flowers may contain small insects, so wash them quickly under cold running water and gently pat dry with kitchen paper. Cut off all but 2.5 cm/1 in of the stems. Courgettes are best sautéed in butter or olive oil flavoured with plenty of chopped garlic and parsley. Courgettes deep fried in a light batter are a favourite accompaniment in Italy. The flowers can be prepared in the same way. To make zucchini a scapece, *slice 1 kg/2¼lb courgettes thickly and brown in hot olive oil. Place in a dish and scatter over about 20 torn mint leaves and 1 finely chopped garlic clove. Season and dress with one part red wine vinegar and two parts olive oil. Mix well and leave the flavours to develop for 2 hours before serving.*

Squashes and pumpkins should be peeled and the seeds and fibrous parts removed. Cut the flesh into chunks or slices. The skin of large pumpkins may be too hard to peel; if so, break open the pumpkin with a hammer or drop it on the floor, and scoop out the flesh, discarding the seeds.

Pumpkin and squash should be blanched in boiling salted water, then sweated in butter until soft and made into soup or stuffing, cooked au gratin or grated raw and added to a risotto. Pumpkin can also be sweetened and used as a pie filling.

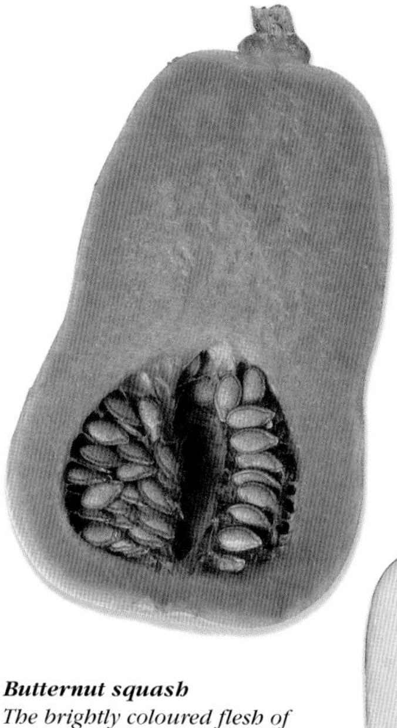

Butternut squash
The brightly coloured flesh of butternut squashes is widely used in northern Italian cooking

Acorn squash
Once halved, these small squashes need to be seeded and peeled before cooking

Salad Leaves

Italians grow salad leaves in profusion and gather them from the wild to create inventive and interesting combinations, such as *misticanza*, a pot-pourri of wild greens and cultivated leaves. In high season, you will find at least a dozen different salad leaves in an Italian market, ranging from fresh green round garden lettuces to bitter dark green grass-like leaves and purplish-red radicchio. Such salads are served after the main course, simply dressed with olive oil and vinegar to cleanse the palate.

Cicoria di campo or dente di leone (dandelion)

Dandelion leaves are rich in iron and vitamins, and are also reputed to be a powerful diuretic. They have a pungent, peppery taste and long, fresh green indented leaves (hence the name "lion's tooth"). They can be picked from the wild before the plant has flowered, but only the young leaves should be eaten. Cultivated dandelion leaves are available. They are more tender than wild leaves, but have a less intense flavour.

Culinary Uses

Young dandelion leaves are usually served raw in salads together with other leaves; they are particularly good with crisply cooked bacon and hard-boiled eggs. They can also be cooked like spinach.

Dandelion leaves
Pick these peppery-tasting leaves from the wild before the plant has flowered

Radicchio

This variety of red-leafed chicory comes originally from Treviso. *Radicchio di Treviso* has elongated purplish-red leaves with pronounced cream-coloured veins. The more familiar round variety is known as *radicchio di Verona*. Both types of red-leafed chicory have a bitter taste, and for salads are best used in small quantities together with other leaves. They look particularly attractive when combined with frilly-leafed curly endive, pale whitish-green chicory leaves, or the darker corn-salad and rocket.

Radicchio di Verona
The more familiar round red-leafed chicory

Radicchio di Treviso
This elongated variety is delicious grilled with olive oil

Culinary Uses

Radicchio can also be eaten as a hot vegetable, either quartered and grilled with olive oil, or stuffed with a mixture of breadcrumbs, anchovies, capers and olives and baked – but it loses its beautiful colour when cooked. A little radicchio added to a risotto made with red wine will add to the pretty pink colour.

Buying and Storing

Radicchio leaves should be fresh-looking with no trace of brown at the edges. *Radicchio di Verona* should be firm with tightly packed leaves. Both types will keep in the fridge for up to a week.

Rucola (rocket)

Rocket has dark green elongated, indented leaves and a hot, pungent flavour and aroma. Like dandelions, it grows wild in the Italian countryside, but it is also cultivated commercially. Home-grown rocket has a much better flavour than the immature leaves usually found in supermarkets, but it bolts easily and should be picked as soon as the leaves are large enough.

Culinary Uses

Rocket adds zest to any green salad and can be eaten on its own with a dressing of olive oil and lemon juice or balsamic vinegar. Combined with radicchio, cornsalad and fresh herbs, rocket makes a good substitute for *misticanza*. It can be added to pasta sauces and risotti, or cooked like spinach, but cooking does diminish the pungent flavour.

Buying and Storing

In Italy, rocket is always sold in small bunches. The leaves should look very fresh with no sign of wilting. Rocket does not keep well unless it has been pre-packaged. To keep it for a day or two, wrap it in damp newspaper or damp kitchen paper and store in the fridge.

Rocket
This hot, pungent salad leaf grows wild in the Italian countryside, but it is also cultivated commercially

Valeriana (cornsalad)

This delicate salad plant, also called lamb's lettuce, has tender green rounded leaves bunched together in a rosette shape. It grows wild in fields in Italy, but is also cultivated and is an essential ingredient of *misticanza*. It has a delicate but distinctive flavour, which adds interest to winter salads.

Culinary Uses

Cornsalad is usually served by itself or in a mixed green salad, but it can also be cooked like spinach. The tender leaves will blacken if damaged, so take care when tossing a salad not to bruise them.

Buying and Storing

Cornsalad should look fresh and green, with no withered or drooping leaves. The smaller and rounder the leaves, the better the flavour. It will keep in the salad drawer of the fridge for several days, but take care not to squash it.

Cornsalad
The delicate but distinctive flavour of this salad plant adds interest to winter salads

Preparing Cornsalad

Cornsalad is sold with the root attached, so it must be washed thoroughly before use. Dunk it in several changes of cold water to remove all the grit, then dab the leaves dry with kitchen paper, handling them very gently.

Mushrooms

Italian country-dwellers have always been passionate collectors of edible wild mushrooms; in spring and autumn, the woods and fields are alive with furtive fungi hunters in search of these flavourful delicacies. Cultivated button mushrooms are rarely eaten in Italy, even when fresh wild varieties are out of season; Italians prefer to use dried or preserved wild fungi with their robust, earthy taste.

The most highly prized mushroom for use in Italian cooking is the *porcino* (cep). Since these are hugely expensive, they are most often dried and used in small quantities to add flavour to field or other wild mushrooms. Drying actually intensifies the flavour of *porcini*, so they are not regarded as inferior to the fresh mushrooms – quite the reverse. Other popular wild fungi include *gallinacci* (chanterelles), *prataioli* (field mushrooooms) and *ovoli* (Caesar's mushrooms).

History

From earliest times, primitive man gathered and ate wild mushrooms. The Greeks and Romans enjoyed many fungi, including *amanita caesarea* (Caesar's mushroom), which was popular with the Emperor Claudius and ultimately his downfall; his wife Agrippina poisoned him by adding deadly *amanita phalloides* (the aptly named deathcap) to a dish of his favourite fungi. The Romans succeeded in cultivating several types of mushrooms, but cultivation on a large scale really began in the 17th century, when a French botanist discovered how to grow mushrooms in compost all year round.

Storing

Never store mushrooms in a plastic bag, as they will sweat and turn mushy. Put them into a paper bag and keep in the vegetable drawer of the fridge for no more than two days.

Preparing and Cooking Mushrooms

Mushrooms should never be washed or they will become waterlogged and mushy. To clean them, cut off the earthy base of the stalk and lightly brush the caps with a soft brush or wipe them clean with a slightly damp cloth.

With very few exceptions (including ceps and Caesar's mushrooms, which can be eaten raw), wild mushrooms should be cooked to destroy any mild toxins they may contain.

All mushrooms can be sliced and sauteéd in hot olive oil or a mixture of butter and olive oil with finely chopped garlic or shallots, a little red chilli and herbs (parsley, marjoram, thyme or mint are particularly good).

Chanterelles
These orangey-yellow mushrooms have a delicious, delicate flavour and a distinct apricot aroma

Cooking Chanterelles

Chanterelles have a delicious, delicate flavour and a slightly chewy texture; they should be cooked slowly or they may become hard. Fry them gently in butter with chopped garlic or shallots for about 10 minutes, adding some finely chopped parsley, marjoram or thyme towards the end of the cooking time. Serve them on hot buttered toast, or add to omelettes or scrambled eggs. They are particularly good with poultry, rabbit or veal and can also be dressed with a herb-flavoured vinaigrette and served warm in a salad.

Ovoli (Caesar's mushrooms; Latin name amanita caesarea)

These large mushrooms with an orangey-yellow cap have an excellent flavour and were a favourite of the Roman emperors. They are still found in Italy, but are very rare elsewhere.

Culinary Uses

Ovoli can be thinly sliced and eaten raw in a salad. They combine very well with hazelnuts.

Dried chanterelles
Dried chanterelles can be used to flavour soups, stew and pasta dishes

Mushroom powder

Well-flavoured dried mushrooms can be crushed to a powder and used to flavour sauces, soups and stews. Some Italian delicatessens stock mushroom powder. If you make your own, store it in an airtight container.

Drying Chanterelles

Leave the chanterelles whole, or halve them if they are large.

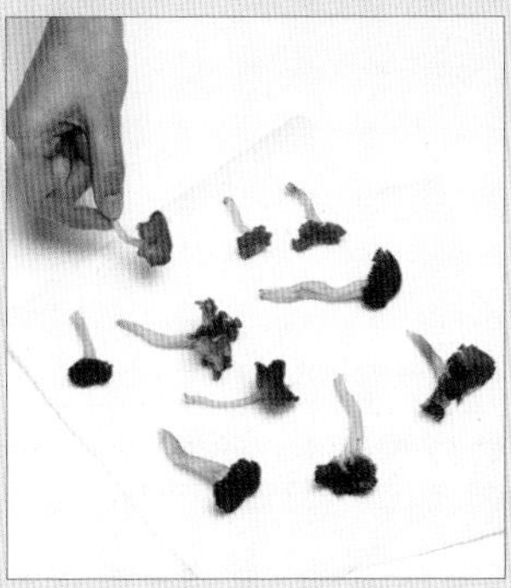

Lay them on a double thickness of newspaper and leave in a very warm, airy place (above the boiler is ideal), turning them over every few hours until they have become completely dry and brittle. Alternatively, string them like necklaces and hang them up to dry, or place in a very cool fan oven (maximum 130°C/250°F/ gas ½), leaving the door ajar. When the chanterelles are completely dry, store them in jars or paper bags. All mushrooms can be dried in this way; slice them thinly before drying. It is only worth drying perfect specimens.

Reconstituting Dried Mushrooms

Soak 25 g/1 oz dried mushrooms in 250 ml/8 fl oz/1 cup hot water for about 20 minutes until soft, then drain and use like fresh mushrooms. Keep the soaking water to use in sauces, stocks or soups; it will have an intense mushroom flavour.

Mushrooms

Porcini (ceps)

These are the king of mushrooms in Italian cooking. Their Italian name means "little piglets", which aptly describes their bulbous stalks and rounded brown caps. In autumn, they are found in woodlands, where they can grow to an enormous size, weighing more than 500 g/1¼ lb each (although mushroom-hunters rarely leave them for long enough to grow to these proportions). There are many different varities of *porcini*, all of which have a fine flavour and meaty texture.

Culinary Uses

All ceps can be cooked in the same way as other mushrooms. Young ones can be thinly sliced and eaten raw, dressed with extra virgin olive oil. Larger caps are delicious brushed with olive oil, grilled and served with a grinding of salt and pepper. Don't discard the stalks, which have an excellent flavour; chop them and cook with the caps, or use them for sauces, stocks and soups; just trim off the earthy bits from the base.

Drying

Ceps can be thinly sliced and dried in the same way as *gallinacci*. Dried *porcini* are commercially available. They are very expensive, but a little goes a long way. Just 25 g/1 oz dried porcini, soaked and drained, will enhance the flavour of 500 g/1¼ lb cultivated mushrooms beyond recognition. Don't be tempted to buy cheap packets of dried *porcini*, which may contain a high proportion of inferior dried mushrooms and bits of twig from the forest floor.

Storing

Fresh *porcini* can be kept in the vegetable drawer of the fridge for up to two days. Dried mushrooms will keep in an airtight container for at least a year.

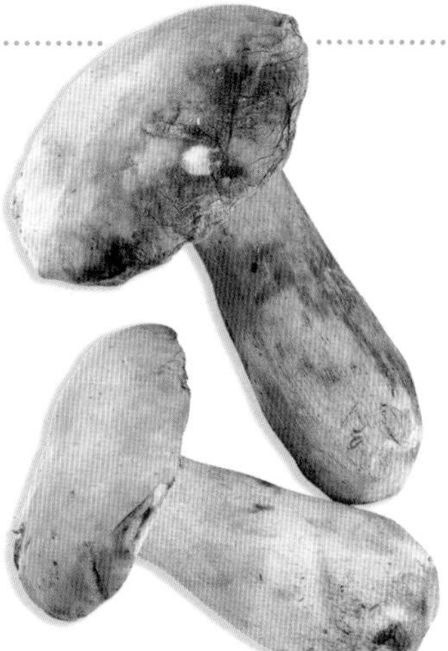

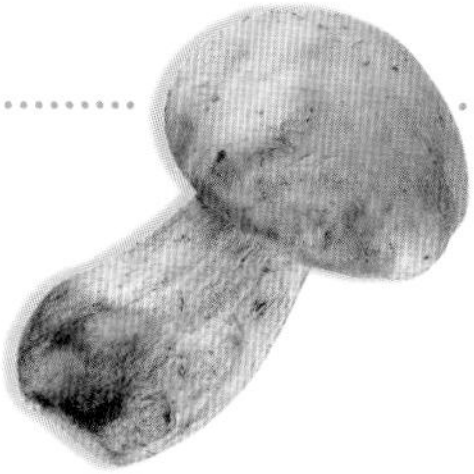

Porcini *(ceps)*
Italian cooks consider these to be the king of mushrooms

Freezing

Small *porcini* in perfect condition can be frozen whole. Large or blemished specimens should be sliced and lightly sautéed in butter, then drained and frozen. Do not defrost before use, or they will become mushy. Simply cook the mushrooms from frozen in hot olive oil or butter. Frozen mushrooms will only keep for about one month.

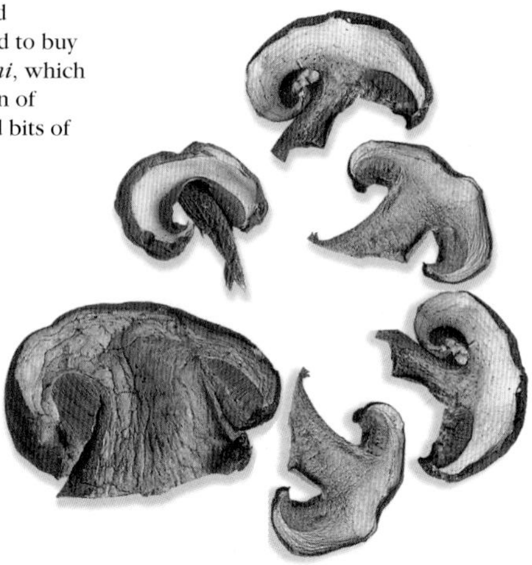

Pickling *Porcini*

Unblemished fresh porcini *can be preserved by pickling. Choose unblemished funghi (if you haven't enough* porcini, *use a mixture of mushrooms), leaving small ones whole and slicing or quartering large ones.*

1 kg/2¼ lb mushrooms
500 ml/17 fl oz/ generous 2 cups white wine vinegar
500 ml/17 fl oz/ generous 2 cups water
10 ml/2 tsp salt
5 ml/1 tsp peppercorns, lightly crushed
2 bay leaves
10 ml/2 tsp coriander seeds
2 garlic cloves, peeled and halved
4 small dried red chillies
olive oil

1 *Put the mushrooms in a saucepan with all the ingredients except the olive oil. Bring to the boil and simmer for 5-10 minutes until the mushrooms are tender but still firm. Drain them, reserving the pickling aromatics, and leave to cool completely.*

2 *Spoon the mushrooms and aromatics into a sterilized preserving jar and fill up the jar with olive oil. Seal and leave for at least a month. Pickled mushrooms will keep for at least six months.*

Dried* porcini *(ceps)
These dried porcini *are expensive to buy, but since drying actually accentuates their flavour, a little goes a long way*

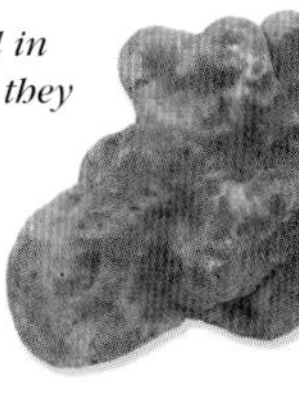

Black truffles
No one has succeeded in cultivating truffles so they remain rare and expensive - the black variety are more highly prized than the white

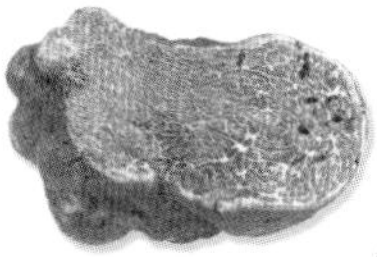

White truffles
Found in Piedmont, northern Italy, these delicately flavoured truffles are usually served raw

Chiodini (honey fungus; Latin name armarilla mellea)

No gardener welcomes the sight of honey fungus (the Italian name means "little nails"), as it is a parasitic fungus that destroys the trees on whose roots it grows. However, the caps of these small golden mushrooms are good to eat (the fibrous stalks should be discarded). In their raw state they are mildly toxic, but once they have been blanched in very hot oil or boiling water, then stewed in butter with a little garlic, seasoning and parsley, they make good eating.

Culinary Uses

Honey fungus makes a good filling for a *frittata* (Italian omelette). Allow 150 g/5 oz *chiodini* caps and 4 large eggs for two people. Season the eggs and beat them lightly with 25 g/1 oz grated Parmesan. Heat 30 ml/2 tbsp olive oil in a frying pan and sauté the blanched mushroom caps with 1 chopped garlic clove and 15 ml/1 tbsp chopped parsley for about 3 minutes. Season with salt and pepper, pour in the eggs and stir well. Cook the *frittata* until set on the bottom, then sprinkle with a little more Parmesan and place under a hot grill until golden brown. Cut into wedges and serve hot or cold.

Tartufi (truffles)

Truffles grow about 20 cm/8 in underground, usually near oak trees. They are in season from October to late December. Their irregular, knobbly, round shape conceals a pungent, earthy and delicious aroma and flavour. There are two main varieties, black and white. The more highly prized black truffles (*tuber melanosporum*) grow mostly in the Périgord region of France, but they are also found in northern Italy, in Tuscany and Piedmont. The more common Piedmont truffle is the white variety (*tuber magnatum*), which has a more delicate flavour.

No one has yet succeeded in cultivating truffles commercially, so they remain rare and expensive. They are sniffed out by trained pigs or dogs, who can detect their subterranean scent. In order to develop their full aroma and flavour, the truffles must be left to mature, so truffle-hunters often cover up those which the animals have unearthed (praying that nobody else will find their buried treasure) until they reach full maturity.

History

Truffles have been eaten since ancient times. They were a favourite dish of the ancient Egyptians. The Greeks and Romans believed them to have aphrodisiac properties, but in the Middle Ages they were thought to be manifestations of the devil. Louis XIV of France, however, subscribed to the earlier theory, and from his reign on truffles were enthusiastically consumed by all those rich enough to afford this luxury food.

Culinary Uses

Truffles can be eaten raw or cooked. White Piedmont truffles are usually served raw, shaved very thinly over fresh pasta, a *fonduta* or eggs. They can be heated briefly in butter and seasoned with salt, white pepper and nutmeg. Black or white truffles are delicious with all poultry and white meat. A few slivers of truffle will add a touch of luxury to almost any savoury sauce. A classic rich Italian dish using truffles is *vincigrassi*, sheets of fresh pasta layered with butter, cream, slivers of truffle, ham and chicken livers. It is a speciality of the Marches and the Abruzzi.

Buying and Storing

If you are lucky enough to find a fresh truffle, use it as soon as possible, as the flavour is volatile. Brush off the earth from the skin and peel the truffle (keep the peelings to use in a sauce). To give whole fresh eggs the most wonderful flavour, put them in a bowl with the truffle, cover and leave overnight; they will absorb the superb musty aroma.

You are more likely to buy canned or bottled truffles than fresh. Whole ones are extremely expensive, but cheaper pieces and even peelings are available. The most economical way to enjoy the flavour of truffles is to buy Italian oil scented with white truffles. A drop or two of this added to a dish will transform it into something really special.

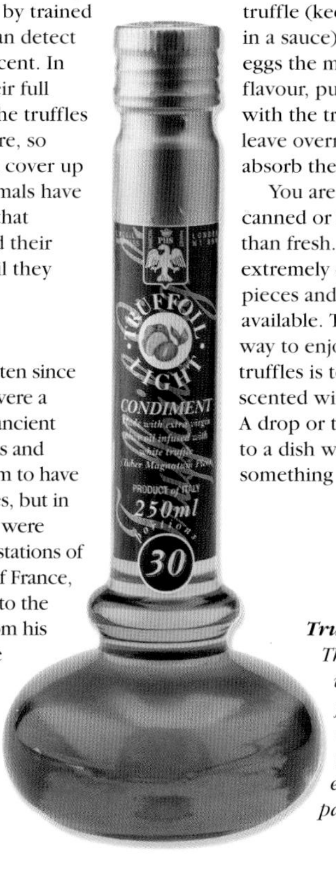

Truffle oil
The most economical way to enjoy the flavour of truffles - a drop or two of this scented oil will enhance sauces, pastas and salads

Fruit & Nuts

Italians prefer to buy only those fruits and nuts that are in season, and who can blame them? Italy produces an abundance of soft, stone and citrus fruits, all bursting with flavour and often available fresh from the tree. There are apples and pears from the orchards of the northern regions; nuts, peaches, plums and figs from the central plains; while the south and Sicily produce almost every kind of fruit - grapes, cherries, oranges and lemons - as well as pistachio nuts and almonds. Many of these fruits are indigenous to Italy and have been grown there since time immemorial.

After a full meal of *antipasto*, pasta and a *secondo* (main course), it is hardly surprising that Italian desserts very often consist of nothing but a bowl of seasonal fresh fruit served on its own or made into a refreshing *macedonia* (fruit salad). Soft fruits form the basis of ice creams, sorbets, *granite* and *frullati* (fresh fruit milkshakes), while nuts and winter fruits (often dried or candied) are baked into tarts and pastries.

Amarena (Morello cherry)

Although Italy does produce sweet dessert cherries, it is best known for the bitter Morello variety, which are preserved in syrup or brandy, or made into ice cream and Maraschino liqueur. These cherries are small, with dark red skins and firm flesh. They are in season from late June to early July, and can be eaten raw, although they have quite a sharp flavour.

Culinary Uses

Morello cherries can be poached in sugar syrup and served whole, or puréed and made into a rich, dark, cherry syrup. Stone the cherries and purée them. Strain the cherries through a fine sieve and leave the juice at room temperature for about 24 hours. Strain through muslin and add 750 g/1 lb 10 oz caster sugar per 500 ml/17 fl oz/generous 2 cups cherry juice. Heat gently. When the sugar has dissolved, bring the cherry syrup to the boil, strain again and pour into airtight bottles or containers. These cherries also make excellent jam. A popular Venetian dish is Morello cherries poached in a red wine syrup flavoured with cinnamon. Bottled cherries in vinegar can be used in sauces for meat, duck and game.

Buying and Storing

Choose fresh cherries with unwrinkled and unblemished skins, which look shiny and feel firm. Stored in a plastic bag, they will keep in the fridge for up to a week.

Morello cherries
These dark red cherries are usually preserved in syrup and used for desserts. Those bottled in vinegar can be used for savoury recipes

Arancia (orange)

Many varieties of oranges are grown in Sicily and southern Italy. The best-known Sicilian oranges are the small blood oranges with their bright ruby-red flesh. Other types of sweet oranges include seedless navels, which take their name from the umbilical-like end which contains an embryonic orange, and seeded late oranges, which have paler flesh and are available throughout the winter. Bitter oranges (*arance amare*) are also grown; these rough-skinned varieties are made into preserves (although rarely marmalade in Italy), candied peel and *liquore all'arancia* (orange liqueur).

History

Oranges originated in China, but bitter oranges may possibly have been known in Ancient Greece; the mythical "golden apples of the Hesperides" are said to have been Seville oranges, although this seems historically far-fetched. They were certainly brought to Italy by Arab traders during the Roman Empire and over the centuries became a symbol of wealth and opulence - so much so that the Medici family incorporated them into their coat of arms as five golden balls. Sweet oranges did not arrive in Italy until the 17th century.

Oranges
Sweet varieties are used for both sweet and savoury recipes - they are a favourite addition to salads

Bitter oranges
This rough-skinned variety can be used to add zest to savoury dishes - it combines well with white fish, liver, duck and game - and is used for preserves

Culinary Uses

A favourite Sicilian recipe is *insalata di arance alla siciliana*, a salad of thinly sliced oranges and red onion rings dressed with black olives and their oil. Oranges also combine well with raw fennel and chicory. They can be sliced and served *alla veneziana*, coated with caramel, or simply macerated in a little lemon juice with a sliver of lemon peel for a refreshing dessert. They can be squeezed for juice, or made into sorbet and *granita*. Bitter oranges combine well with white fish, calf's liver, duck or game, and add zest to a tomato sauce.

Buying and Storing

Oranges are available all year round, but are at their best in winter. They should have unblemished shiny skins and feel heavy for their size (this indicates that they contain plenty of juice and that the flesh is not dry). If you intend to candy the peel or incorporate it into a recipe, choose unwaxed oranges. Oranges will keep at room temperature for a week and for at least two weeks in the fridge. Bring them back to room temperature or warm them slightly before eating them.

Preparing Fresh Oranges

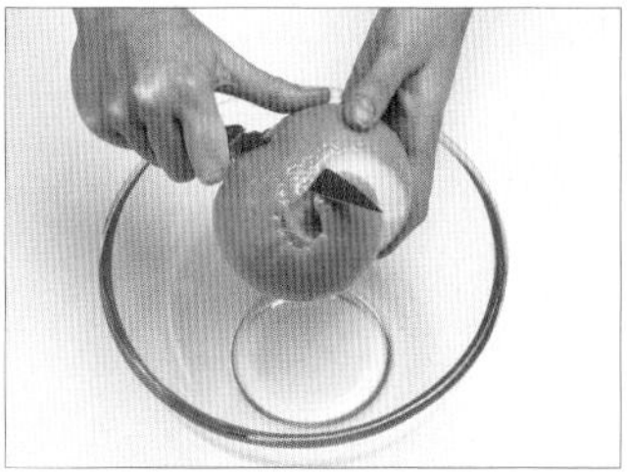

1 When peeling an orange it is important to remove all the bitter white pith and membrane. Hold the orange over a bowl to catch the juice and use a very sharp knife to cut off the peel, pith and the membrane enclosing the flesh.

2 To segment the orange, cut down between the membranes of the segments and ease out the flesh. Squeeze the membranes into the bowl to extract the juice.

3 To remove strips of orange rind, run a cannelle knife down the orange, or use a zester for finer shreds. If you cannot find unwaxed fruit, wash the oranges in warm water, rinse and dry well before removing strips of rind.

Fruit

Purple figs
The sweet succulent flesh of this variety makes a perfect partner to nuts of all kinds

Fico (fig)

Figs are grown all over Italy, but thanks to the hot climate Sicilian figs are perhaps the most luscious of all. During the summer months you will often find Italian farmers at the roadside selling punnets of ripe figs from their own trees. There are two types of Italian figs, green and purple. Both have thin, tender skins and very sweet, succulent, red flesh, and are rich in vitamins A, B and C. They are in season from July to October and are best eaten straight off the tree when they are perfectly ripe.

HISTORY

Figs were said to grow in the Garden of Eden, where Adam and Eve used the leaves to cover their nakedness. In fact they probably originated in Asia Minor, although the oldest fig tree in the world is reputed to be growing in a garden in Palermo in Sicily. The Greeks and Romans certainly enjoyed figs, which are still as highly prized today.

Green figs
Delicious served raw with Parma ham or salami as an antipasto

CULINARY USES

Fresh figs are delicious served on their own, but they have an affinity with nuts such as walnuts, pistachios and almonds. They can be served raw with Parma ham or salami as an *antipasto*, or stuffed with raspberry coulis or mascarpone as a dessert. Poached in a little water or wine flavoured with cinnamon or nutmeg, they make an excellent accompaniment to duck, game or lamb.

BUYING AND STORING

Ripe figs are extremely delicate and do not travel well, so it is hard to find imported fruit at a perfect stage of maturity. In season in Italy, however, you can find local figs that are just ripe for eating; they should be soft and yielding, but not squashy. Sometimes the skin may have split, revealing the luscious red or pink flesh. As long as you are going to eat the fig immediately, this does not matter. Take great care not to squash the figs on your way home, or you will end up with a squishy, inedible mess.

Under-ripe figs can be kept at room temperature for a day or two until the skin softens, but they will never develop the fine flavour of tree-ripened figs. Ripe figs should be eaten on the day they are bought.

PREPARING AND COOKING FIGS

Wash the figs briefly and gently pat dry. Discard the stalk and peel the figs, if you wish.

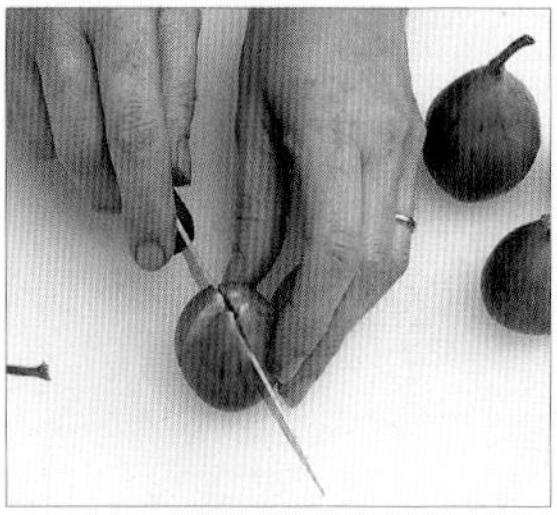

To serve as an antipasto or dessert, cut them downwards from the stalk end into quarters, leaving them attached at the base. Open them out like flowers.

Perfectly ripe figs are best eaten raw, but less perfect specimens can be improved by cooking. They can be gently poached in syrup or red wine flavoured with a cinnamon stick or vanilla pod, or rolled in caster sugar and baked in the oven until caramelized. Barely ripe figs also make excellent jam.

Limone (lemon)

Lemons are grown all over Italy, even in the northern regions. Lake Garda even boasts a town called Limone, named for its abundance of lemon trees. But the most famous Italian lemons come from the Amalfi coast, where they grow to an extraordinary size and have such a sweet flavour that they can almost be eaten as a dessert fruit. Their aromatic flavour enhances almost any dish, and they have the added advantage of being rich in vitamin C.

History

Lemons originated in India or Malaysia and were brought by the Assyrians to Greece, which in turn took them to Italy. The Greeks and Romans greatly appreciated their culinary and medicinal qualities. Later seafarers ate them in large quantities to protect against scurvy, and society ladies used them as a beauty treatment to whiten their skin, bleach their hair and redden their lips.

Culinary Uses

Lemons are extraordinarily versatile. The juice can be squeezed to make a refreshing *spremuta di limone*, or it can be added to other cold drinks or tea. It is an anti-oxidant, which prevents discoloration when applied to other fruits and vegetables. The juice is used for dressings and for flavouring all sorts of drinks and sauces. A squeeze of lemon juice adds a different dimension to intrinsically bland foods, such as fish, poultry, veal or certain vegetables. Its acidity also helps to bring out the flavour of other fruits. The zest makes a wonderfully aromatic flavouring for cakes and pastries, and is an essential ingredient of *gremolata*, a topping of grated zest, garlic and parsley for *osso buco*. Quartered lemons are always served with *fritto misto di mare* (mixed fried fish) and other foods fried in batter.

Preparing Lemons

Before squeezing a lemon, warm it gently: either put it in a bowl, pour boiling water over the top and leave to stand for about 5 minutes or, if you prefer, microwave the lemon on full power for about 30 seconds; this will significantly increase the quantity of juice you will obtain.

For sweet dishes, when you want to add the flavour of lemons, but not the grated rind, rub a sugar lump over the skin of the lemon to absorb the oil, then use the sugar as part of the recipe.

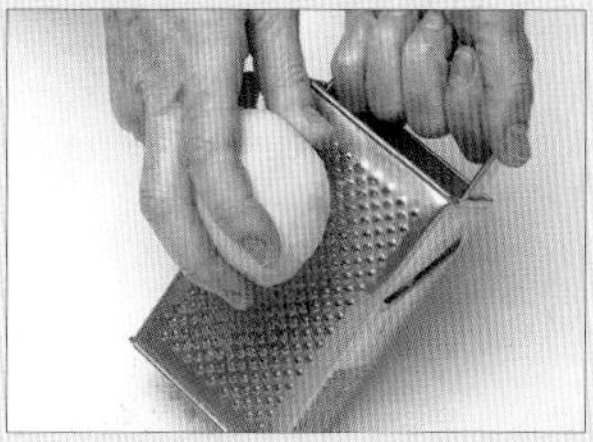

To prepare grated lemon rind, thoroughly wash and dry unwaxed lemons. Grate the rind or peel it off with a zester, taking care not to include any white pith.

Buying and Storing

Depending on the variety, lemons may have thick indented skin, or be perfectly smooth. Their appearance does not affect the flavour, but they should feel heavy for their size. If you intend to use the zest, buy unwaxed lemons. Lemons will keep in the fridge for up to two weeks.

Lemons
Lemons are grown all over Italy - their aromatic flavour enhances almost any dish

Fruit

Melone (melon)

Many different varieties of sweet, aromatic melons are grown in Italy, and each has its own regional name. *Napoletana* melons have a smooth pale green rind and delicately scented orange flesh. *Cantalupo* (cantaloupe) melons have a warty skin, which is conveniently marked into segments, and highly scented deep yellow flesh. A similar Tuscan melon with grey-green rind and orange flesh is called *popone*. These melons are all perfect for eating with Parma ham or salami as an *antipasto*.

Watermelons (*anguria* or *cocomero*) are grown in Tuscany. These huge green melons with their refreshing bright pink or red flesh and edible brown seeds can be round or sausage-shaped. In Florence, the feast of San Lorenzo, the patron saint of cooks, is celebrated with an orgy of watermelons on August 10th. During this season, roadside stalls groan under the weight of hundreds of these gigantic fruit.

Culinary Uses

Italians eat melon as a starter, usually accompanied by wafer-thin *prosciutto crudo* or cured meats. Melons and watermelons are occasionally served as a dessert fruit on their own, but more often appear in a *macedonia* (fruit salad).

Buying and Storing

The best way to tell whether a melon is ripe is to smell it; it should have a mild, sweet scent. If it smells highly perfumed and musky, it will be over-ripe. The fruit should feel heavy for its size and the skin should not be bruised or damaged. Gently press the rind with your thumbs at the stalk end; it should give a little. Melons will ripen quickly at room temperature and should be eaten within two or three days. Wrap cut melon tightly in clear film before storing in the fridge, or its scent may permeate other foods.

Preparing Melon

For serving as an antipasto, *cut the melon into wedges, scoop out the seeds and run a flexible knife between the rind and flesh. Remove the rind before serving.*

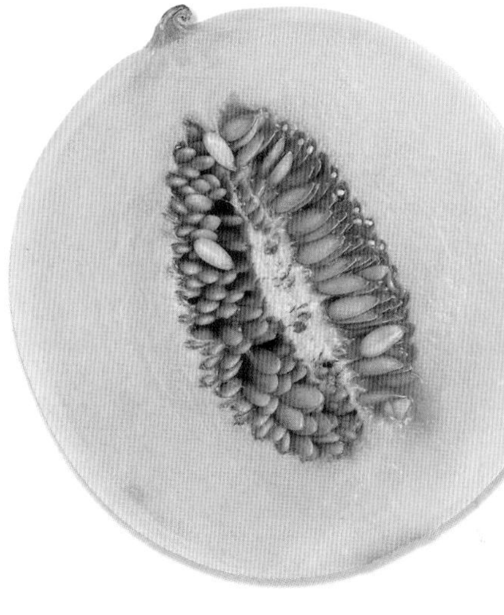

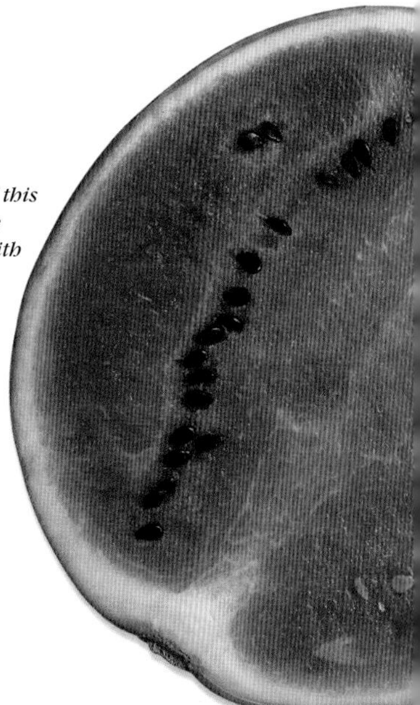

Napoletana melon
The sweet scented flesh of this and the similar cantaloupe melon is perfect for eating with Parma ham as an antipasto

Pesche (peaches) and pesche noci (nectarines)

Peaches, with their velvety skin and sweet, juicy flesh, are a summer fruit grown in central and southern Italy. The most common variety is the *pesca gialla* (yellow peach), which has succulent, yellow flesh. More highly prized are the *pesche bianche* (white peaches), whose pink-tinted flesh is full of juice and flavour.

Nectarines have smooth plum-like skins and taste very similar to peaches. They also come in yellow and white varieties and, like peaches, the white nectarines have a finer flavour. Some people prefer nectarines as a dessert fruit because they do not require peeling. Peaches and nectarines are interchangeable in cooked dishes.

Culinary Uses

Peaches and nectarines are delicious served as a dessert fruit, but can also be macerated in fortified wine or spirits or poached in white wine and syrup. They have a particular affinity with almonds; a favourite Italian dessert is *pesche ripiene alla piemontese*, halved peaches stuffed with crumbled almond-flavoured amaretti biscuits and baked in white wine. They are also delicious served with raspberries, or made into fruit drinks (the famous Bellini cocktail is made with fresh peach juice) and ice creams and sorbets.

Buying and Storing

Peaches are in season from June to September. Make sure they are ripe, but not too soft, with unwrinkled and unblemished skins. They should have a sweet, intense scent. Peaches and nectarines bruise very easily, so try to buy those that have been kept in compartmented trays rather than piled into punnets.

Do not keep peaches and nectarines for more than a day or two. If they are very ripe, store them in the fridge; under-ripe fruit will ripen in a couple of days if kept in a brown paper bag at room temperature.

Preparing Peaches

To peel peaches, place them in a heatproof bowl and pour boiling water over them. Leave for 15–30 seconds (depending on how ripe they are), then refresh in very cold water; the skins will slip off easily.

Peaches
This summer fruit is grown in central and southern Italy

Watermelon
Occasionally served on its own in wedges as a dessert, this vibrant red fruit is more usually chopped and added to a fruit salad

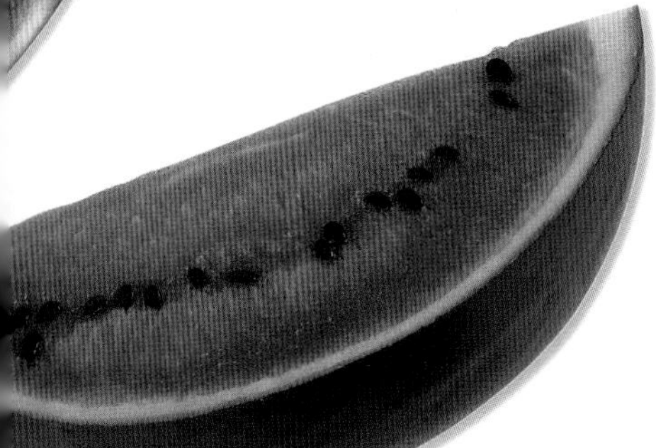

Nectarines
These smooth-skinned fruits are delicious served as a dessert fruit

Fruit

Uva (grapes)

Italy is the world's largest producer of grapes of all kinds. Almost every rural property boasts an expanse of vineyards, some producing wine-making grapes intended only for home consumption. Others (particularly in Chianti and the south) are destined for the enormous Italian wine-making industry. But Apulia, Abruzzo and Sicily produce sweet dessert grapes on a vast commercial scale, from large luscious Italia, with their fine muscat flavour, to Cardinal, named for its deep red colour, purple Alphonse Lavallé, and various small seedless varieties.

Despite their high calorific value, grapes are extremely good for you, since they are rich in potassium, iron and vitamins.

History

Wild grapes grew in the Caucasus as early as the Stone Age, and early man soon discovered the secret of cultivating vineyards and making wine. The Greeks and Romans discovered that drying grapes transformed them into sweet raisins and sultanas. The Gauls invented the wooden wine cask, and from that time wine production became a major industry.

Culinary Uses

Dessert grapes are best eaten on their own or as an accompaniment to cheese, but they can be used in pastries or as a garnish for cooked quails, guinea fowl or other poultry. The seeds are pressed into grapeseed oil, which has a neutral taste and is high in polyunsaturated fatty acids.

Buying and Storing

Choosing white, black or red grapes is a matter of preference; beneath the skin, the flesh is always pale green and juicy. Buy bunches of grapes with fruit which is of equal size and not too densely packed on the stalk. Check that none is withered or bad. The skin should have a delicate bloom and be firm to the touch. Try to eat one grape from a bunch to see how they taste. The flesh should be firm and very juicy and refreshing.

Grapes should be washed immediately after purchase, then placed in a bowl and kept in the fridge for up to three days. Keeping them in a plastic bag causes them to become over-ripe very quickly.

Preparing Grapes

Grapes used for cooking should be peeled and deseeded. Put them in a bowl, pour over boiling water and leave for 10–20 seconds, depending on the ripeness of the grapes. Peel off the skin. To remove the seeds, halve the grapes and scoop out the pips with the tip of a pointed knife.

Italia grapes
These luscious red and white grapes have a wonderful Muscat flavour

Nuts

Many different kinds of nuts are grown in Italy – chestnuts and hazelnuts in the north, pine nuts in the coastal regions, and almonds, pistachios and walnuts in the south. They are used in a wide variety of savoury dishes, cakes and pastries, or served as a dessert with a glass of *vin santo* (sweet white wine).

Castagne (chestnuts)

These are a mainstay of Tuscan and Sardinian cooking, dating back to the days when the peasants could not afford wheat to make flour, so they ground up the chestnuts that grow in abundance throughout the region instead. Most varieties of sweet chestnut contain two or three separate nuts inside the spiky green husk, but commercially grown varieties contain a single, large nut, which is easier to peel and better for serving whole.

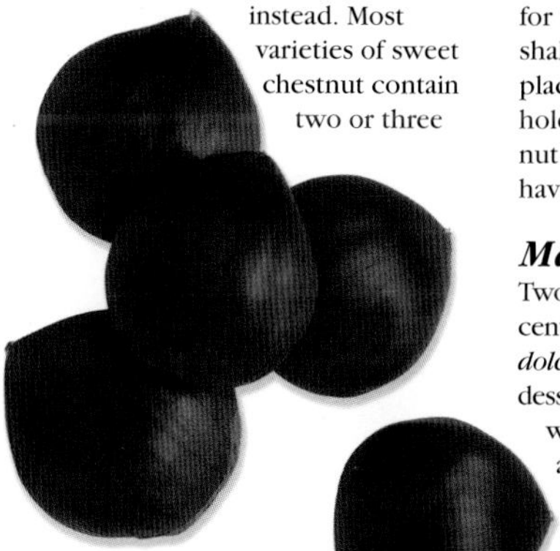

Chestnuts
A mainstay of Tuscan and Sardinian cooking

Chestnuts have shiny, rich reddish-brown shells with a wrinkled, thin skin beneath, which can be very hard to remove. They cannot be eaten raw, but once cooked, the starchy nuts are highly nutritious and very sustaining.

Culinary Uses

Chestnuts roasted over an open fire conjure up the spirit of autumn. Peeled chestnuts can be boiled, poached in red wine or milk or fried in butter as a garnish. They make hearty soups, or can be puréed into sauces for game. In Piedmont, they are candied to make marrons glacés, and a favourite Italian dessert is *monte bianco*, a rich concoction of puréed chestnuts and cream.

Chestnut flour is still widely used in Tuscany and Liguria, where it is baked into cakes and pastries, such as *castagnaccio*, a confection with pine nuts and herbs.

Buying and Storing

The nicest chestnuts are those you gather yourself, but if you are buying them, look for large, shiny specimens, with no tiny maggot holes in the shells. The chestnuts should feel heavy for their size and not rattle when you shake them. They will keep in a cool place for at least two weeks. If any holes appear in the shells, discard the nut immediately, or you will very soon have an infestation of maggots.

Preparing Chestnuts

There are three possible ways to peel chestnuts.

Slit the domed side of the shells with a very sharp knife, then drop them into boiling water for 5 minutes, or put them in a roasting pan with a little hot water and cook in a very hot oven for about 10 minutes. Shell and skin the chestnuts as soon as they are cool enough to handle. Alternatively, shell the raw chestnuts and boil them in their skins for about 20 minutes, then peel off the skins.

Mandorle (almonds)

Two varieties of almonds are grown in central and southern Italy. *Mandorle dolci* (sweet almonds) are eaten as a dessert or used in cooking and baking, while *mandorle amare* (bitter almonds) are used to flavour liqueurs like amaretto or bittersweet confections such as amaretti bicuits. These almonds are not edible in their raw state; in fact, they are poisonous if consumed in large quantities. Both types of almonds have a velvety pale green outer casing; the hard light brown shell within encloses one or two oval nuts.

Culinary Uses

Early in the season (late May), sweet almonds can be eaten raw as a dessert. They have a delicious fresh flavour and the brown skin is still soft enough to be palatable. Later, dried sweet almonds are blanched, slivered or ground to be used for cakes, pastries and all sorts of confectionery, including *marzapane* (marzipan) and *croccante* (almond brittle). They can be devilled or salted as an appetizing snack with an *aperitivo*. Toasted almonds are the classic garnish for trout, and go well with chicken or rabbit. Dried bitter almonds are used in small quantities to add a more intense flavour to biscuits and cakes.

Almonds
In Italy in early spring, fresh almonds are eaten raw as a dessert

Nuts

Buying and Storing

Fresh almonds in the shell are available from late May to late June. They are difficult to crack, so you may prefer to buy ready-shelled nuts. They should look plump, and the skins should not feel too dry. Pre-blanched almonds can often be a disappointment; buy the nuts with their skins on and blanch them yourself. Store shelled almonds in an airtight container for no longer than a month.

Shelled almonds
These dried almonds are used for cakes, pastries and confectionery

Nocciole (hazelnuts)

Fresh hazelnuts are harvested in August and September and during these months are always sold in their frilled green husks. The small round nuts have a very sweet flavour and a milky texture when fresh. In Italy, they are generally dried and used in confectionery and cakes.

Culinary Uses

Hazelnuts are used in all sorts of confectionery, including *torrone* (a sort of nougat) and *gianduiotti*, a delicious fondant chocolate from Piedmont. The famous chocolate *baci* ("kisses") from Perugia contain a whole hazelnut in the centre. Hazelnuts are finely ground to make cakes and biscuits, and are excellent in stuffings for poultry and game.

Buying and Storing

If hazelnuts are sold in their fresh green husks, you can be sure they are fresh and juicy. Otherwise, look for shiny shells which are not too thick and unblemished; cracked shells will cause the nut to shrivel and dry out. Shelled hazelnuts should be kept in an airtight container for no longer than one month.

Shelled hazelnuts
These dried nuts are used for confectionery and cakes

Hazelnuts
When fresh, these small nuts have a very sweet flavour

Noci (walnuts)

Walnuts grow in abundance throughout central and southern Italy. The kernels, shaped like the two halves of a brain, grow inside a pale brown, heavily indented shell enclosed by a smooth green fleshy husk or "shuck". Fresh walnuts have a delicious milky sweetness and a soft texture, which hardens as the nuts mature. Walnuts do not need to be skinned before eating.

Walnuts
In Italy, fresh walnuts are very often eaten straight from the shell as a dessert

Preparing Almonds

To blanch almonds, place them in a strainer and plunge into boiling water for a few seconds. As soon as the skin begins to loosen, transfer the almonds to a bowl of cold water and slip off the skins. Dry thoroughly before storing.

CULINARY USES

Fresh walnuts are usually eaten straight from the shell as a dessert. They can be ground or chopped and used in cakes and desserts, or halved and used for decoration. They are used to make savoury sauces for pasta, such as *salsa di noce*, a rich combination of ground walnuts, butter and cream. Walnut oil has a distinctive flavour and, used sparingly, makes an excellent salad dressing. Unripe walnuts can be pickled, and they are used to make sweet, sticky liqueurs.

BUYING AND STORING

Fresh "wet" walnuts are available from late September to late October. They should be kept in a wicker basket and eaten within a week. Dried walnuts should not have cracked or broken shells. They will keep for at least two months. Never store walnuts in the fridge, as the oil they contain will harden and ruin the flavour. Dried walnut kernels will have the flavour and texture of fresh nuts if they are soaked in milk for at least 4 hours.

Pinoli (pine nuts)

Pine nuts (more accurately known as pine kernels) are actually the seeds from the stone pine trees that grow in profusion along the Adriatic and Mediterranean coasts of Italy. The small, oblong, cream-coloured seeds grow inside a hard husk and are extracted from between the scales of the pine cones. The soft-textured kernels, which have an oily, slightly resinous flavour, are always sold de-husked. They can be eaten raw, but are usually toasted before use to bring out the flavour.

CULINARY USES

Pine nuts are used in many Italian dishes, both sweet and savoury, but they are best known as an essential ingredient of pesto. They go well with meat and game, and make exceptionally delicious biscuits and tarts.

Pine nuts
The oily, slightly resinous flavour is accentuated by toasting

Pistachio nuts
Grown in southern Italy, these sweet, delicately flavoured nuts are used in mortadella

PREPARING PINE NUTS

For most recipes and when used as a garnish, they should be lightly toasted. Heat a dry, heavy frying pan, put in the pine nuts and toss quickly until they turn pale golden. Do not allow them to brown, or they will taste unpleasant.

BUYING AND STORING

Pine nuts are always sold out of the husk. Because they are very oily, they go rancid quite quickly, so buy only as much as you need at any one time. Store them in an airtight container in the fridge for not more than a week.

Pistacchi (pistachios)

Pistachios are native to the Near East, but are grown in southern Italy, particularly Sicily. The small, bright green nut has a yellowish-red skin and is enclosed in a smooth, pale shell. Pistachios have a sweet, delicate flavour, which makes them ideal for desserts, but they are also used to stud mortadella and other pale cooked meat products.

CULINARY USES

Pistachios can be eaten raw or roasted and salted as a snack with an *aperitivo*. Their colour enhances most white meats and poultry. They make deliciously rich ice cream and are used in *cassata gelata*, the famous Sicilian dessert.

BUYING AND STORING

If possible, buy pistachios still in their shells. These will be easier to open if they are already slightly ajar; once open, the nut is very easy to remove. Shelled, blanched pistachios are also available. They are useful for cooking, but lack the fine flavour of whole nuts. Store blanched pistachios in an airtight container for up to two weeks. Whole nuts will keep for well over a month.

Herbs & Seasonings

Herbs are vital to Italian cooking. Their aromatic flavour adds depth and interest to what is essentially plain cooking, based on fine, fresh ingredients. It is impossible to imagine roast chicken or veal without rosemary or sage, or tomatoes or pesto without basil. Many wild herbs grow in the Italian countryside, and these are often incorporated into Italian recipes. One of the most popular is mentuccia, *a wild mint with tiny leaves and the delicate flavour of marjoram. If a recipe specifies* mentuccia *or its close relative* nepitella, *substitute a smaller quantity of mint.*

Basil
More than any other, this pungent, intensely flavoured herb is associated with Italian cooking – it is an essential ingredient in many dishes, including pesto

Always use fresh herbs whenever you can; the dried varieties have a stronger and often quite different taste, and lack the subtlety of fresh herbs. If you must use dried herbs, try to buy them freeze-dried; these taste much closer to the real thing. As a general rule, you will need only about one-third as much dried herb as fresh – in other words, allow about 5 ml/1 tsp dried herbs for every 15 ml/1 tbsp fresh.

Basilico (basil)

Basil, with its intense aroma and fresh, pungently sweet flavour, is associated with Italian cooking more than any other herb. It is an essential ingredient of pesto, but it also finds its way into soups, salads and almost all dishes based on tomatoes, with which it has an extraordinary affinity. There are over 50 varieties of this annual herb, but the one most commonly used in Italy is sweet basil, with its fresh broad green leaves and wonderfully spicy aroma.

Culinary Uses

Basil has a volatile flavour, so it is best added to dishes at the end of cooking. It can be used in any dish that contains tomatoes and is delicious sprinkled on to a pizza.
It adds a pungent, sweet note to almost all salads and is particularly good with white fish and seafood.
It makes an excellent flavouring for omelettes and is often added to minestrone. The most famous of all basil dishes is pesto, the fragrant Genoese sauce made by pounding together fresh basil, garlic, Parmesan, pine nuts and olive oil.

Buying and Storing

In sunny climates, such as southern Italy, basil grows outdoors all through the summer. In other places it is available cut or growing in pots all year round, so there really is no reason to use dried basil. Look for sweet basil with bright green leaves – the larger the better. If you have grown your own and have a glut, you can freeze basil leaves to preserve the flavour, but they lose their fresh texture and darken in colour. Alternatively, put a bunch of basil in a jar and top up with olive oil for a fragrant flavoured oil for dressings. To store fresh cut basil, wrap it in damp kitchen paper and keep in the vegetable drawer of the fridge for up to two days.

Preparing Basil

Basil leaves are tender and bruise easily, so never chop them with a knife, but tear them lightly with your fingers immediately before using.

Pesto

To make enough pesto for 4–6 servings of pasta, put 115 g/4 oz basil leaves in a mortar with 25 g/1 oz pine nuts, 2 fat peeled garlic cloves and a large pinch of coarse salt, and crush to a paste with a pestle. Work in 50 g/2 oz freshly grated Parmesan. Gradually add about 120 ml/4 fl oz extra virgin olive oil, working it in thoroughly with a wooden spoon to make a thick, creamy sauce. Put the pesto in a screwtop jar; it will keep for several weeks in the fridge.

Maggiorana (sweet marjoram) and origano *(oregano)*

These two highly aromatic herbs are closely related (oregano is the wild variety), but marjoram has a much milder flavour. Marjoram is more commonly used in northern Italy, while oregano is widely used in the south to flavour tomato dishes, vegetables and pizzas. Drying greatly intensifies the flavour of both herbs, so they should be used very sparingly.

Culinary Uses

In northern Italy, sweet marjoram is used to flavour meat, poultry, vegetables and soups; the flavour goes particularly well with carrots and cucumber. Despite its rather pungent aroma, marjoram has a delicate flavour, so it should be added to long-cooked foods towards the end of cooking.

Oregano is used exclusively in southern Italian cooking, especially in tomato-based dishes. It is a classic flavouring for pizza, but should always be used in moderation.

Buying and Storing

Marjoram and oregano are in season throughout the summer, but cut fresh herbs are available all year round in supermarkets. The leaves dry out quickly, so store them in plastic bags in the fridge; they will keep for up to a week. Dried oregano should be stored in small airtight jars away from the light. It loses its pungent flavour after a few months, so only buy a little at a time.

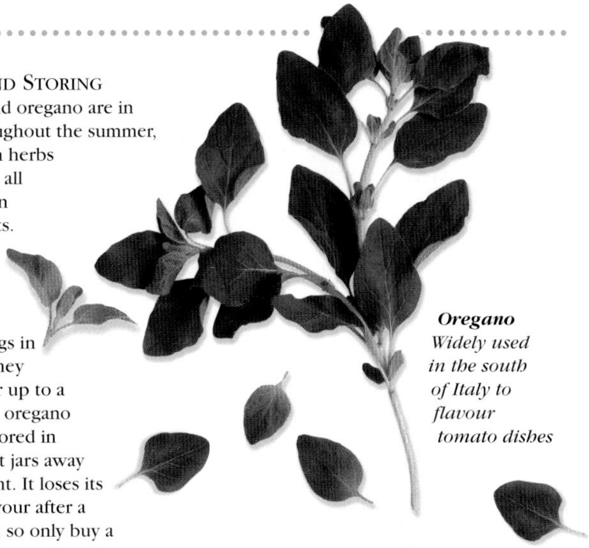

Oregano
Widely used in the south of Italy to flavour tomato dishes

Prezzemolo (parsley)

Italian parsley is the flat leaf variety, which has a more robust flavour than curly parsley. It has attractive dark green leaves, which resemble coriander. It is used as a flavouring in innumerable cooked dishes, but rarely as a garnish. If flat leaf parsley is not available, curly parsley makes a perfectly adequate substitute. Parsley is an extremely nutritious herb, rich in iron and potassium and vitamin C.

Marjoram
The aromatic flavour of this herb is very similar to that of oregano, but much milder

Parsley
Italian parsley is the flat leafed variety. It has a strong, robust flavour

Herbs & Seasonings

CULINARY USES
Parsley can be used to flavour innumerable savoury dishes. It adds colour and flavour to sauces, soups and risotti. The stalks can be used to flavour stocks and stews. Chopped parsley can be sprinkled over cooked savoury dishes; whole leaves are rarely used as a garnish in Italy.

BUYING AND STORING
Parsley is available all year round, so it should never be necessary to use the dried variety. A large bunch of parsley will keep for up to a week in the fridge if washed and wrapped in damp kitchen paper. Chopped parsley freezes very well and can be added to cooked dishes straight from the freezer.

Rosmarino (rosemary)

Spiky evergreen rosemary bushes, with their attractive blue flowers, grow wild all over Italy. The herb has a delicious, highly aromatic flavour, which is intensifed when it is dried. The texture of rosemary leaves is quite hard and the flavour very pungent, so it is never used raw, but only in cooking. It can easily overpower a dish, so only a few leaves should be used in a dish.

CULINARY USES
Rosemary combines extremely well with roast or grilled lamb, veal and chicken. A few needles will enhance the flavour of baked fish or any tomato dish, and it adds a wonderful flavour to roast potatoes and onions. Some rosemary branches added to the charcoal on a barbecue impart a superb flavour to whatever is being cooked. Dried rosemary can always be substituted for fresh; it is extremely pungent, so should be used very sparingly.

Salvia (sage)

Wild sage grows in profusion in the Italian countryside. There are several varieties, including the common garden sage, with furry silvery-grey leaves and spiky purple flowers, and clary sage, with hairy curly leaves, which is used to make dry vermouth. All sages have a slightly bitter aromatic flavour, which contrasts well with fatty meats such as pork. In northern Italy, particularly Tuscany, it is used to flavour veal and chicken. It is an excellent medicinal herb (the Latin name means "good health"); an infusion of sage leaves makes a good gargle for a sore throat.

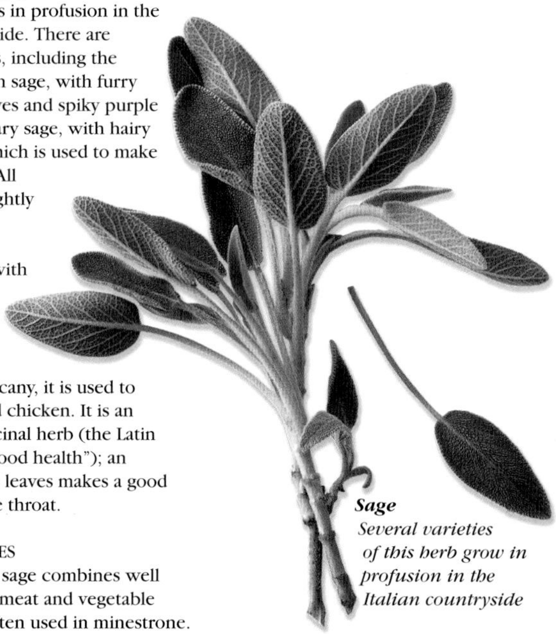

Sage
Several varieties of this herb grow in profusion in the Italian countryside

CULINARY USES
Used sparingly, sage combines well with almost all meat and vegetable dishes and is often used in minestrone. It has a particular affinity with veal (such as *osso buco*, *piccata* and, of course, calf's liver) and is an essential ingredient of *saltimbocca alla romana*, veal escalopes and *prosciutto crudo* topped with sage leaves and sautéed in butter and white wine. In Tuscany, white haricot beans (*fagioli*) are often flavoured with sage.

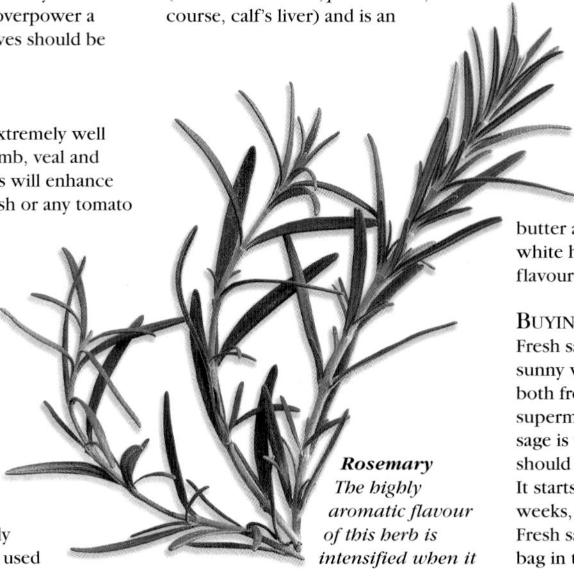

Rosemary
The highly aromatic flavour of this herb is intensified when it is dried

BUYING AND STORING
Fresh sage is very easy to grow on a sunny windowsill. It is available in both fresh and dried forms from supermarkets all year round. Dried sage is very strongly flavoured, so should be used in tiny quantities. It starts to taste musty after a few weeks, so replace it fairly frequently. Fresh sage should be stored in a plastic bag in the fridge; it will keep for up to a week.

Aceto (vinegar)

Like all wine-making countries, Italy produces excellent red and white wine vinegar as a by-product. The best vinegar is made from good wines, which are fermented in oak casks to give a depth of flavour. Good vinegar should be clean-tasting and aromatic, with no trace of bitterness and it should be transparent, not cloudy. White wine vinegar is pale golden with a pinkish tinge; red wine vinegar ranges from deep pink to dark red.

Aceto balsamico (balsamic vinegar)

Balsamic vinegar is the king of vinegars. Its name means "balm-like", reflecting its digestive qualities. Indeed, the best has a flavour so mellow and sweet that it can be drunk on its own as a *digestivo*. Balsamic vinegar is made in the area around Modena; the boiled and concentrated juice of local *trebbiano* grapes is aged in a series of barrels of decreasing size and different woods over a very long period – sometimes as long as 50 years – which gives it a slightly syrupy texture and a rich, deep mahogany colour. Like Parmigiano Reggiano and Parma ham, genuine balsamic vinegar (*aceto balsamico tradizionale di Modena*) is strictly controlled by law; it must have been aged in the wood for at least 12 years. Vinegar aged 20 years or more is called *stravecchio*.

Culinary Uses

Red and white wine vinegars are principally used to make salad dressings and marinades, or to preserve vegetables *sott'aceto* for *antipasti*. They also add the requisite sharpness to sauces like *agrodolce* (sweet and sour). Good balsamic vinegar is also used as a dressing, sometimes on its own. It can be used to finish a delicate sauce for white fish, poultry or calf's liver. A few drops sprinkled over ripe strawberries will enhance their flavour.

Buying and Storing

Price is usually an indication of quality where vinegar is concerned, so always buy the best you can afford. Genuine balsamic vinegar must be labelled *aceto balsamico tradizionale di Modena*; products that purport to be the real thing but are not labelled as such have either not been aged for long enough or, worse, are just red wine vinegar coloured and flavoured with caramel. Proper balsamic vinegar is expensive, but the flavour is so concentrated that a little goes a long way, and it is worth paying more for the genuine article. Vinegar will keep in a cool dark place for many months.

Balsamic vinegar
This is the king of vinegars and has a wonderfully sweet and mellow flavour

Red and white wine vinegars
These vinegars have a sharp flavour and are used principally for salad dressings

Herbs & Seasonings

Aglio (garlic)

Garlic is not, as you might suppose, a type of onion, but is a member of the lily family. The bulb or "head" is a collection of cloves held together by a papery white or purplish skin. When crushed or chopped it releases a pungent, slightly acrid oil with a very distinctive flavour and smell. Freshly picked garlic is milder than older, dried garlic, and the large, mauve-tinged variety has a more delicate flavour than the smaller white variety.

Garlic finds its way into many Italian dishes, but it is generally used with discretion so as not to flavour the food too aggressively. It is indispensable to certain dishes like *bagna cauda* (hot anchovy and garlic dip), *spaghetti all'aglio e olio* (garlic and olive oil) and pesto. In the south, garlic is used to flavour tomato sauces and fish soups.

Culinary Uses

Used in small quantities, garlic enlivens almost any sauce, soup or stew. It can be roasted with lamb and potatoes, or baked in its skin for a mellower flavour. Blanched, crushed garlic will aromatize olive oil to make an excellent dressing for salads or to use in cooking where only a hint of garlic flavour is required. Raw skinned garlic cloves can be rubbed over toasted croutons to make flavourful br*uschetta* bases.

Buying and Storing

Garlic sold loose by the head or kilo is usually fresher and better than pre-packaged varieties. The heads should feel firm and the skin should not be too papery. Do not buy garlic that is sprouting green shoots; the cloves will be soft and of no culinary value.

Stored in a cool dry place, garlic will keep for many months. If possible, hang the heads in bunches to keep them aerated. Once garlic has become soft or wizened, it is useless, so throw it away.

Garlic
Italian cooks prefer to use garlic with discretion, but it is indispensable to many dishes. The purple-skinned variety has a more delicate flavour than the white variety

Preparing and Cooking Garlic

To peel garlic, cut off the root end with a small sharp knife and peel the skin upwards.

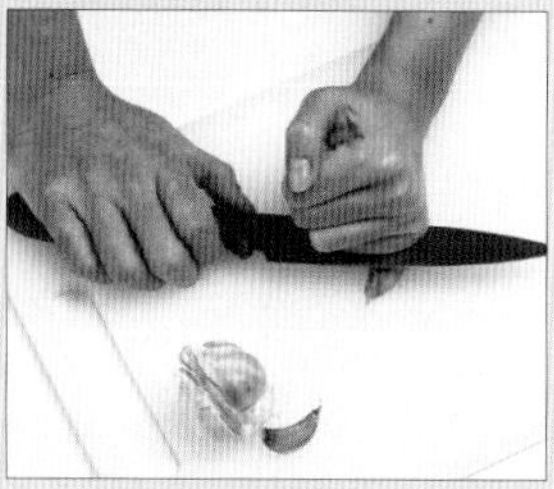

Alternatively, lay a garlic clove on the work surface, place the flat side of a heavy knife blade on top and bring the side of your fist sharply down on to the blade. This will flatten the garlic and split the skin.

To chop garlic, halve the clove and remove the bitter-tasting green shoot. Chop the garlic as finely as possible.

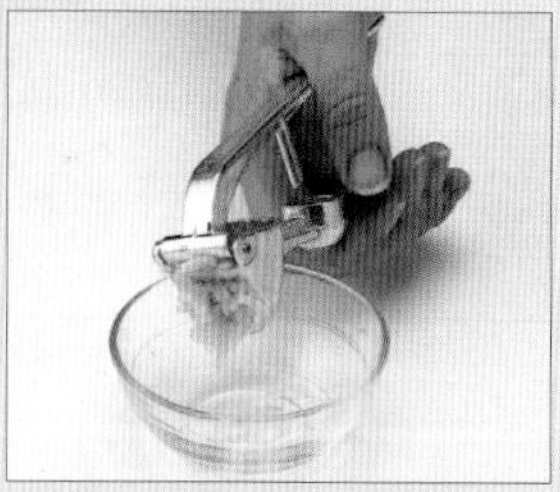

For very fine garlic, crush it in a garlic press.

Garlic should be softened gently in oil or butter; it will become very bitter if allowed to brown. For a subtle flavour, heat a whole clove of garlic in the oil, then remove it before adding the other ingredients. The flavour of garlic dissipates quite quickly during cooking, so for long-cooked dishes add it towards the end of the cooking time.

Olive (olives)

A wide variety of olives is cultivated all over Italy. Most are destined to be pressed into oil (nearly 20 per cent of their weight is oil), but some are kept as table olives to be salted, pickled or marinated, and served as part of an *antipasto* or used in cooking. There are two main types of olive, green (immature) and black (mature); both are bitter and inedible in their natural state. All olives have a high calorific content and are rich in iron, potassium and vitamins.

Green olives are the unripe fruit, which are picked in October or November. They have a sharper flavour and crunchier texture than black olives, which continue to ripen on the tree and are not harvested until December. Among the best Italian table olives are the small, shiny black Gaeta olives from Liguria. Wrinkled black olives from Lazio have a strong, salty flavour, while Sardinian olives are semi-ripened and are brown or purplish in colour. The largest olives come from Apulia and Sicily, where giant, green specimens are grown. These are sometimes stoned and stuffed with pimento, anchovy or almonds. Cured olives can be flavoured with all sorts of aromatics, such as garlic, local herbs, orange or lemon zest and dried chillies.

Black olives
Olives are among the oldest fruits known to man. They are grown all over Italy

History

Olive trees have been grown in the Mediterranean since biblical times, when they were brought there from the East by the Romans. Ancient civilizations venerated the olive tree; the Egyptians believed that the goddess Isis discovered the secret of extracting oil from the fruit.

Culinary Uses

Olives can be served on their own or as a garnish or topping for pizza. They are used as an ingredient in many Italian recipes, such as *caponata*. Sicilian *caponata* is a dome-shaped salad of fried aubergines with celery, onions, tomatoes, capers and green olives, while the Ligurian dish of the same name consists of stale biscuits or bread soaked in olive oil and topped with a mixture of chopped olives, garlic, anchovies and oregano. Olives combine well with Mediterranean ingredients like tomatoes, aubergines, anchovies and capers and are used in sauces for rabbit, chicken and firm-fleshed fish. Made into a paste with red wine vinegar, garlic and olive oil, they make an excellent topping for *crostini*.

Buying and Storing

Cured olives vary enormously in flavour, so ask to taste one before making your selection. Loose olives can be kept in an airtight container in the fridge for up to a week.

Green olives
These unripe olives have a sharper flavour than black olives

Capperi (capers)

Capers are the immature flower buds of a wild Mediterranean shrub. They are pickled in white wine vinegar or preserved in brine which gives them a piquant, peppery flavour. Sicilian capers are packed in whole salt, which should be rinsed off before using the capers. Bottled nasturtium flower buds are sometimes sold as a cheaper alternative to true capers. Caper berries look like large, fat capers on a long stalk, but they are actually the fruit of the caper shrub. They can be served as a cocktail snack or in a salad.

Caper berries
The pickled fruit of the caper shrub can be served as a cocktail snack

Herbs & Seasonings

Culinary Uses
Capers are mainly used as a condiment or garnish, but they also add zest to seafood and fish dishes, salads, pizzas and pasta sauces like the famous Sicilian *pasta colle sarde*, a mixture of sardines, parsley, tomatoes, pine nuts and raisins.

Buying and Storing
Choosing pickled or brined capers is a matter of taste, as is whether or not you should rinse them before use. Large capers are usually cheaper than small ones; there is no difference in flavour, but small capers make a more attractive garnish. Salt-packed capers are always sold loose by the *etto* (100 g/3½ oz); they should be used as soon as possible. Once opened, jars of capers should be kept in the fridge. Make sure any capers left in the jar are covered with the preserving liquid.

Salted capers
These are used to add zest to fish dishes, salads and pasta sauces

Pickled capers
Rinsing these capers before use softens their sharp, piquant flavour

Olio di oliva (olive oil)
Unlike other oils, which are extracted from the seeds or dried fruits of plants, olive oil is pressed from the pulp of ripe olives, which gives it an inimitable richness and flavour. Different regions of Italy produce distinctively different olive oils; Tuscan oil (considered the best) is pungent and peppery, Ligurian oil is lighter and sweeter, while the oils from the south and Sicily are powerful and nutty.

The best olive oil is *extra vergine*, which is strictly controlled and regulated like wine. This is made simply by pressing the olives to extract the oil, with no further processing. Extra virgin olive oil must have an acidity level of less than 1 per cent. The distinctive fruity flavour of this oil makes it ideal for dressings and using raw. Virgin olive oil is pressed in the same way, but has a higher acidity level and a less refined flavour. It, too, can be used as a condiment, but is also suitable for cooking. Unclassified olive oil is refined, then blended with virgin oil to add flavour. It has an undistinguished taste, but is ideal for cooking; it should not be used as a condiment.

Buying and Storing
The best olive oil comes from Lucca in Tuscany and is very expensive. It is made with slightly under-ripe olives, which give it a luminous green colour. If your budget does not stretch to this, buy the best extra virgin oil you can afford to use "neat" or in dressings. Experiment with small bottles of different extra virgin oils to see which you prefer. For cooking, pure olive oil is fine. Once opened, olive oil should be kept in a cool place away from the light. The best oil will soon lose its savour, so use it within six months.

Cooking with Olive Oil

Olive oil can be heated to very high temperatures without burning or smoking, which makes it ideal for frying, sauce-making and other cooking. Extra virgin olive oil should be saved for dressing fish, vegetables and salads.

Extra virgin olive oil
The distinctive fruity flavour makes this oil ideal for salad dressings

Peperoncini (dried red chillies)

Hot flakes of dried chillies are added to many southern Italian dishes, such as *arrabiata* sauce and the famous *pasta all'aglio, olio e peperoncino* (dressed with garlic, oil and chillies). Chillies are unusual in that their "hotness" is usually in inverse proportion to their size, so larger dried varieties are generally milder than the smaller ones. In summer, bunches of tiny fresh red chillies can be bought in Italian markets. These can be used fresh, preserved in olive oil to make a spicy dressing or to drizzle over a pizza, or hung up to dry and crumbled to add "oomph" to a dish. Crushed chilli flakes are available in jars.

Culinary Uses

A small pinch of dried chilli flakes spices up stews and sauces, particularly those made with tomatoes. For a really hot pizza, crumble a few flakes over the top. Dried chillies are extremely fiery and should be used very sparingly.

Buying and Storing

Dried chillies will last for years, but they do lose their savour over a period of time, so buy only small quantities. Whole *peperoncini* should be hung up in bunches and crumbled directly into the dish you are cooking.

Dried red chilli flakes
Just a small pinch of these fiery flakes spices up stews and sauces

Zafferano (saffron)

Saffron consists of the dried stigmas of the saffron crocus. It takes about 80,000 crocuses to produce about 500 g/1¼ lb of spice and these have to be hand-picked, so it is hardly surprising that saffron is the world's most expensive spice. Saffron stigmas or threads are a vivid orangey-red colour with a pungent aroma. They are also sold ground into powder. Saffron has a highly aromatic flavour and will impart a wonderful, rich golden colour to risotti and sauces.

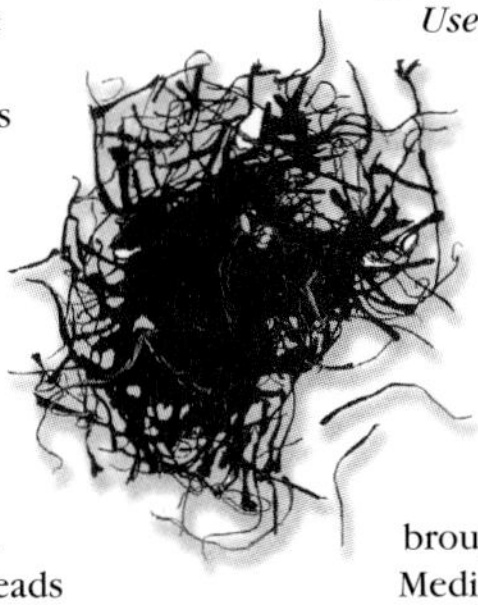

Saffron threads
Used to flavour and colour the classic risotto alla milanese

Dried chillies
These are often used in fiery southern Italian dishes, such as arrabbiata *sauce*

History

Saffron originated in Asia Minor, where it was used by ancient civilizations as a flavouring, as a dye, in perfumery and for medicinal purposes. Arab traders brought the spice to the Mediterranean in the 10th century; for centuries it was so highly prized that stealing or adulterating it was punishable by death. The best saffron is nowadays cultivated in Spain, but it is also grown in Italy.

Culinary Uses

In Italy, saffron is mainly used to flavour and colour risotti, like the classic *risotto alla milanese*. It is excellent in sauces for fish and poultry and can be used to flavour biscuits and cakes.

Buying and Storing

Saffron threads are sold in small boxes or jars containing only a few grams. The wiry threads should be a deep orangey-red in colour; paler yellowish-orange threads are probably the much cheaper and less desirable safflower, which will add colour but not flavour to a dish. Powdered saffron is convenient to use, but less reliable, as it may have been adulterated with safflower. Stored in small, airtight containers, saffron will keep for months.

Cooking with Saffron

Do not add saffron directly to a dish. Infuse threads in a little hot water for at least 5 minutes before blending into a dish to bring out the flavour and ensure even colouring. Add the soaking water together with the threads. Never fry saffron in hot oil or butter; this will ruin the flavour.

Cakes, Biscuits & Breads

In Italy it is perfectly normal and acceptable for a hostess to buy a dolce *(cake or dessert) to serve at the end of a meal, rather than make it herself. Pastry shops and bakeries sell a wide variety of traditional tarts, spiced yeast cakes and biscuits to be enjoyed with coffee or a glass of vin santo, sweet dessert wine or a liqueur. Some of these, like* panettone *and* pastiera napoletana, *are reserved for special occasions like Christmas and Easter, and almost every town has its own speciality for its local saint's day.*

Amaretti (macaroons)

Amaretti biscuits are made from ground almonds, egg whites and sugar. They have a distinctive flavour, which comes from the addition of bitter almonds. They originated in Venice during the Renaissance and their English name of macaroons comes from the Venetian macerone, meaning "fine paste". They come in dozens of different forms, from the famous crunchy sugar-encrusted biscuits wrapped in pairs in twists of crisp white paper to soft-centred macaroons wrapped in brightly-coloured foil. Amaretti are delicious dipped into hot coffee. They can also be crumbled to make a stuffing for baked peaches or apricots.

Panettone
This light-textured yeast cake is a speciality of Milan

Amaretti
These crunchy sugar-encrusted biscuits are delicious dipped into hot coffee

Cantucci

These hard, high-baked lozenge-shaped biscuits from Tuscany are designed to be dipped into *espresso* coffee or *vin santo*. When moistened, they become deliciously soft and crumbly. They are usually studded with almonds or other nuts and flavoured with aniseed or vanilla.

Cantucci

Panettone

Literally meaning "big bread", *panettone* is a light-textured spiced yeast bread containing sultanas and candied fruit. Originally a speciality of Milan, it is now sold all over Italy as a Christmas delicacy and is traditionally given as a gift. *Panettoni* can vary in size from small to enormous. They are sometimes sold in pastel-coloured dome-shaped boxes, which are often hung from the ceiling of bakeries and delicatessens, and look very festive. At Easter, they are baked into the shape of a lamb (*agnello*) or a dove (*colomba*). *Panettone* is sliced into wedges and eaten like cake.

Crumiri

These sweet elbow-shaped biscuits are a speciality of Piedmont. The rich golden brown dough is made with polenta and honey and piped through a fluted nozzle to give the biscuits their characteristic ridged texture. Although the biscuits seem hard on the outside, the polenta flour gives the *crumiri* a pleasantly crunchy texture. *Crumiri* are good teatime biscuits, but they are also excellent dipped in hot coffee.

Panforte

Somewhat resembling a Christmas pudding in flavour, but shaped like a flat disc, *panforte* is a rich, dark spiced cake crammed with dried fruit and toasted nuts. It is a speciality of Siena and is sold in a colourful glossy wrapping, often depicting Sienese scenes. It is extremely rich, so can only be eaten in small quantities, which is just as well, since it is also quite expensive.

Panettone
The characteristic box often hangs from the ceiling in Italian delicatessens

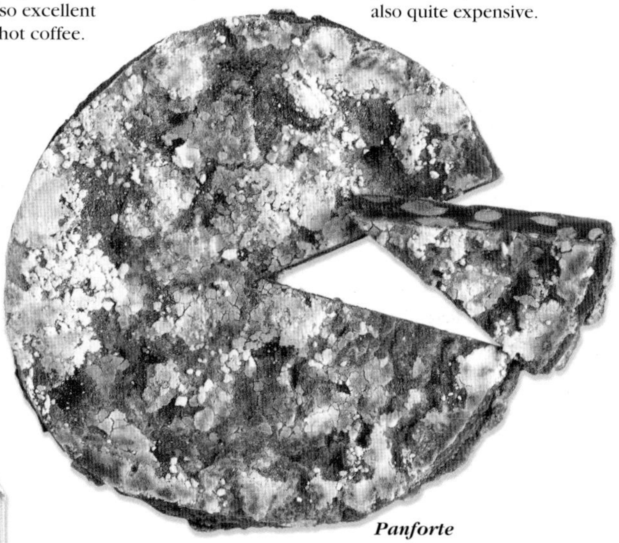

Panforte
This Italian spice cake is packed full of fruit and nuts

Savoiardi
These soft-textured, Italian sponge finger biscuits are used as a base for tiramisu

Savoiardi (sponge biscuits)

As their name suggests, *savoiardi* come from the Savoy region of Piedmont. They are plumper and wider than sponge fingers and have a softer texture. They are excellent dunked into tea or coffee, and are traditionally served with zabaglione; but they are best of all used as a base for tiramisu, the wickedly rich Italian coffee and mascarpone dessert.

Pane (Bread)

No Italian meal is ever served without bread to accompany the food. Indeed, it often constitutes one of the dishes in a meal in the form of *crostini* and *bruschetta* (toasted canapés), soups like *pancotto*, *panzanella* (bread salad) or pizza. In Tuscany, bread plays a more important part in the food of the region than pasta. A favourite antipasto is *fettunta*, toasted or grilled bread rubbed with garlic, anointed with plenty of olive oil and sprinkled with coarse salt. When a topping is added, it becomes *bruschetta*.

Italians buy or make fresh bread every day, but stale or leftover loaves are never wasted. Instead they are made into breadcrumbs and used for thickening sauces and stews, or for stuffings, salads or wonderfully sustaining soups.

There are hundreds of different types of Italian bread with many regional variations to suit the local food. Traditional Tuscan country bread is made without salt, since it is designed to be served with salty cured meats like salami and *prosciutto crudo*. (If you prefer salted bread, ask for *pane salato*.) Southern Italian breads often contain olive oil, which goes well with tomatoes. *Pane integrale* (wholemeal bread) is traditionally baked in a wood oven. The texture and flavour of the bread depends on the type of flour used and the amount of seasoning, but nearly all Italian breads are firm-textured with substantial crusts. You will never find flabby damp white sandwich loaves in an Italian bakery, although the inside of traditional white *panini* (bread rolls) can sometimes resemble cotton wool.

Ciabatta

These flattish, slipper-shaped loaves with squared or rounded ends are made with olive oil and are often flavoured with fresh or dried herbs, olives or sun-dried tomatoes. They have an airy texture inside and a pale, crisp crust. *Ciabatta* is delicious served warm, and is excellent for sandwiches.

Ciabatta
These popular loaves are available plain or flavoured with olives or sun-dried tomatoes

Wholemeal bread
In Italy this bread is traditionally baked in a wooden oven

Focaccia

A dimpled flat bread similar to pizza dough, *focaccia* is traditionally oiled and baked in a wood oven. A whole *focaccia* from a bakery weighs several kilos and is sold by weight, cut into manageable pieces. A variety of ingredients can be worked into the dough or served as a topping – onions, *pancetta*, rosemary or oregano, ham, cheese or olives. *Focaccine* are small versions, which are split and served with fillings like a sandwich. In Apulia, *focaccia del Venerdi Santo*, with its topping of fennel, chicory, anchovies, olives and capers, is traditionally served on Good Friday.

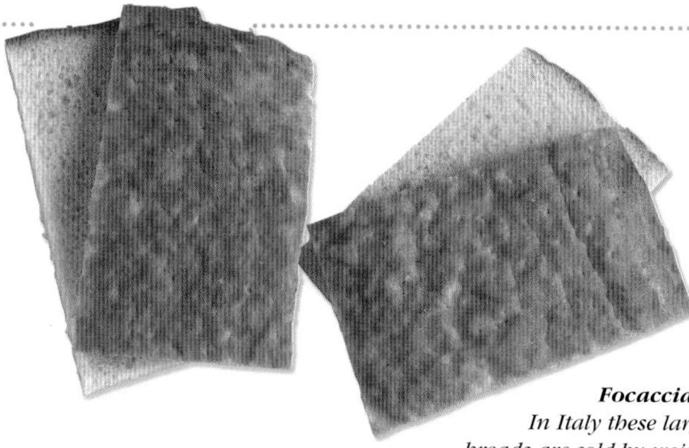

Focaccia
In Italy these large flat breads are sold by weight, cut into manageable pieces. It can be plain, as here, or flavoured with herbs, sun-dried tomatoes or olives

White bread
Like nearly all Italian breads, this one is firm-textured, with a substantial crust

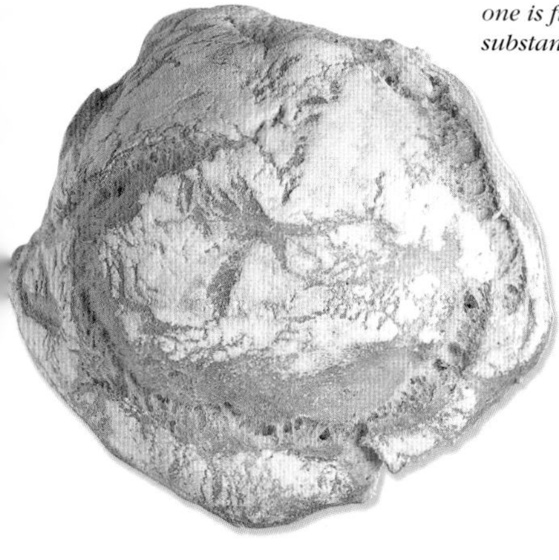

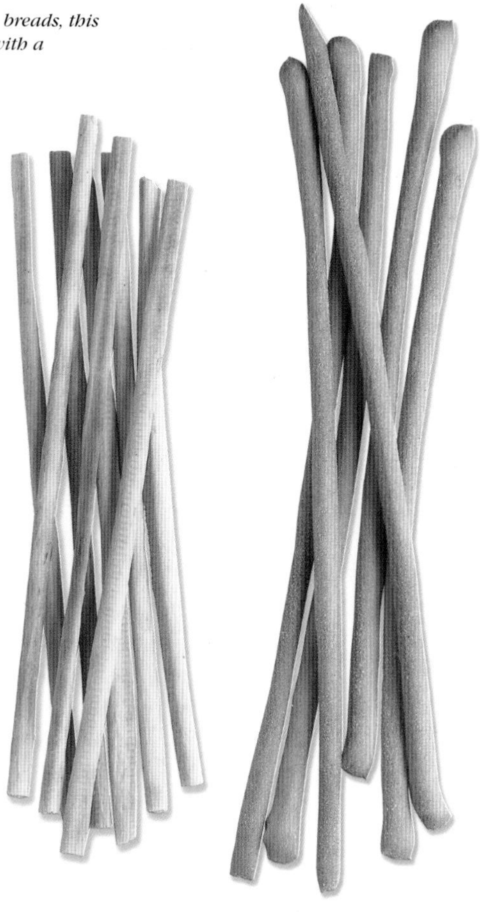

Grissini
The cover charge in every Italian restaurant invariably includes packets of bread sticks

Grissini

These crisp golden bread sticks originated in Turin, but are now found in almost every Italian restaurant, packed in long envelopes. They range in size from matchstick-thin to hefty, knobbly, home-baked batons. Italian bakers often use up any leftover dough to make *grissini*, which are sold loose by weight. They can be rolled in sesame or poppy seeds for extra flavour.

Store Cupboard

One of the great joys of Italian food is that you can create a delicious meal almost instantly using ingredients from your store cupboard. Rice and pasta can be combined with any number of bottled or tinned vegetables, seafood or sauces to make a speedy and nutritious meal. Unopened jars and cans last for months, if not years, so it is worth keeping a selection in your store cupboard for an impromptu meal that you can rustle up in moments.

Pesto

Although nothing is as good as home-made pesto, there are some excellent bottled varieties of this fragrant green basil sauce. Traditional pesto is made with basil, pine nuts, Parmesan or Pecorino cheese and olive oil, but you may also find a red version based on sweet red peppers.

Culinary Uses

Pesto can be used as an instant dressing for any type of pasta or potato gnocchi. It gives a lift to risotti and tomato sauces, and is delicious stirred into minestrone or tomato-based soups. A spoonful of pesto will add a new dimension to bottled mayonnaise, creating a rich, pungent *maionese verde*. For a quick, attractive cocktail snack, halve some cherry tomatoes, scoop out the seeds and fill the tomatoes with pesto.

Pesto
Both the traditional green version shown here and a red type based on sweet red peppers are used to flavour sauces and pasta

Pomodori secchi (sun-dried tomatoes)

Sun-drying tomatoes intensifies their flavour to an astonishing sweetness and pungency and allows you to enjoy the full savour of tomatoes even in winter. If you are extremely lucky, you may still find in markets in southern Italy locally grown tomatoes that have been spread out to dry in the sun, but the commercially produced "sun-dried" varieties are actually air-dried by machine. Wrinkled red dried tomatoes are available dry in packets or preserved in olive oil. Dry tomatoes are brick-red in colour and have a chewy texture. They can be eaten on their own as a snack, but for cooking they should be soaked in hot water until soft (the tomato-flavoured soaking water can be used for a soup or sauce). Bottled sun-dried tomatoes are sold in chunky pieces or as a paste.

Dried tomatoes
Dried tomatoes should always be softened in water before use

Sun-dried tomatoes
These strong-flavoured tomatoes add extra piquancy to dishes

Culinary Uses

Sun-dried tomatoes add piquancy to vegetable dishes, soups or sauces. They can be chopped and added to a simple *sugo di pomodori* or a meaty *ragù* for extra flavour. They make an excellent *antipasto* combined with sliced fresh tomatoes, mozzarella and basil or with other preserved or pickled vegetables. They go well with fresh Mediterranean vegetables like fennel, aubergines and courgettes, and add a special something to egg dishes, such as *frittata*. Use the oil in which the tomatoes are preserved for salad dressings or for sweating vegetables for a soup or sauce.

The paste can be used in small quantities for sauces and soups, or used on its own or with a little butter as a dressing for pasta.

Passata
This rich tomato pureé varies in fineness from the ultra-smooth to the chunkier sugocasa

Passata (*tomato pulp*)

Rich red passata is simply sieved ripe tomatoes, a wonderfully convenient short-cut wherever tomato pulp is required. Depending on the degree of sieving, it can be perfectly smooth or slightly chunky (*polpa di pomodoro* or *passata rustica*: "rustic passata"). The chunky variety is sold in tall jars, while the smoothest type is available in cartons or jars. More highly concentrated tomato paste or purée (*concentrato di pomodoro*) is packed in small cans or tubes. This product is extremely strong and should only be used in small quantities.

Culinary Uses

Passata can be used as a basis for soups and sauces, and as a substitute for fresh tomatoes in all recipes where they require long cooking. For a very quick pasta sauce, sweat some finely chopped onion and garlic in olive oil, add a jar of passata and bubble the sauce while the pasta is cooking. Flavour with fresh basil, oregano, parsley or some chopped olives, capers and/or anchovies. For more body and depth and a richer colour, stir in a spoonful or two of tomato concentrate.

Black olive paste

Green olive paste

Pasta di olive (*olive paste*)

Green or, more usually, black olives are pounded to a paste with salt and olive oil and packed in small jars. Olive paste tends to be very salty and rich, so a little goes a long way.

Culinary Uses

Olive paste can be spread very thinly over pizza bases, or scraped on to toasted croûtons and topped with tomatoes or mushrooms to make *crostini*. Mixed with olive oil and a little lemon juice, it can be a dip for raw vegetables. For an interesting *antipasto*, mash a little olive paste into the yolks of halved hard-boiled eggs, spoon the mixture back into the cavity and top with a few capers.

A little olive paste adds a rich flavour to a tomato sauce, while a spoonful stirred into a vinaigrette makes a good dressing for a robust salad. If you are a real olive lover, stir a small amount into hot pasta for the simplest of dressings.

Legumi sott'olio (*vegetables preserved in oil*)

Italians produce a wide variety of vegetables preserved in olive or sunflower oil, or a mixture of both. The choicest are often cooked *alla brace* (grilled) before being packed in the best olive oil - tiny *carciofini* (artichokes), *funghi* and *porcini* (button and wild mushrooms), *peperoni* (red and yellow peppers) and *melanzane* (aubergines) - which look as beautiful as they taste. You will sometimes find large bulbous jars containing colourful layers of different vegetables in oil; these are packed by hand and are extremely expensive.

Culinary Uses

A mixture of oil-preserved vegetables combined with a selection of cured meats makes a wonderful *antipasto*. They can also be chopped or sliced and used to dress hot or cold pasta, or stirred into rice for a substantial cold salad. They make a delicious topping for *crostini* or pizza.

Artichoke hearts
These olive oil-packed vegetables are often combined with sliced cured meats to make an antipasto

Store Cupboard

Giardiniera (pickled vegetables)

Mixed pickled vegetables are sold packed *in agrodolce* (vinegar and oil). Single varieties like peeled or unpeeled aubergines and courgettes are available, but a mixture of these vegetables along with artichokes, baby onions, carrots, celery and peppers is more colourful. These vegetables are sometimes described as *alla contadina* (peasant-style).

Culinary Uses

Pickled vegetables can be served with salami and ham as an *antipasto*, or drained and mixed with raw vegetables and mayonnaise for a piquant version of *insalata russa* (Russian salad). Their vinegary taste makes an excellent counterpoint to plain cold roast meats or poultry.

Peppers
The vinegary flavour of these pickled vegetables goes well with cold roast meats

Filetti di acciughe (anchovy fillets)

Anchovy fillets are available preserved in salt or oil. The salted fillets have a superior flavour, but they are are only available in catering tins to be sold by the *etto* (100 g/3$^1/_2$ oz) in delicatessens. You can buy these and soak them for 30 minutes, then dry them thoroughly and pack them in olive oil, but it is more practical to buy ready canned or bottled anchovies.

Culinary Uses

Anchovies can be chopped and added to tomato sauces and salad dressings. They can be stirred into a fish risotto, or mixed with tomatoes and capers for a topping for pizzas or *crostini*. They are best of all made into *bagna cauda*, a delicious and quick hot dip for raw vegetables. For six people, heat 150 ml/5 fl oz/$^2/_3$ cup olive oil with 50 g/2 oz/4 tbsp unsalted butter. As soon as it begins to foam, add 3 finely chopped garlic cloves and soften but do not brown. Drain and roughly chop a 50 g/2 oz can of anchovy fillets, add to the pan and stir over low heat until they have disintegrated to a paste. Keep the sauce hot and dip in the vegetables.

Anchovy fillets
Usually chopped and added to sauces or salads for extra flavour. These are available packed in oil or salt – the salted variety have a better flavour

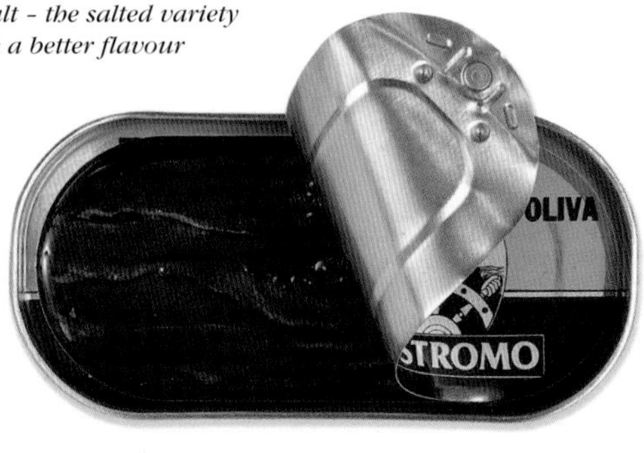

Bottarga (salted roe)

The pressed, salted and dried roe of the grey mullet or tuna, also known as *buttariga, butarega and ovotarica*, is a speciality of Sardinia, Sicily and the Veneto, where it is regarded as a great delicacy. It is usually packed in a sausage shape inside a skin that should be removed before preparing. Wrapped in clear film or polythene, it will keep for several months.

Culinary Uses

Bottarga can be served as an *antipasto* thinly sliced and dressed with a little extra virgin olive oil and lemon juice. In Sicily, it is served with *caponata*, a dome-shaped salad of fried aubergines and celery. It is delicious simply grated over hot pasta with a knob of unsalted butter and a little chopped fresh parsley or dried chilli flakes.

Baccalà (salted dried cod)

Air-drying is the oldest known method of preserving fish. Before the days of deep-freezing, dried fish was invaluable for people who wished to observe meatless days, but who lived far from the sea, because the salting and drying process ensures that it remains edible for many months. The most popular dried fish in Italy is salt cod, which is traditionally eaten on Good Friday. It is sometimes known confusingly as *stoccafisso* (although true stockfish is unsalted). It looks rather unappealing, like a flat, greyish board, but once it has been soaked and reconstituted it is absolutely delicious. Unlike other store cupboard ingredients, *baccalà* must be prepared a day in advance, but it is worth the effort.

Clams in brine

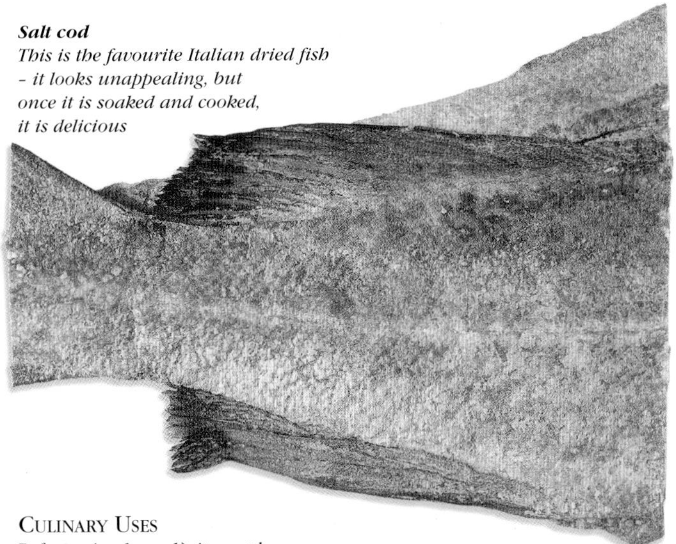

Salt cod
This is the favourite Italian dried fish - it looks unappealing, but once it is soaked and cooked, it is delicious

Culinary Uses

Before using *baccalà*, it must be soaked under cold running water for at least 8 hours to rehydrate it and remove the excess salt. Once this has been done, it can be creamed with olive oil, garlic, cream and parsley to make *baccalà mantecato*, a famous Venetian dish, which is served on fried polenta. In the Florentine version, the salt cod is cut into chunks, coated with flour and fried with tomatoes and onions. *Baccalà* combines well with all Mediterranean flavours and can be stewed or baked with red peppers, potatoes, fennel or celery, capers, olives and anchovies. Many recipes also include pine nuts and raisins or sultanas. For a simple pasta sauce, mix some flaked salt cod with cream and chopped herbs and stir it into the hot pasta.

Vongole (clams)

Tiny clams are sold packed in brine in glass jars. These miniature golden nuggets need no further cooking and can be simply heated through and tossed into hot pasta or risotto, or combined with tomato sauce. If you have time, drain the clams and reduce the juice in which they are packed with finely chopped garlic and a few dried chilli flakes to make a more intense sauce.

Mostarda di Cremona (mustard fruit chutney)

This sweet crystallized fruit chutney with its piquant undertone of the mustard was first produced over a hundred years ago in Cremona and Venice. Its vibrant multi-colour comes from the assortment of candied fruits from which it is made - cherries, pears, melons, figs, apricots and clementines, infused in mustard seed oil. Also known as *mostarda di frutta*, the chutney is traditionally served with sausages like zampone and cotechino, or roast and boiled beef, veal and pork. For an unusual and delicious dessert, serve the chutney as a topping for creamy mascarpone.

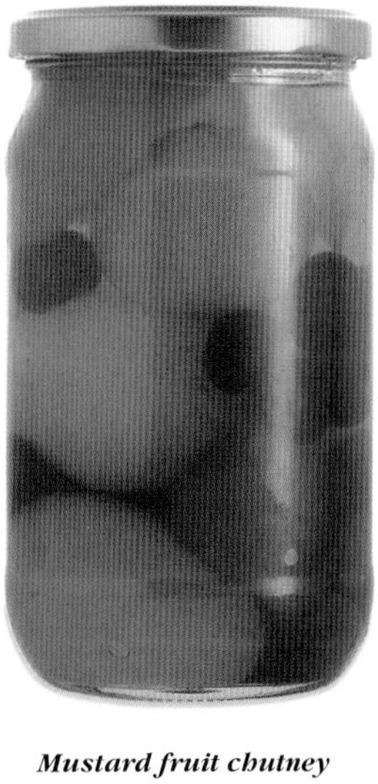

Mustard fruit chutney

Aperitifs & Liqueurs

Behind every bar in Italy is displayed row upon row of bottles containing dozens of different aperitivi *and* digestivi, *many of them never found outside Italy. They are consumed at any hour of the day; a favourite Italian morning drink is* caffè corretto, *espresso coffee laced with grappa or* Stock *(Italian brandy). Many of the vermouths and spirits are made from local ingredients, like herbs, nuts, lemons, artichokes or regional wines. The Italians have an unshakeable belief in the digestive properties of such drinks, many of which are so bitter that most non-Italians find them completely unpalatable. At the end of a restaurant meal, you will always find the men clustered around the bar aiding their digestion with a small glass of spirit or liqueur.*

Amaro

A very bitter *aperitivo* much beloved of the Italians, *amaro* is flavoured with gentian, herbs and orange peel and contains quinine and iron. Marginally less bitter than straight *amaro* are the wine-based *amari* like Campari, which is usually mixed with soda water and drunk before a meal to stimulate the appetite and cleanse the palate. Others, like Fernet-Branca, are served as a pick-me-up and cure for stomach upsets. *Amaro* is reputed to have excellent digestive and tonic properties, to cure hangovers and to have aphrodisiac qualities, which probably explains its popularity in Italy.

Campari

A bright crimson *aperitivo* from the *amaro* family, wine-based Campari has a bitter, astringent flavour. It was first produced in the 19th century by the Campari brothers from Milan, and has been produced by the same family ever since. Campari is sold in triangular single-portion bottles ready-mixed with soda (Campari soda). The neat bitters are an essential ingredient of cocktails like *Negroni* and *Americano*.

Campari soda

Amaro

Fernet-Branca

Cynar

This dark brown, intensely bitter, aperitif with an alcoholic content of 17 per cent is made from artichokes. Too bitter to swallow on its own, it is usually served as a long drink with ice and soda water.

Punt e Mes

The name of this intensely bitter red *aperitivo* means "point and a half". It is said to have been created by the Carpano distillery when customers ordered their drinks to be mixed according to their own specification. Punt e Mes is usually drunk on its own, but can be served with ice and soda.

Cynar

Vermouth

All vermouths, both white and red, are made from white wine flavoured with aromatic herbal extracts and spices. The first vermouth was made in Turin in the 18th century, and vermouth is still produced there. Red vermouths, like Cinzano and sweet Martini, are sweetened with sugar and tinted with caramel to give them a deep red colour. These sweet red varieties are generically called "Italian" vermouth - the "it" in a Gin and It cocktail. Dry vermouth is white and contains less sugar. It is known as "French", but is also produced in Italy by companies such as Martini and Rossi. Other well-known brands include Riccadonna and Gancia.

Punt e Mes

Culinary Uses

Although the Italians tend to use white wine rather than vermouth in their cooking, dry white vermouth can be substituted in sauces and veal, rabbit or poultry dishes. It adds a touch of dryness and intensity.

Extra-dry white Vermouth

Fortified Wines

Marsala

This rich brown fortified wine has a sweet, musky flavour and an alcoholic content of about 18 per cent. It is made in the west of Sicily, near the town from which it takes its name. The best Marsala (*vergine*) has been matured for at least five years to give an intensity of flavour and colour. Although sweet Marsala is better known, dry varieties (*ambra secco*) are also produced; their flavour is reminiscent of medium sherry. The sweetest version is *Marsala all'uovo*, an intensely rich and sticky dessert wine enriched with egg yolks, which can only be drunk in tiny quantities. Dry Marsala is generally served as an *aperitivo*, while the sweet version is served after a meal, usually with little biscuits to dip into the wine. Unlike sherry, sweet Marsala does not deteriorate once the bottle is opened, so it makes a very useful standby in the kitchen.

Vin santo

This "holy wine" from Tuscany is made from semi-dried grapes with a long slow fermentation, followed by many years ageing to produce a syrupy golden wine. Although not a fortified wine, its intense flavour has some similarity to sherry and it is drunk in much the same way. Vin santo can be dry or sweet, but the sweet version is more common. It is generally served with a plate of *cantucci* or *biscotti di Prato*, hard slipper-shaped biscuits studded with nuts. These are dunked into the wine to make a delicious dessert.

Vin santo

Culinary Uses

Sweet Marsala is probably best known as an essential ingredient of *zabaglione*, a light frothy dessert made from whisked egg yolks, sugar and Marsala. It is used in *zuppa inglese* (trifle) and many other desserts. Dry Marsala is widely used in Italian cooking, particularly in veal dishes like *scaloppine* and *piccata alla Marsala* and sautéed chicken livers. A few spoonfuls of Marsala added to the pan in which veal or poultry has been sautéed will mingle with the pan juices to make a delicious syrupy sauce. It adds extra flavour to wild mushrooms or a mushroom risotto.

Marsala *The sweet variety is used to flavour* zabaglione

Dry Marsala *Widely used by Italian cooks for flavouring veal and poultry dishes*

Liqueurs & Digestivi

Amaretto

This sweet liqueur is made from apricot kernels and flavoured with almonds and aromatic extracts. There are several brands produced, but the best is Disaronno Amaretto, which comes in a distinctive squarish rippled glass bottle with a square cap.

Culinary Uses

The distinctive almond flavour of Amaretto enhances many desserts, such as *macedonia* (fruit salad), *zuppa inglese* (trifle) and *panna* (whipped cream).

Galliano

A bright yellow liqueur from Lombardy, Galliano is flavoured with herbs and spices and tastes a little like a bittersweet Chartreuse. It is occasionally drunk on its own as a *digestivo*, but is best known as an ingredient for cocktails like Harvey Wallbanger or Golden Cadillac.

Amaretto

Galliano

Liqueurs & Digestivi

Grappa

A pungent colourless brandy with an alcoholic content of about 40 per cent, distilled from the pressed skins and pips of the grapes left after wine-making. At its crudest, grappa tastes of raw spirit, but after maturing the taste becomes refined and the best grappa can be as good as a fine French *marc*. Grappa is made in many regions, usually from local grapes, which lend each variety its characteristic flavour. On the whole, you get what you pay for; cheap grappa is fiery and pungent, while expensive, well-matured varieties can be very smooth. The very best grappa often comes in exquisite hand-blown bottles. The spirit can be flavoured with various aromatics, including rose petals and lemon peel.

CULINARY USES

Grappa is not widely used in Italian cooking, except in *capretto alla piemontese* (braised kid). It can be used for flambéeing and for preserving soft fruits. The spirit takes on the flavour of the fruits and can be drunk as a *digestivo* after the fruits have been eaten.

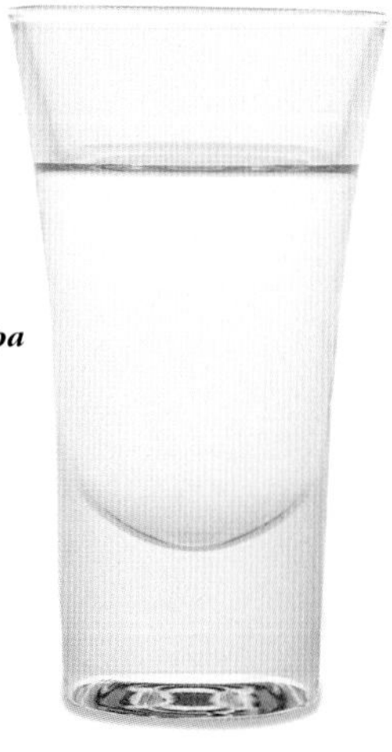

Grappa

Liquore al limone or *Cedro*

This sticky sweet liqueur is made from the peel of the lemons that grow in profusion around the Amalfi coast. Almost every delicatessen in the region sells a home-made version of this opaque yellow drink, whose sweetness is tempered by the tangy citrus fruit. It should be served ice-cold straight from the fridge or freezer and makes a refreshing *aperitivo* or *digestivo*.

Liquore al limone

Maraschino

This sweet, colourless cherry liqueur is made from fermented bitter Maraschino cherries. It can be drunk on its own as a *digestivo*, but is more commonly used for flavouring cocktails or sweet dishes.

Maraschin

Nocino

This sticky, dark brown liqueur from Emilia-Romagna is made from unripe green walnuts steeped in spirit. It has an aromatic but bittersweet flavour.

Sambuca

A colourless liqueur with a strong taste of aniseed, although it is actually distilled from witch elder. Traditionally it is served in a schooner-shaped glass, flambéed and with a coffee bean floating on top. The coffee bean is crunched as the Sambuca is drunk, so that its bitterness counteracts the intense sweetness of the liqueur. This method of serving Sambuca is known as *colla mosca* ("with the fly"), the "fly" being the coffee bean.

Strega

A bright yellow liqueur made from herbs and flowers, strega (meaning "witch"), has a bittersweet flavour and is definitely an acquired taste!

Nocino

Sambuca

Strega

ACETO
BALSAMICO
di Modena
Mazzetti
6%
0586

The Recipes

The recipes in this collection cover a range of styles, from regional specialities to popular modern classics. More unusual, innovative offerings are here too, destined to become future favourites. All of the recipes use ingredients that can be found easily outside Italy, and all are as delicious to eat as they are easy to make.

Buon Appetito.

Antipasti

Antipasto means "before the meal", and no respectable Italian meal would start without it. The recipes in this chapter are typical of Italian antipasti – appetizing and easy on the eye, light and tasty. Vegetables, fish and salads are the mainstay, not only for their lightness and freshness, but also for their colour.

Roasted Pepper Salad

Insalata di peperoni arrostiti

Jars of Italian mixed peppers in olive oil are now a common sight in many supermarkets. None, however, can compete with this colourful, freshly made version, perfect as a starter on its own, or with thinly sliced Italian salami and cold meats.

Ingredients
3 red peppers
2 yellow or orange peppers
2 green peppers
50 g/2 oz/½ cup sun-dried tomatoes in oil, drained
1 garlic clove
30 ml/2 tbsp balsamic vinegar
75 ml/5 tbsp olive oil
few drops of chilli sauce
4 canned artichoke hearts, drained and sliced
salt and freshly ground black pepper
basil leaves, to garnish
serves 4

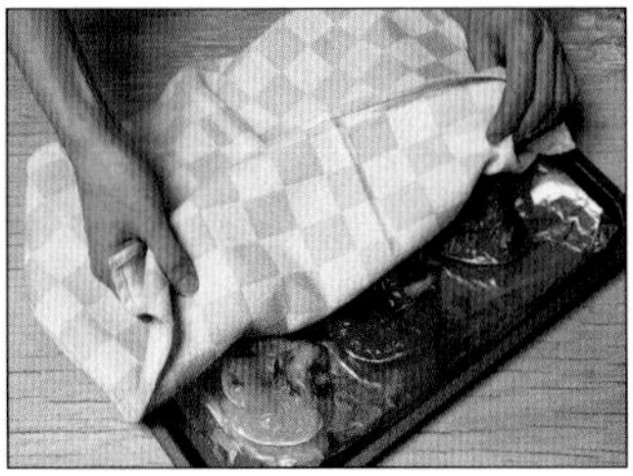

1 ▲ Preheat the oven to 200°C/400°F/Gas 6. Lightly oil a foil-lined baking sheet and place the whole peppers on the foil. Bake for about 45 minutes until beginning to char. Cover with a dish towel and leave to cool for about 5 minutes.

2 ▲ Cut the sun-dried tomatoes into thin strips and thinly slice the garlic. Set the tomatoes and garlic aside.

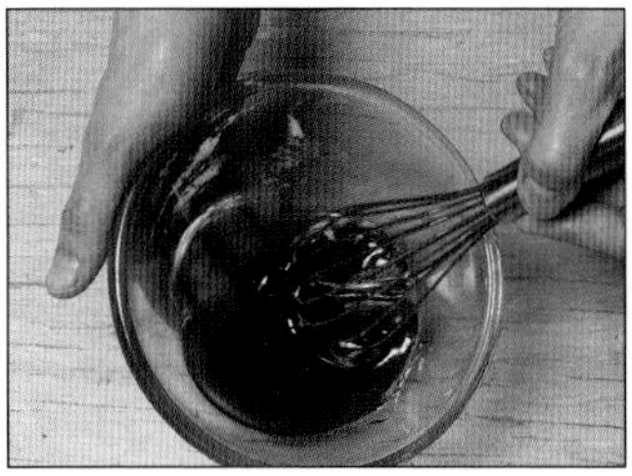

3 ▲ Beat together the vinegar, oil and chilli sauce, then season with a little salt and pepper.

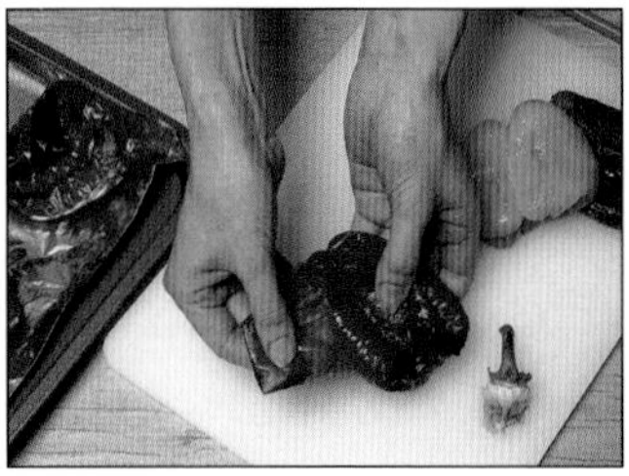

4 ▲ Peel, seed and slice the peppers. Mix with the artichokes, tomatoes and garlic. Pour over the dressing and scatter with the basil leaves.

Fontina Cheese Dip *Fonduta*

Fontina is an Italian medium-fat cheese with a rich salty flavour, a little like Gruyère, which makes a good substitute. This delicious cheese dip need only some warm ciabatta or focaccia, a herby salad and some robust red wine for a thoroughly enjoyable meal.

Ingredients
250 g/9 oz Fontina cheese, diced
250 ml/8 fl oz/1 cup milk
15 g/½ oz/1 tbsp butter
2 eggs, lightly beaten
freshly ground black pepper
bread, to serve
serves 4

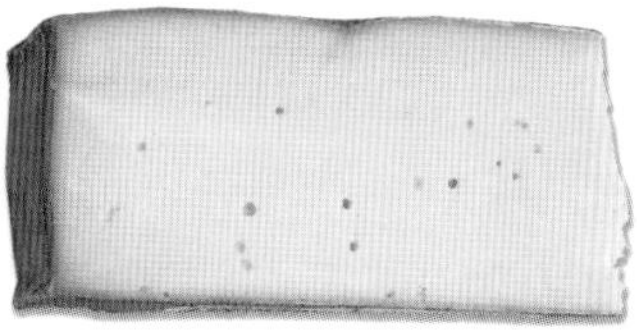

Cook's Tip
This sauce needs to be cooked over a very gentle heat - don't overheat it, or the eggs might curdle. Cook slowly, stirring all the time.

1 ▲ Put the cheese in a bowl with the milk and leave to soak for 2–3 hours. Transfer to a double boiler or a heatproof bowl set over a pan of simmering water.

2 ▲ Add the butter and eggs and cook gently, stirring until the cheese has melted to a smooth sauce with the consistency of custard.

3 Remove from the heat and season with pepper. Transfer to a serving dish and serve immediately with chunks of bread.

Sautéed Mussels with Garlic

Cozze in padella all'aglio

These mussels are served without their shells in a delicious sauce flavoured with garlic and paprika. Eat them with cocktail sticks or small forks.

Ingredients
900 g/2 lb fresh mussels
1 lemon slice
90 ml/6 tbsp olive oil
2 shallots, finely chopped
1 garlic clove, finely chopped
15 ml/1 tbsp chopped fresh parsley
2.5 ml/½ tsp sweet paprika
1.5 ml/¼ tsp dried chilli flakes
serves 4

1 Scrub the mussels. Discard any that do not close when tapped sharply with the back of a knife.

2 ▲ Put the mussels in a large pan, with 250 ml/8 fl oz/1 cup water and the slice of lemon. Bring to the boil and cook for 3–4 minutes; remove the mussels as they open. Discard any that remain closed. Take the mussels out of the shells and drain on kitchen paper.

3 ▲ Heat the oil in a sauté pan, add the mussels and cook, stirring, for a minute. Remove from the pan. Add the shallots and garlic and cook, covered, over a low heat, for about 5 minutes, until soft. Remove from the heat and stir in the parsley, paprika and chilli. Return to the heat and stir in the mussels with any juices. Cook briefly to heat through, then serve at once.

Chicken Liver and Prawn Toasts

Crostini

Crostini are Italian canapés, consisting of toasted slices of bread, spread with various toppings. The following recipes are for a chicken liver pâté and a prawn butter.

Ingredients
12 slices crusty Italian bread, cut 1 cm/½ in thick
75 g/3 oz/6 tbsp butter, melted
salt and ground black pepper
sage leaves and flat leaf parsley, to garnish

For the chicken liver pâté
150 g/5 oz/⅔ cup butter
1 small onion, finely chopped
1 garlic clove, crushed
225 g/8 oz chicken livers
4 sage leaves, chopped

For the prawn butter
225 g/8 oz cooked, peeled prawns
2 drained canned anchovies
115 g/4 oz/¼ cup butter, softened
15 ml/1 tbsp lemon juice
15 ml/1 tbsp chopped fresh parsley
serves 6

1 ▲ To make the chicken liver pâté, melt half the butter in a frying pan, add the onion and garlic, and fry gently until soft. Add the chicken livers and chopped sage and sauté for about 8 minutes, until the livers are brown and firm. Cool slightly, then season with salt and pepper and process in a blender or food processor with the remaining butter.

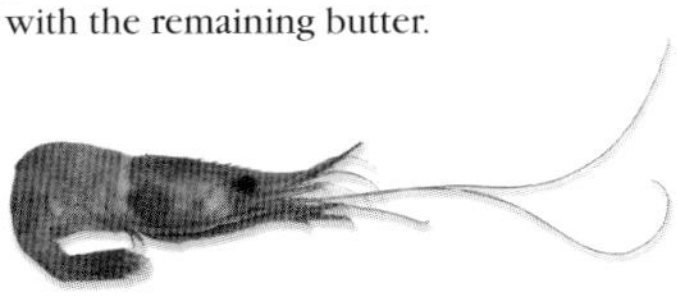

2 ▲ To make the prawn butter, chop the prawns and anchovies finely. Place in a bowl with the butter and beat together until well blended. Add the lemon juice and parsley and season with salt and pepper. Preheat the oven to 200°C/400°F/Gas 6. Place the bread slices on baking sheets and brush with the melted butter.

3 Bake for 8-10 minutes, until pale golden. Spread half the hot crostini with the pâté and the rest with the prawn butter, garnishing with sage and parsley, respectively. Serve the crostini at once.

Cook's Tip
Both the chicken liver pâté and the prawn butter can be made ahead, but should be used within two days. Cover both toppings closely and store them in the fridge.

Crostini with Cheese

Crostini con formaggio

Crostini are small pieces of toasted bread. They can be made with various toppings, and are served hot or cold with drinks. This cheese-topped version is always popular.

Ingredients
4–6 slices day-old white or brown bread
75 g/3 oz/$^3/_4$ cup thinly sliced cheese (fontina, Cheddar or gruyère)
anchovy fillets
strips of grilled red pepper
freshly ground black pepper
serves 6

1 ▲ Cut the bread into small shapes (triangle, circle, oval etc). Preheat the oven to 190°C/375°F/gas 5.

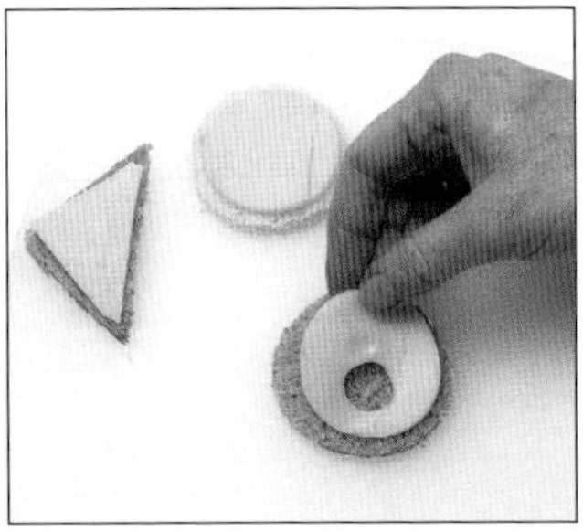

2 ▲ Place a thin slice of cheese on each piece of bread, cutting it to fit.

~ VARIATION ~

For a colourful addition use strips of green or yellow pepper.

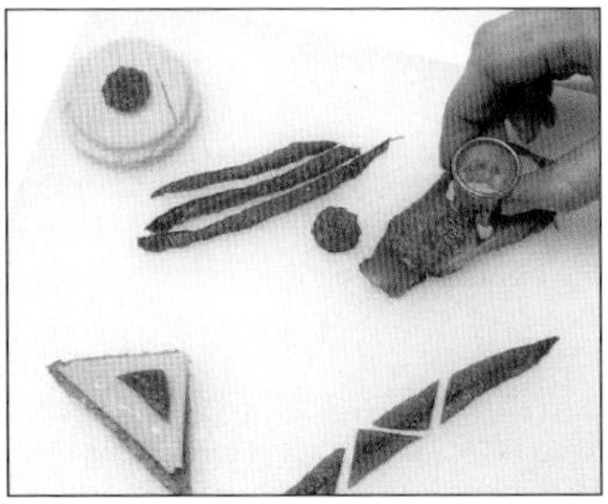

3 ▲ Cut the anchovy fillets and strips of pepper into small decorative shapes and place on top of the cheese. Grind a little pepper on each.

4 ▲ Butter a baking sheet. Place the crostini on it, and bake for 10 minutes, or until the cheese has melted. Serve straight from the oven, or allow to cool before serving.

Crostini with Mussels or Clams

Crostini con cozze o vongole

Each of these seafood crostini is topped with a mussel or clam, and then baked. This recipe comes from Genoa. Use fresh seafood whenever possible.

Ingredients

16 large mussels or clams, in their shells
4 large slices bread, 2.5 cm/1 in thick
40 g/1½ oz/3 tbsp butter
30 ml/2 tbsp chopped fresh parsley
1 shallot, very finely chopped
olive oil, for brushing
lemon sections, to serve
makes 16

1 ▲ Wash the mussels or clams well in several changes of water. Cut the "beards" off the mussels. Place the shellfish in a pan with a cupful of water, and heat until the shells open. (Discard any that do not open.) As soon as they open, lift the molluscs out of the pan. Spoon out of their shells, and set aside. Preheat the oven to 190°C/375°F/gas 5.

2 ▲ Cut the crusts off the bread. Cut each slice into quarters. Scoop out a hollow from the top of each piece large enough to hold a mussel or clam. Do not cut through to the bottom.

3 ▲ Break the scooped-out bread into crumbs, and reserve. In a small frying pan, heat the butter. Cook the parsley with the shallot and the breadcrumbs until the shallot softens.

4 ▲ Brush each piece of bread with olive oil. Place one mussel or clam in each hollow. Spoon a small amount of the parsley and shallot mixture onto each mollusc. Place on an oiled baking sheet. Bake for 10 minutes. Serve at once, while still hot, with the lemon sections.

Grilled Aubergine Parcels

Pacchetti di melanzane alla griglia

These are delicious and flavourful bundles of plum tomatoes, mozzarella cheese and fresh basil, wrapped up smartly in thin slices of aubergine.

Ingredients

2 large, long aubergines
225 g/8 oz mozzarella cheese
2 plum tomatoes
16 large basil leaves
30 ml/2 tbsp olive oil
salt and freshly ground black pepper
30 ml/2 tbsp toasted pine nuts and torn basil leaves, to garnish

For the dressing

60 ml/4 tbsp extra virgin olive oil
5 ml/1 tsp balsamic vinegar
15 ml/1 tbsp sun-dried tomato paste or tomato purée
15 ml/1 tbsp lemon juice

serves 4

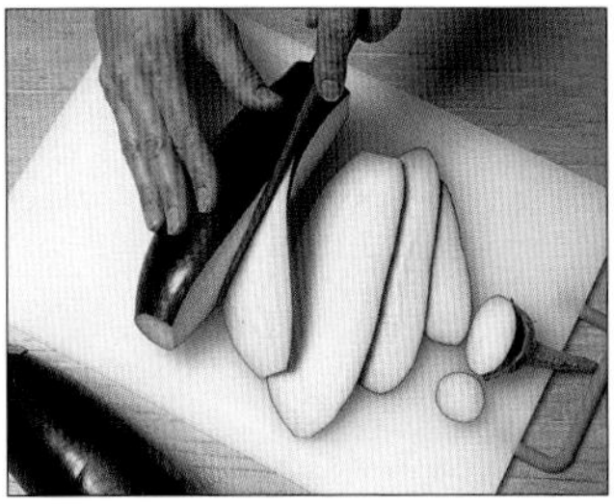

1 ▲ Remove the stalks from the aubergines and cut the aubergines lengthways into thin slices – the aim is to get 16 slices in total, disregarding the first and last slices (each about 5 mm/¼ in thick). If you have a mandolin, it will cut perfect, even slices for you. Otherwise, use a long-bladed, sharp knife.

2 Bring a large pan of salted water to the boil, add the aubergine slices and cook for about 2 minutes, until just softened. Drain the sliced aubergines, then dry them on kitchen paper.

3 Cut the mozzarella into eight slices. Cut each tomato into eight thin slices, not counting the first and last slices.

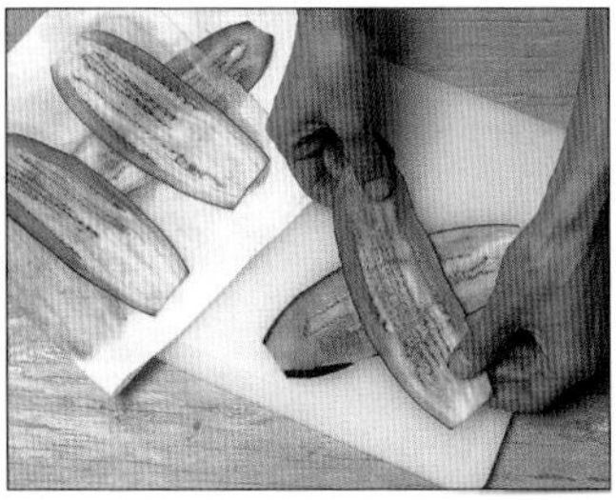

4 ▲ Take two aubergine slices and place on a flameproof tray or dish, in a cross. Place a slice of tomato in the centre, season with salt and pepper, then add a basil leaf, followed by a slice of mozzarella, another basil leaf, a slice of tomato and a little more seasoning.

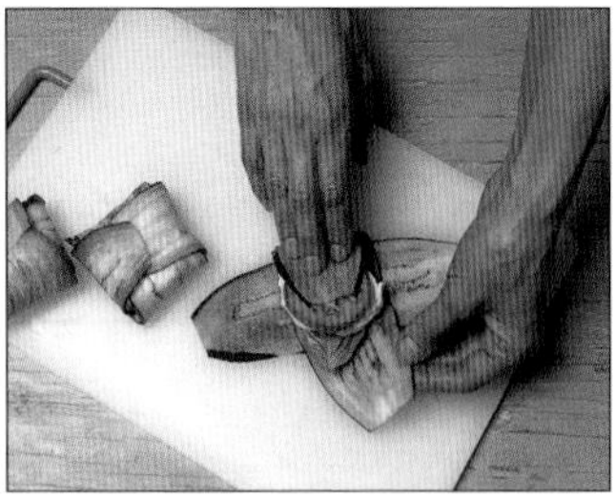

5 ▲ Fold the ends of the aubergine slices around the mozzarella and tomato filling to make a neat parcel. Repeat the process with the rest of the assembled ingredients to make eight parcels. Chill the parcels for 20 minutes.

6 To make the tomato dressing, whisk together the olive oil, vinegar, sun-dried tomato paste and lemon juice. Season to taste.

7 Preheat the grill. Brush the parcels with olive oil and cook them for about 5 minutes on each side, until golden. Serve hot, with the dressing, sprinkled with toasted pine nuts and torn basil leaves.

Cook's Tip

If the aubergines are very large they may have a slightly bitter flavour. To draw out the bitter juices, spread out the raw slices on a tray and sprinkle lightly with salt. Set aside for about 30 minutes, then rinse the aubergine slices thoroughly under cold running water before cooking.

Roasted Peppers with Tomatoes

Insalata di peperoni arrostiti

This is a Sicilian-style salad, using some typical ingredients from the Italian island. The flavour improves if the salad is made and dressed an hour or two before serving.

Ingredients
1 red pepper
1 yellow pepper
4 sun-dried tomatoes in oil, drained
4 ripe plum tomatoes, sliced
2 canned anchovies, drained and chopped
15 ml/1 tbsp capers, drained
15 ml/1 tbsp pine nuts
1 garlic clove, very thinly sliced

For the dressing
75 ml/5 tbsp extra virgin olive oil
15 ml/1 tbsp balsamic vinegar
5 ml/1 tsp lemon juice
chopped fresh mixed herbs
salt and freshly ground black pepper
serves 4

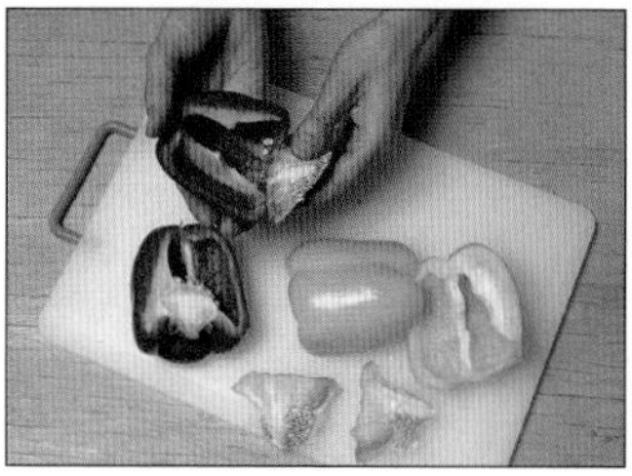

1 ▲ Cut the peppers in half, and remove the seeds and stalks. Cut into quarters and cook, skin side up, under a hot grill until the skin chars. Transfer to a bowl, and cover with a plate. Leave to cool. Peel the peppers and cut into strips.

2 ▲ Thinly slice the sun-dried tomatoes. Arrange the pepper strips and fresh tomatoes on a serving dish. Scatter the anchovies, sun-dried tomatoes, capers, pine nuts and garlic over the top.

3 To make the dressing, mix together the olive oil, vinegar, lemon juice, herbs and seasoning. Pour over the salad just before serving.

Sweet-and-sour Onion Salad

Inslata di cipolle in agrodolce

The best Italian onions are grown in Piedmont. Baby onions are traditionally cooked in this piquant sugar and vinegar sauce and served either warm or cold.

Ingredients

450 g/1 lb baby onions, peeled
50 ml/2 fl oz/¼ cup wine vinegar
45 ml/3 tbsp olive oil
40 g/1½ oz/3 tbsp caster sugar
45 ml/3 tbsp tomato purée
1 bay leaf
2 parsley sprigs
65 g/2½ oz/½ cup raisins
salt and freshly ground black pepper
serves 6

1 ▲ Put the onions in a pan with the wine vinegar, olive oil, sugar, tomato pureé, herbs, raisins, salt and pepper and 300 ml/½ pint/1¼ cups water. Bring to the boil and simmer gently, uncovered, for 45 minutes, or until the onions are tender and most of the liquid has evaporated.

2 ▲ Remove the bay leaf and parsley, check the seasoning, and transfer to a serving dish. Serve at room temperature.

Frittata with Sun-dried Tomatoes

Frittata con pomodori secchi

Adding just a few sun-dried tomatoes gives this frittata a distinctly Mediterranean flavour.

Ingredients

6 sun-dried tomatoes, dry or in oil and drained
60 ml/4 tbsp olive oil
1 small onion, finely chopped
pinch of fresh thyme leaves
salt and freshly ground black pepper
6 eggs
50 g/2 oz/$^1/_2$ cup freshly grated Parmesan cheese
serves 3–4

1 ▲ Place the tomatoes in a small bowl, and pour on enough hot water to just cover them. Soak for about 15 minutes. Lift the tomatoes out of the water, and slice them into thin strips. Reserve the soaking water.

2 ▲ Heat the oil in a large non-stick or heavy frying pan. Stir in the onion, and cook for 5–6 minutes or until soft and golden. Add the tomatoes and thyme, and stir over moderate heat for about 2–3 minutes. Season with salt and pepper.

3 ▲ Break the eggs into a bowl and beat lightly with a fork. Stir in 45–60 ml/3–4 tbsp of the tomato soaking water and the grated Parmesan. Raise the heat under the pan. When the oil is sizzling pour in the eggs. Mix them quickly into the other ingredients, and stop stirring. Lower the heat to moderate, and cook for about 4–5 minutes, or until the frittata is puffed and golden brown.

4 ▲ Take a large plate, place it upside down over the pan, and holding it firmly with oven gloves, turn the pan and the frittata over onto it. Slide the frittata back into the pan, and continue cooking until golden brown on the second side, 3–4 minutes more. Remove from the heat. The frittata can be served hot, at room temperature, or cold. Cut it into wedges to serve.

Tomato and Basil Tart

Torta di pomodoro e basilico

This tart is similar to a pizza, but uses shortcrust pastry instead of yeast dough for the base.

Ingredients
175 g/6 oz/1 $^1/_2$ cups flour
$^1/_2$ tsp salt, plus more to sprinkle
115 g/4 oz/$^1/_2$ cup butter or margarine, chilled
45-75 ml/3–5 tbsp cold water
30 ml/2 tbsp extra-virgin olive oil
For the filling
175 g/6 oz/1 cup mozzarella cheese, sliced as thinly as possible
12 leaves fresh basil
4–5 medium tomatoes, cut into 5 mm/ $^1/_4$in slices
salt and freshly ground black pepper
60 ml/4 tbsp freshly grated Parmesan cheese
serves 6–8

1 ▲ Make the pastry by placing the flour and salt in a mixing bowl. Using a pastry blender, cut the butter or margarine into the dry ingredients until the mixture resembles coarse meal. Add 45 ml/3 tbsp of water, and combine with a fork until the dough holds together. If it is too crumbly, mix in a little more water.

2 Gather the dough into a ball and flatten it into a disc. Wrap in greaseproof paper and refrigerate for at least 40 minutes. Preheat the oven to 190°C/375°F/gas 5.

3 Roll the pastry out between two sheets of greaseproof paper to a thickness of 5 mm/$^1/_4$ inch. Line a 28 cm/11 in a tart or pie pan, trimming the edges evenly. Chill for 20 minutes. Prick the bottom all over with a fork.

4 ▲ Line the pastry with a sheet of baking parchment. Fill with dried beans. Place the pie pan on a baking tray and bake about 15 minutes. Remove from the oven.

5 Remove the beans and paper. Brush the pastry with oil. Line with the mozzarella. Tear half of the basil into pieces, and sprinkle on top.

6 ▲ Arrange the tomato slices over the cheese. Dot with the remaining whole basil leaves. Sprinkle with salt and pepper, Parmesan and oil. Bake for about 35 minutes. If the cheese exudes a lot of liquid during baking, tilt the pan and spoon it off to keep the pastry from becoming soggy. Serve hot or at room temperature.

Potato Pizza

Pizza di patate

This "pizza", made of mashed potatoes with a filling of anchovies, capers and tomatoes, is a speciality of Puglia.

Ingredients
1 kg/2 lb potatoes, scrubbed
100 ml/4 fl oz/$^1/_2$ cup extra-virgin olive oil
salt and freshly ground black pepper
2 cloves garlic, finely chopped
350 g/12 oz tomatoes, diced
3 anchovy fillets, chopped
30 ml/2 tbsp capers, rinsed
serves 4

1 ▲ Boil the potatoes in their skins until tender. Peel and mash or pass through a food mill. Beat in 45 ml/3 tbsp of the oil, and season.

2 Heat another 45 ml/3 tbsp of the oil in a medium saucepan. Add the garlic and the chopped tomatoes, and cook over moderate heat until the tomatoes soften and begin to dry out, 12–15 minutes. Meanwhile, preheat the oven to 200°C/400°F/gas 6.

3 ▲ Oil a shallow baking dish. Spread half the mashed potatoes into the dish in an even layer. Cover with the tomatoes, and dot with the chopped anchovies and the capers.

4 ▲ Spread the rest of the potatoes in a layer on top of the filling. Brush the top with the remaining oil. Bake in the preheated oven for 20–25 minutes, or until the top is golden brown. Serve hot, directly from the baking dish.

~ VARIATION ~

For a vegetarian version of this dish, omit the anchovies. A few stoned and chopped olives may be added to the filling instead.

Bruschetta with Tomato

Bruschetta con pomodoro

Bruschetta is toasted or grilled bread, rubbed with garlic and sprinkled with olive oil or chopped fresh tomatoes. It is eaten as an appetizer or accompaniment.

Ingredients
3–4 medium tomatoes, chopped
salt and freshly ground black pepper
a few leaves fresh basil, torn
8 slices crusty white bread
2 or 3 cloves garlic, peeled and cut in half
90 ml/6 tbsp extra-virgin olive oil
serves 4

1 Place the chopped tomatoes with their juice in a small bowl. Season with salt and pepper, and stir in the basil. Allow to stand for 10 minutes.

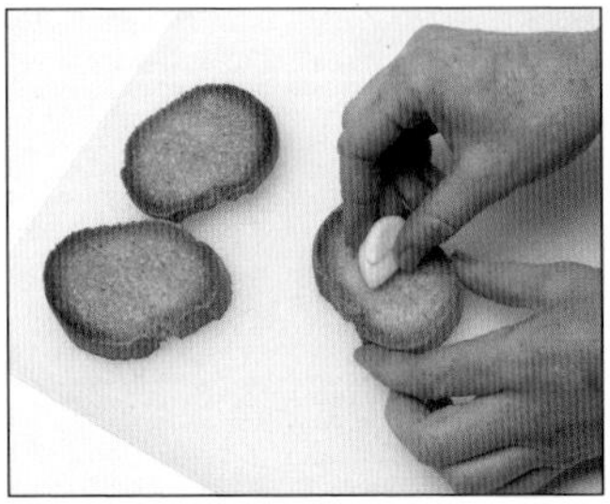

2 ▲ Toast or grill the bread until it is crisp on both sides. Rub one side of each piece of toast with the cut garlic.

3 ▲ Arrange on a platter. Sprinkle with the olive oil. Spoon on the chopped tomatoes, and serve at once.

Grilled Cheese Sandwiches

Panini alla griglia

Garlic, herbs and tomatoes make these open sandwiches very Mediterranean.

Ingredients

45 ml/3 tbsp olive oil
4 or 5 canned plum tomatoes, finely chopped
a few leaves fresh basil, torn into pieces
salt and freshly ground black pepper
4–6 medium slices of Italian or crusty bread
1 clove garlic, peeled and cut in half
75 g/3 oz/$^1/_2$ cup scamorza, mozzarella or Cheddar cheese, sliced
serves 4

1 Heat the oil in a small frying pan. Add the tomatoes and basil, and season with salt and pepper. Cook over low to moderate heat for about 8–10 minutes, or until the tomatoes start to dry out. Preheat the grill.

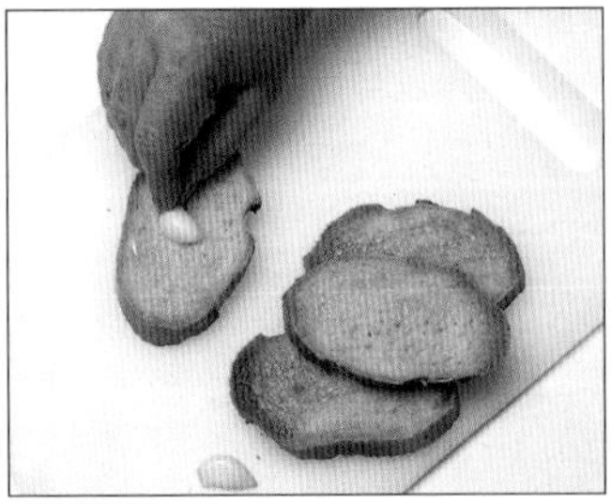

2 ▲ Lightly toast the bread. When it has cooled slightly rub it on one side with the garlic.

3 ▲ Spread some of the tomatoes on each piece of bread, and top with the sliced cheese. Place under the hot grill until the cheese melts and begins to bubble, 5–8 minutes.
Serve hot.

Mozzarella, Tomato and Basil Salad

Insalata caprese

This very popular and easy salad is considered rather patriotic in Italy, as its three ingredients are the colours of the national flag.

Ingredients

4 large tomatoes
400 g/14 oz/2 cups mozzarella cheese, from cow or buffalo milk
8–10 leaves fresh basil
60 ml/4 tbsp extra-virgin olive oil
salt and freshly ground black pepper
serves 4

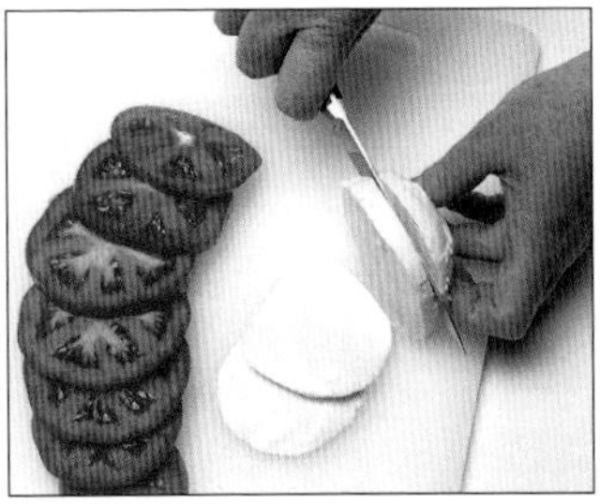

1 ▲ Slice the tomatoes and mozzarella into thick rounds.

2 ▲ Arrange the tomatoes and cheese in overlapping slices on a serving dish. Decorate with basil.

3 ▲ Sprinkle with olive oil and a little salt. Serve with the black pepper passed separately.

~ COOK'S TIP ~

In Italy the most sought-after mozzarella is made from the milk of water buffalo. It is found mainly in the south and in Campania.

Fonduta with Steamed Vegetables

Fonduta con verdure

Fonduta is a creamy cheese sauce from the mountainous Val d'Aosta region. Traditionally it is garnished with slices of white truffles and eaten with toasted bread rounds.

Ingredients

assorted vegetables, such as fennel, broccoli, carrots, cauliflower and courgettes
115 g/4 oz/$^1/_2$ cup butter
12–16 rounds of Italian or French baguette

For the fonduta

300 g/11 oz/1$^2/_3$ cups fontina cheese
15 ml/ 1 tbsp flour
milk, as required
50 g/2 oz/$^1/_4$ cup butter
50 g/2 oz/$^1/_2$ cup freshly grated Parmesan cheese
pinch of grated nutmeg
salt and freshly ground black pepper
2 egg yolks, at room temperature
a few slivers of white truffle (optional)

serves 4

1 ▲ About 6 hours before you want to serve the fonduta, cut the fontina into chunks and place in a bowl. Sprinkle with the flour. Pour in enough milk to barely cover the cheese, and set aside in a cool place. If you put the bowl in the refrigerator, take it out at least 1 hour before cooking the fonduta. It should be at room temperature before being cooked.

2 Just before preparing the fonduta, steam the vegetables until tender. Cut into pieces. Place on a serving platter, dot with butter, and keep warm.

3 Butter the bread rounds and toast lightly in the oven or under the grill.

4 ▲ For the fonduta, melt the butter in a mixing bowl set over a pan of simmering water, or in the top of a double boiler. Strain the fontina and add it, with 45–60 ml/3–4 tbsp of its soaking milk. Cook, stirring, until the cheese melts. When it is hot, and has formed a homogeneous mass, add the Parmesan and stir until melted. Season with nutmeg, salt and pepper.

5 ▲ Remove from the heat and immediately beat in the egg yolks which have been passed through the strainer. Spoon into warmed individual serving bowls, garnish with the white truffle if using, and serve with the vegetables and toasted bread.

Fried Mozzarella

Mozzarella fritta

These cheese slices make a good informal lunch. They originate from the Neapolitan area, where much mozzarella is produced. They must be made just before serving.

Ingredients
300 g/11 oz/1$^{3}/_{4}$ cups mozzarella cheese
oil, for deep-frying
2 eggs
flour seasoned with salt and freshly ground black pepper, for coating
plain dry breadcrumbs, for coating
serves 2–3

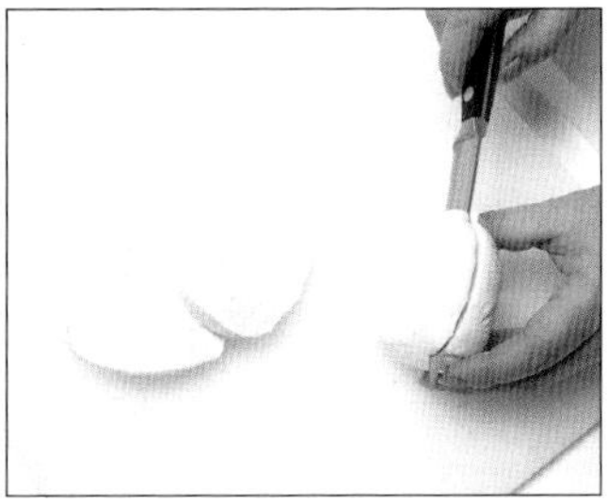

1 ▲ Cut the mozzarella into slices about 1 cm/$^{1}/_{2}$ inch thick. Gently pat off any excess moisture with a paper towel.

2 ▲ Heat the oil until a small piece of bread sizzles as soon as it is dropped in (about 185°C/360°F). While the oil is heating beat the eggs in a shallow bowl. Spread some flour on one plate, and some breadcrumbs on another.

3 ▲ Press the cheese slices into the flour, coating them evenly with a thin layer of flour. Shake off any excess. Dip them into the egg, then into the breadcrumbs. Dip them once more into the egg, and then again into the breadcrumbs.

4 ▲ Fry immediately in the hot oil until golden brown. (You may have to do this in two batches but do not let the breaded cheese wait for too long or the breadcrumb coating will separate from the cheese while it is being fried.) Drain quickly on paper towels, and serve hot.

Baked Eggs with Tomatoes

Uova al piatto con pomodori

These eggs simply baked over a fresh tomato sauce make an easy dish for a light supper. Allow 1 or 2 eggs per person.

Ingredients

60 ml/4 tbsp olive oil
1 small onion, finely chopped
450 g/1 lb tomatoes, peeled, seeded and chopped
30 ml/2 tbsp chopped fresh basil
6 eggs
salt and freshly ground black pepper
15 g/1 tbsp butter
chopped fresh parsley, to garnish

3 large or 6 small servings

1 ▲ Heat the oil in a shallow flameproof dish. Add the onion, and cook until soft and golden.

2 ▲ Preheat the oven to 190°C/375°F/ gas 5. When the onion is soft and golden, add the tomatoes and cook for 5–10 minutes, or until the tomatoes are very soft. Stir in the chopped basil.

~ VARIATION ~

Sprinkle 30–45 ml/2–3 tbsp of freshly grated Parmesan cheese over the eggs before baking for a richer, tastier dish.

3 ▲ Break the eggs one at a time and slip them into the dish in one layer on top of the tomatoes. Season with salt and pepper. Dot with butter. Cover the dish, and bake in the oven for 7–10 minutes, or until the egg whites have just set, but the yolks are still soft. Serve at once.

Baked Eggs with Cheese

Uova al piatto alla parmigiana

Grated Parmesan makes a tasty addition to this simple dish.

Ingredients

6 eggs
salt and freshly ground black pepper
35 g/$1\frac{1}{2}$ oz/3 tbsp ham, cut into thin matchsticks
90 ml/6 tbsp freshly grated Parmesan cheese
25 g/1 oz/2 tbsp butter
3–4 leaves fresh parsley, to garnish
rounds of crusty bread, warmed, to serve

3 large or 6 small servings

1 Preheat the oven to 200°C/400°F/ gas 6. Butter a shallow ovenproof dish (or dishes, if you prefer to bake the eggs individually).

2 ▲ Break the eggs into the dish. Season with salt and pepper. Sprinkle the ham over the whites. Sprinkle the top with the Parmesan.

3 ▲ Dot with butter. Cover the dish, and bake for 7–10 minutes, or until the whites have set and the cheese has melted. Garnish with the parsley. Serve hot with warmed bread.

Frittata with Spinach and Ham

Frittata con spinaci e prosciutto

In Italy, frittate are often used as fillings for sandwiches.

Ingredients
200 g/7 oz/1 cup cooked leaf spinach, fresh or frozen
45 ml/3 tbsp olive oil
4 spring onions, finely sliced
1 clove garlic, finely chopped
50 g/2 oz/$^{1}/_{3}$ cup ham or prosciutto, cut into small dice
salt and freshly ground black pepper
8 eggs
serves 6

1 ▲ Squeeze any excess moisture out of the spinach with your hands. Chop it roughly and set aside.

2 ▲ Heat the oil in a large non-stick or heavy frying pan. Stir in the spring onions, and cook for 3–4 minutes. Add the garlic and ham, and stir over moderate heat until just golden. Stir in the spinach, and cook for 3–4 minutes, or until just heated through. Season with salt and pepper.

3 ▲ Break the eggs into a bowl and beat lightly with a fork. Raise the heat under the vegetables. After about 1 minute pour in the eggs. Mix them quickly into the other ingredients, and stop stirring. Cook over moderate heat for about 5–6 minutes, or until the frittata is puffed and golden brown underneath. If the frittata seems to be sticking to the pan, shake the pan backwards and forwards to release it.

4 ▲ Take a large plate, place it upside down over the pan and, holding it firmly with oven gloves, turn the pan and the frittata over onto it. Slide the frittata back into the pan, and continue cooking until golden brown on the second side, 3–4 minutes more. Remove from the heat. The frittata can be served hot, at room temperature, or cold. Cut it into wedges to serve.

Sliced Frittata Salad

Frittata fredda in insalata

This dish – cold frittata with a tomato sauce – is ideal for a light summer lunch.

Ingredients

6 eggs
30 ml/2 tbsp mixed fresh herbs, finely chopped, such as basil, parsley, thyme or tarragon
35 g/1½ oz/¼ cup freshly grated Parmesan cheese
salt and freshly ground black pepper
45 ml/3 tbsp olive oil

For the tomato sauce

30 ml/2 tbsp olive oil
1 small onion, finely chopped
350 g/12oz fresh tomatoes, or 1x 400 g/14oz can tomatoes, chopped
1 clove garlic, chopped
60 ml/4 tbsp water
salt and freshly ground black pepper

serves 3–4

1 To make the frittata, break the eggs into a bowl, and beat them lightly with a fork. Beat in the herbs and cheese. Season with salt and pepper. Heat the oil in a large non-stick or heavy frying pan until hot but not smoking.

2 ▲ Pour in the egg mixture. Cook, without stirring, until the frittata is puffed and golden brown underneath.

3 Take a large plate, place it upside down over the pan, and holding it firmly with oven gloves, turn the pan and the frittata over onto it. Slide the frittata back into the pan, and continue cooking until golden brown on the second side, 3–4 minutes more. Remove from the heat and allow to cool completely.

4 ▲ To make the tomato sauce, heat the oil in a medium heavy pan. Add the onion, and cook slowly until it is soft. Add the tomatoes, garlic and water, and season with salt and pepper. Cover the pan and cook over moderate heat until the tomatoes are soft, about 15 minutes.

5 Remove from the heat, and cool slightly before passing the sauce through a food mill or strainer. Leave to cool completely.

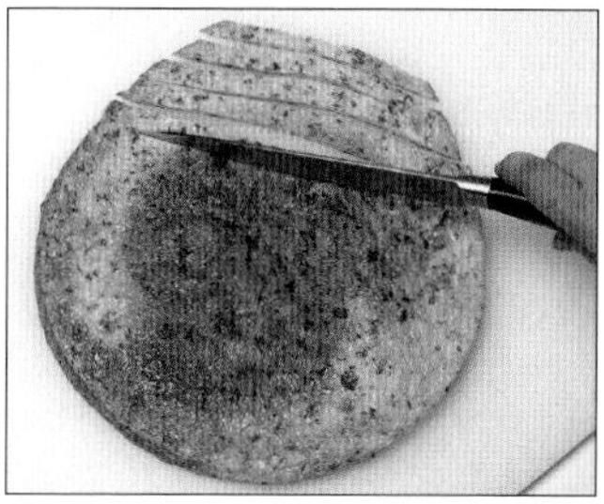

6 ▲ To assemble the salad, cut the frittata into thin slices. Place them in a serving bowl and toss lightly with the sauce. Serve the salad at room temperature or chilled.

Frittata of Leftover Pasta

Frittata di pasta avanzata

This is a great way to use up cold leftover pasta, whatever the sauce.

Ingredients
5–6 eggs
225–275 g/8–10 oz/1 $^{1}/_{2}$–2 cups cold cooked pasta, with any sauce
50 g/2 oz/$^{1}/_{2}$ cup freshly grated Parmesan cheese
salt and freshly ground black pepper
65 g/2 $^{1}/_{2}$ oz/5 tbsp butter
serves 4

1 ▲ In a medium bowl beat the eggs lightly with a fork. Stir in the pasta and the Parmesan. Season to taste.

2 ▲ Heat half the butter in a large non-stick or heavy frying pan. As soon as the foam subsides pour in the pasta mixture. Cook over moderate heat, without stirring, for 4–5 minutes, or until the bottom is golden brown. Loosen the frittata by shaking the pan backwards and forwards.

3 ▲ Take a large plate, place it upside down over the pan and, holding it firmly with oven gloves, turn the pan and the frittata over onto it. Add the remaining butter to the pan. As soon as it stops foaming slide the frittata back into the pan, and continue cooking until golden brown on the second side, 3–4 minutes more. Remove from the heat. The frittata can be served hot, at room temperature, or cold. Cut it into wedges to serve.

Frittata with Onions

Frittata con cipolle

Gently cooked onions add a sweet flavour to the basic frittata mixture.

Ingredients
60 ml/4 tbsp olive oil
2 medium onions, thinly sliced
salt and freshly ground black pepper
30 ml/2 tbsp chopped fresh parsley
6 eggs
serves 3–4

1 Heat the oil in a large non-stick or heavy frying pan. Stir in the onions, and cook over low heat until they are soft and golden. This may take 10–15 minutes. Season with salt and pepper. Stir in the herbs.

2 Break the eggs into a bowl, and beat them lightly with a fork. Raise the heat under the onions to moderate, and when they are sizzling pour in the eggs. Quickly stir them into the onions to distribute them. Stop stirring.

3 ▲ Cook for about 5 minutes, or until the frittata is puffed and golden brown underneath. If the frittata seems to be sticking to the pan, shake the pan back and forth to release it.

4 ▲ Take a large plate, place it upside down over the pan and, holding it firmly with oven mitts, turn the pan and the frittata over onto it. Slide the frittata back into the pan, and continue cooking until golden brown on the second side, 3–4 minutes more. Remove from the heat. Cut it into wedges to serve.

Roast Pepper Terrine

Torta di peperoni al forno

This terrine is perfect for a dinner party because it tastes better if made ahead. Prepare the salsa on the day of serving. Serve with hot Italian bread.

Ingredients

8 peppers (red, yellow and orange)
675 g/1½ lb/3 cups mascarpone cheese
3 eggs, separated
30 ml/2 tbsp each roughly chopped flat leaf parsley and shredded basil
2 large garlic cloves, roughly chopped
2 red, yellow or orange peppers, seeded and roughly chopped
30 ml/2 tbsp extra virgin olive oil
10 ml/2 tsp balsamic vinegar
a few basil sprigs
pinch of sugar
salt and freshly ground black pepper
serves 8

1 Place the peppers under a hot grill for 8 - 10 minutes, turning them frequently until the skins are charred and blistered on all sides. Put the hot peppers in polythene bags, seal and leave until cold.

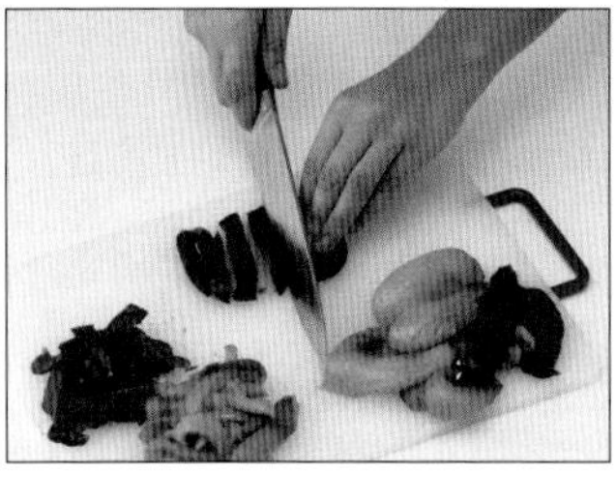

2 ▲ Rub off the pepper skins under cold running water. Break open the flesh and rub out the cores and seeds. Drain the peppers, dry them on kitchen paper, then cut seven of them lengthways into thin, even-size strips. Reserve the remaining pepper for the salsa.

Variation

For a low-fat version of this terrine, use ricotta cheese instead of the mascarpone.

3 Put the mascarpone cheese in a bowl with the egg yolks, herbs and half the garlic. Add salt and pepper to taste. Beat well. In a separate bowl, whisk the egg whites to a soft peak, then fold into the cheese mixture until evenly incorporated.

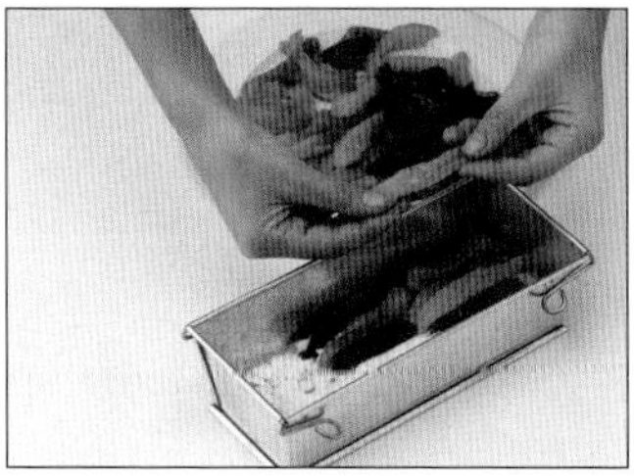

4 ▲ Preheat the oven to 180°C/350°F/Gas 4. Line the base of a lightly oiled 900 g/2 lb loaf tin. Put one-third of the cheese mixture in the tin and spread level. Arrange half the pepper strips on top in an even layer. Repeat until all the cheese and peppers are used.

5 Cover the tin with foil and place in a roasting tin. Pour in boiling water to come halfway up the sides of the tin. Bake for 1 hour. Leave to cool in the water bath, then lift out and chill overnight.

6 A few hours before serving, make the salsa. Place the remaining roast pepper and fresh peppers in a food processor. Add the remaining garlic, oil and vinegar. Set aside a few basil leaves for garnishing and add the rest to the processor. Process until finely chopped. Tip the mixture into a bowl, add salt and pepper to taste and mix well. Cover and chill until ready to serve.

7 Turn out the terrine, peel off the paper and slice thickly. Garnish with the basil leaves and serve cold, with the sweet pepper salsa.

Pan-fried Chicken Liver Salad

Insalata di fegatini

This Florentine salad uses vin santo, a sweet dessert wine from Tuscany, but this is not essential - any dessert wine will do, or a sweet or cream sherry.

Ingredients
75 g/3 oz fresh baby spinach leaves
75 g/3 oz lollo rosso leaves
75 ml/5 tbsp olive oil
15 ml/1 tbsp butter
225 g/8 oz chicken livers, trimmed and thinly sliced
45 ml/3 tbsp vin santo
50–75 g/2–3 oz fresh Parmesan cheese, shaved into curls
salt and freshly ground black pepper
serves 4

1 ▲ Wash and dry the spinach and lollo rosso. Tear the leaves into a large bowl, season with salt and pepper to taste and toss gently to mix.

2 ▲ Heat 30 ml/2 tbsp of the oil with the butter in a large heavy-based frying pan. When foaming, add the chicken livers and toss over a medium to high heat for 5 minutes or until the livers are browned on the outside but still pink in the centre. Remove from the heat.

3 ▲ Remove the livers from the pan with a slotted spoon, drain them on kitchen paper, then place on top of the spinach.

4 ▲ Return the pan to a medium heat, add the remaining oil and the vin santo and stir until sizzling.

5 Pour the hot dressing over the spinach and livers and toss to coat. Put the salad in a serving bowl and sprinkle over the Parmesan shavings. Serve at once.

Salad Leaves with Gorgonzola

Insalata verde con gorgonzola

Crispy fried pancetta makes tasty croûtons, which contrast well in texture and flavour with the softness of mixed salad leaves and the sharp taste of Gorgonzola.

Ingredients
225 g/8 oz pancetta rashers, any rinds removed, coarsely chopped
2 large garlic cloves, roughly chopped
75 g/3 oz rocket leaves
75 g/3 oz radicchio leaves
50 g/2 oz/½ cup walnuts, roughly chopped
115 g/4 oz Gorgonzola cheese
60 ml/4 tbsp olive oil
15 ml/1 tbsp balsamic vinegar
salt and freshly ground black pepper
serves 4

Variation
Use walnut oil instead of olive oil, or hazelnuts and hazelnut oil instead of walnuts and olive oil.

1 ▲ Put the chopped pancetta and garlic in a non-stick or heavy-based frying pan and heat gently, stirring constantly, until the pancetta fat runs. Increase the heat and fry until the pancetta and garlic are crisp. Remove with a slotted spoon and drain on kitchen paper. Leave the pancetta fat in the pan, off the heat.

2 ▲ Tear the rocket and radicchio leaves into a salad bowl. Sprinkle over the walnuts, pancetta and garlic. Add salt and pepper and toss to mix. Crumble the Gorgonzola on top.

3 Return the frying pan to a medium heat and add the oil and balsamic vinegar to the pancetta fat. Stir until sizzling, then pour over the salad. Serve at once, to be tossed at the table.

Tomato and Mozzarella Toasts

Bruschetta casalinga

These resemble mini pizzas and are good with drinks before a dinner party. Prepare them several hours in advance and pop them in the oven just as your guests arrive.

Ingredients
3 *sfilatini* (thin ciabatta)
about 250 ml/8 fl oz/1 cup sun-dried tomato paste
3 x 150 g/5 oz packets mozzarella cheese, drained
about 10 ml/2 tsp dried oregano or mixed herbs
30–45 ml/2–3 tbsp olive oil
freshly ground black pepper
serves 6–8

Variations
Use red or green pesto instead of the sun-dried tomato paste – a combination of colours is especially effective if the toasts are served on a large platter. Halved olives can be pressed into the cheese, or criss-cross strips of anchovy.

1 ▲ Cut each *sfilatino* on the diagonal into 12–15 slices, discarding the ends. Toast lightly on both sides.

2 Preheat the oven to 220°C/425°F/Gas 7. Spread sun-dried tomato paste on one side of each slice of toast. Cut the mozzarella into small pieces and arrange over the tomato paste.

3 ▲ Put the toasts on baking sheets, sprinkle with herbs and pepper to taste and drizzle with oil. Bake for 5 minutes or until the mozzarella has melted and is bubbling. Leave the toasts to settle for a few minutes before serving.

Genoese Squid Salad

Calamari in insalata alla genovese

This is a good salad for summer, when French beans and new potatoes are at their best. Serve it for a first course or light lunch.

Ingredients
450 g/1 lb prepared squid, cut into rings
4 garlic cloves, roughly chopped
300 ml/½ pint/1¼ cups Italian red wine
450 g/1 lb waxy new potatoes, scrubbed clean
225 g/8 oz French beans, trimmed and cut into short lengths
2–3 drained sun-dried tomatoes in oil, thinly sliced lengthways
60 ml/4 tbsp extra virgin olive oil
15 ml/1 tbsp red wine vinegar
salt and freshly ground black pepper
serves 4–6

Cook's Tips
The French potato called Charlotte is perfect for this type of salad because it retains its shape and does not break up when boiled. Prepared squid can be bought from supermarkets with fresh fish counters, and from fishmongers.

1 ▲ Preheat the oven to 180°C/350°F/Gas 4. Put the squid rings in an earthenware dish with half the garlic, the wine and pepper to taste. Cover and cook for 45 minutes or until the squid is tender.

2 Put the potatoes in a saucepan, cover with cold water and add a good pinch of salt. Bring to the boil, cover and simmer for 15–20 minutes or until tender. Using a slotted spoon, lift out the potatoes and set aside. Add the beans to the boiling water and cook for 3 minutes. Drain.

3 ▲ When the potatoes are cool enough to handle, slice them thickly on the diagonal and place them in a bowl with the warm beans and sun-dried tomatoes. Whisk the oil, wine vinegar and the remaining garlic in a jug and add salt and pepper to taste. Pour over the potato mixture.

4 Drain the squid and discard the wine and garlic. Add the squid to the potato mixture and fold very gently to mix. Arrange the salad on individual plates and grind pepper liberally all over. Serve warm.

Tuna Carpaccio

Carpaccio di tonno

Fillet of beef is most often used for carpaccio, but meaty fish like tuna – and swordfish – make an unusual change. The secret is to slice the fish wafer thin, made possible by freezing the fish first, a technique used by the Japanese for making sashimi.

Ingredients

2 fresh tuna steaks, about 450 g/1 lb total weight
60 ml/4 tbsp extra virgin olive oil
15 ml/1 tbsp balsamic vinegar
5 ml/1 tsp caster sugar
30 ml/2 tbsp drained bottled green peppercorns or capers
salt and freshly ground black pepper
lemon wedges and green salad, to serve

serves 4

Cook's Tip

Raw fish is safe to eat as long as it is very fresh, so check with your fishmonger before purchase, and make and serve carpaccio on the same day. Do not buy fish that has been frozen and thawed.

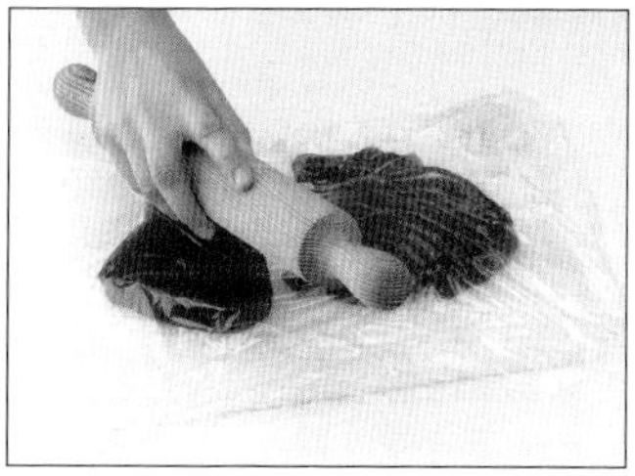

1 ▲ Remove the skin from each tuna steak and place each steak between two sheets of clear film or non-stick baking paper. Pound with a rolling pin until flattened slightly.

2 Roll up the tuna as tightly as possible, then wrap tightly in clear film and place in the freezer for 4 hours or until firm.

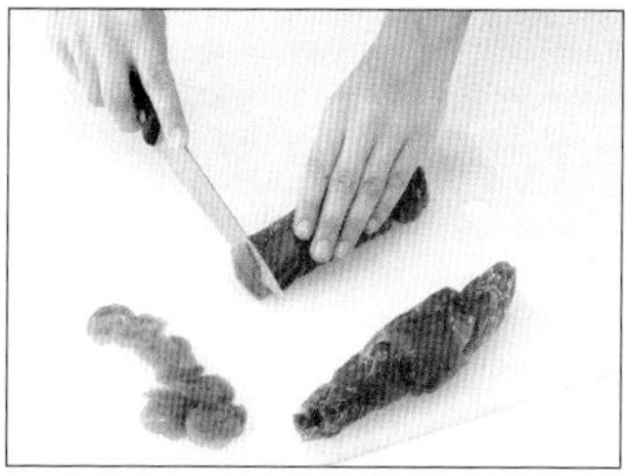

3 ▲ Unwrap the tuna and cut crossways into the thinnest possible slices. Arrange on individual plates.

4 Whisk together the remaining ingredients, season and pour over the tuna. Cover and allow to come to room temperature for 30 minutes before serving with lemon wedges and green salad.

Marinated Vegetable Antipasto

Verdura marinata per antipasto

Antipasto means "before the meal" and traditionally consists of a selection of marinated vegetable dishes served with good Italian salami and thin slices of Parma ham. Serve in attractive bowls, with plenty of fresh crusty bread.

Ingredients

For the peppers

3 red peppers
3 yellow peppers
4 garlic cloves, sliced
handful fresh basil, plus extra to garnish
extra virgin olive oil
salt and freshly ground black pepper

For the mushrooms

450 g/1 lb open cap mushrooms
60 ml/4 tbsp extra virgin olive oil
1 large garlic clove, crushed
15 ml/1 tbsp chopped fresh rosemary
250 ml/8 fl oz/1 cup dry white wine
fresh rosemary sprigs, to garnish

For the olives

1 dried red chilli, crushed
grated rind of 1 lemon
120 ml/4 fl oz/½ cup extra virgin olive oil
225 g/8 oz/1⅓ cups Italian black olives
30 ml/2 tbsp chopped fresh flat leaf parsley
1 lemon wedge, to serve

serves 4

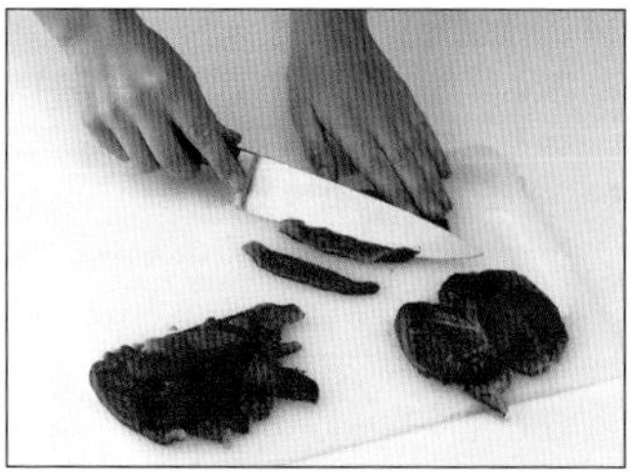

1 ▲ Place the peppers under a hot grill. Turn occasionally until they are blackened and blistered all over. Remove from the heat and place in a large plastic bag. When cool, remove the skin, halve the peppers and remove the seeds. Cut the flesh into strips lengthways and place them in a bowl with the sliced garlic and basil leaves. Add salt, to taste, cover with oil and marinate for 3–4 hours before serving, tossing occasionally. When serving, garnish with more basil leaves.

2 Thickly slice the mushrooms and place in a large bowl. Heat the oil in a small pan and add the garlic and rosemary. Pour in the wine. Bring the mixture to the boil, then lower the heat and simmer for 3 minutes. Add salt and pepper to taste.

3 ▲ Pour the mixture over the mushrooms. Mix well and leave until cool, stirring occasionally. Cover and marinate overnight. Serve at room temperature, garnished with rosemary sprigs.

4 ▲ Prepare the olives. Place the chilli and lemon rind in a small pan with the oil. Heat gently for about 3 minutes. Add the olives and heat for 1 minute more. Tip into a bowl and leave to cool. Marinate overnight. Sprinkle the parsley over just before serving with the lemon wedge.

Cook's Tip

The pepper antipasto can be stored in the fridge for up to 2 weeks covered in olive oil in a screw-top jar.

Stuffed Roast Peppers with Pesto

Peperoni arrostiti con pesto

Serve these scallop- and pesto-filled sweet red peppers with Italian bread, such as ciabatta or focaccia, to mop up the garlicky juices.

Ingredients
4 squat red peppers
2 large garlic cloves, cut into thin slivers
60 ml/4 tbsp olive oil
4 shelled scallops
45 ml/3 tbsp pesto
salt and freshly ground black pepper
freshly grated Parmesan cheese, to serve
salad leaves and fresh basil sprigs, to garnish
serves 4

Cook's Tip
Scallops are available from most fishmongers and supermarkets with fresh fish counters. Never cook scallops for longer than the time stated in the recipe or they will be tough and rubbery.

1 Preheat the oven to 180°C/350°F/ Gas 4. Cut the peppers in half lengthways, through their stalks. Scrape out and discard the cores and seeds. Wash the pepper shells and pat dry.

2 ▲ Put the peppers, cut-side up, in an oiled roasting tin. Divide the slivers of garlic equally among them and sprinkle with salt and pepper to taste. Spoon the oil into the peppers, then roast for 40 minutes.

3 ▲ Cut each of the shelled scallops in half to make two flat discs. Remove the peppers from the oven and place a scallop half in each pepper half. Top with pesto.

4 Return the tin to the oven and roast for 10 minutes more. Transfer the peppers to individual serving plates, sprinkle with grated Parmesan and garnish each plate with a few salad leaves and fresh basil sprigs. Serve warm.

Mozzarella Skewers

Spiedini alla romana

Stacks of flavour – layers of oven-baked mozzarella, tomatoes, basil and bread.

Ingredients

12 slices white country bread, each about 1 cm/½ in thick
45 ml/3 tbsp olive oil
225 g/8 oz mozzarella cheese, cut into 5 mm/¼ in slices
3 plum tomatoes, cut into 5 mm/¼ in slices
15 g/½ oz/½ cup fresh basil leaves, plus extra to garnish
salt and freshly ground black pepper
30 ml/2 tbsp chopped fresh flat leaf parsley, to garnish

serves 4

Cook's Tip

If you use wooden skewers, soak them in water first, to prevent scorching.

1 ▲ Preheat the oven to 220°C/425°F/Gas 7. Trim the crusts from the bread and cut each slice into four equal squares. Arrange on a baking sheet and brush on one side (or both sides) with half the olive oil. Bake for 3–5 minutes until the squares are pale golden.

2 Remove from the oven and place the bread squares on a board with the other ingredients.

3 ▲ Make 16 stacks, each starting with a square of bread, then a slice of mozzarella topped with a slice of tomato and a basil leaf. Sprinkle with salt and pepper, then repeat, ending with the bread. Push a skewer through each stack and place on the baking sheet. Drizzle with the remaining oil and bake for 10–15 minutes until the cheese begins to melt. Garnish with fresh basil leaves and serve scattered with chopped fresh flat leaf parsley.

Aubergine Fritters

Frittelle di melanzane

These simply delicious fritters make a superb starter or vegetarian supper dish.

Ingredients

1 large aubergine, about 675 g/1½ lb, cut into 1 cm/½ in thick slices
30 ml/2 tbsp olive oil
1 egg, lightly beaten
2 garlic cloves, crushed
60 ml/4 tbsp chopped fresh parsley
130 g/4½ oz/2¼ cups fresh white breadcrumbs
90 g/3½ oz/generous 1 cup grated Parmesan cheese
90 g/3½ oz/generous 1 cup feta cheese, crumbled
45 ml/3 tbsp plain flour
sunflower oil, for shallow frying
salt and freshly ground black pepper

To serve

natural yogurt, flavoured with fried red chillies and cumin seeds
lime wedges

serves 4

1 ▲ Preheat the oven to 190°C/375°F/Gas 5. Brush the aubergine slices with the olive oil, then place them on a baking sheet and bake for about 20 minutes until golden and tender. Chop the slices finely and place them in a bowl with the egg, garlic, parsley, breadcrumbs, Parmesan and feta. Add salt and pepper to taste, and mix well. Leave the mixture to rest for about 20 minutes. If the mixture looks very sloppy, add more breadcrumbs.

2 ▲ Divide the mixture into eight balls and flatten them slightly. Place the flour on a plate and season with salt and pepper. Coat the fritters in the flour, shaking off any excess.

3 Shallow fry the fritters in batches for 1 minute on each side, until golden brown. Drain on kitchen paper and serve with the flavoured yogurt and lime wedges.

Raw Vegetables with Olive Oil Dip

Pinzimonio

Use a combination of any fresh seasonal vegetables for this colourful antipasto from Rome, where the dip usually consists only of olive oil and salt. The vegetables should be raw or lightly blanched, and the olive oil of the best quality available.

Ingredients
3 large carrots, peeled
2 fennel bulbs
6 tender stalks celery
1 pepper
12 radishes, trimmed of roots
2 large tomatoes, or 12 cherry tomatoes
8 spring onions
12 small cauliflower florets
For the dip
125 ml/4 fl oz/$^1/_2$ cup extra-virgin olive oil
salt and freshly ground black pepper
45 ml/3 tbsp fresh lemon juice (optional)
4 leaves fresh basil, torn into small pieces (optional)
serves 6–8

1 Prepare the vegetables by slicing the carrots, fennel, celery and pepper into small sticks.

2 ▲ Cut the large tomatoes into sections if using. Trim the roots and dark green leaves from the spring onions. Arrange the vegetables on a large platter, leaving a space in the centre for the dip.

3 ▲ Make the dip by pouring the olive oil into a small bowl. Add salt and pepper. Stir in the lemon juice and basil, if using. Place the bowl in the centre of the vegetable platter.

Celery Stuffed with Gorgonzola

Sedano ripieno di Gorgonzola

These celery sticks are very easy to make. Serve them with drinks, or take them to a picnic.

Ingredients
12 crisp sticks celery, leaves left on
75 g/3 oz/$^1/_2$ cup Gorgonzola
75 g/3 oz/$^1/_2$ cup cream cheese
fresh chives, to garnish
serves 4–6

1 ▲ Wash and dry the celery sticks, and trim the root ends.

2 ▲ In a small bowl, mash the cheeses together until smooth.

3 ▲ Fill the celery sticks with the cheese mixture, using a spatula to smooth the filling. Chill before serving. Garnish with chopped chives.

Grilled Vegetable Terrine

Terrina di verdure alla griglia

A colourful, layered terrine, using the flavourful vegetables associated with the south of Italy: red and yellow peppers, courgettes and aubergines.

Ingredients

2 large red peppers, quartered, cored and seeded
2 large yellow peppers, quartered, cored and seeded
1 large aubergine, sliced lengthways
2 large courgettes, sliced lengthways
90 ml/6 tbsp olive oil
1 large red onion, thinly sliced
75 g/3 oz/½ cup raisins
15 ml/1 tbsp tomato purée
15 ml/1 tbsp red wine vinegar
400 ml/14 fl oz/1⅔ cups tomato juice
15 g/½ oz/2 tbsp powdered gelatine
fresh basil leaves, to garnish

For the dressing

90 ml/6 tbsp extra virgin olive oil
30 ml/2 tbsp red wine vinegar
salt and freshly ground black pepper
serves 6

1 Place the prepared red and yellow peppers skin side up under a hot grill and cook until the skins are blackened. Transfer to a bowl and cover with a plate. Leave to cool.

2 ▲ Preheat the grill. Arrange the aubergine and courgette slices on separate baking sheets. Brush them with a little oil and cook under the grill, in batches if necessary, turning occasionally, until tender and golden.

3 When the peppers are cool, peel off the skins and then rinse the peppers under running water. Cut into thick strips and set aside.

4 ▲ Heat the remaining olive oil in a frying pan, and add the sliced onion, raisins, tomato purée and red wine vinegar. Cook gently until soft and syrupy. Leave the mixture to cool in the frying pan.

5 Line a 1.75 litre/3 pint/7½ cup terrine with clear film, (it helps to lightly oil the terrine first) leaving a little hanging over the slides.

6 Pour half the tomato juice into a small saucepan and sprinkle the gelatine over the top. Dissolve gently over a low heat, stirring occasionally. Do not allow the gelatine mixture to boil or it may not set properly.

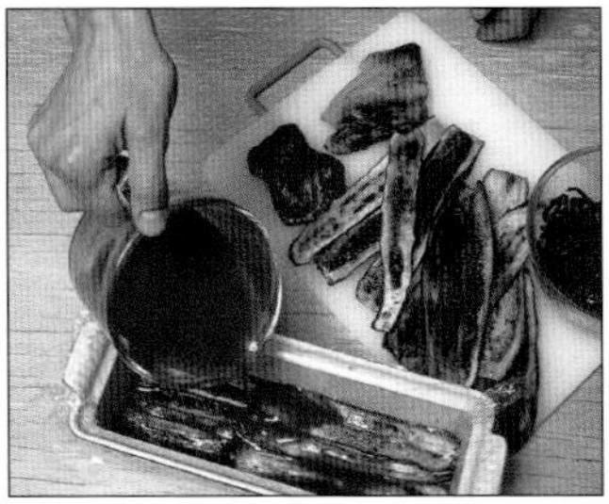

7 ▲ Place a thin layer of red peppers in the bottom of the terrine, and pour in enough of the tomato juice and gelatine mixture to cover. Continue layering the aubergine, courgettes, yellow peppers and onion mixture, finishing with another layer of red peppers. Pour a little of the tomato juice and gelatine mixture over each layer of vegetables.

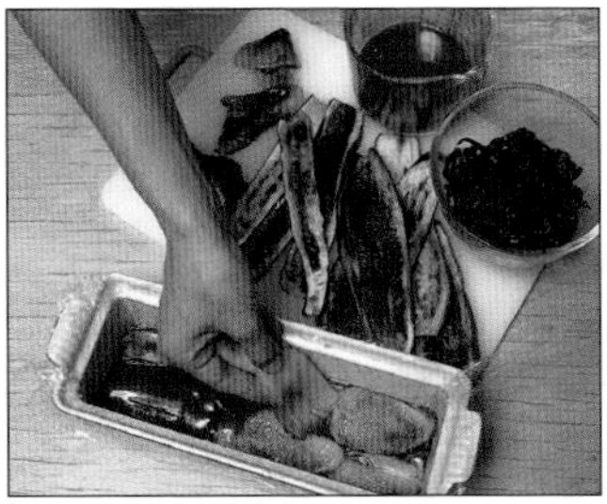

8 ▲ Add the remaining tomato juice to any left in the pan, and pour into the terrine. Give the terrine a sharp tap, to disperse the juice, then cover and transfer to the fridge to set.

9 To make the dressing, whisk together the oil and vinegar, and season. Turn out the terrine and remove the clear film. Cut the terrine into thick slices and serve, drizzled with a little of the dressing. Garnish with basil leaves.

Mixed Seafood Salad

Insalata di frutti di mare

All along Italy's coasts versions of this salad appear. Use fresh seafood that is in season, or use a combination of fresh and frozen.

Ingredients

350 g/12oz small squid
1 small onion, cut into quarters
1 bay leaf
200 g/7oz prawns, in their shells
750 g/1 $^1/_2$lb fresh mussels, in their shells
450 g/1lb fresh small clams
175 ml/6 fl oz $^3/_4$ cup white wine
1 fennel bulb

For the dressing

75 ml/5 tbsp extra-virgin olive oil
45 ml/3 tbsp fresh lemon juice
1 garlic clove, finely chopped
salt and freshly ground black pepper

serves 6–8

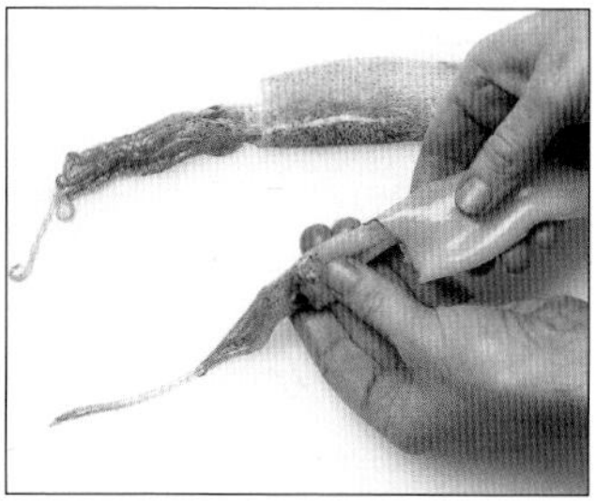

1 ▲ Working near the sink, clean the squid by first peeling off the thin skin from the body section. Rinse well. Pull the head and tentacles away from the sac section. Some of the intestines will come away with the head. Remove and discard the translucent quill and any remaining insides from the sac. Sever the tentacles from the head. Discard the head and intestines. Remove the small hard beak from the base of the tentacles. Rinse the sac and tentacles well under cold running water. Drain.

2 Bring a large pan of water to the boil. Add the onion and bay leaf. Drop in the squid and cook for about 10 minutes, or until tender. Remove with a slotted spoon, and allow to cool before slicing into rings 1 cm/$^1/_2$ in wide. Cut each tentacle section into 2 pieces. Set aside.

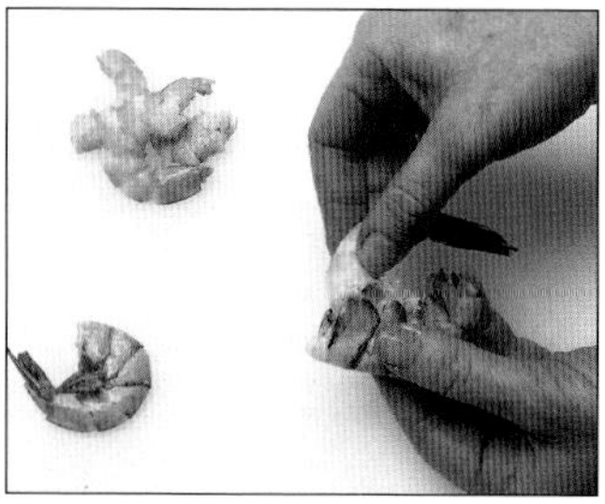

3 ▲ Drop the prawns into the same boiling water, and cook until they turn pink, about 2 minutes. Remove with a slotted spoon. Peel and devein. (The cooking liquid may be strained and kept for soup.)

4 ▲ Cut off the "beards" from the mussels. Scrub and rinse the mussels and clams well in several changes of cold water. Place in a large pan with the wine. Cover, and steam until all the shells have opened. (Discard any that do not open.) Lift the clams and mussels out.

5 ▲ Remove all the clams from their shells with a small spoon. Place in a large serving bowl. Remove all but 8 of the mussels from their shells, and add them to the clams in the bowl. Leave the remaining mussels in their half shells, and set aside. Cut the green, ferny part of the fennel away from the bulb. Chop finely and set aside. Chop the bulb into bite-size pieces, and add it to the serving bowl with the squid and prawns.

6 ▲ Make a dressing by combining the oil, lemon juice, garlic and chopped fennel green in a small bowl. Add salt and pepper to taste. Pour over the salad, and toss well. Decorate with the remaining mussels in the half shell. This salad may be served at room temperature or slightly chilled.

Prosciutto with Figs

Prosciutto crudo con fichi

The hams cured in the region of Parma are held to be the finest in Italy. Prosciutto makes an excellent appetizer sliced paper-thin and served with fresh figs or melon.

Ingredients
8 ripe green or black figs
12 paper-thin slices prosciutto crudo
crusty bread, to serve
unsalted butter, to serve
serves 4

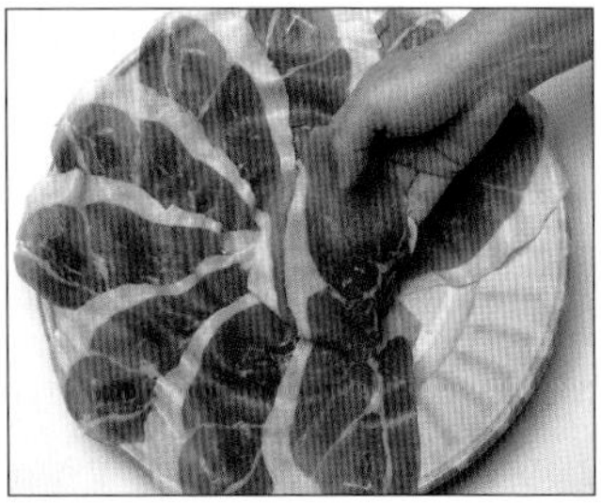

1 ▲ Arrange the slices of prosciutto on a serving plate.

2 ▲ Wipe the figs with a damp cloth. Cut them almost into quarters but do not cut all the way through the base. If the skins are tender, they may be eaten along with the inner fruit. If you prefer, you may peel each quarter carefully by pulling the peel gently away from the pulp.

3 ▲ Arrange the figs on top of the prosciutto. Serve with bread and unsalted butter.

Cherry Tomatoes with Pesto

Pomodorini con pesto

These make a colourful and tasty appetizer to go with drinks, or as part of a buffet. Make the pesto when fresh basil is plentiful, and freeze it in batches.

Ingredients
450 g/1 lb cherry tomatoes (about 36)
For the pesto
90 g/3½ oz/1 cup fresh basil
3–4 garlic cloves
60 ml/4 tbsp pine nuts
5 ml/1 tsp salt, plus extra to taste
100 ml/4 fl oz/½ cup olive oil
50 ml/3 tbsp freshly grated parmesan cheese
90 ml/6 tbsp freshly grated pecorino cheese
freshly ground black pepper
serves 8–10 as an appetizer

1 Wash the tomatoes. Slice off the top of each tomato, and carefully scoop out the seeds with a melon baller or small spoon.

2 ▲ Place the basil, garlic, pine nuts, salt and olive oil in a blender or food processor and process until smooth. Remove the contents to a bowl with a rubber spatula. If desired, the pesto may be frozen at this point, before the cheeses are added. To use when frozen, allow to thaw, then proceed to step 3.

3 Fold in the grated cheeses (use all parmesan if pecorino is not available). Season with pepper, and more salt if necessary.

4 ▲ Use a small spoon to fill each tomato with a little pesto. This dish is at its best if chilled for about an hour before serving.

Hard-boiled Eggs with Tuna Sauce

Uova sode tonnate

The combination of eggs with a tasty tuna mayonnaise makes a nourishing first course that is quick and easy to prepare.

Ingredients
6 extra large eggs
1 x 200g/7 oz can tuna in olive oil
3 anchovy fillets
15 ml/1 tbsp capers, drained
30 ml/2 tbsp fresh lemon juice
60 ml/4 tbsp olive oil
salt and freshly ground black pepper
For the mayonnaise
1 egg yolk, at room temperature
5 ml/1 tsp Dijon mustard
5 ml/1 tsp white wine vinegar or fresh lemon juice
150 ml/$^1/_4$ pint/$^2/_3$ cup olive oil
capers and anchovy fillets, to garnish (optional)
serves 6

1 Boil the eggs for 12–14 minutes. Drain under cold water. Peel carefully and set aside.

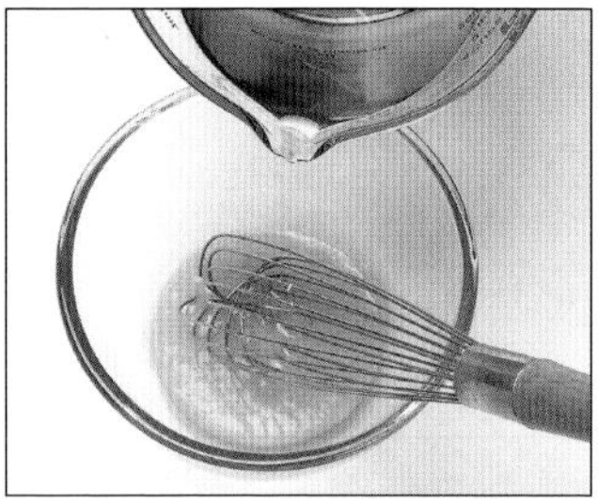

2 ▲ Make the mayonnaise by whisking the egg yolk, mustard and vinegar or lemon juice together in a small bowl. Whisk in the oil a few drops at a time until 3 or 4 tablespoons of oil have been incorporated. Pour in the remaining oil in a slow stream, whisking constantly.

3 Place the tuna with its oil, the anchovies, capers, lemon juice and olive oil in the bowl of a blender or food processor. Process until smooth.

4 ▲ Fold the tuna sauce into the mayonnaise. Season with black pepper, and extra salt if necessary. Refrigerate for at least 1 hour.

5 ▲ To serve, cut the eggs in half lengthwise. Arrange on a serving platter. Spoon on the sauce, and garnish with capers and anchovy fillets, if desired. Serve chilled.

Tuna and Bean Salad

Tonno e fagioli

This substantial salad makes a good light meal, and can be very quickly assembled from canned ingredients.

Ingredients

2 × 400 g/14 oz cans cannellini or borlotti beans
2 × 200 g/7oz cans tuna fish, drained
60 ml/4 tbsp extra-virgin olive oil
30 ml/2 tbsp fresh lemon juice
salt and freshly ground black pepper
15 ml/1 tbsp chopped fresh parsley
3 spring onions, thinly sliced
serves 4–6

1 ▲ Pour the beans into a large strainer and rinse under cold water. Drain well. Place in a serving dish.

2 ▲ Break the tuna into fairly large flakes and arrange over the beans.

3 ▲ In a small bowl make the dressing by combining the oil with the lemon juice. Season with salt and pepper, and stir in the parsley. Mix well. Pour over the beans and tuna.

4 ▲ Sprinkle with the spring onions. Toss well before serving.

Carpaccio with Rocket

Carpaccio con rucola

Carpaccio is a fine dish of raw beef in lemon juice and olive oil. It is traditionally served with flakes of fresh Parmesan cheese. Use very fresh meat of the best quality.

Ingredients
1 garlic clove, peeled and cut in half
$1^1/_2$ lemons
50 ml/2 fl oz/$^1/_4$ cup extra-virgin olive oil
salt and freshly ground black pepper
2 bunches rocket
4 very thin slices of beef top round
115g/4 oz/1 cup Parmesan cheese, thinly shaved
serves 4

1 Rub a small bowl all over with the cut side of the garlic. Squeeze the lemons into the bowl. Whisk in the olive oil. Season with salt and pepper. Allow the sauce to stand for at least 15 minutes before using.

2 ▲ Carefully wash the rocket and tear off any thick stalks. Spin or pat dry. Arrange the rocket around the edge of a serving platter, or divide on 4 individual plates.

3 ▲ Place the beef in the centre of the platter, and pour on the sauce, spreading it evenly over the meat. Arrange the shaved Parmesan on top of the meat slices. Serve at once.

Tuna in Rolled Red Peppers

Peperoni rossi ripieni di tonno

This savoury combination originated in southern Italy. Grilled peppers have a sweet, smoky taste that combines particularly well with fish.

Ingredients
3 large red peppers
1 x 200 g/7oz can tuna fish, drained
30 ml/2 tbsp fresh lemon juice
45 ml/3 tbsp olive oil
6 green or black olives, pitted and chopped
30 ml/2 tbsp chopped fresh parsley
1 garlic clove, finely chopped
1 medium stalk celery, very finely chopped
salt and freshly ground black pepper
serves 4–6

1 Place the peppers under a hot grill, and turn occasionally until they are black and blistered on all sides. Remove from the heat and place in a paper bag.

2 ▲ Leave for 5 minutes, and then peel. Cut the peppers into quarters, and remove the stems and seeds.

3 Meanwhile, flake the tuna and combine with the lemon juice and oil. Stir in the remaining ingredients. Season with salt and pepper.

4 ▲ Lay the pepper segments out flat, skin side down. Divide the tuna mixture equally between them. Spread it out, pressing it into an even layer. Roll the peppers up. Place the pepper rolls in the refrigerator for at least 1 hour. Just before serving, cut each roll in half with a sharp knife.

Stuffed Mussels

Cozze gratinate

This tasty appetizer is a speciality of southern Italy. It can be made equally well using large clams. Always use the freshest seafood available.

Ingredients

750 g/1 1/2 lb large fresh mussels in their shells
75 g/3 oz/1/3 cup unsalted butter, at room temperature
25g/1 oz/1/4 cup dry breadcrumbs
2 garlic cloves, finely chopped
45 ml/3 tbsp chopped fresh parsley
25 g/1 oz/1/4 cup freshly grated Parmesan cheese
salt and freshly ground black pepper
serves 4

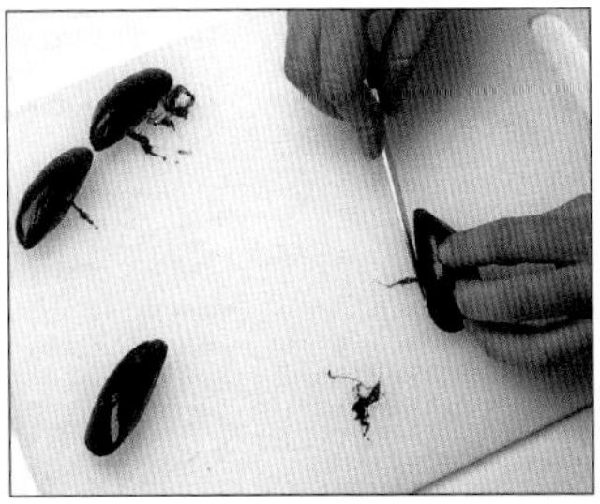

1 ▲ Scrub the mussels well under cold running water, cutting off the "beard" with a small knife. Preheat the oven to 230°C/450°F/Gas 8.

2 ▲ Place the mussels with a cupful of water in a large saucepan over a moderate heat. As soon as they open, lift them out one by one. Remove and discard the empty half shells, leaving the meat in the other half. (Discard any mussels that do not open.)

3 ▲ Combine all the remaining ingredients in a small bowl. Blend well. Place in a small pan and heat gently until the stuffing mixture begins to soften.

4 ▲ Arrange the mussel halves on a flat baking tray. Spoon a small amount of the stuffing over each mussel. Bake for about 7 minutes, or until lightly browned. Serve hot or at room temperature.

Lemon and Herb Risotto Cake

Budino di riso al limone

This unusual dish can be served as a main course with salad, or as a satisfying side dish. It is also good served cold, and packs well for picnics.

Ingredients
1 small leek, thinly sliced
600 ml/1 pint/2½ cups chicken stock
225 g/8 oz/1 cup short grain rice
finely grated rind of 1 lemon
30 ml/2 tbsp chopped fresh chives
30 ml/2 tbsp chopped fresh parsley
75 g/3 oz/¾ cup grated mozzarella cheese
salt and freshly ground black pepper
parsley and lemon wedges, to garnish
serves 4

1 Preheat the oven to 200°C/400°F/Gas 6. Lightly oil a 22 cm/8½ in round loose-based cake tin.

2 ▲ Cook the leek in a large pan with 45 ml/3 tbsp stock, stirring over a moderate heat, to soften. Add the rice and the remaining stock.

3 ▲ Bring to the boil. Cover the pan and simmer gently, stirring occasionally for about 20 minutes, or until all the liquid is absorbed.

◀ 4 Stir in the lemon rind, herbs, cheese and seasoning. Spoon the mixture into the tin, cover with foil and bake for 30-35 minutes or until lightly browned. Turn out and serve in slices, garnished with parsley and lemon wedges.

Cook's Tip
The best type of rice to choose is one of the round grain risotto rices, such as Arborio.

Soups

The Italians are great soup eaters, and some of the best soups in the world come from Italy. Clear broth, brodo, *and delicate puréed soups are served as a first course before a main meal. More substantial chunky soups,* minestre, *are often main meals in themselves, usually served in the evening if the main meal of the day has been at lunchtime.*

Wild Mushroom Soup

Zuppa di porcini

Wild mushrooms are expensive. Dried porcini have an intense flavour, so only a small quantity is needed. The beef stock may seem unusual in a vegetable soup, but it helps to strengthen the earthy flavour of the mushrooms.

Ingredients

25 g/1 oz/2 cups dried porcini mushrooms
30 ml/2 tbsp olive oil
15 g/½ oz/1 tbsp butter
2 leeks, thinly sliced
2 shallots, roughly chopped
1 garlic clove, roughly chopped
225 g/8 oz/3 cups fresh wild mushrooms
about 1.2 litres/2 pints/5 cups beef stock
2.5 ml/½ tsp dried thyme
150 ml/¼ pint/⅔ cup double cream
salt and freshly ground black pepper
fresh thyme sprigs, to garnish
serves 4

Cook's Tip

Porcini are ceps. Italian cooks would make this soup with a combination of fresh and dried ceps, but if fresh ceps are difficult to obtain, you can use other wild mushrooms, such as chanterelles.

1 ▲ Put the dried porcini in a bowl, add 250 ml/8 fl oz/1 cup warm water and leave to soak for 20 – 30 minutes. Lift out of the liquid and squeeze over the bowl to remove as much of the soaking liquid as possible. Strain all the liquid and reserve to use later. Finely chop the porcini.

2 Heat the oil and butter in a large saucepan until foaming. Add the sliced leeks, chopped shallots and garlic and cook gently for about 5 minutes, stirring frequently, until softened but not coloured.

3 ▲ Chop or slice the fresh mushrooms and add to the pan. Stir over a medium heat for a few minutes until they begin to soften. Pour in the stock and bring to the boil. Add the porcini, soaking liquid, dried thyme and salt and pepper. Lower the heat, half cover the pan and simmer gently for 30 minutes, stirring occasionally.

4 ▲ Pour about three-quarters of the soup into a blender or food processor and process until smooth. Return to the soup remaining in the pan, stir in the cream and heat through. Check the consistency and add more stock if the soup is too thick. Taste for seasoning. Serve hot, garnished with thyme sprigs.

Cream of Courgette Soup

Vellutata di zucchini

The beauty of this soup is its delicate colour, rich and creamy texture and subtle taste. If you prefer a more pronounced cheese flavour, use Gorgonzola instead of Dolcelatte.

Ingredients
30 ml/2 tbsp olive oil
15 g/½ oz/1 tbsp butter
1 medium onion, roughly chopped
900 g/2 lb courgettes, trimmed and sliced
5 ml/1 tsp dried oregano
about 600 ml/1 pint/2½ cups vegetable or chicken stock
115 g/4 oz Dolcelatte cheese, rind removed, diced
300 ml/½ pint/1¼ cups single cream
salt and freshly ground black pepper
fresh oregano and extra Dolcelatte, to garnish
serves 4–6

1 ▲ Heat the oil and butter in a large saucepan until foaming. Add the onion and cook gently for about 5 minutes, stirring frequently, until softened but not brown.

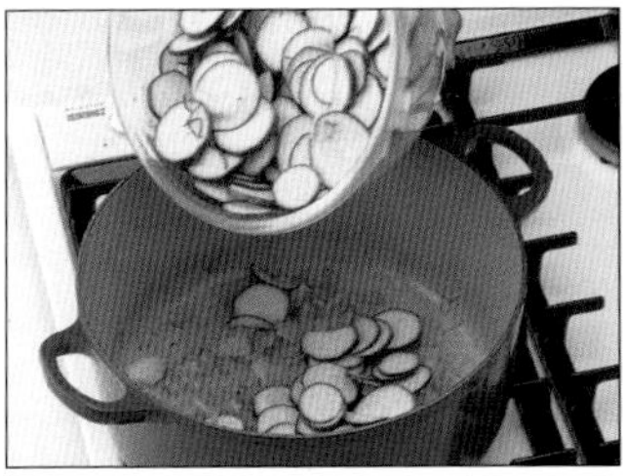

2 ▲ Add the courgettes and oregano, with salt and pepper to taste. Cook over a medium heat for 10 minutes, stirring frequently.

3 ▲ Pour in the stock and bring to the boil, stirring. Lower the heat, half cover the pan and simmer gently, stirring occasionally, for about 30 minutes. Stir in the diced Dolcelatte until melted.

Cook's Tip
To save time, trim off and discard the ends of the courgettes, cut them into thirds, then chop in a food processor fitted with the metal blade.

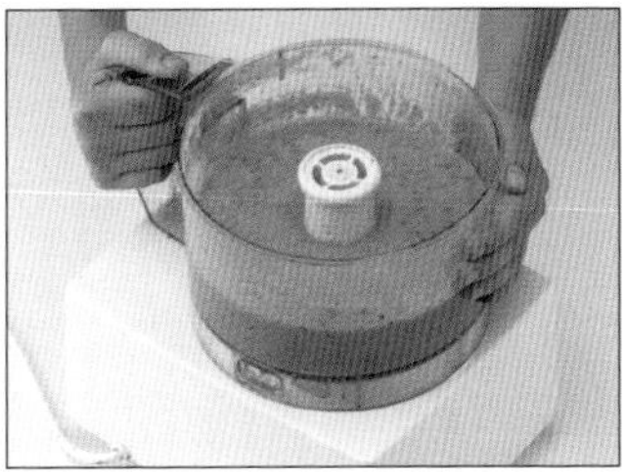

4 ▲ Process the soup in a blender or food processor until smooth, then press through a sieve into a clean pan.

5 Add two-thirds of the cream and stir over a low heat until hot, but not boiling. Check the consistency and add more stock if the soup is too thick. Taste for seasoning, then pour into heated bowls. Swirl in the remaining cream. Garnish with oregano and extra cheese and serve.

Minestrone with Pasta and Beans

Minestrone alla milanese

This classic minestrone from Lombardy includes pancetta for a pleasant touch of saltiness. Milanese cooks vary the recipe according to what is on hand, and you can do the same.

Ingredients

45 ml/3 tbsp olive oil
115 g/4 oz pancetta, any rinds removed, roughly chopped
2–3 celery sticks, finely chopped
3 medium carrots, finely chopped
1 medium onion, finely chopped
1–2 garlic cloves, crushed
2 x 400 g/14 oz cans chopped tomatoes
about 1 litre/1¾ pints/4 cups chicken stock
400 g/14 oz can cannellini beans, drained and rinsed
50 g/2 oz/½ cup short–cut macaroni
30–60 ml/2–4 tbsp chopped flat leaf parsley, to taste
salt and freshly ground black pepper
shaved Parmesan cheese, to serve
serves 4

Variation

Use long-grain rice instead of the pasta, and borlotti beans instead of cannellini.

1 ▲ Heat the oil in a large saucepan. Add the pancetta, celery, carrots and onion and cook over a low heat for 5 minutes, stirring constantly, until the vegetables are softened.

2 Add the garlic and tomatoes, breaking them up well with a wooden spoon. Pour in the stock. Add salt and pepper to taste and bring to the boil. Half cover the pan, lower the heat and simmer gently for about 20 minutes, until the vegetables are soft.

3 ▲ Drain the beans and add them to the pan with the macaroni. Bring to the boil again. Cover, lower the heat and continue to simmer for about 20 minutes more. Check the consistency and add more stock if necessary. Stir in the parsley and taste for seasoning.

4 Serve hot, sprinkled with plenty of Parmesan cheese. This makes a meal in itself if served with chunks of crusty Italian bread.

Summer Minestrone

Minestrone estivo

This brightly coloured, fresh-tasting soup makes the most of summer vegetables.

Ingredients

45 ml/3 tbsp olive oil
1 large onion, finely chopped
15 ml/1 tbsp sun-dried tomato paste
450 g/1 lb ripe Italian plum tomatoes, peeled and finely chopped
225 g/8 oz green courgettes, trimmed and roughly chopped
225 g/8 oz yellow courgettes, trimmed and roughly chopped
3 waxy new potatoes, diced
2 garlic cloves, crushed
about 1.2 litres/2 pints/5 cups chicken stock or water
60 ml/4 tbsp shredded fresh basil
50 g/2 oz/⅔ cup grated Parmesan cheese
salt and freshly ground black pepper
serves 4

1 ▲ Heat the oil in a large saucepan, add the onion and cook gently for about 5 minutes, stirring constantly, until softened. Stir in the sun-dried tomato paste, chopped tomatoes, courgettes, diced potatoes and garlic. Mix well and cook gently for 10 minutes, uncovered, shaking the pan frequently to stop the vegetables sticking to the base.

2 ▲ Pour in the stock. Bring to the boil, lower the heat, half cover the pan and simmer gently for 15 minutes or until the vegetables are just tender. Add more stock if necessary.

3 Remove the pan from the heat and stir in the basil and half the cheese. Taste for seasoning. Serve hot, sprinkled with the remaining cheese.

Clam and Pasta Soup

Zuppa alle vongole

This soup is a play on the pasta dish – spaghetti alle vongole – using store cupboard ingredients. Serve it with hot focaccia or ciabatta for an informal supper with friends.

Ingredients

30 ml/2 tbsp olive oil
1 large onion, finely chopped
2 garlic cloves, crushed
400 g/14 oz can chopped tomatoes
15 ml/1 tbsp sun-dried tomato paste
5 ml/1 tsp granulated sugar
5 ml/1 tsp dried mixed herbs
about 750 ml/1¼ pints/3 cups fish or vegetable stock
150 ml/¼ pint/⅔ cup red wine
50 g/2 oz/½ cup small pasta shapes
150 g/5 oz jar or can clams in natural juice
30 ml/2 tbsp finely chopped flat leaf parsley, plus a few whole leaves, to garnish
salt and freshly ground black pepper
serves 4

1 ▲ Heat the oil in a large saucepan. Cook the onion gently for 5 minutes, stirring frequently, until softened.

2 ▲ Add the garlic, tomatoes, tomato paste, sugar, herbs, stock and wine, with salt and pepper to taste. Bring to the boil. Lower the heat, half cover the pan and simmer for 10 minutes, stirring occasionally.

3 ▲ Add the pasta and continue simmering, uncovered, for about 10 minutes or until *al dente*. Stir occasionally, to prevent the pasta shapes from sticking together.

Cook's Tip

This soup has a fuller flavour if it is made the day before and reheated.

4 ▲ Add the clams and their juice to the soup and heat through for 3–4 minutes, adding more stock if required. Do not let it boil or the clams will be tough. Remove from the heat, stir in the parsley and taste the soup for seasoning. Serve hot, sprinkled with coarsely ground black pepper and parsley leaves.

Tuscan Bean Soup

Zuppa di fagioli alla toscana

There are lots of versions of this wonderful soup. This one uses cannellini beans, leeks, cabbage and good olive oil – and tastes even better reheated.

Ingredients
45 ml/3 tbsp extra virgin olive oil
1 onion, roughly chopped
2 leeks, roughly chopped
1 large potato, peeled and diced
2 garlic cloves, finely chopped
1.2 litres/2 pints/5 cups vegetable stock
400 g/14 oz can cannellini beans, drained, liquid reserved
175 g/6 oz Savoy cabbage, shredded
45 ml/3 tbsp chopped fresh flat leaf parsley
30 ml/2 tbsp chopped fresh oregano
75 g/3 oz/1 cup Parmesan cheese, shaved
salt and freshly ground black pepper

For the garlic toasts
30–45 ml/2–3 tbsp extra virgin olive oil
6 thick slices country bread
1 garlic clove, peeled and bruised
serves 4

1 ▲ Heat the oil in a large saucepan and gently cook the onion, leeks, potato and garlic for 4–5 minutes.

2 ▲ Pour on the stock and liquid from the beans. Cover and simmer for 15 minutes.

3 ▲ Stir in the cabbage and beans, with half the herbs, season and cook for 10 minutes more. Spoon about one-third of the soup into a food processor or blender and process until fairly smooth. Return to the soup in the pan, taste for seasoning and heat through for 5 minutes.

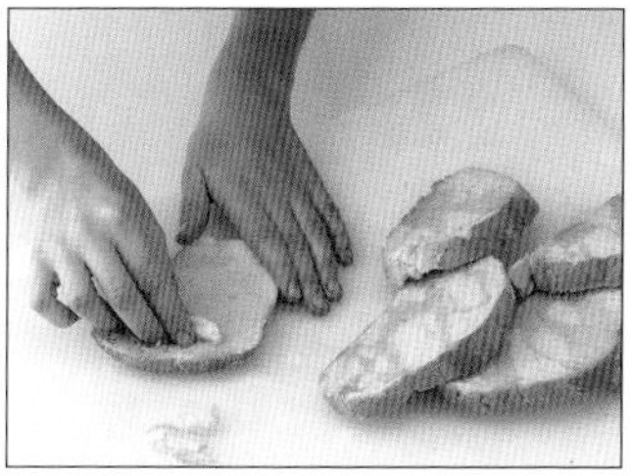

4 ▲ Meanwhile make the garlic toasts. Drizzle a little oil over the slices of bread, then rub both sides of each slice with the garlic. Toast until browned on both sides. Ladle the soup into bowls. Sprinkle with the remaining herbs and the Parmesan shavings. Add a drizzle of olive oil and serve with the toasts.

Lentil Soup with Tomatoes

Minestra di lenticchie

A classic rustic Italian soup flavoured with rosemary, delicious served with garlic bread.

Ingredients

225 g/8 oz/1 cup dried green or brown lentils
45 ml/3 tbsp extra virgin olive oil
3 rindless streaky bacon rashers, cut into small dice
1 onion, finely chopped
2 celery sticks, finely chopped
2 carrots, finely diced
2 rosemary sprigs, finely chopped
2 bay leaves
400 g/14 oz can chopped plum tomatoes
1.75 litres/3 pints/7½ cups vegetable stock
salt and freshly ground black pepper
bay leaves and rosemary sprigs, to garnish

serves 4

Cook's Tip

Look out for the small green lentils in Italian groceries or delicatessens.

1 Place the lentils in a bowl and cover with cold water. Leave to soak for 2 hours. Rinse and drain well.

2 ▲ Heat the oil in a large saucepan. Add the bacon and cook for about 3 minutes, then stir in the onion and cook for 5 minutes until softened. Stir in the celery, carrots, rosemary, bay leaves and lentils. Toss over the heat for 1 minute until thoroughly coated in the oil.

3 ▲ Tip in the tomatoes and stock and bring to the boil. Lower the heat, half cover the pan, and simmer for about 1 hour, or until the lentils are perfectly tender.

4 Remove the bay leaves, add salt and pepper to taste and serve with a garnish of fresh bay leaves and rosemary sprigs.

Spinach and Rice Soup

Minestra di riso e spinaci

Use very fresh, young spinach leaves to prepare this light and fresh-tasting soup.

Ingredients

675 g/1½ lb fresh spinach, washed
45 ml/3 tbsp extra virgin olive oil
1 small onion, finely chopped
2 garlic cloves, finely chopped
1 small fresh red chilli, seeded and finely chopped
115 g/4 oz/generous 1 cup risotto rice
1.2 litres/2 pints/5 cups vegetable stock
60 ml/4 tbsp grated Pecorino cheese
salt and freshly ground black pepper

serves 4

1 Place the spinach in a large pan with just the water that clings to its leaves after washing. Add a large pinch of salt. Heat gently until the spinach has wilted, then remove from the heat and drain, reserving any liquid.

2 ▲ Either chop the spinach finely using a large knife or place in a food processor and process to a fairly coarse purée.

3 ▲ Heat the oil in a large saucepan and gently cook the onion, garlic and chilli for 4–5 minutes until softened. Stir in the rice until well coated, then pour in the stock and reserved spinach liquid. Bring to the boil, lower the heat and simmer for 10 minutes. Add the spinach, with salt and pepper to taste. Cook for 5–7 minutes more, until the rice is tender. Check the seasoning and serve with the Pecorino cheese.

Onion Soup

La cipollata

This warming winter soup comes from Umbria, where it is sometimes thickened with beaten eggs and lots of grated Parmesan cheese. It is then served on top of hot toasted croûtes – rather like savoury scrambled eggs.

Ingredients

115 g/4 oz pancetta rashers, any rinds removed, roughly chopped
30 ml/2 tbsp olive oil
15 g/½ oz/1 tbsp butter
675 g/1½ lb onions, thinly sliced
10 ml/2 tsp granulated sugar
about 1.2 litres/2 pints/5 cups chicken stock
350 g/12 oz ripe Italian plum tomatoes, peeled and roughly chopped
a few basil leaves, shredded
salt and freshly ground black pepper
freshly grated Parmesan cheese, to serve

serves 4

1 ▲ Put the chopped pancetta in a large saucepan and heat gently, stirring constantly, until the fat runs. Increase the heat to medium, add the oil, butter, onions and sugar and stir well to mix.

2 ▲ Half cover the pan and cook the onions gently for about 20 minutes until golden. Stir frequently and lower the heat if necessary.

3 ▲ Add the stock, tomatoes and salt and pepper and bring to the boil, stirring. Lower the heat, half cover the pan and simmer, stirring occasionally, for about 30 minutes.

4 Check the consistency of the soup and add a little more stock or water if it is too thick.

5 Just before serving, stir in most of the basil and taste for seasoning. Serve hot, garnished with the remaining shredded basil. Hand round the freshly grated Parmesan separately.

Cook's Tip

Look for Vidalia onions to make this soup. They are available at large supermarkets, and have a very sweet flavour and attractive yellowish flesh.

Tomato and Fresh Basil Soup

Crema di pomodori al basilico

A soup for late summer when fresh tomatoes are at their most flavoursome.

Ingredients

15 ml/1 tbsp olive oil
25 g/1 oz/2 tbsp butter
1 medium onion, finely chopped
900 g/2 lb ripe Italian plum tomatoes, roughly chopped
1 garlic clove, roughly chopped
about 750 ml/1 ¼ pints/3 cups chicken or vegetable stock
120 ml/4 fl oz/½ cup dry white wine
30 ml/2 tbsp sun-dried tomato paste
30 ml/2 tbsp shredded fresh basil, plus a few whole leaves, to garnish
150 ml/¼ pint/ ⅔ cup double cream
salt and freshly ground black pepper

serves 4–6

1 ▲ Heat the oil and butter in a large saucepan until foaming. Add the onion and cook gently for about 5 minutes, stirring frequently, until softened but not brown.

2 ▲ Stir in the chopped tomatoes and garlic, then add the stock, white wine and sun-dried tomato paste, with salt and pepper to taste. Bring to the boil, then lower the heat, half cover the pan and simmer gently for 20 minutes, stirring occasionally to stop the tomatoes sticking to the base of the pan.

3 ▲ Process the soup with the shredded basil in a blender or food processor, then press through a sieve into a clean pan.

4 ▲ Add the double cream and heat through, stirring. Do not allow the soup to approach boiling point. Check the consistency and add more stock if necessary and then taste for seasoning. Pour into heated bowls and garnish with basil. Serve at once.

Variation

The soup can also be served chilled. Pour it into a container after sieving and chill for at least 4 hours. Serve in chilled bowls.

Mediterranean Broth

Minestrone con prosciutto salato

This delicious main meal soup is very similar to the warming, chunky meat and potato broths of cooler climates. For extra colour, a few onion skins can be added when cooking the gammon, but remember to remove them before serving.

Ingredients

450 g/3 lb gammon, in one piece
2 bay leaves
2 onions, sliced
10 ml/2 tsp paprika
675 g/1$^{1}/_{2}$ lb potatoes, cut into large chunks
225g/8 oz spring greens
425 g/15 oz can haricot or cannellini beans, drained
salt and freshly graound black pepper
serves 4

1 Soak the gammon overnight in cold water. Drain and put in a large saucepan with the bay leaves and onions. Pour over 1.5 litres/2$^{1}/_{2}$ pints/ 6$^{1}/_{4}$ cups cold water.

2 Bring to the boil, then reduce the heat and simmer very gently for about 1$^{1}/_{2}$ hours until the meat is tender. Keep an eye on the pan to make sure it doesn't boil over.

Cook's Tip

Bacon knuckles can be used instead of the gammon. The bones will give the juices a delicious flavour.

3 ▲ Drain the meat, reserving the cooking liquid and leave to cool slightly. Discard the skin and any excess fat from the meat and cut into small chunks. Return to the pan with the paprika and potatoes. Cover and simmer gently for 20 minutes.

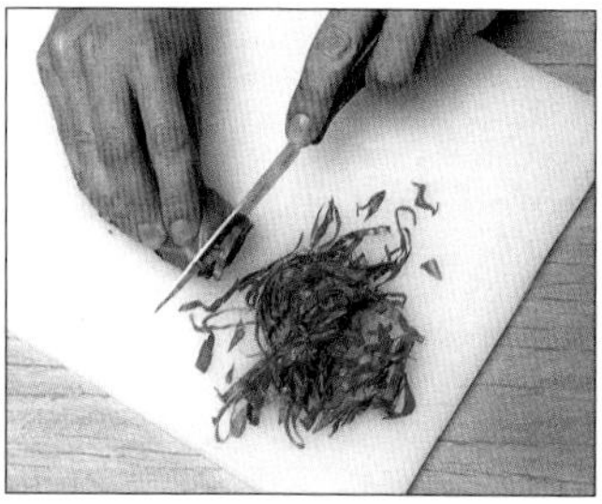

4 ▲ Cut away the cores from the spring greens. Roll up the leaves and cut into thin shreds. Add to the pan with the beans and simmer for about 10 minutes. Season with salt and pepper to taste and serve hot.

Egg and Cheese Soup

Stracciatella

In this classic Roman soup, eggs and cheese are beaten into hot broth, producing a slightly "curdled" texture characteristic of the dish.

Ingredients
3 eggs
45 ml/3 tbsp fine semolina
90 ml/6 tbsp freshly grated Parmesan cheese
pinch of nutmeg
1.5 litres/2$^1/_2$ pints/6$^1/_4$ cups meat or chicken broth
salt and freshly ground black pepper
12 rounds of French bread, to serve
serves 6

1 ▲ Beat the eggs in a bowl with the semolina and the cheese. Add the nutmeg. Beat in 1 cupful of the cool broth.

2 ▲ Meanwhile heat the remaining broth to simmering point in a large saucepan.

3 ▲ When the broth is hot, and a few minutes before you are ready to serve the soup, whisk the egg mixture into the broth. Raise the heat slightly, and bring it barely to the boil. Season with salt and pepper. Cook for 3–4 minutes. As the egg cooks, the soup will not be completely smooth.

4 ▲ To serve, toast the rounds of French bread and place 2 in the bottom of each soup plate. Ladle on the hot soup, and serve immediately.

Minestrone with Pesto

Minestrone con pesto

Minestrone is a thick mixed vegetable soup using almost any combination of seasonal vegetables. Short pasta or rice may also be added. This version includes pesto sauce.

Ingredients

1.5 litres/2½ pints/6¼ cups broth or water, or a combination of both
45 ml/3 tbsp olive oil
1 large onion, finely chopped
1 leek, sliced
2 carrots, finely chopped
1 stalk celery, finely chopped
2 cloves garlic, finely chopped
2 potatoes, peeled and cut into small dice
1 bay leaf
1 sprig fresh thyme, or 1 ml/¼ tsp dried thyme leaves
salt and freshly ground black pepper
115g/4 oz/¾ cup peas, fresh or frozen
2–3 courgettes, finely chopped
3 medium tomatoes, peeled and finely chopped
425 g/15 oz/2 cups cooked or canned beans such as cannellini
45 ml/3 tbsp pesto sauce
freshly grated Parmesan cheese, to serve

serves 6

1 In a medium pan, heat the broth or water to simmering.

2 ▲ In a saucepan heat the olive oil in a large pan. Stir in the onion and leek, and cook for 5-6 minutes, or until the onion softens. Add the carrots, celery and garlic, and cook over moderate heat, stirring often, for another 5 minutes. Add the potatoes and cook for 2-3 minutes more.

3 Pour in the hot broth or water, and stir well. Add the herbs and seasonwith salt and pepper. Bring to the boil, reduce the heat slightly, and cook for 10-12 minutes.

4 Stir in the peas, if fresh, and the courgettes. Simmer for 5 minutes more. Add the frozen peas, if using, and the tomatoes. Cover the pan, and boil for 5-8 minutes.

5 ▲ About 10 minutes before serving the soup, uncover, and stir in the beans. Simmer for 10 minutes. Stir in the pesto sauce. Taste for seasoning. Simmer for another 5 minutes then remove from the heat. Allow the soup to stand for a few minutes, then serve with the grated Parmesan.

Pumpkin Soup

Minestrone di zucca

This beautifully coloured soup would be perfect for an autumn dinner.

Ingredients

450 g/1lb piece of peeled pumpkin
50g/2 oz/¼ cup butter
1 medium onion, finely chopped
750 ml/1¼ pints/3½ cups chicken broth or water
475 ml/16 fl oz/2 cups milk
pinch of grated nutmeg
salt and freshly ground black pepper
40 g/1½oz/ 7 tbsp spaghetti, broken into small pieces
90 ml/6 tbsp freshly grated Parmesan cheese

serves 4

1 Chop the piece of pumpkin into 2.5 cm/1 in cubes.

2 ▲ Heat the butter in a saucepan. Add the onion, and cook over moderate heat until it softens, 6-8 minutes. Stir in the pumpkin, and cook for 2-3 minutes more.

3 Add the broth or water, and cook until the pumpkin is soft, about 15 minutes. Remove from the heat.

4 Purée the soup in a blender or food processor. Return it to the pan. Stir in the milk and nutmeg. Season with salt and pepper. Bring the soup back to a boil.

5 Stir the broken spaghetti into the soup. Cook until the pasta is done. Stir in the Parmesan and serve at once.

Broccoli Soup

Zuppa di broccoletti

Around Rome broccoli grows abundantly and is served in this soup with garlic toasts.

Ingredients
675 g/1 1/2 lb broccoli spears
1.75 litres/3 pints/7 1/2 cups chicken or vegetable broth
salt and freshly ground black pepper
30 ml/1 tbsp fresh lemon juice

To serve
6 slices white bread
1 large clove garlic, cut in half
freshly grated Parmesan cheese (optional)

serves 6

1 Using a small sharp knife, peel the broccoli stems, starting from the base of the stalks and pulling gently up towards the florets. (The peel comes off very easily.) Chop the broccoli into small chunks.

2 Bring the stock to the boil in a large pan. Add the broccoli and simmer for 30 minutes, or until soft.

3 ▲ Purée about half of the soup and mix into the rest of the soup. Season with salt, pepper and lemon juice.

4 ▲ Just before serving, reheat the soup to just below boiling point. Toast the bread, rub with garlic and cut into quarters. Place 3 or 4 pieces of toast in the bottom of each soup plate. Ladle on the soup. Serve at once, with Parmesan if desired.

Tomato and Bread Soup

Pappa al pomodoro

This colorful Florentine recipe was created to use up stale bread. It can be made with very ripe fresh or canned plum tomatoes.

Ingredients
90 ml/6 tbsp olive oil
small piece of dried chilli, crumbled (optional)
175 g/6 oz/1 1/2 cups stale bread, cut into 2.5 cm/1 in cubes
1 medium onion, finely chopped
2 cloves garlic, finely chopped
675 g/1 1/2 lb ripe tomatoes, peeled and chopped, or 2 x 400 g/14 oz cans peeled plum tomatoes, chopped
45 ml/3 tbsp chopped fresh basil
1.5 litres/2 1/2 pints/6 1/4 cups light meat broth or water, or a combination of both
salt and freshly ground black pepper
extra-virgin olive oil, to serve (optional)

serves 4

1 Heat 60 ml/4 tbsp of the oil in a large saucepan. Add the chilli, if using, and stir for 1–2 minutes. Add the bread cubes and cook until golden. Remove to a plate and drain on kitchen paper.

2 ▲ Add the remaining oil, the onion and garlic, and cook until the onion softens. Stir in the tomatoes, bread and basil. Season with salt. Cook over moderate heat, stirring occasionally, for about 15 minutes.

3 Meanwhile, heat the broth or water to simmering. Add it to the pan with the tomato mixture, and mix well. Bring to the boil. Lower the heat slightly and simmer for 20 minutes.

4 ▲ Remove the soup from the heat. Use a fork to mash the tomatoes and the bread together. Season with pepper, and more salt if necessary. Allow to stand for 10 minutes. Just before serving swirl in a little extra-virgin olive oil, if desired.

White Bean Soup

Minestrone di fagioli

A thick purée of cooked dried beans is at the heart of this substantial country soup from Tuscany. It makes a warming winter lunch or supper dish.

Ingredients

350 g/12 oz/1 1/2 cups dried cannellini or other white beans
1 bay leaf
75 ml/5 tbsp olive oil
1 medium onion, finely chopped
1 carrot, finely chopped
1 stalk celery, finely chopped
3 medium tomatoes, peeled and finely chopped
2 cloves garlic, finely chopped
1 tsp fresh thyme leaves, or 1/2 tsp dried thyme
750 ml/1 1/4 pints/3 1/2 cups boiling water
salt and freshly ground black pepper
extra-virgin olive oil, to serve

serves 6

1 ▲ Pick over the beans carefully, discarding any stones or other particles. Soak the beans in a large bowl of cold water overnight. Drain. Place the beans in a large saucepan of water, bring to a boil, and cook for 20 minutes. Drain. Return the beans to the pan, cover with cold water, and bring to a boil again. Add the bay leaf, and cook until the beans are tender, 1–2 hours. Drain again. Remove the bay leaf.

2 Purée about three-quarters of the beans in a food processor, or pass through a food mill, adding a little water if necessary.

3 Heat the oil in a large saucepan. Stir in the onion, and cook until it softens. Add the carrot and celery, and cook for 5 minutes more.

4 ▲ Stir in the tomatoes, garlic and thyme. Cook for 6–8 minutes more, stirring often.

5 ▲ Pour in the boiling water. Stir in the beans and the bean purée. Season with salt and pepper. Simmer for 10–15 minutes. Serve in individual soup bowls, sprinkled with a little extra-virgin olive oil.

Fish Soup

Ciuppin

Liguria is famous for its fish soups. In this one the fish are cooked in a broth with vegetables and then puréed. This soup can also be used to dress pasta.

Ingredients

1 kg/2 lb mixed fish or fish pieces (such as pollock, whiting, red mullet, red or white snapper, cod etc)
90 ml/6 tbsp olive oil, plus extra to serve
1 medium onion, finely chopped
1 stick celery, chopped
1 carrot, chopped
60 ml/4 tbsp chopped fresh parsley
175 ml/6 fl oz/¾ cup dry white wine
3 medium tomatoes, peeled and chopped
2 cloves garlic, finely chopped
1.5 litres/2½ pints/6¼ cups boiling water
salt and freshly ground black pepper
rounds of French bread, to serve

serves 6

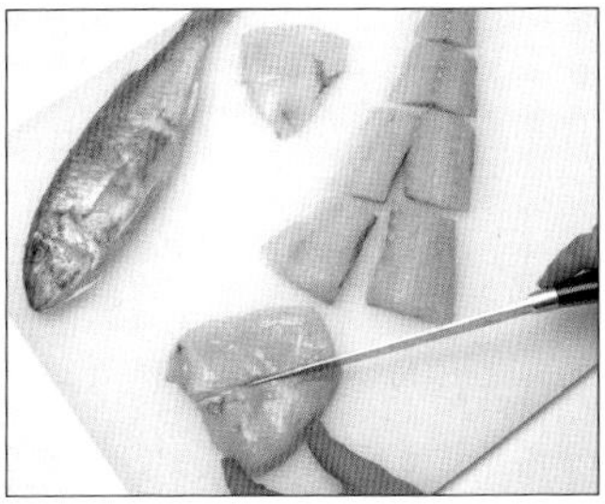

1 ▲ Scale and clean the fish, discarding all innards, but leaving the heads on. Cut into large pieces. Rinse well in cool water.

2 Heat the oil in a large saucepan and add the onion. Cook over low to moderate heat until it begins to soften. Stir in the celery and carrot, and cook for 5 minutes more. Add the parsley.

3 ▲ Pour in the wine, raise the heat, and cook until it reduces by about half. Stir in the tomatoes and garlic. Cook for 3–4 minutes, stirring occasionally. Pour in the boiling water, and bring back to a boil. Cook over moderate heat for 15 minutes.

4 Stir in the fish, and simmer for 10–15 minutes, or until the fish are tender. Season with salt and pepper.

5 ▲ Remove the fish from the soup with a slotted spoon. Discard any bones. Purée in a food processor. Taste for seasoning. If the soup is too thick, add a little more water.

6 To serve, heat the soup to simmering. Toast the rounds of bread, and sprinkle with olive oil. Place 2 or 3 in each soup plate before pouring over the soup.

~ VARIATION ~

To use the soup as a pasta dressing, cook until it reduces to the consistency of a sauce.

Barley and Vegetable Soup

Minestrone d'orzo

This soup comes from the Alto Adige region, in Italy's mountainous north. It is a thick, nourishing and warming winter soup. Serve with crusty bread.

Ingredients

225 g/8 oz/1 cup pearl barley, preferably organic
2 litres/3½ pints/9 cups mat broth or water, or a combination of both
45 ml/3 tbsp olive oil
2 carrots, finely chopped
1 large onion, finely chopped
2 sticks celery, finely chopped
1 leek, thinly sliced
1 large potato, finely chopped
115 g/4 oz/½ cup diced ham
1 bay leaf
45 ml/3 tbsp chopped fresh parsley
1 small sprig fresh rosemary
salt and freshly ground black pepper
freshly grated Parmesan cheese, to serve (optional)

serves 6–8

1 Pick over the barley, and discard any stones or other particles. Wash it in cold water. Put the barley to soak in cold water for at least 3 hours.

2 Drain the barley and place in a large saucepan with the stock or water. Bring to a boil, lower the heat and simmer for 1 hour. Skim off any scum.

3 ▲ Stir in the oil, all the vegetables and the ham. Add the herbs. If necessary add more water. The ingredients should be covered by at least 2.5 cm/1 in. Simmer for 1-1½ hours, or until the vegetables and barley are very tender.

4 ▲ Taste for seasoning, adding salt and pepper as necessary. Serve hot with grated Parmesan, if desired.

~ VARIATION ~

An excellent vegetarian version of this soup can be made by using vegetable broth instead of beef broth, and omitting the ham.

Rice and Broad Bean Soup

Minestra di riso e fave

This thick soup makes the most of fresh broad beans while they are in season. It works well with frozen beans for the rest of the year.

Ingredients

1 kg/2 lb broad beans in their pods, or 400g/14oz shelled frozen fava beans, thawed
90 ml/6 tbsp olive oil
1 medium onion, finely chopped
salt and freshly ground black pepper
2 medium tomatoes, peeled and finely chopped
225 g/8 oz/1 cup risotto or other non-parboiled rice
25 g/1 oz/2 tbsp butter
1 litre/1¾ pints/4 cups boiling water
freshly grated Parmesan cheese, to serve (optional)

serves 4

1 ▲ Shell the beans if they are fresh. Bring a large pan of water to a boil, and blanch the beans, fresh or frozen, for 3-4 minutes. Rinse under cold water, and peel off the skins.

2 Heat the oil in a large saucepan. Add the chopped onion, and cook over low to moderate heat until it softens. Stir in the broad beans, and cook for about 5 minutes, stirring often to coat them with the oil. Season with salt and pepper. Add the tomatoes, and cook for 5 minutes more, stirring often.

3 Stir in the rice. After 1-2 minutes add the butter, and stir until it melts. Pour in the water, a little at a time, until the whole amount has been added. Taste for seasoning. Continue cooking the soup until the rice is tender. Serve hot, with grated Parmesan if desired.

Pasta and Dried Bean Soup

Pasta e fagioli

This peasant soup is very thick. In Italy it is made with dried or fresh beans, never canned, and served hot or at room temperature.

Ingredients

300 g/11 oz/$1^{1}/_{2}$ cups dried borlotti or cannellini beans
1 x 400g/14 oz can plum tomatoes, chopped, with their juice
3 cloves garlic, crushed
2 bay leaves
pinch coarsely ground black pepper
90 ml/6 tbsp olive oil, plus extra to serve (optional)
750 ml/ $1^{1}/_{4}$ pint/$3^{1}/_{2}$ cups water
10 ml/2 tsp salt
200 g/7 oz/$2^{1}/_{4}$ cups ditalini or other small pasta
45 ml/3 tbsp chopped fresh parsley
freshly grated Parmesan cheese, to serve

serves 4–6

1 Soak the beans in water overnight. Rinse and drain well.

2 Place the beans in a large saucepan and cover with water. Bring to a boil and cook for 10 minutes. Rinse and drain again.

3 ▲ Return the beans to the pan. Add enough water to cover them by 2.5 cm/1 in. Stir in the coarsely chopped tomatoes with their juice, the garlic, bay leaves, black pepper and the oil. Simmer for $1^{1}/_{2}$–2 hours, or until the beans are tender. If necessary, add more water.

4 ▲ Remove the bay leaves. Pass about half of the bean mixture through a food mill, or purée in a food processor. Stir into the pan with the remaining bean mixture. Add the water, and bring the soup to the boil.

5 ▲ Add the salt and the pasta. Stir, and cook until the pasta is just done. Stir in the parsley. Allow to stand for at least 10 minutes before serving. Serve with grated Parmesan passed separately. In Italy a little olive oil is poured into each serving.

Pasta and Lentil Soup

Pasta e lenticchie

The small brown lentils which are grown in central Italy are usually used in this wholesome soup, but green lentils may be substituted if preferred.

Ingredients

225g/8 oz/1 cup dried green or brown lentils
90 ml/6 tbsp olive oil
50g/2 oz/$^1/_4$ cup ham or salt pork, cut into small dice
1 medium onion, finely chopped
1 stick celery, finely chopped
1 carrot, finely chopped
2 litres/3$^1/_2$ pints/9 cups chicken broth or water, or a combination of both
1 leaf fresh sage or $^1/_8$ tsp dried
1 sprig fresh thyme or $^1/_4$ tsp dried
salt and freshly ground black pepper
175 g/6 oz/2$^1/_2$ cups ditalini or other small soup pasta

serves 4–6

1 ▲ Carefully check the lentils for small stones. Place them in a bowl, covered with cold water, and soak for 2-3 hours. Rinse and drain well.

2 ▲ In a large saucepan, heat the oil and sauté the ham or salt pork for 2-3 minutes. Add the onion, and cook gently until it softens.

3 ▲ Stir in the celery and carrot, and cook for 5 minutes more, stirring frequently. Add the lentils, and stir to coat them in the fats.

4 ▲ Pour in the broth or water and the herbs, and bring the soup to a boil. Cook over moderate heat for about 1 hour or until the lentils are tender. Add salt and pepper to taste.

5 Stir in the pasta, and cook it until it is just done. Allow the soup to stand for a few minutes before serving.

Pasta and Chickpea Soup

Pasta e ceci

Another thick soup from central Italy. The addition of a sprig of fresh rosemary provides a typically Mediterranean flavour.

Ingredients

200 g/7 oz/1 cup dried chickpeas
3 cloves garlic, peeled
1 bay leaf
90 ml/6 tbsp olive oil
pinch of freshly ground black pepper
50 g/2 oz/$^1/_4$ cup salt pork, pancetta or bacon, diced
1 sprig fresh rosemary
600 ml/1 pint/2$^1/_2$ cups water
150 g/5 oz ditalini or other short hollow pasta
salt, to taste
freshly grated Parmesan cheese, to serve (optional)

serves 4–6

1 ▲ Soak the chickpeas in water overnight. Rinse well and drain. Place the chickpeas in a large saucepan with water to cover. Boil for 15 minutes. Rinse and drain.

~ COOK'S TIP ~

Allow the soup to stand for about 10 minutes before serving. This will allow the flavour and texture to develop.

2 ▲ Return the chickpeas to the pan. Add water to cover, 1 clove of garlic, the bay leaf, 45 ml/3 tbsp of the oil and the ground pepper.

3 ▲ Simmer until tender, about 2 hours, adding more water as necessary. Remove the bay leaf. Pass about half the chickpeas through a food mill or purée in a food processor with a few tablespoons of the cooking liquid. Return the purée to the pan with the rest of the peas and the remaining cooking water.

4 ▲ Sauté the diced pork gently in the remaining oil with the rosemary and 2 cloves of garlic until just golden. Discard the rosemary and garlic.

5 ▲ Stir the pork with its oils into the chickpea mixture.

6 ▲ Add 600 ml/1 pint/2$^1/_2$ cups of water to the chickpeas, and bring to a boil. Correct the seasoning if necessary. Stir in the pasta, and cook until just *al dente*. Pass the Parmesan separately, if desired.

Pasta & Gnocchi

In Italy, pasta and gnocchi are traditionally served as first courses after the antipasti *and before the second course of fish or meat. Everyday dishes are often simple, served with nothing more than olive oil or butter, grated Parmesan and basil. Outside of Italy there are no hard-and-fast rules, and nowadays people eat pasta and gnocchi whenever they like.*

How to Make Egg Pasta by Hand

This classic recipe for egg noodles from Emilia-Romagna calls for just three ingredients: flour and eggs, with a little salt. In other regions of Italy water, milk or oil are sometimes added. Use plain unbleached white flour, and large eggs. As a general guide, use 70 g/2½ oz/½ cup of flour to each egg. Quantities will vary with the exact size of the eggs.

To serve 3–4
2 eggs, salt
140 g/5 oz/1 cup flour

To serve 4–6
3 eggs, salt
210 g/7½ oz/1½ cups flour

To serve 6–8
4 eggs, salt
280 g/10 oz/2 cups flour

1 Place the flour in the centre of a clean smooth work surface. Make a well in the middle. Break the eggs into the well. Add a pinch of salt.

2 ▲ Start beating the eggs with a fork, gradually drawing the flour from the inside walls of the well. As the paste thickens, continue the mixing with your hands. Incorporate as much flour as possible until the mixture forms a mass. It will still be lumpy. If it still sticks to your hands, add a little more flour. Set the dough aside. Scrape off all traces of the dough from the work surface until it is perfectly smooth. Wash and dry your hands.

About Pasta

Most pasta is made from durum wheat flour and water – durum is a special kind of wheat with a very high protein content. Egg pasta, *pasta all'uova*, contains flour and eggs, and is used for flat noodles such as tagliatelle, or for lasagne. Very little whole wheat pasta is eaten in Italy, but it is quite popular in other countries.

All these types of pasta are available dried in packets, and will keep almost indefinitely. Fresh pasta is now more widely available and can be bought in most supermarkets. It can be very good, but can never compare to home-made egg pasta.

Pasta comes in countless shapes and sizes. It is very difficult to give a definite list, as the names for the shapes vary from country to country. In some cases, just within Italy, the same shape can appear with several different names, depending upon which region it is in. The pasta shapes called for in this book, as well as many others, are illustrated in the introduction. The most common names have been listed.

Most of the recipes in this book specify the pasta shape most appropriate for a particular sauce. They can, of course, be replaced with another kind. A general rule is that long pasta goes better with tomato or thinner sauces, while short pasta is best for chunkier, meatier sauces. But this rule should not be followed too rigidly. Part of the fun of cooking and eating pasta is in the endless combinations of sauce and pasta shapes.

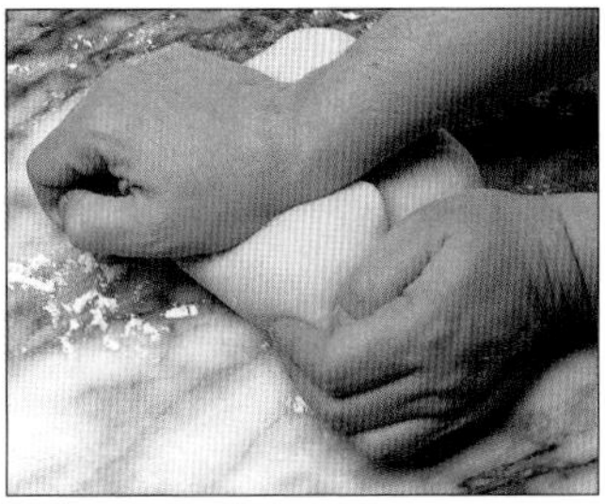

3 ▲ Lightly flour the work surface. Knead the dough by pressing it away from you with the heel of your hands, and then folding it over towards you. Repeat this action over and over, turning the dough as you knead. Work for about 10 minutes, or until the dough is smooth and elastic.

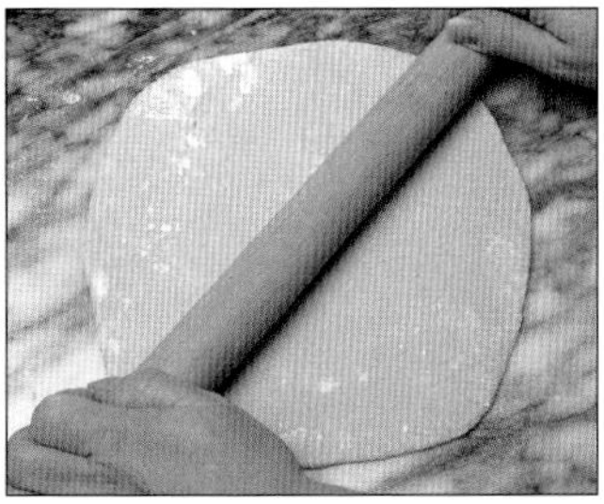

4 ▲ If you are using more than 2 eggs, divide the dough in half. Flour the rolling pin and the work surface. Pat the dough into a disc and begin rolling it out into a flat circle, rotating it one quarter turn after each roll to keep its shape round. Roll until the disc is about 3mm/$^{1}/_{8}$ in thick.

5 ▲ Roll out the dough until it is paper-thin by rolling up onto the rolling pin and simultaneously giving a sideways stretching with the hands. Wrap the near edge of the dough around the center of the rolling pin, and begin rolling the dough up away from you. As you roll back and forth, slide your hands from the center towards the outer edges of the pin, stretching and thinning out the pasta.

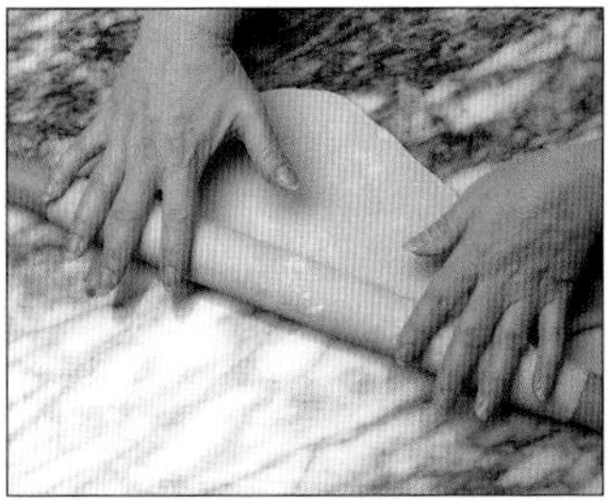

6 ▲ Quickly repeat these movements until about two-thirds of the sheet of pasta is wrapped around the pin. Lift and turn the wrapped pasta sheet about 45° before unrolling it. Repeat the rolling and stretching process, starting from a new point of the sheet each time to keep it evenly thin. By the end (this process should not last more than 8 to 10 minutes or the dough will lose its elasticity) the whole sheet should be smooth and almost transparent. If the dough is still sticky, lightly flour your hands as you continue rolling and stretching.

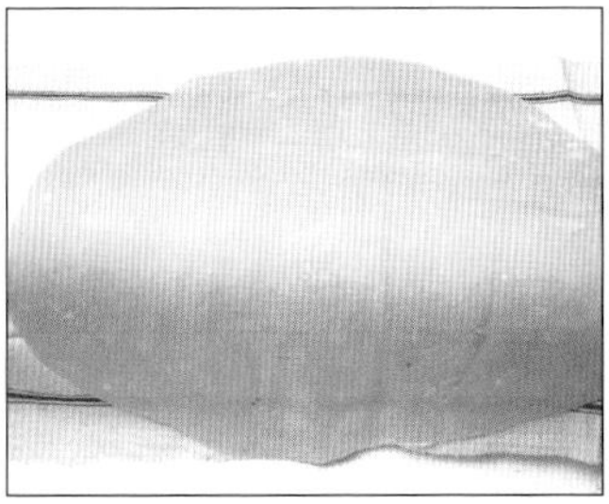

7 ▲ If you are making noodles (tagliatelle, fettuccine etc.) lay a clean dish towel on a table or other flat surface, and unroll the pasta sheet on it, letting about a third of the sheet hang over the edge of the table. Rotate the dough every 10 minutes. Roll out the second sheet of dough if you are using more than 2 eggs. After 25–30 minutes the pasta will have dried enough to cut. Do not overdry or the pasta will crack as it is cut.

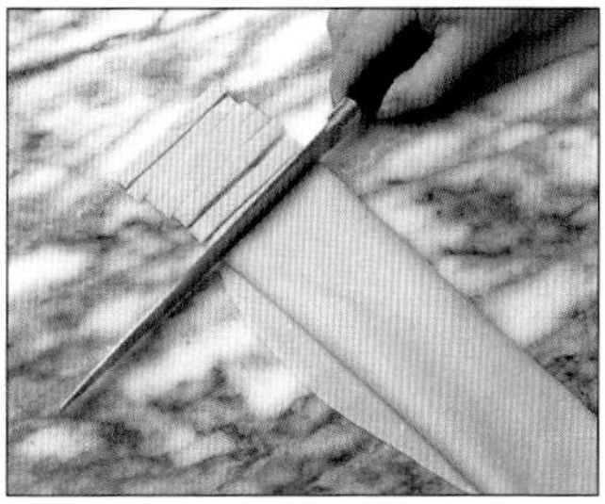

8 ▲ To cut tagliatelle, fettuccine or tagliolini, fold the sheet of pasta into a flat roll about 10 cm/4 in wide. Cut across the roll to form noodles of the desired width. Tagliolini is 3 mm/$^{1}/_{8}$ in; Fettuccine is 4 mm/$^{1}/_{6}$ in; Tagliatelle is 6 mm/$^{1}/_{4}$ in. After cutting, open out the noodles, and let them dry for about 5 minutes before cooking. These noodles may be stored for some weeks without refrigeration. Let dry completely before storing them, uncovered, in a dry cupboard, and use as required.

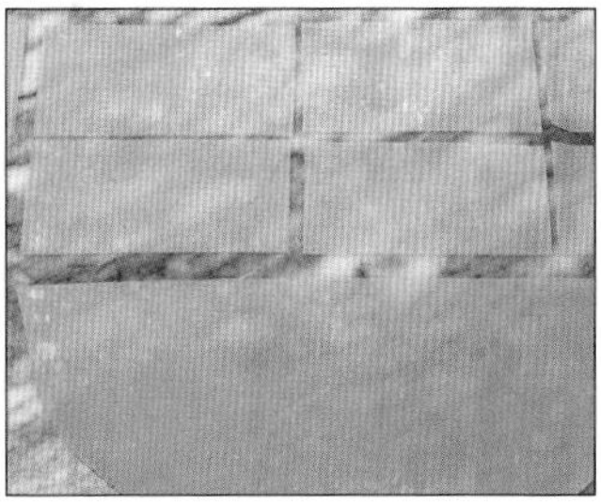

9 ▲ To cut the pasta for lasagne or pappardelle, do not fold or dry the rolled out dough. Lasagne is made by cutting rectangles about 13 cm/5 in by 9 cm/3$^{1}/_{2}$ in. Pappardelle are large noodles cut with a fluted pastry wheel. They are about 2 cm/$^{3}/_{4}$ in wide.

Egg Pasta Made by Machine

Making pasta with a machine is quick and easy. The results are perhaps not quite as fine as with handmade pasta, but they are certainly better than store-bought pastas.

You will need a pasta-making machine, either hand-cranked or electric. Use the same proportions of eggs, flours and salt as for Handmade Egg Pasta.

1 ▲ Place the flour in the centre of a clean smooth work surface. Make a well in the middle. Break the eggs into the well. Add a pinch of salt. Start beating the eggs with a fork, gradually drawing the flour from the inside walls of the well. As the paste thickens, continue mixing with your hands. Incorporate as much flour as possible until the mixture forms a mass. It will still be lumpy. If it sticks to your hands, add a little more flour. Set the dough aside and scrape the work surface clean.

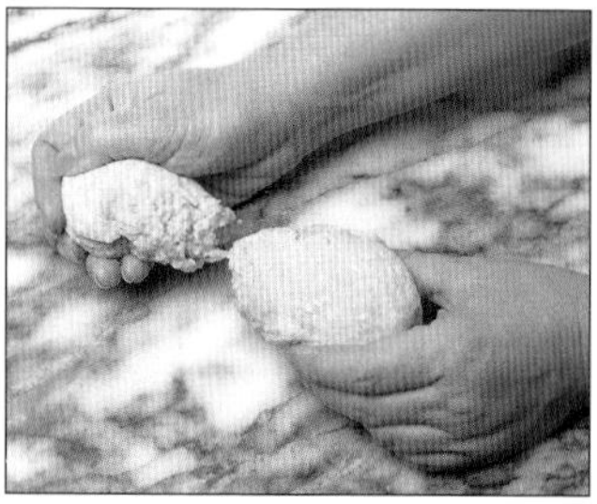

2 ▲ Set the machine rollers at their widest (kneading) setting. Pull off a piece of dough the size of a small orange. Place the remaining dough between two soup plates. Feed the dough through the rollers. Fold it in half, end to end, and feed it through again 7 or 8 times, turning it and folding it over after each kneading. The dough should be smooth and fairly evenly rectangular. If it sticks to the machine, brush with flour. Lay it out on a lightly floured work surface or on a clean dish towel, and repeat with the remaining dough, broken into pieces the same size.

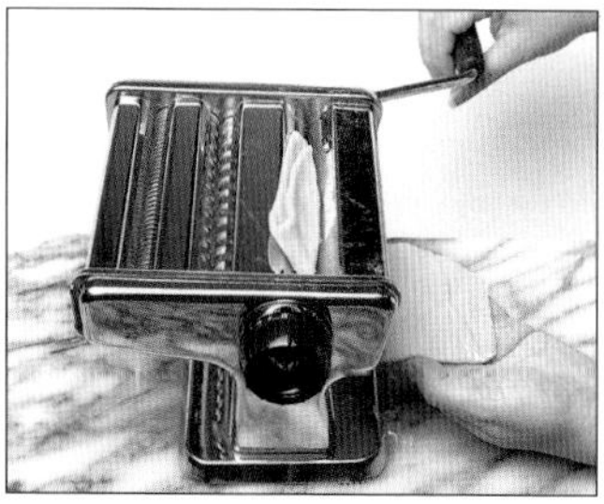

3 ▲ Adjust the machine to the next line setting. Feed each strip through once only, and replace on the drying surface. Keep them in the order in which they were first kneaded.

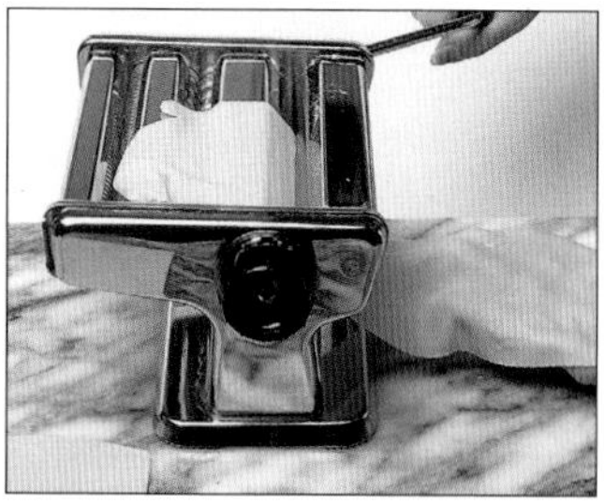

4 ▲ Reset the machine to the next setting. Repeat, passing each strip through once. Repeat for each remaining roller setting until the pasta is the right thickness - for most purposes this is given by the next to last setting, except for very delicate strips such as tagliolini, or for ravioli. If the pasta strips get too long, cut them in half to facilitate handling.

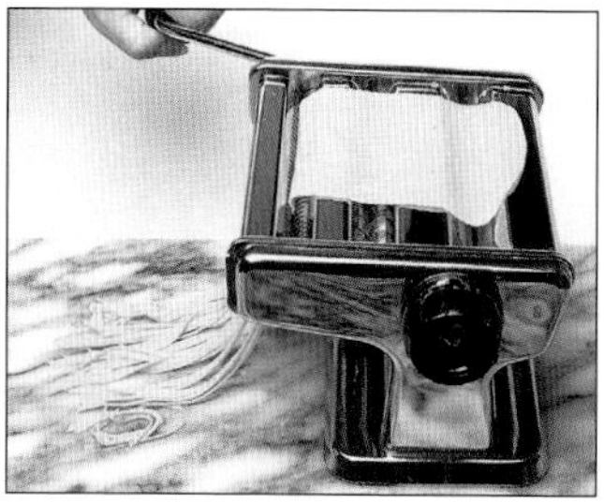

5 ▲ When all the strips are the desired thickness they may be machine-cut into noodles, or hand-cut for lasagne or pappardelle, as described for handmade pasta earlier. When making noodles, be sure the pasta is fairly dry, but not brittle, or the noodles may stick togther when cut. Select the desired width of cutter, and feed the strips through.

6 Separate the noodles, and leave to dry for at least 15 minutes before using. They may be stored for some weeks without refrigeration. Allow them to dry completely before storing them, uncovered, in a dry cupboard. They may also be frozen, first loose on trays and then packed together.

7 If you are making stuffed pasta (ravioli, cannelloni etc.) do not let the pasta strips dry out before filling them, but proceed immediately with the individual recipes.

~ PASTA VERDE ~

Follow the same recipe, adding 50 g/2 oz/$^1/_4$ cup cooked, very finely chopped spinach (after having been squeezed very dry) to the eggs and flour. You may have to add a little more flour to absorb the moisture from the spinach. This pasta is very suitable for stuffed recipes, as it seals better than plain egg pasta.

How to Cook Dried Pasta

Store-bought and home-made pasta are cooked in the same way, though the timings vary greatly. Home-made pasta cooks virtually in the time it takes for the water to return to a boil after it is put in.

1 Always cook pasta in a large amount of rapidly boiling water. Use at least 1 litre/2 pints/5 cups of water to each 115 g/4 oz/ $^1/_2$ cup pasta.

2 ▲ The water should be salted at least 2 minutes before the pasta is added, to give the salt time to dissolve. Add about 20 g/$1^1/_2$ tbsp salt per 2 cups of pasta. You may want to vary the saltiness of the cooking water.

3 ▲ Drop the pasta into the boiling water all at once. Use a wooden spoon to help ease long pasta in as it softens, to prevent it from breaking. Stir frequently to prevent the pasta sticking to itself or to the pan. Cook the pasta at a fast boil, but be prepared to lower the heat if it boils over.

4 Timing is critical in pasta cooking. Follow package indications for store-bought pasta, but it is best in all cases to test for doneness by tasting, several times if necessary. In Italy pasta is always eaten *al dente*, which means firm to the bite. Cooked this way it is just tender, but its "soul" (the innermost part) is still firm. Overcooked pasta will be mushy.

5 ▲ Place a colander in the sink before the pasta has finished cooking. As soon as the pasta tastes done, tip it all into the colander (you may first want to reserve a cupful of the hot cooking water to add to the sauce if it needs thinning). Shake the colander lightly to remove most but not all of the cooking water. Pasta should never be over-drained.

6 ▲ Quickly turn the pasta into a warmed serving dish, and immediately toss it with a little butter or oil, or the prepared sauce. Alternatively, turn it into the cooking pan with the sauce, where it will be cooked for 1–2 minutes more as it is mixed into the sauce. Never allow pasta to sit undressed, as it will stick together and become unpalatable.

How to Cook Egg Pasta

Fresh egg pasta, especially home-made, cooks very much faster than dried pasta. Make sure everything is ready (the sauce, serving dishes etc) before you start boiling egg pasta, as there will not be time once the cooking starts, and egg pasta becomes soft and mushy very quickly.

1 Always cook pasta in a large pot with a generous amount of rapidly boiling water. Use at least 1 litre/2 pints/5 cups of water to a quantity of pasta made with 115 g/4 oz/1 cup of flour. Salt the water as for dried pasta.

2 ▲ Drop the pasta into the boiling water all at once. Stir gently to prevent the pasta sticking to itself or to the pan. Cook the pasta at a fast boil.

3 ▲ Freshly made pasta can be done as little as 15 seconds after the cooking water comes back to a boil. Stuffed pasta takes a few minutes longer. When done, turn the pasta into the colander and proceed as for dried pasta.

Basic Tomato Sauce

Sugo di pomodoro alla napoletana

Tomato sauce is without a doubt the most popular dressing for pasta in Italy. This sauce is best made with fresh tomatoes, but works well with canned plum tomatoes.

Ingredients
60 ml/4 tbsp olive oil
1 medium onion, very finely chopped
1 clove garlic, finely chopped
450 g/1lb tomatoes, fresh or canned, chopped, with their juice
salt and freshly ground black pepper
a few leaves fresh basil or sprigs parsley
for 4 servings of pasta

1 Heat the oil in a medium pan. Add the chopped onion, and cook over a moderate heat until it is translucent, 5–8 minutes.

2 ▲ Stir in the garlic and the tomatoes with their juice (add 45 ml/3 tbsp of water if you are using fresh tomatoes). Season with salt and pepper. Add the herbs. Cook for 20–30 minutes.

3 ▲ Pass the sauce through a food mill or purée in a food processor. To serve, reheat gently, correct the seasoning and pour over the drained pasta.

Special Tomato Sauce

Sugo di pomodoro

The tomatoes in this sauce are enhanced by the addition of extra vegetables. It is good served with all types of pasta or could be served as an accompaniment to stuffed vegetables.

Ingredients
700g/1 $^{2}/_{3}$lb tomatoes, fresh or canned, chopped
1 carrot, chopped
1 stick celery, chopped
1 medium onion, chopped
1 clove garlic, crushed
75 ml/5 tbsp olive oil
salt and freshly ground black pepper
a few leaves fresh basil or a small pinch dried oregano
for 6 servings of pasta

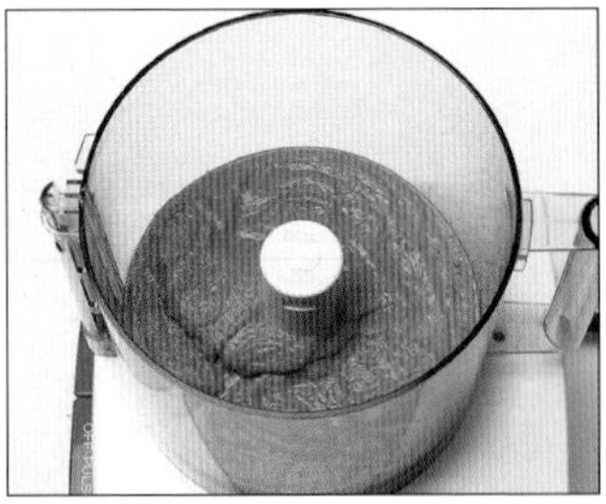

1 Place all the ingredients in a medium heavy saucepan, and simmer together for 30 minutes.

2 ▲ Purée the sauce in a food processor, or press through a sieve.

3 ▲ Return the sauce to the pan, correct the seasoning, and simmer again for about 15 minutes.

~ COOK'S TIP ~

This sauce may be spooned into freezer bags and frozen until required. Allow to thaw to room temperature before re-heating.

Linguine with Pesto Sauce

Linguine con pesto

Pesto originates in Liguria, where the sea breezes are said to give the local basil a particularly fine flavour. It is traditionally made with a mortar and pestle, but it is easier to make in a food processor or blender. Freeze any spare pesto in an ice cube tray.

Ingredients

65 g/2$^1/_2$ oz/$^3/_4$ cup fresh basil leaves
3–4 cloves garlic, peeled
45 ml/3 tbsp pine nuts
$^1/_2$ tsp salt
75 ml/5 tbsp olive oil
50 g/2 oz/$^1/_2$ cup freshly grated Parmesan cheese
60 ml/4 tbsp freshly grated pecorino cheese
freshly ground black pepper
500 g/1$^1/_4$lb linguine
serves 5–6

1 ▲ Place the basil, garlic, pine nuts, salt and olive oil in a blender or food processor and process until smooth. Remove to a bowl. (If desired, the sauce may be frozen at this point, before the cheeses are added.)

2 ▲ Stir in the cheeses (use all Parmesan if pecorino is not available). Taste for seasoning.

3 ▲ Cook the pasta in a large pan of rapidly boiling salted water until it is *al dente*. Just before draining it, take about 60 ml/4 tbsp of the cooking water and stir it into the sauce.

4 ▲ Drain the pasta and toss with the sauce. Serve immediately.

Bologneses Meat Sauce

Ragù alla bolognese

This great meat sauce is a speciality of Bologna. It is delicious with tagliatelle or short pastas such as penne or conchiglie as well as spaghetti, and is indispensable in baked lasagne. It keeps well in the refrigerator for several days and can also be frozen.

Ingredients
25 g/1 oz/2 tbsp butter
60 ml/4 tbsp olive oil
1 medium onion, finely chopped
25 g/1 oz/2 tbsp pancetta or unsmoked bacon, finely chopped
1 carrot, finely sliced
1 stick celery, finely sliced
1 garlic clove, finely chopped
350 g/12oz lean ground beef
salt and freshly ground black pepper
150 ml/$^1/_4$ pint/$^2/_3$ cup red wine
125 ml/4 fl oz/$^1/_2$ cup milk
1 x 400 g/14oz can plum tomatoes, chopped, with their juice
1 bay leaf
$^1/_4$ tsp fresh thyme leaves
for 6 servings of pasta

1 ▲ Heat the butter and oil in a heavy saucepan or earthenware pot. Add the onion, and cook over moderate heat for 3–4 minutes. Add the pancetta, and cook until the onion is translucent. Stir in the carrot, celery and garlic. Cook for 3–4 minutes more.

2 Add the beef, and crumble it into the vegetables with a fork. Stir until the meat loses its red colour. Season with salt and pepper.

3 ▲ Pour in the wine, raise the heat slightly, and cook until the liquid evaporates, 3–4 minutes. Add the milk, and cook until it evaporates.

4 ▲ Stir in the tomatoes with their juice, and the herbs. Bring the sauce to a boil. Reduce the heat to low, and simmer, uncovered for $1^1/_2$–2 hours, stirring occasionally. Correct the seasoning before serving.

Spaghetti with Garlic and Oil

Spaghetti con aglio e olio

This is one of the simplest and most satisfying pasta dishes of all. It is very popular throughout Italy. Use the best quality oil available for this dish.

Ingredients

400 g/14 oz spaghetti
60 ml/6 tbsp extra-virgin olive oil
3 cloves garlic, chopped
60 ml/4 tbsp chopped fresh parsley
salt and freshly ground black pepper
freshly grated Parmesan cheese, to serve (optional)

serves 4

1 Drop the spaghetti into a large pan of rapidly boiling salted water.

2 ▲ In a large frying pan heat the oil and gently sauté the garlic until it is barely golden. Do not let it brown or it will taste bitter. Stir in the parsley. Season with salt and pepper. Remove from the heat until the pasta is ready.

3 ▲ Drain the pasta when it is barely *al dente*. Add it to the pan with the oil and garlic, and cook together for 2–3 minutes, stirring well to coat the spaghetti with the sauce. Serve immediately in a warmed serving bowl, with Parmesan, if desired.

Spaghetti with Walnut Sauce

Spaghetti con salsa di noci

Like pesto, this sauce is traditionally ground in a mortar and pestle, but works just as well made in a food processor. It is also very good on tagliatelle and other noodles.

Ingredients

115 g/4 oz/1 cup walnut pieces or halves
45 ml/3 tbsp plain breadcrumbs
45 ml/3 tbsp olive or walnut oil
45 ml/3 tbsp chopped fresh parsley
1–2 cloves garlic (optional)
50 g/2 oz/$^1/_4$ cup butter, at room temperature
30 ml/2 tbsp cream
salt and freshly ground black pepper
400 g/14oz wholewheat spaghetti
freshly grated Parmesan cheese, to serve

serves 4

1 Drop the nuts into a small pan of boiling water, and cook for 1–2 minutes. Drain. Slip off the skins. Dry on paper towels. Coarsely chop and set aside about a quarter of the nuts.

2 ▲ Place the remaining nuts, the breadcrumbs, oil, parsley and garlic, if using, in a food processor or blender. Process to a paste. Remove to a bowl, and stir in the softened butter and the cream. Season with salt and pepper.

3 ▲ Cook the pasta in a large pan of rapidly boiling salted water until *al dente*. Drain, and toss with the sauce. Sprinkle with the reserved chopped nuts, and pass the Parmesan separately.

Fusilli with Peppers and Onions

Fusilli con peperoni

Peppers are characteristic of southern Italy. When grilled and peeled they have a delicious smoky flavour, and are easily digested.

Ingredients
450 g/1 lb red and yellow peppers (about 2 large ones)
90 ml/6 tbsp olive oil
1 large red onion, thinly sliced
2 cloves garlic, minced
400 g/14 oz/4 cups fusilli or other short pasta
salt and freshly ground black pepper
45 ml/3 tbsp finely chopped fresh parsley
freshly grated Parmesan cheese, to serve
serves 4

1 ▲ Place the peppers under a hot grill and turn occasionally until they are black and blistered on all sides. Remove from the heat, place in a paper bag and leave for 5 minutes.

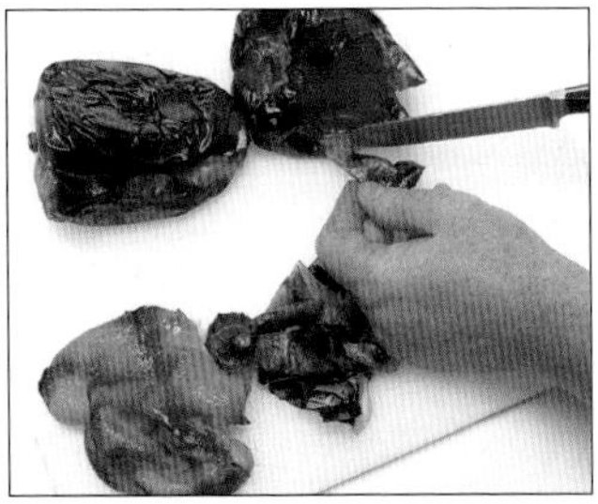

2 ▲ Peel the peppers. Cut them into quarters, remove the stems and seeds, and slice into thin strips. Bring a large pan of water to a boil.

3 ▲ Heat the oil in a large frying pan. Add the onion, and cook over moderate heat until it is translucent, 5–8 minutes. Stir in the garlic, and cook for 2 minutes more.

4 ▲ Add salt and the pasta to the boiling water, and cook until the pasta is just *al dente*.

~ COOK'S TIP ~

Peppers belong to the *Capsicum annuum* species. They were brought to Europe by Columbus who discovered them in Haiti. The large red, yellow and orange peppers are usually sweeter than the green varieties, and have a fuller flavour.

5 ▲ Meanwhile, add the peppers to the onions, and mix together gently. Stir in about 45 ml/3 tbsp of the pasta cooking water. Season with salt and pepper. Stir in the parsley.

6 ▲ Drain the pasta. Tip it into the pan with the vegetables, and cook over moderate heat for 3–4 minutes, stirring constantly to mix the pasta into the sauce. Serve with the Parmesan passed separately.

Orecchiette with Broccoli

Pasta e broccoli

Puglia, in southern Italy, specializes in imaginative pasta and vegetable combinations. Using the broccoli cooking water for boiling the pasta gives it more of the vegetable's flavour.

Ingredients

800 g/1¾lb broccoli
450 g/1lb orecchiette or penne
90 ml/6 tbsp olive oil
3 cloves garlic, finely chopped
6 anchovy fillets in oil
salt and freshly ground black pepper

serves 6

1 Peel the stems of the broccoli, starting from the base and pulling up towards the florets with a knife. Discard the woody parts of the stem. Cut florets and stems into 5 cm/2 in pieces.

2 ▲ Bring a large pan of water to the boil. Drop in the broccoli, and boil until barely tender, about 5–8 minutes. Remove the broccoli pieces from the pan to a serving bowl. Do not discard the cooking water.

3 ▲ Add salt to the broccoli cooking water. Bring it back to a boil. Drop in the pasta, stir well, and cook until it is *al dente*.

4 ▲ While the pasta is boiling, heat the oil in a small pan. Add the garlic and, after 2–3 minutes, the anchovy fillets. Using a fork, mash the anchovies and garlic to a paste. Cook for 3–4 minutes more.

5 ▲ Before draining the pasta, ladle 1–2 cupfuls of the cooking water over the broccoli. Add the drained pasta and the hot anchovy and oil mixture. Mix well, and season with salt and pepper if necessary. Serve at once.

Spaghetti with Eggs and Bacon

Spaghetti alla carbonara

One of the classic pasta sauces, about which a debate remains: whether or not it should contain cream. Purists believe that it should not.

Ingredients

30 ml/2 tbsp olive oil
150 g/5 oz/generous $^1/_2$ cup bacon, cut into matchsticks
1 clove garlic, crushed
400 g/14 oz spaghetti
3 eggs, at room temperature
75 g/3 oz/$^3/_4$ cup freshly grated Parmesan cheese
salt and freshly ground black pepper
serves 4

1 ▲ Bring a large pan of water to the boil. In a medium frying pan, heat the oil and sauté the bacon and the garlic until the bacon renders its fat and starts to brown. Remove and discard the garlic. Keep the bacon and its fat hot until needed.

2 ▲ Add salt and the spaghetti to the boiling water, and cook until it is *al dente*.

3 ▲ While the pasta is cooking, warm a large serving bowl and break the eggs into it. Beat in the Parmesan cheese with a fork, and season with salt and pepper.

4 ▲ As soon as the pasta is done, drain it quickly, and mix it into the egg mixture. Pour on the hot bacon and its fat. Stir well. The heat from the pasta and bacon fat will cook the eggs. Serve immediately.

Short Pasta with Cauliflower

Pennoni rigati con cavolfiore

This is a pasta version of cauliflower cheese. The cauliflower water is used to boil the pasta.

Ingredients
1 medium cauliflower
500 ml/16 fl oz/2 cups milk
1 bay leaf
50 g/2 oz/$^1/_4$ cup butter
50 g/2 oz/$^1/_2$ cup flour
salt and freshly ground black pepper
75 g/3 oz/$^3/_4$ cup freshly grated Parmesan or Cheddar cheese
500 g/1 $^1/_4$lb pennoni rigati, or other short pasta
serves 6

1 Bring a large pan of water to the boil. Wash the cauliflower well, and separate it into florets. Boil the florets until they are just tender, about 8–10 minutes. Remove them from the pan with a strainer or slotted spoon. Chop the cauliflower into bite-size pieces and set aside. Do not discard the cooking water.

2 ▲ Make a béchamel sauce by gently heating the milk with the bay leaf in a small saucepan. Do not let it boil. Melt the butter in a medium heavy saucepan. Add the flour, and mix it in well with a wire whisk ensuring there are no lumps. Cook for 2–3 minutes, but do not let the butter burn.

3 Strain the hot milk into the flour and butter mixture all at once, and mix smoothly with the whisk.

4 Bring the sauce to a boil, stirring constantly, and cook for 4–5 minutes more. Season with salt and pepper. Add the cheese, and stir over low heat until it melts. Stir in the cauliflower.

5 ▲ Bring the cooking water back to the boil. Add salt, and stir in the pasta. Cook until it is *al dente*. Drain, and place the pasta in a warm serving bowl. Pour over the sauce. Mix well, and serve at once.

Spaghetti with Bacon and Onion

Spaghetti all'amatriciana

This easy sauce is quickly made from ingredients that are almost always at hand.

Ingredients
30 ml/2 tbsp olive oil or lard
115 g/4 oz/$^1/_2$ cup unsmoked lean bacon, cut into matchsticks
1 small onion, finely chopped
100 ml/4 fl oz/$^1/_2$ cup dry white wine
450 g/1 lb fresh or canned tomatoes, chopped
$^1/_4$ tsp thyme leaves
salt and freshly ground black pepper
600 g/1 lb 5 oz spaghetti
freshly grated Parmesan, to serve
serves 6

1 In a medium frying pan, heat the oil or lard. Add the bacon and onion, and cook over low to moderate heat until the onion is golden and the bacon has rendered its fat and is beginning to brown, about 8–10 minutes. Bring a large pan of water to the boil.

2 ▲ Add the wine to the bacon and onion, raise the heat, and cook rapidly until the liquid boils off. Add the tomatoes, thyme, salt and pepper. Cover, and cook over moderate heat for 10–15 minutes.

3 ▲ Meanwhile, add salt to the boiling water, and cook the pasta until it is *al dente*. Drain, toss with the sauce, and serve with the grated Parmesan.

Spaghetti with Olives and Capers

Spaghetti alla puttanesca

This spicy sauce originated in the Naples area, where it was named for the local women of easy virtue. It can be quickly assembled using a few kitchen cupboard staples.

Ingredients

60 ml/4 tbsp olive oil
2 cloves garlic, finely chopped
small piece of dried chilli, crumbled
50 g/2 oz can of anchovy fillets, chopped
350 g/12 oz tomatoes, fresh or canned, chopped
115 g/4 oz/$^2/_3$ cup pitted black olives
30 g/2 tbsp capers, rinsed
15 ml/1 tbsp tomato paste
400 g/14 oz spaghetti
2 tbsp chopped fresh parsley, to serve
serves 4

1 ▲ Bring a large pan of water to the boil. Heat the oil in a large frying pan. Add the garlic and the dried chilli, and cook for 2–3 minutes until the garlic is just golden.

2 ▲ Add the anchovies, and mash them into the garlic with a fork.

3 ▲ Add the tomatoes, olives, capers and tomato paste. Stir well and cook over moderate heat.

4 Add salt to the boiling water, and put in the spaghetti. Stir, and cook until the pasta is just *al dente*. Drain.

5 ▲ Turn the spaghetti into the sauce. Raise the heat, and cook for 1–2 minutes, turning the pasta constantly. Sprinkle with parsley if desired and serve. Traditionally, no cheese is served with this sauce.

Linguine with Clam and Tomato Sauce

Linguine con vongole

There are two types of traditional Italian clam sauce for pasta: one with and one without tomatoes. This tomato version can be made with bottled clams if fresh are not available.

Ingredients
1 kg/2 lb fresh clams in their shells, or 350 g/12 oz canned clams, with their liquid
90 ml/6 tbsp olive oil
1 clove garlic, crushed
400 g/14 oz tomatoes, fresh or canned, very finely chopped
350 g/12 oz linguine
60 ml/4 tbsp chopped fresh parsley
salt and freshly ground black pepper
serves 4

1 ▲ Scrub and rinse the clams well under cold running water. Place them in a large pan with a cupful of water, and heat until the clams begin to open. Lift each clam out as soon as it opens, and scoop it out of its shell using a small spoon. Place in a bowl.

2 If the clams are large, chop them into 2 or 3 pieces. Reserve any liquids from the shells in a separate bowl. When all the clams have opened (discard any that do not open) pour the cooking liquids into the juices from the clams, and strain them through a piece of paper towel to remove any sand. If using canned clams, use the liquid from the can.

3 Bring a large pan of water to a boil for the pasta. Place the olive oil in a medium saucepan with the crushed garlic. Cook over a moderate heat until the garlic is just golden.

4 ▲ Remove the garlic and discard. Add the chopped tomatoes to the oil, and pour in the clam liquid. Mix well and cook over a low to moderate heat until the sauce begins to dry out and thicken slightly. Add salt and the pasta to the boiling water.

5 ▲ A minute or two before the pasta is ready to be drained, stir the parsley and the clams into the tomato sauce, and raise the heat. Add some freshly ground black pepper, and taste for seasoning. Drain the pasta, and turn it into a serving bowl. Pour on the hot sauce, and mix well before serving.

Spaghetti with Mussels

Spaghetti con cozze

Mussels are popular in all the coastal regions of Italy, and are delicious with pasta. This simple dish is greatly improved by using the freshest mussels available.

Ingredients

1 kg/2 lb fresh mussels, in their shells
75 ml/5 tbsp olive oil
3 cloves garlic, finely chopped
60 ml/4 tbsp finely chopped fresh parsley
60 ml/4 tbsp white wine
400 g/14 oz spaghetti
salt and freshly ground black pepper
serves 4

1 ▲ Scrub the mussels well under cold running water, cutting off the "beard" with a small sharp knife.

2 ▲ Bring a large pan of water to a boil for the pasta. Place the mussels with a cupful of water in another large pan over moderate heat. As soon as they open, lift them out one by one.

3 ▲ When all the mussels have opened (discard any that do not), strain the liquid in the pan through a layer of paper towels and reserve until needed.

4 ▲ Heat the oil in a large frying pan. Add the garlic and parsley, and cook for 2–3 minutes. Add the mussels, their strained juices and the wine. Cook over moderate heat. Meanwhile add salt to the boiling water, and drop in the pasta.

5 ▲ Add a generous amount of freshly ground black pepper to the sauce. Taste for seasoning, adding salt as necessary.

6 ▲ Drain the pasta when it is *al dente*. Add it to the frying pan with the sauce, and stir well over moderate heat for 1–2 minutes more. Serve at once, without cheese.

~ COOK'S TIP ~

Mussels should be firmly closed when fresh. If a mussel is slightly open, pinch it closed. If it remains closed on its own, it is alive. If it remains open, discard it. Fresh mussels should be consumed as soon as possible after being purchased. They may be kept in a bowl of cold water in the refrigerator.

Pasta with Fresh Sardine Sauce

Pasta con sarde

In this classic Sicilian dish, fresh sardines are combined with sultanas and pine nuts.

Ingredients
30 g/1$^1/_4$ oz/3 tbsp sultanas
450 g/1lb fresh sardines
90 ml/6 tbsp breadcrumbs
1 small fennel bulb
90 ml/6 tbsp olive oil
1 medium onion, very thinly sliced
30 g/1$^1/_4$ oz/3 tbsp pine nuts
$^1/_2$ tsp fennel seeds
salt and freshly ground black pepper
400 g/14 oz long hollow pasta such as percatelli, ziti, or bucatini
serves 4

1 Soak the sultanas in warm water for 15 minutes. Drain and pat dry.

2 ▲ Clean the sardines. Open each one out flat and remove the back bone and head. Wash well and shake dry. Sprinkle with breadcrumbs.

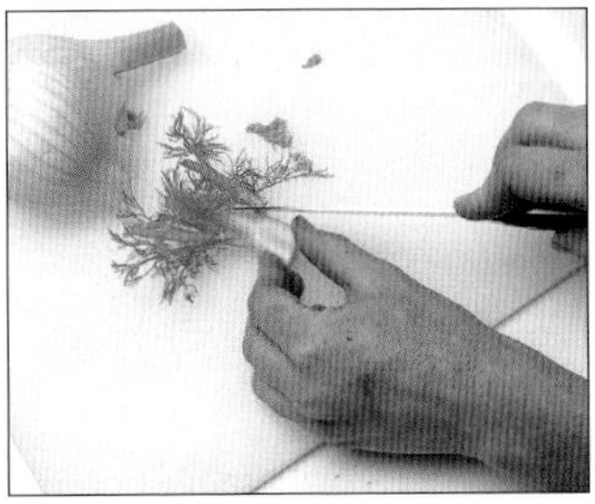

3 ▲ Coarsely chop the top fronds of fennel and reserve. Pull off a few outer leaves and wash. Fill a large pan with enough water to cook the pasta. Add the fennel leaves and bring to a boil.

4 ▲ Heat the oil in a large frying pan and sauté the onion lightly until soft. Remove to a side dish. Add the sardines, a few at a time, and cook over moderate heat until golden on both sides, turning them once carefully. When all the sardines have been cooked, gently return them to the pan. Add the onion, and the sultanas, pine nuts and fennel seeds. Season with salt and pepper.

5 ▲ Take about 60 ml/4 tbsp of the boiling water for the pasta, and add it to the sauce. Add salt to the boiling water, and drop in the pasta. Cook until it is *al dente*. Drain, and remove the fennel leaves. Dress the pasta with the sauce. Divide between individual serving plates, arranging several sardines on each. Sprinkle with the reserved chopped fennel tops before serving.

Baked Macaroni with Cheese

Maccheroni gratinati al forno

This delicious dish is perhaps less common in Italy than other pasta dishes, but has become a family favourite around the world.

Ingredients

500 ml/16 fl oz/2 cups milk
1 bay leaf
3 blades mace, or pinch of grated nutmeg
50 g/2 oz/4 tbsp butter
35 g/1½ oz/⅓ cup flour
salt and freshly ground black pepper
175 g/6 oz/1½ cups grated Parmesan or Cheddar cheese, or a combination of both
40 g/1¾ oz/⅓ cup breadcrumbs
450 g/1 lb macaroni or other short hollow pasta

serves 6

1 Make a béchamel sauce by gently heating the milk with the bay leaf and mace in a small saucepan. Do not let it boil. Melt the butter in a medium heavy saucepan. Add the flour, and mix it in well with a wire whisk. Cook for 2–3 minutes, but do not let the butter burn. Strain the hot milk into the flour and butter mixture all at once, and mix smoothly with the whisk. Bring the sauce to the boil, stirring constantly, and cook for another 4–5 minutes.

2 ▲ Season with salt and pepper, and the nutmeg if no mace has been used. Add all but 30 ml/2 tbsp of the cheese, and stir over low heat until it melts. Place a layer of plastic wrap right on the surface of the sauce to stop a skin from forming, and set aside.

3 ▲ Bring a large pan of water to a boil. Preheat the oven to 200°C/400°F/gas 6. Grease an ovenproof dish, and sprinkle with some breadcrumbs. Add salt and the pasta to the boiling water, and cook until it is barely *al dente*. Do not overcook, as the pasta will get a second cooking in the oven.

4 ▲ Drain the pasta, and combine it with the sauce. Pour it into the prepared ovenproof dish. Sprinkle the top with the remaining breadcrumbs and grated cheese, and place in the centre of the preheated oven. Bake for 20 minutes.

Penne with Tuna and Mozzarella

Penne con tonno e mozzarella

This tasty sauce is quickly made from store-cupboard ingredients, with the addition of fresh mozzarella. If possible, use tuna canned in olive oil.

Ingredients
400 g/14 oz penne, or other short pasta
15 ml/1 tbsp capers, in brine or salt
2 cloves garlic
45 g/3 tbsp chopped fresh parsley
1 x 200 g/7oz can of tuna, drained
75 ml/5 tbsp olive oil
salt and freshly ground black pepper
115 g/4 oz/$^2/_3$ cup mozzarella cheese, cut into small dice
serves 4

1 Bring a large pan of salted water to a boil and drop in the pasta.

2 ▲ Rinse the capers well in water. Chop them finely with the garlic. Combine with the parsley and the tuna. Stir in the oil, and season with salt and pepper, if necessary.

3 ▲ Drain the pasta when it is just *al dente*. Turn it into a large frying pan. Add the tuna sauce and the diced mozzarella, and cook over a moderate heat, stirring constantly, until the cheese just begins to melt. Serve at once.

Spaghettini with Vodka and Caviar

Spaghettini con vodka e caviale

This is an elegant yet easy way to serve spaghettini. In Rome it is an after-theatre favourite.

Ingredients
60 ml/4 tbsp olive oil
3 spring onions, thinly sliced
1 clove garlic, finely chopped
100 ml/4 fl oz/$^1/_2$ cup vodka
150 ml/$^1/_4$ pint/$^2/_3$ cup heavy cream
75 g/3 oz/$^1/_2$ cup black or red caviar
salt and freshly ground black pepper
400 g/14 oz spaghettini
serves 4

1 ▲ Heat the oil in a small frying pan. Add the spring onions and garlic, and cook gently for 4-5 minutes.

2 ▲ Add the vodka and cream, and cook over low heat for about 5-8 minutes more.

~ COOK'S TIP ~

The finest caviar is salted sturgeon roe. Red "caviar" is salmon roe, cheaper and often saltier than sturgeon roe, as is the black-dyed lump fish roe.

3 ▲ Remove from the heat and stir in half the caviar. Season with salt and pepper as necessary.

4 Meanwhile, cook the spaghettini in a large pan of rapidly boiling salted water until *al dente*. Drain the pasta, and toss with the sauce. Spoon the remaining caviar on top and serve immediately.

Pasta Bows with Prawns and Peas

Farfalle con gamberetti e piselli

A small amount of saffron in the sauce gives this dish a lovely golden colour.

Ingredients
45 ml/3 tbsp olive oil
25 g/1 oz/2 tbsp butter
2 spring onions, chopped
350 g/12oz fresh or frozen peeled prawns
225 g/8 oz/$1^1/_4$ cups frozen petits pois or peas, thawed
400 g/14 oz farfalle
250 ml/8 fl oz/1 cup dry white wine
a few whole strands saffron or $^1/_8$ tsp powdered saffron
salt and freshly ground black pepper
30 ml/2 tbsp chopped fresh fennel or dill, to serve
serves 4

1 Bring a large pan of water to a boil. Heat the oil and butter in a large frying pan and sauté the spring onions lightly. Add the peas, and cook for 2-3 minutes.

2 ▲ Add salt and the pasta to the boiling water. Add the prawns, wine and saffron to the peas. Raise the heat and cook until the wine is reduced by about half. Add salt and pepper to taste. Cover the pan and reduce the heat to low.

3 ▲ Drain the pasta when it is *al dente*. Add it to the pan with the sauce. Stir over high heat for 1-2 minutes, coating the pasta with the sauce. Sprinkle with the fresh herbs, and serve at once.

Short Pasta with Spring Vegetables

Pasta primavera

This colourful sauce makes the most of new crops of fresh tender spring vegetables.

Ingredients
1 or 2 small young carrots
2 spring onions
150 g/6 oz/1 cup courgettes
2 tomatoes
75 g/3 oz/$^1/_2$ cup shelled peas, fresh or frozen
75 g/3 oz/$^1/_2$ cup green beans
1 yellow pepper
60 ml/4 tbsp olive oil
25 g/1 oz/2 tbsp butter
1 clove garlic, finely chopped
5–6 leaves fresh basil, torn into pieces
salt and freshly ground black pepper
500 g/$1^1/_4$
lb/5 cups short coloured or plain pasta such as fusilli, penne or farfalle
freshly grated Parmesan, to serve
serves 6

1 Cut all the vegetables into small, bite-size pieces.

2 ▲ Heat the oil and butter in a large frying pan. Add the chopped vegetables, and cook over moderate heat for 5-6 minutes, stirring occasionally. Add the garlic and the basil, and season with salt and pepper. Cover the pan, and cook for 5-8 minutes more, or until the vegetables are just tender.

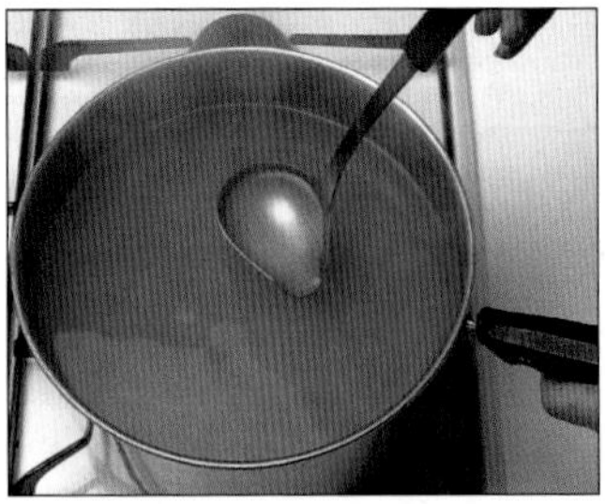

3 ▲ Meanwhile, cook the pasta in a large pan of rapidly boiling salted water until *al dente*. Before draining it, reserve a cupful of the pasta water.

4 Turn the pasta into the pan with the sauce, and mix well to distribute the vegetables. If the sauce seems too dry, add a few tablespoons of the reserved pasta water. Serve with the Parmesan passed separately.

Baked Seafood Spaghetti

Spaghetti cartoccio

In this dish, each portion is baked and served in an individual packet which is then opened at the table. Use parchment paper or aluminium foil to make the packets.

Ingredients

450 g/1lb fresh mussels
100 ml/4 fl oz/$^{1}/_{2}$ cup dry white wine
60 ml/4 tbsp olive oil
2 cloves garlic, finely chopped
450 g/1 lb tomatoes, fresh or canned, peeled and finely chopped
400 g/14 oz spaghetti or other long pasta
225 g/8 oz peeled and deveined prawns, fresh or frozen
30 ml/2 tbsp chopped fresh parsley
salt and freshly ground black pepper
serves 4

1 ▲ Scrub the mussels well under cold running water, cutting off the "beard" with a small sharp knife. Place the mussels and the wine in a large saucepan and heat until they open.

2 ▲ Lift out the mussels and remove to a side dish. (Discard any that do not open.) Strain the cooking liquid through paper towels, and reserve until needed. Preheat the oven to 150°C/300°F/gas 2.

3 ▲ Bring a large pan of water to a boil. In a medium pan, heat the olive oil and garlic together for 1–2 minutes. Add the tomatoes, and cook over moderate to high heat until they soften. Stir in 150 ml/6 fl oz/ $^{3}/_{4}$ cup of the cooking liquid from the mussels. Add salt and the pasta to the boiling water, and cook until it is just *al dente*.

4 ▲ Just before draining the pasta, add the prawns and parsley to the tomato sauce. Cook for 2 minutes. Taste for seasoning, adding salt and pepper as desired. Remove from the heat.

~ VARIATION ~

Bottled mussels or clams may be substituted for fresh shellfish in this recipe. Add them to the tomato sauce with the prawns.

5 ▲ Prepare 4 pieces of parchment paper or foil approximately 30 cm × 45 cm (12 in × 18 in). Place each sheet in the center of a shallow bowl. Turn the drained pasta into a mixing bowl. Add the tomato sauce and mix well. Stir in the mussels.

6 ▲ Divide the pasta and seafood between the four pieces of paper, placing a mound in the center of each, and twisting the paper ends together to make a closed packet. (The bowl under the paper will stop the sauce from spilling while the paper parcels are being closed.) Arrange on a large baking tray, and place in the centre of the preheated oven. Bake for 10 minutes. Place one unopened packet on each individual serving plate.

Tuna Pasta Salad

Insalata di pasta con tonno

This easy pasta salad uses canned beans and tuna for a quick main dish.

Ingredients

450 g/1 lb short pasta, such as ruote, macaroni or farfalle
60 ml/4 tbsp olive oil
2 × 200 g/7 oz cans tuna, drained
2 × 400 g/14 oz cans cannellini or borlotti beans, rinsed and drained
1 small red onion
2 sticks celery
juice of 1 lemon
30 ml/2 tbsp chopped fresh parsley
salt and freshly ground black pepper
serves 6–8

1 Cook the pasta in a large pan of rapidly boiling salted water until it is *al dente*. Drain, and rinse under cold water to stop cooking. Drain well and turn into a large bowl. Toss with the olive oil, and set aside. Allow to cool completely before mixing with the other ingredients.

2 ▲ Mix the flaked tuna and the beans into the cooked pasta. Slice the onion and celery very thinly and add them to the pasta.

3 ▲ Combine the lemon juice with the parsley. Mix into the other ingredients. Season with salt and pepper. Allow the salad to stand for at least 1 hour before serving.

Chicken Pasta Salad

Insalata di pasta con pollo

This salad uses leftover chicken from a roast, or a cold poached chicken breast.

Ingredients

350 g/12 oz short pasta, such as mezze rigatoni, fusilli or penne
45 ml/3 tbsp olive oil
225 g/8 oz/$1\frac{1}{2}$ cups cold cooked chicken
2 small red and yellow peppers (about 200 g/7 oz)
50 g/2 oz/$\frac{1}{3}$ cup pitted green olives
4 spring onions, chopped
45 ml/3 tbsp mayonnaise
1 tsp Worcestershire sauce
15 ml/1 tbsp wine vinegar
salt and freshly ground black pepper
a few leaves fresh basil, to garnish
serves 4

1 Cook the pasta in a large pan of rapidly boiling salted water until it is *al dente*. Drain, and rinse under cold water to stop the cooking. Drain well and turn into a large bowl. Toss with the olive oil, and set aside. Allow to cool completely.

2 ▲ Cut the chicken into bite-size pieces, removing any bones. Cut the peppers into small pieces, removing the seeds and stems.

3 ▲ Combine all the ingredients except the pasta in a medium bowl. Taste for seasoning, then mix into the pasta. Garnish with the basil, and serve chilled.

Wholewheat Pasta Salad

Insalata di pasta integrale

This substantial vegetarian salad is easily assembled from any combination of seasonal vegetables. Use raw or lightly blanched vegetables, or a mixture of both.

Ingredients

450 g/1 lb short wholewheat pasta, such as fusilli or penne
45 ml/3 tbsp olive oil
2 medium carrots
1 small bunch broccoli, halved
175 g/6 oz/1 cup shelled peas, fresh or frozen
1 red or yellow pepper
2 sticks celery
4 spring onions
1 large tomato
75 g/3 oz/$^1/_2$ cup stoned olives, halved

For the dressing

45 ml/3 tbsp wine or balsamic vinegar
60 ml/4 tbsp olive oil
15 ml/1 tbsp Dijon style mustard
15 ml/1 tbsp sesame seeds
10 ml/2 tsp finely chopped mixed fresh herbs, such as parsley, thyme and basil
salt and freshly ground black pepper
115 g/4 oz/$^2/_3$ cup diced Cheddar or mozzarella, or a combination of both

serves 8

1 Cook the pasta in a large pan of rapidly boiling salted water until it is *al dente*. Drain, and rinse under cold water to stop the cooking. Drain well and turn into a large bowl. Toss with 45ml/3 tbsp of the olive oil, and set aside. Allow to cool completely before mixing with the other ingredients.

2 ▲ Lightly blanch the carrots, broccoli and peas in a large pan of boiling water. Refresh under cold water. Drain well.

3 ▲ Chop the carrots and broccoli into bite-size pieces and add to the pasta with the peas. Slice the pepper, celery, spring onions and tomato into small pieces. Add them to the salad with the olives.

4 ▲ Make the dressing in a small bowl by combining the vinegar with the oil and mustard. Stir in the sesame seeds and herbs. Mix the dressing into the salad. Taste for seasoning, adding salt, pepper or more oil and vinegar as necessary. Stir in the cheese. Allow the salad to stand for 15 minutes before serving.

Pasta Salad with Olives

Insalata di pasta con olive

This delicious salad combines all the flavours of the Mediterranean. It is an excellent way of serving pasta and is particularly nice on hot summer days.

Ingredients

450 g/1 lb short pasta, such as medium shells, farfalle or penne
60 ml/4 tbsp extra-virgin olive oil
10 sun-dried tomatoes, thinly sliced
30 ml/2 tbsp capers, in brine or salted
115 g/4 oz/$^2/_3$ cup black olives, pitted
2 cloves garlic, finely chopped
45 ml/3 tbsp balsamic vinegar
salt and freshly ground black pepper
45 ml/3 tbsp chopped fresh parsley
serves 6

1 ▲ Cook the pasta in a large pan of rapidly boiling salted water until it is *al dente*. Drain, and rinse under cold water to stop the cooking. Drain well and turn into a large bowl. Toss with the olive oil, and set aside.

2 ▲ Soak the tomatoes in a bowl of hot water for 10 minutes. Do not discard the water. Rinse the capers well. If they have been preserved in salt, soak them in a little hot water for 10 minutes. Rinse again.

3 ▲ Combine the olives, tomatoes, capers, garlic and vinegar in a small bowl. Season with salt and pepper.

4 ▲ Stir this mixture into the pasta, and toss well. Add 2 or 3 spoons of the tomato soaking water if the salad seems too dry. Toss with the parsley, and allow to stand for 15 minutes before serving.

Cannelloni with Tuna

Cannelloni sorpresa

Children love this pasta dish. Fontina cheese has a sweet, nutty flavour and very good melting qualities. Look for it in large supermarkets and Italian delicatessens.

Ingredients

50 g/2 oz/¼ cup butter
50 g/2 oz/½ cup plain flour
about 900 ml/1½ pints/3 ¾ cups hot milk
2 x 200 g/7 oz cans tuna, drained
115 g/4 oz/1 cup Fontina cheese, grated
1.5 ml/¼ tsp grated nutmeg
12 no-precook cannelloni tubes
50 g/2 oz/⅔ cup grated Parmesan cheese
salt and freshly ground black pepper
fresh herbs, to garnish

serves 4–6

1 ▲ Melt the butter in a heavy-based saucepan, add the flour and stir over a low heat for 1–2 minutes. Remove the pan from the heat and gradually add 350 ml/12 fl oz/1½ cups of the milk, beating vigorously after each addition. Return the pan to the heat and whisk for 1–2 minutes until the sauce is very thick and smooth. Remove from the heat.

2 ▲ Mix the drained tuna with about 120 ml/4 fl oz/½ cup of the warm white sauce in a bowl. Add salt and black pepper to taste. Preheat the oven to 180°C/350°F/Gas 4.

3 ▲ Gradually whisk the remaining milk into the rest of the sauce, then return to the heat and simmer, whisking constantly, until thickened. Add the grated Fontina and nutmeg, with salt and pepper to taste. Simmer for a few more minutes, stirring frequently. Pour about one-third of the sauce into a baking dish and spread to the corners.

4 ▲ Fill the cannelloni tubes with the tuna mixture, pushing it in with the handle of a teaspoon. Place the cannelloni in a single layer in the dish. Thin the remaining sauce with a little more milk if necessary, then pour it over the cannelloni. Sprinkle with Parmesan cheese and bake for 30 minutes or until golden. Serve hot, garnished with herbs.

Seafood Lasagne

Lasagne alla marinara

Rich and creamy, this flavoursome lasagne makes a good supper-party dish.

Ingredients

65 g/2 ½ oz/5 tbsp butter
450 g/1 lb monkfish fillets, skinned and diced small
225 g/8 oz fresh prawns, shelled, deveined and roughly chopped
225 g/8 oz/3 cups button mushrooms, chopped
40 g/1½ oz/3 tbsp plain flour
600 ml/1 pint/2 ½ cups hot milk
300 ml/½ pint/1¼ cups double cream
400 g/14 oz can chopped tomatoes
30 ml/2 tbsp shredded fresh basil
8 sheets no-precook lasagne
75 g/3 oz/1 cup grated Parmesan cheese
salt and freshly ground black pepper
fresh herbs, to garnish

serves 6

1 ▲ Melt 15 g/½ oz/1 tbsp of the butter in a large, deep sauté pan, add the monkfish and prawns and sauté over a medium to high heat for 2–3 minutes. As soon as the prawns turn pink, remove them with a slotted spoon and place in a bowl.

2 Add the mushrooms to the pan and sauté for about 5 minutes until the juices run and the mushrooms are soft. Remove with a slotted spoon and add to the fish in the bowl.

3 Melt the remaining butter in a saucepan, add the flour and stir over a low heat for 1–2 minutes. Remove the pan from the heat and gradually whisk in the milk. Return to the heat and bring to the boil, whisking. Lower the heat and simmer for 2–3 minutes, whisking occasionally, until thick. Whisk in the cream and cook over a low heat for 2 minutes more.

4 ▲ Remove the sauce from the heat and stir in the fish and mushroom mixture with all the juices that have collected in the bowl. Add salt to taste, and plenty of pepper. Preheat the oven to 190°C/375°F/Gas 5.

5 Spread half the chopped tomatoes over the bottom of a baking dish. Sprinkle with half the basil and add salt and pepper to taste. Ladle one-third of the sauce over the tomatoes.

6 ▲ Cover the sauce with four lasagne sheets. Spread the remaining tomatoes over the lasagne and sprinkle with the remaining basil and salt and pepper to taste. Ladle half the remaining sauce over. Arrange the remaining lasagne sheets on top, top with the remaining sauce and cover with the cheese. Bake for 30–40 minutes until golden and bubbling. Serve hot, garnished with fresh herbs.

Fettuccine with Ham and Cream

Fettuccine con prosciutto

Prosciutto is perfect for this rich and delicious dish, which makes an elegant first course.

Ingredients

115 g/4 oz/1/2 cup slice prosciutto crudo or other unsmoked ham (raw or cooked)
50 g/2 oz/1/4 cup butter
2 shallots, very finely chopped
salt and freshly ground black pepper
150 ml/1/4 pint/3/4 cup heavy cream
350 g/12 oz fettuccine (made with 3 eggs)
50 g/2 oz/1/2 cup grated Parmesan cheese
sprig fresh parsley, to garnish
serves 4

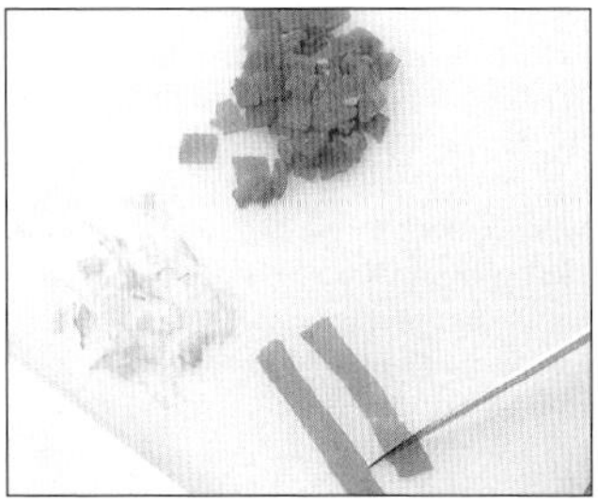

1 ▲ Cut the fat from the ham, and chop both lean and fat parts separately into small squares.

2 ▲ Melt the butter in a medium frying pan, and add the shallots and the squares of ham fat. Cook until golden. Add the lean ham, and cook for 2 minutes more. Season with black pepper. Stir in the cream, and keep warm over low heat while the pasta is cooking.

3 ▲ Boil the pasta in a large pan of rapidly boiling salted water. Drain when *al dente*. Turn into a warmed serving bowl, and toss with the sauce. Stir in the cheese and serve at once, garnished with a sprig of parsley.

~ VARIATION ~

Substitute 170 g/6 oz fresh or frozen peas for the ham. Add to the pan with the shallots.

Tagliatelle with Smoked Salmon

Tagliatelle con salmone affumicato

In Italy smoked salmon is imported, and quite expensive. This elegant creamy sauce makes a little go a long way. Use a mixture of green and white pasta if you wish.

Ingredients

115 g/4 oz/3/4 cup smoked salmon slices or ends, fresh or frozen
300 ml/1/2 pint/1 1/4 cups single cream
pinch of ground mace or nutmeg
350g/12 oz green and white tagliatelle (made with 3 eggs)
salt and freshly ground black pepper
45 ml/3 tbsp chopped fresh chives, to garnish
serves 4–5

1 Cut the salmon into thin strips about 5 cm/2 in long. Place in a bowl with the cream and the mace or nutmeg. Stir, cover, and allow to stand for at least 2 hours in a cool place.

2 ▲ Bring a large pan of water to a boil for the pasta. While the water is heating, gently warm the cream and salmon mixture in a small saucepan without boiling it.

3 ▲ Add salt to the boiling water. Drop in the pasta all at once. Drain when it is just *al dente*. Pour the sauce over the pasta and mix well. Season and garnish with the chives.

Spaghetti with Clams and White Wine *Spaghetti alle vongole*

Raid the pantry to make this quick and easy pasta dish with an intense flavour.

Ingredients
30 ml/2 tbsp olive oil
1 onion, very finely chopped
2 garlic cloves, crushed
400 g/14 oz can chopped tomatoes
150 ml/¼ pint/⅔ cup dry white wine
150 g/5 oz jar or can clams in natural juice, drained with juice reserved
350 g/12 oz dried spaghetti
30 ml/2 tbsp finely chopped fresh flat leaf parsley, plus extra to garnish
salt and freshly ground black pepper
serves 4

Cook's Tip
The tomato sauce can be made several days ahead of time and kept in the fridge. Add the clams and heat them through at the last minute - but don't let them boil or they will toughen.

1 Heat the oil in a saucepan, add the onion and cook gently, stirring frequently, for about 5 minutes until softened, but not brown.

2 ▲ Stir in the garlic, tomatoes, wine and reserved clam juice, with salt to taste. Add a generous grinding of black pepper. Bring to the boil, stirring, then lower the heat. Cover the pan and simmer the sauce gently for about 20 minutes, stirring from time to time.

3 ▲ Meanwhile, coil the spaghetti into a large saucepan of rapidly boiling salted water and cook for 12 minutes or until it is *al dente*.

4 Drain the spaghetti thoroughly. Add the clams and finely chopped parsley to the tomato sauce and heat through, then taste for seasoning. Tip the drained spaghetti into a warmed serving bowl, pour over the tomato sauce and toss to mix. Serve at once, sprinkled with more parsley.

Pasta with Cream and Parmesan *Pasta Alfredo*

This popular classic originated in Rome. It is incredibly quick and simple, perfect for a midweek supper.

Ingredients
350 g/12 oz dried fettuccine
25 g/1 oz/2 tbsp butter
300 ml/½ pint/1¼ cups double cream
50 g/2 oz/⅔ cup grated Parmesan cheese, plus extra to serve
30 ml/2 tbsp finely chopped fresh flat leaf parsley, plus extra to garnish
salt and freshly ground black pepper
serves 3–4

Variation
In Rome, fettuccine would traditionally be served with this sauce, but tagliatelle can be used if you prefer. Pasta shapes, such as penne, rigatoni or farfalle, are also suitable.

1 Cook the fettuccine in a large pan of rapidly boiling salted water for 8–10 minutes or until *al dente*.

2 ▲ Meanwhile, melt the butter in a large flameproof casserole and add the cream and Parmesan, with salt and pepper to taste. Stir over a medium heat until the cheese has melted and the sauce has thickened.

3 ▲ Drain the fettuccine thoroughly and add it to the sauce with the chopped parsley. Fold the pasta and sauce together over a medium heat until the strands of pasta are generously coated. Grind more black pepper over and garnish with the extra chopped parsley. Serve at once, with a bowl of grated Parmesan handed round separately.

Tagliatelle with Bolognese Sauce

Tagliatelle alla bolognese

Most people think of bolognese sauce, the famous ragù from Bologna, as being served with spaghetti. To be absolutely correct, it should be served with tagliatelle.

Ingredients
30 ml/2 tbsp olive oil
1 onion, finely chopped
1 carrot, finely chopped
1 celery stick, finely chopped
1 garlic clove, crushed
350 g/12 oz minced beef
150 ml/¼ pint/⅔ cup red wine
250 ml/8 fl oz/1 cup milk
400 g/14 oz can chopped tomatoes
15 ml/1 tbsp sun-dried tomato paste
350 g/12 oz dried tagliatelle
salt and freshly ground black pepper
shredded fresh basil, to garnish
grated Parmesan cheese, to serve
serves 4

1 ▲ Heat the oil in a large saucepan. Add the onion, carrot, celery and garlic and cook gently, stirring frequently, for about 10 minutes until softened. Do not allow the vegetables to colour.

2 ▲ Add the minced beef to the pan with the vegetables and cook over a medium heat until the meat changes colour, stirring constantly and breaking up any lumps with a wooden spoon.

3 ▲ Pour in the wine. Stir frequently until it has evaporated, then add the milk and continue cooking and stirring until this has evaporated, too.

Cook's Tip
Don't skimp on the cooking time – it is essential for a full-flavoured bolognese sauce. Some Italian cooks insist on cooking it for 3–4 hours, so the longer the better.

4 ▲ Stir in the tomatoes and tomato paste, with salt and pepper to taste. Simmer the sauce uncovered, over the lowest possible heat for at least 45 minutes.

5 Cook the tagliatelle in a large pan of rapidly boiling salted water for 8–10 minutes or until *al dente*. Drain thoroughly and tip into a warmed large bowl. Pour over the sauce and toss to combine. Garnish with basil and serve at once, with Parmesan cheese handed separately.

Penne with Pancetta and Cream

Penne alla carbonara

This makes a gloriously rich supper dish. Follow it with a simple salad.

Ingredients

300 g/11 oz dried penne
30 ml/2 tbsp olive oil
1 small onion, finely chopped
175 g/6 oz pancetta rashers, any rinds removed, cut into bite-size strips
1–2 garlic cloves, crushed
5 egg yolks
175 ml/6 fl oz/¾ cup double cream
115 g/4 oz/1⅓ cups grated Parmesan cheese, plus extra to serve
salt and freshly ground black pepper
serves 3–4

1 ▲ Cook the penne in a large pan of rapidly boiling salted water for about 10 minutes or until *al dente*.

2 Meanwhile, heat the oil in a large flameproof casserole. Add the onion and cook gently for about 5 minutes, stirring frequently, until softened. Add the pancetta and garlic. Cook over a medium heat until the pancetta is cooked but not crisp. Remove the pan from the heat and set aside.

3 ▲ Put the egg yolks in a jug and add the cream and Parmesan cheese. Grind in plenty of black pepper. Beat well to mix.

4 ▲ Drain the penne thoroughly, tip into the casserole and toss over a medium to high heat until the pancetta mixture is evenly mixed with the pasta.

5 Remove from the heat, pour in the egg yolk mixture and toss well to combine. Spoon into a large shallow serving dish, grind a little black pepper over and sprinkle with some of the extra Parmesan. Serve the rest of the Parmesan separately.

Cook's Tip

Serve this dish the moment it is ready or it will not be hot enough. Having added the egg yolks, don't return the pan to the heat or attempt to reheat the pasta and sauce together or the egg yolks will scramble and give the pasta a curdled appearance.

Baked Lasagne with Meat Sauce

Lasagne al forno

This lasagne made from egg pasta with home-made meat and béchamel sauces is exquisite.

Ingredients

1 recipe Bolognese Meat Sauce
egg pasta sheets made with 3 eggs, or 400 g/14 oz dried lasagne
115 g/4 oz/1 cup grated Parmesan cheese
40 g/3 tbsp butter

For the béchamel sauce

700 ml/1 $^1/_4$ pints/3 cups milk
1 bay leaf
3 blades mace
115 g/4 oz/$^1/_2$ cup butter
75 g/3 oz/$^3/_4$ cup flour
salt and freshly ground black pepper

serves 8–10

1 Prepare the meat sauce and set aside. Butter a large shallow baking dish, preferably rectangular or square.

2 Make the béchamel sauce by gently heating the milk with the bay leaf and mace in a small saucepan. Melt the butter in a medium heavy pan. Add the flour, and mix it in well with a wire whisk. Cook for 2–3 minutes. Strain the hot milk into the flour and butter mixture, and combine smoothly with the whisk. Bring the sauce to a boil, stirring constantly, and cook for 4–5 minutes more. Season with salt and pepper, and set aside.

3 ▲ Make the pasta. Do not let it dry out before cutting it into rectangles approximately 11 cm/4$^1/_2$ in wide and the same length as the baking dish (this will make it easier to assemble). Preheat the oven to 200°C/400°F/gas 6.

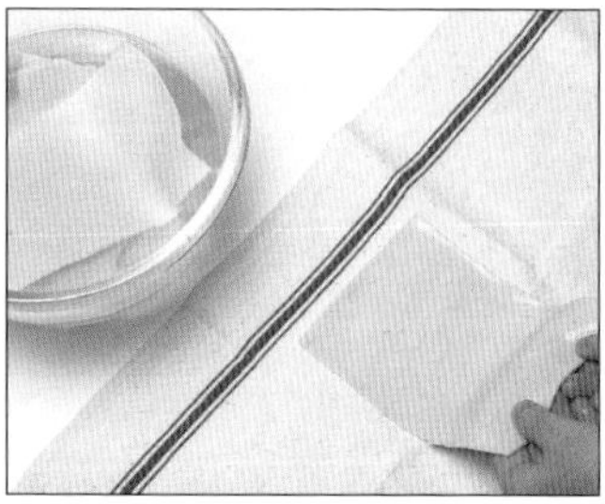

4 ▲ Bring a very large pan of water to a boil. Place a large bowl of cold water near the stove. Cover a large work surface with a tablecloth. Add salt to the rapidly boiling water. Drop in 3 or 4 of the egg pasta rectangles. Cook very briefly, about 30 seconds. Remove them from the pan using a slotted spoon, and drop them into the bowl of cold water for about 30 seconds. Pull them out of the water, shaking off the excess water. Lay them out flat without overlapping on the tablecloth. Continue with all the remaining pasta and trimmings.

5 ▲ To assemble the lasagne, have all the elements at hand: the baking dish, béchamel and meat sauces, pasta strips, grated Parmesan and butter. Spread one large spoonful of the meat sauce over the bottom of the dish. Arrange a layer of pasta in the dish, cutting it with a sharp knife so that it fits well inside the dish.

6 ▲ Cover with a thin layer of meat sauce, then one of béchamel. Sprinkle with a little cheese. Repeat the layers in the same order, ending with a layer of pasta coated with béchamel. Do not make more than about 6 layers of pasta. (If you have a lot left over, make another small lasagne in a little ovenproof dish.) Use the pasta trimmings to patch any gaps in the pasta. Sprinkle the top with Parmesan, and dot with butter.

7 Bake in the preheated oven for 20 minutes or until brown on top. Remove from the oven and allow to stand for 5 minutes before serving. Serve directly from the baking dish, cutting out rectangular or square sections for each helping.

~ VARIATION ~

If you are using dried or bought pasta, follow step 4, but boil the lasagne in just two batches, and stop the cooking about 4 minutes before the recommended cooking time on the package has elapsed. Rinse in cold water and lay the pasta out the same way as for the egg pasta.

Tagliolini with Asparagus

Tagliolini con asparagi

Tagliolini are very thin home-made egg noodles, more delicate in texture than spaghetti. They go well with this subtle cream sauce flavoured with asparagus.

Ingredients
450 g/1 lb fresh asparagus
egg pasta sheets made with 2 eggs, or 350 g/12 oz fresh tagliolini or other egg noodles
50 g/2 oz/$^1/_4$ cup butter
3 spring onions, finely chopped
3–4 leaves fresh mint or basil, finely chopped
150 ml/$^1/_4$ pint/$^2/_3$ cup double cream
salt and freshly ground black pepper
50 g/2 oz/$^1/_2$ cup freshly grated Parmesan cheese
serves 4

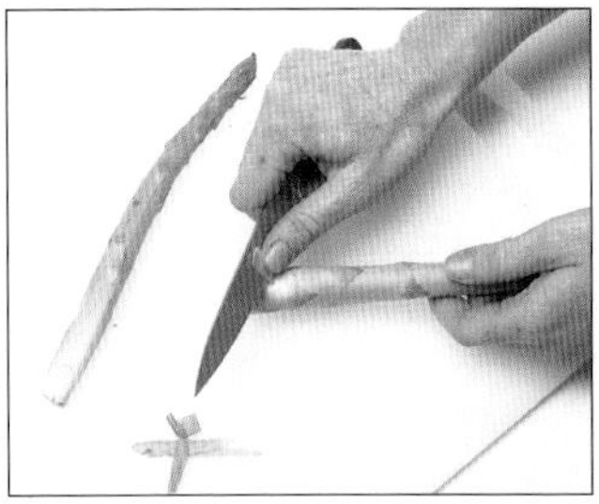

1 ▲ Peel the asparagus by inserting a small sharp knife at the base of the stalks and pulling upwards towards the tips. Drop them into a large pan of rapidly boiling water, and boil until just tender, 4–6 minutes.

2 ▲ Remove from the water, reserving the cooking water. Cut the tips off, and then cut the stalks into 4 cm/1$^1/_2$ in pieces. Set aside.

3 Make the egg pasta sheets, and fold and cut into thin noodles, or feed them through the narrowest cutters of a machine. Open the noodles out, and let them dry for at least 5–10 minutes.

4 ▲ Melt the butter in a large frying pan. Add the spring onions and herbs, and cook for 3–4 minutes. Stir in the cream and asparagus, and heat gently, but do not boil. Season to taste.

5 Bring the asparagus cooking water back to the boil. Add salt. Drop the noodles in all at once. Cook until just tender (freshly made noodles will cook in a few seconds). Drain.

6 ▲ Turn the pasta into the pan with the sauce, raise the heat slightly, and mix well. Stir in the Parmesan. Mix well and serve at once.

Ravioli with Ricotta and Spinach

Ravioli ripieni di magro

Home-made ravioli are fun to make, and can be stuffed with different meat, cheese or vegetable fillings. This filling is easy to make, and lighter than the normal meat variety.

Ingredients
400 g/14 oz fresh spinach or 175 g/6oz frozen spinach
175 g/6 oz/$^3/_4$ cup ricotta cheese
1 egg
50 g/2 oz/$^1/_2$ cup grated Parmesan cheese
pinch of grated nutmeg
salt and freshly ground black pepper
egg pasta sheets made with 3 eggs

For the sauce
75 g/3 oz/$^1/_3$ cup butter
5–6 sprigs fresh sage

serves 4

1 Wash fresh spinach well in several changes of water. Place in a saucepan with only the water that is clinging to the leaves. Cover, and cook until tender, about 5 minutes. Drain. Cook frozen spinach according to the instructions on the package. When the spinach is cool, squeeze out as much moisture as possible. Chop finely.

2 Combine the chopped spinach with the ricotta, egg, Parmesan and nutmeg. Mix well. Season with salt and pepper. Cover the bowl and set aside.

3 Prepare the sheets of egg pasta. Roll out very thinly by hand or machine. Do not let the pasta dry out.

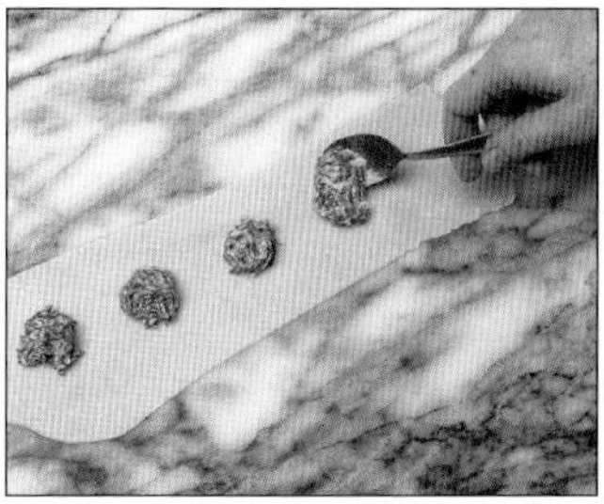

4 ▲ Place small teaspoons of filling along the pasta in rows 5 cm/2 in apart. Cover with another sheet of pasta, pressing down gently to avoid forming air pockets.

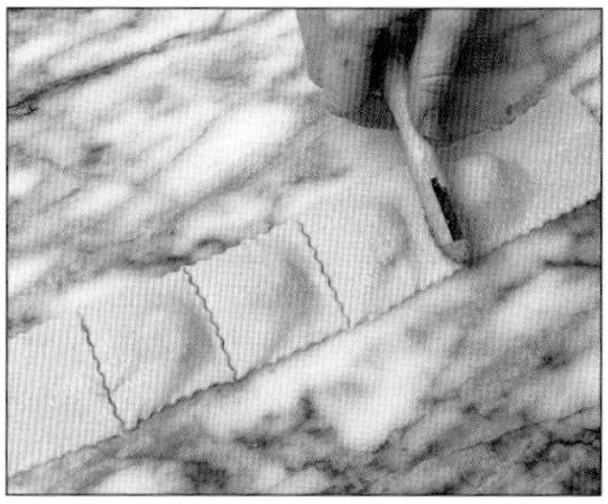

5 ▲ Use a fluted pastry wheel to cut between the rows to form small squares with filling in the center of each. If the edges do not stick well, moisten with milk or water, and press together with a fork. Place the ravioli on a lightly floured surface, and allow to dry for at least 30 minutes. Turn occasionally so they dry on both sides. Bring a large pan of salted water to the boil.

6 Heat the butter and sage together over very low heat, taking care that the butter melts but does not darken.

7 ▲ Drop the ravioli into the boiling water. Stir gently to prevent them from sticking. They will be cooked in very little time, about 4-5 minutes. Drain carefully and arrange in individual serving dishes. Spoon on the sauce, and serve at once.

Tagliatelle with Hazelnut Pesto

Tagliatelle al pesto di nocciale

Hazelnuts make an interesting addition to this variation on the classic pesto.

Ingredients

2 garlic cloves, crushed
25 g/1 oz/1 cup fresh basil leaves
25 g/1 oz/¼ cup shelled hazelnuts
200 g/7 oz/scant 1 cup skimmed milk soft cheese
225 g/8 oz dried tagliatelle
salt and freshly ground black pepper
serves 4

Cook's Tip

If you buy fresh tagliatelle instead of dried, cook in boiling salted water for only 2-3 minutes until *al dente*.

1 Place the crushed garlic, basil leaves, hazelnuts and cheese in a blender or food processor and process to a thick paste.

2 ▲ Meanwhile, cook the tagliatelle in lightly salted boiling water for about 10 minutes until *al dente*, then drain well.

3 ▲ Spoon the pesto into the hot pasta and toss lightly until melted. Grind over plenty of black pepper and serve hot.

Spaghetti with Tuna Sauce

Spaghetti al sugo di tonno

This delicious pasta dish combines some of the simplest, but most delicious Italian ingredients, along with a little extra zing from the chilli sauce.

Ingredients

225 g/8 oz dried spaghetti
1 garlic clove, crushed
400 g/14 oz can chopped tomatoes
425 g/15 oz can tuna fish in brine, drained
2.5 ml/½ tsp chilli sauce
4 black olives, stoned and chopped
salt and freshly ground black pepper
serves 4

Cook's Tip

If fresh tuna steaks are available, use 450 g/1 lb. Cut the steaks into small chunks and add to the sauce after step 2. Simmer for 6-8 minutes, then add the chilli, olives and pasta.

1 ▲ Cook the spaghetti in lightly salted boiling water for about 10 minutes or until *al dente*. Drain well and keep hot.

2 ▲ Add the garlic and tomatoes to the pan and bring to the boil. Simmer uncovered for 2-3 minutes.

3 Add the tuna, chilli sauce, olives and spaghetti to the pan. Heat well, season to taste with salt and plenty of black pepper and serve hot.

Farfalle with Mushrooms and Cheese

Farfalle boscaiole

Fresh wild mushrooms are very good in this sauce, but they are expensive. To cut the cost, use half wild and half cultivated, or as many wild as you can afford - even a small handful will intensify the mushroom flavour.

Ingredients

15 g/½ oz/1 cup dried porcini mushrooms
25 g/1 oz/2 tbsp butter
1 small onion, finely chopped
1 garlic clove, crushed
225 g/8 oz/3 cups fresh mushrooms, thinly sliced
a few fresh sage leaves, very finely chopped, plus a few whole leaves, to garnish
150 ml/¼ pint/⅔ cup dry white wine
225 g/8 oz/2 cups dried farfalle
115 g/4 oz/½ cup mascarpone cheese
115 g/4 oz/1 cup Gorgonzola or torta di Gorgonzola cheese, crumbled
salt and freshly ground black pepper

serves 4

1 ▲ Put the dried porcini in a small bowl with 250 ml/8 fl oz/1 cup warm water and leave to soak for 20–30 minutes. Remove from the liquid and squeeze the porcini over the bowl to extract as much liquid as possible. Strain the liquid and set it aside. Finely chop the porcini.

2 Melt the butter in a large saucepan, add the onion and chopped porcini and cook gently, stirring for about 3 minutes until the onion is soft. Add the garlic and fresh mushrooms, chopped sage, salt and plenty of black pepper. Cook over a medium heat, stirring frequently, for about 5 minutes or until the mushrooms are soft and juicy. Stir in the soaking liquid and the wine and simmer.

3 ▲ Cook the farfalle in a large saucepan of rapidly boiling salted water, for about 10 minutes or until *al dente*.

Variation

For a lighter sauce, use crème fraîche instead of mascarpone.

4 ▲ Meanwhile, stir the mascarpone and Gorgonzola into the mushroom sauce. Heat through, stirring, until melted. Taste for seasoning. Drain the pasta thoroughly, add to the sauce and toss to mix. Serve at once, with black pepper ground liberally on top. Garnish with sage leaves.

Pasta with Tomato and Chilli Sauce

Pasta all'arrabbiata

This is a speciality of Lazio – the word arrabbiata means rabid or angry, and describes the heat that comes from the chilli. This quick version is made with bottled sugocasa.

Ingredients
500 g/1 lb sugocasa (see Cook's Tip)
2 garlic cloves, crushed
150 ml/¼ pint/⅔ cup dry white wine
15 ml/1 tbsp sun-dried tomato purée
1 fresh red chilli
300 g/11 oz penne or tortiglioni
60 ml/4 tbsp finely chopped fresh flat leaf parsley
salt and freshly ground black pepper
freshly grated Pecorino cheese, to serve
serves 4

1 ▲ Put the sugocasa, garlic, wine, tomato paste and whole chilli in a saucepan and bring to the boil. Cover and simmer gently.

2 ▲ Drop the pasta into a large saucepan of rapidly boiling salted water and simmer for 10–12 minutes or until *al dente*.

Cook's Tip
Sugocasa is sold in bottles sometimes labelled "crushed Italian tomatoes". It is finer than canned chopped tomatoes and coarser than passata, and so is ideal for pasta sauces, soups and stews.

3 ▲ Remove the chilli from the sauce and add half the parsley. Taste for seasoning. If you prefer a hotter taste, chop some or all of the chilli and return it to the sauce.

4 ▲ Drain the pasta and tip into a warmed large bowl. Pour the sauce over the pasta and toss to mix. Serve at once, sprinkled with grated Pecorino and the remaining parsley.

Baked Vegetable Lasagne

Lasagne al forno con funghi e pomodori

Following the principles of the classic meat sauce lasagne, other combinations of ingredients can be used most effectively. This vegetarian lasagne uses fresh vegetables and herbs.

Ingredients

egg pasta sheets made with 3 eggs
30 ml/2 tbsp olive oil
1 medium onion, very finely chopped
500 g/1 $^{1}/_{4}$lb tomatoes, fresh or canned, chopped
salt and freshly ground black pepper
675 g/1 $^{1}/_{2}$ lb cultivated or wild mushrooms, or a combination of both
75 g/3 oz/$^{1}/_{3}$ cup butter
2 cloves garlic, finely chopped
juice of $^{1}/_{2}$ lemon
1 litre/1$^{3}/_{4}$ pints/4$^{1}/_{2}$ cups béchamel sauce
1$^{1}/_{2}$ cups freshly grated Parmesan or Romano cheese, or a combination

serves 8

1 Butter a large shallow baking dish, preferably rectangular or square.

2 ▲ Make the egg pasta. Do not let it dry out before cutting it into rectangles approximately 11 cm/4$^{1}/_{2}$in wide and the same length as the baking dish (this will make it easier to assemble).

3 In a small frying pan heat the oil and sauté the onion until translucent. Add the chopped tomatoes, and cook for 6–8 minutes, stirring often. Season with salt and pepper, and set aside.

4 ▲ Wipe the mushrooms carefully with a damp cloth. Slice finely. Heat 35 g/1$^{1}/_{2}$ oz/2 tbsp of the butter in a frying pan, and when it is bubbling, add the mushrooms. Cook until the mushrooms start to exude their juices. Add the garlic and lemon juice, and season with salt and pepper. Cook until the liquids have almost all evaporated and the mushrooms are starting to brown. Set aside.

5 ▲ Preheat the oven to 200°C/400°F/ gas 6. Bring a very large pan of water to the boil. Place a large bowl of cold water near the stove. Cover a large work surface with a tablecloth. Add salt to the rapidly boiling water. Drop in 3 or 4 of the egg pasta rectangles. Cook very briefly, about 30 seconds. Remove them from the pan using a slotted spoon, and drop them into the bowl of cold water for about 30 seconds. Remove and lay out to dry. Continue with the remaining pasta.

6 ▲ To assemble the lasagne have all the elements at hand: the baking dish, fillings, pasta, cheeses and butter. Spread one large spoonful of the béchamel sauce over the bottom of the dish. Arrange a layer of pasta in the dish, cutting it with a sharp knife so that it fits well. Cover the pasta with a thin layer of mushrooms, then one of béchamel sauce. Sprinkle with a little cheese.

7 ▲ Make another layer of pasta, spread with a thin layer of tomatoes, and then one of béchamel. Sprinkle with cheese. Repeat the layers in the same order, ending with a layer of pasta coated with béchamel. Do not make more than about 6 layers of pasta. Use the pasta trimmings to patch any gaps in the pasta. Sprinkle with cheese, and dot with butter.

8 Bake for 20 minutes. Remove from the oven and allow to stand for 5 minutes before serving.

Tortelli with Pumpkin Stuffing

Tortelli di zucca

During autumn and winter the northern Italian markets are full of bright orange pumpkins, which are used to make soups and pasta dishes. This dish is a speciality of Mantua.

Ingredients
1 kg/2 lb pumpkin (weight with shell)
75 g/3 oz/1 $^1/_2$ cups amaretti, finely crushed
2 eggs
75 g/3 oz/$^3/_4$ cup freshly grated Parmesan cheese
pinch of grated nutmeg
salt and freshly ground black pepper
plain breadcrumbs, as required
egg pasta sheets made with 3 eggs

To serve
115 g/4 oz/1/2 cup butter
75 g/3 oz/$^3/_4$ cup freshly grated Parmesan cheese

serves 6–8

1 Preheat the oven to 190°C/375°F/gas 5. Cut the pumpkin into 10 cm/4 in pieces. Leave the skin on. Place the pumpkin pieces in a covered casserole, and bake for 45–50 minutes. When cool, cut off the skins. Purée the flesh in a food mill or food processor or press through a sieve.

2 ▲ Combine the pumpkin purée with the biscuit crumbs, eggs, Parmesan and nutmeg. Season with salt and pepper. If the mixture is too wet, add 15–30 g/1–2 tbsp of breadcrumbs. Set aside.

3 Prepare the sheets of egg pasta. Roll out very thinly by hand or machine. Do not let the pasta dry out before filling it.

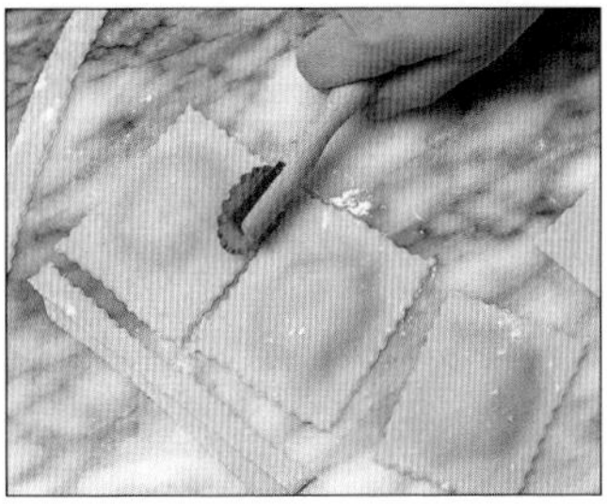

4 ▲ Place tablespoons of filling every 6–7 cm/2$^1/_2$ in along the pasta in rows 5 cm/2 in apart. Cover with another sheet of pasta, and press down gently. Use a fluted pastry wheel to cut between the rows to form rectangles with filling in the center of each. Place the tortelli on a lightly floured surface, and allow to dry for at least 30 minutes. Turn them occasionally so they dry on both sides.

5 Bring a large pan of salted water to a boil. Gently heat the butter over very low heat, taking care that it does not darken.

6 ▲ Drop the tortelli into the boiling water. Stir to prevent from sticking. They will be cooked in 4–5 minutes. Drain and arrange in individual dishes. Spoon on the melted butter, sprinkle with Parmesan or Romano, and serve.

Stuffed Pasta Half-moons

Mezzelune ripiene di formaggi

These stuffed egg pasta half-moons are filled with a delicate mixture of cheeses. They make an elegant first course.

Ingredients
225 g/8 oz/1 1/4 cups fresh ricotta or curd cheese
225 g/8 oz/1 1/4 cups mozzarella cheese
115 g/4 oz/1 cup freshly grated Parmesan cheese
2 eggs
45 ml/3 tbsp finely chopped fresh basil
salt and freshly ground black pepper
egg pasta sheets made with 3 eggs
milk

For the sauce
450 g/1 lb fresh tomatoes
30 ml/2 tbsp olive oil
1 small onion, very finely chopped
90 ml/6 tbsp cream

serves 6–8

1 ▲ Press the ricotta or curd cheese through a sieve or strainer. Chop the mozzarella into very small cubes. Combine all three cheeses in a bowl. Beat in the eggs and basil, season and set aside.

2 Make the sauce by dropping the tomatoes into a small pan of boiling water for 1 minute. Remove, and peel using a small sharp knife to pull the skins off. Chop the tomatoes finely. Heat the oil in a medium pan. Add the onion and cook over moderate heat until soft and translucent. Add the tomatoes and cook until soft, about 15 minutes. Season with salt and pepper. (The sauce may be pressed through a sieve to make it smooth.) Set aside.

3 Prepare the sheets of egg pasta. Roll out very thinly by hand or machine. Do not let the pasta dry out.

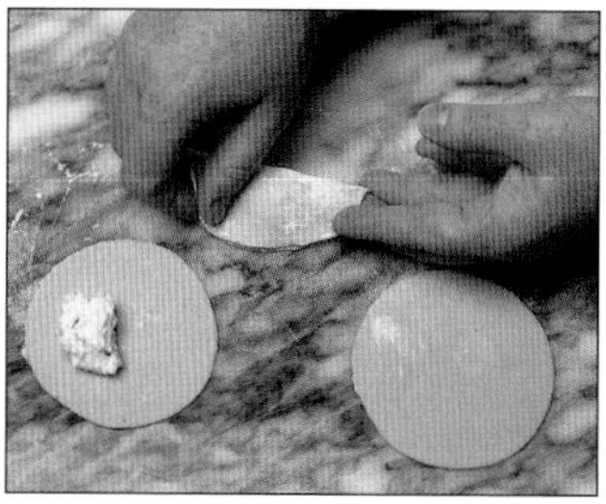

4 ▲ Using a water glass or pastry cutter, cut out rounds approximately 10 cm/4in in diameter. Spoon one large tablespoon of the filling onto one half of each pasta round and fold over.

5 Press the edges closed with a fork. Re-roll any trimmings and use to make more rounds. Allow the half-moons to dry for at least 10–15 minutes. Turn them over so they dry evenly.

6 Bring a large pan of salted water to a boil. Place the tomato sauce in a small saucepan and heat gently while the pasta is cooking. Stir in the cream. Do not boil.

7 Gently drop the stuffed pasta into the boiling water, and stir carefully to prevent them from sticking. Cook for 5–7 minutes. Scoop them out of the water, drain carefully, and arrange in individual dishes. Spoon on some of the sauce, and serve at once.

Cannelloni Stuffed with Meat

Cannelloni ripieni di carne

Cannelloni are rectangles of egg pasta which are spread with a filling, rolled up and baked in a sauce. In this recipe, they are baked in a béchamel sauce.

Ingredients

30 ml/2 tbsp olive oil
1 medium onion, very finely chopped
225 g/8 oz/$1\frac{1}{2}$ cups very lean minced beef
75 g/3 oz/$\frac{1}{2}$ cup cooked ham (either boiled or baked), finely chopped
15 ml/1 tbsp chopped fresh parsley
30 ml/2 tbsp tomato paste, softened in 15 ml/1 tbsp warm water
1 egg
salt and freshly ground black pepper
egg pasta sheets made with 2 eggs
750 ml/$1\frac{1}{4}$ pints/$3\frac{1}{4}$ cups béchamel sauce
50 g/2 oz/$\frac{1}{2}$ cup freshly grated Parmesan cheese
40 g/$1\frac{1}{2}$ oz/3 tbsp butter

serves 6–8

1 ▲ Prepare the meat filling by heating the oil in a medium saucepan. Add the onion, and sauté gently until translucent. Stir in the beef, crumbling it with a fork, and stirring constantly until it has lost its raw red colour. Cook for 3–4 minutes.

2 ▲ Remove from the heat, and turn the beef mixture into a bowl with the ham and parsley. Add the tomato paste and the egg, and mix well. Season with salt and pepper. Set aside.

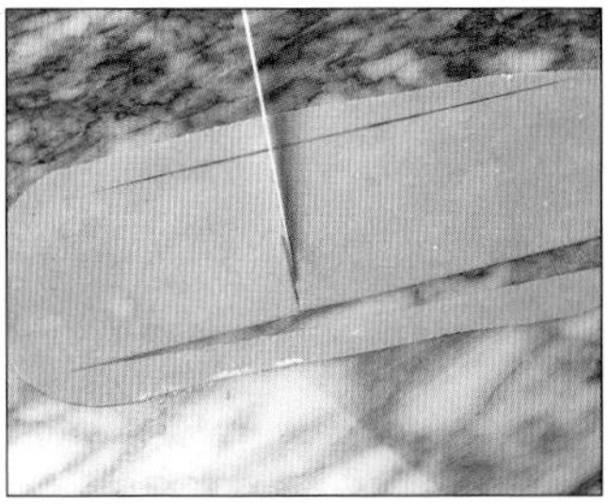

3 ▲ Make the egg pasta sheets with a machine or by hand. Do not let the pasta dry before cutting it into rectangles 12-13 cm/5-6 in long and as wide as they come from the machine (8-9 cm/3 in if you are not using a machine).

4 Bring a very large pan of water to a boil. Place a large bowl of cold water near the stove. Cover a large work surface with a tablecloth. Add salt to the rapidly boiling water. Drop in 3 or 4 of the egg pasta rectangles. Cook very briefly, about 30 seconds. Remove and drop them into the bowl of cold water for about 30 seconds more. Pull them out of the water, shaking off the excess water. Lay them out flat on the tablecloth. Continue with the remaining pasta.

5 Preheat the oven to 220°C/425°F/gas 7. Select a shallow baking dish large enough to accommodate all the cannelloni in one layer. Butter the dish, and smear 2-3 tbsp of béchamel sauce over the bottom.

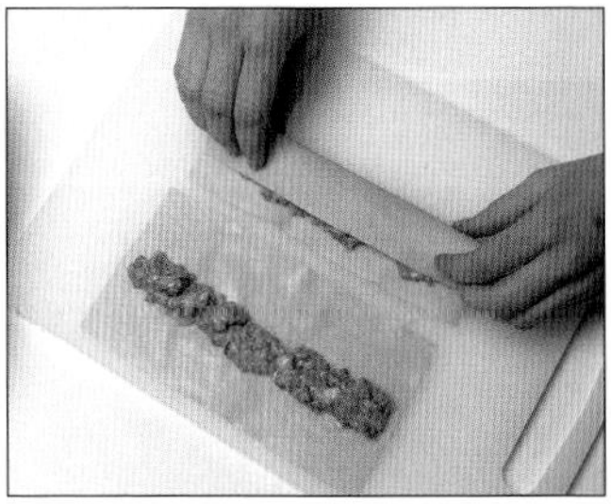

6 ▲ Stir about one-third of the béchamel into the meat filling. Spread a thin layer of filling on each pasta rectangle. Roll the rectangles up loosely starting from the long side, Swiss-roll style. Place the cannelloni into the baking dish with their open edges down.

7 ▲ Spoon the rest of the sauce over the cannelloni, pushing a little down between each pasta roll. Sprinkle the top with the grated Parmesan, and dot with butter. Bake for about 20 minutes. Allow to rest for 5–8 minutes before serving.

Three-cheese Lasagne

Lasagne ai tre formaggi

The cheese makes this lasagne quite expensive, so reserve it for a special occasion.

Ingredients
30 ml/2 tbsp olive oil
1 onion, finely chopped
1 carrot, finely chopped
1 celery stick, finely chopped
1 garlic clove, crushed
675 g/1½ lb minced beef
400 g/14 oz can chopped tomatoes
300 ml/½ pint/1¼ cups beef stock
300 ml/½ pint/1¼ cups red wine
30 ml/2 tbsp sun-dried tomato paste
10 ml/2 tsp dried oregano
9 sheets no-precook lasagne
3 x 150 g/5 oz packets mozzarella cheese, thinly sliced
450 g/1 lb/2 cups ricotta cheese
115 g/4 oz Parmesan cheese, grated
salt and freshly ground black pepper
serves 6–8

1 Heat the oil and gently cook the onion, carrot, celery and garlic, stirring for 10 minutes until softened.

2 Add the beef and cook until it changes colour, stirring constantly and breaking up the meat.

3 ▲ Add the tomatoes, stock, wine, tomato paste, oregano and salt and pepper and bring to the boil, stirring. Cover, lower the heat and simmer gently for 1 hour, stirring occasionally.

4 ▲ Preheat the oven to 190°C/375°F/Gas 5. Check for seasoning, then ladle one-third of the meat sauce into a 23 x 33 cm/9 x 13 in baking dish and cover with 3 sheets of lasagne. Arrange one-third of the mozzarella slices over the top, dot with one-third of the ricotta, then sprinkle with one-third of the Parmesan.

5 Repeat these layers twice, then bake for 40 minutes. Leave to cool for 10 minutes before serving.

Tortiglioni with Spicy Sausage Sauce

Tortiglioni alla siciliana

This heady pasta dish is not for the faint-hearted. Serve it with a robust Sicilian red wine.

Ingredients
30 ml/2 tbsp olive oil
1 onion, finely chopped
1 celery stick, finely chopped
2 large garlic cloves, crushed
1 fresh red chilli, seeded and chopped
450 g/1 lb ripe Italian plum tomatoes, peeled and finely chopped
30 ml/2 tbsp tomato purée
150 ml/¼ pint/⅔ cup red wine
5 ml/1 tsp sugar
300 g/11 oz dried tortiglioni
175 g/6 oz spicy salami, rind removed
salt and freshly ground black pepper
30 ml/2 tbsp chopped fresh parsley, to garnish
grated Parmesan cheese, to serve
serves 4

Cook's Tip
Buy the salami for this dish in one piece so that you can chop it into large chunks.

1 ▲ Heat the oil, then add the onion, celery, garlic and chilli and cook gently, stirring frequently, for about 10 minutes until softened.

2 Add the tomatoes, tomato purée, wine, sugar and salt and pepper to taste and bring to the boil, stirring. Lower the heat, cover and simmer gently, stirring occasionally, for about 20 minutes. Add a few spoonfuls of water from time to time if the sauce becomes too thick.

3 ▲ Meanwhile, drop the pasta into a large saucepan of rapidly boiling salted water and simmer, uncovered, for 10 - 12 minutes.

4 Chop the salami into bite-size chunks and add to the sauce. Heat through, then taste for seasoning.

5 Drain the pasta, tip it into a large bowl, then pour the sauce over and toss to mix. Scatter over the parsley and serve with grated Parmesan.

Pasta and Bolognese Bake

Pasticcio

Pasticcio is Italian for pie, and in some regions this is made with a pastry topping. This simple version makes a great family supper because it's such a favourite with children.

Ingredients

225 g/8 oz dried conchiglie
1 quantity hot Bolognese Sauce (see Tagliatelle with Bolognese Sauce page 158)
salt and freshly ground black pepper

For the white sauce

50 g/2 oz/¼ cup butter
50 g/2 oz/½ cup plain flour
750 ml/1¼ pints/3 cups milk
75 g/3 oz/1 cup grated Parmesan cheese
1 egg, beaten
good pinch of grated nutmeg
mixed salad leaves, to serve

serves 4

1 Cook the conchiglie in a large pan of rapidly boiling salted water for 10–12 minutes or until *al dente*.

2 Meanwhile, make the white sauce. Melt the butter in a saucepan until foaming, add the flour and stir over a low heat for 1–2 minutes. Remove the pan from the heat and gradually whisk in the milk. Return the pan to the heat and bring to the boil, whisking all the time. Lower the heat and simmer for 2–3 minutes, whisking occasionally, until the sauce thickens. Remove the pan from the heat.

3 ▲ Preheat the oven to 190°C/375°F/ Gas 5. Drain the pasta thoroughly, tip it into a 20 x 30 cm/8 x 12 in baking dish and mix in the hot bolognese sauce. Level the surface.

4 ▲ Stir about two-thirds of the Parmesan into the white sauce, then stir in the beaten egg and nutmeg, with salt and pepper to taste. Pour over the pasta and sauce and sprinkle with the remaining Parmesan. Bake for 20 minutes or until golden and bubbling. Serve hot, straight from the dish. Add a salad garnish to each plate.

Cook's Tip

This is a good way of using up leftover bolognese sauce and cooked pasta – the quantities do not need to be exact.

Pasta with Aubergines

Pasta alla Norma

This Sicilian recipe is traditionally made from fried aubergines. This version is lighter.

Ingredients

2 medium aubergines, about 225 g/8 oz each, diced small
45 ml/3 tbsp olive oil
275 g/10 oz dried macaroni or fusilli
50 g/2 oz/$^{2}/_{3}$ cup grated Pecorino cheese
salt and freshly ground black pepper
shredded fresh basil leaves, to garnish
crusty bread, to serve

For the tomato sauce

30 ml/2 tbsp olive oil
1 onion, finely chopped
400 g/14 oz can chopped tomatoes or 400 g/14 oz passata

serves 4

Cook's Tip

In Sicily, a cheese called ricotta salata is used for this recipe. This is a matured salted ricotta that is grated like Pecorino and Parmesan. It is unlikely that you will find ricotta salata outside Sicily; Pecorino is the best substitute because it tastes slightly saltier than Parmesan.

1 Soak the diced aubergine in a bowl of cold salted water for 30 minutes.

2 Meanwhile, preheat the oven to 220°C/425°F/Gas 7. Make the sauce. Heat the oil in a large saucepan, add the onion and cook gently for about 3 minutes until softened. Add the tomatoes, with salt and pepper to taste. Bring to the boil, lower the heat, cover and simmer for about 20 minutes. Stir the sauce and add a few spoonfuls of water from time to time, to prevent it from becoming too thick. Remove from the heat.

3 ▲ Drain the aubergines and pat dry. Spread the pieces out in a roasting tin, add the oil and toss to coat. Bake for 20–25 minutes, turning the aubergines every 4–5 minutes with a fish slice so that they brown evenly.

4 Cook the pasta in a large pan of rapidly boiling salted water for 10–12 minutes or until *al dente*. Reheat the tomato sauce.

5 ▲ Drain the pasta thoroughly and add it to the tomato sauce, with half the roasted aubergines and half the Pecorino. Toss to mix, then taste for seasoning.

6 Spoon the pasta and sauce mixture into a warmed large serving dish and top with the remaining roasted aubergines. Scatter the shredded fresh basil leaves over the top, followed by the remaining Pecorino. Serve at once, with generous chunks of crusty bread.

Semolina Gnocchi

Gnocchi di semola

This famous Roman dish is made with coarsely ground semolina, which is cooked in a similar way to polenta. The rich paste is cut into flat discs, and baked with butter and cheese.

Ingredients
1 litre/$1^3/_4$ pints/$4^1/_2$ cups milk
pinch of salt
35 g/$1^1/_2$ oz/3 tbsp butter
250 g/9 oz/generous 2 cups coarsely ground semolina
3 egg yolks
3 tbsp freshly grated Parmesan cheese

For baking
60 g/$2^1/_4$ oz/5 tbsp butter, melted
60 g/$2^1/_4$ oz/$^1/_2$ cup freshly grated Parmesan cheese
pinch of grated nutmeg

serves 4

1 ▲ Heat the milk with the salt and a third of the butter in a heavy or non-stick saucepan. When it boils sprinkle in the semolina, stirring with a wire whisk to prevent lumps from forming. Bring the mixture to the boil. Lower the heat and simmer for 15–20 minutes, stirring occasionally. The mixture will be very thick.

~ COOK'S TIP ~

Semolina is ground durum wheat, which is the kind used to make dried pasta. Buy semolina in small batches and store in an air-tight container as it goes stale when kept for too long.

2 ▲ Remove from the heat and beat in the remaining butter, and then the egg yolks one at a time. Stir in the grated Parmesan. Season with salt. Sprinkle a little cold water onto a work surface. Spread the hot semolina mixture out onto it in an even layer about 1 cm/$^1/_2$ inch thick. Allow to cool for at least 2 hours.

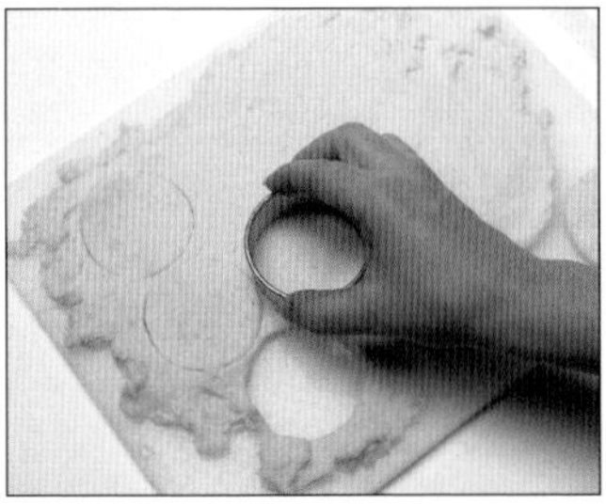

3 ▲ Preheat the oven to 220°C/425°F/gas 7. Butter a shallow baking dish. Use a biscuit cutter to cut the semolina into 6 cm/$2^1/_2$in rounds.

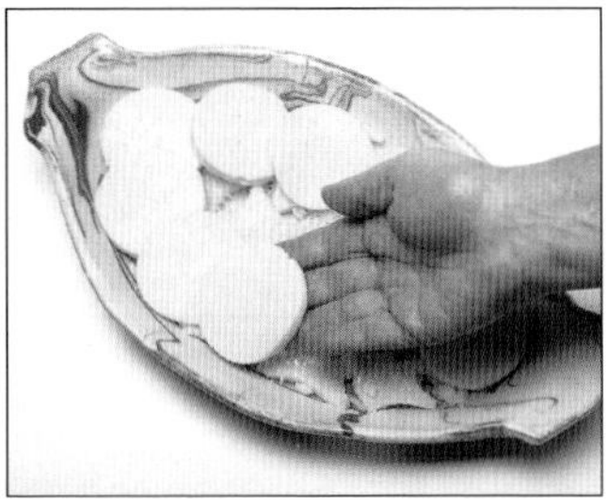

4 ▲ Place the trimmings in an even layer in the bottom of the dish. Pour over a little melted butter, and sprinkle with cheese. Cover with a layer of the cut-out circles, overlapping them slightly. Sprinkle with nutmeg, cheese and butter. Continue the layering until all the ingredients have been used up.

5 Bake for about 20 minutes, or until the top is browned. Remove from the oven and allow to stand for 5 minutes before serving.

Potato Gnocchi

Gnocchi di patate

Gnocchi are little dumplings made either with mashed potato and flour, as here, or with semolina. They should be light in texture, and must not be overworked while being made.

Ingredients

1 kg/2 lb waxy potatoes, scrubbed
15 ml/1 tbsp salt
250–300 g/9–11 oz/2–2$^1/_2$ cups flour
1 egg
pinch of grated nutmeg
25 g/1 oz/2 tbsp butter
freshly grated Parmesan, to serve
serves 4–6

1 Place the unpeeled potatoes in a large pan of salted water. Bring to a boil, and cook until the potatoes are tender but not falling apart. Drain. Peel as soon as possible, while the potatoes are still hot.

2 On a work surface spread out a layer of flour. Mash the hot potatoes with a food mill, dropping them directly onto the flour, dropping them directly onto the flour. Sprinkle with about half of the remaining flour and mix very lightly into the potatoes. Break the egg into the mixture, add the nutmeg, and knead lightly, drawing in more flour as necessary. When the dough is light to the touch and no longer moist or sticky it is ready to be rolled. Do not overwork or the gnocchi will be heavy.

3 ▲ Divide the dough into 4 parts. On a lightly floured board form each into a roll about 2 cm/$^3/_4$ inch in diameter. Cut the rolls crosswise into pieces about 2 cm/$^3/_4$ inch long.

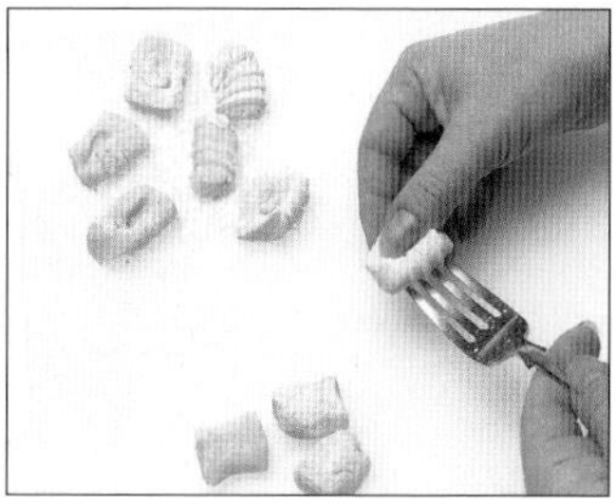

4 ▲ Hold an ordinary table fork with long tines sideways, leaning on the board. One by one press and roll the gnocchi lightly along the tines of the fork towards the points, making ridges on one side, and a depression from your thumb on the other.

5 Bring a large pan of water to a fast boil. Add salt, and drop in about half the gnocchi.

6 ▲ When the gnocchi rise to the surface, after 3–4 minutes, they are cooked. Scoop them out of the water, allow to drain, and place in a warmed serving bowl. Dot with butter. Keep warm while the remaining gnocchi are boiling. As soon as they are cooked, toss the gnocchi with the butter or a heated sauce, sprinkle with grated Parmesan, and serve.

Potato and Spinach Gnocchi

Gnocchi di patate e spinaci

These green gnocchi are made in the same way as potato gnocchi, with the addition of fresh or frozen spinach. Serve tossed with butter or with a tomato sauce.

Ingredients

750 g/1 1/2 lb fresh spinach, or 400 g/ 14 oz frozen leaf spinach
1 kg/2 lb waxy potatoes, scrubbed
salt, to taste
250–300 g/9–11 oz/2–2 1/2 cups flour
1 egg
pinch of grated nutmeg
50 g/2 oz/1/4 cup butter
freshly grated Parmesan cheese, to serve

serves 6

1 Wash fresh spinach in several changes of cold water. Pull off any tough stalks. Place in a large saucepan with only the water that is clinging to the leaves. Cover the pan, and cook over moderate heat, stirring occasionally, until the spinach is tender, about 5-8 minutes. Cook uncovered for the last 2-3 minutes to boil off some of the water. Remove from the heat. Drain.

2 ▲ Cook frozen spinach according to the instructions on the packet. Spread the spinach over a clean dish towel, roll it up and wring out all excess moisture. Chop the spinach finely with a sharp knife.

3 Place the unpeeled potatoes in a large pan of salted water. Bring to a boil, and cook until the potatoes are tender but not falling apart. Drain. Peel as soon as possible, while the potatoes are still hot.

4 ▲ On a work surface spread out a layer of flour. Mash the hot potatoes with a food mill, dropping them directly onto the flour. Add the spinach, and mix lightly into the potatoes. Sprinkle with about half of the remianing flour and mix in lightly.

5 Break the egg into the mixture, add the nutmeg, and knead lightly, drawing in more flour as necessary. When the dough is light to the touch and no longer moist or sticky it is ready to be rolled. Do not overwork or the gnocchi will be heavy.

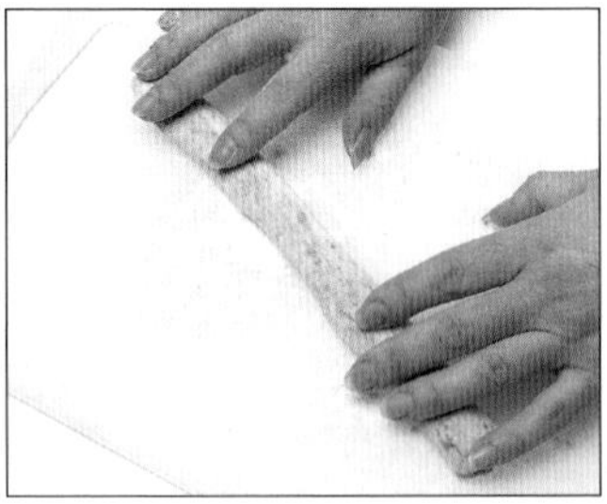

6 ▲ Divide the dough into 4 parts. On a lightly floured board form each into a roll about 2 cm/3/4 inch in diameter. Cut the rolls crosswise into pieces about 2 cm/3/4 inch long.

7 ▲ Hold an ordinary table fork with long tines sideways, leaning on the board. One by one press and roll the gnocchi lightly along the tines of the fork towards the points, making ridges on one side, and a depression from your thumb on the other.

8 ▲ Bring a large pan of water to a fast boil. Add salt and drop about half the gnocchi in. They will sink to the bottom of the pan. When they rise to the surface, after 3-4 minutes, the gnocchi are done. Scoop them out with a large slotted spoon, and place in a warmed serving bowl. Keep warm while the remaining gnocchi are boiling. As soon as they are cooked, toss the gnocchi with the butter or a heated sauce, sprinkle with grated Parmesan, and serve.

Spinach and Ricotta Gnocchi

Gnocchi de spinaci e ricotta

The mixture for these tasty little herb dumplings needs to be handled very carefully to achieve light and fluffy results. Serve with a sage butter and grated Parmesan.

Ingredients

6 garlic cloves, unpeeled
25 g/1 oz mixed fresh herbs, such as parsley, basil, thyme, coriander and chives, finely chopped
225 g/8 oz fresh spinach leaves
250 g/9 oz/generous 1 cup ricotta cheese
1 egg yolk
50 g/2 oz/$^{2}/_{3}$ cup grated Parmesan cheese
75 g/3 oz/$^{2}/_{3}$ cup plain flour
50 g/2 oz/$^{1}/_{4}$ cup butter
30 ml/2 tbsp fresh sage, chopped
salt and freshly ground black pepper
serves 4

1 Cook the garlic cloves in boiling water for 4 minutes. Drain and pop out of the skins. Place in a food processor with the herbs and blend to a purée or mash the garlic with a fork and add the herbs to mix well.

2 ▲ Place the spinach in a large pan with just the water that clings to the leaves and cook gently until wilted. Leave to cool then squeeze out as much liquid as possible. Chop finely.

3 Place the ricotta in a bowl and beat in the egg yolk, spinach, herbs and garlic. Stir in half the Parmesan, sift in the flour and mix well.

Cook's Tip

Squeeze the spinach dry to ensure the gnocchi are not wet and to give a lighter result. The mixture should be fairly soft and will be easier to handle if chilled for an hour before preparing the dumplings.

4 ▲ Using floured hands, break off pieces of the mixture slightly smaller than a walnut and roll into small dumplings.

5 Bring a large pan of salted water to the boil and carefully add the gnocchi. When they rise to the top of the pan they are cooked, this should take about 3 minutes.

6 ▲ The gnocchi should be light and fluffy all the way through. If not, simmer for a further minute. Drain well. Meanwhile, melt the butter in a frying pan and add the sage. Simmer gently for 1 minute. Add the gnocchi to the frying pan and toss in the butter over a gentle heat for 1 minute, then serve sprinkled with the remaining Parmesan.

Gnocchi with Gorgonzola Sauce

Gnocchi alla gorgonzola

Gnocchi are prepared all over Italy with different ingredients used in different regions. These are gnocchi di patate, *potato dumplings.*

Ingredients
450 g/1 lb potatoes, unpeeled
1 large egg
115 g/4 oz/1 cup plain flour
fresh thyme sprigs, to garnish
salt and freshly ground black pepper

For the sauce
115 g/4 oz Gorgonzola cheese
60 ml/4 tbsp double cream
15 ml/1 tbsp fresh thyme, chopped
60 ml/4 tbsp freshly grated Parmesan cheese, to serve

serves 4

1 Cook the potatoes in boiling salted water for about 20 minutes until they are tender. Drain and, when cool enough to handle, remove the skins.

2 ▲ Force the potatoes through a sieve, pressing through using the back of a spoon, into a mixing bowl. Add plenty of seasoning and then beat in the egg until completely incorporated. Add the flour a little at a time, stirring well with a wooden spoon after each addition until you have a smooth dough. (You may not need all the flour.)

3 Turn the dough out on to a floured surface and knead for about 3 minutes, adding more flour if necessary, until it is smooth and soft and not sticky to the touch.

Cook's Tips
Choose dry, floury potatoes. Avoid new or red-skinned potatoes which do not have the right dry texture.

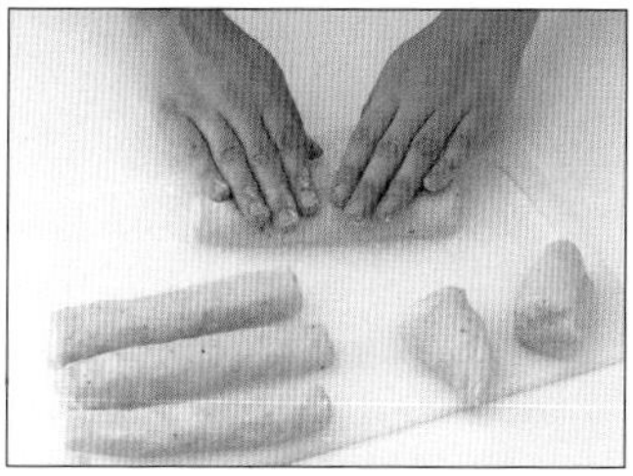

4 ▲ Divide the dough into 6 equal pieces. Flour your hands and gently roll each piece between your hands into a log shape measuring 15–20 cm/ 6–8 in long and 2.5 cm/1 in around. Cut each log into 6–8 pieces, about 2.5 cm/1 in long, then gently roll each piece in the flour. Form into gnocchi by gently pressing each piece on to the floured surface with the tines of a fork to leave ridges in the dough.

5 ▲ To cook, drop the gnocchi into a pan of boiling water about 12 at a time. Once they rise to the surface, after about 2 minutes, cook for 4–5 minutes more. Remove and drain.

6 Place the Gorgonzola, cream and thyme in a large frying pan and heat gently until the cheese melts to form a thick, creamy consistency and heat through. Add the drained gnocchi and toss well to combine. Serve with Parmesan and garnish with thyme.

Rice, Polenta & Pizzas

In the north of Italy, rice is served as a first course, as creamy risotto, but you can serve it as a main dish, with a salad and Italian bread. Polenta, also from the north of Italy, is most often served with the main course, especially with meaty casseroles. Pizzas hail from the south, where they are eaten at any time of day, the ultimate convenience food.

Risotto with Parmesan Cheese

Risotto alla parmigiana

Risotto is distinguished from other rice dishes by its unique cooking method.

Ingredients

1.1 litres/2 pints/5$^1/_2$ cups meat, chicken or vegetable broth, preferably home-made
65 g/5 tbsp butter
1 small onion, finely chopped
275 g/10 oz/1$^1/_2$ cups medium-grain risotto rice, such as arborio
100 ml/4 fl oz/$^1/_2$ cup dry white wine
salt and freshly ground black pepper
$^3/_4$ cup freshly grated Parmesan cheese
serves 3–4

1 Heat the stock in a medium saucepan, and keep it simmering until it is needed.

2 In a large heavy frying pan, melt two-thirds of the butter. Stir in the onion, and cook gently until it is soft and golden. Add the rice, mixing it well to coat it with butter. After 1–2 minutes pour in the wine.

3 ▲ Raise the heat slightly, and cook until the wine evaporates. Add one small ladleful of the hot stock. Over moderate heat cook until the stock is absorbed or evaporates, stirring the rice with a wooden spoon to prevent it from sticking to the pan. Add a little more stock, and stir until the rice dries out again. Continue stirring and adding the liquid a little at a time. After about 20 minutes of cooking time, taste the rice. Add salt and pepper.

4 Continue cooking, stirring and adding the liquid until the rice is *al dente*, or tender but still firm to the bite. The total cooking time of the risotto may be from 20–35 minutes. If you run out of stock, use hot water, but do not worry if the rice is done before you have used up all the stock.

5 ▲ Remove the risotto pan from the heat. Stir in the remaining butter and the cheese. Taste again for seasoning. Allow the risotto to rest for 3–4 minutes before serving.

Risotto with Prawns

Risotto con gamberi

This prawn risotto is given a soft pink colour by the addition of a little tomato purée.

Ingredients

325 g/12oz fresh prawns in their shells
1.1 litres/2 pints/5 cups water
1 bay leaf
1–2 sprigs of parsley
5 ml/1 tsp whole peppercorns
2 cloves garlic, peeled
65 g/2$^1/_2$ oz/5 tbsp butter
2 shallots, finely chopped
275 g/10 oz/1$^1/_2$ cups medium-grain risotto rice, such as arborio
15 ml/1 tbsp tomato purée softened in 100 ml/4 fl oz/$^1/_2$ cup dry white wine
salt and freshly ground black pepper
serves 4

1 Place the prawns in a large saucepan with the water, herbs, peppercorns and garlic. Bring to a boil and cook for about 1 minute. Remove the prawns, peel, and return the shells to the saucepan. Boil the shells for another 10 minutes. Strain. Return the broth to a pan, and simmer until needed.

2 Slice the prawns in half lengthwise, removing the dark vein along the back. Set 4 halves aside for garnish and roughly chop the rest.

3 Heat two-thirds of the butter in a casserole. Add the shallots and cook until golden. Stir in the prawns. Cook for 1–2 minutes.

4 ▲ Add the rice, mixing well to coat it with butter. After 1–2 minutes pour in the tomato paste and wine. Follow steps 3–5 for Risotto with Parmesan, omitting the cheese and garnishing with the reserved prawn halves.

Risotto with Mushrooms

Risotto con funghi

The addition of wild mushrooms gives this risotto a wonderful woodsy flavour.

Ingredients

25 g/1 oz/$^1/_3$ cup dried wild mushrooms, preferably porcini
175 g/6 oz/1 $^1/_2$ cups fresh cultivated mushrooms
juice of $^1/_2$ lemon
75 g/3 oz/$^1/_3$ cup butter
30 ml/2 tbsp finely chopped parsley
900 ml/1 $^2/_3$ pints/4 cups meat or chicken broth, preferably home-made
30 ml/2 tbsp olive oil
1 small onion, finely chopped
275 g/10 oz/1 $^1/_2$ cups medium-grain risotto rice, such as arborio
100 ml/4 fl oz/$^1/_2$ cup dry white wine
salt and freshly ground black pepper
45 ml/3 tbsp freshly grated Parmesan cheese

serves 3–4

1 Place the dried mushrooms in a small bowl with about 350 ml/12 fl oz/1 $^1/_2$ cups warm water. Soak for at least 40 minutes. Rinse the mushrooms thoroughly. Filter the soaking water through a strainer lined with paper towels, and reserve.

2 ▲ Wipe the fresh mushrooms with a damp cloth, and slice finely. Place in a bowl and toss with the lemon juice. In a large heavy frying pan or casserole melt one-third of the butter. Stir in the fresh sliced mushrooms and cook over moderate heat until they give up their juices, and begin to brown. Stir in the parsley, cook for 30 seconds more, and remove to a side dish.

3 Place the broth in a saucepan. Add the soaking water from the mushrooms, and simmer until needed.

4 ▲ Heat another third of the butter with the olive oil in the same pan the mushrooms were cooked in. Stir in the onion, and cook until it is soft and golden. Add the rice, stirring for 1–2 minutes to coat it with the oils. Add the soaked and sautéed mushrooms, and mix well.

5 ▲ Pour in the wine, and cook over moderate heat until it evaporates. Follow steps 3–4 for Risotto with Parmesan Cheese.

6 Remove the risotto pan from the heat. Stir in the remaining butter and the Parmesan or Romano. Grind in a little black pepper, and taste again for salt. Allow the risotto to rest for about 3–4 minutes before serving.

Risotto with Asparagus

Risotto con asparagi

This is an elegant risotto to make when asparagus is in season.

Ingredients
225 g/8 oz asparagus, lower stalks peeled
700 ml/1 $^{1}/_{4}$ pints/3 cups vegetable or meat broth, preferably home-made
65 g/2 $^{1}/_{2}$ oz/5 tbsp butter
1 small onion, finely chopped
400 g/14 oz/2 cups medium-grain risotto rice, such as arborio
salt and freshly ground black pepper
75 g/3 oz/ $^{3}/_{4}$ cup freshly grated Parmesan cheese
serves 4–5

1 Bring a large pan of water to the boil. Add the asparagus. Bring the water back to the boil, and blanch for 5 minutes. Lift the asparagus out, reserving the cooking water. Rinse the asparagus under cold water. Drain. Cut the asparagus diagonally into 4 cm/1 $^{1}/_{2}$ in pieces. Keep the tip and next-highest sections separate from the stalk sections.

2 Place the broth in a saucepan. Measure out 850 ml/1 $^{1}/_{2}$ pints/3 $^{3}/_{4}$ cups of the asparagus cooking water, and add it to the broth. Heat the liquid to simmering, and keep it hot until it is needed.

3 ▲ Heat two-thirds of the butter in a large heavy frying pan or casserole. Add the chopped onion and cook until it is soft and golden. Stir in all the asparagus except the top two sections. Cook for 2–3 minutes. Add the rice, mixing well to coat it with butter for 1–2 minutes.

4 ▲ Stir in half a ladleful of the hot liquid. Using a wooden spoon, stir constantly until the liquid has been absorbed or evaporated. Add another half ladleful of the liquid, and stir until it has been absorbed. Continue stirring and adding the liquid, a little at a time, for about 10 minutes.

5 ▲ Add the remaining asparagus sections, and proceed as for step 4 of Risotto with Parmesan Cheese.

6 Remove the risotto pan from the heat. Stir in the remaining butter and the Parmesan. Grind in a little black pepper, and taste again for salt. Serve at once.

Timballo of Rice with Peas

Timballo di riso con piselli

The timballo is named because it looks like an inverted kettledrum (timballo or timpano). It is made like a risotto, but is given a final baking in the oven, and then unmoulded.

Ingredients

75 g/3 oz/$^1/_3$ cup butter
30 ml/2 tbsp olive oil
1 small onion, finely chopped
50 g/2 oz/$^1/_3$ cup ham, cut into small dice
45 ml/3 tbsp finely chopped fresh parsley, plus a few sprigs to garnish
2 cloves garlic, very finely chopped
225 g/8 oz/1 cup shelled peas, fresh or frozen and thawed
salt and freshly ground black pepper
60 ml/4 tbsp water
1.25 litres/2$^1/_4$ pints/5$^1/_2$ cups meat or vegetable broth, preferably home-made
275 g/10 oz/1$^1/_2$ cups medium-grain risotto rice, such as arborio
75 g/3 oz/$^3/_4$ cup freshly grated Parmesan cheese
175 g/6 oz/$^3/_4$ cup fontina cheese, very thinly sliced
a few sprigs parsley, to garnish

serves 4

1 ▲ Heat half the butter and all the oil in a large heavy frying pan or casserole. Add the chopped onion, and cook for a few minutes until it softens. Add the diced ham, and stir over moderate heat for 3–4 minutes. Stir in the parsley and garlic. Cook for 1 or 2 minutes. Add the peas, mix well, season with salt and pepper and add the water. Cover the pan, and cook for about 8 minutes for fresh peas, 4 minutes for frozen peas. Remove the cover, and cook until all the liquid has evaporated. Remove half the pea mixture to a dish.

2 Heat the broth, and keep it simmering until needed. Butter a round, flat-bottomed ovenproof dish and line the bottom with a round of buttered greaseproof paper.

3 ▲ Stir the rice into the pea mixture remaining in the pan. After 1–2 minutes, add a small ladleful of the hot broth. Cook over moderate heat until the broth is absorbed, stirring the rice with a wooden spoon to prevent it from sticking. Add a little more stock, and stir until the rice dries out again. Continue stirring and adding the liquid.

4 ▲ Preheat the oven to 180°C/350°F. After about 20 minutes of cooking time, taste the rice. As soon as the rice is just *al dente*, or tender but still firm to the bite, remove the pan from the heat. Correct the seasoning. Mix most of the remaining butter and half the grated Parmesan into the rice.

5 Assemble by sprinkling a little Parmesan into the bottom of the dish. Spoon about half the rice into the dish. Follow with a thin layer of the fontina and a layer of reserved cooked peas and ham. Sprinkle with grated Parmesan.

6 ▲ Cover with the remaining fontina slices and end with the rice. Sprinkle with Parmesan, and dot with butter. Bake in the preheated oven for 10–15 minutes. Remove from the oven, and allow to stand for 10 minutes.

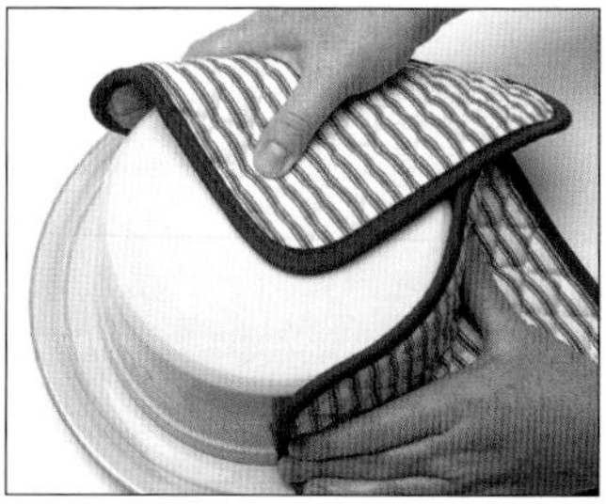

7 ▲ To unmould, slip a knife around between the rice and the dish. Place a serving plate upside down on top of the dish. Wearing oven mitts, pick up the dish and turn it over while still holding the plate. If the rice does not drop down, give it a sharp knock with your gloved hand. Peel off the greaseproof paper. Garnish with parsley. Serve by cutting the timballo into wedges.

Risotto with Spring Vegetables

Risotto primavera

This is one of the prettiest risottos, especially if you can get yellow courgettes.

Ingredients

150 g/5 oz/1 cup shelled fresh peas
115 g/4 oz/1 cup French beans, cut into short lengths
30 ml/2 tbsp olive oil
75 g/3 oz/6 tbsp butter
2 small yellow courgettes, cut into matchsticks
1 onion, finely chopped
275 g/10 oz/1½ cups risotto rice
120 ml/4 fl oz/½ cup Italian dry white vermouth
about 1 litre/1¾ pints/4 cups boiling chicken stock
75 g/3 oz/1 cup grated Parmesan cheese
a small handful of fresh basil leaves, finely shredded, plus a few whole leaves, to garnish
salt and freshly ground black pepper

serves 4

1 Blanch the peas and beans in a large saucepan of lightly salted boiling water for 2-3 minutes until just tender. Drain, refresh under cold running water, drain again and set aside for later.

2 ▲ Heat the oil and 25 g/1 oz/2 tbsp of the butter in a medium saucepan until foaming. Add the courgettes and cook gently for 2-3 minutes or until just softened. Remove with a slotted spoon and set aside. Add the onion to the pan and cook gently for about 3 minutes, stirring frequently, until it is softened.

3 ▲ Stir in the rice until the grains start to swell and burst, then add the vermouth. Stir until the vermouth stops sizzling and most of it has been absorbed by the rice, then add a few ladlefuls of the stock, with salt and pepper to taste. Stir over low heat until the stock has been absorbed.

4 Continue cooking and stirring for 20-25 minutes, adding the remaining stock a few ladlefuls at a time. The rice should be *al dente* and the risotto should have a moist and creamy appearance.

5 ▲ Gently stir in the vegetables, the remaining butter and about half the grated Parmesan. Heat through, then stir in the shredded basil and taste for seasoning. Garnish with a few whole basil leaves and serve hot, with the remaining grated Parmesan handed separately.

Variations

Shelled broad beans can be used instead of the peas and asparagus tips instead of the French beans. Use green courgettes if yellow ones are unavailable.

Rice with Peas, Ham and Cheese

Risi e bisi

A classic risotto from the Veneto. Although it is traditionally served as a starter in Italy, risi e bisi makes an excellent supper dish with hot crusty bread.

Ingredients
75 g/3 oz/6 tbsp butter
1 small onion, finely chopped
about 1 litre/1¾ pints/4 cups boiling chicken stock
275 g/10 oz/1½ cups risotto rice
150 ml/¼ pint/⅔ cup dry white wine
225 g/8 oz/2 cups frozen petits pois, thawed
115 g/4 oz cooked ham, diced
salt and freshly ground black pepper
50 g/2 oz/⅔ cup Parmesan cheese, to serve
serves 4

1 ▲ Melt 50 g/2 oz/4 tbsp of the butter in a saucepan until foaming. Add the onion and cook gently for about 3 minutes, stirring frequently, until softened. Have the hot stock ready in an adjacent pan.

2 ▲ Add the rice to the onion mixture. Stir until the grains start to burst, then pour in the wine. Stir until it stops sizzling and most of it has been absorbed, then pour in a little hot stock, with salt and pepper to taste. Stir over a low heat until the stock has been absorbed.

3 ▲ Add the remaining stock, a little at a time, allowing the rice to absorb all the liquid before adding more, and stirring constantly. Add the peas towards the end. After 20–25 minutes, the rice should be *al dente* and the risotto moist and creamy.

4 ▲ Gently stir in the diced cooked ham and the remaining butter. Heat through until the butter has melted, then taste for seasoning. Transfer to a warmed serving bowl. Grate or shave a little Parmesan over the top and hand the rest separately.

Risotto with Four Cheeses

Risotto ai quattro formaggi

This is a very rich dish. Serve it for a dinner-party first course, with sparkling white wine.

Ingredients

- 40 g/1½ oz/3 tbsp butter
- 1 small onion, finely chopped
- 1 litre/1¾ pints/4 cups boiling chicken stock
- 350 g/12 oz/1¾ cups risotto rice
- 200 ml/7 fl oz/scant 1 cup sparkling dry white wine
- 50 g/2 oz/½ cup grated Gruyère cheese
- 50 g/2 oz/½ cup Fontina cheese, diced small
- 50 g/2 oz/½ cup Gorgonzola cheese, crumbled
- 50 g/2 oz/⅔ cup grated Parmesan cheese
- salt and freshly ground black pepper
- fresh flat leaf parsley, to garnish

serves 6

Cook's Tip

If you're feeling extravagant you can use champagne for this risotto, although asti spumante is more often used.

1 Melt the butter in a saucepan until foaming. Add the onion and cook gently, stirring frequently, for about 3 minutes until softened. Have the hot stock ready in an adjacent pan.

2 ▲ Add the rice and stir until the grains start to swell and burst, then add the sparkling wine. Stir until it stops sizzling and most of it has been absorbed by the rice, then pour in a little of the hot stock. Add salt and pepper to taste. Stir over a low heat until the stock has been absorbed.

3 Add more stock, a little at a time, allowing the rice to absorb it before adding more, and stirring constantly. After 20 – 25 minutes the rice will be *al dente* and the risotto creamy.

4 ▲ Turn off the heat under the pan, then add the Gruyère, Fontina, Gorgonzola and 30 ml/2 tbsp of the Parmesan. Stir gently until the cheeses have melted, then taste for seasoning. Tip into a serving bowl and garnish with parsley. Serve the remaining Parmesan separately.

Fried Rice Balls Stuffed with Cheese

Supplì

These deep-fried balls of risotto are stuffed with an inner filling of mozzarella cheese. They are very popular snacks in Rome and central Italy.

Ingredients
1 recipe Risotto with Parmesan Cheese or Risotto with Mushrooms
3 eggs
115 g/4 oz/⅔ cup mozzarella cheese, cut into small dice
plain breadcrumbs, as required
oil, for deep-frying
flour, to coat
serves 4

1 ▲ Allow the risotto to cool completely. (These are even better when formed from risotto made the day before.) Beat 2 of the eggs, and mix them well into the cold risotto.

2 ▲ Use your hands to form the rice mixture into balls the size of a large egg. If the mixture is too moist to hold its shape well, stir in a few tablespoons of breadcrumbs as necessary. Poke a hole into the centre of each ball, fill it with a few small cubes of mozzarella, and close the hole over again with the rice mixture.

3 Heat the oil until a small piece of bread sizzles as soon as it is dropped in (about 185°C/360°F).

4 ▲ Spread some flour on a plate. Beat the remaining egg in a shallow bowl. Sprinkle another plate with breadcrumbs. Roll the balls in the flour, then in the egg, and finally in the breadcrumbs.

5 ▲ Fry them a few at a time in the hot oil until golden and crisp. Drain on paper towels while the remaining balls are frying. Serve hot.

Saffron Risotto

Risotto alla milanese

This classic risotto is always served with osso buco, but makes a delicious first course or light supper dish in its own right.

Ingredients
about 1.2 litres/2 pints/5 cups beef or chicken stock
good pinch of saffron threads or 1 sachet of saffron powder
75 g/3 oz/6 tbsp butter
1 onion, finely chopped
275 g/10 oz/1½ cups risotto rice
75 g/3 oz/1 cup grated Parmesan cheese
salt and freshly ground black pepper
serves 4

1 Bring the stock to the boil, then reduce to a low simmer. Ladle a little stock into a small bowl. Add the saffron threads or powder and leave to infuse.

2 Melt 50 g/2 oz/4 tbsp of the butter in a large saucepan until foaming. Add the onion and cook gently for about 3 minutes, stirring frequently, until softened.

3 Add the rice. Stir until the grains start to swell and burst, then add a few ladlefuls of the stock, with the saffron liquid and salt and pepper to taste. Stir over a low heat until the stock is absorbed. Add the remaining stock, a few ladlefuls at a time, allowing the rice to absorb all the liquid before adding more, and stirring constantly. After 20–25 minutes, the rice should be *al dente* and the risotto golden yellow, moist and creamy.

4 ▲ Gently stir in about two-thirds of the grated Parmesan and the remaining butter. Heat through until the butter has melted, then taste for seasoning. Transfer the risotto to a warmed serving bowl or platter and serve hot, with the remaining grated Parmesan sprinkled on top.

Polenta Elisa

Polenta Elisa

This dish comes from the valley around Lake Como. Serve it solo as a starter, or with a mixed salad and some sliced salami or prosciutto for a midweek supper.

Ingredients
250 ml/8 fl oz/1 cup milk
225 g/8 oz/2 cups pre-cooked polenta
115 g/4 oz/1 cup grated Gruyère cheese
115 g/4 oz/1 cup torta di Dolcelatte cheese, crumbled
50 g/2 oz/¼ cup butter
2 garlic cloves, roughly chopped
a few fresh sage leaves, chopped
salt and freshly ground black pepper
prosciutto, to serve
serves 4

1 Preheat the oven to 200°C/400°F/Gas 6. Lightly butter a 20–25 cm/8–10 in baking dish.

Cook's Tip
Pour the polenta into the boiling liquid in a continuous stream, stirring constantly with a wooden spoon or balloon whisk. If using a whisk, change to a wooden spoon once the polenta thickens.

2 ▲ Bring the milk and 750ml/1¼ pints/3 cups water to the boil in a large saucepan, add 5 ml/1 tsp salt, then tip in the polenta. Cook for about 8 minutes or according to the instructions on the packet.

3 Spoon half the polenta into the baking dish and level. Cover with half the grated Gruyère and crumbled Dolcelatte. Spoon the remaining polenta evenly over the top and sprinkle with the remaining cheeses.

4 Melt the butter in a small saucepan until foaming, add the garlic and sage and fry, stirring, until the butter turns golden brown.

5 ▲ Drizzle the butter mixture over the polenta and cheese and grind black pepper liberally over the top. Bake for 5 minutes. Serve hot, with slices of prosciutto.

Polenta

Polenta

Polenta is a form of cornmeal. It is eaten in northern Italy in place of rice or pasta.

Ingredients
1.5 litres/2½ pints/6¼ cups water
15 ml/1 tbsp salt
350 g/12 oz/2½ cups polenta flour
serves 4–6

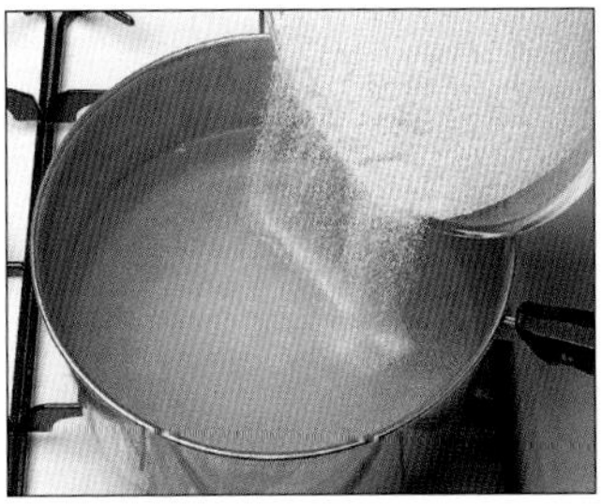

1 ▲ Bring the water to a boil in a large heavy saucepan. Add the salt. Reduce the heat to a simmer, and begin to add the polenta flour in a fine rain. Stir constantly with a whisk until the polenta has all been incorporated.

2 ▲ Switch to a long-handled wooden spoon, and continue to stir the polenta over low to moderate heat until it is a thick mass, and pulls away from the sides of the pan. This may take from 25–50 minutes, depending on the type of polenta used. For best results, never stop stirring the polenta until you remove it from the heat.

3 ▲ When the polenta is cooked, spoon it into a large slightly wet bowl, wait 5 minutes, and turn it out onto a serving platter. Serve it with a meat or tomato sauce, or follow the instructions given in the recipes on the following pages.

Fried Polenta

Polenta fritta

Leftover polenta can be fried, making a crispy appetizer to serve with drinks or antipasti.

Ingredients
cold leftover polenta
oil, for deep-frying
flour, for dredging
salt and freshly ground black pepper
serves 6–8 as an appetizer

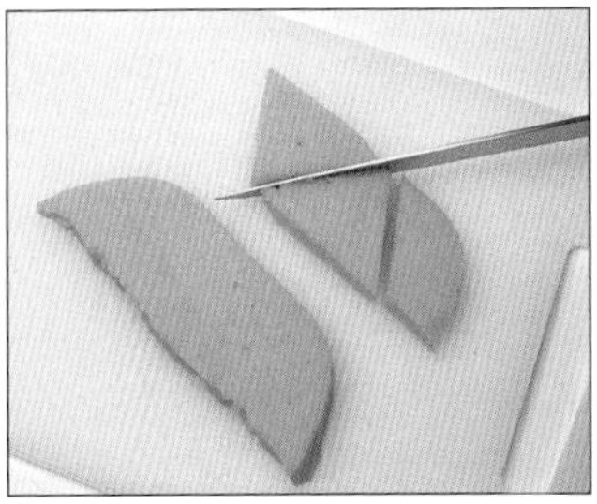

1 ▲ Cut the polenta into slices about 1 cm/½ inch thick. Cut the slices into triangles or rounds.

2 Heat the oil until a small piece of bread sizzles as soon as it is dropped in (about 185°C/360°F).

3 ▲ Season the flour with salt and pepper. Dredge the pieces lightly in the flour, shaking off any excess.

4 ▲ Fry the polenta, a few pieces at a time, until golden and crisp. Drain on paper towels while the remaining pieces are frying. Serve at once.

Baked Polenta with Tomato Sauce

Polenta al forno

Polenta, or cornmeal, is a staple food in Italy, fulfilling much the same role as rice, bread or potatoes by providing the starchy base for a meal. It is cooked like a sort of porridge, and eaten soft, or – as here – set, cut into shapes, then baked or grilled.

Ingredients
5ml/1 tsp salt
250 g/9 oz/2¼ cups quick-cook polenta
5 ml/1 tsp paprika
2.5 ml/½ tsp ground nutmeg
30 ml/2 tbsp olive oil
1 large onion, finely chopped
2 garlic cloves, crushed
2 x 400 g/14 oz cans chopped tomatoes
15 ml/1 tbsp tomato purée
5 ml/1 tsp sugar
75 g/3 oz Gruyère cheese, grated
salt and freshly ground black pepper
serves 4

1 Preheat the oven to 200°C/400°F/ Gas 6. Line a baking tin (28 x 18 cm/ 11 x 7 in) with clear film. Bring 1 litre/1¾ pints/4 cups water to the boil with the salt.

2 ▲ Pour in the polenta in a steady stream and cook, stirring continuously, for 5 minutes. Beat in the paprika and nutmeg, then pour into the prepared tin and smooth the surface. Leave to cool.

3 Heat the oil in a pan and cook the onion and garlic until soft. Add the tomatoes, tomato purée and sugar. Season. Simmer for 20 minutes.

4 ▲ Turn out the polenta on to a chopping board, and cut into about 12 squares. Place half the squares in a greased ovenproof dish. Spoon over half the tomato sauce, and sprinkle with half the cheese. Repeat the layers. Bake in the oven for about 25 minutes, until golden.

Polenta with Mushroom Sauce

Polenta con salsa di funghi

Polenta, made from maize flour, fulfils the same function as rice, bread or potatoes in forming the starchy base for a meal. Here, it is cooked until it forms a soft dough, then flavoured with Parmesan. Its subtle taste works well with the rich mushroom sauce.

Ingredients

1.2 litres/2 pints/5 cups vegetable stock
350 g/12 oz/3 cups polenta
50 g/2 oz/ $^2/_3$ cup grated Parmesan cheese
salt and freshly ground black pepper

For the sauce

15 g/$^1/_2$ oz/1 cup dried porcini mushrooms
15 ml/1 tbsp olive oil
50 g/2 oz/$^1/_4$ cup butter
1 onion, finely chopped
1 carrot, finely chopped
1 celery stick, finely chopped
2 garlic cloves, crushed
450 g/1 lb/6 cups mixed chestnut and large flat mushrooms, roughly chopped
120 ml/4 fl oz/$^1/_2$ cup red wine
400 g/14 oz can chopped tomatoes
5 ml/1 tsp tomato purée
15 ml/1 tbsp chopped fresh thyme leaves

serves 4

1 ▲ Make the sauce. Put the dried mushrooms in a bowl, add 150 ml/$^1/_4$ pint/$^2/_3$ cup of hot water and soak for 20 minutes. Drain the mushrooms, reserving the liquid, and chop roughly.

2 Heat the oil and butter in a saucepan and add the onion, carrot, celery and garlic. Cook over a low heat for about 5 minutes until the vegetables are beginning to soften, then raise the heat and add the fresh and soaked dried mushrooms to the pan of vegetables. Cook for 8 - 10 minutes until the mushrooms are softened and golden.

3 ▲ Pour in the wine and cook rapidly for 2-3 minutes until reduced, then tip in the tomatoes and reserved mushroom liquid. Stir in the tomato purée with the thyme and plenty of salt and pepper. Lower the heat and simmer for 20 minutes until the sauce is rich and thick.

Cook's Tip

The polenta will spit during cooking, so use a long-handled spoon and wrap a towel around your hand to protect it while stirring.

4 ▲ Meanwhile, heat the stock in a large heavy saucepan. Add a generous pinch of salt. As soon as it simmers, tip in the polenta in a fine stream, whisking until the mixture is smooth. Cook for 30 minutes, stirring constantly, until the polenta comes away from the pan. Remove from the heat and stir in half the Parmesan and some black pepper, to taste.

5 Divide among four heated bowls and top each with sauce. Sprinkle with the remaining Parmesan.

Polenta with Mushrooms

Polenta con funghi

This dish is delicious made with a mixture of wild and cultivated mushrooms. Just a few dried porcini mushrooms will help to give cultivated mushrooms a more interesting flavour.

Ingredients

10 g/$^{1}/_{4}$ oz/2 tbsp dried porcini mushrooms (omit if using wild mushrooms)
60 ml/4 tbsp olive oil
1 small onion, finely chopped
700 g/1$^{1}/_{2}$lb mushrooms, wild or cultivated, or a combination of both
2 cloves garlic, finely chopped
45 ml/3 tbsp chopped fresh parsley
3 medium tomatoes, peeled and diced
15 ml/1 tbsp tomato paste
175 ml/6 fl oz/$^{3}/_{4}$ cup warm water
$^{1}/_{4}$ tsp fresh thyme leaves, or $^{1}/_{8}$ tsp dried thyme
1 bay leaf
salt and freshly ground black pepper
a few sprigs fresh parsley, to garnish

For the polenta

1.5 litres/2$^{1}/_{2}$ pints/6$^{1}/_{4}$ cups water
15 ml/1 tbsp salt
350 g/12 oz/2$^{1}/_{2}$ cups polenta flour

serves 6

1 ▲ Soak the dried mushrooms, if using, in a small cup of warm water for 20 minutes. Remove the mushrooms with a slotted spoon, and rinse them well in several changes of cool water. Filter the soaking water through a layer of paper towels placed in a sieve, and reserve.

2 In a large frying pan heat the oil, and sauté the onion over low heat until soft and golden.

3 ▲ Clean the fresh mushrooms by wiping them with a damp cloth. Cut into slices. When the onion is soft add the mushrooms to the pan. Stir over moderate to high heat until they give up their liquid. Add the garlic, parsley and diced tomatoes. Cook for 4–5 minutes more.

4 ▲ Soften the tomato paste in the warm water (use only 100 ml/4 fl oz/$^{1}/_{2}$ cup water if you are using dried mushrooms). Add it to the pan with the herbs. Add the dried mushrooms and soaking liquid, if using them. Mix well and season with salt and pepper. Lower the heat to low to moderate and cook for 15–20 minutes. Set aside while you make the polenta.

5 ▲ Bring the water to a boil in a large heavy saucepan. Add the salt. Reduce the heat to a simmer, and begin to add the polenta in a fine rain. Stir constantly with a whisk until the polenta has all been incorporated.

6 Switch to a long-handled wooden spoon, and continue to stir the polenta over low to moderate heat until it is a thick mass, and pulls away from the sides of the pan. This may take from 25–50 minutes, depending on the type of polenta used. For best results, never stop stirring the polenta until you remove it from the heat.

7 ▲ When the polenta has almost finished cooking, gently reheat the mushroom sauce. To serve, spoon the polenta onto a warmed serving platter. Make a well in the centre. Spoon some of the mushroom sauce into the well, and garnish with parsley. Serve at once, passing the remaining sauce in a separate bowl.

Grilled Polenta with Gorgonzola

Polenta alla griglia

Grilled polenta is delicious, and is a good way of using up cold polenta. Try it with any soft flavourful cheese. Plain grilled polenta is a good accompaniment to stews and soups.

Ingredients

1.5 litres/2$^1/_2$ pints/6$^1/_4$ cups water
15 ml/1 tbsp salt
350 g/12 oz/2$^1/_2$ cups polenta flour
225 g/8 oz/1$^1/_4$ cups Gorgonzola or other cheese, at room temperature

serves 6–8 as a snack or appetizer

1 ▲ Bring the water to a boil in a large heavy-bottomed saucepan. Add the salt. Reduce the heat to a simmer, and begin to add the polenta in a fine rain. Stir constantly with a whisk until the polenta has all been incorporated.

2 ▲ Switch to a long-handled wooden spoon, and continue to stir the polenta over low to moderate heat until it is a thick mass, and pulls away from the sides of the pan. This may take from 25–50 minutes, depending on the type of polenta used. For best results, never stop stirring the polenta until you remove it from the heat.

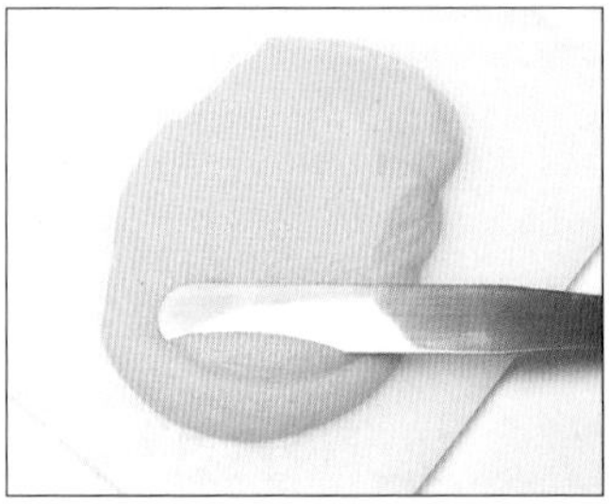

3 ▲ When the polenta is cooked, sprinkle a work surface or large board with a little water. Spread the polenta out on to the surface in a layer 1.5 cm/ $^3/_4$ in thick. Allow to cool completely. Preheat the grill.

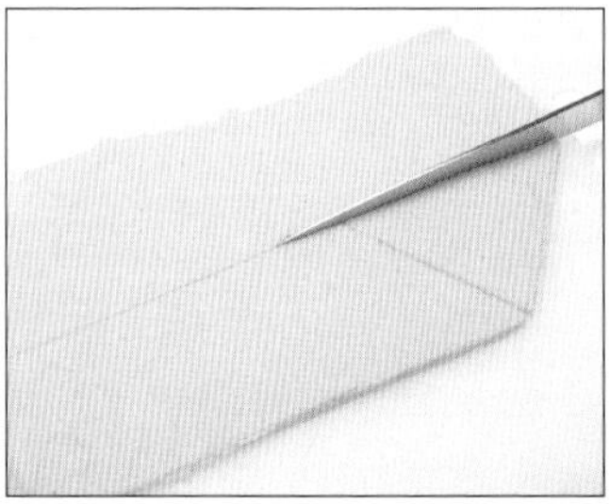

4 ▲ Cut the polenta into triangles. Grill until hot and speckled with brown on both sides. Spread with the Gorgonzola or other cheese. Serve immediately.

Polenta Baked with Cheese

Polenta pasticciata

Cold polenta can be cut into slices and baked in layers with cheese and other ingredients. The traditional way of cutting it is with a wooden knife or a piece of thick thread.

Ingredients

75 g/3 oz/generous $^1/_3$ cup butter
warm cooked polenta, made with 250 g/9 oz/2 cups polenta flour
45 ml/3 tbsp olive oil
2 medium onions, thinly sliced
pinch of grated nutmeg
salt and freshly ground black pepper
150 g/5 oz/$^3/_4$ cup mozzarella or sharp Cheddar cheese, cut into thin slices
45 ml/3 tbsp finely chopped fresh parsley
$^1/_3$ cup freshly grated Parmesan cheese

serves 4–6

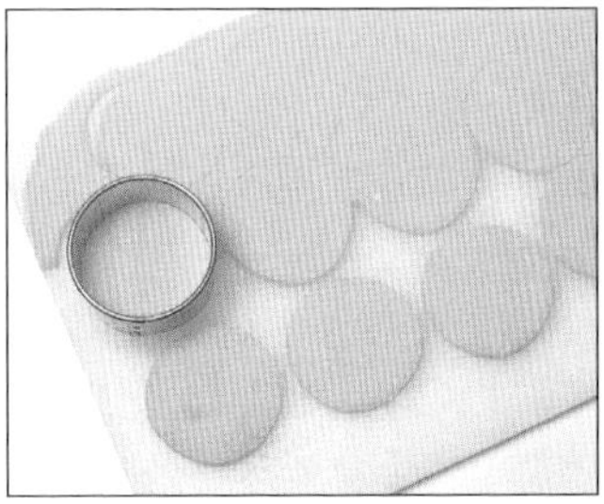

1 ▲ Stir a third of the butter into the cooked polenta. Sprinkle a work surface with a little water. Spread the polenta out in a layer 1 cm/$^1/_2$in thick. Allow to cool. Cut into 6 cm/2$^1/_2$in rounds.

2 ▲ Heat the oil in a medium pan with 15 g/$^1/_2$ oz/1 tbsp of the remaining butter. Add the onions, and stir over low heat until soft.

3 ▲ Season the onions with nutmeg, salt and pepper. Preheat the oven to 190°C/375°F. Butter an oven-proof dish. Spread a few of the onion slices in the bottom of the dish. Cover with a layer of polenta rounds. Dot with butter.

4 ▲ Add a layer of the sliced mozzarella or Cheddar, and a sprinkling of parsley and Parmesan. Season with salt and pepper. Make another layer of the onions, and continue the layers in order, ending with the Parmesan. Dot the top with butter and bake for 20–25 minutes, or until the cheese has melted. Serve from the baking dish.

Basic Pizza Dough

Pizza dough is leavened with yeast. It usually rises once before being rolled out and filled. The dough can be baked in pizza pans or baked directly on a flat baking sheet.

Ingredients

25 g/1 oz/2½ tbsp fresh bread yeast or 15 g/½ oz/1½ tbsp active dried yeast
250 ml/ 8 fl oz/1 cup lukewarm water
pinch of sugar
5 ml/1 tsp salt
350–400 g/12–14 oz/3–3½ cups plain flour, preferably strong

serves 4 as a main course or 8 as an appetizer

1 ▲ Warm a medium mixing bowl by swirling some hot water in it. Drain. Place the yeast in the bowl, and pour on the warm water. Stir in the sugar, mix with a fork, and allow to stand until the yeast has dispersed and starts to foam, 5-10 minutes.

2 ▲ Use a wooden spoon to mix in the salt and about one-third of the flour. Mix in another third of the flour, stirring with the spoon until the dough forms a mass and begins to pull away from the sides of the bowl.

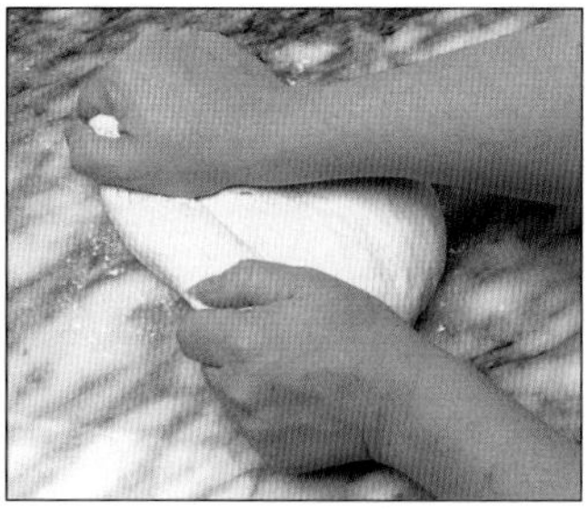

3 ▲ Sprinkle some of the remaining flour onto a smooth work surface. Remove the dough from the bowl and begin to knead it, working in the remaining flour a little at a time. Knead for 8-10 minutes. By the end the dough should be elastic and smooth. Form it into a ball.

4 Lightly oil a mixing bowl. Place the dough in the bowl. Stretch a moistened and wrung-out dish towel across the top of the bowl, and leave it to stand in a warm place until the dough has doubled in volume, about 40-50 minutes or more, depending on the type of yeast used. (If you do not have a warm enough place, turn the oven on to medium heat for 10 minutes before you knead the dough. Turn it off. Place the bowl with the dough in it in the turned-off oven with the door closed and let it rise there.) To test whether the dough has risen enough, poke two fingers into the dough. If the indentations remain, the dough is ready.

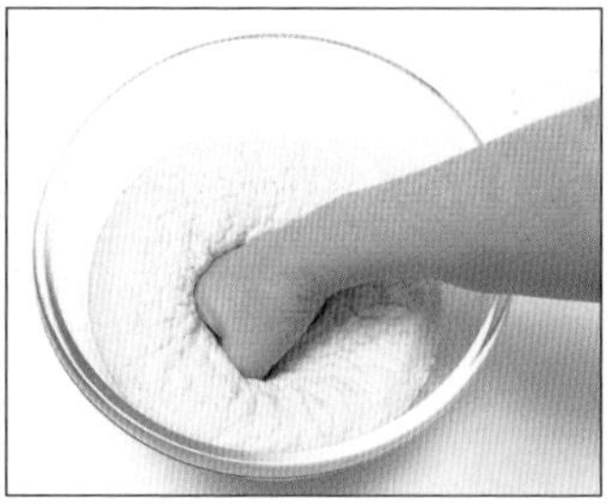

5 ▲ Punch the dough down with your fist to release the air. Knead the dough for 1-2 minutes.

6 If you want to make 2 medium pizzas, divide the dough into 2 balls. If you want to make 4 individual pizzas (in pans 26 cm/10½ in in diameter), divide the dough into 4 balls. Pat the ball of dough out into a flat circle on a lightly floured surface. With a rolling pin, roll it out to a thickness of about 5-7 mm/⅜-¼in. If you are using a pizza pan, roll the dough out about 7 mm/¼ in larger than the size of the pan to allow for the rim of the crust.

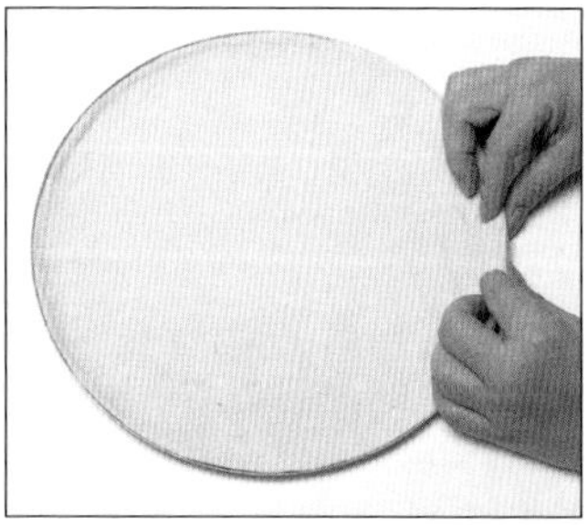

7 ▲ Place in the lightly oiled pan, folding the extra dough under to make a thicker rim around the edge. If you are baking the pizza without a round pan, press some of the dough from the center of the circle towards the edge, to make a thicker rim. Place it on a lightly oiled flat baking sheet. The dough is now ready for filling.

~ COOK'S TIP ~

This basic dough can be used for other recipes in this book, such as Focaccia, Breadsticks, Calzone and Sicilian Closed Pizza. The dough may be frozen at the end of step 7, and thawed before filling.

Wholewheat Pizza Dough

Pizza dough can also be made with wholewheat flour, although it is easier to handle and more elastic if a proportion of white flour is used. This dough can be used in any recipe calling for Basic Pizza Dough.

Ingredients

25 g/1 oz/2½ tbsp fresh bread yeast or 15 g/½ oz/1½ tbsp active dried yeast
250 ml/8 fl oz/1 cup lukewarm water
pinch of sugar
30 ml/2 tbsp olive oil
5 ml/1 tsp salt
150 g/5 oz/1¼ cups plain white flour
250 g/ 9 oz/2 cups stoneground wholewheat flour

serves 4 as a main course or 8 as an appetizer

1 Warm a medium mixing bowl by swirling some hot water in it. Drain. Place the yeast in the bowl, and pour on the warm water. Stir in the sugar, mix with a fork, and allow to stand until the yeast has dispersed and starts to foam, 5–10 minutes.

2 ▲ Use a wooden spoon to mix in the olive oil and the salt, and the white flour. Mix in about half of the wholewheat flour, stirring with the spoon until the dough forms a mass and begins to pull away from the sides of the bowl.

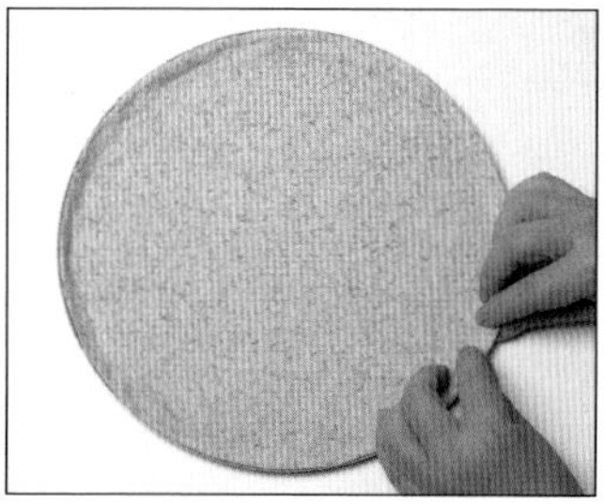

3 ▲ Proceed with steps 3–7 as for Basic Pizza Dough, punching down the risen dough, and kneading until ready to roll out and place in a pan.

To Make the Dough in a Food Processor

1 ▲ Have all the ingredients ready and measured out. In a small pitcher or bowl add the yeast to the warm water. Stir in the sugar, and allow to stand until the yeast has dissolved, 5–10 minutes.

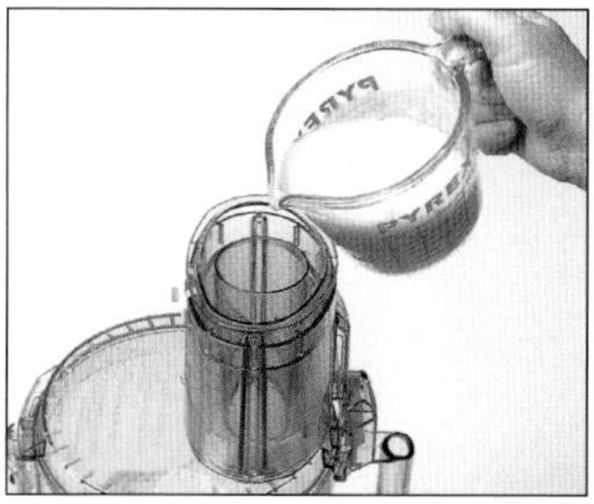

2 ▲ Fit the food processor with the metal blades. Place the salt and three-quarters of the flour in the bowl of the food processor. Turn it on, and pour in the yeast mixture and olive oil through the opening at the top. Continue processing until the dough forms one or two balls. Turn the machine off, open it, and touch the dough. If it still feels sticky, add a little more flour, and process again until it is incorporated.

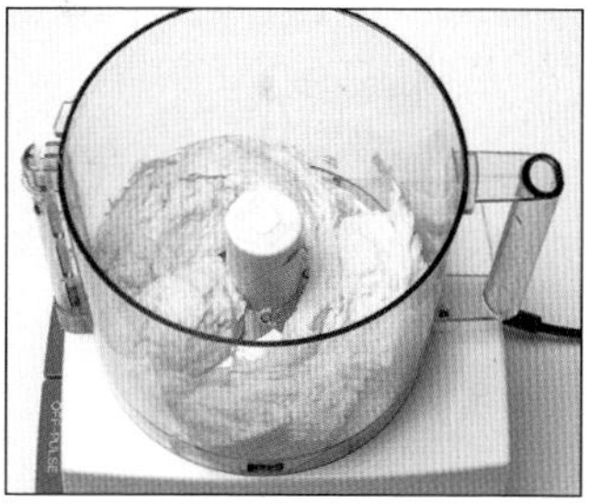

3 ▲ Remove the dough from the processor. Knead it for about 2–3 minutes on a surface dusted with the remaining flour. Form the dough into a ball, and proceed with Step 4 of Basic Pizza Dough.

Cheese and Tomato Pizza

Pizza alla Margherita

The Margherita is named after the nineteenth-century Queen of Italy, and is one of the most popular of all pizzas.

Ingredients
450 g/1 lb peeled plum tomatoes, fresh or canned, weighed whole, without extra juice
1 recipe Basic Pizza Dough, rolled out
350 g/12 oz/1 3/4 cups mozzarella cheese, cut into small dice
10–12 leaves fresh basil, torn
60 ml/4 tbsp freshly grated Parmesan cheese (optional)
salt and freshly ground black pepper
45 ml/3 tbsp olive oil
serves 4

1 Preheat the oven to 250°C/475°F/ gas 9 for at least 20 minutes before baking. Strain the tomatoes through the medium holes of a food mill placed over a bowl, scraping in all the pulp.

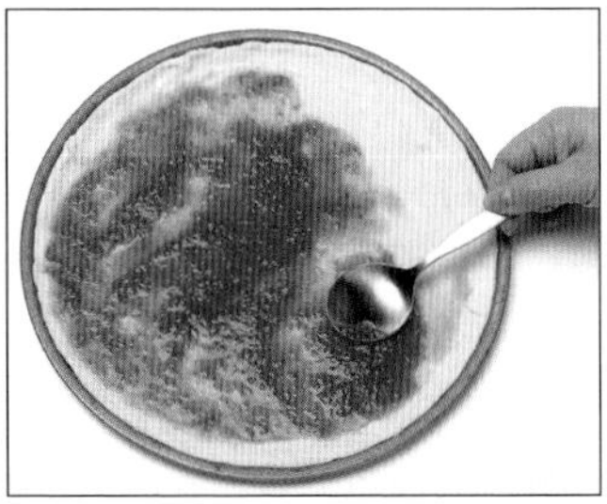

2 ▲ Spread the puréed tomatoes onto the prepared pizza dough, leaving the rim uncovered.

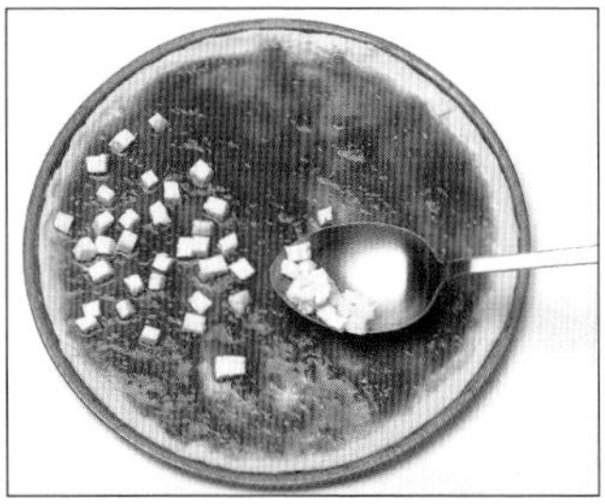

3 ▲ Sprinkle evenly with the mozzarella. Dot with basil. Sprinkle with Parmesan if using, salt and pepper and olive oil. Immediately place the pizzas in the oven. Bake for about 15–20 minutes, or until the crust is golden brown and the cheeses are melted and bubbling.

Pizza with Mozzarella and Anchovies

Pizza alla napoletana

If you ask for a pizza in the Neapolitan manner anywhere in Italy other than in Naples, you will be given this pizza with anchovies.

Ingredients
450 g/1 lb peeled plum tomatoes, fresh or canned, weighed whole, without extra juice
1 recipe Basic Pizza Dough, rolled out
40 g/1 1/2 oz/3 tbsp anchovy fillets in oil, drained and cut into pieces
350 g/12 oz/1 3/4 cups mozzarella cheese, cut into small dice
5 ml/1 tsp oregano leaves, fresh or dried
salt and freshly ground black pepper
45 ml/3 tbsp olive oil
serves 4

1 Preheat the oven to 250°C/475°F/ gas 9 for at least 20 minutes before baking. Strain the tomatoes through the medium holes of a food mill placed over a bowl, scraping in all the pulp.

2 ▲ Spread the puréed tomatoes on the pizza dough, leaving the rim uncovered. Dot with the anchovy pieces and the mozzarella.

3 ▲ Sprinkle with oregano, salt and pepper, and olive oil. Immediately place the pizza in the oven. Bake for about 15–20 minutes, or until the crust is golden brown and the cheese is bubbling.

Four Seasons Pizza

Pizza quattro stagioni

The topping on this pizza is divided into four quarters, one for each "season". You may replace the suggested ingredients with any other seasonal favourites.

Ingredients

450 g/1lb peeled plum tomatoes, fresh or canned, weighed whole, without extra juice
75 ml/5 tbsp olive oil
115 g/4 oz/1 cup mushrooms, thinly sliced
1 clove garlic, finely chopped
1 recipe Basic Pizza Dough, rolled out
350 g/12 oz/1$^{3}/_{4}$ cups mozzarella cheese, cut into small dice
4 thin slices of ham, cut into 5 cm/2in squares
32 black olives, stoned and halved
8 artichoke hearts marinated in oil, drained and cut in half
5 ml/1 tsp oregano leaves, fresh or dried
salt and freshly ground black pepper
serves 4

1 ▲ Preheat the oven to 250°C/475°F/ gas 9 for at least 20 minute before baking the pizza. Strain the tomatoes through the medium holes of a food mill placed over a bowl, scraping in all the pulp.

2 Heat 2 tbsp of the oil in a frying pan and lightly sauté the mushrooms. Stir in the garlic and set aside.

3 ▲ Spread the puréed tomato on the prepared pizza dough, leaving the rim uncovered. Sprinkle evenly with the mozzarella. Spread mushrooms over one-quarter of each pizza.

4 ▲ Arrange the ham on another quarter, and the olives and artichoke hearts on the two remaining quarters. Sprinkle with oregano, salt and pepper, and the remaining olive oil. Immediately place the pizza in the oven. Bake for about 15–20 minutes, or until the crust is golden brown and the topping is bubbling.

Pizza with Fresh Vegetables

Pizza all'ortolana

This pizza can be made with any combination of fresh vegetables. Most will benefit from being blanched or sautéed before being baked on the pizza.

Ingredients
400 g/14 oz peeled plum tomatoes, fresh or canned, weighed whole, without extra juice
2 medium broccoli spears
225 g/8oz fresh asparagus
2 small courgettes
75 ml/5 tbsp olive oil
50 g/2 oz/$^{1}/_{3}$ cup shelled peas, fresh or frozen
4 spring onions, sliced
1 recipe Basic Pizza Dough, rolled out
75 g/3 oz/$^{1}/_{2}$ cup mozzarella cheese, cut into small dice
10 leaves fresh basil, torn
2 cloves garlic, finely chopped
salt and freshly ground black pepper
serves 4

1 Preheat the oven to 250°C/475°F/ gas 9 for at least 20 minutes before baking the pizza. Strain the tomatoes through the medium holes of a food mill placed over a bowl, scraping in all the pulp.

2 ▲ Peel the broccoli stems and the lower parts of the asparagus, and blanch with the courgette in a large pan of boiling water for 4–5 minutes. Drain. Cut into bite-size pieces.

3 Heat 30 ml/2 tbsp of the olive oil in a small pan. Stir in the peas and spring onions, and cook for 5-6 minutes, stirring often. Remove from the heat.

4 ▲ Spread the puréed tomatoes on to the pizza dough, leaving the rim uncovered. Add the other vegetables, spreading them evenly over the tomatoes.

5 ▲ Sprinkle with the mozzarella, basil, garlic, salt and pepper, and remaining olive oil. Immediately place the pizza in the oven. Bake for about 20 minutes, or until the crust is golden brown and the cheese has melted.

Pizza with Sausage

Pizza con salsicce

Use sausages with a high meat content for this topping.

Ingredients
450 g/1 lb peeled plum tomatoes, fresh or canned, weighed whole, without extra juice
1 recipe Basic Pizza Dough, rolled out
350 g/12 oz/1$^{3}/_{4}$ cups mozzarella cheese, cut into small dice
225 g/8 oz/1$^{1}/_{2}$ cups sausage meat, removed from the casings and crumbled
5 ml/1 tsp oregano leaves, fresh or dried
salt and freshly ground black pepper
45 ml/3 tbsp olive oil
serves 4

1 Preheat the oven to 250°C/475°F/ gas 9 for at least 20 minutes before baking the pizza. Strain the tomatoes through the medium holes of a food mill placed over a bowl, scraping in all the pulp.

2 ▲ Spread some of the puréed tomatoes on the prepared pizza dough, leaving the rim uncovered. Sprinkle evenly with the mozzarella. Add the sausage meat in a layer.

3 ▲ Sprinkle with oregano, salt and pepper, and olive oil. Immediately place the pizza in the preheated oven. Bake for about 15–20 minutes, or until the crust is golden brown and the cheese is bubbling.

Pizza with Four Cheeses

Pizza con quattro formaggi

Any combination of cheeses can be used, but choose cheeses which are different in character.

Ingredients
1 recipe Basic Pizza Dough, rolled out
75 g/3 oz/$^{1}/_{2}$ cup Gorgonzola or other blue cheese, thinly sliced
75 g/3 oz/$^{1}/_{2}$ cup mozzarella cheese, finely diced
75 g/3 oz/$^{1}/_{2}$ cup goat's cheese, thinly sliced
75 g/3 oz/$^{1}/_{2}$ cup sharp Cheddar cheese, coarsely grated
4 leaves fresh sage,torn into pieces, or 45 ml/3 tbsp chopped fresh parsley
salt and freshly ground black pepper
45 ml/3 tbsp olive oil
serves 4

1 Preheat the oven to 250°C/475°F/ gas 9 for at least 20 minutes before baking the pizza. Arrange the Gorgonzola on one quarter of the pizza and the mozzarella on another, leaving the edge free.

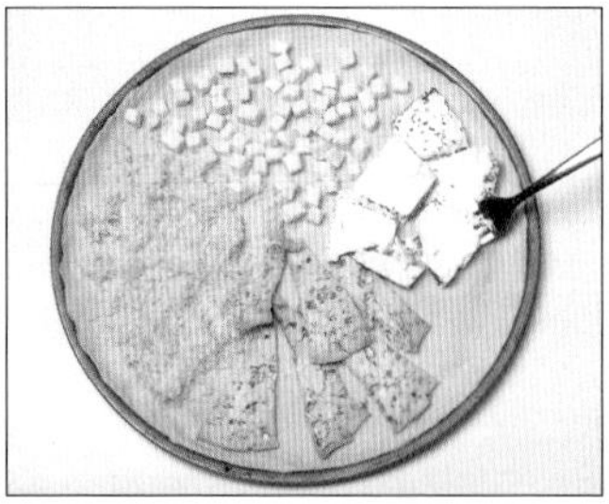

2 ▲ Arrange the goat's and Cheddar cheeses on the remaining two quarters.

~ VARIATION ~

For an unusual taste, substitute 75 g/3oz sliced smoked cheese for one of the cheeses.

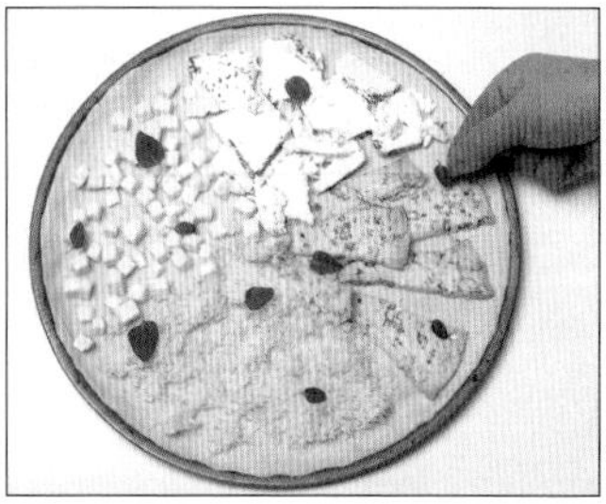

3 ▲ Sprinkle with the herbs, salt and pepper, and olive oil. Immediately place the pizza in the oven. Bake for about 15–20 minutes, or until the crust is golden brown and the cheeses are bubbling.

Mediterranean Pizza

Pizza mediterranea

The combination of favourite Mediterranean ingredients makes a delicious modern pizza topping.

Ingredients

12 sun-dried tomatoes, dry or in oil, drained
350 g/12 oz/$1^{3}/_{4}$ cups goat's cheese, sliced as thinly as possible
1 recipe Basic Pizza Dough, rolled out
30 g/2 tbsp capers in brine or salt, rinsed
10 leaves fresh basil
salt and freshly ground black pepper
60 ml/3 tbsp olive oil
serves 4

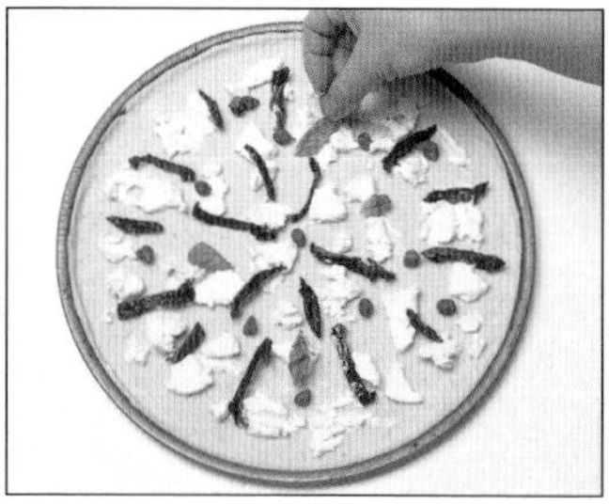

1 Preheat the oven to 250°C/475°F/ gas 9 for at least 20 minutes before baking the pizza. Place the tomatoes in a small bowl, cover with hot water, and leave to soak for 15 minutes. Drain and cut into thin slices. (The soaking water may be saved to add to a pasta sauce or soup.)

2 ▲ Arrange the cheese on the prepared pizza dough, leaving the rim uncovered. Dot the pizza with the tomato slices.

3 ▲ Sprinkle with the capers and basil leaves. Allow to rise for 10 minutes before baking.

4 Sprinkle with salt, pepper and olive oil. Place the pizza in the oven. Bake for about 15–20 minutes, or until the crust is golden brown.

Pizza with Onions and Olives

Pizza con cipolle e olive

Onions cooked slowly to release their sweetness contrast with the salty bitterness of the olives.

Ingredients

90 ml/6 tbsp olive oil
4 medium onions, finely sliced
salt and freshly ground black pepper
1 recipe Basic Pizza Dough, rolled out
350 g/12 oz/$1^{3}/_{4}$ cups mozzarella cheese, cut into small dice
32 black olives, pitted and halved
60 ml/3 tbsp chopped fresh parsley
serves 4

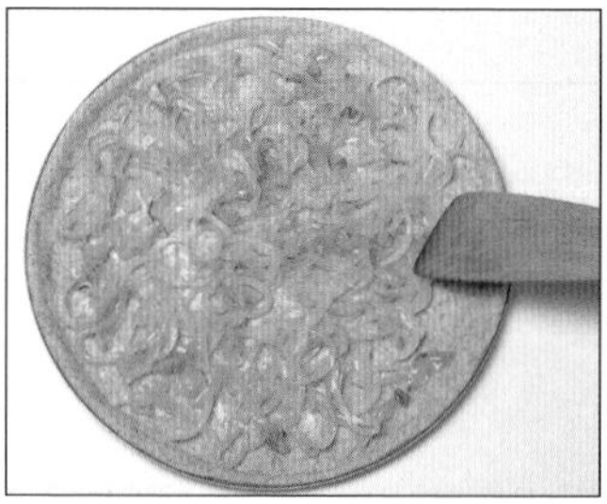

1 Preheat the oven to 250°C/475°F/ gas 9 for at least 20 minutes before baking the pizza.Heat half the olive oil in a large frying pan.Add the sliced onions, and cook over low heat until soft, translucent, and just beginning to turn brown, 12–15 minutes. Season with salt and pepper, and remove from the heat.

2 ▲ Spread the onions over the prepared pizza dough in an even layer, leaving the rim uncovered. Sprinkle with the mozzarella.

3 ▲ Dot with the olives. Sprinkle with parsley and the remaining olive oil. Immediately place the pizza in the oven. Bake for about 15–20 minutes, or until the crust is golden brown and the cheese is bubbling.

Pizza with Seafood

Pizza con frutti di mare

Any combination of shellfish or other seafood can be used as a pizza topping.

Ingredients

450 g/1 lb peeled plum tomatoes, fresh or canned, weighed whole, without extra juice
175 g/6 oz small squid
225 g/8 oz fresh mussels
1 recipe Basic Pizza Dough, rolled out
175 g/6 oz prawns, raw or cooked, peeled and deveined
2 cloves garlic, finely chopped
45 ml/3 tbsp chopped fresh parsley
salt and freshly ground black pepper
45 ml/3 tbsp olive oil
serves 4

1 ▲ Preheat the oven to 250°C/475°F/gas 6 for at least 20 minutes before baking the pizza. Strain the tomatoes through the medium holes of a food mill placed over a bowl, scraping in all the pulp.

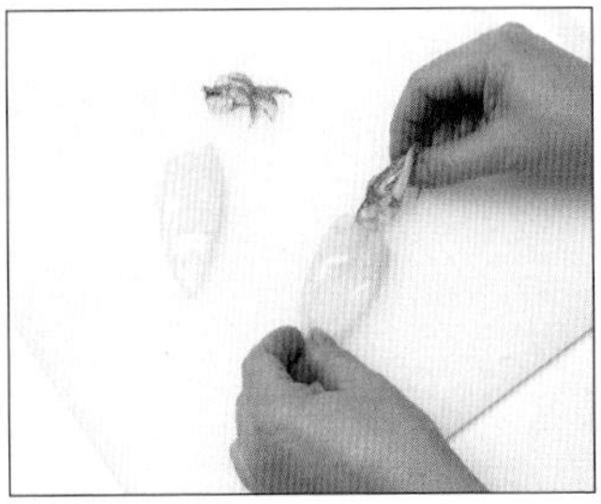

2 ▲ Working near the sink, clean the squid by first peeling off the thin skin from the body section. Rinse well. Pull the head and tentacles away from the sac section. Some of the intestines will come away with the head.

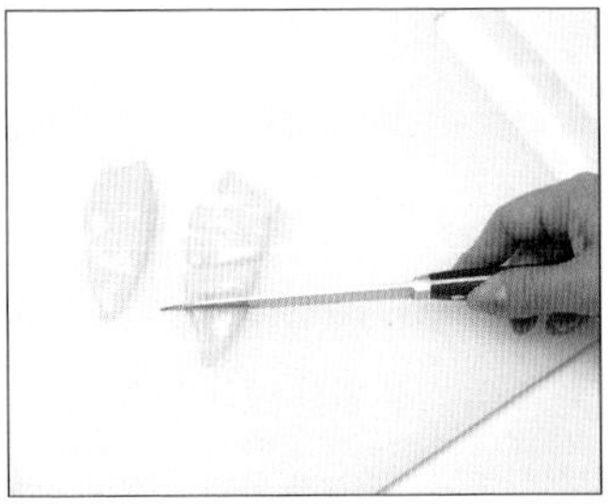

3 ▲ Remove and discard the translucent quill and any remaining insides from the sac. Sever the tentacles from the head, and discard the head and intestines. Remove the small hard beak from the base of the tentacles. Rinse the sac and tentacles under running water. Drain. Slice the sacs into rings 5mm/$^1/_4$ in thick.

4 ▲ Scrape any barnacles off the mussels, and scrub well with a stiff brush. Rinse in several changes of cold water. Place the mussels in a saucepan and heat until they open. Lift them out with a slotted spoon, and remove to a side dish. (Discard any that do not open.) Break off the empty half shells, and discard.

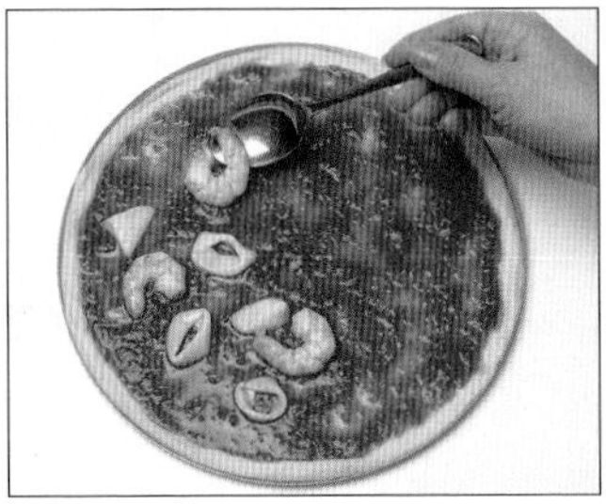

5 ▲ Spread the puréed tomatoes on the prepared pizza dough, leaving the rim uncovered. Dot evenly with the prawns and squid rings and tentacles. Sprinkle with the garlic, parsley, salt and pepper, and olive oil. Immediately place the pizza in the oven. Bake for about 8 minutes.

6 ▲ Remove from the oven, and add the mussels in the half shells. Return to the oven and bake for 7–10 minutes more, or until the crust is golden.

~ VARIATION ~

Fresh clams may be added to this pizza. Scrub them well under cold running water, then cook them in the same way as the mussels. Discard any that do not open. Break off the empty half shells, and discard. Add the clams to the pizza after 8 minutes of baking.

Pizza with Herbs

Pizza in bianco con erbe aromatiche

This simple topping of mixed fresh herbs, olive oil and salt makes a delicious hot pizza which can also be eaten as a bread. In Italy it is often served in pizzerias as an appetizer.

Ingredients
1 recipe Basic Pizza Dough, rolled out
60 ml/4 tbsp chopped mixed fresh herbs, such as thyme, rosemary, basil, parsley or sage
salt, to taste
90 ml/6 tbsp extra-virgin olive oil
serves 4

1 ▲ Preheat the oven to 250°C/475°F/ gas 9 for at least 20 minutes before baking the pizza. Sprinkle the prepared dough with the herbs, and salt.

2 ▲ Sprinkle with olive oil. Immediately place the pizza in the oven. Bake for about 20 minutes, or until the crust is golden brown.

Sicilian Closed Pizza

Sfinciuni

These can be stuffed with any pizza topping.

Ingredients
1 recipe Basic Pizza Dough, risen once
30 ml/2 tbsp coarse cornmeal
3 hard-boiled eggs, peeled and sliced
50 g/2 oz/$^1/_4$ cup anchovy fillets, drained and chopped
12 olives, stoned and halved
8 leaves fresh basil, torn into pieces
6 medium tomatoes, peeled, seeded and diced
2 cloves garlic, finely chopped
freshly ground black pepper
175 g/6 oz/1$^1/_2$ cups grated caciocavallo or Pecorino cheese
olive oil, for brushing
serves 4–6

1 Preheat the oven to 230°C/450°F/ gas 8. Punch the dough and knead lightly for 3–4 minutes. Divide the dough into two pieces, one slightly larger than the other. Lightly oil a round pizza pan 38 cm/15 inches in diameter. Sprinkle with the cornmeal. Roll or press the larger piece of dough into a round slightly bigger than the pan.

2 ▲ Transfer to the pan, bringing the dough up the sides of the pan to the rim. Fill the pie by placing the sliced eggs in the bottom in a layer, leaving the edges of the dough uncovered. Dot with the anchovies, olives and basil.

3 Spread the diced tomatoes over the other ingredients. Sprinkle with garlic and pepper. Top with the grated cheese.

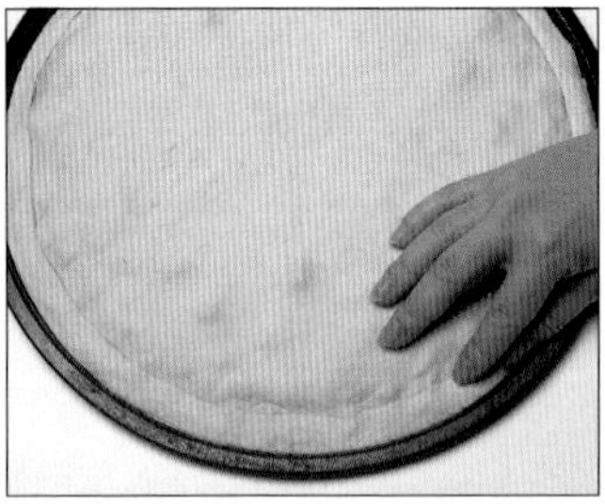

4 ▲ Roll or press the other piece of dough into a circle the same size as the pan. Place it over the filling. Roll the edge of the bottom dough over it, and crimp together to make a border.

5 Brush the top and edges of the pie with olive oil. Bake for 30–40 minutes, or until the top is golden brown. Allow to stand for 5–8 minutes before slicing into wedges.

Calzones

Calzone

A calzone is a pizza folded over to enclose its filling. It can be made large or small, and stuffed with any of the flat pizza fillings. Calzones can be eaten hot or cold.

Ingredients

1 recipe Basic Pizza Dough, risen once
350 g/12 oz/$1^{1}/_{2}$ cups ricotta cheese
175 g/6 oz/$^{3}/_{4}$ cup ham, cut into small dice
6 medium tomatoes, peeled, seeded and diced
8 leaves fresh basil, torn into pieces
175 g/6 oz/1 cup mozzarella cheese, cut into small dice
60 ml/4 tbsp freshly grated Parmesan cheese
salt and freshly ground black pepper
olive oil, for brushing
serves 4

1 ▲ Preheat the oven to 250°C/475°F/gas 9 for at least 20 minutes before baking the calzoni. Punch the dough down and knead it lightly. Divide the dough into 4 balls.

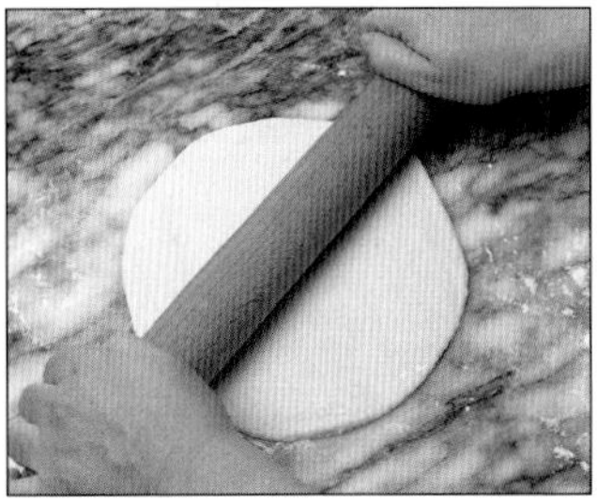

2 ▲ Roll each ball out into a flat circle about 5 mm/$^{1}/_{4}$ in thick.

3 ▲ Combine all the filling ingredients in a bowl, and mix well. Season with salt and pepper.

4 ▲ Divide the filling between the 4 circles of dough, placing it on half of each circle and allowing a border of 2 cm/1 in all around.

~ COOK'S TIP ~

The calzone is a speciality of Naples. Calzone means "trouser leg" in Italian. This pizza was so named because it resembled a leg of the baggy trousers worn by Neapolitan men in the 18th and 19th centuries. Calzones are now usually round but were traditionally made from rectangular pieces of dough folded over a long central filling.

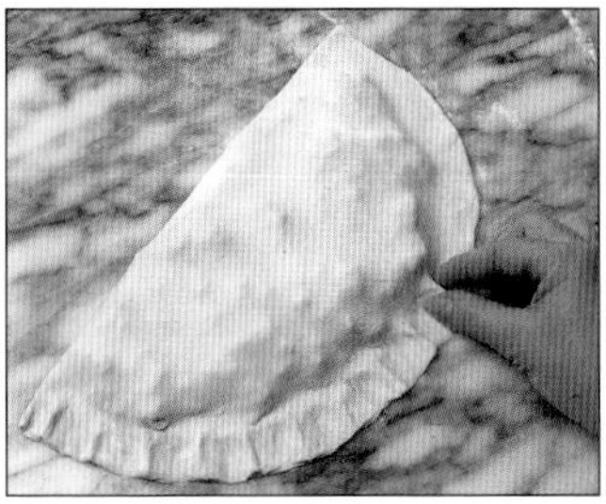

5 ▲ Fold the other half of the circle over. Crimp the edges of the dough together with your fingers to seal.

6 ▲ Place the calzones on lightly oiled baking sheets. Brush the tops lightly with olive oil. Bake in the preheated oven for about 15–20 minutes, or until the tops are golden brown and the dough is puffed.

Butternut Squash and Sage Pizza

Pizza con zucca e salvia

The combination of the sweet butternut squash, sage and sharp goat's cheese works wonderfully on this pizza. Pumpkin and winter squashes are popular in northern Italy.

Ingredients
15 g/½ oz/1 tbsp butter
30 ml/2 tbsp olive oil
2 shallots, finely chopped
1 butternut squash, peeled, seeded and cubed, about 450 g/1 lb prepared weight
16 sage leaves
1 quantity risen Pizza Dough
1 quantity Tomato Sauce
115 g/4 oz/1 cup mozzarella cheese, sliced
115 g/4 oz/½ cup firm goat's cheese
salt and freshly ground black pepper
serves 4

1 ▲ Preheat the oven to 200°C/400°F/Gas 6. Oil four baking sheets. Put the butter and oil in a roasting tin and heat in the oven for a few minutes. Add the shallots, squash and half the sage leaves. Toss to coat. Roast for 15–20 minutes until tender.

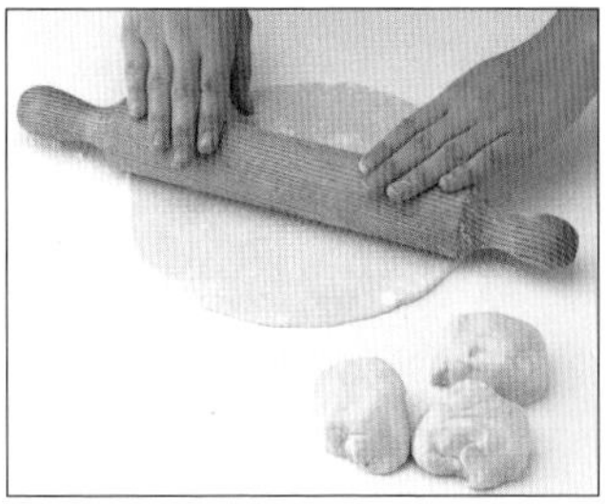

2 ▲ Raise the oven temperature to 220°C/425°F/Gas 7. Divide the pizza dough into four equal pieces and roll out each piece on a lightly floured surface to a 25 cm/10 in round.

3 ▲ Transfer each round to a baking sheet and spread with the tomato sauce, leaving a 1 cm/½ in border all around. Spoon the squash and shallot mixture over the top.

4 ▲ Arrange the slices of mozzarella over the squash mixture and crumble the goat's cheese over. Scatter the remaining sage leaves over and season with plenty of salt and pepper. Bake for 15–20 minutes until the cheese has melted and the crust on each pizza is golden.

Ricotta and Fontina Pizza

Pizza con ricotta e fontina

The earthy mixed mushrooms' flavours are delicious with the creamy cheeses.

Ingredients

For the pizza dough

2.5 ml/½ tsp active dried yeast
pinch of granulated sugar
450 g/1 lb/4 cups strong white flour
5 ml/1 tsp salt
30 ml/2 tbsp olive oil

For the tomato sauce

400 g/14 oz can chopped tomatoes
150 ml/¼ pint/⅔ cup passata
1 large garlic clove, finely chopped
5 ml/1 tsp dried oregano
1 bay leaf
10 ml/2 tsp malt vinegar
salt and freshly ground black pepper

For the topping

30 ml/2 tbsp olive oil
1 garlic clove, finely chopped
350 g/12 oz/4 cups mixed mushrooms (chestnut, flat or button), sliced
30 ml/2 tbsp chopped fresh oregano, plus whole leaves, to garnish
250 g/9 oz/generous 1 cup ricotta cheese
225 g/8 oz Fontina cheese, sliced

makes 4 x 25 cm/10 in thin crust pizzas

1 ▲ Make the dough. Put 300 ml/½ pint/1¼ cups warm water in a measuring jug. Add the yeast and sugar and leave for 5–10 minutes until frothy. Sift the flour and salt into a large bowl and make a well in the centre. Gradually pour in the yeast mixture and the olive oil. Mix to make a smooth dough. Knead on a lightly floured surface for about 10 minutes until smooth, springy and elastic. Place the dough in a floured bowl, cover and leave to rise in a warm place for 1½ hours.

2 Meanwhile, make the tomato sauce. Place all the ingredients in a saucepan, cover and bring to the boil. Lower the heat, remove the lid and simmer for 20 minutes, stirring occasionally, until reduced.

3 ▲ Make the topping. Heat the oil in a frying pan. Add the garlic and mushrooms, with salt and pepper to taste. Cook, stirring, for about 5 minutes or until the mushrooms are tender and golden. Set aside.

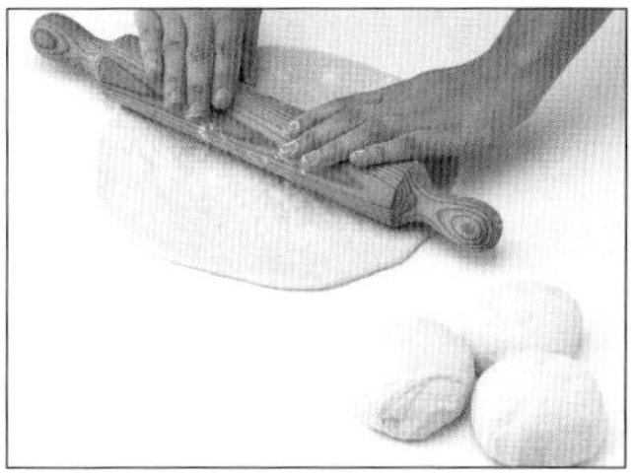

4 ▲ Preheat the oven to 220°C/425°F/Gas 7. Brush four baking sheets with oil. Knead the dough for 2 minutes, then divide into four equal pieces. Roll out each piece to a 25 cm/10 in round and place on a baking sheet.

5 Spoon the tomato sauce over each dough round. Brush the edge with a little olive oil. Add the mushrooms, oregano and cheese. Bake for about 15 minutes until golden brown and crisp. Scatter the oregano leaves over.

Fried Pizza Pasties

Panzerotti

These tasty little morsels are served all over central and southern Italy as a snack food or as part of a hot antipasti. Although similar to calzone they are fried instead of baked.

Ingredients
½ quantity Pizza Dough
½ quantity Tomato Sauce
225 g/8 oz mozzarella cheese, chopped
115 g/4 oz Italian salami, thinly sliced
handful of fresh basil leaves, roughly torn
sunflower oil, for deep frying
salt and freshly ground black pepper
serves 4

Cook's Tip
To test that the oil is ready, carefully drop a piece of bread into the oil. If it sizzles instantly, the oil is ready.

1 Preheat the oven to 200°C/400°F/ Gas 6. Brush two baking sheets with oil. Divide the dough into 12 and roll out each piece on a lightly floured surface to a 10 cm/4 in round.

2 ▲ Spread the centre of each round with a little of the tomato sauce, leaving sufficient border all round for sealing the pasty, then top with a few pieces of mozzarella and salami slices. Sprinkle with salt and freshly ground black pepper and add a few fresh basil leaves to each round.

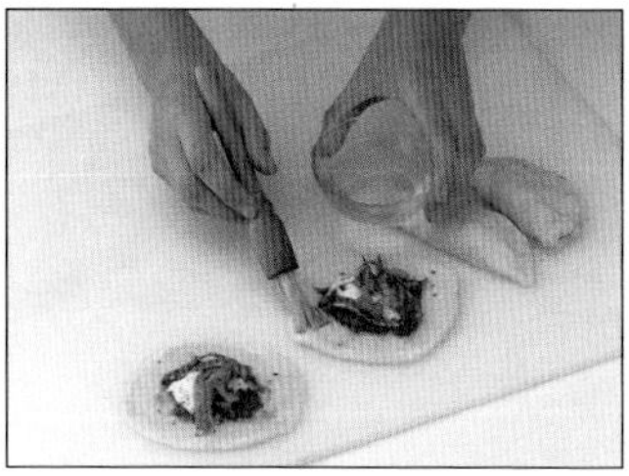

3 ▲ Brush the edges of the dough rounds with a little water, then fold over and press together to seal.

4 Heat oil to a depth of about 10 cm/ 4 in in a heavy-based pan. When hot, deep-fry the pasties, a few at a time, for 8 - 10 minutes until golden. Drain on kitchen paper and serve hot.

Sicilian Pizza

Pizza alla siciliana

This robust-flavoured pizza is topped with mozzarella and Pecorino cheeses.

Ingredients
1 small aubergine, cut into thin rounds
30 ml/2 tbsp olive oil
½ quantity risen Pizza Dough
½ quantity Tomato Sauce
175 g/6 oz mozzarella cheese, sliced
50 g/2 oz/½ cup pitted black olives
15 ml/1 tbsp drained capers
60 ml/4 tbsp grated Pecorino cheese
salt and freshly ground black pepper
serves 2

Cook's Tip
For best results choose olives that have been marinated in extra virgin olive oil and flavoured with herbs and garlic.

1 ▲ Preheat the oven to 200°C/400°F/ Gas 6. Brush one or two baking sheets with oil. Brush the aubergine rounds with olive oil and arrange them on the baking sheet(s). Bake for 10 - 15 minutes, turning once, until browned and tender. Remove the aubergine slices from the baking sheet(s) and drain on kitchen paper.

2 Raise the oven temperature to 220°C/425°F/Gas 7. Roll out the pizza dough to two 25 cm/10 in rounds. Transfer to baking sheets and spread with the tomato sauce.

3 ▲ Pile the aubergine slices on top of the tomato sauce and cover with the mozzarella. Dot with the black olives and capers. Sprinkle the Pecorino cheese liberally over the top, and season with plenty of salt and pepper. Bake for 15-20 minutes until the crust on each pizza is golden.

Fish & Shellfish

Italy has such an extensive coastline – and so many lakes, rivers and streams – that it is small wonder that fish and shellfish are so popular. Of course there are many different types that are unique to the country itself, but the most common varieties are available outside Italy. Cooking methods are very simple and quick, and any accompanying sauces light and fresh.

Sole with Sweet and Sour Sauce

Sfogi in saor

This Venetian dish should be prepared 1–2 days before it is to be eaten.

Ingredients

3–4 fillets of sole, about 500 g/1 1/4 lb total, divided in half
60 ml/4 tbsp flour
salt and freshly ground black pepper
pinch of ground cloves
90–120 ml/6–8 tbsp olive oil
35 g/1 1/2 oz/generous 1/4 cup pine nuts
3 bay leaves
pinch of ground cinnamon
pinch of grated nutmeg
4 cloves
1 small onion, very finely sliced
50 ml/2 fl oz/1/4 cup dry white wine
50 ml/2 fl oz/1/4 cup white wine vinegar
50 g/2 oz/1/3 cup sultanas

serves 4

1 Dredge the sole fillets in the flour seasoned with salt and pepper and the ground cloves.

2 Heat 45 ml/3 tbsp of the oil in a heavy frying pan or skillet. Cook the sole fillets a few at a time until golden, about 3 minutes on each side. Add more oil as necessary.

3 ▲ Remove with a slotted spatula to a large shallow serving dish. Sprinkle with the pine nuts, bay leaves, cinnamon, nutmeg and whole cloves.

4 ▲ Heat the remaining oil in a pan. Add the onion, and cook over low heat until golden. Add the wine, vinegar and sultanas, and boil for 4–5 minutes. Pour over the fish. Cover the dish with foil, and leave in a cool place for 24–48 hours. Remove 2 hours before serving. This dish is traditionally eaten at room temperature.

Salt Cod with Parsley and Garlic

Baccalà alla bolognese

Salt cod is very popular all over Italy. For centuries it has been imported from Scandinavia. The very salty fish must be soaked for 24 hours in water to reduce its salt content.

Ingredients

750 g/1 1/2 lb boneless and skinless salt cod, preferably in one piece
flour seasoned with freshly ground black pepper, for dredging
30 ml/2 tbsp extra-virgin olive oil
45 ml/3 tbsp finely chopped fresh parsley
2 cloves garlic, finely chopped
25 g/1 oz/2 tbsp butter, cut into small pieces

serves 4–5

1 Cut the salt cod into 5 cm/2in squares. Place them in a large bowl and cover with cold water. Allow to stand for at least 24 hours, changing the water several times.

2 ▲ Preheat the oven to 190°C/375°F/gas 5. Drain the fish, shaking out the excess moisture. Remove any remaining bones or skin. Dredge lightly in the seasoned flour.

3 Spread 15 ml/1 tbsp of the oil over the bottom of a baking dish large enough to hold the fish in one layer.

4 ▲ Place the fish in the dish. Combine the chopped parsley and garlic, and sprinkle evenly over the fish. Sprinkle with the remaining oil, and dot with butter. Bake for 15 minutes. Turn the fish, and bake for 15–20 minutes more, or until tender. Serve at once, with the lemon wedges.

Fresh Tuna and Tomato Stew

Tonno e pomodori in umido

A deliciously simple dish that relies on good basic ingredients. For real Italian flavour serve with polenta or pasta.

Ingredients
12 baby onions, peeled
900 g/2 lb ripe tomatoes
675 g/1½ lb fresh tuna
45 ml/3 tbsp olive oil
2 garlic cloves, crushed
45 ml/3 tbsp chopped fresh herbs
2 bay leaves
2.5 ml/½ tsp caster sugar
30 ml/2 tbsp sun-dried tomato paste
150 ml/¼ pint/⅔ cup dry white wine
salt and freshly ground black pepper
baby courgettes and fresh herbs, to garnish
serves 4

1 Leave the onions whole and cook in a pan of salted boiling water for 4–5 minutes until softened. Drain.

2 Plunge the tomatoes into boiling water for 30 seconds, then refresh in cold water. Peel away the skins and chop roughly.

3 ▲ Cut the tuna into 2.5 cm/1 in chunks. Heat the oil in a large frying or sauté pan and quickly fry the tuna until browned. Drain.

4 ▲ Add the onions, garlic, tomatoes, chopped herbs, bay leaves, sugar, tomato paste and wine and bring to the boil, breaking up the tomatoes with a wooden spoon.

5 Reduce the heat and simmer gently for 5 minutes. Return the fish to the pan and cook for a further 5 minutes. Season, and serve hot, garnished with baby courgettes and fresh herbs.

Variation
Two large mackerel make a more readily available alternative to the tuna. Fillet them and cut into chunks or simply lay the whole fish over the sauce and cook, covered with a lid, until the mackerel is cooked through. Fresh sage, rosemary or oregano all go extremely well with this dish. Choose whichever you prefer, or use a mixture of two.

Red Mullet with Tomatoes

Triglie con pomodoro

Red mullet is a popular fish in Italy, and this recipe accentuates both its flavour and colour.

Ingredients

4 red mullet or red snapper, about 175–200 g/6–7oz each
450 g/1 lb tomatoes, peeled, or
1 x 400 g/14 oz can plum tomatoes
60 ml/4 tbsp olive oil
60 ml/4 tbsp finely chopped fresh parsley
2 cloves garlic, finely chopped
salt and freshly ground black pepper
100 ml/4 fl oz/$^1/_2$ cup white wine
4 thin lemon slices, cut in half

serves 4

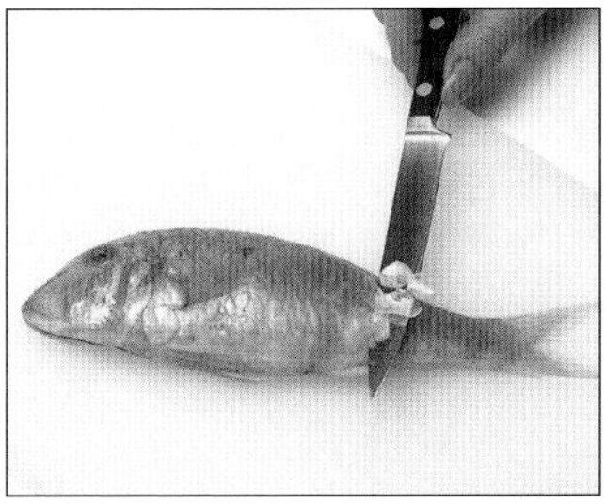

1 ▲ Scale and clean the fish without removing the liver. Wash and pat dry with paper towels.

2 ▲ Chop the tomatoes into small pieces. Heat the oil in a pan large enough to hold the fish in one layer. Add the parsley and garlic, and sauté for 1 minute. Stir in the tomatoes and cook over moderate heat for 15–20 minutes. Season with salt and pepper.

3 ▲ Add the fish to the tomato sauce and cook over moderate to high heat for 5 minutes. Add the wine and the lemon slices. Bring the sauce back to the boil, and cook for about 5 minutes more. Turn the fish over, and cook for 4–5 minutes more, until tender. Remove the fish to a warmed serving platter and keep warm until needed.

4 ▲ Boil the sauce for 3–4 minutes to reduce it slightly. Spoon it over the fish, and serve.

~ VARIATION ~

Small sea bass may be substituted.

Baked Cod with Garlic Mayonnaise

Merluzzo al forno

Because cod is not native to the Mediterranean, a similar species is used for this dish.

Ingredients
4 anchovy fillets
45 ml/3 tbsp finely chopped fresh parsley
coarsely ground black pepper
90 ml/6 tbsp olive oil
4 cod fillets, about 750 g/1 $^1/_2$ lb total, skinned
40 g/1 $^1/_2$ oz/$^1/_3$ cup plain breadcrumbs
For the mayonnaise
2 cloves garlic, finely chopped
1 egg yolk
5 ml/1 tsp Dijon mustard
175 ml/6 fl oz/$^3/_4$ cup vegetable oil
salt and freshly ground black pepper
serves 4

1 Make the mayonnaise. first put the garlic in a mortar or small bowl. Mash it to a paste. Beat in the egg yolk and mustard. Add the oil in a thin stream while whisking vigorously with a small wire whisk. When the mixture is thick and smooth, season with salt and pepper. Cover the bowl and keep cool.

2 ▲ Preheat the oven to 200°C/400°F/ gas 6. Chop the anchovy fillets with the parsley very finely. Place in a small bowl, and add pepper and 45 ml/3 tbsp of the oil. Stir to a paste.

3 ▲ Place the cod fillets in one layer in an oiled baking dish. Spread the anchovy paste on the top of the cod fillets. Sprinkle with the breadcrumbs and the remaining oil. Bake for 20–25 minutes, or until the breadcrumbs are golden. Serve hot with the garlic mayonnaise.

Monkfish Medallions with Thyme

Pescatrice con timo

Monkfish has a sweet flesh that combines well with Mediterranean flavours.

Ingredients
600 g/1 $^1/_4$ lb monkfish fillet, preferably in one piece
45 ml/3 tbsp extra-virgin olive oil
75 g/3 oz/$^1/_2$ cup small black olives, preferably from the Riviera, stoned
1 large or 2 small tomatoes, seeded and diced
1 sprig fresh thyme, or 1 tsp dried thyme leaves
salt and freshly ground black pepper
15 ml/1 tbsp very finely chopped fresh parsley, to serve
serves 4

1 Preheat the oven to 200°C/400°F/ gas 6. Remove the grey membrane from the monkfish, if necessary. Cut the fish into slices 1 cm/$^1/_2$ in thick.

2 Heat a non-stick frying pan quite hot, without oil. Sear the fish quickly on both sides. Remove to a side dish.

3 ▲ Spread 15 ml/1 tbsp of the olive oil in the bottom of a shallow baking dish. Arrange the fish in one layer. Distribute the olives and diced tomato on top of the fish.

4 Sprinkle the fish with thyme, salt and pepper, and the remaining oil. Bake for 10–12 minutes.

5 ▲ To serve, divide the medallions between 4 warmed plates. Spoon on the vegetables and any cooking juices. Sprinkle with the chopped parsley.

Grilled Salmon Steaks with Fennel

Salmone alla griglia

Fennel grows wild all over the south of Italy. Its mild aniseed flavour goes well with fish.

Ingredients

juice of 1 lemon
45 g/3 tbsp chopped fresh fennel herb, or the green fronds from the top of a fennel bulb
5 ml/1 tsp fennel seeds
45 ml/3 tbsp olive oil
4 salmon steaks of the same thickness, about 700 g/1 $^{1}/_{2}$ lb total
salt and freshly ground black pepper
lemon slices, to garnish
serves 4

1 Combine the lemon juice, chopped fennel and fennel seeds with the olive oil in a bowl. Add the salmon steaks, turning them to coat them with the marinade. Sprinkle with salt and pepper. Cover and place in the refrigerator. Allow to stand for 2 hours.

2 ▲ Preheat the grill. Arrange the fish in one layer on a grill pan or baking tray. Grill about 10 cm/4 in from the heat source for 3–4 minutes.

3 ▲ Turn. Spoon on the remaining marinade and grill for 3–4 minutes on the other side, or until the edges begin to brown. Serve hot, garnished with lemon slices.

Octopus with Lemon and Garlic

Polpo con limone e aglio

Octopus is widely appreciated in Italy. Dressed with oil and lemon it is delicious.

Ingredients

1 kg/2 lb octopus (young and small if possible)
30 ml/2 tbsp capers
2 cloves garlic, very finely chopped
60 ml/4 tbsp extra-virgin olive oil
45 ml/3 tbsp fresh lemon juice
freshly ground black pepper
serves 3–4

1 Beat the octopus repeatedly against a strong table or marble surface. Clean, removing the eyes, beak and sacs. (Or ask your fishmonger to do this.) Wash carefully under cold running water.

2 Place the octopus in a large pan with cold water to cover. Bring to the boil, cover the pan tightly, and simmer gently until tender, 45 minutes for small octopus and up to 2 hours for larger ones. Skim off any scum which rises to the surface.

3 ▲ Remove from the pan, and allow to cool slightly. Rub the octopus lightly with a clean cloth to remove any loose dark skin. Slice the warm octopus into rounds 1 $^{1}/_{2}$ cm/ $^{3}/_{4}$ inch wide.

~ COOK'S TIP ~

In Italy, a wine cork is placed in the pan with the octopus to reduce the scum.

4 ▲ Place the octopus pieces in a serving bowl. Toss with the parsley, garlic, olive oil and lemon juice. Sprinkle with pepper. Mix well. Allow to stand for at least 20 minutes before serving at room temperature.

Roast Sea Bass

Branzino al forno

Sea bass has meaty flesh. It is an expensive fish, best cooked as simply as possible. Avoid elaborate sauces, which would mask its delicate flavour.

Ingredients

1 fennel bulb with fronds, about 275 g/10 oz
2 lemons
120 ml/4 fl oz/½ cup olive oil
1 small red onion, diced
2 sea bass, about 500 g/1¼ lb each, cleaned with heads left on
120 ml/4 fl oz/½ cup dry white wine
salt and freshly ground black pepper
lemon slices, to garnish

serves 4

1 ▲ Preheat the oven to 190°C/375°F/ Gas 5. Cut the fronds off the top of the fennel and reserve for the garnish. Cut the fennel bulb lengthways into thin wedges, then into dice. Cut one half lemon into four slices. Squeeze the juice from the remaining lemon half and the other lemon.

2 ▲ Heat 30 ml/2 tbsp of the oil in a frying pan, add the diced fennel and onion and cook gently, stirring frequently, for about 5 minutes until softened. Remove from the heat.

3 ▲ Make three diagonal slashes on both sides of each sea bass with a sharp knife. Brush a roasting tin generously with oil, add the fish and tuck two lemon slices in each cavity. Scatter the softened fennel and onion over the fish.

Cook's Tip

Farmed or wild sea bass are available all year round from the fishmonger. They are expensive, but well worth buying for a special main course. Sizes vary from the ones used here, which are a very good size for two servings, to 1.5–1.75 kg/ 3–4½ lb, which take up to 50 minutes to cook.

4 ▲ Whisk the remaining oil, the lemon juice and salt and pepper to taste and pour over the fish. Cover with foil and roast for 30 minutes or until the flesh flakes, removing the foil for the last 10 minutes. Discard the lemon slices, transfer the fish to a heated serving platter and keep hot.

5 Put the roasting tin on top of the stove. Add the wine and stir over a medium heat to incorporate all the pan juices. Bring to the boil, then spoon the juices over the fish. Garnish with the reserved fennel fronds and lemon slices and serve at once.

Stuffed Swordfish Rolls

Involtini di pesce spada

This is a very tasty dish, with strong flavours from the tomato, olive and caper sauce – and from the salty Pecorino cheese. If you like, substitute Parmesan cheese, which is milder.

Ingredients

30 ml/2 tbsp olive oil
1 small onion, finely chopped
1 celery stick, finely chopped
450 g/1 lb ripe Italian plum tomatoes, chopped
115 g/4 oz stoned green olives, half roughly chopped, half left whole
45 ml/3 tbsp drained bottled capers
4 large swordfish steaks, each about 1 cm / ½ in thick and 115 g/4 oz in weight
1 egg
50 g/2 oz/⅔ cup grated Pecorino cheese
25 g/1 oz/½ cup fresh white breadcrumbs
salt and freshly ground black pepper
sprigs of fresh parsley, to garnish

serves 4

Cook's Tip

This dish is not for the inexperienced cook because the pounding, stuffing and rolling of the fish is quite tricky. If you prefer, you can omit the stuffing and simply cook the swordfish steaks in the sauce.

1 ▲ Heat the oil in a large heavy-based frying pan. Add the onion and celery and cook gently for about 3 minutes, stirring frequently. Stir in the tomatoes, olives and capers, with salt and pepper to taste. Bring to the boil, then lower the heat, cover and simmer for about 15 minutes. Stir occasionally and add a little water if the sauce becomes too thick.

2 Remove the fish skin and place each steak between two sheets of clear film. Pound lightly with a rolling pin until each steak is reduced to about 5 mm/¼ in thick.

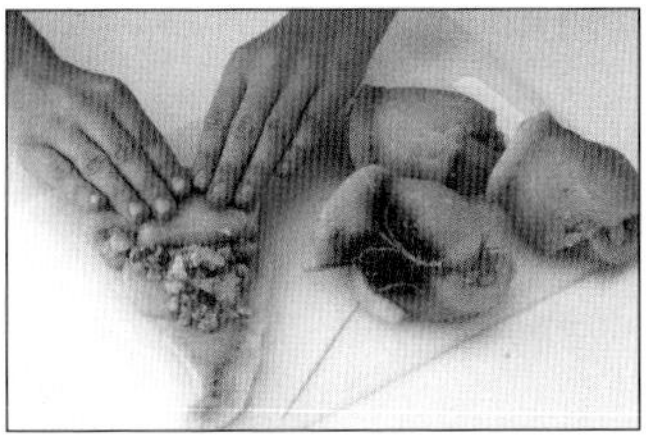

3 ▲ Beat the egg in a bowl and add the cheese, breadcrumbs and a few spoonfuls of the sauce. Stir well to mix to a moist stuffing. Spread one-quarter of the stuffing over each swordfish steak, then roll up into a sausage shape. Secure with wooden cocktail sticks.

4 ▲ Add the rolls to the sauce in the pan and bring to the boil. Lower the heat, cover and simmer for about 30 minutes, turning once. Add a little water as the sauce reduces.

5 Remove the rolls from the sauce and discard the cocktail sticks. Place on warmed dinner plates and spoon the sauce over and around. Garnish with the parsley and serve hot.

Pan-fried Sole with Lemon

Sogliole al limone

The delicate flavour and texture of sole is brought out in this simple, classic recipe. Lemon sole is used here because it is easier to obtain - and less expensive - than Dover sole.

Ingredients

30–45 ml/2–3 tbsp plain flour
4 lemon sole fillets
45 ml/3 tbsp olive oil
50 g/2 oz/¼ cup butter
60 ml/4 tbsp lemon juice
30 ml/2 tbsp rinsed bottled capers
salt and freshly ground black pepper
fresh flat leaf parsley and lemon wedges, to garnish

serves 2

Cook's Tip

It is important to cook the pan juices to the right colour after removing the fish. Too pale, and they will taste insipid, too dark, and they may taste bitter. Take great care not to be distracted at this point so that you can watch the colour of the juices change to a golden brown.

1 ▲ Season the flour with salt and black pepper. Coat the sole fillets evenly on both sides. Heat the oil with half the butter in a large shallow pan until foaming. Add two sole fillets and fry over a medium heat for 2–3 minutes on each side.

2 Lift out the sole fillets with a fish slice and place on a warmed serving platter. Keep hot. Fry the remaining sole fillets.

3 ▲ Remove the pan from the heat and add the lemon juice and remaining butter. Return the pan to a high heat and stir vigorously until the pan juices are sizzling and beginning to turn golden brown. Remove from the heat and stir in the capers.

4 Pour the pan juices over the sole, sprinkle with salt and pepper to taste and garnish with the parsley. Add the lemon wedges and serve at once.

Three-colour Fish Kebabs

Spiedini tricolore

Don't let the fish marinate for more than an hour. The lemon juice will start to break down the fibres of the fish after this time and it will be difficult not to overcook it.

Ingredients
120 ml/4 fl oz/½ cup olive oil
finely grated rind and juice of 1 large lemon
5 ml/1 tsp crushed chilli flakes
350 g/12 oz monkfish fillet, cubed
350 g/12 oz swordfish fillet, cubed
350 g/12 oz thick salmon fillet or steak, cubed
2 red, yellow or orange peppers, cored, seeded and cut into squares
30 ml/2 tbsp finely chopped fresh flat leaf parsley
salt and freshly ground black pepper

For the sweet tomato and chilli salsa
225 g/8 oz ripe tomatoes, finely chopped
1 garlic clove, crushed
1 fresh red chilli, seeded and chopped
45 ml/3 tbsp extra virgin olive oil
15 ml/1 tbsp lemon juice
15 ml/1 tbsp finely chopped fresh flat leaf parsley
pinch of sugar
serves 4

1 ▲ Put the oil in a shallow glass or china bowl and add the lemon rind and juice, the chilli flakes and pepper to taste. Whisk to combine, then add the fish chunks. Turn to coat evenly.

2 Add the pepper squares, stir, then cover and marinate in a cool place for 1 hour, turning occasionally.

Variation
Use tuna instead of swordfish. It has a similar meaty texture.

3 ▲ Thread the fish and peppers on to eight oiled metal skewers, reserving the marinade. Barbecue or grill the skewered fish for 5–8 minutes, turning once.

4 Meanwhile, make the salsa by mixing all the ingredients in a bowl, and seasoning to taste with salt and pepper. Heat the reserved marinade in a small pan, remove from the heat and stir in the parsley, with salt and pepper to taste. Serve the kebabs hot, with the marinade spooned over, accompanied by the salsa.

Seafood Stew

Zuppa di pesce

"Soups" - really stews - of mixed fish and shellfish are specialities of the Mediterranean.

Ingredients
45 ml/3 tbsp olive oil
1 medium onion, sliced
1 carrot, sliced
$^1/_2$ stick celery, sliced
2 cloves garlic, chopped
1 x 400 g/14 oz can plum tomatoes, chopped, with their juice
225 g/8 oz fresh prawns, peeled and deveined (reserve the shells)
450 g/1 lb white fish bones and heads, gills removed
1 bay leaf
1 sprig fresh thyme, or $^1/_4$ tsp dried thyme leaves
a few peppercorns
salt and freshly ground black pepper
750 g/1$^1/_2$ lb fresh mussels, in their shells, scrubbed and rinsed
500 g/1 lb fresh small clams, in their shells, scrubbed and rinsed
250 ml/8 fl oz/1 cup white wine
1 kg/2 lb mixed fish fillets, such as cod, monkfish, red snapper or hake, bones removed and cut into chunks
45 ml/3 tbsp finely chopped fresh parsley
rounds of French bread, toasted, to serve
serves 6–8

1 ▲ Heat the olive oil in a medium saucepan. Add the sliced onion, and cook slowly until soft. Stir in the carrot and celery, and cook gently for 5 minutes more. Add the chopped garlic, the tomatoes and their juice, and 250 ml/8 fl oz/1 cup of water. Cook over moderate heat until the vegetables are soft, about 15 minutes. Purée in a food processor or pass through a food mill. Set aside.

2 ▲ Place the prawn shells in a large pan with the fish bones and heads. Add the herbs and peppercorns, and pour in 700 ml/1$^1/_4$ pints/3 cups of water. Bring to the boil, reduce the heat, and simmer for 25 minutes, skimming off any scum that rises to the surface. Strain and pour into a pan with the tomato sauce. Season.

3 Place the mussels and clams in a saucepan with the wine. Cover, and steam until all the shells have opened. (Discard any that do not open.)

4 Lift the clams and mussels out and set aside. Filter the cooking liquid through a layer of paper towel and add it to the stock and tomato sauce. Check the seasoning.

5 ▲ Bring the sauce to a boil. Add the fish, and boil for 5 minutes. Add the prawns and boil for 3–4 minutes. Stir in the mussels and clams and cook for 2–3 minutes more. Transfer the stew to a warmed casserole. Sprinkle with parsley, and serve with the toasted rounds of French bread.

Trout Baked in Paper with Olives

Trota in cartoccio con olive

Baking fish in paper packets keeps in all the flavour and moisture.

Ingredients
4 medium trout, about 275 g/10 oz each, gutted
75 ml/5 tbsp olive oil
4 bay leaves
salt and freshly ground black pepper
4 slices pancetta or bacon
60 ml/4 tbsp chopped shallots
60 ml/4 tbsp chopped fresh parsley
100 ml/4 fl oz/$^1/_2$ cup dry white wine
24 green olives, stoned
serves 4

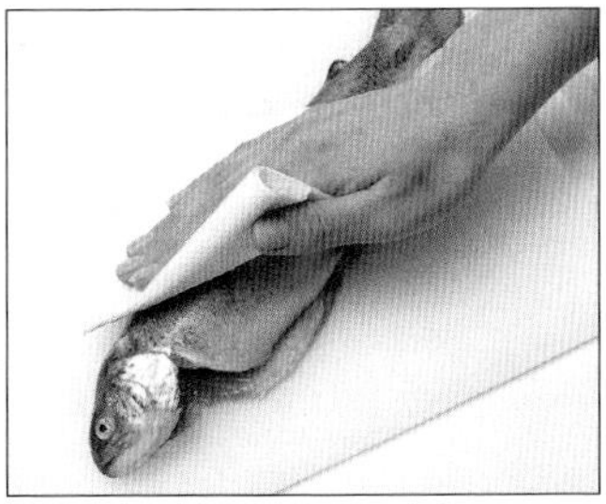

1 ▲ Preheat the oven to 200°C/400°F/ gas 6. Wash the trout well in cold running water. Drain. Pat dry with paper towels.

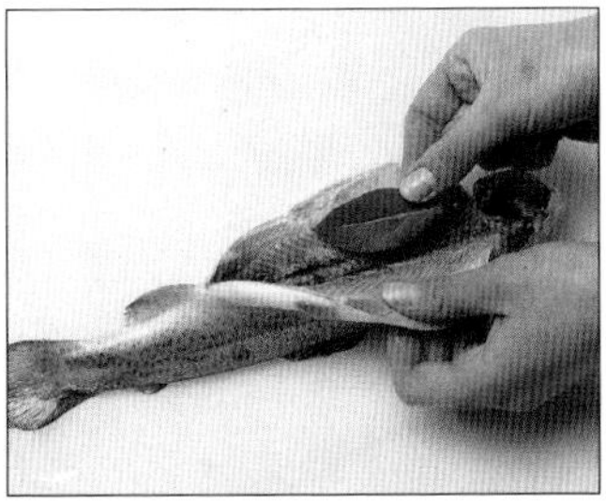

2 ▲ Lightly brush oil onto 4 pieces of baking parchment each large enough to enclose one fish. Lay one fish on each piece of oiled paper. Place a bay leaf in each cavity, and sprinkle with salt and pepper.

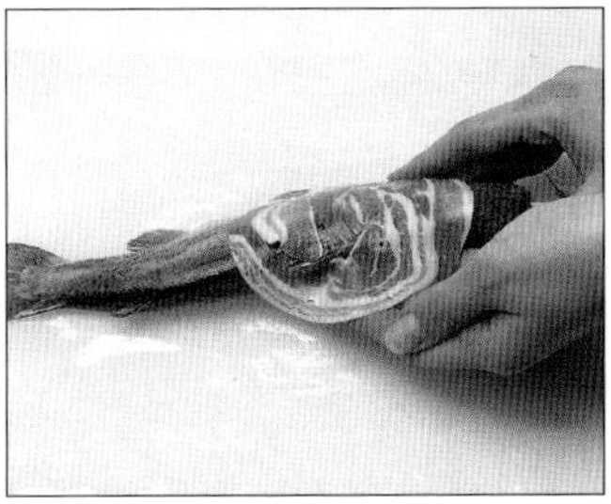

3 ▲ Wrap a slice of pancetta or bacon around each fish. Sprinkle with 1 tbsp each of chopped shallots and parsley. Drizzle each fish with 15 ml/1 tbsp of oil and 30 ml/2 tbsp of white wine. Add 6 olives to each packet.

4 ▲ Close the paper loosely around the fish, rolling the edges together to seal them completely. Bake for 25 minutes. Place each packet on an individual plate and open at the table.

Stuffed Squid

Calamari ripieni

Squid are popular in all the coastal regions of Italy. They are very tender and easy to cook.

Ingredients
900 g/2 lb fresh squid (about 16 medium)
juice of 1/2 lemon
2 anchovy fillets, chopped
2 cloves garlic, finely chopped
3 medium tomatoes, peeled, seeded and finely chopped
30 ml/2 tbsp chopped fresh parsley
50 g/2 oz/1/2 cup plain breadcrumbs
1 egg
salt and freshly ground black pepper
30 ml/2 tbsp olive oil
100 ml/4 fl oz/1/2 cup dry white wine
few sprigs fresh parsley, to garnish
serves 4

1 Working near the sink, clean the squid by first peeling off the thin skin from the body section. Rinse well. Pull the head and tentacles away from the body sac. Some of the intestines will come away with the head. Remove and discard the translucent quill and any remaining insides from the sac. Sever the tentacles from the head. Discard the head and intestines.

2 Remove and discard the small hard beak from the base of the tentacles. Place the tentacles in a bowl of water with the lemon juice. Rinse the sacs well under cold running water. Pat the insides dry with paper towels.

3 ▲ Preheat the oven to 180°C/350°F/gas 4. Drain the tentacles. Chop them coarsely and place in a mixing bowl. Stir in the next 6 ingredients and season. Use this mixture to loosely stuff the squid sacs. Close the opening to the sacs with wooden toothpicks.

4 ▲ Oil a shallow baking dish large enough to accommodate the squid in one layer. Arrange the squid sacs in the dish. Pour over the oil and wine. Bake uncovered for 35–45 minutes, or until tender. Remove the toothpicks and serve garnished with parsley.

~ COOK'S TIP ~

Do not overstuff the squid sacs or they may burst during cooking.

Deep-fried Prawns and Squid

Fritto misto

The Italian name of this recipe means "mixed fry". Any mixture of seafood can be used.

Ingredients
vegetable oil, for deep-frying
600 g/1 lb 5 oz medium-sized fresh prawns, shelled and deveined
600 g/1 lb 5 oz squid (about 12 medium) cleaned and cut into bite-size pieces
115 g/1 cup flour
lemon wedges, to serve
For the batter
2 egg whites
30 ml/2 tbsp olive oil
15 ml/1 tbsp white wine vinegar
100 g/3 1/2 oz/scant 1 cup flour
10 ml/2 tsp baking soda
75 g/3 oz/1/3 cup cornflour
salt and freshly ground black pepper
250 ml/8 fl oz/1 cup water
serves 6

1 Make the batter in a large bowl by beating the egg whites, olive oil and vinegar together lightly with a wire whisk. Beat in the dry ingredients, and whisk until well blended. Beat in the water, a little at a time. Cover the bowl, and allow to stand 15 minutes.

2 Heat the oil for deep-frying until a small piece of bread sizzles as soon as it is dropped in (about 185°C/360°F).

3 Dredge the prawns and squid pieces in the flour, shaking off any excess. Dip them quickly into the batter. Fry in small batches for about 1 minute, stirring with a slotted spoon to keep them from sticking to each other.

4 ▲ Remove and drain on paper towels. Allow the oil to come back up to the correct temperature between batches. Sprinkle lightly with salt, and serve hot with lemon wedges.

Pan-fried Red Mullet with Citrus

Triglie agli agrumi

Red mullet is extremely popular all over the Mediterranean. This recipe combines it with oranges and lemons, which grow in abundance in Italy.

Ingredients

4 red mullet, about 225 g/8 oz each, filleted
90 ml/6 tbsp extra virgin olive oil
10 black peppercorns, crushed
2 medium oranges, one peeled and sliced and one squeezed
1 lemon
30 ml/2 tbsp plain flour
15 g/½ oz/1 tbsp butter
2 drained canned anchovies, chopped
60 ml/4 tbsp shredded fresh basil or chopped fresh parsley
salt and freshly ground black pepper

serves 4

1 ▲ Place the fish fillets in a shallow dish in a single layer. Pour over the olive oil and sprinkle with the crushed peppercorns. Lay the orange slices on top of the fish. Cover the dish, and leave to marinate in the fridge for at least 4 hours, or overnight, if you prefer.

Cook's Tip

Ask the fishmonger to fillet the red mullet for you. If red mullet is not available, use other small fish fillets for this dish, such as lemon sole, red bream, trout, haddock or hake.

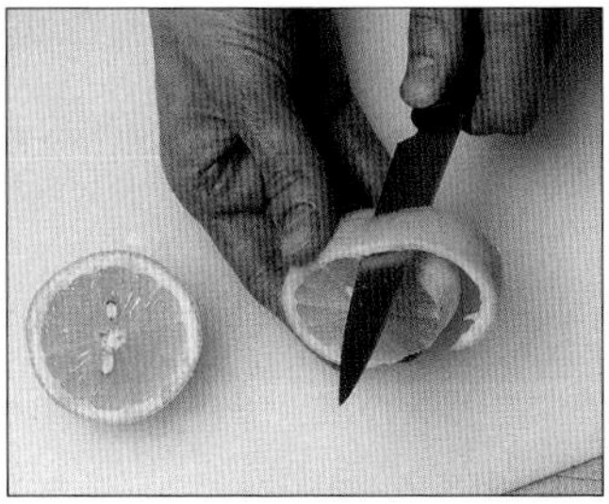

2 ▲ Cut the lemon in half. Remove the skin and pith from one half using a small sharp knife. Discard the pith and peel, then slice the lemon thinly. Squeeze the juice from the other lemon half.

3 ▲ Lift the fish out of the marinade, and pat dry on kitchen paper. Reserve the marinade and orange slices. Season the fish with salt and pepper and dust lightly with flour.

4 Heat about 45 ml/3 tbsp of the marinade in a large frying pan. Add the fish and fry for 2 minutes on each side until the fish is just cooked through. Carefully remove the fish fillets from the pan and keep them warm. Discard the marinade that is left in the pan.

5 Melt the butter in the frying pan with any of the remaining original marinade. Add the chopped anchovies to the pan and cook until they are completely softened.

6 Stir in the orange and lemon juice, then season to taste with salt and pepper. Reduce the heat and simmer until the cooking juices are slightly reduced. Stir in the shredded basil or chopped parsley.

7 To serve, pour the sauce over the fish, garnish with the reserved orange slices and lemon slices and serve at once.

Black Pasta with Squid Sauce

Pasta nera con Calamari

Tagliatelle flavoured with squid ink looks amazing and tastes deliciously of the sea. You'll find it in good Italian delicatessens.

Ingredients

105 ml/7 tbsp olive oil
2 shallots, chopped
3 garlic cloves, crushed
45 ml/3 tbsp chopped fresh parsley
675 g/1½ lb cleaned squid, cut into rings and rinsed
150 ml/¼ pint/⅔ cup dry white wine
400 g/14 oz can chopped tomatoes
2.5 ml/½ tsp dried chilli flakes or chili powder
450 g/1 lb dried squid ink tagliatelle
salt and freshly ground black pepper

serves 4

1 ▲ Heat the oil in a pan and add the shallots. Cook until pale golden, then add the garlic. When the garlic colours a little, add 30 ml/2 tbsp of the parsley, stir, then add the squid and stir again. Cook for 3 - 4 minutes, then add the wine. Simmer for a few seconds, then add the tomatoes.

2 ▲ Add the chilli flakes or powder and seasoning. Cover and simmer for 1 hour, or until the squid is tender. Add more water if necessary. Cook the tagliatelle in plenty of boiling, salted water, for 10 minutes or until *al dente*. Drain and return the tagliatelle to the pan. Add the squid sauce and mix well. Sprinkle each serving with the remaining chopped parsley and serve at once.

Sicilian Spaghetti with Sardines

Spaghetti alle sarde

A traditional dish from Sicily, made with fresh ingredients and flavourings that are common to many parts of the Mediterranean.

Ingredients
12 fresh sardines, cleaned and boned
250 ml/8 fl oz/1 cup extra virgin olive oil
1 onion, chopped
25 g/1 oz/¼ cup dill sprigs
50 g/2 oz/½ cup pine nuts
25 g/1 oz/2 tbsp raisins, soaked in water
50 g/2 oz/½ cup fresh breadcrumbs
450 g/1 lb dried spaghetti
flour, for dusting
salt
serves 4

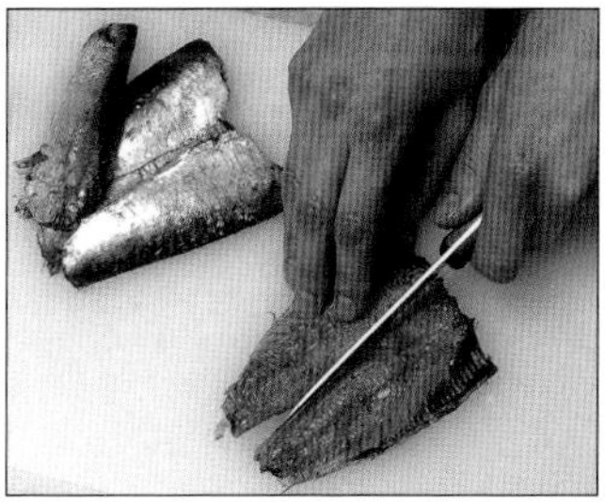

1 ▲ Wash the sardines and pat dry on kitchen paper. Open them out flat, then cut in half lengthways.

2 Heat 30 ml/2 tbsp of the oil in a pan, add the onion and fry until golden. Add the dill and cook gently for a minute or two. Add the pine nuts and raisins and season with salt. Dry-fry the breadcrumbs in a frying pan until golden. Set aside.

3 ▲ Cook the spaghetti in boiling salted water according to the instructions on the packet, until *al dente*. Heat the remaining oil in a pan. Dust the sardines with flour and fry in the hot oil for 2–3 minutes. Drain on kitchen paper.

4 Drain the spaghetti and return to the pan. Add the onion mixture and toss well. Transfer the spaghetti mixture to a serving platter and arrange the fried sardines on top. Sprinkle with the toasted breadcrumbs and serve immediately.

Grilled Fresh Sardines

Sarde alla griglia

Fresh sardines are flavourful and firm-fleshed, and quite different in taste and consistency from those canned in oil. They are excellent simply grilled and served with lemon.

Ingredients

1 kg/2 lb very fresh sardines, gutted and with heads removed
olive oil, for brushing
salt and freshly ground black pepper
45 ml/3 tbsp chopped fresh parsley, to serve
lemon wedges, to garnish
serves 4–6

1 Preheat the grill. Rinse the sardines in water. Pat dry with paper towels.

2 ▲ Brush the sardines lightly with olive oil and sprinkle generously with salt and pepper. Place the sardines in one layer on the grill pan. Grill for about 3–4 minutes.

3 ▲ Turn, and cook for 3–4 minutes more, or until the skin begins to brown. Serve immediately, sprinkled with parsley and garnished with lemon wedges.

Baked Aromatic Sea Bass

Branzino aromatizzato al forno

Sea bass is a firm white-fleshed fish which benefits from simple cooking. Use fresh herbs for this recipe, if possible.

Ingredients

1 large sea bass, about 1.5 kg/3 lb
4 bay leaves
few sprigs fresh thyme
8–10 sprigs fresh parsley
few sprigs fresh fennel, tarragon or basil
15 ml/1 tbsp peppercorns
135 ml/9 tbsp extra-virgin olive oil
salt and freshly ground black pepper
flour, for coating
lemon wedges, to garnish
serves 5–6

1 Gut the fish, leaving the head on. Wash carefully in cold water. Pat dry with paper towels. Place half the herbs and peppercorns in the bottom of a shallow platter, and lay the fish on top. Arrange the remaining herbs on top of the fish and in its cavity. Sprinkle with 45 ml/3 tbsp of the oil. Cover lightly with foil, and refrigerate for 2 hours.

2 ▲ Preheat the oven to 205°C/400°F/gas 6. Remove and discard all the herbs from around the fish, and pat it dry with paper towels. Spread a little flour in a platter and season it with salt and pepper. Roll the fish in the flour, then shake off the excess.

3 ▲ Heat the remaining olive oil in a flameproof dish just large enough to hold the fish comfortably. When the oil is hot, add the fish, and brown it quickly on both sides. Transfer the dish to the oven, and bake for 25–40 minutes, depending on the size of the fish. The fish is cooked when the dorsal fin (in the middle of the backbone) comes out easily when pulled. Serve garnished with sprigs of herbs or lemon wedges.

Monkfish with Tomato and Olive Sauce

Pesce alla calabrese

This dish comes from the coast of Calabria in southern Italy. Garlic-flavoured mashed potato is delicious with its robust sauce.

Ingredients

450 g/1 lb fresh mussels, scrubbed
a few fresh basil sprigs
2 garlic cloves, roughly chopped
300 ml/½ pint/1¼ cups dry white wine
30 ml/2 tbsp olive oil
15 g/½ oz/1 tbsp butter
900 g/2 lb monkfish fillets, skinned and cut into large chunks
1 onion, finely chopped
500 g/1¼ lb jar sugocasa or passata
15 ml/1 tbsp sun-dried tomato paste
115 g/4 oz/1 cup stoned black olives
salt and freshly ground black pepper
extra fresh basil leaves, to garnish

serves 4

1 ▲ Put the mussels in a flameproof casserole with some basil leaves, the garlic and the wine. Cover and bring to the boil. Lower the heat and simmer for 5 minutes, shaking the pan frequently. Remove the mussels, discarding any that fail to open. Strain the cooking liquid and reserve.

2 ▲ Heat the oil and butter until foaming, add the monkfish pieces and sauté over a medium heat until they just change colour. Remove.

3 ▲ Add the onion to the juices in the casserole and cook gently for about 5 minutes, stirring frequently, until softened. Add the sugocasa or passata, the reserved cooking liquid from the mussels and the tomato paste. Season with salt and pepper to taste. Bring to the boil, stirring, then lower the heat, cover and simmer for 20 minutes, stirring occasionally.

4 ▲ Pull off and discard the top shells from the mussels. Add the monkfish pieces to the tomato sauce and cook gently for 5 minutes. Gently stir in the olives and remaining basil, then taste for seasoning. Place the mussels in their half shells on top of the sauce, cover the pan and heat the mussels through for 1–2 minutes. Serve at once, garnished with basil.

Chargrilled Squid

Grigliata di calamari

If you like your food hot, chop some – or all – of the chilli seeds with the flesh. If not, cut the chillies in half lengthways, scrape out the seeds and discard them before chopping the flesh.

Ingredients
2 whole prepared squid, with tentacles
75 ml/5 tbsp olive oil
30 ml/2 tbsp balsamic vinegar
2 fresh red chillies, finely chopped
60 ml/4 tbsp dry white wine
salt and freshly ground black pepper
hot cooked risotto rice, to serve
sprigs of fresh parsley, to garnish
serves 2

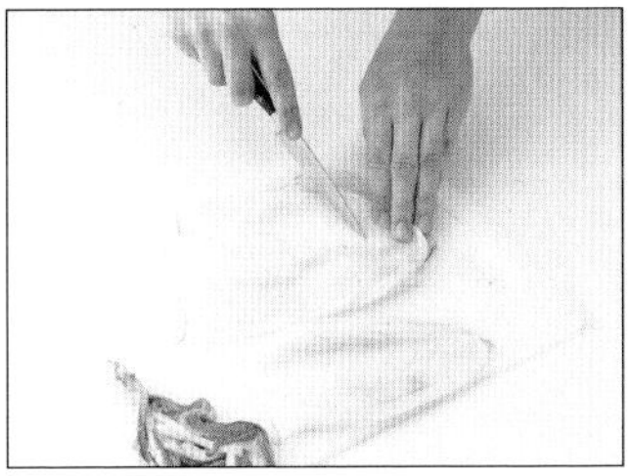

1 ▲ Make a lengthways cut down the body of each squid, then open out the body flat. Score the flesh on both sides of the bodies in a criss-cross pattern with the tip of a sharp knife. Chop the tentacles. Place all the squid in a china or glass dish. Whisk the oil and vinegar in a small bowl. Add salt and pepper to taste and pour over the squid. Cover and leave to marinate for about 1 hour.

2 ▲ Heat a ridged cast-iron pan until hot. Add the body of one of the squid. Cook over a medium heat for 2–3 minutes, pressing the squid with a fish slice to keep it flat. Repeat on the other side. Cook the other squid body in the same way.

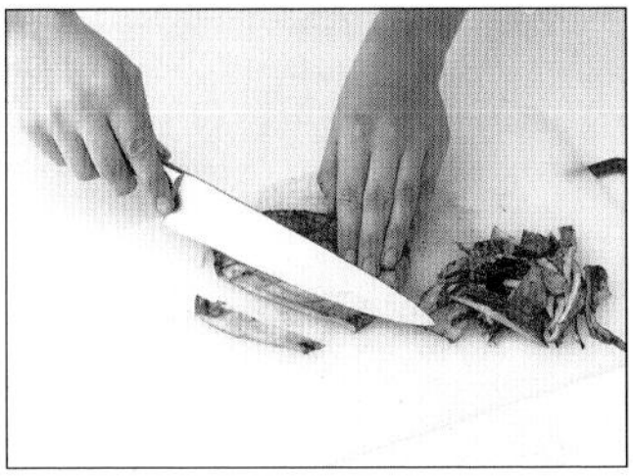

3 ▲ Cut the squid bodies into diagonal strips. Pile the hot risotto rice in the centre of heated soup plates and top with the strips of squid, arranging them criss-cross fashion. Keep hot.

4 ▲ Add the chopped tentacles and chillies to the pan and toss over a medium heat for 2 minutes. Stir in the wine, then drizzle over the squid and rice. Garnish with the parsley and serve at once.

Pan-fried Prawns in their Shells

Gamberi fritti in padella

Although expensive, this is a very quick and simple dish, ideal for an impromptu supper with friends. Serve with hot crusty Italian bread to scoop up the juices.

Ingredients

60 ml/4 tbsp extra virgin olive oil
32 large fresh prawns, in their shells
4 garlic cloves, finely chopped
120 ml/4 fl oz/½ cup Italian dry white vermouth
45 ml/3 tbsp passata
salt and freshly ground black pepper
chopped fresh flat leaf parsley, to garnish
crusty bread, to serve

serves 4

Cook's Tip

Prawns in their shells are sweet and juicy, and fun to eat with your fingers. They can be quite messy though, so provide guests with finger bowls and napkins.

1 ▲ Heat the olive oil in a large heavy-based frying pan until just sizzling. Add the prawns and toss over a medium to high heat until their shells just begin to turn pink. Sprinkle the garlic over the prawns in the pan and toss again, then add the vermouth and let it bubble, tossing the prawns constantly so that they cook evenly and absorb the flavours of the garlic and vermouth.

2 ▲ Keeping the pan on the heat, add the passata, with salt and pepper to taste. Stir until the prawns are thoroughly coated in the sauce. Serve at once, sprinkled with the parsley and accompanied by plenty of hot crusty bread.

Grilled Red Mullet with Rosemary

Triglie al rosmarino

This recipe is very simple – the taste of grilled red mullet is so good in itself that it needs very little to bring out the flavour.

Ingredients

4 red mullet, cleaned, about 275 g/10 oz each
4 garlic cloves, cut lengthways into thin slivers
75 ml/5 tbsp olive oil
30 ml/2 tbsp balsamic vinegar
10 ml/2 tsp very finely chopped fresh rosemary or 5 ml/1 tsp dried rosemary
freshly ground black pepper
coarse sea salt, to serve
fresh rosemary sprigs and lemon wedges, to garnish

serves 4

Variation

Red mullet are extra delicious cooked on the barbecue. If possible, enclose them in a basket grill so that they are easy to turn over.

1 ▲ Cut three diagonal slits in both sides of each fish. Push the garlic slivers into the slits. Place the fish in a single layer in a shallow dish. Whisk the oil, vinegar and rosemary, with ground black pepper to taste.

2 ▲ Pour over the fish, cover with clear film and leave to marinate in a cool place for about 1 hour. Put the fish on the rack of a grill pan and grill for 5–6 minutes on each side, turning once and brushing with the marinade. Serve hot, sprinkled with coarse sea salt and garnished with fresh rosemary sprigs and lemon wedges.

Baked Mussels and Potatoes

Cozze in tortiera con patate

This dish originates from Puglia, noted for its imaginative baked casseroles.

Ingredients

750 g/1 ½lb large mussels, in their shells
225 g/8oz potatoes, unpeeled
75 ml/5 tbsp olive oil
2 cloves garlic, finely chopped
8 leaves fresh basil, torn
225 g/8oz tomatoes, peeled and thinly sliced
45 ml/3 tbsp plain breadcrumbs
freshly ground black pepper
serves 2–3

1 Cut off the "beards" from the mussels. Scrub and soak in several changes of cold water. Discard any with broken shells. Place the mussels with a cupful of water in a large saucepan over moderate heat. As soon as they open, lift them out. Remove and discard the empty half shells, leaving the mussels in the other half. (Discard any mussels that do not open.) Strain any liquid in the pan through a layer of paper towels, and reserve.

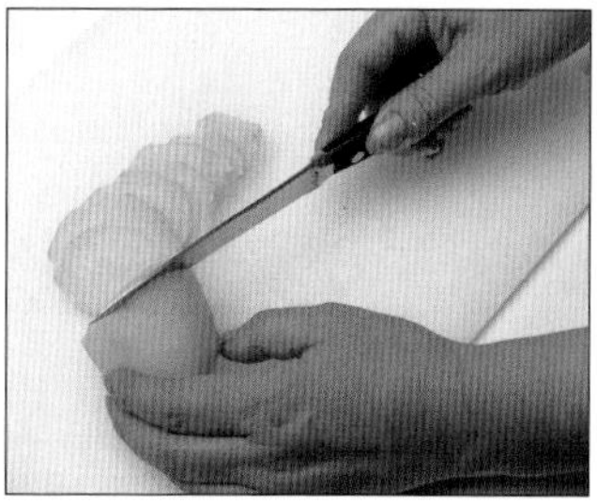

2 ▲ Boil the potatoes. Remove them from the water when they are still quite firm and peel and slice them.

3 ▲ Preheat the oven to 180°C/350°F/gas 4. Spread 30 ml/2 tbsp of the olive oil in the bottom of a shallow ovenproof dish. Cover with the potato slices in one layer. Add the mussels in their half shells in one layer. Sprinkle with garlic and pieces of basil.

4 ▲ Cover with a layer of the tomato slices. Sprinkle with breadcrumbs and black pepper, the filtered mussel liquid and the remaining olive oil. Bake for about 20 minutes, or until the tomatoes are soft and the breadcrumbs golden. Serve directly from the baking dish.

Prawns in Spicy Tomato Sauce

Gamberi alla marinara

The tomato sauce base can be sharpened up by adding hot chillies.

Ingredients
90 ml/6 tbsp olive oil
1 medium onion, finely chopped
1 stick celery, finely chopped
1 small red pepper, seeded and chopped
100 ml/4 fl oz/$^1/_2$ cup red wine
15 ml/1 tbsp wine vinegar
1 x 400 g/14 oz can plum tomatoes, chopped, with their juice
salt and freshly ground black pepper
1 kg/2 lb fresh prawns, in their shells
2–3 cloves garlic, finely chopped
45 ml/3 tbsp finely chopped fresh parsley
1 piece dried chilli, crumbled or chopped (optional)
serves 6

1 In a heavy saucepan, heat half of the oil. Add the chopped onion, and cook over low heat until soft. Stir in the celery and pepper, and cook gently for 5 minutes more. Raise the heat to medium high, and add the wine, vinegar and tomatoes. Season with salt and pepper. Bring to a boil and cook for about 5 minutes.

2 ▲ Lower the heat, cover the pan, and simmer until the vegetables are soft, about 30 minutes. Purée the sauce through a food mill.

3 Shell the prawns and devein them, either by using a deveiner or by making a shallow incision with a small sharp knife down the centre of the back to disclose the long black vein. Remove and discard.

4 ▲ Heat the remaining oil in a clean heavy saucepan. Stir in the garlic, parsley and chilli, if using. Cook over moderate heat, stirring constantly, until the garlic is golden. Do not let it brown. Add the tomato sauce and bring to the boil. Taste for seasoning.

5 ▲ Stir in the prawns. Bring the sauce back to a boil. Reduce the heat slightly and simmer until the prawns are pink and stiff, 6–8 minutes, depending on their size. Remove from the heat and serve.

Stewed Mussels and Clams

Zuppa di cozze e vongole

Casseroles of mixed shellfish are very popular on the Ligurian coast.

Ingredients

750 g/1½lb fresh mussels, in their shells
750 g/1½lb fresh clams, in their shells
75 ml/5 tbsp olive oil
3 cloves garlic, peeled and crushed
300 ml/½ pint/1¼ cups dry white wine
75 ml/5 tbsp chopped fresh parsley
freshly ground black pepper
rounds of crusty bread, toasted, to serve
serves 4

1 Cut off the "beards" from the mussels. Scrub and rinse the mussels and clams in cold water. Discard any with broken shells.

2 Heat the oil in a large saucepan with the garlic. As soon as this is golden, add the mussels, clams and the wine. Cover, and steam until all the shells have opened, about 5–8 minutes. (Discard any that do not open.)

3 Lift the clams and mussels out, pouring any liquid in the shells back into the saucepan. Place in a warmed serving bowl. Discard the garlic.

4 ▲ Strain the liquid in the saucepan through a layer of paper towels held in a sieve, pouring it over the clams and mussels in the bowl. Sprinkle with parsley and black pepper.

5 ▲ To serve, place rounds of toasted bread in the bottom of individual soup bowls, and ladle in the mussels and clams with some of the hot liquid.

Broiled Prawns with Herbs

Gamberi con erbe aromatiche

Large prawns are delicious marinated with fresh herbs, lemon and garlic. They can be grilled or cooked on a barbecue.

Ingredients

24 large raw prawns, in their shells
3 cloves garlic, finely chopped
45 ml/3 tbsp finely chopped fresh basil
15 ml/1 tbsp fresh thyme leaves
30 ml/2 tbsp finely chopped fresh parsley
15 ml/1 tbsp coarsely crushed black pepper
juice of 1 lemon
60 ml/4 tbsp olive oil
8 bay leaves
50 g/2 oz/¼ cup salt pork or pancetta, cut into 8 small squares
serves 4

1 Shell the prawns and devein them either by using a deveiner, or by making a shallow incision with a small sharp knife down the center of the back to disclose the long black vein. Remove and discard this.

2 ▲ Place the prawns in a bowl with the garlic, chopped herbs, pepper, lemon juice and olive oil. Mix well, cover, and leave to marinate in the refrigerator for at least 6 hours, or preferably overnight.

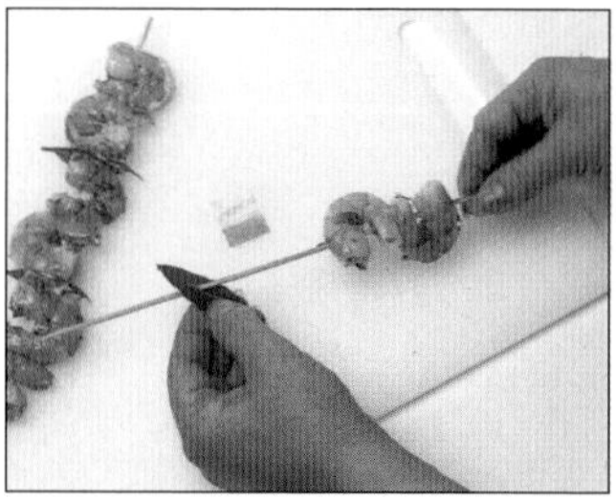

3 ▲ Preheat the grill. Arrange 6 prawns on each of 4 skewers so that they lie flat, threading a bay leaf and a square of salt pork between every 2 shrimp. Brush with the remaining marinade. Place in one layer under the grill or on a barbecue. Cook for about 3 minutes. Turn, and cook for 3 minutes more.

Poultry & Meat

The Italians eat a wide variety of different meats, and tastes vary according to region. Veal, pork and poultry are popular all over the country, while beef is farmed and eaten more in the north, and lamb is a great Roman speciality. All meats are eaten as a second course – secondo piatto *– usually simple and served solo, with vegetables to follow.*

Pizzaiola Steak

Bistecchine alla pizzaiola

This dish comes from Naples, where tomato sauces are used in all kinds of dishes.

Ingredients
450 g/1 lb beef steaks, preferably rump or chuck, thinly sliced
45 ml/3 tbsp flour, for dredging
45 ml/3 tbsp olive oil
3 cloves garlic, peeled and crushed
400 g/14 oz can plum tomatoes, with their juice, passed through a food mill
30 ml/2 tbsp chopped fresh basil
salt and freshly ground black pepper
serves 4

1 Trim any excess fat from the steaks, and notch the edges slightly with a sharp knife to prevent them from curling during cooking. Pat the steaks dry with paper towels, and dredge lightly in the flour.

2 ▲ In a large heavy frying pan or skillet, heat 30 ml/2 tbsp of the oil with the garlic cloves. As soon as they are golden, raise the heat, push them to the side of the pan, and add the steaks. Brown quickly on both sides. Remove the meat to a dish.

3 ▲ Add the tomatoes, the remaining oil, and the herbs to the pan. Season with salt and pepper. Cook over moderate heat for about 15 minutes. Discard the garlic cloves. Return the steaks to the pan, stir to cover them with the sauce, and cook for 4-5 minutes more.

Herbed Burgers

Polpette

Dress up minced beef with fresh herbs and a tasty tomato sauce.

Ingredients
750 g/1 $^1/_2$ lb lean minced beef
1 clove garlic, finely chopped
1 spring onion, very finely chopped
45 ml/3 tbsp chopped fresh basil
45 ml/2 tbsp chopped fresh parsley
salt and freshly ground black pepper
40 g/1 $^1/_2$ oz/3 tbsp butter
For the tomato sauce
45 ml/3 tbsp olive oil
1 medium onion, finely chopped
300 g/11oz tomatoes, chopped
a few leaves fresh basil
45–60 ml/3–4 tbsp water
5 ml/1 tsp sugar
15 ml/1 tbsp white wine vinegar
salt and freshly ground black pepper
serves 4

1 To make the tomato sauce, heat the oil in a large pan and sauté the onion gently until translucent. Add the tomatoes and cook for 2-3 minutes. Add the basil, cover the pan, and cook for 7-8 minutes over moderate heat.

2 Add the water, sugar and vinegar, and cook for 2-3 minutes more. Season with salt and pepper. Remove from the heat, allow to cool slightly, and pass the sauce through a food mill or strainer. Check the seasoning.

3 ▲ Combine the meat with the garlic, spring onion and herbs in a mixing bowl. Season with salt and pepper. Form into 4 burgers, patting the meat as lightly as possible.

4 ▲ Heat the butter in a frying pan. When the foam subsides add the burgers, and cook over moderate heat until brown on the underside. Turn the burgers over, and continue cooking until done. Remove to a warmed plate.

5 Tilt the frying pan, and spoon off any surface fat. Pour in the sauce, raise the heat and bring to a boil, scraping up the meat residue from the bottom of the pan. Serve with the burgers.

Meatballs

Polpettine

These meatballs are delicious served hot with pasta or rice. They are also good cold.

Ingredients

7.5 g/¼ oz/2 tbsp dried porcini mushrooms
150 ml/¼ pint/⅔ cup warm water
450 g/1 lb lean ground beef
2 cloves garlic, finely chopped
60 ml/4 tbsp chopped fresh parsley
45 ml/3 tbsp chopped fresh basil
1 egg
4 tbsp/6 tbsp plain breadcrumbs
30 ml/2 tbsp freshly grated Parmesan cheese
salt and freshly ground black pepper
60 ml/4 tbsp olive oil
1 medium onion, very finely chopped
50 ml/2 fl oz/¼ cup dry white wine
chopped fresh parsley, to garnish

serves 3–4

1 Soak the dried mushrooms in the warm water for 15 minutes. Lift them out of the water and chop finely. Filter the soaking water through paper towels and reserve.

2 ▲ In a mixing bowl, combine the meat with the chopped mushrooms, garlic and herbs. Stir in the egg. Add the breadcrumbs and Parmesan, and season with salt and pepper. Form the mixture into small balls 3.5 cm/1½ in in diameter.

3 ▲ In a large heavy frying pan or skillet, heat the oil. Add the onion and cook over low heat until soft. Raise the heat and add the meatballs, rolling them often to brown them evenly on all sides. After about 5 minutes add the filtered mushroom soaking water. Cook for 5–8 minutes more, or until the meatballs are cooked through.

4 ▲ Remove the meatballs to a heated serving plate with a slotted spoon or spatula. Add the wine to the pan, and cook for 1–2 minutes, stirring to scrape up any residues on the bottom of the pan. Pour the sauce over the meatballs. Sprinkle with parsley, and serve at once.

Meatballs with Peperonata

Polpette di manzo

These taste very good with creamed potatoes. Use a potato ricer to get them really smooth.

Ingredients
400 g/14 oz minced beef
115 g/4 oz/2 cups fresh white breadcrumbs
50 g/2 oz/$^2/_3$ cup grated Parmesan cheese
2 eggs, beaten
pinch of paprika
pinch of grated nutmeg
5 ml/1 tsp dried mixed herbs
2 thin slices of mortadella or prosciutto (total weight about 50 g/2 oz), chopped
vegetable oil, for shallow frying
salt and freshly ground black pepper
snipped fresh basil leaves, to garnish

For the peperonata
30 ml/2 tbsp olive oil
1 small onion, thinly sliced
2 yellow peppers, cored, seeded and cut lengthways into thin strips
2 red peppers, cored, seeded and cut lengthways into thin strips
275 g/10 oz/1$^1/_4$ cups finely chopped tomatoes or passata
15 ml/1 tbsp chopped fresh parsley
serves 4

1 ▲ Put the minced beef in a bowl. Add half the breadcrumbs and all the remaining ingredients, including salt and ground black pepper to taste. Mix well with clean wet hands. Divide the mixture into 12 equal portions and roll each into a ball. Flatten the meat balls slightly so they are about 1 cm/$^1/_2$ in thick.

2 Put the remaining breadcrumbs on a plate and roll the meatballs in them, a few at a time, until they are evenly coated. Place on a plate, cover with clear film and chill for about 30 minutes to firm up.

3 ▲ Meanwhile, make the peperonata. Heat the oil in a medium saucepan, add the onion and cook gently for about 3 minutes, stirring frequently, until softened. Add the pepper strips and cook for 3 minutes, stirring constantly. Stir in the tomatoes or passata and parsley, with salt and pepper to taste. Bring to the boil, stirring. Cover and cook for about 15 minutes, then remove the lid and continue to cook, stirring frequently, for 10 minutes more, or until reduced and thick. Taste for seasoning. Keep hot.

4 ▲ Pour oil into a frying pan to a depth of about 2.5 cm/1 in. When hot but not smoking, shallow fry the meatballs for 10–12 minutes, turning them 3–4 times and pressing them flat with a fish slice. Remove and drain on kitchen paper. Serve hot, with the peperonata alongside. Garnish with the basil.

Variation
Instead of minced beef, used half minced pork and half minced veal.

Beef Stew with Tomatoes, Wine and Peas

Spezzatino

It seems there are as many spezzatino recipes as there are Italian cooks. This one is very traditional, perfect for a winter lunch or dinner. Serve it with boiled or mashed potatoes to soak up the deliciously rich sauce.

Ingredients

30 ml/2 tbsp plain flour
10 ml/2 tsp chopped fresh thyme or 5 ml/1 tsp dried thyme
1 kg/2¼ lb braising or stewing steak, cut into large cubes
45 ml/3 tbsp olive oil
1 medium onion, roughly chopped
450 g/1 lb jar sugocasa or passata
250 ml/8 fl oz/1 cup beef stock
250 ml/8 fl oz/1 cup red wine
2 garlic cloves, crushed
30 ml/2 tbsp tomato purée
275 g/10 oz/2 cups shelled fresh peas
5 ml/1 tsp sugar
salt and freshly ground black pepper
fresh thyme, to garnish

serves 4

1 ▲ Preheat the oven to 160°C/325°F/ Gas 3. Put the flour in a shallow dish and season with the thyme and salt and pepper. Add the beef cubes and coat evenly.

2 ▲ Heat the oil in a large flameproof casserole, add the beef and brown on all sides over a medium to high heat. Remove with a slotted spoon and drain on kitchen paper.

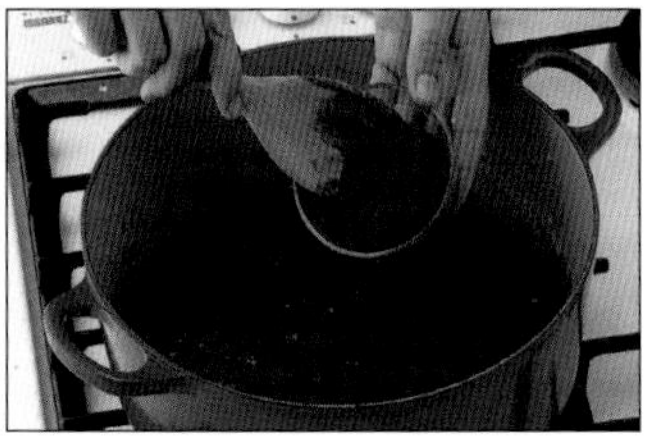

3 ▲ Add the onion to the pan, scraping the base of the pan to mix in any sediment. Cook gently for about 3 minutes, stirring frequently, until softened, then stir in the sugocasa or passata, stock, wine, garlic and tomato purée. Bring to the boil, stirring. Return the beef to the pan and stir well to coat with the sauce. Cover and cook in the oven for 1½ hours.

4 ▲ Stir in the peas and sugar. Return the casserole to the oven and cook for 30 minutes more, or until the beef is tender. Taste for seasoning. Garnish with fresh thyme before serving.

Variation

Use thawed frozen peas instead of fresh. Add them 10 minutes before the end of cooking.

Beef Stew with Red Wine

Spezzatino di manzo con vino rosso

This rich, hearty dish should be served with mashed potatoes or polenta.

Ingredients

75 ml/5 tbsp olive oil
1.2 kg/2½ lb boneless beef chuck, cut into 3 cm/1½ in cubes
1 medium onion, very finely sliced
2 carrots, chopped
45 ml/3 tbsp finely chopped fresh parsley
1 clove garlic, chopped
1 bay leaf
a few sprigs fresh thyme, or pinch of dried thyme leaves
pinch of grated nutmeg
250 ml/8 fl oz/1 cup red wine
400 g/14 oz can plum tomatoes, chopped, with their juice
100 ml/4 fl oz/½ cup beef or chicken broth
about 15 black olives, stoned and halved
salt and freshly ground black pepper
1 large red sweet pepper, cut into strips

serves 6

1 ▲ Preheat the oven to 180°C/350°F/gas 4. Heat 45 ml/3 tbsp of the oil in a large, heavy casserole. Brown the meat a little at a time, turning it to colour on all sides. Remove to a side plate while the remaining meat is being browned.

2 When all the meat has been browned and removed, add the remaining oil, the onion and carrots. Cook over low heat until the onion softens. Add the parsley and garlic, and cook for 3–4 minutes more.

3 ▲ Return the meat to the pan, raise the heat, and stir well to mix the vegetables with the meat. Stir in the bay leaf, thyme and nutmeg. Add the wine, bring to a boil and cook, stirring, for 4–5 minutes. Stir in the tomatoes, stock and olives, and mix well. Season with salt and pepper, and return to the boil. Cover the casserole, and place in the centre of the preheated oven. Bake for 1½ hours.

4 ▲ Remove the casserole from the oven. Stir in the strips of pepper. Return the casserole to the oven and cook, uncovered, for 30 minutes more, or until the beef is tender.

Corsican Beef Stew with Macaroni *Stufato di manzo alla corsa*

Pasta is eaten in many parts of Italy. In Corsica, it is often served with gravy as a sauce and, in this case, a rich beef stew.

Ingredients
25 g/1 oz dried porcini mushrooms
6 garlic cloves
900 g/2 lb stewing beef, cut into 5 cm/2 in cubes
115 g/4 oz lardons, or thick streaky bacon cut into strips
45 ml/3 tbsp olive oil
2 onions, sliced
300 ml/½ pint/1¼ cups dry white wine
30 ml/2 tbsp passata
pinch of ground cinnamon
sprig of rosemary
1 bay leaf
225 g/8 oz/2 cups large macaroni
50 g/2 oz/⅔ cup freshly grated Parmesan cheese
salt and freshly ground black pepper
serves 4

1 ▲ Soak the dried mushrooms in warm water for 30 minutes. Drain, set the mushrooms aside and reserve the liquid. Cut three of the garlic cloves into thin strips and insert into the pieces of the beef by making little slits with a sharp knife. Push the lardons or pieces of bacon into the beef with the garlic. Season the meat with salt and pepper.

2 ▲ Heat the oil in a heavy-based pan, add half the beef and brown well on all sides. Repeat with the remaining beef. Transfer to a plate. Add the sliced onions to the pan and cook until lightly browned. Crush the remaining garlic and add to the onions with the meat.

3 ▲ Stir in the white wine, passata, mushrooms, cinnamon, rosemary and bay leaf and season with salt and pepper. Cook gently for 30 minutes, stirring often. Strain the mushroom liquid and add to the stew with enough water to cover. Bring to the boil, cover and simmer the stew very gently for about 3 hours, or until the meat is very tender.

4 ▲ Cook the macaroni in a large pan of boiling, salted water for 10 minutes, or until *al dente*. Lift the pieces of meat out of the gravy and transfer to a warmed serving platter. Drain the pasta and layer in a serving bowl with the gravy and cheese. Serve with the meat.

Cook's Tip
This recipe calls for 30 ml/2 tbsp passata, thick puréed tomatoes. If you haven't a jar already open, substitute tomato purée or a tablespoon or two of sun-dried tomato paste.

Roast Lamb with Herbs

Arrosto d'agnello con erbe e aglio

This dish originates from southern Italy, where lamb is roasted with garlic and wild herbs.

Ingredients

1.5 kg/3 lb leg of lamb
45–60 ml/3–4 tbsp olive oil
4 cloves garlic, peeled and halved
2 sprigs fresh sage, or pinch of dried sage leaves
2 sprigs fresh rosemary, or 5 ml/1 tsp dried rosemary leaves
2 bay leaves
2 sprigs fresh thyme, or $^1/_2$ tsp dried
salt and freshly ground black pepper
175 ml/6 fl oz/$^3/_4$ cup dry white wine

serves 4–6

1 Cut any excess fat from the lamb. Rub with olive oil. Using a sharp knife, make small cuts just under the skin all around the meat. Insert the garlic pieces in some of the cuts, and a few of the fresh herbs in the others. (If using dried herbs, sprinkle them over the surface of the meat.)

2 Rub the remaining fresh herbs all over the lamb, and allow it to stand in a cool place for at least 2 hours before cooking. Preheat the oven to 190°C/375°F/gas 5.

3 ▲ Place the lamb in a baking pan, surrounded by the herbs. Pour on 30 ml/2 tbsp of the oil. Season. Place in the oven and roast for 35 minutes, basting occasionally.

4 ▲ Pour the wine over the lamb. Roast for 15 minutes more, or until the meat is cooked. Remove the lamb to a heated serving dish. Tilt the pan, spooning off any fat on the surface. Strain the pan juices into a gravy boat. Slice the meat, and serve with the sauce handed separately.

Lamb Stewed with Tomatoes and Garlic

Spezzatino d'agnello

This rustic stew comes from the plateau of Puglia, where sheep graze alongside vineyards.

Ingredients

2 large cloves garlic
1 sprig fresh rosemary, or 45 ml/3 tbsp chopped fresh parsley if fresh rosemary is not available
90 ml/6 tbsp olive oil
1.3 kg/2$^1/_2$ lb stewing lamb, trimmed of fat and gristle and cut into chunks
flour seasoned with freshly ground black pepper, for dredging
175 ml/6 fl oz/$^3/_4$ cup dry white wine
10 ml/2 tsp salt
450 g/1 lb fresh tomatoes, chopped, or 1 x 400g/14oz can tomatoes, chopped
100 ml/$^1/_2$ cup beef stock, heated

serves 5–6

1 Preheat the oven to 180°C/350°F/gas 4. Chop the garlic with the parsley, if using. Heat 60 ml/4 tbsp of the oil in a wide casserole.

2 Add the garlic and rosemary or parsley and cook over moderate heat, until the garlic is golden.

3 ▲ Dredge the lamb in the flour. Add a batch of lamb chunks to the pan in one layer, turning to brown them evenly. When brown, remove them to a side plate. Add a little more oil, and brown the remaining lamb.

4 ▲ When all the lamb has been browned, return it to the casserole with the wine. Raise the heat and bring to the boil, scraping up any residues from the bottom. Sprinkle with the salt. Stir in the tomatoes and the stock. Stir well. Cover the casserole, and place in the centre of the oven. Bake for 1$^3/_4$–2 hours, or until the meat is tender.

Roast Lamb with Rosemary

Agnello al rosmarino

In Italy, lamb is traditionally served at Easter. This simple roast with potatoes owes its wonderful flavour to the fresh rosemary and garlic. It makes the perfect Sunday lunch at any time of year, served with one or two lightly cooked fresh vegetables, such as broccoli, spinach or baby carrots.

Ingredients

½ leg of lamb, about 1.4 kg/3 lb
2 garlic cloves, cut lengthways into thin slivers
leaves from 4 sprigs of fresh rosemary, finely chopped
105 ml/7 tbsp olive oil
about 250 ml/8 fl oz/1 cup lamb or vegetable stock
675 g/1½ lb potatoes, cut into 2.5 cm/1 in cubes
a few fresh sage leaves, chopped
salt and freshly ground black pepper
lightly cooked baby carrots, to serve

serves 4

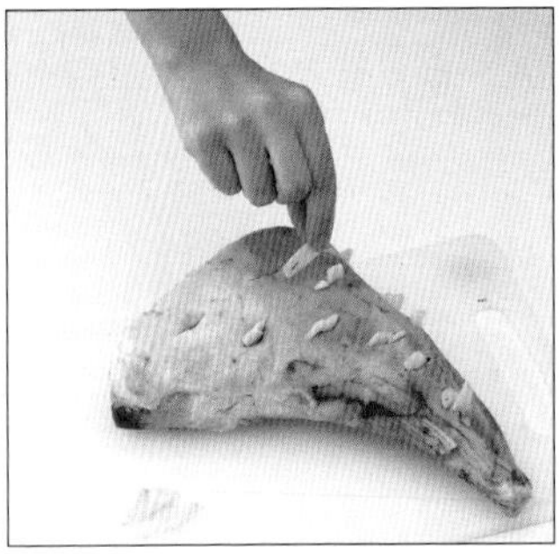

1 ▲ Preheat the oven to 230°C/450°F/Gas 8. Using the point of a sharp knife, make deep incisions in the lamb, especially near the bone, and insert the slivers of garlic.

2 ▲ Put the lamb in a roasting tin and rub it all over with 45 ml/3 tbsp of the oil. Sprinkle over about half of the chopped rosemary, patting it on firmly, and season with plenty of salt and pepper. Roast for 30 minutes, turning once.

3 ▲ Lower the oven temperature to 190°C/375°F/Gas 5. Turn the lamb over again and add 120 ml/4 fl oz/½ cup of the stock.

4 Roast for a further 1¼–1½ hours until the lamb is tender, turning the joint two or three times more and adding the rest of the stock in two or three batches. Baste the lamb each time it is turned.

5 ▲ Meanwhile, put the potatoes in a separate roasting tin and toss with the remaining oil and rosemary and the sage. Roast, on the same oven shelf if possible, for 45 minutes, turning the potatoes several times until they are golden and tender.

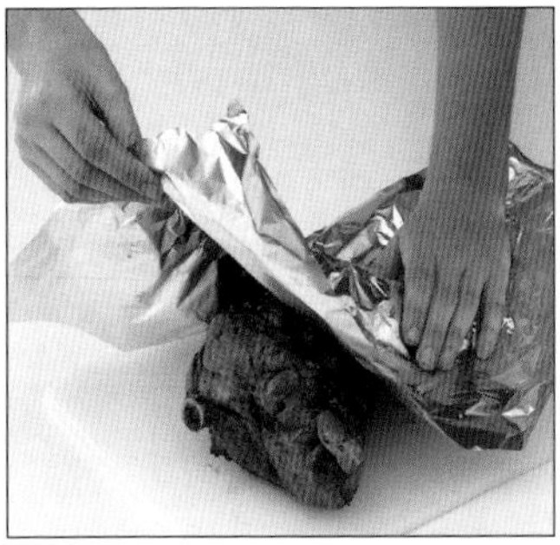

6 ▲ Transfer the lamb to a carving board, tent with foil and leave in a warm place for 10 minutes so that the flesh firms for easier carving. Serve whole or carved into thin slices, surrounded by the potatoes and accompanied by baby carrots.

Cook's Tip

If you like, the cooking juices can be strained and used to make a thin gravy with stock and red wine.

Pork in Sweet and Sour Sauce

Scaloppine di maiale in agrodolce

The combination of sweet and sour flavours is popular in Venetian cooking, especially with meat and liver. This recipe is given extra bite with the addition of crushed mixed peppercorns. Served with shelled broad beans tossed with grilled bacon – it is delectable.

Ingredients

1 whole pork fillet, about 350 g/12 oz
25 ml/1½ tbsp plain flour
30–45 ml/2–3 tbsp olive oil
250 ml/8 fl oz/1 cup dry white wine
30 ml/2 tbsp white wine vinegar
10 ml/2 tsp granulated sugar
15 ml/1 tbsp mixed peppercorns, coarsely ground
salt and freshly ground black pepper
broad beans tossed with grilled bacon, to serve

serves 2

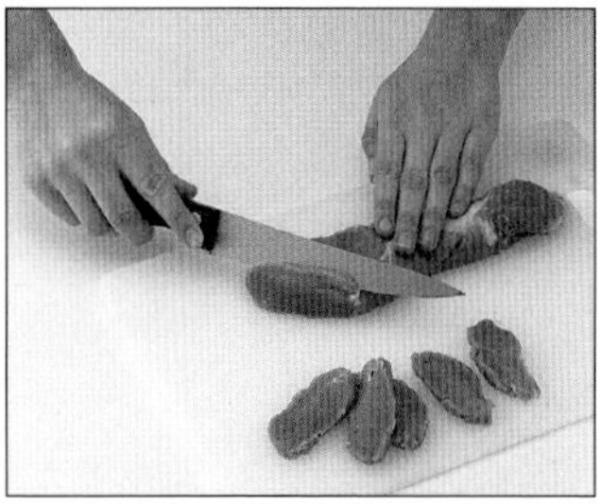

1 ▲ Cut the pork diagonally into thin slices. Place between two sheets of clear film and pound lightly with a rolling pin to flatten them evenly.

2 ▲ Spread out the flour in a shallow bowl. Season well and coat the meat.

Cook's Tip
Grind the peppercorns in a pepper grinder, or crush them with a mortar and pestle.

3 ▲ Heat 15 ml/1 tbsp of the oil in a wide heavy-based saucepan or frying pan and add as many slices of pork as the pan will hold. Fry over a medium to high heat for 2–3 minutes on each side until crispy and tender. Remove with a fish slice and set aside. Repeat with the remaining pork, adding more oil as necessary.

4 ▲ Mix the wine, wine vinegar and sugar in a jug. Pour into the pan and stir vigorously over a high heat until reduced, scraping the pan to incorporate the sediment. Stir in the peppercorns and return the pork to the pan. Spoon the sauce over the pork until it is evenly coated and heated through.

Pork with Marsala and Juniper

Maiale al marsala

Although most frequently used in desserts, Sicilian marsala gives savoury dishes a rich, fruity and alcoholic tang. Use good-quality butcher's pork, which won't be overwhelmed by the richly aromatic flavour of the sauce.

Ingredients

25 g/1 oz dried porcini mushrooms
4 pork escalopes
10 ml/2 tsp balsamic vinegar
8 garlic cloves
15 g/½ oz/1 tbsp butter
45 ml/3 tbsp marsala
several sprigs of rosemary
10 juniper berries, crushed
salt and freshly ground black pepper
noodles and green vegetables, to serve
serves 4

1 Put the dried mushrooms in a bowl and just cover with hot water. Leave to stand.

2 ▲ Brush the pork with 5 ml/1 tsp of the vinegar and season with salt and pepper. Put the garlic cloves in a small pan of boiling water and cook for 10 minutes until soft. Drain and set aside.

3 ▲ Melt the butter in a large frying pan. Add the pork and fry quickly until browned on the underside. Turn the meat over and cook for another minute.

4 Add the marsala, rosemary, mushrooms, 60 ml/4 tbsp of the mushroom juices, the garlic cloves, juniper and remaining vinegar.

5 Simmer gently for about 3 minutes until the pork is cooked through. Season lightly and serve hot with noodles and green vegetables.

Pork Braised in Milk with Carrots

Lonza al latte con carote

This method of slowly cooking a joint of pork produces a deliciously creamy gravy. It is a speciality of the Veneto region.

Ingredients

750 g/1 1/2 lb lean loin of pork
45 ml/3 tbsp olive oil
25 g/2 tbsp butter
1 small onion, finely chopped
1 stick celery, finely chopped
8 carrots, cut into 5 cm/2 in strips
2 bay leaves
15 ml/1 tbsp peppercorns
salt, to taste
500 ml/2 cups milk, scalded
serves 4–5

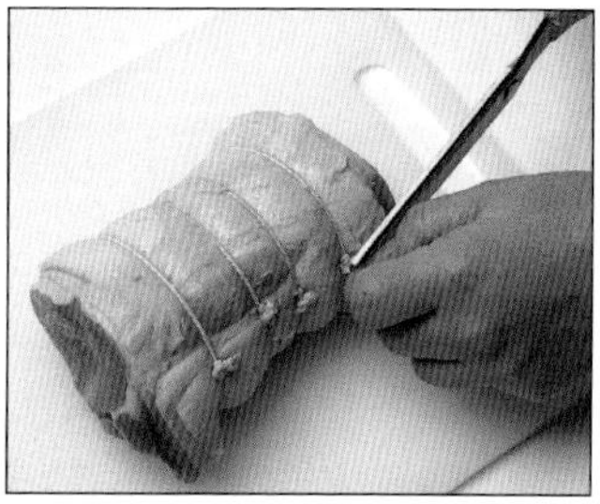

1 ▲ Trim any excess fat from the pork, and tie it into a roll with string.

2 ▲ Preheat the oven to 180°C/350°F/gas 4. Heat the oil and butter in a large casserole. Add the vegetables, and cook over low heat until they soften, 8–10 minutes. Raise the heat, push the vegetables to one side and add the pork, browning it on all sides. Add the bay leaves and peppercorns, and season with salt.

3 ▲ Pour in the hot milk. Cover the casserole and place it in the centre of the oven. Bake for about 90 minutes, turning and basting the pork with the sauce about once every 20 minutes. Remove the cover for the last 20 minutes of baking.

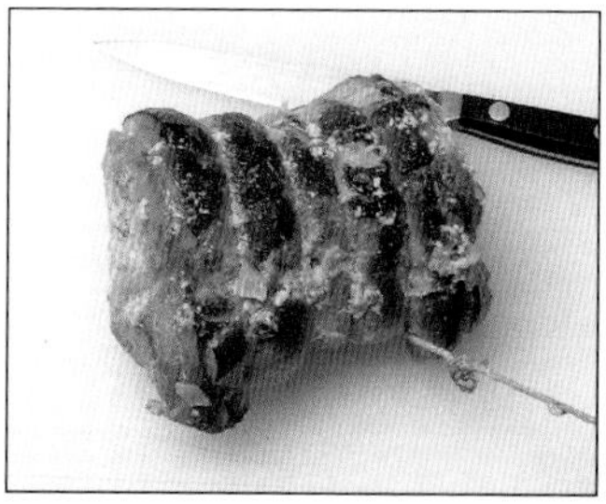

4 ▲ Remove the meat from the casserole, and cut off the string. Place the meat on a warmed serving platter and cut into slices.

~ VARIATION ~

This dish can also be made using a joint of veal. Substitute a piece of boneless veal and proceed as in the recipe. This dish is delicious served hot or cold.

5 ▲ Discard the bay leaves. Press about one-third of the carrots and all the liquids in the pan through a strainer. Arrange the remaining carrots around the meat.

6 ▲ Place the sauce in a small saucepan, taste for seasoning, and bring to the boil. If it seems too thin, boil it for a few minutes to reduce it slightly. Serve the sliced meat with the carrots, and pass the hot sauce separately.

Pork Fillet with Caper Sauce

Fettine di maiale con salsa di capperi

The caper sauce can be made in advance and reheated while the pork is sautéed.

Ingredients
450 g/1 lb pork fillet, cut into thin slices
flour seasoned with freshly ground black pepper, for dredging
25 g/1 oz/2 tbsp butter
30 ml/2 tbsp olive oil
For the caper sauce
30 ml/2 tbsp olive oil
50 g/2 oz/$^1/_4$ cup butter
$^1/_2$ small onion, very finely chopped
1 anchovy fillet, rinsed and chopped
15 ml/1 tbsp flour
30 ml/2 tbsp capers, rinsed
15 ml/1 tbsp finely chopped fresh parsley
60 ml/4 tbsp wine vinegar
60 ml/4 tbsp water
60 ml/4 tbsp balsamic vinegar
serves 4–5

1 Make the sauce by heating the oil and 25 g/1 oz/2 tbsp of the butter in a small saucepan (not aluminum) and slowly cooking the onion. When it is soft, add the anchovy, mashing it into the onion with a wooden spoon.

2 ▲ Stir in the flour and, when it is well amalgamated, the capers and parsley. Add the wine vinegar and water, stirring constantly over low heat to thicken the sauce. Just before serving stir in another 25 g/1 oz/2 tbsp of butter, and the balsamic vinegar.

3 Meanwhile, flatten the pork fillets with a meat pounder until thin. Dredge lightly in the seasoned flour, shaking off any excess.

4 ▲ Heat 25 g/ 1 oz/2 tbsp of butter and the oil in a large frying pan, and when hot add some of the pork slices in one layer. Brown the meat on both sides, cooking it for a total of 5–6 minutes. Remove to a heated serving dish, and repeat with the remaining pork slices. Serve hot, with the sauce.

Pork Chops with Mushrooms

Costolette di maiale con funghi

The addition of dried porcini mushrooms gives fresh cultivated mushrooms a richer flavour.

Ingredients
15 g/$^1/_2$ oz/3 tbsp dried porcini mushrooms, soaked in 250 ml/8 fl oz/ 1 cup warm water and drained (reserve the soaking water)
75 g/3 oz/$^1/_3$ cup butter
2 cloves garlic, peeled and crushed
300 g/11oz fresh cultivated mushrooms, thinly sliced
salt and freshly ground black pepper
15 ml/1 tbsp olive oil
4 pork chops, trimmed of excess fat
$^1/_2$ tsp fresh thyme leaves, or $^1/_4$ tsp dried
100 ml/$^1/_2$ cup dry white wine
75 ml/$^1/_3$ cup light cream
serves 4

1 Filter the mushroom soaking water through a layer of paper towels and reserve. Melt two-thirds of the butter in a large frying pan. Add the garlic. When the foam subsides, stir in all the mushrooms. Season and cook over moderate heat until the mushrooms give up their liquid, 8–10 minutes.

2 Remove the mushrooms to a side dish. Add the remaining butter and the oil to the frying pan. When hot, add the pork in one layer and sprinkle with thyme. Cook over moderate to high heat for about 3 minutes per side to seal. Reduce the heat, and cook for 15–20 minutes more. Remove to a warmed plate.

3 ▲ Spoon off any fat in the pan. Pour in the wine and the mushroom water. Cook over high heat until reduced by about half, stirring to scrape up the residues at the bottom. Add the mushrooms and the cream, and cook for 4–5 minutes more. Serve the sauce poured over the chops.

Milanese Veal Chops

Costolette alla milanese

This famous dish depends on the chops being cooked carefully in butter.

πIngredients
2 veal chops or cutlets, on the bone
1 egg
salt and freshly ground black pepper
90–120 ml/ 6–8 tbsp plain breadcrumbs
50 g/2 oz/$^1/_4$ cup butter
15 ml/1 tbsp vegetable oil
lemon wedges, to serve
serves 2

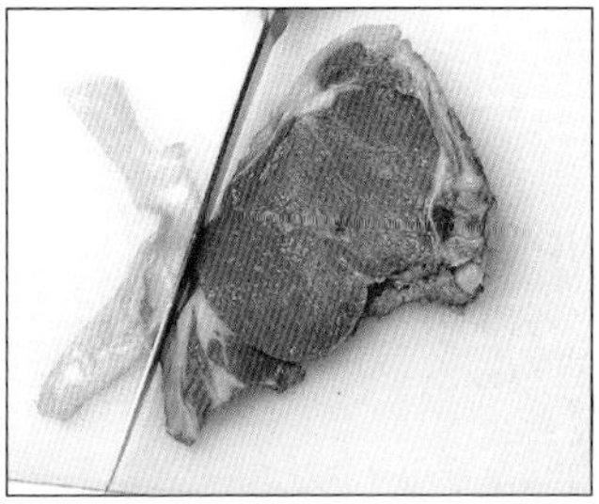

1 ▲ Trim any gristle or thick fat from the chops. Cut along the rib bone, if necessary, to free the meat on one side. Pound the meat slightly to flatten.

2 ▲ Beat the egg in a shallow bowl and season it with salt and pepper. Spread the breadcrumbs over a plate. Dip the chops into the egg, and then into the breadcrumbs. Pat the breadcrumbs to help them to stick.

~ COOK'S TIP ~

Milanese cooks sometimes soak the chops in milk for about an hour to soften the meat.

3 ▲ Heat the butter with the oil in a heavy frying pan large enough to hold both chops side by side. Do not let it brown. Add the chops to the pan, and cook them slowly over low to moderate heat until the breadcrumbs are golden and the meat is cooked through. The timing will depend on the thickness of the chops. The important thing is not to overcook the breadcrumb coating while undercooking the meat. Serve hot with lemon wedges.

Veal Rolls with Sage and Ham

Saltimbocca

These rolls are so good that, as their Italian name implies, they "jump into your mouth".

Ingredients
8 small veal escalopes
8 small slices prosciutto
8 leaves fresh sage
salt and freshly ground black pepper
40 g/1$^1/_2$ oz/3 tbsp butter
100 ml/4 fl oz/$^1/_2$ cup meat broth or stock, warmed
serves 3-4

1 Gently pound the veal slices with a mallet until thin. Lay a piece of prosciutto over each slice. Top with a sage leaf, and season with salt and pepper. Roll the escalopes around the filling and secure each roll with a wooden toothpick.

2 ▲ Heat half the butter in a frying pan just large enough to hold the rolls in one layer. When the butter is bubbling add the veal, turning the rolls to brown them on all sides. Cook for about 7–10 minutes, or until the veal is cooked. Remove to a warmed plate.

3 ▲ Add the remaining butter and the hot broth or stock to the frying pan, and bring to the boil, scraping up the brown residue on the bottom of the pan with a wooden spoon. Pour the sauce over the veal rolls, and serve.

Veal Escalopes with Marsala

Scaloppine di vitello con Marsala

This quick and delicious dish enlivens the mild flavour of veal with the sweetness of Marsala.

Ingredients

450 g/1 lb veal escalopes, preferably cut across the grain, about 5 mm/$^1/_4$ in thick
50 g/2 oz/$^1/_2$ cup flour seasoned with salt and freshly ground black pepper, for dredging
50 g/2 oz/$^1/_4$ cup butter
75 ml/5 tbsp Marsala
75 ml/5 tbsp stock or water
serves 4

1 Pound the escalopes flat to a thickness of about 4 mm/$^1/_4$in. If they have not been cut across the grain or from one muscle, cut small notches around the edges to stop them from curling during cooking.

2 ▲ Spread the flour out on a plate. Heat the butter in a large frying pan. Lightly dredge the veal slices in the flour, shaking off any excess. As soon as the foam from the butter subsides, put the veal into the pan in one layer, and brown the slices quickly on both sides, in two batches if necessary. Remove to a warmed serving plate.

3 ▲ Pour in the Marsala and the stock. Cook over moderate to high heat for 3–4 minutes, scraping up any meat residues from the bottom of the pan. Pour the sauce over the meat, and serve at once.

Ham and Cheese Veal Escalopes

Scaloppine alla bolognese

This dish from Bologna can be made with Parmesan or Gruyère cheese.

Ingredients

8 veal escalopes, about 450 g/1 lb total, preferably cut across the grain
50 g/2 oz/$^1/_2$ cup flour seasoned with salt and freshly ground black pepper, for dredging
25 ml/1 oz/2 tbsp butter
30 ml/2 tbsp olive oil
45 ml/3 tbsp dry white wine
8 thin slices ham
50 g/2 oz/$^1/_2$ cup freshly grated Parmesan cheese, or 8 small slices Gruyère cheese
serves 4

1 Preheat the oven to 200°C/400°F/gas 6. Pound the escalopes flat. If they have not been cut across the grain or from one muscle, cut small notches around the edges to prevent them from curling during cooking. Spread the seasoned flour over a plate.

2 ▲ Heat the butter with the oil in a large frying pan. Lightly dredge the veal slices in the flour, shaking off any excess. As soon as the foam from the butter subsides, put the veal into the pan in one layer, and brown the slices quickly on both sides. Remove to a shallow oven dish. Add the wine to the pan and cook for 1–2 minutes, scraping up the brown residue from the bottom of the pan with a wooden spoon. Pour over the escalopes.

3 ▲ Place one slice of ham on top of each escalope. Sprinkle with one tablespoon of Parmesan, or top with one slice of Gruyère. Place in the oven and cook until the cheese melts, 5–7 minutes. Serve hot.

Cold Veal with Tuna Sauce

Vitello tonnato

This classic summer dish is best when prepared in advance and refrigerated for a few hours before serving. The dish can be kept for up to 3 days in the refrigerator.

Ingredients
800 g/1$^3/_4$ lb boneless roasting veal, in one piece
1 carrot, peeled
1 stick celery
1 small onion, peeled and quartered
1 bay leaf
1 clove
5 ml/1 tsp whole peppercorns

For the tuna sauce
400 g/14 oz canned tuna, preferably in olive oil
4 anchovy fillets
10 ml/2 tsp capers, rinsed and drained
45 ml/3 tbsp fresh lemon juice
300 ml/$^1/_2$ pint/1$^1/_4$ cups mayonnaise
salt and freshly ground black pepper
capers and pickled gherkins, to garnish

serves 6–8

1 ▲ Place the veal, vegetables and flavourings in a medium saucepan (not aluminium or copper). Cover with water. Bring to a boil and simmer for 50–60 minutes. Skim off any scum that rises to the surface. Do not overcook, or the veal will fall apart when sliced. Allow it to cool in its cooking liquid for several hours, or overnight.

2 Drain the tuna. Place it in a food processor or blender, and add the anchovies, capers and lemon juice. Process to a creamy paste. If it seems too thick, add 30–45 ml/2–3 tbsp of the cool veal broth and process again.

3 ▲ Scrape the tuna purée into a bowl. Fold in the mayonnaise. Check the seasoning and adjust as necessary.

4 Slice the veal as thinly as possible. Spread a little of the tuna sauce over the bottom of a serving platter.

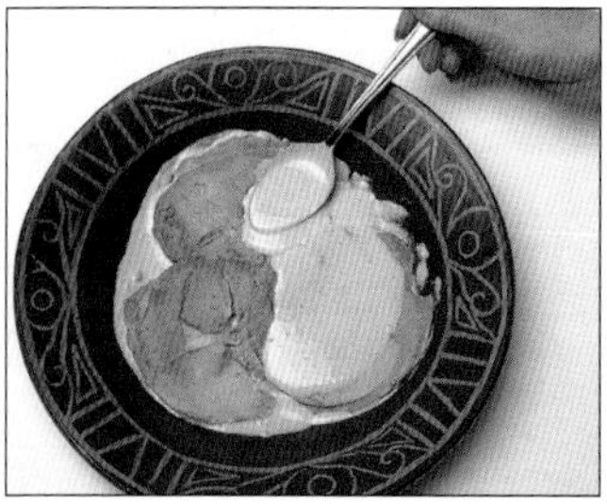

5 ▲ Arrange a layer of the veal slices on top of the sauce. Cover with a thin layer of sauce. Make another layer or two of veal slices and sauce, ending with the sauce. Garnish with capers and gherkins. Cover with plastic wrap and refrigerate until needed.

Liver with Onions

Fegato alla veneziana

This classic Venetian dish is very good served with grilled polenta. Allow enough time for the onions to cook very slowly, to produce a sweet flavour.

Ingredients
75 g/3 oz/$^1/_3$ cup butter
45 ml/3 tbsp olive oil
750 g/1$^1/_2$ lb onions, very finely sliced
salt and freshly ground black pepper
800 g/1$^3/_4$ lb calf's liver, sliced thinly
45 ml/3 tbsp finely chopped fresh parsley, to garnish
grilled polenta wedges, to serve (optional)
serves 6

1 ▲ Heat two-thirds of the butter with the oil in a large heavy frying pan. Add the onions, and cook over low heat until soft and tender, about 40–50 minutes, stirring often. Season with salt and pepper. Remove to a side dish.

2 ▲ Heat the remaining butter in the pan over moderate to high heat. When it has stopped bubbling add the liver, and brown it on both sides. Cook for about 5 minutes, or until done. Remove to a warmed side dish.

3 ▲ Return the onions to the pan. Raise the heat slightly, and stir the onions to mix them into the liver cooking juices.

4 ▲ When the onions are hot, turn them out onto a heated serving platter. Arrange the liver on top, and sprinkle with parsley. Serve with grilled polenta wedges, if desired.

Veal Shanks with Tomatoes and White Wine

Osso buco

This famous Milanese dish is rich and hearty. It is traditionally served with risotto alla milanese, but plain boiled rice goes equally well. The lemony gremolata garnish helps to cut the richness of the dish, as does a crisp green salad - serve it after the osso buco and before the dessert, to refresh the palate.

Ingredients

30 ml/2 tbsp plain flour
4 pieces of osso buco
2 small onions
30 ml/2 tbsp olive oil
1 large celery stick, finely chopped
1 medium carrot, finely chopped
2 garlic cloves, finely chopped
400 g/14 oz can chopped tomatoes
300 ml/½ pint/1¼ cups dry white wine
300 ml/½ pint/1¼ cups chicken or veal stock
1 strip of thinly pared lemon rind
2 bay leaves, plus extra for garnishing (optional)
salt and freshly ground black pepper

For the gremolata

30 ml/2 tbsp finely chopped fresh flat leaf parsley
finely grated rind of 1 lemon
1 garlic clove, finely chopped

serves 4

1 ▲ Preheat the oven to 160°C/325°F/Gas 3. Season the flour with salt and pepper and spread it out in a shallow bowl. Add the pieces of veal and turn them in the flour until evenly coated. Shake off any excess flour.

2 ▲ Slice one of the onions and separate it into rings. Heat the oil in a large flameproof casserole, then add the veal, with the onion rings, and brown the veal on both sides over a medium heat. Remove the veal shanks with tongs and set aside on kitchen paper to drain.

3 ▲ Chop the remaining onion and add it to the pan with the celery, carrot and garlic. Stir the bottom of the pan to incorporate the pan juices and sediment. Cook gently, stirring frequently, for about 5 minutes until the vegetables soften slightly.

4 ▲ Add the chopped tomatoes, wine, stock, lemon rind and bay leaves, then season to taste with salt and pepper. Bring to the boil, stirring. Return the veal to the pan and coat with the sauce. Cover and cook in the oven for 2 hours or until the veal feels tender when pierced with a fork.

5 Meanwhile, make the gremolata. In a small bowl, mix together the chopped parsley, lemon rind and chopped garlic. Remove the casserole from the oven and lift out and discard the strip of lemon rind and the bay leaves. Taste the sauce for seasoning. Serve the osso buco hot, sprinkled with the gremolata and garnished with extra bay leaves, if you like.

Cook's Tip

Osso buco is available from large supermarkets and good butchers. Choose pieces about 2 cm/¾ in thick.

Calf's Liver with Balsamic Vinegar

Fegato all'aceto balsamico

This sweet and sour liver dish is a speciality of Venice. Serve it very simply, with green beans sprinkled with browned breadcrumbs.

Ingredients

15 ml/1 tbsp plain flour
2.5 ml/½ tsp finely chopped fresh sage
4 thin slices of calf's liver, cut into serving pieces
45 ml/3 tbsp olive oil
25 g/1 oz/2 tbsp butter
2 small red onions, sliced and separated into rings
150 ml/¼ pint/⅔ cup dry white wine
45 ml/3 tbsp balsamic vinegar
pinch of granulated sugar
salt and freshly ground black pepper
fresh sprigs of sage, to garnish
green beans sprinkled with browned breadcrumbs, to serve

serves 2

Cook's Tip

Never overcook calf's liver, because it quickly turns tough. Its delicate flesh is at its most tender when it is served slightly underdone and pink – like a rare steak.

1 ▲ Spread out the flour in a shallow bowl. Season it with the sage and plenty of salt and pepper. Turn the liver in the flour until well coated.

2 Heat 30 ml/2 tbsp of the oil with half of the butter in a wide heavy-based saucepan or frying pan until foaming. Add the onion rings and cook gently, stirring frequently, for about 5 minutes until softened but not coloured. Remove with a fish slice and set aside.

3 ▲ Heat the remaining oil and butter in the pan until foaming, add the liver and cook over medium heat for 2–3 minutes on each side. Transfer to heated dinner plates and keep hot.

4 Add the wine and vinegar to the pan, then stir to mix with the pan juices and any sediment. Add the onions and sugar and heat through, stirring. Spoon the sauce over the liver, garnish with sage sprigs and serve at once with the green beans.

Veal Escalopes with Lemon

Scaloppine al limone

Popular in Italian restaurants, this dish is very easy to make at home.

Ingredients

4 veal escalopes
30–45 ml/2–3 tbsp plain flour
50 g/2 oz/¼ cup butter
60 ml/4 tbsp olive oil
60 ml/4 tbsp Italian dry white vermouth or dry white wine
45 ml/3 tbsp lemon juice
salt and freshly ground black pepper
lemon wedges and fresh parsley, to garnish
green beans and peperonata, to serve
serves 4

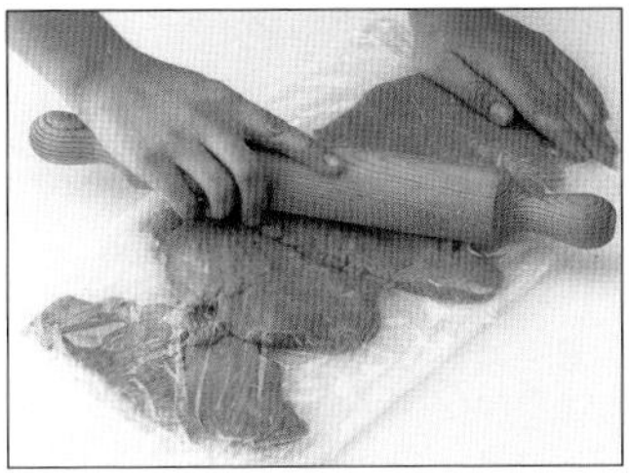

1 ▲ Put each escalope between two sheets of clear film and pound until very thin.

2 Cut the pounded escalopes in half or quarters, if you like, and coat in the flour, seasoned with salt and pepper.

3 ▲ Melt the butter with half the oil in a large, heavy frying pan until sizzling. Add as many escalopes as the pan will hold. Fry over a medium to high heat for 1-2 minutes on each side until lightly coloured. Remove with a fish slice and keep hot. Add the remaining oil and cook the remaining escalopes in the same way.

4 Remove the pan from the heat and add the vermouth or wine and the lemon juice. Stir vigorously to mix with the pan juices, then return to the heat and return all the veal to the pan. Spoon the sauce over the veal. Shake the pan over a medium heat until all of the escalopes are coated in the sauce and heated through.

5 Serve at once, garnished with lemon wedges and parsley. Lightly cooked green beans and peperonata make a delicious accompaniment.

Variation

Use skinless boneless chicken breasts instead of the veal. If they are thick, cut them in half before pounding.

Chicken with Chianti

Pollo al chianti

Together the robust, full-flavoured red wine and red pesto give this sauce a rich colour and almost spicy flavour, while the grapes add a delicious sweetness. Serve the stew with grilled polenta or warm crusty bread, and accompany with a piquant salad, such as rocket or watercress, tossed with a tasty dressing.

Ingredients
45 ml/3 tbsp olive oil
4 part-boned chicken breasts, skinned
1 medium red onion
30 ml/2 tbsp red pesto
300 ml/½ pint/1¼ cups Chianti
300 ml/½ pint/1¼ cups water
115 g/4 oz red grapes, halved lengthways and seeded if necessary
salt and freshly ground black pepper
fresh basil leaves, to garnish
rocket salad, to serve
serves 4

1 ▲ Heat 30 ml/2 tbsp of the oil in a large frying pan, add the chicken breasts and sauté over a medium heat for about 5 minutes until they have changed colour on all sides. Remove with a slotted spoon and drain on kitchen paper.

Cook's Tip

Use part-boned chicken breasts, if you can get them, in preference to boneless chicken for this dish as they have a better flavour. Chicken thighs or drumsticks could also be cooked in this way.

2 Cut the onions in half, through the root. Trim off the root, then slice the onion halves lengthways to create thin wedges.

3 ▲ Heat the remaining oil in the pan, add the onion wedges and red pesto and cook gently, stirring constantly, for about 3 minutes until the onion is softened, but not browned.

4 ▲ Add the Chianti and water to the pan and bring to the boil, stirring, then return the chicken to the pan and add salt and pepper to taste.

5 Reduce the heat, then cover the pan and simmer gently for about 20 minutes or until the chicken is tender, stirring occasionally.

6 ▲ Add the grapes to the pan and cook over a low to medium heat until heated through, then taste the sauce for seasoning. Serve the chicken hot, garnished with basil and accompanied by the rocket salad.

Variations

Use green pesto instead of red, and substitute a dry white wine such as pinot grigio for the Chianti, then finish with seedless green grapes. A few spoonfuls of mascarpone cheese can be added at the end if you like, to enrich the sauce.

Hunter's Chicken

Pollo alla cacciatora

This traditional dish sometimes has strips of green pepper in the sauce for extra colour and flavour instead of the fresh mushrooms.

Ingredients
15 g/½ oz/1 cup dried porcini mushrooms
30 ml/2 tbsp olive oil
15 g/½ oz/1 tbsp butter
4 chicken pieces, on the bone, skinned
1 large onion, thinly sliced
400 g/14 oz can chopped tomatoes
150 ml/¼ pint/⅔ cup red wine
1 garlic clove, crushed
leaves of 1 sprig of fresh rosemary, finely chopped
115 g/4 oz/1¾ cups fresh field mushrooms, thinly sliced
salt and freshly ground black pepper
fresh rosemary sprigs, to garnish
serves 4

1 ▲ Put the porcini in a bowl, add 250 ml/8 fl oz/1 cup warm water and soak for 20–30 minutes. Remove from the liquid and squeeze the porcini over the bowl. Strain the liquid and reserve. Finely chop the porcini.

2 ▲ Heat the oil and butter in a large flameproof casserole until foaming. Add the chicken. Sauté over a medium heat for 5 minutes, or until golden. Remove and drain on kitchen paper.

3 ▲ Add the onion and chopped mushrooms to the pan. Cook gently, stirring frequently, for about 3 minutes until the onion has softened but not browned. Stir in the chopped tomatoes, wine and reserved mushroom soaking liquid, then add the crushed garlic and chopped rosemary, with salt and pepper to taste. Bring to the boil, stirring all the time.

4 ▲ Return the chicken to the pan and coat with the sauce. Cover and simmer gently for 30 minutes.

5 Add the fresh mushrooms and stir well to mix into the sauce. Continue simmering gently for 10 minutes or until the chicken is tender. Taste for seasoning. Serve hot, with creamed potato or polenta, if you like. Garnish with rosemary.

Chicken with Tomatoes and Prawns

Pollo alla marengo

This Piedmontese dish was created especially for Napoleon after the battle of Marengo. Versions of it appear in both Italian and French recipe books.

Ingredients

120 ml/4 fl oz/½ cup olive oil
8 chicken thighs on the bone, skinned
1 onion, finely chopped
1 celery stick, finely chopped
1 garlic clove, crushed
350 g/12 oz ripe Italian plum tomatoes, peeled and roughly chopped
250 ml/8 fl oz/1 cup dry white wine
2.5 ml/½ tsp finely chopped fresh rosemary
15 ml/1 tbsp butter
8 small triangles of thinly sliced white bread, without crusts
175 g/6 oz large raw prawns, shelled
salt and freshly ground black pepper
finely chopped flat leaf parsley, to garnish

serves 4

1 ▲ Heat about 30 ml/2 tbsp of the oil in a frying pan, add the chicken thighs and sauté over a medium heat for about 5 minutes until they have changed colour on all sides. Transfer to a flameproof casserole.

2 ▲ Add the onion and celery to the frying pan and cook gently, stirring frequently, for about 3 minutes until softened. Add the garlic, tomatoes, wine, rosemary and salt and pepper to taste. Bring to the boil, stirring.

3 Pour the tomato sauce over the chicken. Cover and cook gently for 40 minutes or until the chicken is tender when pierced.

4 ▲ About 10 minutes before serving, add the remaining oil and the butter to the frying pan and heat until hot but not smoking. Add the triangles of bread and shallow fry until crisp and golden on each side. Drain on kitchen paper.

5 ▲ Add the prawns to the tomato sauce and heat until the prawns are cooked. Taste the sauce for seasoning. Dip one of the tips of each fried bread triangle in parsley. Serve the dish hot, garnished with the bread triangles.

Variation

To make the dish look more like its original, authentic version, garnish it with a few large crayfish or prawns in their shells.

Chicken with Parma Ham and Cheese

Pollo alla valdostana

The name Valdostana is derived from Val d'Aosta, home of the Fontina cheese used here.

Ingredients
2 thin slices of prosciutto
2 thin slices of Fontina cheese
4 part-boned chicken breasts
4 sprigs of basil
30 ml/2 tbsp olive oil
15 g/½ oz/1 tbsp butter
120 ml/4 fl oz/½ cup dry white wine
salt and freshly ground black pepper
tender young salad leaves, to serve
serves 4

Cook's Tip
There is nothing quite like the buttery texture and nutty flavour of Fontina cheese, and it also has superb melting qualities, but you could use a Swiss or French mountain cheese, such as Gruyère or Emmental. Ask for the cheese to be sliced thinly on the machine slicer, as you will find it difficult to slice it thinly yourself.

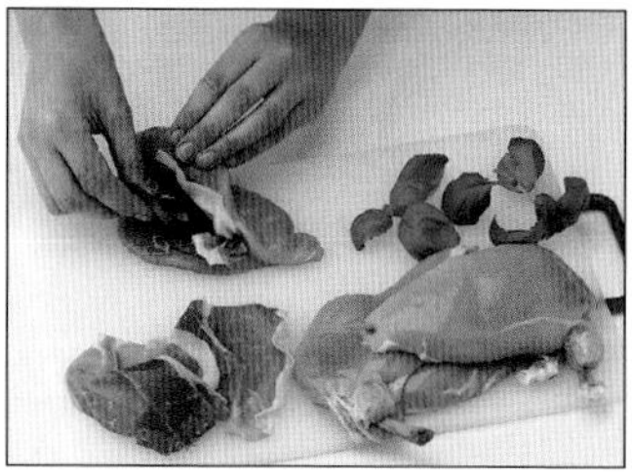

1 ▲ Preheat the oven to 200°C/400°F/Gas 6. Lightly oil a baking dish. Cut the prosciutto and Fontina slices in half crossways. Skin the chicken breasts, open out the slit in the centre of each one, and fill each cavity with half a ham slice and a basil sprig.

2 ▲ Heat the oil and butter in a wide heavy-based frying pan until foaming. Cook the chicken breasts over a medium heat for 1–2 minutes on each side until they change colour. Transfer to the baking dish. Add the wine to the pan juices, stir until sizzling, then pour over the chicken and season to taste.

3 Top each chicken breast with a slice of Fontina. Bake for 20 minutes or until the chicken is tender. Serve hot, with tender young salad leaves.

Devilled Chicken

Pollo alla diavola

You can tell this spicy, barbecued chicken dish comes from southern Italy because it has dried red chillies in the marinade. Versions without the chillies are just as good.

Ingredients
120 ml/4 fl oz/½ cup olive oil
finely grated rind and juice of 1 large lemon
2 garlic cloves, finely chopped
10 ml/2 tsp finely chopped or crumbled dried red chillies
12 skinless, boneless chicken thighs, each cut into 3 or 4 pieces
salt and freshly ground black pepper
flat leaf parsley leaves, to garnish
lemon wedges, to serve
serves 4

Cook's Tip
Thread the chicken pieces spiral-fashion on the skewers so they do not fall off during cooking.

1 ▲ Make a marinade by mixing the oil, lemon rind and juice, garlic and chillies in a large, shallow glass or china dish. Add salt and pepper to taste. Whisk well, then add the chicken pieces, turning to coat with the marinade. Cover and marinate in the fridge for at least 4 hours, or preferably overnight.

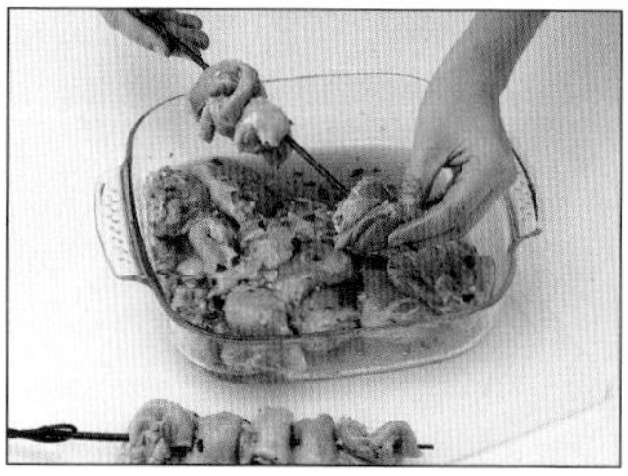

2 ▲ When ready to cook, prepare the barbecue or preheat the grill and thread the chicken pieces on to eight oiled metal skewers. Cook on the barbecue or under a hot grill for 6–8 minutes, turning frequently, until tender. Garnish with parsley leaves and serve hot, with lemon wedges for squeezing.

Chicken with Peppers

Pollo con peperoni

This colourful dish comes from the south of Italy, where sweet peppers are plentiful.

Ingredients

1.5 kg/3 lb chicken, cut into serving pieces
3 large peppers, red, yellow, or green
90 ml/6 tbsp olive oil
2 medium red onions, finely sliced
2 cloves garlic, finely chopped
small piece of dried chilli, crumbled (optional)
100 ml/4 fl oz/$^1/_2$ cup white wine
salt and freshly ground black pepper
2 tomatoes, fresh or canned, peeled and chopped
45 g/3 tbsp chopped fresh parsley
serves 4

1 Trim any fat off the chicken, and remove all excess skin. Wash the peppers. Prepare by cutting them in half, scooping out the seeds, and cutting away the stem. Slice into strips.

2 ▲ Heat half the oil in a large heavy saucepan or casserole. Add the onion, and cook over low heat until soft. Remove to a side dish. Add the remaining oil to the pan, raise the heat to moderate, add the chicken and brown on all sides, 6–8 minutes. Return the onions to the pan, and add the garlic and dried chilli, if using.

3 ▲ Pour in the wine, and cook until it has reduced by half. Add the peppers. Season. After 3–4 minutes, stir in the tomatoes. Lower the heat, cover the pan and cook until the peppers are soft, and the chicken is cooked, approximately 25–30 minutes. Stir occasionally. Stir in the parsley and serve.

Chicken Breasts Cooked in Butter

Petti di pollo alla fiorentina

This simple and delicious way of cooking chicken brings out all of its delicacy.

Ingredients

4 small chicken breasts, skinned and boned
flour seasoned with salt and freshly ground black pepper, for dredging
75 g/3 oz/$^1/_3$ cup butter
1 sprig fresh parsley, to garnish
serves 4

1 Separate the two fillets of each breast. They come apart very easily; one is large, the other small. Pound the large fillets lightly to flatten them. Dredge the chicken in the seasoned flour, shaking off any excess.

~ COOK'S TIP ~

This chicken dish should be accompanied by delicately flavoured vegetables so that its subtle taste is not overpowered.

2 ▲ Heat the butter in a large heavy frying pan until it bubbles. Place all the chicken fillets in the pan, in one layer if possible. Cook over moderate to high heat for 3–4 minutes until they are golden brown.

3 ▲ Turn the chicken over. Reduce the heat to low to moderate, and continue cooking until the fillets are cooked through but still springy to the touch, about 9–12 minutes in all. If the chicken begins to brown too much, cover the pan for the final minutes of cooking. Serve immediately, garnished with a little parsley.

Roast Chicken with Fennel

Pollo con finocchio

In Italy this dish is prepared with wild fennel. Cultivated fennel bulb works just as well.

Ingredients

1.8 kg/3$^1/_2$ lb roasting chicken
salt and freshly ground black pepper
1 onion, quartered
100 ml/4 fl oz/$^1/_2$ cup olive oil
2 medium fennel bulbs
1 clove garlic, peeled
pinch of grated nutmeg
3–4 thin slices pancetta or bacon
100 ml/4 fl oz/$^1/_2$ cup dry white wine
serves 4–5

1 Preheat the oven to 180°C/350°F/gas 4. Rinse the chicken in cold water. Pat it dry inside and out with paper towels. Sprinkle the cavity with salt and pepper. Place the onion quarters in the cavity. Rub the chicken with about 45 ml/3 tbsp of the olive oil. Place in a roasting pan.

2 Cut the green fronds from the tops of the fennel bulbs. Chop the fronds with the garlic. Place in a small bowl and mix with the nutmeg. Season with salt and pepper.

3 ▲ Sprinkle the fennel mixture over the chicken, pressing it onto the oiled skin. Cover the breast with the slices of pancetta or bacon. Sprinkle with 30 ml/2 tbsp of oil. Place in the oven and roast for 30 minutes.

4 Meanwhile, boil or steam the fennel bulbs until barely tender. Remove from the heat and cut into quarters or sixths lengthwise. After the chicken has been cooking for 30 minutes, remove the pan from the oven. Baste the chicken with any oils in the pan.

5 Arrange the fennel pieces around the chicken. Sprinkle the fennel with the remaining oil. Pour about half the wine over the chicken, and return the pan to the oven.

6 ▲ After 30 minutes more, baste the chicken again. Pour on the remaining wine. Cook for 15–20 minutes more. To test, prick the thigh with a fork. If the juices run clear, the chicken is cooked. Transfer the chicken to a serving platter, and arrange the fennel around it.

Chicken with Ham and Cheese

Petti di pollo alla bolognese

This tasty combination comes from Emilia-Romagna, where it is also prepared with veal.

Ingredients

4 small chicken breasts, skinned and boned
flour seasoned with salt and freshly ground black pepper, for dredging
50 g/2 oz/$^1/_4$ cup butter
3–4 leaves fresh sage
4 thin slices prosciutto crudo, or cooked ham, cut in half
50 g/2 oz/$^1/_2$ cup freshly grated Parmesan cheese
serves 4

1 Cut each chicken breast in half lengthwise to make two flat fillets of approximately the same thickness. Dredge the chicken in the seasoned flour, and shake off the excess.

2 ▲ Preheat the grill. Heat the butter in a large heavy frying pan or skillet with the sage leaves. Add the chicken in one layer, and cook over low to moderate heat until golden brown on both sides, turning as necessary. This will take about 15 minutes.

3 ▲ Remove the chicken from the heat, and arrange on a flameproof serving dish or grill pan. Place one piece of ham on each chicken fillet, and top with the grated Parmesan. Grill for 3–4 minutes, or until the cheese has melted. Serve at once.

Mediterranean Turkey Skewers

Spiedini di tacchino

These skewers are delicious, and can be cooked on a grill or on a charcoal barbecue.

Ingredients

90 ml/6 tbsp olive oil
45 ml/3 tbsp fresh lemon juice
1 clove garlic, finely chopped
30 ml/2 tbsp chopped fresh basil
salt and freshly ground black pepper
2 medium courgettes
1 long thin aubergine
300 g/11oz boneless turkey, cut into 5 cm/2in cubes
12–16 pickled onions
1 pepper, red or yellow, cut into 5 cm/2in squares

serves 4

1 ▲ In a small bowl mix the oil with the lemon juice, garlic and basil. Season with salt and pepper.

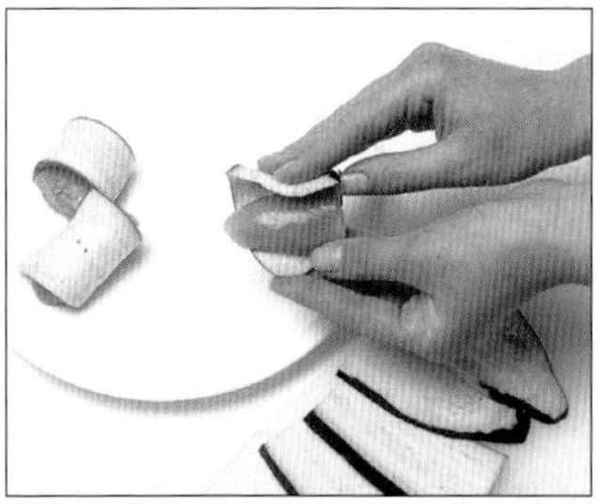

2 ▲ Slice the courgettes and aubergine lengthwise into strips 5mm/$^1/_4$ inch thick. Cut them crosswise about two-thirds of the way along their length. Discard the shorter length. Wrap half the turkey pieces with the courgette slices, and the other half with the aubergine slices.

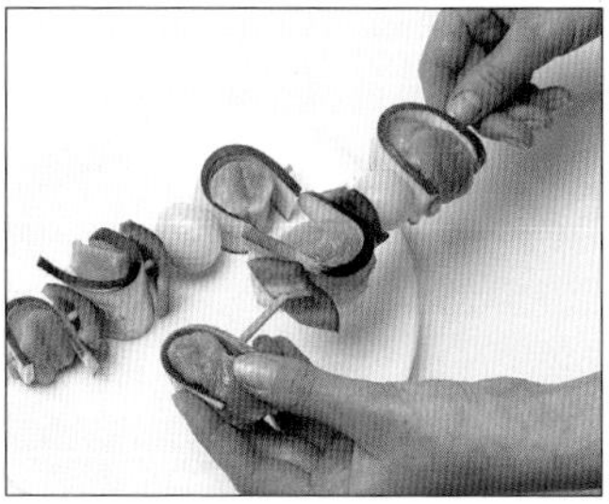

3 ▲ Prepare the skewers by alternating the turkey, onions, and pepper pieces. Lay the prepared skewers on a platter, and sprinkle with the flavored oil. Leave to marinate for at least 30 minutes. Preheat the grill, or prepare a barbecue.

4 ▲Grill for about 10 minutes, or until the vegetables are tender, turning the skewers occasionally. Serve hot.

Turkey Cutlets with Olives

Petto di tacchino con olive

This quick and tasty dish makes a good light main course.

Ingredients
90 ml/6 tbsp olive oil
1 clove garlic, peeled and lightly crushed
1 dried chilli, lightly crushed
500 g/1 $^1/_4$ lb boneless turkey breast, cut into 5 mm/ $^1/_4$ in slices
salt and freshly ground black pepper
100 ml/4 fl oz/$^1/_2$ cup dry white wine
4 tomatoes, peeled and seeded, cut into thin strips
about 24 black olives
6–8 leaves fresh basil, torn into pieces
serves 4

1 ▲ Heat 60 ml/4 tbsp of the olive oil in a large frying pan. Add the garlic and dried chilli, and cook over low heat until the garlic is golden.

2 ▲ Raise the heat to moderate. Place the turkey slices in the pan, and brown them lightly on both sides. Season with salt and pepper. The turkey will be cooked after about 2 minutes. Remove the turkey to a heated dish.

3 ▲ Discard the garlic and chilli. Add the wine, tomato strips and olives. Cook over moderate heat for 3–4 minutes, scraping up any meat residue from the bottom of the pan.

4 ▲ Return the turkey to the pan. Sprinkle with the basil. Heat for about 30 seconds, and serve.

Stuffed Turkey Breast with Lemon

Petto di tacchino ripieno

This elegant dish of rolled turkey breast makes an impressive but economical main course.

Ingredients

750 g/1 $^{1}/_{2}$ lb turkey breast, in one piece
1 carrot, cut into matchsticks
1 medium courgette, cut into matchsticks
75 g/3 oz/ $^{1}/_{3}$ cup ham, cut into matchsticks
115 g/4 oz/2 thick slices white bread, crusts removed, softened in a little milk
10 green olives, stoned and finely chopped
1 large clove garlic, finely chopped
60 ml/4 tbsp chopped fresh parsley
60 ml/4 tbsp finely chopped fresh basil
1 egg
$^{1}/_{8}$ tsp grated lemon zest
30 ml/2 tbsp freshly grated Parmesan cheese
salt and freshly ground black pepper
60 ml/4 tbsp olive oil
250 ml/8 fl oz/1 cup chicken broth or stock, warmed
$^{1}/_{2}$ lemon, cut into thin wedges
25 g/1 oz/2 tbsp butter
serves 4–5

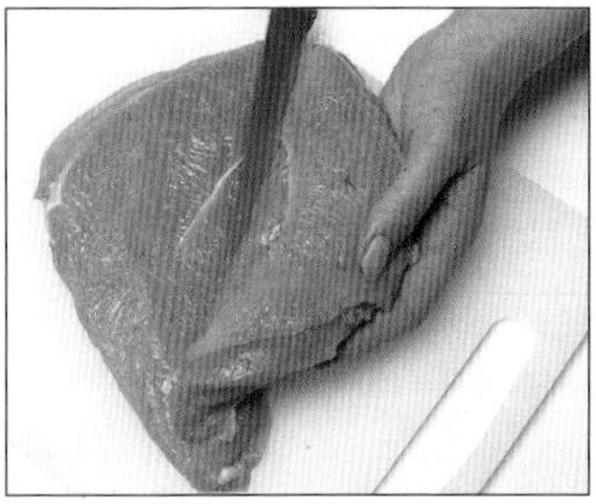

1 ▲ Remove any bones, skin or fat from the turkey. Using a sharp knife, cut part of the way through the turkey breast and open the two halves out like a book.

~ VARIATION ~

Substitute 75 g/3 oz sliced mushrooms sautéed lightly in 45 g/1 $^{1}/_{2}$ oz/3 tbsp butter for the ham in step 3. Omit the lemon wedges during cooking.

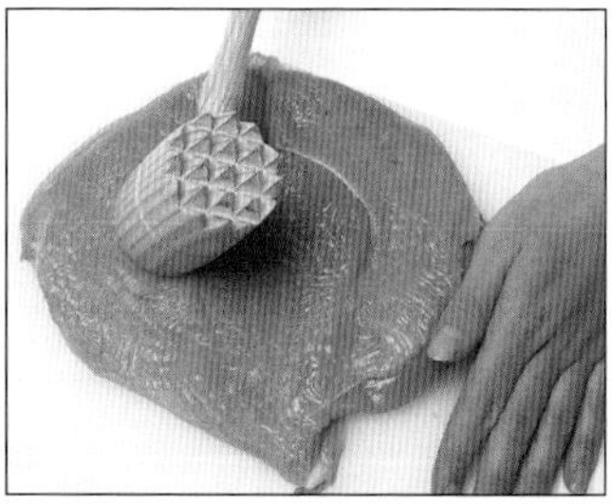

2 ▲ Pound the meat with a mallet to obtain one large piece of meat of as even a thickness as possible.

3 ▲ Preheat the oven to 200°C/400°F/ gas 6. Blanch the carrot and courgette pieces in a small saucepan of boiling water for 2 minutes. Drain. Combine with the matchsticks of ham.

4 ▲ Squeeze the bread, and place in a mixing bowl, breaking it into small pieces with a fork. Stir in the olives, garlic and herbs, and the egg. Add the lemon zest and grated Parmesan. Season with salt and pepper.

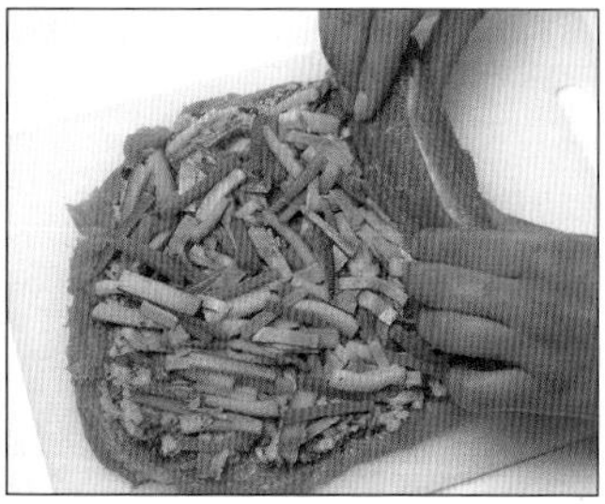

5 ▲ Spread the bread mixture in one layer over the meat, leaving a small border all around. Cover with the ham and vegetable mixture. Roll the turkey up. Tie the roll in several places with string.

6 ▲ Heat the oil in a ovenproof casserole. When the oil is hot, brown the meat on all sides. Remove from the heat, add the broth or stock, and arrange the lemon wedges around the meat. Cover and place in the oven.

7 After 15 minutes remove the cover, discard the lemon and baste the meat. Continue cooking, uncovered, for a further 25–30 minutes, basting occasionally. Allow the roll to stand for at least 10 minutes before slicing.

8 Strain the sauce. Stir in the butter and taste for seasoning. Serve the sliced roll warm with the sauce. If you wish to serve it cold, slice the roll just before serving and omit the sauce.

Turkey with Marsala Cream Sauce

Tacchino al marsala

Marsala makes a very rich and tasty sauce. The addition of lemon juice gives it a sharp edge, which helps to offset the richness.

Ingredients
6 turkey breast steaks
45 ml/3 tbsp plain flour
30 ml/2 tbsp olive oil
25 g/1 oz/2 tbsp butter
175 ml/6 fl oz/¾ cup dry Marsala
60 ml/4 tbsp lemon juice
175 ml/6 fl oz/¾ cup double cream
salt and freshly ground black pepper
lemon wedges, and chopped fresh parsley, to garnish
mangetouts and French beans, to serve
serves 6

1 ▲ Put each turkey steak between two sheets of clear film and pound with a rolling pin to flatten and stretch. Cut each steak in half or into quarters, cutting away and discarding any sinew.

2 ▲ Spread out the flour in a shallow bowl. Season well and coat the meat.

Variation
Veal or pork escalopes or chicken breast fillets can be used instead of the turkey, and 50 g/2 oz/¼ cup mascarpone cheese instead of the double cream.

3 ▲ Heat the oil and butter in a wide heavy-based saucepan or frying pan until sizzling. Add as many pieces of turkey as the pan will hold and sauté over a medium heat for about 3 minutes on each side until crispy and tender. Transfer to a warmed serving dish with tongs and keep hot. Repeat with the remaining turkey.

4 ▲ Lower the heat. Mix the Marsala and lemon juice in a jug, add to the pan and raise the heat. Bring to the boil, stirring in the sediment, then add the cream. Simmer, stirring constantly, until the sauce is reduced and glossy. Taste for seasoning. Spoon over the turkey, garnish with the lemon wedges and parsley and serve at once with the mangetouts and French beans.

Duck with Chestnut Sauce

Petti di anatra con salsa di castagne

This autumnal dish makes use of the sweet chestnuts that are gathered in Italian woods.

Ingredients
1 sprig fresh rosemary
1 clove garlic, thinly sliced
30 ml/2 tbsp olive oil
4 duck breasts, boned and fat removed

For the sauce
450 g/1 lb chestnuts
5 ml/1 tsp oil
350 ml/12 fl oz/$1\frac{1}{2}$ cups milk
1 small onion, finely chopped
1 carrot, finely chopped
1 small bay leaf
salt and freshly ground black pepper
30 ml/2 tbsp cream, warmed

serves 4–5

1 ▲ Pull the leaves from the sprig of rosemary. Combine them with the garlic and oil in a shallow bowl. Pat the duck breasts dry with paper towels. Brush the duck breasts with the marinade. Allow to stand for at least 2 hours before cooking.

2 Preheat the oven to 180°C/350°F/ gas 4. Cut a cross in the flat side of each chestnut with a sharp knife.

~ COOK'S TIP ~

The chestnut sauce may be prepared in advance and kept in the refrigerator for up to 2 days, or it may be made when chestnuts are in season and frozen. Allow to thaw to room temperature before re-heating.

3 ▲ Place the chestnuts in a baking pan with the oil, and shake the pan until the nuts are coated with the oil. Bake for about 20 minutes, then peel.

4 Place the peeled chestnuts in a heavy pan with the milk, onion, carrot and bay leaf. Cook slowly for about 10–15 minutes until the chestnuts are very tender. Season with salt and pepper. Discard the bay leaf. Press the mixture through a strainer.

5 Return the sauce to the saucepan. Heat gently while the duck is cooking. Just before serving, stir in the cream. If the sauce is too thick, add a little more cream. Preheat the grill, or prepare a barbecue.

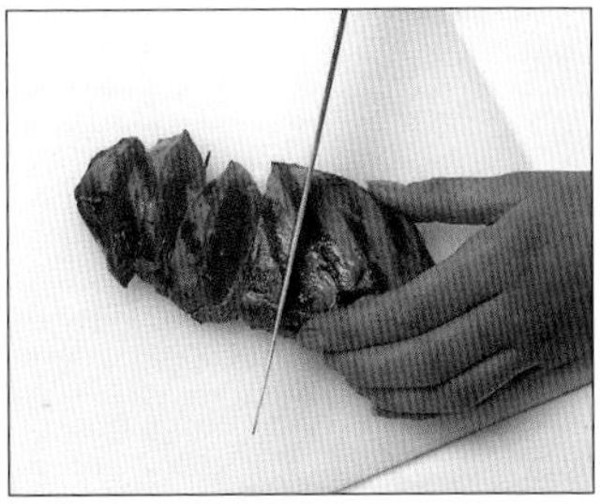

6 ▲ Grill the duck breasts until medium rare, about 6–8 minutes. The meat should be pink when sliced. Slice into rounds and arrange on warm plates. Serve with the heated sauce.

Pan-Fried Marinated Poussin

Galletti marinati in padella

These small birds are full of flavour when marinated for several hours before cooking.

Ingredients
2 poussins, about 450 g/1 lb each
5–6 leaves fresh mint, torn into pieces
1 leek, sliced into thin rings
1 clove garlic, finely chopped
salt and coarsely ground black pepper
60 ml/4 tbsp olive oil
30 ml/2 tbsp fresh lemon juice
50 ml/2 fl oz/$^1/_4$ cup dry white wine
mint leaves, to garnish
serves 3–4

1 Cut the poussins in half down the backbone, dividing the breast. Flatten the 4 halves with a mallet. Place them in a bowl with the mint, leek, garlic and pepper. Sprinkle with oil and half the lemon juice, cover, and allow to stand in a cool place for 6 hours.

2 ▲ Heat a large heavy frying pan or skillet. Place the poussins and their marinade in the pan. Cover and cook over moderate heat for about 45 minutes, turning occasionally. Season with salt during the cooking. Remove to a warm serving platter.

3 ▲ Tilt the pan and spoon off any fat on the surface. Pour in the wine and remaining lemon juice, and cook until the sauce reduces. Strain the sauce, pressing the vegetables to extract all the juices. Place the poussins on individual dishes, and spoon over the sauce. Sprinkle with mint, and serve.

Quail with Grapes

Quaglie con uva

Small birds often feature in Italian recipes. Use the most flavourful grapes for this dish.

Ingredients
6–8 fresh quail, gutted
salt and freshly ground black pepper
60 ml/4 tbsp olive oil
50 g/2 oz/$^1/_4$ cup pancetta or bacon, cut into small dice
250 ml/8 fl oz/1 cup dry white wine
250 ml/8 fl oz/1 cup chicken broth, warmed
350 g/12 oz green grapes
serves 4

1 Wash the quail carefully inside and out with cold water. Pat dry with paper towels. Sprinkle salt and pepper into the cavities.

2 Heat the oil in a heavy sauté pan or casserole large enough to accommodate all the quail in one layer. Add the pancetta or bacon, and cook over low heat for 5 minutes.

3 ▲ Raise the heat to moderate to high, and place the quail in the pan. Brown them evenly on all sides. Pour in the wine, and cook over moderate heat until it reduces by about half. Turn the quail over. Cover the pan, and cook for about 10–15 minutes. Add the stock, turn the quail again, cover, and cook for 15–20 minutes more, or until the birds are tender. Remove to a warmed serving platter and keep warm while the sauce is being finished.

4 ▲ Meanwhile drop the grapes into a pan of boiling water, and blanch for about 3 minutes. Drain and reserve.

5 Strain the pan juices into a small cup. If bacon has been used, allow the fat to separate and rise to the top. Spoon off the fat and discard. Pour the strained gravy into a small saucepan. Add the grapes and warm them gently for 2–3 minutes. Spoon around the quail and serve.

Roast Pheasant with Juniper Berries

Fagiano arrosto

Sage and juniper are often used in Italian cooking to flavour pheasant and other game.

Ingredients
1.2-1.4 kg/$2^1/_2$-3 lb pheasant with liver, finely chopped (optional)
45 ml/3 tbsp olive oil
2 sprigs fresh sage
3 shallots, chopped
1 bay leaf
2 lemon quarters, plus 5 ml/1 tsp juice
30 g/2 tbsp juniper berries, lightly crushed
salt and freshly ground black pepper
4 thin slices pancetta or bacon
90 ml/6 tbsp dry white wine
250 ml/8 fl oz/1 cup fresh chicken broth or stock, heated
25 g/1 oz/2 tbsp butter, at room temperature
30 ml/2 tbsp flour
30 ml/2 tbsp brandy
serves 3–4

1 ▲ Wash the pheasant under cool water. Drain well, and pat dry with paper towels. Rub with 15 ml/1 tbsp of the olive oil. Place the remaining oil, sage leaves, shallots, and bay leaf in a shallow bowl. Add the lemon juice and juniper berries. Place the pheasant and lemon quarters in the bowl with the marinade, and spoon it over the bird. Allow to stand for several hours in a cool place, turning the pheasant occasionally. Remove the lemon.

2 Preheat the oven to 180°C/350°F/ gas 4. Place the pheasant in a roasting pan, reserving the marinade. Sprinkle the cavity with salt and pepper, and place the lemon quarters and bay leaf inside.

3 Arrange some of the sage leaves on the breast of the pheasant, and lay the pancetta or bacon over the top. Secure with string.

4 ▲ Spoon the remaining marinade on top of the pheasant, and roast until tender, about 30 minutes per 450 g/1 lb. Baste frequently with the pan juices and with the white wine. Transfer the pheasant to a warmed serving platter, discarding the string and pancetta.

5 Tilt the baking pan and skim off any surface fat. Pour in the stock. Stir over moderate heat, scraping up any meat residues from the bottom of the pan. Add the pheasant liver, if using. Bring to a boil and cook for 2–3 minutes Strain into a saucepan.

6 ▲ Blend the butter to a paste with the flour. Stir into the gravy a little at a time. Boil for 2–3 minutes, stirring to smooth out any lumps. Remove from the heat, stir in the brandy, and serve.

Rabbit with Tomatoes

Coniglio con pomodori

Rabbit is very popular in Italy, and is prepared in many ways. This is a hearty dish with strong and robust flavours.

Ingredients

750 g/1 $^{1}/_{2}$lb boned rabbit, cut into chunks
2 cloves garlic, thinly sliced
115 g/4 oz/$^{1}/_{2}$ cup thinly sliced pancetta or bacon
750 g/1 $^{1}/_{2}$ lb tomatoes, peeled, seeded and roughly chopped
45 ml/3 tbsp chopped fresh basil
salt and freshly ground black pepper
60 ml/4 tbsp olive oil

serves 4–5

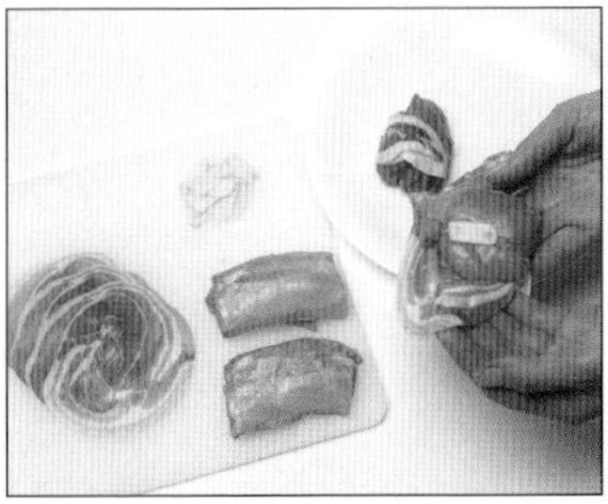

1 ▲ Preheat the oven to 200°C/400°F/ gas 6. Pat the rabbit pieces dry with paper towels. Place a thin slice of garlic on each piece. Wrap a slice of pancetta or bacon around it, making sure the garlic is held in place.

2 ▲ Place the tomatoes in a non-stick pan, and cook them for a few minutes until they give up some of their liquid and begin to dry out. Stir in the basil, and season with salt and pepper.

3 ▲ Place the tomatoes in a layer in the bottom of a baking dish. Arrange the rabbit pieces on top of the tomatoes. Sprinkle with olive oil and place, uncovered, in the oven. Roast for 40–50 minutes.

4 ▲ Baste the rabbit occasionally with any fat in the dish. After the rabbit has cooked for about 25 minutes the dish may be covered with foil for the remaining time if the sauce seems to be too dry.

Vegetables & Salads

There is no shortage of fresh and delicious vegetables in Italy, and the dishes are imaginative and varied. Most Italian cooks buy only when the vegetables are in season and at their best, so you will rarely find winter and summer vegetables together in one dish. The list of irresistible salad combinations, however, is endless, often with roasted ingredients stirred into crisp green leaves.

Stuffed Artichokes

Carciofi ripieni

Artichokes grow almost wild in southern Italy and they are cooked in many different ways. In this recipe the artichokes are stuffed and baked whole.

Ingredients
1 lemon
6 large globe artichokes
For the stuffing
2 slices white bread, crusts removed (about 50 g/2 oz)
3 anchovy fillets, finely chopped
2 cloves garlic, finely chopped
30 ml/2 tbsp capers, rinsed and finely chopped
45 ml/3 tbsp finely chopped fresh parsley
60 ml/4 tbsp plain dry breadcrumbs
60 ml/4 tbsp olive oil
salt and freshly ground black pepper
For baking
1 garlic clove, cut into 3 or 4 pieces
1 sprig fresh parsley
45 ml/3 tbsp olive oil
serves 6

1 Prepare the stuffing. Soak the white bread in a little water for 5 minutes. Squeeze dry. Place in a bowl with the other stuffing ingredients and mix.

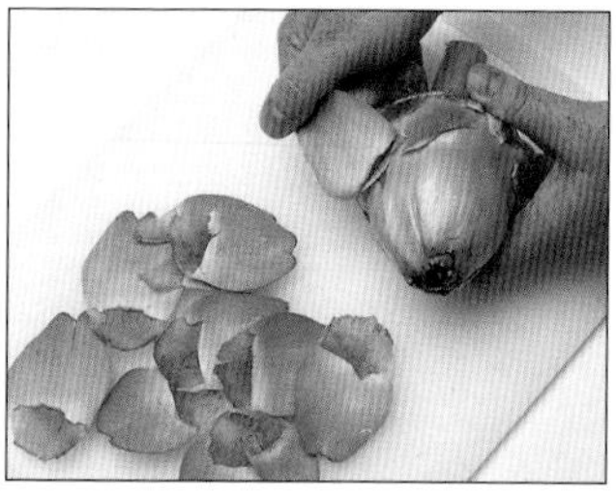

2 ▲ Squeeze the lemon, and put the juice and the squeezed halves in a large bowl of cold water. Wash the artichokes and prepare them one at a time. Cut off only the tip from the stem. Peel the stem with a small knife, pulling upwards towards the leaves. Pull off the small leaves around the stem, and continue snapping off the upper part of the dark outer leaves until you reach the taller inner leaves. Cut off the topmost part of these leaves with a sharp knife.

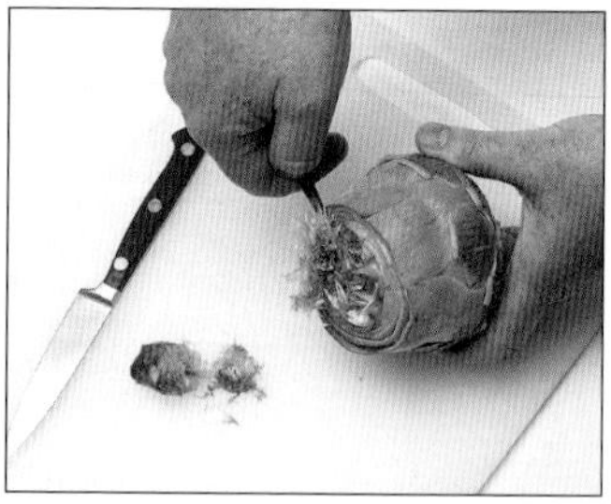

3 ▲ Open the artichoke slightly by spreading the leaves apart to get at the inner bristly "choke". Cut around it with the knife, and scrape it out with a small spoon. This forms a cavity inside the artichoke leaves. As soon as each artichoke has been prepared, place it in the bowl of acidulated water. This will prevent it from darkening. Preheat the oven to 190C°/375°F/gas 5.

4 ▲ Place the garlic and the parsley leaves in a baking dish large enough to hold the artichokes upright in one layer. Pour in cold water to a depth of 1 cm/$^1/_2$ inch. Remove the artichokes from the bowl, drain quickly, and fill the cavities with the stuffing. Place the artichokes upside down in the dish. Pour a little oil over each. Cover the dish tightly with foil. Bake for about 1 hour, or until tender.

Asparagus with Eggs

Asparagi alla milanese

The addition of fried eggs and grated Parmesan turns asparagus into something special. Peeling enables the asparagus to cook evenly, and makes the whole spear edible.

Ingredients

450 g/1 lb fresh asparagus
65 g/2$^1/_2$ oz/5 tbsp butter
4 eggs
60 ml/4 tbsp freshly grated Parmesan cheese
salt and freshly ground black pepper
serves 4

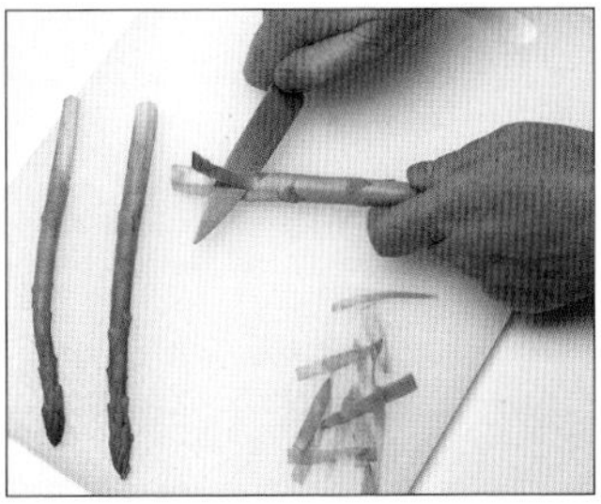

1 ▲ Cut off any woody ends from the asparagus. Peel the lower half of the asparagus spears by inserting a knife under the thick skin at the base, and pulling upwards towards the tip. Wash the asparagus in cold water.

2 Bring a large pan of water to a boil. Boil the asparagus until just tender when pierced with a knife.

3 ▲ While the asparagus is cooking, melt about a third of the butter in a frying pan. When it is bubbling, gently break in each egg, and cook until the whites have set but the yolks are still slightly soft.

4 ▲ As soon as the asparagus is cooked, remove it from the water with two slotted spoons. Place it on a cake rack covered with a clean dish towel to drain. Divide the spears between warmed individual serving plates. Place a fried egg on each, and sprinkle with the grated Parmesan.

5 ▲ Melt the remaining butter in the frying pan. As soon as it is bubbling pour it over the cheese and eggs on the asparagus. Serve at once with salt and pepper.

Stewed Artichokes

Carciofi in umido

Artichokes are eaten in many ways in Italy, sometimes sliced paper-thin and eaten raw as a salad, sometimes cut up and stewed lightly with garlic, parsley and wine, as in this recipe.

Ingredients
1 lemon
4 large or 6 small globe artichokes
25 g/1 oz/2 tbsp butter
60 ml/4 tbsp olive oil
2 cloves garlic, finely chopped
60 ml/4 tbsp chopped fresh parsley
salt and freshly ground black pepper
45 ml/3 tbsp water
90 ml/6 tbsp milk
90 ml/6 tbsp white wine
serves 6

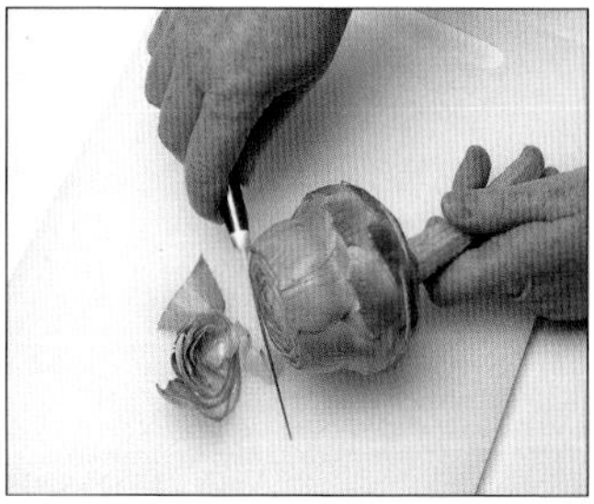

1 Squeeze the lemon, and put the juice and the squeezed halves in a large bowl of cold water. Wash the artichokes and prepare them one at a time. Cut off only the tip from the stem. Peel the stem with a small knife, pulling upwards towards the leaves. Pull off the small leaves around the stem, and continue snapping off the upper part of the dark outer leaves until you reach the taller inner leaves.

2 ▲ Slice the topmost part of the leaves off. Cut the artichoke into 4 or 6 segments.

3 Cut out the bristly "choke" from each segment. Place in the acidulated water to prevent the artichokes from darkening while you prepare the rest.

4 Blanch the artichokes in a large pan of rapidly boiling water for 4–5 minutes. Drain.

5 ▲ Heat the butter and olive oil in a large pan. Add the garlic and parsley, and cook for 2–3 minutes. Stir in the artichokes. Season with salt and pepper. Add the water and the milk, and cook for about 10 minutes, or until the liquid has evaporated. Stir in the wine, cover and cook until the artichokes are tender. Serve hot or at room temperature.

Green Beans with Tomatoes

Fagiolini verdi con pomodori

This dish is particularly good when fresh tomatoes are used.

Ingredients
450 g/1 lb fresh green beans
45 ml/3 tbsp olive oil
1 medium onion, preferably red, very finely sliced
350 g/12oz plum tomatoes, fresh or canned, peeled and finely chopped
125 ml/4 fl oz/$^1/_2$ cup water
salt and freshly ground black pepper
5–6 leaves of fresh basil torn into pieces
serves 4–6

1 Snap or cut the stem ends off the beans, and wash well in plenty of cold water. Drain.

2 ▲ Heat the oil in a large frying pan with a cover. Add the onion slices and cook until just soft, 5–6 minutes. Add the tomatoes and cook over moderate heat until they soften, about 6–8 minutes. Stir in the water. Season with salt and pepper, and add the basil.

3 ▲ Stir in the beans, turning them in the pan to coat with the sauce. Cover the pan, and cook over moderate heat until tender, about 15–20 minutes. Stir occasionally, and add a little more water if the sauce dries out too much. Serve hot or cold.

Aubergine Baked with Cheeses

Parmigiana di melanzane

This famous dish is a speciality of Italy's southern regions.

Ingredients

1 kg/2 lb aubergines
flour, for coating
oil, for frying
35 g/1 $^1/_2$ oz/$^1/_3$ cup freshly grated Parmesan cheese
400g/14 oz/2 cups mozzarella cheese, sliced very thinly
salt and freshly ground black pepper

For the tomato sauce

60 ml/4 tbsp olive oil
1 medium onion, very finely chopped
1 clove garlic, finely chopped
450 g/1 lb tomatoes, fresh or canned, chopped, with their juice
salt and freshly ground black pepper
a few leaves fresh basil or sprigs parsley

serves 4–6

1 Wash the aubergines. Cut into rounds about 1 cm/$^1/_2$ inch wide, sprinkle with salt, and leave to drain for about 1 hour.

2 ▲ Meanwhile make the tomato sauce. Heat the olive oil in a medium saucepan. Add the chopped onion, and cook over moderate heat until it is translucent, 5–8 minutes. Stir in the chopped garlic and the tomatoes (add 45 ml/3 tbsp water if you are using fresh tomatoes). Season with salt and pepper. Add the fresh basil or parsley. Cook for 20–30 minutes. Purée in a food mill or a food processor.

3 Pat the aubergine slices dry with paper towels. Coat lightly in flour. Heat a little oil in a large frying pan (preferably non-stick). Add one layer of aubergines, and cook over low to moderate heat with the pan covered until they soften. Turn, and cook on the other side. Remove from the pan, and repeat with the remaining slices.

4 Preheat the oven to 180°C/350°F/gas 4. Grease a wide shallow baking dish or tin. Spread a little tomato sauce in the bottom. Cover with a layer of aubergine. Sprinkle with a few teaspoons of Parmesan, season with salt and pepper, and cover with a layer of mozzarella. Spoon on some tomato sauce. Repeat until all the ingredients are used up, ending with a covering of tomato sauce and a sprinkling of Parmesan. Sprinkle with a little olive oil, and bake for about 45 minutes.

Sweet and Sour Aubergines

Caponata

This delicious Sicilian dish combines aubergines and celery in a piquant sauce.

Ingredients

700 g/1 $^1/_2$ lb aubergines
30 ml/2 tbsp olive oil
1 medium onion, finely sliced
1 clove garlic, finely chopped
1 x 225g/8 oz can plum tomatoes, peeled and finely chopped
125 ml/4 fl oz/$^1/_2$ cup white wine vinegar
30 ml/2 tbsp sugar
salt and freshly ground black pepper
tender central sticks of a head of celery (about 175 g/6 oz)
30 ml/2 tbsp capers, rinsed
75 g/3 oz/$^1/_2$ cup green olives, pitted
oil, for deep-frying
30 ml/2 tbsp chopped fresh parsley

serves 4

1 Wash the aubergines and cut into small cubes. Sprinkle with salt, and leave to drain in a colander for 1 hour.

2 ▲ Heat the oil in a large pan. Stir in the onion, and cook until soft. Stir in the garlic and tomatoes, and fry over moderate heat for 10 minutes. Stir in the vinegar, sugar and pepper. Simmer until the sauce reduces, 10 minutes more. Blanch the celery sticks in boiling water until tender. Drain, and chop into 2 cm/1 in pieces. Add to the sauce with the capers and olives.

3 ▲ Pat the aubergine cubes dry with paper towels. Heat the oil to 185°C/360°F/gas 5, and deep-fry the aubergine in batches until golden. Drain on paper towels.

4 Add the aubergine to the sauce. Stir gently and season. Stir in the parsley. Allow to stand for 30 minutes. Serve at room temperature.

Carrots with Marsala

Carote al Marsala

The sweet flavour of Marsala goes surprisingly well with carrots in this Sicilian dish.

Ingredients
50 g/2 oz/4 tbsp butter
450 g/1 lb carrots, cut into sticks
5 ml/1 tsp sugar
$^1/_2$ tsp salt
50 ml/2 fl oz/$^1/_4$ cup Marsala
serves 4

1 Melt the butter in a medium saucepan, and add the carrots. Stir well to cover well with the butter. Add the sugar and salt, and mix well.

2 ▲ Stir in the Marsala, and simmer for 4–5 minutes.

3 ▲ Pour in enough water to barely cover the carrots. Cover the pan, and cook over low to moderate heat until the carrots are tender. Remove the cover, and cook until the liquids reduce almost completely. Serve hot.

Broccoli with Oil and Garlic

Broccoletti saltati con aglio

This is a very simple way of transforming steamed or blanched broccoli into a succulent Mediterranean dish. Peeling the broccoli stalks is easy, and allows for even cooking.

Ingredients
1 kg/2 lb fresh broccoli
90 ml/6 tbsp olive oil
2–3 cloves garlic, finely chopped
salt and freshly ground black pepper
serves 6

1 ▲ Wash the broccoli. Cut off any woody parts at the base of the stems. Use a small sharp knife to peel the broccoli stems. Cut any very long or wide stalks in half.

2 ▲ Boil water in the bottom of a saucepan equipped with a steamer, or bring a large pan of water to a boil. If steaming the broccoli, put it in the steamer and cover tightly. Cook for 8–12 minutes or until the stems are just tender when pierced with the point of a knife. Remove from the heat. If blanching, drop the broccoli into the pan of boiling water and blanch until just tender, 5–6 minutes. Drain.

3 ▲ In a frying pan large enough to hold all the broccoli pieces, gently heat the oil with the garlic. When the garlic is light golden (do not let it brown or it will be bitter) add the broccoli, and cook over moderate heat for 3–4 minutes, turning carefully to coat it with the hot oil. Season with salt and pepper. Serve hot or cold.

Meat-stuffed Cabbage Rolls

Involtini di verza ripieni di carne

Stuffed cabbage leaves are a good way of using up cooked meats. These rolls are quite substantial, and make a satisfying luncheon dish.

Ingredients

1 head Savoy cabbage
75 g/3 oz/$^2/_3$ cup white bread
milk, to soak bread
350 g/12 oz/1$^1/_2$ cups cooked meat, very finely chopped, or fresh minced lean beef
1 egg
30 ml/2 tbsp finely chopped fresh parsley
1 clove garlic, finely chopped
50 g/2 oz/$^1/_2$ cup freshly grated Parmesan cheese
pinch of grated nutmeg
salt and freshly ground black pepper
75 ml/5 tbsp olive oil
1 medium onion, finely chopped
250 ml/8 fl oz/1 cup dry white wine

serves 4–5

1 ▲ Cut the leaves from the cabbage. Save the innermost part for soup. Blanch the leaves a few at a time in a large pan of boiling water for 4–5 minutes. Refresh under cold water. Spread the leaves out on clean dish towels to dry.

~ VARIATION ~

Serve the rolls with a tomato sauce, spooned over just before serving.

2 ▲ Cut the crusts from the bread, and discard. Soak the bread in a little milk for about 5 minutes. Squeeze out the excess moisture with your hands.

3 ▲ In a mixing bowl combine the chopped or minced meat with the egg and soaked bread. Stir in the parsley, garlic and Parmesan. Season with nutmeg, salt and pepper.

4 ▲ Divide any very large cabbage leaves in half, discarding the rib. Lay the leaves out on a flat surface.

Form little sausage-shaped mounds of stuffing, and place them at the edge of each leaf. Roll up the leaves, tucking the ends in as you roll. Squeeze each roll lightly in the palm of your hand to help the leaves to stick.

5 ▲ In a large, shallow, flameproof casserole or deep frying pan large enough to hold all the cabbage rolls in one layer, heat the olive oil. Add the onion, and cook gently until it softens. Raise the heat slightly, and add the cabbage rolls, turning them over carefully with a large spoon as they begin to cook.

6 ▲ Pour in half of the wine. Cook over low to moderate heat until the wine has evaporated. Add the rest of the wine, cover the pan, and cook for 10–15 minutes more. Remove the cover, and cook until all the liquid has evaporated. Remove from the heat, and allow to rest for about 5 minutes before serving.

Tuscan Baked Beans

Fagioli al forno alla toscana

Beans, both dried and fresh, are particularly popular in Tuscany, where they are cooked in many different ways. In this vegetarian dish the beans are flavoured with fresh sage leaves.

Ingredients

600 g/1lb 6oz dried beans, such as cannellini
60 ml/4 tbsp olive oil
2 cloves garlic, crushed
3 leaves fresh sage (if fresh sage is not available use 60 ml/4 tbsp chopped fresh parsley)
1 leek, finely sliced
1 x 400g/14oz can plum tomatoes, chopped, with their juice
salt and freshly ground black pepper

serves 6–8

1 ▲ Carefully pick over the beans, discarding any stones or other particles. Place the beans in a large bowl and cover with water. Soak for at least 6 hours, or overnight. Drain.

2 ▲ Preheat the oven to 180°C/350°F/gas 4. In a small saucepan heat the oil and sauté the garlic cloves and sage leaves for 3–4 minutes. Remove from the heat.

3 ▲ In a large deep baking dish combine the beans with the leek and tomatoes. Stir in the oil with the garlic and sage. Add enough fresh water to cover the beans by 2 cm/1 inch. Mix well. Cover the dish with a lid or foil, and place in the centre of the preheated oven. Bake for $1^3/_4$ hours.

4 ▲ Remove the dish from the oven, stir the beans, and season with salt and pepper. Return the beans to the oven, uncovered, and cook for another 15 minutes, or until the beans are tender. Remove from the oven and allow to stand for 7–8 minutes before serving. Serve hot or at room temperature.

Stewed Lentils

Lenticchie in umido

In Italy lentils are very often eaten as an accompaniment to duck and to zampone or cotechino sausages, but they are also good by themselves.

Ingredients
450 g/1 lb/2 cups green or brown lentils
45 ml/3 tbsp olive oil
50 g/2 oz/$^1/_4$ cup pancetta or salt pork
1 medium onion, very finely chopped
1 stick celery, very finely sliced
1 carrot, very finely chopped
1 clove garlic
1 bay leaf
45 g/3 tbsp chopped fresh parsley
salt and freshly ground black pepper
serves 6

1 ▲ Carefully pick over the lentils, removing any stones or other particles. Place them in a large bowl and cover with water. Soak for several hours. Drain.

2 ▲ In a large heavy saucepan heat the oil. Add the pancetta or salt pork and cook for 3 or 4 minutes. Stir in the onion, and cook over low heat until it is soft.

3 ▲ Add the celery and carrot and cook for 3–4 minutes more.

4 ▲ Add the lentils to the pan, stirring to coat them with the fat. Pour in enough boiling water just to cover the lentils. Stir well, adding the whole garlic clove, the bay leaf and the parsley. Season with salt and pepper. Cook over moderate heat until the lentils are tender, about 1 hour. Discard the garlic and bay leaf. Serve hot or at room temperature.

Broad Bean Purée with Ham

Purea di fave con prosciutto

Peeling broad beans leaves them tender and sweet. They go particularly well with the saltiness of prosciutto crudo in this Tuscan combination.

Ingredients

1 kg/2 lb fresh broad beans in their pods, or 400 g/14oz shelled broad beans, thawed if frozen
1 medium onion, finely chopped
2 small potatoes, peeled and diced
50 g/2 oz/$^1/_4$ cup prosciutto crudo
45 ml/3 tbsp extra-virgin olive oil
salt and freshly ground black pepper
serves 4

1 Place the shelled beans in a saucepan and cover with water. Bring to a boil and cook for 5 minutes. Drain. When they are cool enough to handle, peel the beans.

2 ▲ Place the peeled beans in a saucepan with the onion and potatoes. Add enough water just to cover the vegetables. Bring to the boil. Lower the heat slightly, cover, and simmer until the vegetables are very soft, 15–20 minutes. Check occasionally that all the water has not evaporated. If necessary add a few tablespoons more.

3 Chop the ham into very small dice. Heat the oil and sauté until the ham is just golden.

4 ▲ Mash or purée the bean mixture. Return it to the pan. If it is very moist, cook it over moderate heat until it reduces slightly. Stir in the oil with the ham. Season and cook for 2 minutes.

Deep-fried Cauliflower

Cavolfiore fritto

Deep-frying is very popular in Italy, and everything from cheese to fruit may be fried. The cauliflower may be eaten as a side dish or as an antipasto.

Ingredients

1 large cauliflower
1 egg
salt and freshly ground black pepper
100 g/3$^1/_2$ oz/scant 1 cup flour
175 ml/6 fl oz/$^3/_4$ cup dry white wine
oil, for deep-frying
serves 4

1 Soak the cauliflower in a bowl of salted water. In a mixing bowl, beat the egg. Season and beat in the flour. The mixture will be very thick. Add the wine. If necessary add more to make a fairly runny batter. Cover, and allow to rest for 30 minutes.

2 Steam or boil the cauliflower until just tender – do not overcook. Cut it into small florets when cool.

3 ▲ Heat the oil until a small piece of bread sizzles as soon as it is dropped in (about 185°C/360°F/gas 5). Dip each cauliflower piece into the batter before deep-frying it until golden.

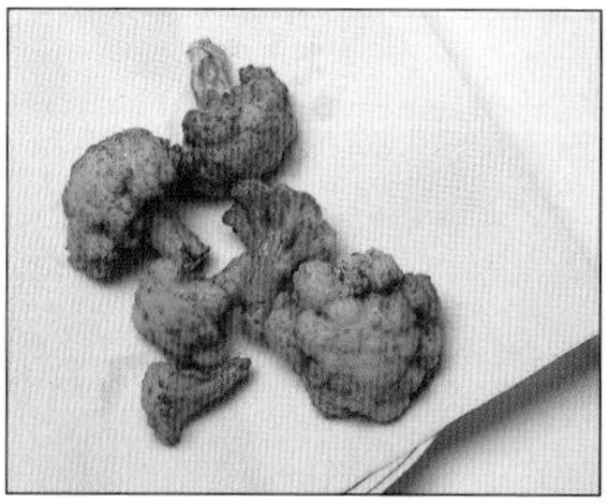

4 ▲ Remove from the oil with a slotted spoon and drain on paper towels. Sprinkle lightly with salt and serve hot.

Baked Fennel with Parmesan Cheese

Finocchio gratinato

Fennel is widely eaten in Italy, both raw and cooked. It is delicious married with the sharpness of Parmesan cheese in this quick and simple dish.

Ingredients

1 kg/2lb fennel bulbs, washed and cut in half
50 g/2 oz/4 tbsp butter
40g/1 1/2 oz/1/3 cup freshly grated Parmesan cheese
serves 4–6

1 ▲ Cook the fennel in a large pan of boiling water until just soft but not mushy. Drain. Preheat the oven to 200°C/400°F/gas 6.

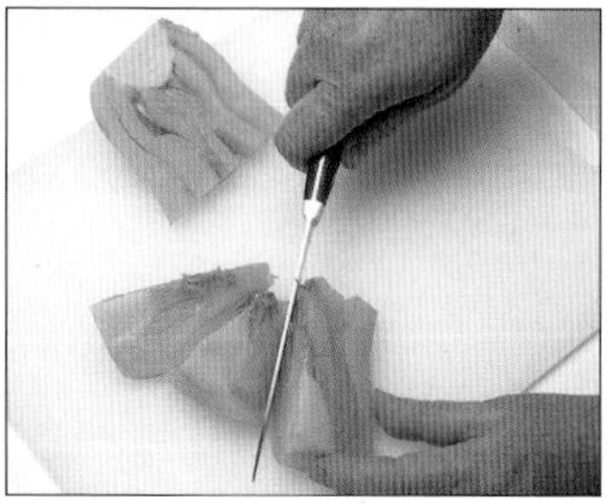

2 ▲ Cut the fennel bulbs lengthwise into 4 or 6 pieces. Place them in a buttered baking dish.

3 ▲ Dot with butter. Sprinkle with the grated Parmesan. Bake in the hot oven until the cheese is golden brown, about 20 minutes. Serve at once.

~ VARIATION ~

For a more substantial version of this dish, sprinkle 75 g/3oz chopped ham over the fennel before topping with the cheese.

Roast Mushroom Caps

Funghi arrosti

Hunting for edible wild mushrooms is one of the Italians' great passions. The most prized are porcini which grow in forests.

Ingredients

4 large mushroom caps, such as porcini or other wild types
2 cloves garlic, chopped
45 ml/3 tbsp chopped fresh parsley
salt and freshly ground black pepper
extra-virgin olive oil, for sprinkling
serves 4

1 Preheat the oven to 190°C/375°F/gas 5. Carefully wipe the mushrooms clean with a damp cloth or paper towel. Cut off the stems. (Save them for soup if they are not too woody). Oil a baking dish large enough to hold the mushrooms in one layer.

2 ▲ Place the mushroom caps in the dish, smooth side down. Mix together the chopped garlic and parsley and sprinkle on the caps.

3 ▲ Season the mushrooms with salt and pepper. Sprinkle the parsley stuffing with oil. Bake for 20-25 minutes. Serve at once.

Roasted Plum Tomatoes and Garlic

Pomodori al forno

These are so simple to prepare yet taste absolutely wonderful. Use a large, shallow earthenware dish that will allow the tomatoes to sear and char in a hot oven.

Ingredients

8 plum tomatoes, halved
12 garlic cloves
60 ml/4 tbsp extra virgin olive oil
3 bay leaves
salt and freshly ground black pepper
45 ml/3 tbsp fresh oregano leaves, to garnish

serves 4

Cook's Tip

Use ripe plum tomatoes for this recipe as they keep their shape and do not fall apart when roasted at such a high temperature. Leave the stalks on, if possible.

1 ▲ Preheat the oven to 230°C/450°F/ Gas 8. Select an ovenproof dish that will hold all the tomatoes snugly in a single layer. Place the tomatoes in the dish and push the whole, unpeeled garlic cloves between them.

2 ▲ Brush the tomatoes with the oil, add the bay leaves and sprinkle black pepper over the top. Bake for about 45 minutes until the tomatoes have softened and are sizzling in the pan. They should be charred around the edges. Season with salt and a little more black pepper, if needed. Garnish with oregano and serve.

Marinated Baby Aubergines

Melanzane in agrodolce

Aubergines are especially popular in the south of Italy. This dish uses ingredients that have been included in recipes since Renaissance times. Make a day in advance, to allow the sour and sweet flavours to develop.

Ingredients

12 baby aubergines, halved lengthways
250 ml/8 fl oz/1 cup extra virgin olive oil
juice of 1 lemon
30 ml/2 tbsp balsamic vinegar
3 cloves
25 g/1 oz/⅓ cup pine nuts
25 g/1 oz/2 tbsp raisins
15 ml/1 tbsp granulated sugar
1 bay leaf
large pinch of dried chilli flakes
salt and freshly ground black pepper

1 Preheat the grill to high. Place the aubergines, cut side up, in a grill pan and brush with a little of the olive oil. Grill for 10 minutes, until slightly blackened, turning them over halfway through cooking.

2 ▲ To make the marinade, put the remaining olive oil, the lemon juice, vinegar, cloves, pine nuts, raisins, sugar and bay leaf in a jug. Add the chilli flakes and salt and pepper and mix well.

3 ▲ Place the hot aubergines in an earthenware or glass bowl and pour the marinade over. Leave to cool, turning the aubergines once or twice. Serve cold.

Fennel Gratin

Finocchi gratinati

This is one of the best ways to eat fresh fennel. The fennel takes on a delicious, almost creamy, flavour, which contrasts beautifully with the sharp, strong Gruyère.

Ingredients

2 fennel bulbs, about 675 g/1½ lb total weight
300 ml/½ pint/1¼ cups milk
15 g/½ oz/1 tbsp butter, plus extra for greasing
15 ml/1 tbsp plain flour
75 g/3 oz Gruyère cheese, grated
25 g/1 oz/scant ½ cup dry white breadcrumbs
salt and freshly ground black pepper

serves 4

Cook's Tip

Instead of the Gruyère, Parmesan, Pecorino or any other strong cheese would work perfectly.

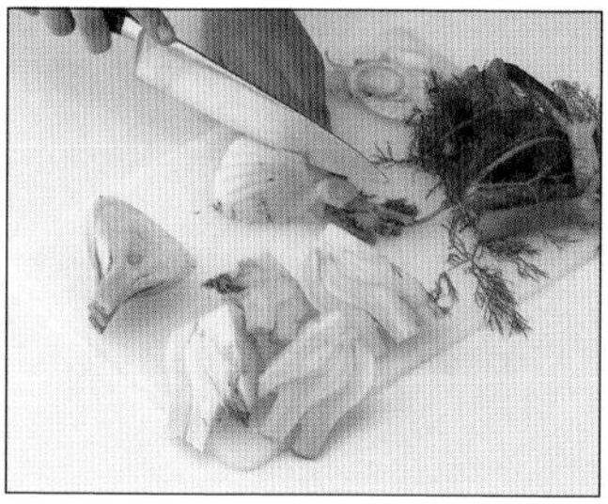

1 ▲ Preheat the oven to 240°C/475°F/Gas 9. Discard the stalks and root ends from the fennel. Slice into quarters and place in a large saucepan. Pour over the milk and simmer for 10–15 minutes until tender. Butter a small baking dish.

2 Remove the fennel pieces with a slotted spoon, reserving the milk and arrange the fennel pieces in the dish.

3 ▲ Melt the butter in a small saucepan and add the flour, stir well, then gradually whisk in the reserved milk. Stir the sauce until thickened.

4 Pour the sauce over the fennel pieces, sprinkle with the white breadcrumbs and grated Gruyère. Season with salt and black pepper and bake for about 20 minutes until browned.

Sweet and Sour Onions

Cipolline in agrodolce

Onions are naturally sweet, and when they are cooked at a high temperature the sweetness intensifies. Serve with roasts and meat dishes or as part of an antipasti.

Ingredients

50 g/2 oz/¼ cup butter
75 ml/5 tbsp sugar
120 ml/4 fl oz/½ cup white wine vinegar
30 ml/2 tbsp balsamic vinegar
675 g/1½ lb small pickling onions, peeled
salt and freshly ground black pepper

serves 4

Cook's Tips

This recipe also looks and tastes delicious when made with either yellow or red onions, which are cut into either thin slices or into chunks. Cooking times will vary, depending on the size of the onion pieces.

1 ▲ Heat the butter in a large saucepan over a gentle heat. Add the sugar and heat until dissolved, stirring constantly.

2 ▲ Add the vinegars to the pan with the onions and mix together well. Season with salt and pepper and cover and cook over a moderate heat for 20–25 minutes until the onions are a golden colour and soft when pierced with a knife. Serve hot.

Courgettes with Sun-dried Tomatoes

Zucchinecon pomodori

One way to preserve tomatoes for winter is to dry them in the sun, as they do all over southern Italy. These tomatoes have a concentrated, sweet flavour that goes well with courgettes.

Ingredients
10 sun-dried tomatoes, dry or preserved in oil and drained
175 ml/6 fl oz/$^3/_4$ cup warm water
75 ml/5 tbsp olive oil
1 large onion, finely sliced
2 cloves garlic, finely chopped
1 kg/2 lb courgettes, cut into thin strips
salt and freshly ground black pepper
serves 6

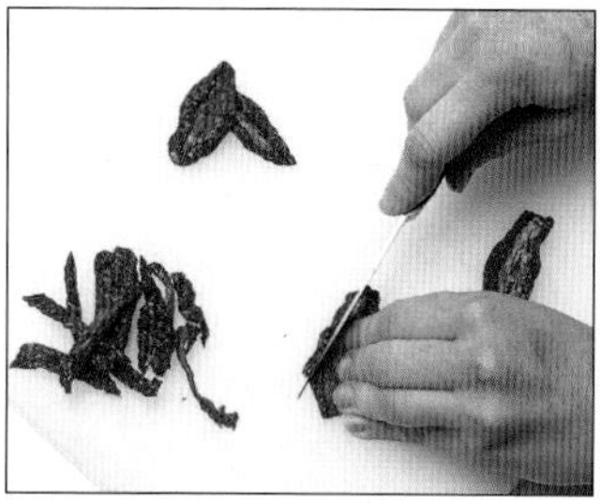

1 ▲ Slice the tomatoes into thin strips. Place in a bowl with the warm water. Allow to stand for 20 minutes.

2 ▲ In a large, deep frying pan or saucepan, heat the oil and stir in the onion. Cook over low to moderate heat until it softens but does not brown.

3 ▲ Stir in the garlic and the courgettes. Cook for about 5 minutes, continuing to stir the mixture.

4 ▲ Stir in the tomatoes and their soaking liquid. Season with salt and pepper. Raise the heat slightly and cook until the courgettes are just tender. Serve hot or cold.

Stuffed Onions

Cipolle ripiene

These savoury onions make a satisfying dish for a light lunch or supper. Small onions could be stuffed and served as an accompaniment to a meat dish.

Ingredients
6 large onions
75 g/3 oz/scant 1/2 cup ham, cut into small dice
1 egg
50 g/2 oz/1/2 cup dry breadcrumbs
45 ml/3 tbsp finely chopped fresh parsley
1 clove garic, finely chopped
pinch of grated nutmeg
75 g/3 oz/3/4 cup grated cheese, such as Parmesan or sharp Cheddar
90 ml/6 tbsp olive oil
salt and freshly ground black pepper
serves 6

1 Peel the onions without cutting through the base. Cook them in a large pan of boiling water for about 20 minutes. Drain, and refresh in plenty of cold water.

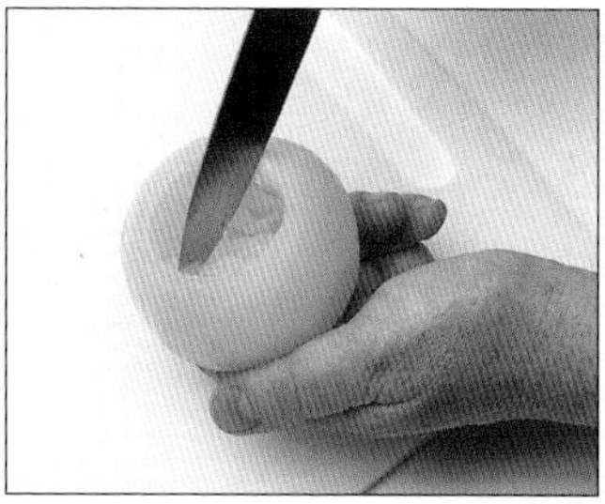

2 ▲ Using a small sharp knife, cut around and scoop out the central section. Remove about half the inside (save it for soup). Lightly salt the empty cavities, and leave the onions to drain upside down.

3 ▲ Preheat the oven to 200°C/400°F/gas 6. In a small bowl, beat the ham into the egg. Stir in the breadcrumbs, parsley, garlic, nutmeg and all but 45 g/3 tbsp of the grated cheese. Add 45 g/3 tbsp of the oil, and season with salt and pepper.

4 Pat the insides of the onions dry with paper towels. Stuff them using a small spoon. Arrange the onions in one layer in an oiled baking dish.

5 ▲ Sprinkle the tops with the remaining cheese, and sprinkle with oil. Bake for 45 minutes, or until the onions are tender and golden on top.

~ VARIATION ~

For a vegetarian version, replace the ham with chopped olives.

Aromatic Stewed Mushrooms

Funghi trifolati

This dish from Piedmont combines both field and cultivated mushrooms, which give a balanced but not overwhelming flavour.

Ingredients

750 g/1$^1/_2$ lb firm fresh mushrooms, field and cultivated
90 ml/6 tbsp olive oil
2 cloves garlic, finely chopped
salt and freshly ground black pepper
45 ml/3 tbsp chopped fresh parsley
serves 6

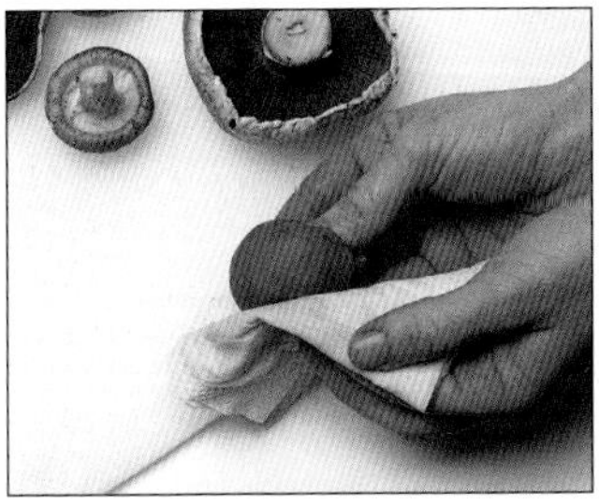

1 ▲ Clean the mushrooms carefully by wiping them with a damp cloth or paper towels.

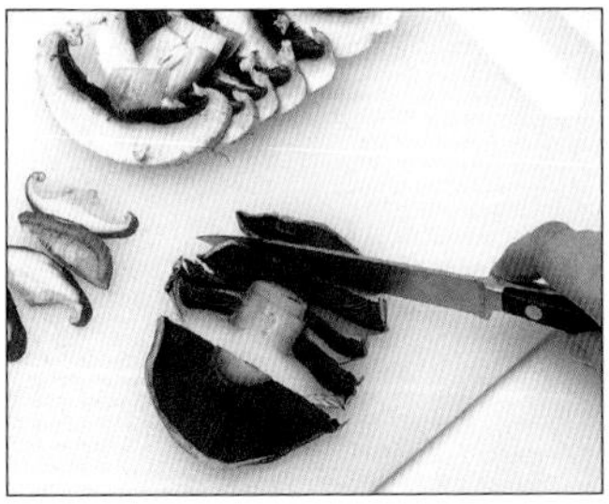

2 ▲ Cut off the woody tips of the stems and discard. Slice the stems and caps fairly thickly.

3 ▲ Heat the oil in a large frying pan. Stir in the garlic and, after about 1 minute, the mushrooms. Cook for 8–10 minutes, stirring occasionally. Season with salt and pepper, and stir in the parsley. Cook for 5 minutes more, and serve at once.

Sautéed Peas with Ham

Piselli alla fiorentina

When fresh peas are in season, they can be stewed with a little ham and onion and served as a substantial side dish.

Ingredients

45 ml/3 tbsp olive oil
115 g/4 oz/$^1/_2$ cup pancetta or ham, finely diced
45 ml/3 tbsp finely chopped onion
1 kg/2 lb whole peas (about 300 g/11oz shelled) or 275 g/ 10 oz frozen petits pois, thawed
30-45 ml/2–3 tbsp water
salt and freshly ground black pepper
a few leaves fresh mint or sprigs parsley
serves 4

1 Heat the oil in a medium saucepan, and sauté the pancetta or ham and onion for 2–3 minutes.

2 ▲ Stir in the shelled fresh or thawed frozen peas. Add the water. Season with salt and pepper and mix well to coat with the oil.

3 ▲ Add the fresh herbs, cover, and cook over moderate heat until tender. This may take from 5 minutes for sweet fresh peas, to 15 for tougher, older peas. Serve as a side dish to meat dishes or frittate.

Roasted Potatoes with Red Onions

Patate al forno

These mouth-watering potatoes are a fine accompaniment to just about anything. The key is to use small firm potatoes; the smaller they are cut, the quicker they will cook.

Ingredients

675 g/1½ lb small firm potatoes
25 g/1 oz/2 tbsp butter
30 ml/2 tbsp olive oil
2 red onions, cut into chunks
8 garlic cloves, unpeeled
30 ml/2 tbsp chopped fresh rosemary
salt and freshly ground black pepper
serves 4

Cook's Tip

To ensure that the potatoes are crisp, make sure they are completely dry before cooking. Resist the urge to turn the potatoes too often. Allow them to brown on one side before turning. Do not salt the potatoes until the end of cooking – salting beforehand encourages them to give up their liquid, making them limp.

1 ▲ Preheat the oven to 230°C/450°F/ Gas 8. Peel and quarter the potatoes, rinse them well and pat thoroughly dry on kitchen paper. Place the butter and oil in a roasting tin and place in the oven to heat.

2 ▲ When the butter has melted and is foaming, add the potatoes, red onions, garlic and rosemary. Toss well then spread out in one layer.

3 Place the tin in the oven and roast for about 25 minutes until the potatoes are golden and tender when tested with a fork. Shake the tin from time to time to redistribute the potatoes. When cooked, season with salt and pepper.

Radicchio and Chicory Gratin

Radicchio e indivia gratinati

Vegetables like radicchio and chicory take on a different flavour when cooked in this way. The creamy béchamel combines wonderfully with the bitter leaves.

Ingredients

2 heads radicchio, quartered lengthways
2 heads chicory, quartered lengthways
25 g/1 oz/½ cup drained sun-dried tomatoes in oil, chopped roughly
25 g/1 oz/2 tbsp butter
15 g/½ oz/1 tbsp plain flour
250 ml/8 fl oz/1 cup milk
pinch grated nutmeg
50 g/2 oz/½ cup grated Emmenthal cheese
salt and freshly ground black pepper
chopped fresh parsley, to garnish
serves 4

1 ▲ Preheat the oven to 180°C/350°F/ Gas 4. Grease a 1.2 litre/2 pint/5 cup baking dish. Trim the radicchio and chicory and pull away, discarding any damaged or wilted leaves. Quarter them lengthways and arrange in the baking dish. Scatter over the sun-dried tomatoes and brush the leaves liberally with the oil from the jar. Sprinkle with salt and pepper and cover with foil. Bake for 15 minutes, then remove the foil and bake for a further 10 minutes until the vegetables are softened.

Cook's Tip

In Italy radicchio and chicory are often grilled on an outside barbecue. To do this, simply prepare the vegetables as above and brush with olive oil. Place cut-side down on the grill for 7–10 minutes until browned. Turn and grill until the other side is browned, about 5 minutes longer.

2 ▲ Make the sauce. Place the butter in a small saucepan and melt over a moderate heat. When the butter is foaming, add the flour and cook for 1 minute, stirring. Remove from the heat and gradually add the milk, whisking all the time. Return to the heat and bring to the boil, simmer for 2–3 minutes to thicken. Season to taste and add the nutmeg.

3 Pour the sauce over the vegetables and sprinkle with the grated cheese. Bake for about 20 minutes until golden. Serve immediately, garnished with parsley.

Potato and Pumpkin Pudding

Tortino di patate e zucca

Serve this savoury pudding with any rich meat dish or simply with a mixed salad.

Ingredients

45 ml/3 tbsp olive oil
1 garlic clove, sliced
675 g/1½ lb pumpkin flesh, cut into 2 cm/¾ in chunks
350 g/12 oz potatoes
25 g/1 oz/2 tbsp butter
90 g/3½ oz/scant ½ cup ricotta cheese
50 g/2 oz/⅔ cup grated Parmesan cheese
pinch grated nutmeg
4 size 3 eggs, separated
salt and freshly ground black pepper
chopped fresh parsley, to garnish

serves 4

1 Preheat the oven to 200°C/400°F/Gas 6. Grease a 1.75 litre/3 pint/7½ cup, shallow, oval baking dish.

Cook's Tip

You may process the vegetables in a food processor for a few seconds, but be careful not to overprocess, as they will become very gluey.

2 ▲ Heat the oil in a large shallow pan, add the garlic and pumpkin and cook, stirring often to prevent sticking, for 15–20 minutes or until the pumpkin is tender. Meanwhile, cook the potatoes in boiling salted water for 20 minutes until tender. Drain, leave until cool enough to handle, then peel off the skins. Place the potatoes and pumpkin in a large bowl and mash well with the butter.

3 Mash the ricotta with a fork until smooth and add to the potato and pumpkin mixture, mixing well.

4 ▲ Stir the Parmesan, nutmeg and plenty of seasoning into the ricotta mixture – it should be smooth and creamy.

5 Add the egg yolks one at a time until mixed thoroughly.

6 Whisk the egg whites with an electric whisk until they form stiff peaks, then fold gently into the mixture. Spoon into the prepared baking dish and bake for 30 minutes until golden and firm. Serve hot, garnished with parsley.

Fried Spring Greens

Cavolo fritto

This dish can be served as a vegetable accompaniment, or it can be enjoyed simply on its own, with some warm crusty bread.

Ingredients

30 ml/2 tbsp olive oil
25 g/1 oz/2 tbsp butter
75 g/3 oz rindless smoked streaky bacon, chopped
1 large onion, thinly sliced
250 ml/8 fl oz/1 cup dry white wine
2 garlic cloves, finely chopped
900 g/2 lb spring greens, shredded
salt and freshly ground black pepper

serves 4

Cook's Tips

This dish would work just as well using shredded red cabbage and red wine. Leave to simmer for 10 minutes longer as red cabbage leaves are slightly tougher than the spring greens.

1 In a large frying pan, heat the oil and butter and add the bacon. Fry for 2 minutes, then add the onions and fry for a further 3 minutes until the onion is beginning to soften.

2 Add the wine and simmer vigorously for 2 minutes to reduce.

3 Reduce the heat and add the spring greens and salt and pepper. Cook over a gentle heat for about 15 minutes until the greens are tender. (Cover the pan so that the greens retain their colour.) Serve hot.

Stuffed Peppers

Peperoni ripieni

Sweet peppers can be stuffed and baked with many different fillings, from leftover cooked vegetables to rice or pasta. Blanching the peppers first helps to make them tender.

Ingredients

6 medium to large peppers, any colour
200 g/7 oz/scant 1 cup rice
60 ml/4 tbsp olive oil
1 large onion, finely chopped
3 anchovy fillets, chopped
2 cloves garlic, finely chopped
3 medium tomatoes, peeled and cut into small dice
60 ml/4 tbsp white wine
45 ml/3 tbsp finely chopped fresh parsley
1/2 cup mozzarella cheese, cut into small dice
90 ml/6 tbsp freshly grated Parmesan cheese
salt and freshly ground black pepper
Basic Tomato Sauce, to serve (optional)

serves 6

1 ▲ Cut the tops off the peppers. Scoop out the seeds and fibrous insides. Blanch the peppers and their tops in a large pan of boiling water for 3–4 minutes. Remove, and stand upside down on racks to drain.

~ COOK'S TIP ~

Choose peppers with sturdy, even bases, so they will stand on end unsupported. This will make them easier to cook and serve.

2 ▲ Boil the rice according to the instructions on the package, but drain and rinse it in cold water 3 minutes before the recommended cooking time has elapsed. Drain again.

3 ▲ In a large frying pan, heat the oil and sauté the onion until soft. Stir in the anchovy pieces and the garlic, and mash them. Add the tomatoes, and the wine, and cook for 5 minutes.

4 ▲ Preheat the oven to 190°C/375°F/gas 5. Remove the tomato mixture from the heat. Stir in the rice, parsley, mozzarella and 60 g/4 tbsp of the Parmesan cheese. Season the mixture with salt and pepper.

5 ▲ Pat the insides of the peppers dry with paper towels. Sprinkle with salt and pepper. Stuff the peppers. Sprinkle the tops with the remaining Parmesan, and sprinkle with a little oil.

6 ▲ Arrange the peppers in a shallow baking dish. Pour in enough water to come 1 cm/1/2 inch up the sides of the peppers. Bake for 25 minutes. Serve at once, with tomato sauce if desired. These peppers are also good served at room temperature.

Stuffed Aubergines

Melanzane alla liguria

This typical Ligurian dish is spiked with paprika and allspice, a legacy from the days when spices from the East came into northern Italy via the port of Genoa.

Ingredients

2 aubergines, about 225 g/8 oz each, stalks removed
275 g/10 oz potatoes, peeled and diced
30 ml/2 tbsp olive oil
1 small onion, finely chopped
1 garlic clove, finely chopped
good pinch of ground allspice and paprika
1 egg, beaten
40 g/1½ oz/½ cup grated Parmesan cheese
15ml/1 tbsp fresh white breadcrumbs
salt and freshly ground black pepper
fresh mint sprigs, to garnish
salad leaves, to serve

serves 4

1 Bring a large saucepan of lightly salted water to the boil. Add the whole aubergines and cook for 5 minutes, turning frequently. Remove with a slotted spoon and set aside. Add the potatoes to the pan and cook for 20 minutes until soft.

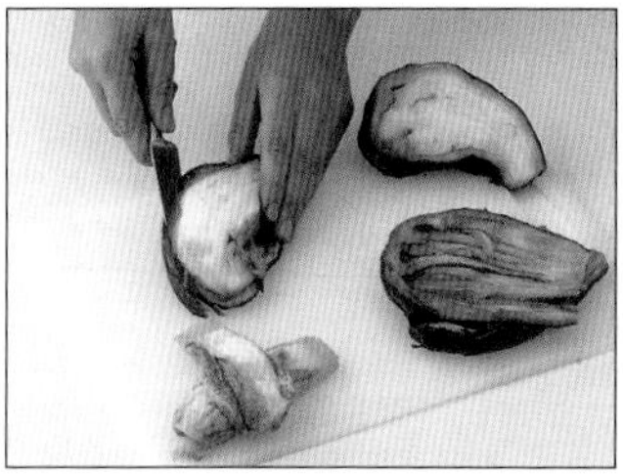

2 ▲ Meanwhile, cut the aubergines in half lengthways and gently scoop out the flesh with a small sharp knife and a spoon, leaving 5 mm/¼ in of the shell intact. Select a baking dish that will hold the aubergine shells snugly in a single layer. Brush it lightly with oil. Put the shells in the baking dish and chop the aubergine flesh roughly.

Cook's Tip

The aubergines can be filled in advance, then covered with foil and kept in the fridge. Add the crumb topping just before baking.

3 ▲ Heat the oil in a frying pan, add the onion and cook gently, stirring frequently, until softened. Add the chopped aubergine flesh and the garlic. Cook, stirring frequently, for 6–8 minutes. Tip into a bowl. Preheat the oven to 190°C/375°F/Gas 5.

4 Drain and mash the potatoes. Add to the aubergine mixture with the spices and beaten egg. Set aside 15 ml/1 tbsp of the Parmesan and add the rest to the aubergine mixture, stir in salt and pepper to taste.

5 ▲ Spoon the mixture into the aubergine shells. Mix the breadcrumbs with the reserved Parmesan cheese and sprinkle the mixture over the aubergines. Bake for 40–45 minutes until the topping is crisp. Garnish with mint and serve with salad leaves.

Pepper Gratin

Peperoni gratinati

Serve this simple but delicious dish as a starter with a small mixed leaf or rocket salad and some good crusty bread to mop up the juices from the peppers.

Ingredients
2 red peppers
30 ml/2 tbsp extra virgin olive oil
60 ml/4 tbsp fresh white breadcrumbs
1 garlic clove, finely chopped
5 ml/1 tsp drained bottled capers
8 stoned black olives, roughly chopped
15 ml/1 tbsp chopped fresh oregano
15 ml/1 tbsp chopped fresh flat leaf parsley
salt and freshly ground black pepper
fresh herbs, to garnish
serves 4

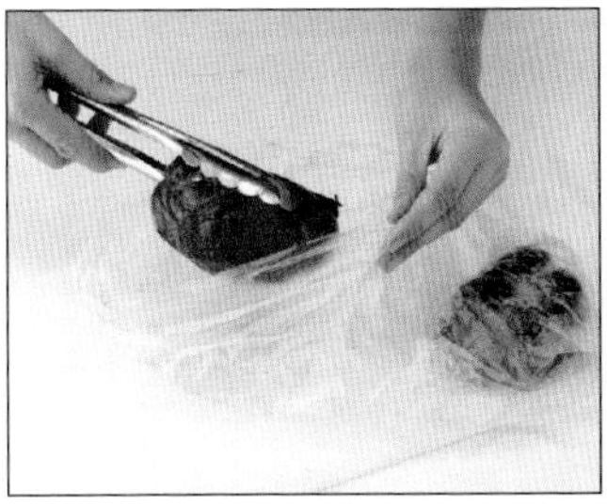

1 ▲ Preheat the oven to 200°C/400°F/Gas 6. Place the peppers under a hot grill. Turn occasionally until they are blackened and blistered all over. Remove from the heat and place in a plastic bag. Seal and leave to cool.

2 ▲ When cool, peel the peppers. (Don't skin them under the tap as the water would wash away some of the delicious smoky flavour.) Halve and remove the seeds, then cut the flesh into large strips.

3 ▲ Use a little of the olive oil to grease a small baking dish. Arrange the pepper strips in the dish.

4 ▲ Scatter the remaining ingredients on top, drizzle with the remaining olive oil and add salt and pepper to taste. Bake for about 20 minutes until the breadcrumbs have browned. Garnish with fresh herbs and serve immediately.

Stewed Peppers

Peperonata

This dish originated in the south of Italy, but has become a popular favourite everywhere. It can be eaten as a side dish or appetizer, and makes a delicious filling for a frittata.

Ingredients
4–5 very ripe peppers, preferably red or yellow, about 750 g/$1^{1}/_{2}$lb
60 ml/4 tbsp olive oil
2 medium onions, thinly sliced
3 cloves garlic, finely chopped
350 g/12oz plum tomatoes, peeled, seeded and chopped
salt and freshly ground black pepper
a few fresh basil leaves
serves 6

1 Wash the peppers. Cut them into quarters, removing the stems and seeds. Slice them into thin strips.

2 ▲ In a large, heavy pan, heat the oil and sauté the onions until soft (covering the pan will prevent the onions from browning). Add the peppers, and cook for 5–8 minutes over moderate heat, stirring frequently.

3 ▲ Stir in the garlic and tomatoes. Cover the pan, and cook for about 25 minutes, stirring occasionally. The peppers should be soft, but should still hold their shape. Season, tear the basil leaves into pieces, and stir into the peppers. Serve hot or cold.

Grilled Radicchio and Courgette

Verdure ai ferri

In Italy radicchio is often eaten grilled or barbecued. It is delicious and very easy to prepare.

Ingredients
2–3 firm heads of radicchio, round or long type
4 medium courgette
90 ml/6 tbsp olive oil
salt and freshly ground black pepper
serves 4

1 ▲ Preheat the grill, or prepare a barbecue. Cut the radicchio in half through the root section or base. If necessary, wash in cold water. Drain.

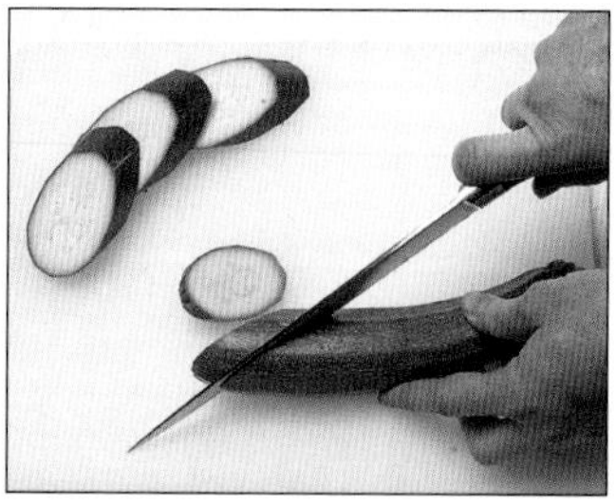

2 ▲ Cut the courgettes into 1 cm/ $^{1}/_{2}$ in diagonal slices.

3 ▲ When the grill or barbecue is hot, brush the vegetables all over with the olive oil, and sprinkle with salt and pepper. Cook for 4–5 minutes on each side. Serve on their own or as an accompaniment to grilled fish or meat.

Potatoes Baked with Tomatoes

Patate e pomodori al forno

This simple, hearty dish from the south of Italy is best when tomatoes are in season, but can also be made with canned plum tomatoes.

Ingredients
2 large red or yellow onions, thinly sliced
1 kg/2 lb potatoes, peeled and thinly sliced
450 g/1 lb tomatoes, fresh or canned, sliced, with their juice
90 ml/6 tbsp olive oil
115 g/4 oz/1 cup freshly grated Parmesan or sharp Cheddar cheese
salt and freshly ground black pepper
a few leaves fresh basil
50 ml/2 fl oz/$^{1}/_{4}$ cup water
serves 6

1 Preheat the oven to 180°C/350°F/ gas 4. Brush a large baking dish generously with oil.

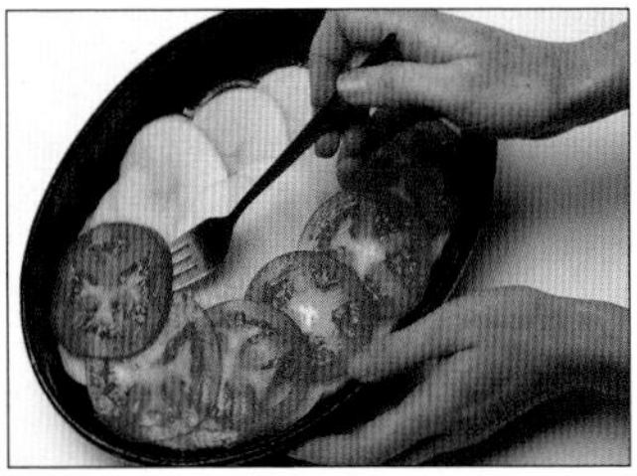

2 ▲ Arrange a layer of onions in the dish, followed by layers of potatoes and tomatoes. Pour on a little of the oil, and sprinkle with a little cheese. Season with salt and pepper.

3 ▲ Repeat until the vegetables are used up, ending with an overlapping layer of potatoes and tomatoes. Tear the basil leaves into pieces, and add them here and there among the vegetables. Sprinkle the top with cheese, and a little oil.

4 ▲ Pour on the water. Bake for 1 hour, or until tender.

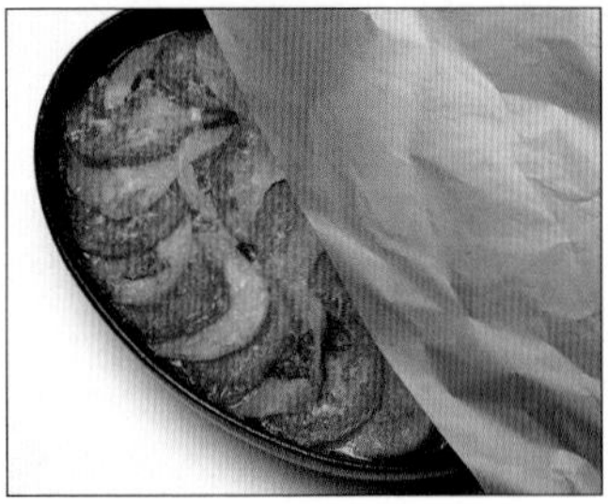

5 ▲ If the top begins to brown too much, place a sheet of foil or a flat baking tray on top of the dish. Serve hot.

Tomatoes with Pasta Stuffing

Pomodori ripieni di pasta

Tomatoes are one of Italy's staple foods, appearing in more than three-quarters of all Italian savoury dishes. They can be baked with various stuffings. This one comes from the south.

Ingredients

8 large tomatoes, firm and ripe
115 g/4 oz/1 1/4 cups small soup pasta
8 black olives, stoned and finely chopped
45 ml/3 tbsp finely chopped mixed fresh herbs, such as chives, parsley, basil and thyme
60 ml/4 tbsp grated Parmesan cheese
60 ml/4 tbsp olive oil
salt and freshly ground black pepper
serves 4

1 ▲ Wash the tomatoes. Slice off the tops, and scoop out the pulp into a strainer with a small spoon. Chop the pulp and turn the tomatoes upside down on a rack to drain.

2 ▲ Leave the pulp in a strainer, and allow the juices to drain off. Meanwhile, boil the pasta in a pan of boiling salted water. Drain it 2 minutes before the recommended cooking time elapses.

3 ▲ Preheat the oven to 190°C/375°F/ gas 5. Combine the pasta with the remaining ingredients in a bowl. Stir in the drained tomato pulp. Season with salt and pepper.

4 ▲ Stuff the tomatoes, and replace the tops. Arrange them in one layer in a well-oiled baking dish. Bake for 15–20 minutes. Peel off the skins, if desired. Serve hot or at room temperature.

Tomato, Pepper and Bread Salad

Panzanella

In this lively classic salad, a tangy blend of tomato juice, olive oil and red wine vinegar is soaked up in a colourful mixture of roasted peppers, anchovies and toasted ciabatta.

Ingredients
225 g/8 oz ciabatta (about ⅔ loaf)
150 ml/¼ pint/⅔ cup olive oil
3 red peppers
3 yellow peppers
50 g/2 oz can anchovy fillets
675 g/1½ lb ripe plum tomatoes
4 garlic cloves, crushed
60 ml/4 tbsp red wine vinegar
50 g/2 oz capers
115 g/4 oz/1 cup pitted black olives
salt and freshly ground black pepper
basil leaves, to garnish
serves 4-6

1 Preheat the oven to 200°C/400°F/Gas 6. Cut the ciabatta into 2 cm/¾ in chunks and drizzle with 50 ml/2 fl oz/¼ cup of the oil. Grill the bread lightly until golden on both sides.

2 Put the peppers on a foil-lined baking sheet and bake for about 45 minutes until the skin begins to char. Remove from the oven, transfer to a large bowl, cover with a plate and leave until the peppers are cool enough to handle.

3 When the peppers are cool, peel off the skins, then cut the peppers into quarters, discarding the stalk ends and seeds. Drain, then roughly chop the anchovies. Set aside.

4 To make the tomato dressing, peel and halve the tomatoes. Scoop the seeds into a sieve set over a bowl.

5 Press the tomato pulp in the sieve to extract the juice. Discard the pulp and add the remaining oil, the garlic, vinegar and seasoning to the juice. Layer the toasted bread, peppers, tomatoes, anchovies, capers and olives in a large bowl. Pour the dressing over and leave to stand for 30 minutes, then serve garnished with plenty of basil leaves.

Radicchio and Artichoke Salad

Insalata di radicchio e topinambur

The distinctive, earthy taste of Jerusalem artichokes makes a lovely contrast to the sharp freshness of radicchio and lemon. Serve warm or cold as an accompaniment to grilled steak or barbecued meats.

Ingredients
1 large radicchio or 150 g/5 oz radicchio leaves
40 g/1½ oz/6 tbsp walnut pieces
45 ml/3 tbsp walnut oil
500 g/1¼ lb Jerusalem artichokes
pared rind and juice of 1 lemon
coarse sea salt and freshly ground black pepper
flat leaf parsley, to garnish (optional)
serves 4

1 ▲ If using a whole radicchio, cut it into 8–10 wedges. Put the wedges or leaves in a shallow flameproof dish. Scatter the walnuts over the top, then pour over the oil and season. Grill for 2–3 minutes.

2 Peel the artichokes and cut up any large ones so the pieces are all roughly the same size. Add the artichokes to a pan of boiling salted water with half the lemon juice and cook for about 5–7 minutes until tender. Drain. Preheat the grill to high.

3 Toss the artichokes into the salad with the remaining lemon juice and the pared rind. Season with coarse sea salt and pepper. Grill until beginning to brown. Serve at once, garnished with flat leaf parsley, if you like.

Roasted Pepper and Tomato Salad *Peperoni arrostiti con pomodori*

This is one of those lovely recipes which brings together perfectly the colours, flavours and textures of southern Italian food. Eat this dish at room temperature with a green salad.

Ingredients
3 red peppers
6 large plum tomatoes
2.5 ml/½ tsp dried red chilli flakes
1 red onion, finely sliced
3 garlic cloves, finely chopped
grated rind and juice of 1 lemon
45 ml/3 tbsp chopped fresh flat leaf parsley
30 ml/2 tbsp extra virgin olive oil
salt and freshly ground black pepper
black and green olives and extra chopped flat leaf parsley, to garnish
serves 4

Cook's Tip
Peppers roasted this way will keep for several weeks. After peeling off the skins, place the pepper pieces in a jar with a tight-fitting lid. Pour enough olive oil over them to cover completely. Store in the fridge.

1 ▲ Preheat the oven to 220°C/425°F/ Gas 7. Place the peppers on a baking sheet and roast, turning occasionally, for 10 minutes or until the skins are almost blackened. Add the tomatoes to the baking sheet and bake for 5 minutes more.

2 Place the peppers in a plastic bag, close the top loosely, trapping in the steam, and then set them aside, with the tomatoes, until they are cool enough to handle.

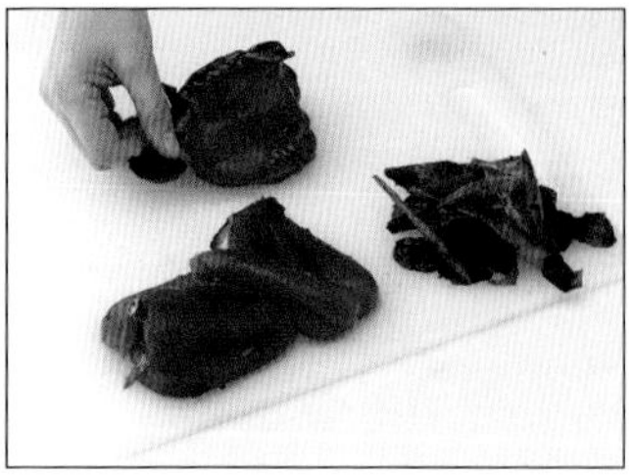

3 ▲ Carefully pull off the skin from the peppers. Remove the seeds, then chop the peppers and tomatoes roughly and place in a mixing bowl.

4 Add the chilli flakes, onion, garlic, lemon rind and juice. Sprinkle over the parsley. Mix well, then transfer to a serving dish. Sprinkle with a little salt, drizzle over the olive oil and scatter olives and extra parsley over the top. Serve at room temperature.

Marinated Courgettes *Zucchini a scapece*

This is a simple vegetable dish which is prepared all over Italy using the best of the season's courgettes. It can be eaten hot or cold.

Ingredients
4 courgettes
60 ml/4 tbsp extra virgin olive oil
30 ml/2 tbsp chopped fresh mint, plus whole leaves, to garnish
30 ml/2 tbsp white wine vinegar
salt and freshly ground black pepper
wholemeal Italian bread and green olives, to serve
serves 4

Cook's Tip
Carrots, French beans, runner beans or onions can also be prepared in this way.

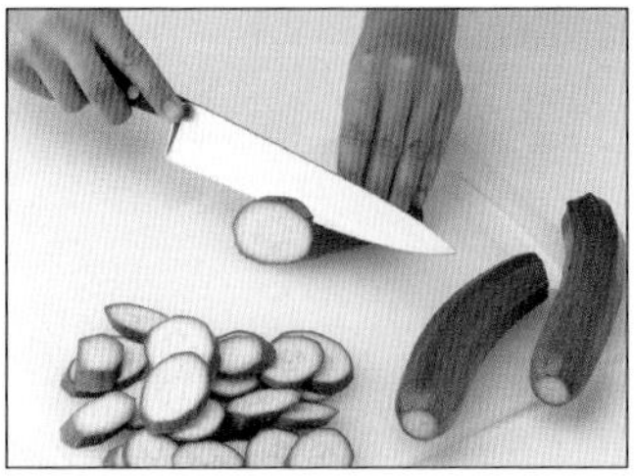

1 ▲ Cut the courgettes into thin slices. Heat 30 ml/2 tbsp of the oil in a wide heavy-based saucepan. Fry the courgettes in batches, for 4–6 minutes, until tender and brown around the edges. Transfer the courgettes to a bowl. Season well.

2 ▲ Heat the remaining oil in the pan, then add the mint and vinegar and let it bubble for a few seconds. Pour over the courgettes. Marinate for 1 hour, then serve garnished with mint and accompanied by bread and olives.

Tomato and Bread Salad

Panzanella

This salad is a traditional peasant dish from Tuscany which was created to use up bread that was several days old. It is best made with sun-ripened tomatoes.

Ingredients
400 g/14 oz/3$^1/_2$ cups stale white or brown bread or rolls
4 large tomatoes
1 large red onion, or 6 spring onions
a few leaves fresh basil, to garnish
For the dressing
60 ml/4 tbsp extra-virgin olive oil
30 ml/2 tbsp white wine vinegar
salt and freshly ground black pepper
serves 4

1 Cut the bread or rolls into thick slices. Place in a shallow bowl, and soak with cold water. Leave for at least 30 minutes.

2 ▲ Cut the tomatoes into chunks. Place in a serving bowl. Finely slice the onion or spring onions, and add them to the tomatoes. Squeeze as much water out of the bread as possible, and add it to the vegetables.

3 ▲ Make a dressing with the oil and vinegar. Season with salt and pepper Pour it over the salad and mix well. Decorate with the basil leaves. Allow to stand in a cool place for at least 2 hours before serving.

Broiled Pepper Salad

Insalata di peperoni

This colourful salad is a southern Italian creation: all the ingredients are sun-lovers which thrive in the hot, dry Mezzogiorno.

Ingredients
4 large peppers, red or yellow or a combination of both
30 ml/2 tbsp capers in salt, vinegar, or brine, rinsed
18–20 black or green olives
For the dressing
90 ml/6 tbsp extra-virgin olive oil
2 cloves garlic, finely chopped
30 ml/2 tbsp balsamic or wine vinegar
salt and freshly ground black pepper
serves 6

1 Place the peppers under a hot grill, and turn occasionally until they are black and blistered on all sides. Remove from the heat and place in a paper bag. Leave for 5 minutes.

2 ▲ Peel the peppers, then cut into quarters. Remove the stems and seeds.

3 Cut the peppers into strips, and arrange them in a serving dish. Distribute the capers and olives evenly over the peppers.

4 ▲ For the dressing, mix the oil and garlic together in a small bowl, crushing the garlic with a spoon to release as much flavor as possible. Mix in the vinegar, and season with salt and pepper. Pour over the dressing, mix well, and allow to stand for at least 30 minutes before serving.

Spinach and Roast Garlic Salad

Insalata di spinaci con aglio arrosto

Don't worry about the amount of garlic in this salad. During roasting, the garlic becomes sweet and subtle and loses its pungent taste.

Ingredients

12 garlic cloves, unpeeled
60 ml/4 tbsp extra virgin olive oil
450 g/1 lb baby spinach leaves
50 g/2 oz/½ cup pine nuts, lightly toasted
juice of ½ lemon
salt and freshly ground black pepper
serves 4

Cook's Tip

If spinach is to be served raw in a salad, the leaves need to be young and tender. Wash them well, drain and pat dry with kitchen paper.

1 ▲ Preheat the oven to 190°C/375°F/ Gas 5. Place the garlic in a small roasting dish, toss in 30 ml/2 tbsp of the olive oil and bake for about 15 minutes until the garlic cloves are slightly charred around the edges.

2 ▲ While still warm, tip the garlic into a salad bowl. Add the spinach, pine nuts, lemon juice, remaining olive oil and a little salt. Toss well and add black pepper to taste. Serve immediately, inviting guests to squeeze the softened garlic purée out of the skin to eat.

Sweet and Sour Artichoke Salad

Carciofi in salsa agrodolce

Agrodolce is a sweet and sour sauce which works perfectly in this salad.

Ingredients

6 small globe artichokes
juice of 1 lemon
30 ml/2 tbsp olive oil
2 medium onions, roughly chopped
175 g/6 oz/1 cup fresh or frozen broad beans (shelled weight)
175 g/6 oz/1½ cups fresh or frozen peas (shelled weight)
salt and freshly ground black pepper
fresh mint leaves, to garnish

For the salsa agrodolce

120 ml/4 fl oz/½ cup white wine vinegar
15 ml/1 tbsp caster sugar
handful fresh mint leaves, roughly torn
serves 4

1 ▲ Peel the outer leaves from the artichokes and cut into quarters. Place the artichokes in a bowl of water with the lemon juice.

2 ▲ Heat the oil in a large saucepan and add the onions. Cook until the onions are golden. Add the beans and stir, then drain the artichokes and add to the pan. Pour in about 300 ml/½ pint/1¼ cups of water and cook, covered, for 10–15 minutes.

3 ▲ Add the peas, season with salt and pepper and cook for a further 5 minutes, stirring from time to time, until the vegetables are tender. Strain through a sieve and place all the vegetables in a bowl, leave to cool, then cover and chill.

4 ▲ To make the salsa agrodolce, mix all the ingredients in a small pan. Heat gently for 2–3 minutes until the sugar has dissolved. Simmer gently for about 5 minutes, stirring occasionally. Leave to cool. To serve, drizzle the salsa over the vegetables and garnish with mint leaves.

Fennel, Orange and Rocket Salad

Insalata di finocchio

This light and refreshing salad is ideal to serve with spicy or rich foods.

Ingredients
2 oranges
1 fennel bulb
115 g/4 oz rocket leaves
50 g/2 oz/⅓ cup black olives

For the dressing
30 ml/2 tbsp extra virgin olive oil
15 ml/1 tbsp balsamic vinegar
1 small garlic clove, crushed
salt and freshly ground black pepper
serves 4

1 With a vegetable peeler, cut strips of rind from the oranges, leaving the pith behind and cut into thin julienne strips. Cook in boiling water for a few minutes. Drain. Peel the oranges, removing all the white pith. Slice them into thin rounds and discard any seeds.

2 Cut the fennel bulb in half lengthways and slice across the bulb as thinly as possible, preferably in a food processor fitted with a slicing disc or using a mandoline.

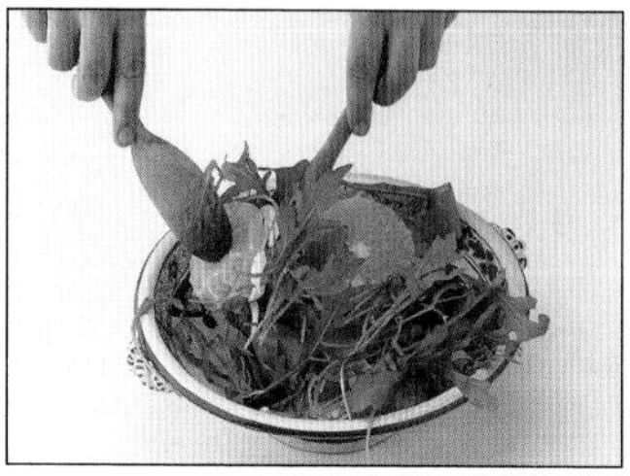

3 ▲ Combine the oranges and fennel in a serving bowl and toss with the rocket leaves.

4 ▲ Mix together the oil, vinegar, garlic and seasoning and pour over the salad, toss together well and leave to stand for a few minutes. Sprinkle with the black olives and julienne strips of orange.

Aubergine, Lemon and Caper Salad

Caponata

This cooked vegetable relish is a classic Sicilian dish, which is delicious served as an accompaniment to cold meats, with pasta or simply on its own with some good crusty bread. Make sure the aubergine is well cooked until it is meltingly soft.

Ingredients
1 large aubergine, about 675 g/1½ lb
60 ml/4 tbsp olive oil
grated rind and juice of 1 lemon
30 ml/2 tbsp capers, rinsed
12 stoned green olives
30 ml/2 tbsp chopped fresh flat leaf parsley
salt and freshly ground black pepper
serves 4

Cook's Tips
This will taste even better when made the day before. Serve at room temperature. It will store, covered in the fridge, for up to 4 days. To enrich this dish to serve it on its own as a main course, add toasted pine nuts and shavings of Parmesan cheese. Serve with crusty bread.

1 ▲ Cut the aubergine into 2.5 cm/1 in cubes. Heat the olive oil in a large frying pan and cook the aubergine cubes over a medium heat for about 10 minutes, tossing regularly, until golden and softened. You may need to do this in two batches. Drain on kitchen paper and sprinkle with a little salt.

2 ▲ Place the aubergine cubes in a large serving bowl, toss with the lemon rind and juice, capers, olives and chopped parsley and season well with salt and pepper. Serve at room temperature.

Artichoke Salad with Eggs

Insalata di carciofi con uova

Artichoke bottoms are best when cut from fresh artichokes, but can also be bought frozen. This salad is easily assembled for a light lunch.

Ingredients
4 large artichokes, or 4 frozen artichoke bottoms, thawed
$\frac{1}{2}$ lemon
4 eggs, hard-boiled and shelled

For the mayonnaise
1 egg yolk
10 ml/2 tsp Dijon mustard
15 ml/1 tbsp white wine vinegar
salt and freshly ground black pepper
250 ml/ 8 fl oz/1 cup olive or vegetable oil
a few sprigs fresh parsley

serves 4

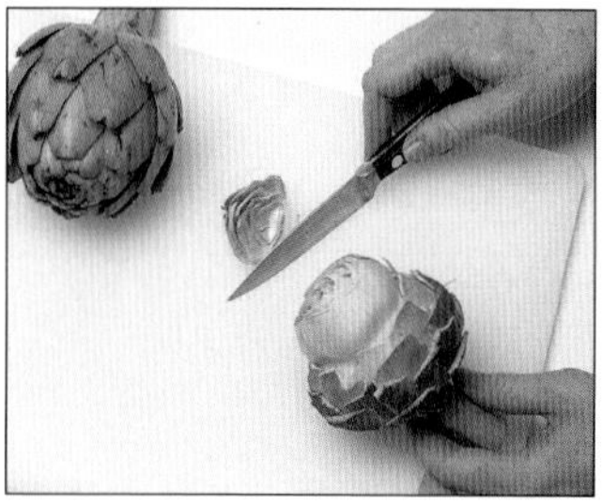

1 ▲ If using fresh artichokes, wash them. Squeeze the lemon, and put the juice and the squeezed half in a bowl of cold water. Prepare the artichokes one at a time. Cut off only the tip from the stem. Peel the stem with a small knife, pulling upwards towards the leaves. Pull off the small leaves around the stem, and continue snapping off the upper part of the dark outer leaves until you reach the taller inner leaves. Cut the tops off the leaves with a sharp knife. Place in the acidulated water. Repeat with the other artichokes.

2 Boil or steam fresh artichokes until just tender (when a leaf comes away quite easily when pulled). Cook frozen artichoke bottoms according to the package instructions. Allow to cool.

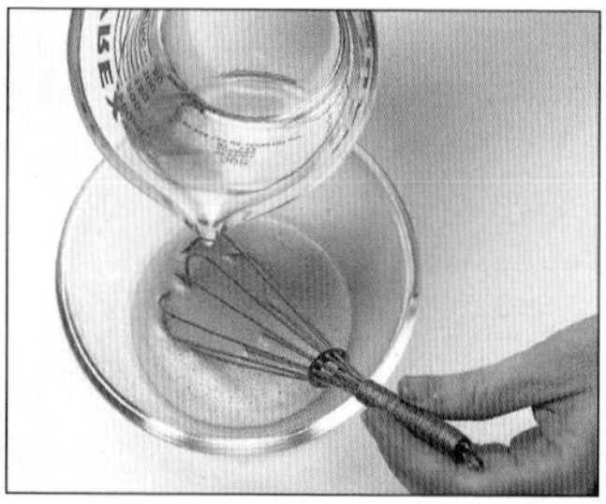

3 ▲ Make the mayonnaise. Combine the egg yolk, mustard and vinegar in a mixing bowl. Add salt and pepper to taste. Add the oil in a thin stream while beating vigorously with a wire whisk. When the mixture is thick and smooth, stir in the parsley. Blend well. Cover and refrigerate until needed.

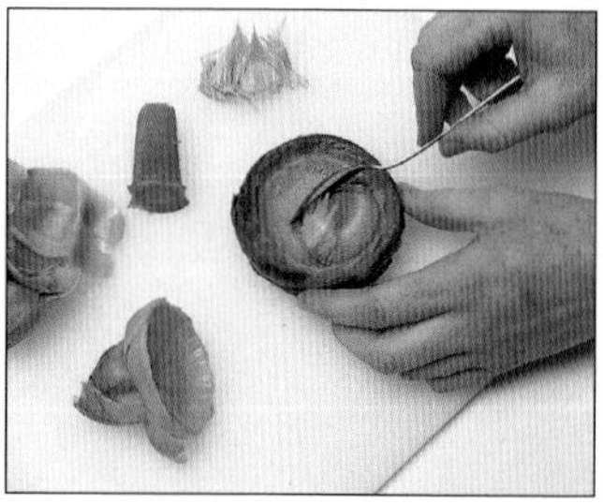

4 ▲ Pull the leaves off the fresh artichokes. Cut the stems off level with the base. Scrape the hairy "choke" off with a knife or spoon.

5 Assemble the salad by cutting the eggs and artichokes into wedges. Arrange on a serving plate, and serve garnished with the mayonnaise.

Fennel and Orange Salad

Insalata di finocchio con arancio

In seventeenth-century Italy fennel was often served at the end of the meal, sprinkled with salt. This refreshing salad originated in Sicily.

Ingredients
2 large fennel bulbs (about 700 g/1$^1/_2$ lb)
2 sweet oranges
2 spring onions, to garnish
For the dressing
60 ml/4 tbsp extra-virgin olive oil
30 ml/2 tbsp fresh lemon juice
salt and freshly ground black pepper
serves 4

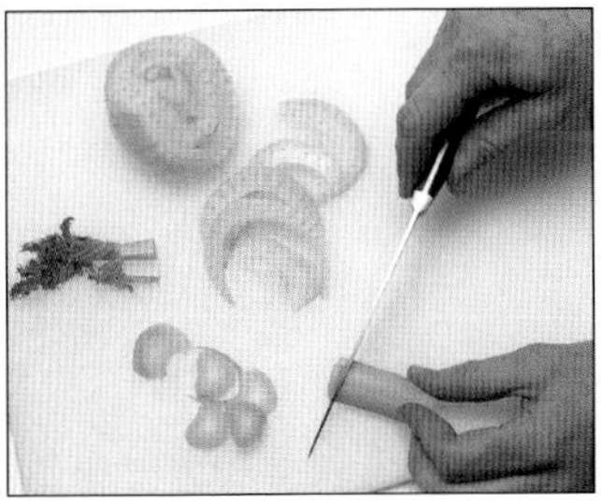

1 ▲ Wash the fennel bulbs and remove any brown or stringy outer leaves. Slice the bulbs and stems into thin pieces. Place in a shallow serving bowl.

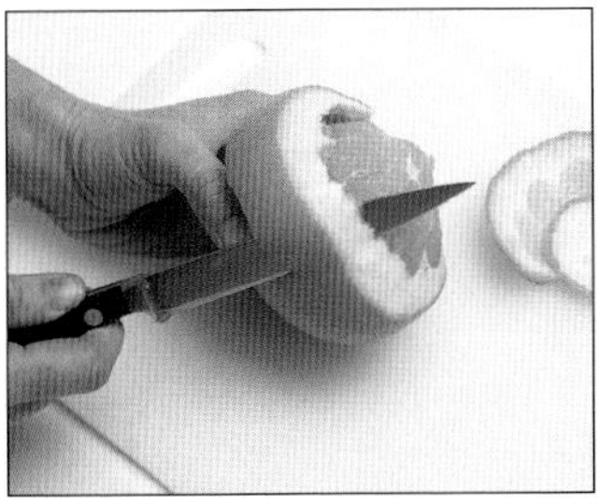

2 ▲ Peel the oranges with a sharp knife, cutting away the white pith. Slice thinly. Cut each slice into thirds. Arrange over the fennel, adding any juice from the oranges.

3 ▲ For the dressing, mix the oil and lemon juice together. Season with salt and pepper. Pour the dressing over the salad. Mix well.

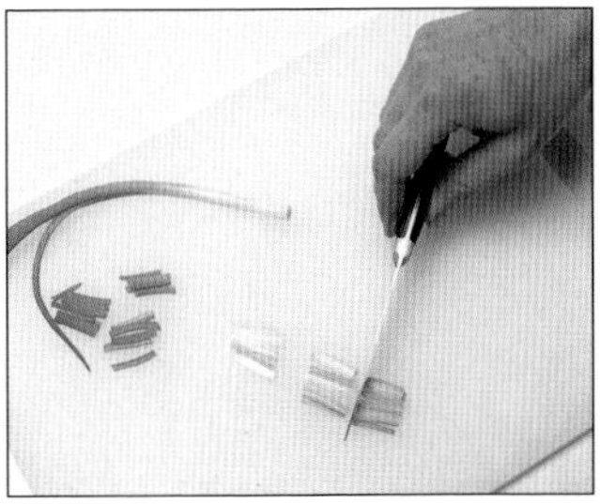

4 ▲ Slice the white and green sections of the spring onions thinly. Sprinkle over the salad.

Potato Salad

Insalata di patate

This salad is dressed while the potatoes are still warm, so the flavours are fully absorbed. Use the best olive oil available.

Ingredients
1 kg/2lb waxy potatoes
For the dressing
90 ml/6 tbsp extra-virgin olive oil
juice of 1 lemon
1 clove garlic, very finely chopped
30 ml/2 tbsp chopped fresh herbs, such as parsley, basil, thyme or oregano
salt and freshly ground black pepper
serves 6

1 Wash the potatoes, but do not peel them. Boil or steam them until tender. When they are cool enough to handle, peel them. Cut the potatoes into dice.

2 ▲ While the potatoes are cooking, mix together all the ingredients for the dressing.

3 ▲ Pour the dressing over the potatoes while they are still warm. Mix well. Serve at room temperature or cold.

Chickpea Salad

Ceci in insalata

This salad makes a good light meal, and is quickly assembled if canned chickpeas are used.

Ingredients
2 × 400 g/14 oz cans chickpeas, or 450 g/1 lb/2 cups cooked chickpeas
6 spring onions, chopped
2 medium tomatoes, cut into cubes
1 small red onion, finely chopped
12 black olives, stoned and cut in half
15 ml/1 tbsp capers, drained
30 g/2 tbsp finely chopped fresh parsley or mint
4 hard-boiled eggs, cut into quarters, to garnish
For the dressing
75 ml/5 tbsp olive oil
45 ml/3 tbsp wine vinegar
salt and freshly ground black pepper
serves 4–6

1 Rinse the chickpeas under cold water. Drain. Place in a serving bowl.

2 ▲ Mix in the other vegetables with the olives and capers.

3 ▲ Mix the dressing ingredients together in a small bowl.

4 ▲ Toss the salad. Pour the dressing over and mix well. Taste for seasoning. Allow to stand for at least 1 hour. Just before serving decorate the salad with the egg wedges.

~ VARIATION ~

Other types of canned cooked beans may be substituted in this salad, such as cannellini or borlotti.

Desserts

An everyday Italian meal usually concludes with fresh fruit. Desserts are reserved for special occasions, and are often bought in from the local pasticceria or gelateria. This is not to say that sweet things are unpopular, but they are usually eaten with a cup of espresso coffee at other times of the day.

Coffee and Chocolate Bombe

Zuccotto

In Italy the commercial ice cream is so good that no one would dream of making their own ice cream for this dessert. Assembling the zuccotto is impressive enough in itself.

Ingredients

15–18 savoiardi (Italian sponge fingers)
about 175 ml/6 fl oz/¾ cup sweet Marsala
75 g/3 oz amaretti biscuits
about 475 ml/16 fl oz/2 cups coffee ice cream, softened
about 475 ml/16 fl oz/2 cups vanilla ice cream, softened
50 g/2 oz bittersweet or plain chocolate, grated
chocolate curls and sifted cocoa powder or icing sugar, to decorate

serves 6–8

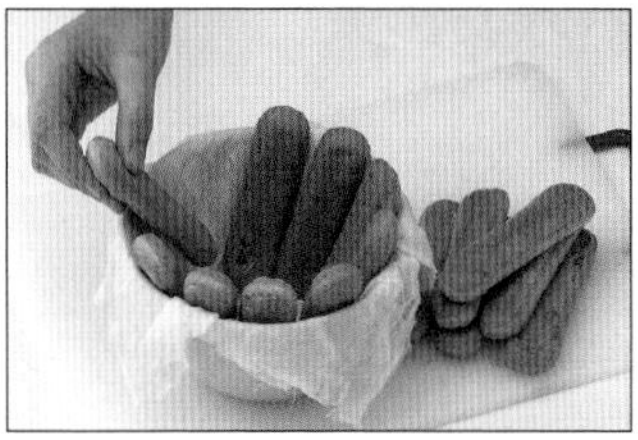

1 ▲ Line a 1 litre/1¾ pint/4 cup pudding basin with a large piece of damp muslin, letting it hang over the top edge. Trim the sponge fingers to fit the basin, if necessary. Pour the Marsala into a shallow dish. Dip a sponge finger in the Marsala, turning it quickly so that it becomes saturated but does not disintegrate. Stand it against the side of the basin, sugared-side out. Repeat with the remaining sponge fingers to line the basin fully.

2 Fill in the base and any gaps around the side with any trimmings and savoiardi cut to fit. Chill for about 30 minutes.

Cook's Tip

In Italy there are special dome-shaped moulds for making this dessert, the name for which comes from the Italian word zucca, meaning pumpkin. The shape will not be quite the same when it is made in a pudding basin.

3 ▲ Put the amaretti biscuits in a large bowl and crush them with a rolling pin. Add the coffee ice cream and any remaining Marsala and beat until mixed. Spoon into the sponge-finger-lined basin.

4 Press the ice cream against the sponge to form an even layer with a hollow. Freeze for 2 hours.

5 Put the vanilla ice cream and grated chocolate in a bowl and beat together until evenly mixed. Spoon into the hollow in the centre of the mould. Smooth the top, then cover with the overhanging muslin. Place in the freezer overnight.

6 To serve, run a palette knife between the muslin and the basin, then unfold the top of the muslin. Invert a chilled serving plate on top of the zuccotto, then invert the two so that the zuccotto is upside down on the plate. Carefully peel off the muslin. Decorate the zuccotto with the chocolate curls, then sift cocoa powder or icing sugar over. Serve at once.

Apple Cake

Torta di mele

This moist cake is best served warm. It comes from Genoa, home of the whisked sponge. When whipping the cream, add grated lemon rind – it tastes delicious.

Ingredients
675 g/1½ lb Golden Delicious apples
finely grated rind and juice of 1 large lemon
4 eggs
150 g/5 oz/¾ cup caster sugar
150 g/5 oz/1¼ cups plain flour
5 ml/1 tsp baking powder
pinch of salt
115 g/4 oz/½ cup butter, melted and cooled, plus extra for greasing
1 sachet of vanilla sugar, for sprinkling
very finely pared strips of citrus rind, to decorate
whipped cream, to serve
serves 6

1 ▲ Preheat the oven to 180°C/350°F/Gas 4. Brush a 23 cm/9 in springform tin with melted butter and line the base with non-stick baking paper. Quarter, core and peel the apples, then slice thinly. Put the slices in a bowl and pour over the lemon juice.

2 ▲ Put the eggs, sugar and lemon rind in a bowl and whisk with a hand-held electric mixture until the mixture is thick and mousse-like. The whisks should leave a trail.

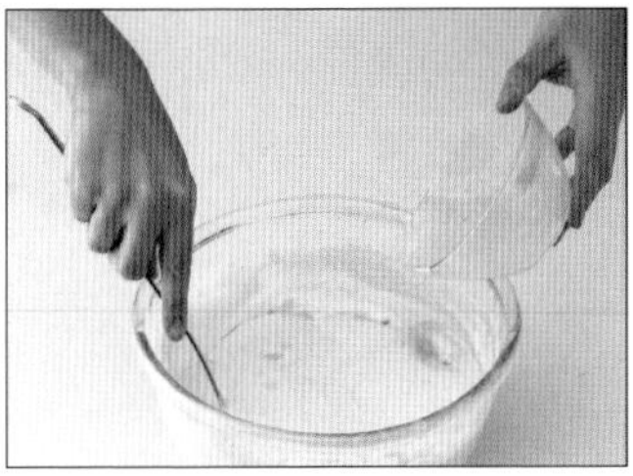

3 ▲ Sift half the flour, all the baking powder and the salt over the egg mousse, then fold in gently with a large metal spoon. Slowly drizzle in the melted butter from the side of the bowl and fold it in gently with the spoon. Sift over the remaining flour, fold it in gently, then add the apples and fold these in equally gently.

4 ▲ Spoon into the prepared tin and level the surface. Bake for 40 minutes or until a skewer comes out clean. Leave to settle in the tin for about 10 minutes, then invert on a wire rack. Turn the cake the right way up and sprinkle the vanilla sugar over the top. Decorate with the citrus rind. Serve warm, with whipped cream.

Lemon Ricotta Cake

Torta di limone e ricotta

This lemony cake from Sardinia is quite different from a traditional cheesecake.

Ingredients

75 g/3 oz/$^1/_3$ tbsp butter
170 g/6 oz/$^3/_4$ cup granulated sugar
75 g/3 oz/generous $^1/_3$ cup ricotta
3 eggs, separated
175 g/6 oz/1$^1/_2$ cups flour
1$^1/_2$ tsp baking powder
grated zest of 1 lemon
45 ml/3 tbsp fresh lemon juice
icing sugar, for dusting
serves 6–8

1 Grease a 22 cm/9in round cake or springform pan. Line the bottom with baking parchment or waxed paper. Grease the paper. Dust with flour. Set aside. Preheat the oven to 180°C/350°F/ gas 4.

2 Cream the butter and sugar together until smooth. Beat in the ricotta.

3 Beat in the egg yolks, one at a time. Add 30 ml/2 tbsp of the flour, and the lemon zest and juice. Sift the baking powder into the remaining flour and beat into the batter until well blended only.

4 ▲ Beat the egg whites until they form stiff peaks. Fold them carefully into the batter.

5 ▲ Turn the mixture into the prepared pan. Bake for 45 minutes, or until a cake tester inserted in the center of the cake comes out clean. Allow the cake to cool for 10 minutes before turning it out onto a rack to cool. Dust the cake generously with icing sugar before serving.

Peaches with Amaretti Stuffing

Pesche alla piemontese

Peaches are plentiful all over Italy. They are sometimes prepared hot, as in this classic dish.

Ingredients

4 ripe fresh peaches
juice of $^1/_2$ lemon
65 g/2$^1/_2$ oz/$^2/_3$ cup crushed amaretti biscuits, or 90 g/31/2 oz/1 cup home-made amaretti (see recipe)
30 ml/2 tbsp Marsala, brandy or peach brandy
25 g/1 oz/2 tbsp butter, at room temperature
$^1/_2$ tsp vanilla extract
30 ml/2 tbsp granulated sugar
1 egg yolk
serves 4

1 Preheat the oven to 180°C/350°F/ gas 4. Wash the peaches. Cut them in half and remove the stones. Enlarge the hollow left by the pits by scooping out some of the peach with a small spoon. Sprinkle the peach halves with the lemon juice.

2 ▲ Soften the amaretti crumbs in the Marsala or brandy for a few minutes. Beat the butter until soft, and then stir in the amaretti mixture and all remaining ingredients.

3 ▲ Arrange the peach halves in a baking dish in one layer, hollow side upwards. Divide the amaretti mixture into 8 parts, and fill the hollows, mounding the stuffing up in the center. Bake for 35–40 minutes, until browned and bubbling. These peaches are delicious served hot or cold.

Chocolate Salami

Salame al cioccolato

This after-dinner sweetmeat resembles a salami in shape, hence its curious name. It is very rich and will serve a lot of people. Slice it very thinly and serve with espresso coffee and amaretto liqueur.

Ingredients

24 Petit Beurre biscuits, broken
350 g/12 oz bittersweet or plain chocolate, broken into squares
225 g/8 oz/1 cup unsalted butter, softened
60 ml/4 tbsp amaretto liqueur
2 egg yolks
50 g/2 oz/½ cup flaked almonds, lightly toasted and thinly shredded lengthways
25 g/1 oz/¼ cup ground almonds

serves 8–12

1 ▲ Place the biscuits in a food processor fitted with a metal blade and process until coarsely crushed.

2 Place the chocolate in a large heatproof bowl. Place the bowl over a saucepan of barely simmering water, add a small chunk of the butter and all the liqueur and heat until the chocolate melts, stirring occasionally.

Cook's Tip

Take care when melting chocolate that it does not overheat or it will form a hard lump. The base of the bowl containing the chocolate must not touch the water, and the chocolate must be melted very slowly and gently. If you think the water is getting too hot, remove the pan from the heat.

3 ▲ Remove the bowl from the heat, allow the chocolate to cool for a minute or two, then stir in the egg yolks followed by the remaining butter, a little at a time. Tip in most of the crushed biscuits, leaving behind a good handful, and stir well to mix. Stir in the shredded almonds. Leave the mixture in a cold place for about 1 hour until it begins to stiffen.

4 ▲ Process the remaining crushed biscuits in the food processor until they are very finely ground. Tip into a bowl and mix with the ground almonds. Cover and set aside until serving time.

5 ▲ Turn the chocolate and biscuit mixture on to a sheet of lightly oiled greaseproof paper, then shape into a 35 cm/14 in sausage with a palette knife, tapering the ends slightly so that the roll looks like a salami. Wrap in the paper and freeze for at least 4 hours until solid.

6 To serve, unwrap the "salami". Spread the ground biscuits and almonds out on a clean sheet of greaseproof paper and roll the salami in them until evenly coated. Transfer to a board and leave to stand for about 1 hour before serving in slices.

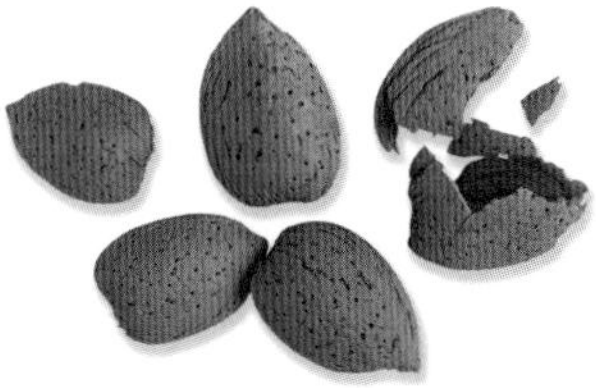

Sicilian Ricotta Cake

Cassata siciliana

The word cassata is often used to describe a layered ice cream cake. In Sicily, however, it is a traditional cake made of layers of sponge, ricotta cheese and candied peel, imbibed with alcohol, and it looks and tastes truly delicious.

Ingredients
675 g/1 1/2 lb/3 cups ricotta cheese
finely grated rind of 1 orange
2 sachets of vanilla sugar
75 ml/5 tbsp orange-flavoured liqueur
115 g/4 oz candied peel
8 trifle sponge cakes
60 ml/4 tbsp freshly squeezed orange juice
extra candied peel, to decorate
serves 8–10

1 ▲ Push the ricotta cheese through a sieve into a bowl, add the orange rind, vanilla sugar and 15 ml/1 tbsp of the liqueur and beat well to mix. Transfer about one-third of the mixture to another bowl, cover and chill until serving time.

2 ▲ Finely chop the candied peel and beat into the remaining ricotta cheese mixture until evenly mixed. Set aside while you prepare the tin.

3 ▲ Line the base of a 1.2 litre/2 pint/5 cup loaf tin with non-stick baking paper. Cut the trifle sponges in half through their thickness. Arrange four pieces of sponge side by side in the bottom of the loaf tin and sprinkle with 15 ml/1 tbsp each of liqueur and orange juice.

4 ▲ Put one-third of the ricotta and fruit mixture in the tin and spread it out evenly. Cover with four more pieces of sponge and sprinkle with another 15 ml/1 tbsp each liqueur and orange juice as before.

5 Repeat the alternate layers of ricotta mixture and sponge until all the ingredients are used, soaking the sponge pieces with liqueur and orange juice each time, and ending with soaked sponge. Cover with a piece of non-stick baking paper.

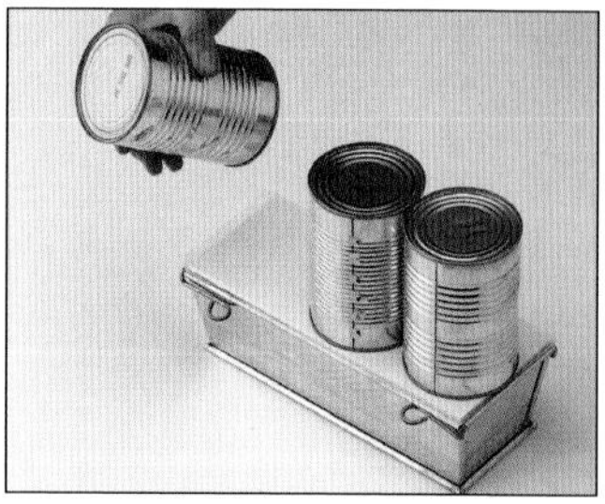

6 ▲ Cut a piece of card to fit inside the tin, place on top of the non-stick baking paper and weight down evenly. Chill for 24 hours.

7 To serve, remove the weights, card and paper and run a palette knife between the sides of the cassata and the tin. Invert a serving plate on top of the cassata, then invert the two so that the cassata is upside down on the plate. Peel off the lining paper.

8 Spread the chilled ricotta mixture over the cassata to cover it completely, then decorate the top with candied peel, cut into fancy shapes. Serve chilled.

Cook's Tip
Don't worry if the cassata has pressed into an uneven shape when turned out. This will be disguised when the cake is covered in the chilled ricotta mixture.

Walnut and Ricotta Cake

Dolce di noci e ricotta

Soft, tangy ricotta cheese is widely used in Italian sweets. Here, it is included along with walnuts and orange to flavour a whisked egg sponge. Don't worry if it sinks slightly after baking – this gives it an authentic appearance.

Ingredients

115 g/4 oz/1 cup walnut pieces
150 g/5 oz/⅔ cup unsalted butter, softened
150 g/5 oz/⅔ cup caster sugar
5 eggs, separated
finely grated rind of 1 orange
150 g/5 oz/⅔ cup ricotta cheese
40 g/1½ oz/6 tbsp plain flour

To finish

60 ml/4 tbsp apricot jam
30 ml/2 tbsp brandy
50 g/2 oz bitter or plain chocolate, coarsely grated

makes 10 slices

1 Preheat the oven to 190°C/375°F/Gas 5. Grease and line the base of a deep 23 cm/9 in round, loose-based cake tin. Roughly chop and lightly toast the walnuts.

2 ▲ Cream together the butter and 115 g/4 oz/½ cup of the sugar until light and fluffy. Add the egg yolks, orange rind, ricotta cheese, flour and walnuts and mix together.

Variation

Use toasted and chopped almonds in place of the walnuts.

3 ▲ Whisk the egg whites in a large bowl until stiff. Gradually whisk in the remaining sugar. Using a large metal spoon, fold a quarter of the whisked whites into the ricotta mixture. Carefully fold in the rest of the whisked whites.

4 Tip the mixture into the prepared tin and carefully level the surface. Bake for about 30 minutes, or until risen and firm. Leave the cake to cool in the tin.

5 ▲ Transfer the cake to a serving plate. Heat the apricot jam in a small saucepan with 15 ml/1 tbsp water. Press through a sieve and stir in the brandy. Use to coat the top and sides of the cake. Scatter the cake generously with grated chocolate.

Chestnut Pudding

Budino di castagne

Sweet chestnuts are found in the mountainous regions of Italy in October and November.

Ingredients
450 g/1lb fresh sweet chestnuts
300 ml/½ pint/1¼ cups milk
115 g/4 oz/½ cup caster sugar
2 eggs, separated, at room temperature
25 g/1 oz/¼ cup unsweetened cocoa powder
½ tsp pure vanilla extract
50 g/2 oz/⅓ cup icing sugar, sifted
butter, for the mould(s)
fresh whipped cream, to garnish
marrons glacés, to garnish
serves 4–5

1 Cut a cross in the side of the chestnuts, and drop them into a pan of boiling water. Cook for 5-6 minutes. Remove with a slotted spoon, and peel while still warm.

2 ▲ Place the peeled chestnuts in a heavy or non-stick saucepan with the milk and half of the caster sugar. Cook over low heat, stirring occasionally, until soft. Remove from the heat and allow to cool. Press the contents of the pan through a strainer.

3 Preheat the oven to 180°C/350°F/gas 4. Beat the egg yolks with the remaining caster sugar until the mixture is pale yellow and fluffy. Beat in the cocoa powder and the vanilla.

4 ▲ In a separate bowl, whisk the egg whites with a wire whisk or electric beater until they form soft peaks. Gradually beat in the sifted icing sugar and continue beating until the mixture forms stiff peaks.

5 ▲ Fold the chestnut and egg yolk mixtures together. Fold in the egg whites. Turn the mixture into one large or several individual buttered pudding moulds. Place on a baking sheet, and bake in the oven until firm, 12-20 minutes depending on the size. Remove from the oven, and allow to cool for 10 minutes before unmolding. Serve garnished with whipped cream and marrons glacés.

Fruit Salad

Macedonia

A really good fruit salad is always refreshing, and in Italy it comes bathed in fresh orange and lemon juices. Use any mixture of fresh seasonal fruits.

Ingredients
juice of 3 large sweet oranges
juice of 1 lemon
1 banana
1–2 apples
1 ripe pear
2 peaches or nectarines
4–5 apricots or plums
115 g/4 oz/$^2/_3$ cup black or green grapes
115 g/4 oz/$^2/_3$ cup berries (strawberries, raspberries etc)
any other fruits in season
sugar, to taste (optional)
30–45 ml/2–3 tbsp Kirsch, maraschino or other liqueur (optional)
serves 4–6

1 Place the fresh orange and lemon juices in a large serving bowl.

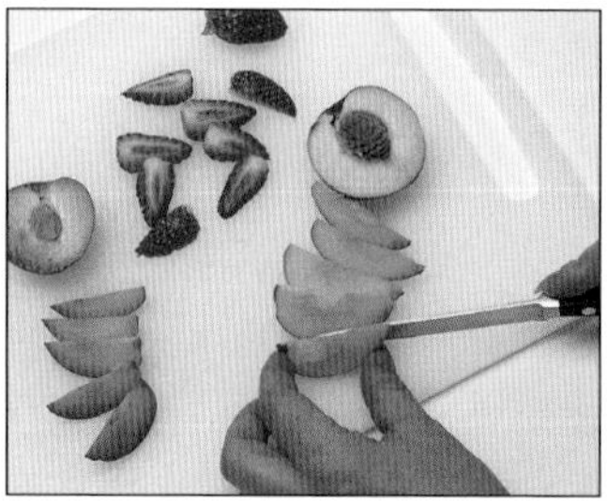

2 ▲ Prepare all the fruits by washing or peeling them as necessary. Cut them into bite-size pieces. Halve the grapes and remove any seeds. Core and slice the apples. Stone and slice soft fruits and leave small berries whole. As soon as each fruit is prepared, put it into the bowl with the juices.

3 ▲ Taste the salad, adding sugar if using. A few tablespoons of liqueur may also be added. Cover the bowl and refrigerate for at least 2 hours. Mix well before serving. In Italy, fruit salad is eaten alone, with vanilla ice cream or with zabaione. It is not usually served with cream.

Baked Apples with Red Wine

Mele al forno

Italian baked apples include a delicious filling of sultanas soaked in spiced red wine.

Ingredients
65 g/ 2$^1/_2$ oz/scant $^1/_2$ cup sultanas
350 ml/12 fl oz/1$^1/_2$ cups red wine
pinch of grated nutmeg
pinch of ground cinnamon
60 g/4 tbsp granulated sugar
pinch of grated lemon zest
6 tart apples of even size
35 g/1$^1/_2$ oz/3 tbsp butter
serves 6

1 In a small bowl, combine the sultanas with the wine. Stir in the spices, sugar and lemon zest. Allow to stand for 1 hour.

2 Preheat the oven to 190°C/375°F/ gas 5. Wash the apples. Use a corer or small, sharp knife to remove the central cores without cutting through to the bottom of the apples.

3 ▲ Divide the filling mixture between the 6 apples, spooning it into the hollow cores. Spoon in a little of the spiced wine.

4 ▲ Arrange the apples in a buttered baking dish. Pour the remaining wine around the apples. Top each core hole with a knob of butter. Bake for 40–50 minutes, or until the apples are soft but not mushy. Serve hot or at room temperature.

Zabaglione

Zabaglione

This sumptuous warm dessert is very quick and easy to make, but it does need to be served straight away. For a dinner party, assemble all the ingredients and equipment ahead of time so that all you have to do is quickly mix everything together once the main course is over.

Ingredients
4 egg yolks
65 g/2 1/2 oz/1/3 cup caster sugar
120 ml/4 fl oz/1/2 cup dry Marsala
savoiardi (Italian sponge fingers), to serve
serves 6

Cook's Tip
When whisking the egg yolks, make sure that the bottom of the bowl does not touch the water or the egg yolks will scramble.

1 ▲ Half fill a pan with water and bring it to simmering point. Put the egg yolks and sugar in a large heatproof bowl and beat with a hand-held electric mixer until pale and creamy.

2 ▲ Put the bowl over the pan and gradually pour in the Marsala, whisking the mixture until it is very thick and has increased in volume.

3 Remove the bowl from the water and pour the zabaglione into six heatproof, long-stemmed glasses. Serve at once, with sponge fingers.

Lovers' Knots

Cenci

The literal translation of cenci is "rags and tatters", but they are often referred to by the more endearing term of lovers' knots. They are eaten at carnival time in February.

Ingredients
150 g/5 oz/1 1/4 cups plain flour
2.5 ml/1/2 tsp baking powder
pinch of salt
30 ml/2 tbsp caster sugar, plus extra for dusting
1 egg, beaten
about 25 ml/1 1/2 tbsp rum
vegetable oil, for deep frying
makes 24

Cook's Tip
If you do not have a deep-fat fryer with a built-in thermostat, or a deep-fat thermometer, test the temperature of the oil before deep frying by dropping in a scrap of the dough trimmings – it should turn crisp and golden in about 30 seconds.

1 ▲ Sift the flour, baking powder and salt into a bowl, then stir in the sugar. Add the egg. Stir with a fork until it is evenly mixed with the flour, then add the rum gradually and continue mixing until the dough draws together. Knead the dough on a lightly floured surface until it is smooth. Divide the dough into quarters.

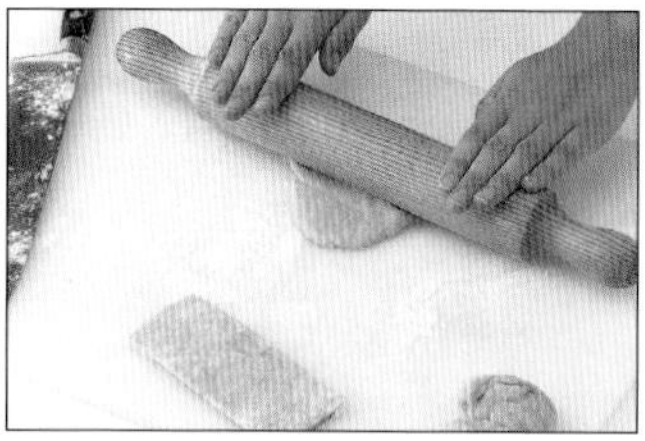

2 ▲ Roll each piece out to a 15 x 7.5 cm/ 6 x 3 in rectangle and trim to make them straight. Cut each rectangle lengthways into six strips, 1 cm/ 1/2 in wide, and tie into a simple knot.

3 Heat the oil in a deep-fat fryer to a temperature of 190°C/375°F. Deep fry the knots in batches for 1–2 minutes until crisp and golden. Transfer to kitchen paper with a slotted spoon. Serve warm, dusted with sugar.

Italian Trifle

Zuppa inglese

Known in Italy as "English Soup", this is a kind of trifle that has little to do with England!

Ingredients
500 ml/16 fl oz/2 cups milk
grated zest of 1/2 lemon
4 egg yolks
75 g/3 oz/1/3 cup superfine sugar
50 g/2 oz/1/2 cup flour, sifted
15 ml/1 tbsp rum or brandy
25 g/1 oz/2 tbsp butter
200 g/7 oz savoyard bicuits or 300 g/11oz sponge cake, sliced into 1 cm/1/2 in slices
75 ml/3 fl oz/1/3 cup Alchermes liqueur or cherry brandy
75 ml/3 fl oz/1/3 cup Strega liqueur
45 ml/3 tbsp apricot jam
fresh whipped cream, to garnish
chopped toasted nuts, to garnish
serves 6–8

1 Heat the milk with the lemon zest in a small saucepan. Remove from the heat as soon as small bubbles form on the surface.

2 ▲ Beat the egg yolks with a wire whisk. Gradually incorporate the sugar, and continue beating until pale yellow. Beat in the flour. Stir in the milk very gradually, pouring it in through a strainer to remove the lemon. When all the milk has been added, pour the mixture into a heavy saucepan. Bring to a boil stirring constantly with a whisk. Simmer for 5–6 minutes, stirring constantly. Remove from the heat and stir in the rum or brandy. Beat in the butter. Allow to cool to room temperature, stirring to prevent a skin from forming.

3 ▲ Brush the biscuits or cake slices with the Alchermes liqueur or cherry brandy on one side, and the Strega liqueur on the other. Spread a thin layer of the custard over the bottom of a serving dish. Line the dish with a layer of biscuits or cake slices. Cover with some of the custard. Add another layer of cookies which have been brushed with liqueur.

4 ▲ Heat the jam in a small saucepan with 30 ml/2 tbsp water. When it is hot, pour or brush it evenly over the biscuits. Continue with layers of custard and liqueur-brushed biscuits until the ingredients have been used up. End with custard. Cover with plastic wrap or foil, and refrigerate for at least 2–3 hours. To serve, decorate the top of the trifle with whipped cream and garnish with chopped nuts.

Stuffed Peaches with Amaretto

Pesche ripiene

Together amaretti biscuits and amaretto liqueur have an intense almond flavour, and they make a natural partner for peaches.

Ingredients
4 ripe but firm peaches
50 g/2 oz amaretti biscuits
25 g/1 oz/2 tbsp butter, softened
25 g/1 oz/2 tbsp caster sugar
1 egg yolk
60 ml/4 tbsp amaretto liqueur
250 ml/8 fl oz/1 cup dry white wine
8 tiny sprigs of basil, to decorate
ice cream or pouring cream, to serve
serves 4

1 ▲ Preheat the oven to 180°C/350°F/Gas 4. Following the natural indentation line on each peach, cut in half down to the central stone, then twist the halves in opposite directions to separate them. Remove the peach stones, then cut away a little of the central flesh to make a larger hole for the stuffing. Chop this flesh finely and set aside.

2 ▲ Put the amaretti biscuits in a bowl and crush them finely with the end of a rolling pin.

3 ▲ Cream the butter and sugar together in a separate bowl until smooth. Stir in the reserved chopped peach flesh, the egg yolk and half the amaretto liqueur with the amaretti crumbs. Lightly butter a baking dish that is just large enough to hold the peach halves in a single layer.

4 ▲ Spoon the stuffing into the peaches, then stand them in the dish. Mix the remaining liqueur with the wine, pour over the peaches and bake for 25 minutes or until the peaches feel tender when tested with a skewer. Decorate with basil and serve at once, with ice cream or cream.

Tiramisu

Tiramisu

The name of this popular dessert translates as "pick me up", which is said to derive from the fact that it is so good that it literally makes you swoon when you eat it. There are many, many versions, and the recipe can be adapted to suit your own taste - you can vary the amount of mascarpone, eggs, sponge fingers, coffee and liqueur.

Ingredients

3 eggs, separated
450 g/1 lb/2 cups mascarpone cheese, at room temperature
1 sachet of vanilla sugar
175 ml/6 fl oz/¾ cup cold, very strong, black coffee
120 ml/4 fl oz/½ cup Kahlúa or other coffee-flavoured liqueur
18 savoiardi (Italian sponge fingers)
sifted cocoa powder and grated bittersweet chocolate, to finish

serves 6–8

1 ▲ Put the egg whites in a grease-free bowl and whisk with an electric mixer until stiff and in peaks.

2 ▲ Mix the mascarpone, vanilla sugar and egg yolks in a separate large bowl and whisk with the electric mixer until evenly combined. Fold in the egg whites, then put a few spoonfuls of the mixture in the bottom of a large serving bowl and spread it out evenly.

3 ▲ Mix the coffee and liqueur together in a shallow dish. Dip a sponge finger in the mixture, turn it quickly so that it becomes saturated but does not disintegrate, and place it on top of the mascarpone in the bowl. Add five more dipped sponge fingers, placing them side by side.

4 ▲ Spoon in about one-third of the remaining mixture and spread it out. Make more layers in the same way, ending with mascarpone. Level the surface, then sift cocoa powder all over. Cover and chill overnight. Before serving, sprinkle with cocoa and grated chocolate.

Ricotta Pudding

Budino di ricotta

This creamy, rich dessert is very easy to make and, as it can be made up to 24 hours ahead, it is ideal for a dinner party. The combination of ricotta cheese and candied fruits is very popular in Sicily, where this recipe originated.

Ingredients
225 g/8 oz/1 cup ricotta cheese
50 g/2 oz/⅓ cup candied fruits
60 ml/4 tbsp sweet Marsala
250 ml/8 fl oz/1 cup double cream
50 g/2 oz/¼ cup caster sugar, plus extra to serve
finely grated rind of 1 orange
350 g/12 oz/2 cups fresh raspberries
strips of thinly pared orange rind, to decorate
serves 4–6

Cook's Tip
Buy candied fruits in large pieces from a good delicatessen - tubs of chopped candied peel are too tough to eat raw, and should only be used in baking.

1 ▲ Press the ricotta through a sieve into a bowl. Finely chop the candied fruits and stir into the sieved ricotta with half of the Marsala. Put the cream, sugar and orange rind in another bowl and whip until the cream is standing in soft peaks.

2 ▲ Fold the whipped cream into the ricotta mixture. Spoon into individual glass serving bowls and top with the raspberries. Chill until serving time. Sprinkle with the remaining Marsala and dust the top of each bowl liberally with caster sugar just before serving. Decorate with the orange rind.

Coffee Granita

Granita di caffè

A granita is a cross between a frozen drink and a flavored ice. The consistency should be slushy, not solid. They can be made at home with the help of a food processor.

Ingredients
500 ml/16 fl oz/2 cups water
115 g/4 oz/$^1/_2$ cup granulated sugar
250 ml/8 fl oz/1 cup very strong espresso coffee, cooled
whipped cream, to garnish (optional)
serves 4–5

1 ▲ Heat the water and sugar together over low heat until the sugar dissolves. Bring to the boil. Remove from the heat and allow to cool.

2 ▲ Combine the coffee with the sugar syrup. Place in a shallow container or freezer tray, and freeze until solid. Plunge the bottom of the frozen container or tray in very hot water for a few seconds. Turn the frozen mixture out, and chop it into large chunks.

3 ▲ Place the mixture in a food processor fitted with metal blades, and process until it forms small crystals. Spoon into serving glasses and top with whipped cream, if desired. If you do not want to serve the granita immediately, pour the processed mixture back into a shallow container or ice tray and freeze until serving time. Allow to thaw for a few minutes before serving, or process again.

Lemon Granita

Granita di limone

Nothing is more refreshing on a hot summer's day than a fresh lemon granita.

Ingredients
500 ml/16 fl oz/2 cups water
115 g/4 oz/$^1/_2$ cup granulated sugar
grated zest of 1 lemon. scrubbed before grating
juice of 2 large lemons
serves 4–5

1 Heat the water and sugar together over low heat until the sugar dissolves. Bring to the boil. Remove from the heat, and allow to cool.

2 Combine the lemon zest and juice with the sugar syrup. Place in a shallow container or freezer tray, and freeze until solid.

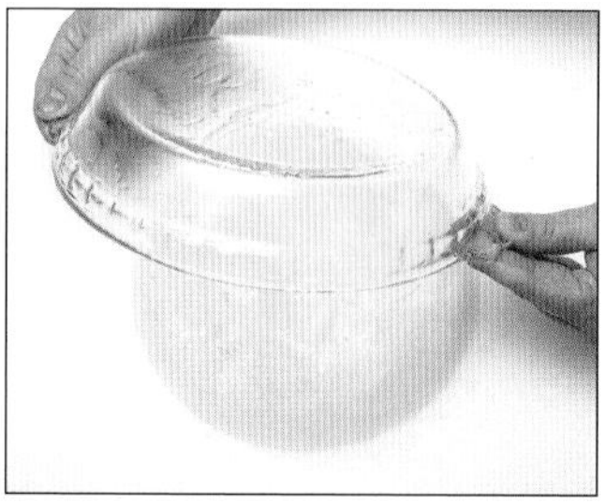

3 ▲ Plunge the bottom of the frozen container or tray in very hot water for a few seconds. Turn the frozen mixture out, and chop it into chunks.

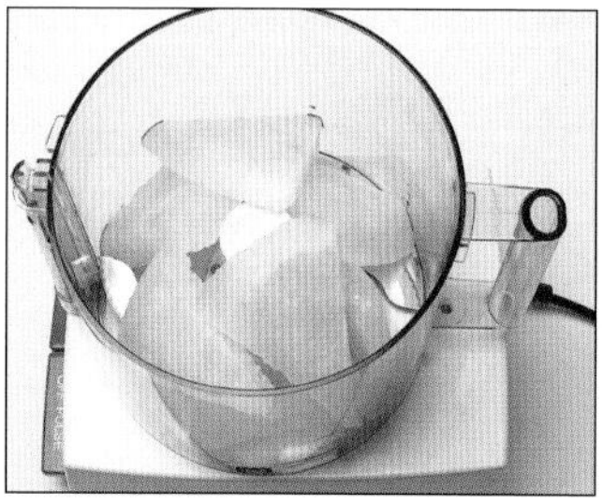

4 ▲ Place the mixture in a food processor fitted with metal blades, and process until it forms small crystals. Spoon into serving glasses.

Custard Ice Cream

Gelato di crema

Italian ice creams are soft in consistency, and should not be over-sweet.

Ingredients
750 ml/24 fl oz/3½ cups milk
½ tsp grated lemon zest
6 egg yolks
150 g/5 oz/½ cup granulated sugar
makes about 850 ml/1½ pints/ 3¾ cups

1 To make the custard, heat the milk with the lemon zest in a small saucepan. Remove from the heat as soon as small bubbles start to form on the surface. Do not let it boil.

2 Beat the egg yolks with a wire whisk or electric beater. Gradually incorporate the sugar, and continue beating for about 5 minutes until the mixture is pale yellow. Strain the milk. Slowly beat it into the egg mixture drop by drop.

3 ▲ When all the milk has been added, pour the mixture into the top of a double boiler, or into a bowl placed over a pan of simmering water. Stir over moderate heat until the water in the pan is boiling, and the custard thickens enough to lightly coat the back of a spoon. Remove from the heat and allow to cool.

4 Freeze in an ice cream maker, following the manufacturer's instructions. The ice cream is ready when it is firm but still soft.

5 ▲ If you do not have an ice cream maker, pour the mixture into a metal or plastic freezer container and freeze until set, about 3 hours. Remove from the container and chop roughly into 7 cm/3in pieces. Place in the bowl of a food processor and process until smooth. Return to the freezer container, and freeze again until firm. Repeat the freezing-chopping process 2 or 3 times, until a smooth consistency is reached.

Chocolate Ice Cream

Gelato al cioccolato

Use good quality plain or cooking chocolate for the best flavour.

Ingredients
750 ml/ 24 fl oz/3½ cups milk
10 cm/4in piece of vanilla pod
225 g/8oz cooking chocolate, melted
4 egg yolks
150 g/5 oz/½ cup granulated sugar
makes about 850 ml/1½ pints/ 3¾ cups

1 Make the custard as for Custard Ice Cream, replacing the lemon with the vanilla.

2 Beat the egg yolks with a wire whisk or electric beater. Gradually incorporate the sugar, and continue beating for about 5 minutes until the mixture is pale yellow. Strain the milk. Slowly add it to the egg mixture drop by drop.

3 ▲ Pour the mixture into a double boiler with the melted chocolate. Stir over moderate heat until the water in the pan is boiling, and the custard thickens enough to lightly coat the back of a spoon. Remove from the heat and allow to cool.

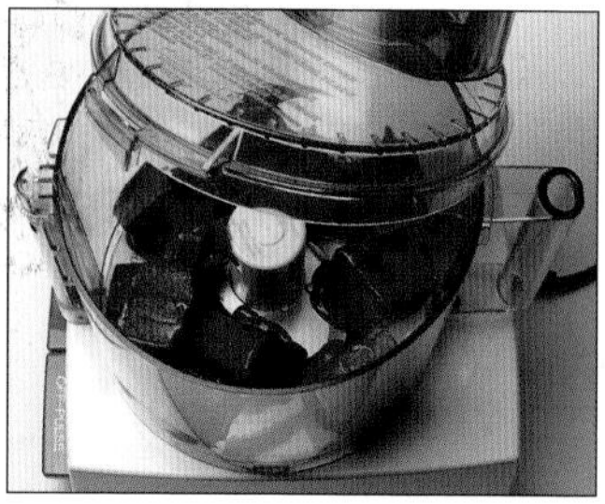

4 ▲ Freeze in an ice cream maker, or follow step 5 of Custard Ice Cream, freezing and processing until a smooth consistency has been reached.

Hazelnut Ice Cream

Gelato di nocciola

This popular flavour goes very well with the chocolate and custard ice creams.

Ingredients
75 g/3 oz/$^1/_2$ cup hazelnuts
500 ml/16 fl oz/2 cups milk
10 cm/4 in piece vanilla bean
4 egg yolks
75 g/3 oz/6 tbsp granulated sugar
serves 4–6

1 Spread the hazelnuts out on a baking tray, and place under a grill for about 5 minutes, shaking the pan frequently to turn the nuts over. Remove from the heat and allow to cool slightly. Place the nuts on a clean dish towel, and rub them with the cloth to remove their dark outer skin. Chop very finely, or grind in a food processor with 30 ml/2 tbsp of the sugar.

2 Make the custard. Heat the milk with the vanilla pod in a small saucepan. Remove from the heat as soon as small bubbles start to form on the surface. Do not let it boil.

3 ▲ Beat the egg yolks with a wire whisk or electric beater. Gradually incorporate the sugar, and continue beating for about 5 minutes until the mixture is pale yellow. Add the milk very gradually, pouring it in through a strainer and discarding the vanilla pod. Stir constantly until all the milk has been added.

4 ▲ Pour the mixture into the top of a double boiler, or into a bowl placed over a pan of simmering water. Add the chopped nuts. Stir over moderate heat until the water in the pan is boiling, and the custard thickens enough to lightly coat the back of a spoon. Remove from the heat and allow to cool.

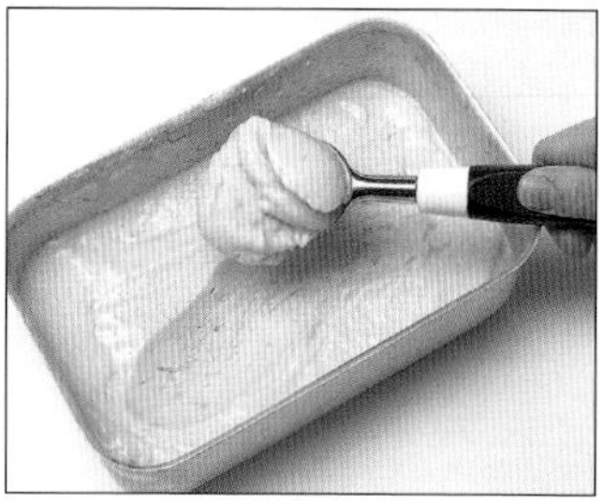

5 ▲ Freeze in an ice cream maker, or follow step 5 of Custard Ice Cream, freezing and processing until a smooth consistency has been reached.

Fresh Orange Granita

Granita all'arancia

A granita is like a water ice, but coarser and quite grainy in texture, hence its name. It makes a refreshing dessert after a rich main course, or a cooling treat on a hot summer's day.

Ingredients
4 large oranges
1 large lemon
150 g/5 oz/ ¾ cup granulated sugar
475 ml/16 fl oz/2 cups water
blanched pared strips of orange and lemon rind, to decorate
dessert biscuits, to serve
serves 6

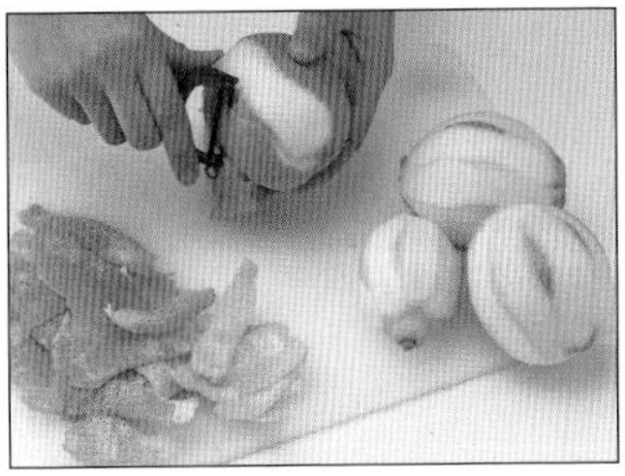

1 ▲ Thinly pare the rind from the oranges and lemon, taking care to avoid the bitter white pith, and set aside for the decoration. Cut the fruit in half and squeeze the juice into a jug. Set aside.

2 Heat the sugar and water in a heavy-based saucepan, stirring over a gentle heat until the sugar dissolves. Bring to the boil, then boil without stirring for about 10 minutes, until a syrup forms.

3 ▲ Remove the syrup from the heat, add the pieces of orange and lemon rind and shake the pan. Cover and allow to cool.

4 ▲ Strain the sugar syrup into a shallow freezer container and add the fruit juice. Stir well to mix, then freeze, uncovered, for about 4 hours until slushy.

Cook's Tip
To make the decoration, slice extra orange and lemon rind into thin strips. Blanch for 2 minutes, refresh under cold water and dry before use.

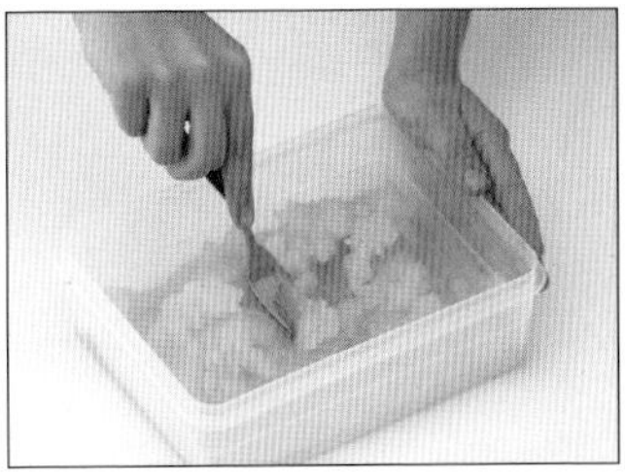

5 ▲ Remove the half-frozen mixture from the freezer and mix with a fork, then return to the freezer and freeze again for 4 hours more or until frozen hard. To serve, turn into a bowl and allow to soften for about 10 minutes, then break up with a fork again and pile into long-stemmed glasses. Decorate with the strips of orange and lemon rind and serve with dessert biscuits.

Baking

The Italian tradition of baking dates back to Roman times, and Italian bakers and pastry chefs today take an enormous pride in their art. Baking at home is generally simple – rustic breads, pies and tarts, the occasional cheesecake or batch of biscuits. Elaborate confections are usually left to the professionals.

Sun-dried Tomato Bread

Pane ai pomodori secchi

In the south of Italy, tomatoes are often dried off in the hot sun. They are then preserved in oil, or hung up in strings in the kitchen, to use in the winter. This recipe uses the former.

Ingredients
675 g/1½ lb/6 cups strong plain flour
10 ml/2 tsp salt
25 g/1 oz/2 tbsp caster sugar
25 g/1 oz fresh yeast
400–475 ml/14–16 fl oz/1⅔–2 cups warm milk
15 ml/1 tbsp tomato purée
75 ml/5 tbsp oil from the jar of sun-dried tomatoes
75 ml/5 tbsp extra virgin olive oil
75 g/3 oz/¾ cup drained sun-dried tomatoes in oil, chopped
1 large onion, chopped
serves 4 small loaves

1 ▲ Sift the flour, salt and sugar into a bowl, and make a well in the centre. Crumble the yeast, mix with ⅔ cup of the warm milk and add to the flour.

2 ▲ Mix the tomato purée into the remaining milk, until evenly blended, then add to the flour with the tomato oil and olive oil.

3 ▲ Gradually mix the flour into the liquid ingredients, until you have a dough. Turn out on to a floured surface, and knead for about 10 minutes, until smooth and elastic. Return to the clean bowl, cover with a cloth, and let rise in a warm place for about 2 hours.

4 ▲ Knock the dough back, and add the tomatoes and onion. Knead until evenly distributed through the dough. Shape into four loaves and place on a greased baking sheet. Cover with a dish towel and allow to rise again for about 45 minutes.

5 Preheat the oven to 190°C/375°F/Gas 5. Bake the bread for 45 minutes, or until the loaves sound hollow when you tap them underneath with your fingers. Allow to cool on a wire rack. Eat warm, or toasted with grated mozzarella cheese sprinkled on top.

Cook's Tip
Use a pair of sharp kitchen scissors to cut up the sun-dried tomatoes.

Olive and Oregano Bread

Pane alle olive ed origano

This makes an excellent accompaniment to salads and soups and is particularly good served warm with a chunk of cheese.

Ingredients

300 ml/10 fl oz/1¼ cups warm water
5 ml/1 tsp dried yeast
pinch of sugar
15 ml/1 tbsp olive oil
1 onion, chopped
450 g/1 lb/4 cups strong white flour
5 ml/1 tsp salt
1.5 ml/¼ tsp freshly ground black pepper
50 g/2 oz/⅓ cup stoned black olives, roughly chopped
15 ml/1 tbsp black olive paste
15 ml/1 tbsp chopped fresh oregano
15 ml/1 tbsp chopped fresh parsley

serves 8–10

1 ▲ Put half of the warm water in a jug. Sprinkle the yeast on top. Add the sugar, mix well and leave to stand for 10 minutes.

2 ▲ Heat the olive oil in a frying pan and fry the onion over a medium heat until golden brown.

3 ▲ Sift the flour into a mixing bowl with the salt and pepper. Make a well in the centre. Add the yeast mixture, the fried onion (with the oil), the olives, olive paste, herbs and remaining water. Gradually incorporate the flour and mix to a soft dough, adding a little extra water if necessary.

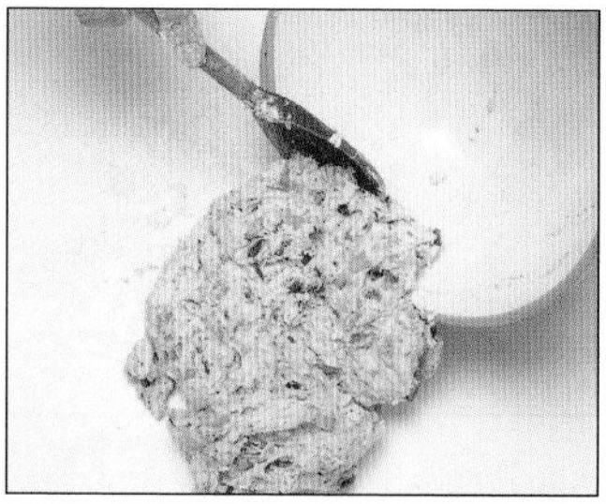

4 ▲ Turn the dough on to a floured work surface and knead for 5 minutes until smooth and elastic. Place in a mixing bowl, cover with a damp dish towel and leave in a warm place to rise for about 2 hours until doubled in bulk. Lightly grease a baking sheet.

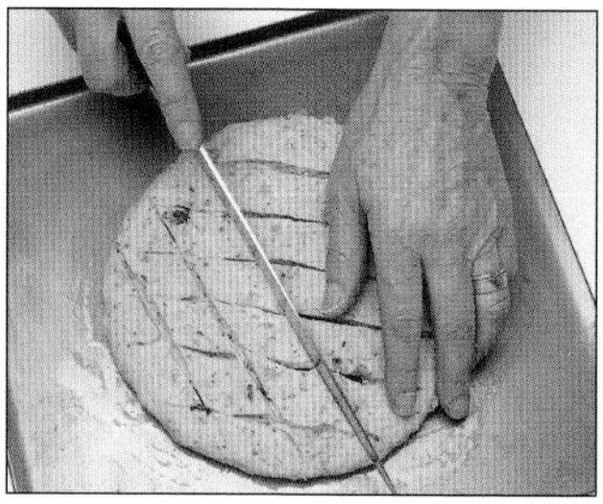

5 ▲ Turn the dough on to a floured surface and knead again for a few minutes. Shape into a 20 cm/8 in round and place on the prepared baking sheet. Using a sharp knife, make criss-cross cuts over the top. Cover and leave in a warm place for 30 minutes until well risen. Preheat the oven to 220°C/425°F/Gas 7.

6 ▲ Dust the loaf with a little flour. Bake for 10 minutes then lower the oven temperature to 200°C/400°F/ Gas 6. Bake for 20 minutes more, or until the loaf sounds hollow when it is tapped underneath. Transfer to a wire rack to cool slightly before serving.

Focaccia

Focaccia

Focaccia is an antique form of flat bread which is oiled before baking. It is traditionally made on a large baking tray, and sold in bakeries cut into squares.

Ingredients
1 recipe Basic Pizza Dough, risen once
45 ml/3 tbsp olive oil
coarse sea salt
serves 6–8 as a side dish

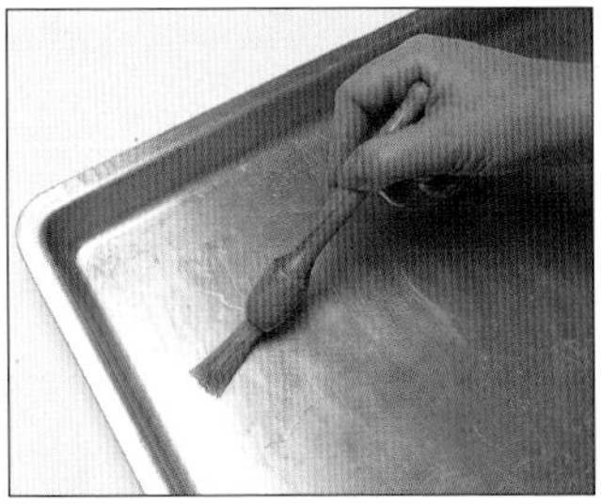

1 ▲ After punching the dough down, knead it for 3–4 minutes. Brush a large shallow baking pan with 15 ml/1 tbsp of oil.

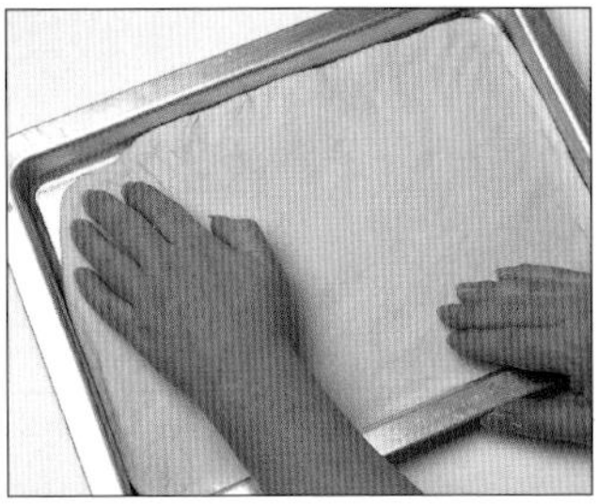

2 ▲ Place the dough in the pan, and use your fingers to press it into an even layer 2 cm/1 in thick. Cover the dough with a cloth, and leave to rise in a warm place for 30 minutes. Preheat the oven to 200°C/400°F/gas 6.

~ COOK'S TIP ~

To freeze, allow to cool to room temperature after baking. Wrap in foil and freeze. Thaw and place in a warm oven before serving.

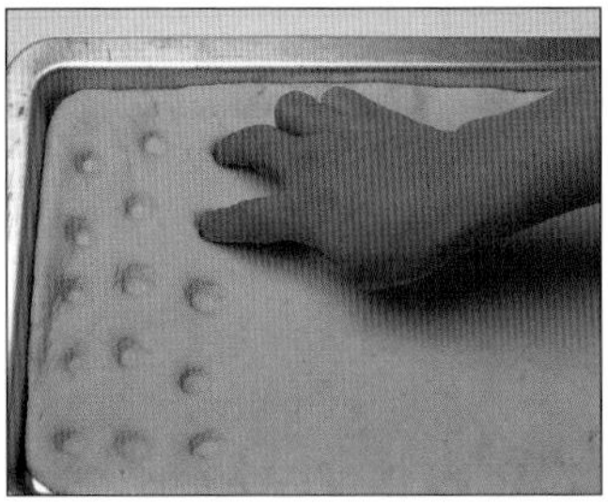

3 ▲ Just before baking, use your fingers to press rows of light indentations into the surface of the focaccia dough.

4 ▲ Brush with the remaining oil, and sprinkle lightly with coarse salt. Bake for about 25 minutes, or until just golden. Cut into squares or wedges and serve as an accompaniment to a meal, or alone, warm or at room temperature.

Focaccia with Onions

Focaccia con cipolle

This appetizing flat bread has a topping of sautéed onions. It can be split and filled with prosciutto or cheese for an unusual sandwich.

Ingredients

1 recipe Basic Pizza Dough, risen once
75 ml/5 tbsp olive oil
1 medium onion, sliced very thinly and cut into short lengths
1/2 tsp fresh thyme leaves
coarse sea salt

serves 6–8 as a side dish

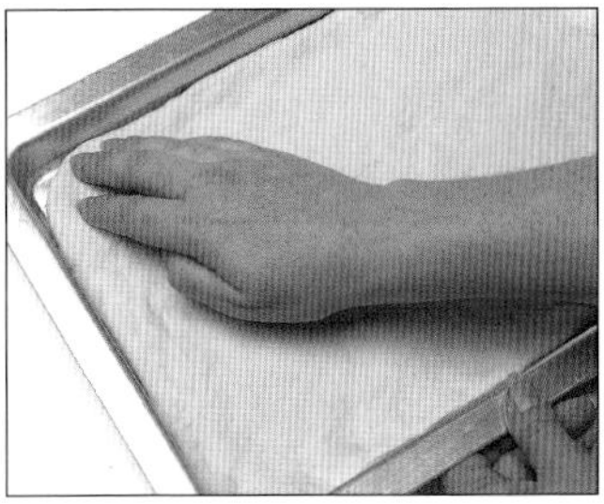

1 ▲ After punching the dough down, knead it for 3–4 minutes. Brush a large shallow baking pan with 15 ml/1 tbsp of the oil. Place the dough in the pan, and use your fingers to press it into an even layer 2 cm/1 inch thick. Cover the dough with a cloth, and leave to rise in a warm place for 30 minutes. Preheat the oven to 200°C/400°F/gas 6 for 30 minutes during this time.

2 ▲ While the focaccia is rising, heat 45 ml/3 tbsp of the oil in a medium frying pan. Add the onion, and cook over low heat until soft. Stir in the thyme.

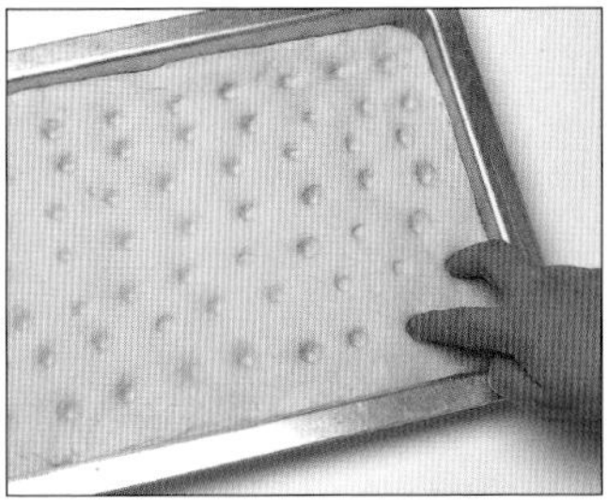

3 ▲ Just before baking, use your fingers to press rows of light indentations into the surface of the focaccia. Brush with the remaining oil.

4 ▲ Spread the onions evenly over the top, and sprinkle lightly with coarse salt. Bake for about 25 minutes, or until just golden. Cut into squares or wedges and serve as an accompaniment to a meal, or alone, either warm or at room temperature.

Focaccia with Olives

Focaccia con olive

For this topping, pieces of pitted green olives are pressed onto the dough before baking.

Ingredients

1 recipe Basic Pizza Dough, risen once
45 ml/3 tbsp olive oil
10–12 large green olives, stoned and cut in half lengthwise
coarse sea salt

serves 6–8 as a side dish

1 After punching the dough down, knead it for 3–4 minutes. Brush a large shallow baking pan with 15 ml/1 tbsp of the oil. Place the dough in the pan, and use your fingers to press it into an even layer 2 cm/1in thick. Cover the dough with a cloth, and leave to rise in a warm place for 30 minutes. Preheat the oven to 200°C/400°F/gas 6 for 30 minutes during this time.

2 ▲ Just before baking, use your fingers to press rows of light indentations into the surface of the focaccia. Brush with the remaining oil.

3 ▲ Dot the bread evenly with the olive pieces, and sprinkle with a little coarse salt. Bake for about 25 minutes, or until just golden. Cut into squares or wedges and serve alone or as an accompaniment to a meal, warm or at room temperature.

Focaccia with Rosemary

Focaccia con rosmarino

One of the most popular breads. If possible, use fresh rosemary for this recipe.

Ingredients

1 recipe Basic Pizza Dough, risen once
45 ml/3 tbsp olive oil
2 medium sprigs fresh rosemary, coarse stalks removed
coarse sea salt

serves 6–8 as a side dish

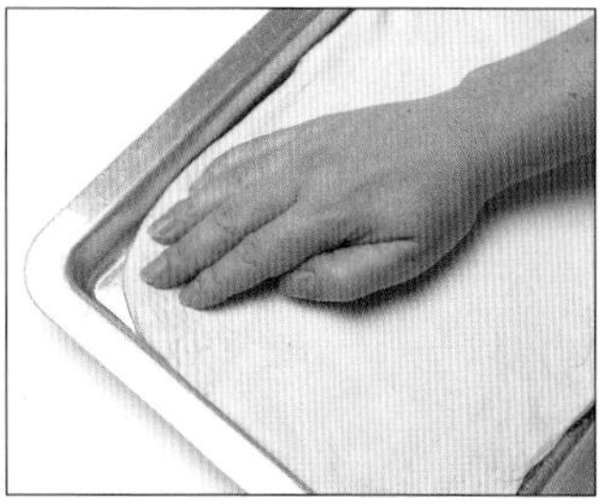

1 ▲ After punching the dough down, knead it for 3–4 minutes. Brush a large shallow baking pan with 15 ml/1 tbsp of the oil. Place the dough in the pan, and use your fingers to press it into an even layer 2 cm/1 inch thick.

2 ▲ Sprinkle with the rosemary leaves. Cover the dough with a cloth, and leave to rise in a warm place for 30 minutes. Preheat the oven to 200°C/400°F/gas 6 for 30 minutes during this time.

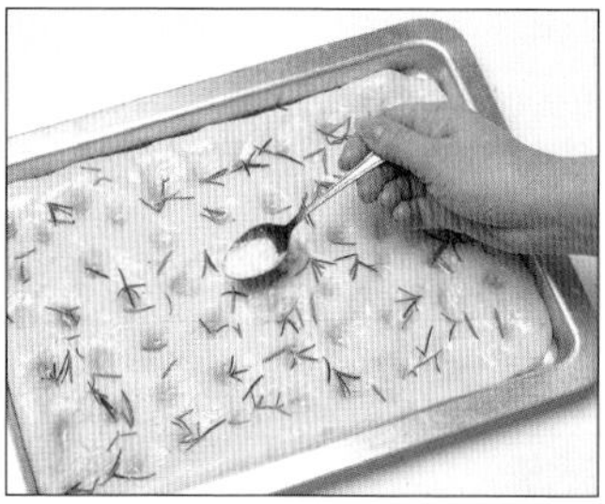

3 ▲ Just before baking, use your fingers to press rows of light indentations into the surface of the focaccia. Brush with the remaining oil, and sprinkle lightly with coarse salt. Bake for about 25 minutes, or until just golden. Cut into squares or wedges and serve as an accompaniment to a meal, or alone, warm or at room temperature.

Italian Bread Sticks

Grissini

These typically Italian bread sticks are especially delicious when hand-made. They are still sold loose in many bakeries in Turin and the north of Italy.

Ingredients
15 g/$^1/_2$ oz/1 tbsp fresh bread yeast or 7 g/$^1/_4$ oz/$^1/_2$ tbsp active dried yeast
100 ml/4 fl oz/$^1/_2$ cup lukewarm water
pinch of sugar
10 ml/2 tsp malt extract (optional)
1 tsp salt
200–225/7–8 oz/1$^3/_4$–2 cups plain flour
makes about 30

1 ▲ Warm a medium mixing bowl by swirling some hot water in it. Drain. Place the yeast in the bowl, and pour on the warm water. Stir in the sugar, mix with a fork, and allow to stand until the yeast has dispersed and starts to foam, 5–10 minutes.

2 ▲ Use a wooden spoon to mix in the malt extract, if using, the salt and about one-third of the flour. Mix in another third of the flour, stirring with the spoon until the dough forms a mass and begins to pull away from the sides of the bowl.

3 ▲ Sprinkle some of the remaining flour onto a smooth work surface. Remove all of the dough from the bowl, and begin to knead it, working in the remaining flour a little at a time. Knead for 8–10 minutes. By the end the dough should be elastic and smooth. Form it into a ball.

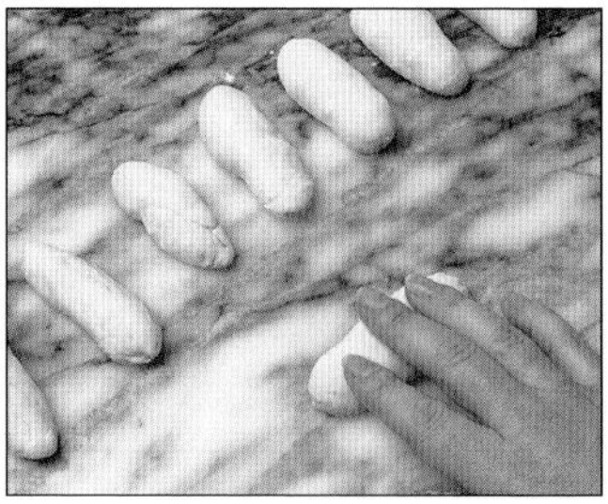

4 ▲ Tear a lump the size of a small walnut from the ball of dough. Roll it lightly between your hands into a small sausage shape. Set it aside on a lightly floured surface. Repeat until all the dough is used up. There should be about 30 pieces.

~ VARIATION ~

Grissini are also good when rolled lightly in poppy or sesame seeds before being baked.

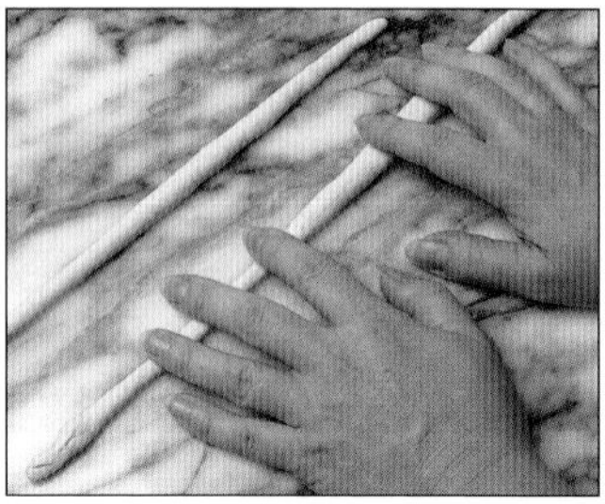

5 ▲ Place one piece of dough on a clean smooth work surface without any flour on it. Roll the dough under the spread-out fingers of both hands, moving your hands backwards and forwards to lengthen and thin the dough into a long strand about 1 cm/$^3/_8$ inch thick. Transfer to a very lightly greased baking tray. Repeat with the remaining dough pieces, taking care to roll all the grissini to about the same thickness.

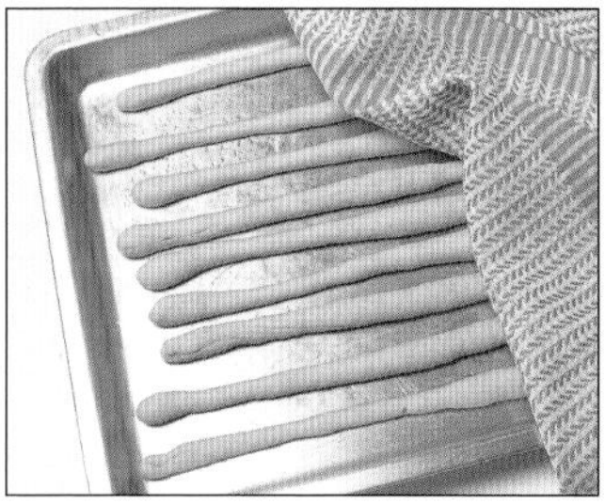

6 ▲ Preheat the oven to 200°C/400°F/gas 6. Cover the tray with a cloth, and place the grissini in a warm place to rise for 10–15 minutes while the oven is heating. Bake for about 8–10 minutes. Remove from the oven. Turn the grissini over, and return them to the oven for 6–7 minutes more. Do not let them brown. Allow to cool. Grissini should be crisp when served. If they lose their crispness on a damp day, warm them in a moderate oven for a few minutes before serving.

Bread with Grapes

Schiacciata con uva

This bread is made to celebrate the grape harvest in central Italy. Use small black grapes with or without seeds; in Italy wine grapes are used.

Ingredients
750 g/1½ lb small black grapes
115 g/4 oz/½ cup sugar
1 recipe Basic Pizza Dough, risen once
30 ml/2 tbsp olive oil
serves 6–8

1 ▲ Remove the grapes from their stems. Wash them well, and pat dry with paper towels. Place in a bowl and sprinkle with the sugar. Set aside until they are needed.

2 ▲ Knead the dough lightly. Divide it into two halves. Roll out or press one half into a circle about 1cm/½ inch thick. Place on a lightly oiled flat baking sheet. Sprinkle with half of the sugared grapes.

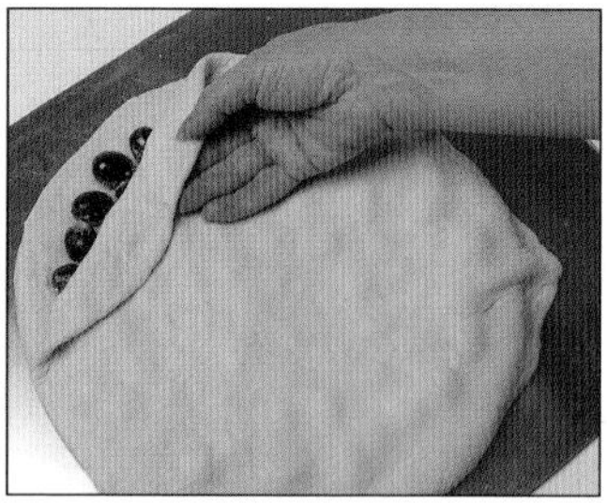

3 ▲ Roll out or press the second half of the dough into a circle the same size as the first. Place it on top of the first.

4 ▲ Crimp the edges together. Sprinkle the top with the remaining grapes. Cover with a dish towel and leave in a warm place to rise for 30 minutes. Preheat the oven to 190°C/375°F/gas 5. Sprinkle the bread with the oil, and bake for 50–60 minutes, until risen and golden. Allow to cool before cutting into wedges.

Spicy Fruit Cake from Siena

Panforte di Siena

This is a delicious flat cake with a wonderful spicy flavour. Panforte is very rich, so should be cut into small wedges - offer a glass of sparkling wine to go with it.

Ingredients
butter for greasing
175 g/6 oz/1 cup hazelnuts, roughly chopped
75 g/3 oz/½ cup whole almonds, roughly chopped
225 g/8 oz/1⅓ cups mixed candied fruits, diced
1.5 ml/¼ tsp ground coriander
4 ml/ ¾ tsp ground cinnamon
1.5 ml/¼ tsp ground cloves
1.5 ml/¼ tsp grated nutmeg
50 g/2 oz/½ cup plain flour
115 g/4 oz/½ cup honey
115 g/4 oz/generous 1 cup granulated sugar
icing sugar, for dusting
serves 12–14

1 Preheat the oven to 180°C/350°F/ Gas 4. Grease a 20 cm/8 in round cake tin with the butter. Line the base of the tin with non-stick baking paper.

2 ▲ Spread the nuts on a baking tray and place in the oven for about 10 minutes until lightly toasted. Remove and set aside. Lower the oven temperature to 150°C/300°F/Gas 2.

3 In a large mixing bowl combine the candied fruits, all the spices and the flour and stir together with a wooden spoon. Add the nuts and stir in thoroughly.

Cook's Tip
This will store in an airtight container for up to 2 weeks.

4 ▲ In a small heavy saucepan, stir together the honey and sugar and bring to the boil. Cook the mixture until it reaches 138°C/280°F on a sugar thermometer or when a small bit forms a hard ball when pressed between fingertips in iced water. Take care when doing this and use a teaspoon to remove a little mixture out of the pan for testing.

5 ▲ At this stage immediately pour the sugar syrup into the dry ingredients and stir in well until evenly coated. Pour into the prepared tin. Dip a spoon into water and use the back of the spoon to press the mixture into the tin. Bake in the preheated oven for 1 hour.

6 When ready, it will still feel quite soft but will harden as it cools. Cool completely in the tin and then turn out on to a serving plate. Dust with icing sugar before serving.

Sultana and Walnut Bread

Pane di uva con noci

This bread is delicious with soup for a first course, or with salami, cheese and salad for lunch. It also tastes good with jam, and toasts extremely well when it is a day or two old.

Ingredients

300 g/11 oz/2¾ cups strong plain flour
2.5 ml/½ tsp salt
15 ml/1 tbsp butter
7.5 ml/1½ tsp easy-blend dried yeast
115 g/4 oz/scant 1 cup sultanas
75 g/3 oz/½ cup walnuts, roughly chopped
melted butter, for brushing
makes 1 loaf

1 ▲ Sift the flour and salt into a bowl, cut in the butter with a knife, then stir in the yeast.

2 ▲ Gradually add 175 ml/6 fl oz/¾ cup tepid water to the flour mixture, stirring with a spoon at first, then gathering the dough together with your hands.

3 Turn the dough out on to a floured surface and knead for about 10 minutes until smooth and elastic.

Cook's Tip

Easy-blend dried yeast is sold in sachets at most supermarkets. It is a real boon for the busy cook because it cuts out the need to let the dough rise before shaping.

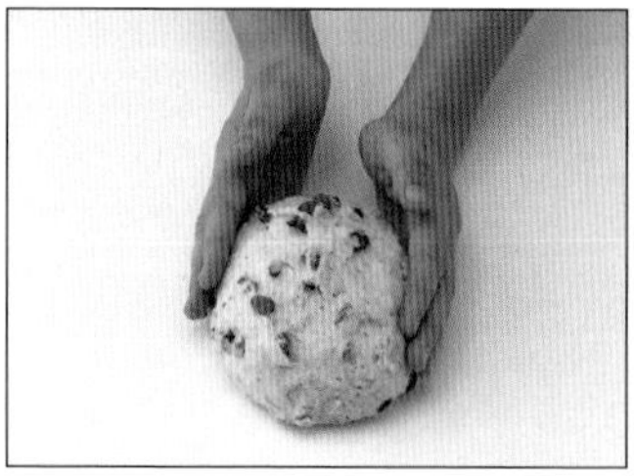

4 ▲ Knead the sultanas and walnuts into the dough until they are evenly distributed. Shape into a rough oval, place on a lightly oiled baking sheet and cover with oiled clear film. Leave to rise in a warm place for 1–2 hours until doubled in bulk. Preheat the oven to 220°C/425°F/Gas 7.

5 Uncover the loaf and bake for 10 minutes, then reduce the oven temperature to 190°C/375°F/Gas 5 and bake for a further 20–25 minutes.

6 ▲ Transfer to a wire rack, brush with melted butter and cover with a tea towel. Cool before slicing.

Chocolate Bread

Pane al cioccolato

In Italy it is the custom to serve this dessert bread as a snack with mascarpone or Gorgonzola cheese and a glass of red wine. Although this combination may sound unusual, it is really delicious. Chocolate bread also tastes good spread with butter at tea time, and is excellent toasted next day for breakfast and served with butter and jam.

Ingredients
450 g/1 lb/4 cups strong plain flour
2.5 ml/½ tsp salt
30 ml/2 tbsp butter
30 ml/2 tbsp caster sugar
10 ml/2 tsp easy-blend dried yeast
30 ml/2 tbsp cocoa powder
75 g/3 oz/½ cup plain chocolate chips
melted butter, for brushing
makes 2 loaves

1 ▲ Sift the flour and salt into a bowl, cut in the butter with a knife, then stir in the sugar, yeast and cocoa powder.

2 Gradually add 300 ml/½ pint/1¼ cups of tepid water to the flour mixture, stirring with a spoon at first, then gathering the dough together with your hands.

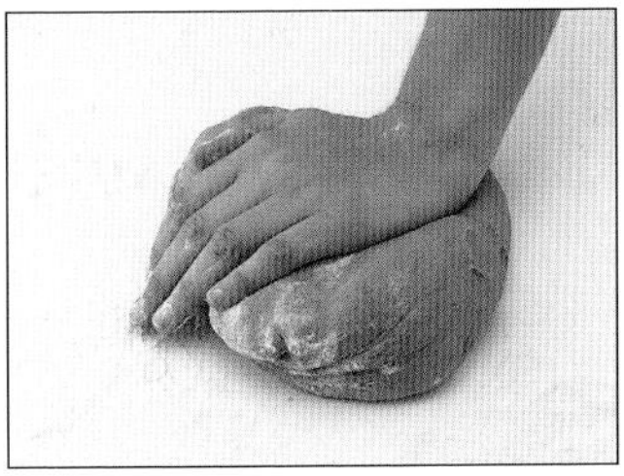

3 ▲ Turn the dough out on to a floured surface and knead for about 10 minutes until smooth and elastic.

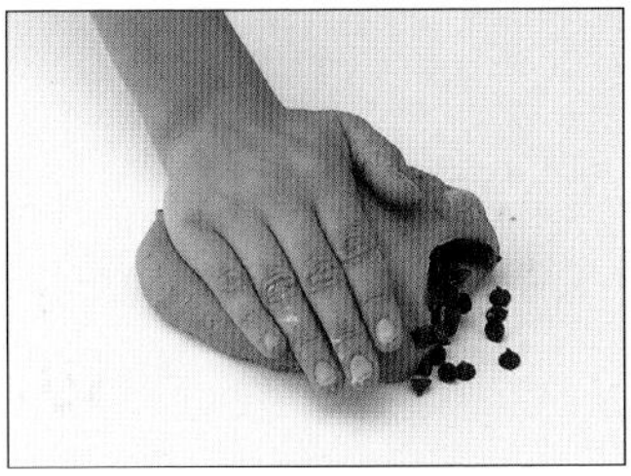

4 ▲ Cut the dough in half and knead half the chocolate chips into each piece of dough until they are evenly distributed. Shape into rounds, place on lightly oiled baking sheets and cover with oiled clear film. Leave to rise in a warm place for 1–2 hours until the dough has doubled in bulk.

5 Preheat the oven to 220°C/425°F/Gas 7. Uncover the loaves and bake for 10 minutes, then reduce the oven temperature to 190°C/375°F/Gas 5 and bake for a further 15–20 minutes.

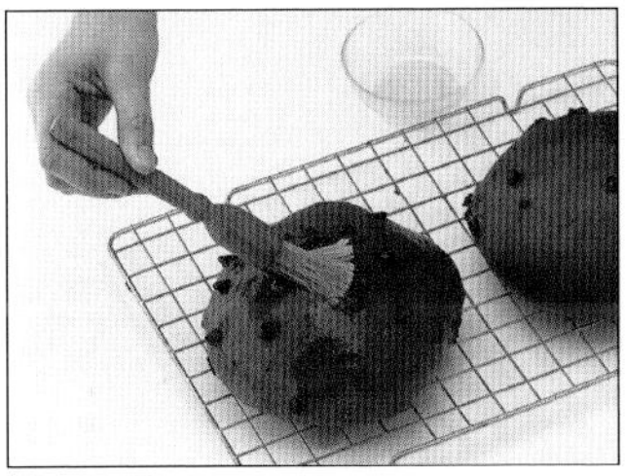

6 ▲ Place the loaves on a wire rack and brush liberally with butter. Cover with a tea towel and leave to cool.

Ricotta Cheesecake

Crostata di ricotta

Low-fat ricotta cheese is excellent for cheesecake fillings because it has a good, firm texture. Here it is enriched with eggs and cream and enlivened with tangy orange and lemon rind to make a Sicilian-style dessert.

Ingredients
450 g/1 lb/2 cups low-fat ricotta cheese
120 ml/4 fl oz/½ cup double cream
2 eggs
1 egg yolk
75 g/3 oz/⅓ cup caster sugar
finely grated rind of 1 orange
finely grated rind of 1 lemon

For the pastry
175 g/6 oz/1½ cups plain flour
45 ml/3 tbsp caster sugar
pinch of salt
115 g/4 oz/8 tbsp chilled butter, diced
1 egg yolk
serves 8

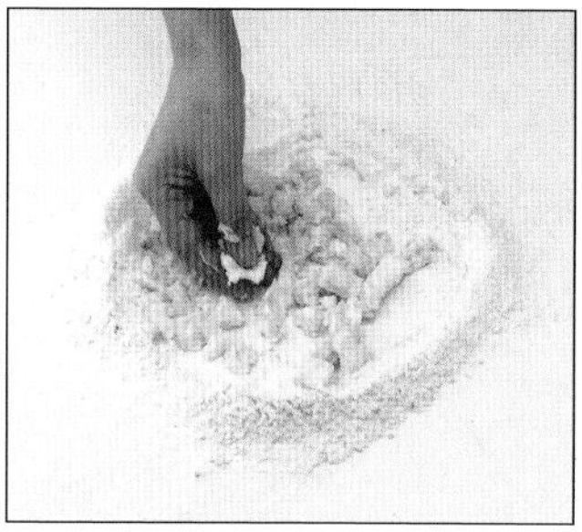

1 ▲ Make the pastry. Sift the flour, sugar and salt on to a cold work surface. Make a well in the centre and put in the diced butter and egg yolk. Gradually work the flour into the diced butter and egg yolk, using your fingertips.

Variations
Add 50–115 g/2–4 oz/⅓–⅔ cup finely chopped candied peel to the filling in step 3, or 50 g/2 oz/⅓ cup plain chocolate chips. For a really rich dessert, you can add both candied peel and some grated plain chocolate.

2 ▲ Gather the dough together, reserve about a quarter for the lattice, then press the rest into a 23 cm/9 in fluted tart tin with a removable base. Chill the pastry case for 30 minutes.

3 ▲ Meanwhile, preheat the oven to 190°C/375°F/Gas 5 and make the filling. Put all the ricotta, cream, eggs, egg yolk, sugar and orange and lemon rinds in a large bowl and beat together until evenly mixed.

4 ▲ Prick the bottom of the pastry case, then line with foil and fill with baking beans. Bake blind for 15 minutes, then transfer to a wire rack, remove the foil and beans and allow the tart shell to cool in the tin.

5 ▲ Spoon the cheese and cream filling into the pastry case and level the surface. Roll out the reserved dough and cut into strips. Arrange the strips on the top of the filling in a lattice pattern, sticking them in place with water.

6 Bake for 30–35 minutes until golden and set. Transfer to a wire rack and leave to cool, then carefully remove the side of the tin, leaving the cheesecake on the tin base.

Jam Tart

Crostata di marmellata di frutta

Jam tarts are popular in northern Italy, traditionally decorated with pastry strips.

Ingredients
200 g/7 oz/1 $^3/_4$ cups flour
pinch of salt
50 g/2 oz/$^1/_4$ cup granulated sugar
115 g/4 oz/$^1/_2$ cup butter or margarine, chilled
1 egg
$^1/_4$ tsp grated lemon zest
350 g/12 oz/1 $^1/_4$ cups fruit jam, such as raspberry, apricot or strawberry
1 egg, lightly beaten with 30 ml/2 tbsp whipping cream, for glazing
serves 6–8

1 ▲ Make the pastry by placing the flour, salt and sugar in a mixing bowl. Using a pastry blender or two knives, cut the butter or margarine into the dry ingredients as quickly as possible until the mixture resembles coarse meal. Beat the egg with the lemon zest in a cup, and pour it over the flour mixture. Combine with a fork until the dough holds together. If it is too crumbly, mix in 15-30 ml/1-2 tbsp of water.

2 Gather the dough into 2 balls, one slightly larger than the other, and flatten into discs. Wrap in greaseproof or waxed paper, and refrigerate for at least 40 minutes.

3 Lightly grease a shallow 23 cm/9 in tart or pie pan, preferably with a removable bottom. Roll out the larger disc of pastry on a lightly floured surface to a thickness of about 3 mm/$^1/_8$ inch.

4 Roll the pastry around the rolling pin and transfer to the prepared pan. Trim the edges evenly with a small knife. Prick the bottom with a fork. Refrigerate for at least 30 minutes.

5 ▲ Preheat the oven to 190°C/375°F/ gas 5. Spread the jam evenly over the base of the pastry. Roll out the remaining pastry.

6 ▲ Cut the pastry into strips about 1 cm/$^1/_2$ inch wide using a ruler as a guide. Arrange them over the jam in a lattice pattern. Trim the edges of the strips even with the edge of the pan, pressing them lightly onto the pastry shell. Brush the pastry with the egg and cream glaze. Bake for about 35 minutes, or until the crust is golden brown. Allow to cool before serving.

Chocolate Nut Tart

Crostata di cioccolata con nocciole

This is a luxurious relative of the simple tart in the previous recipe.

Ingredients
200 g/7 oz/$1^{3}/_{4}$ cups flour
50 g/2 oz/$^{1}/_{4}$ cup granulated sugar
pinch of salt
115 g/4 oz/$^{1}/_{2}$ cup butter or margarine, chilled
1 egg
15 ml/1 tbsp Marsala
$^{1}/_{4}$ tsp grated lemon zest
For the filling
200 g/7 oz/$1^{3}/_{4}$ cups dry amaretti biscuits or 300 g/11 oz/2 cups home-made amaretti (see recipe)
100 g/31/2 oz/$^{3}/_{4}$ cup blanched almonds
50 g/2 oz/$^{1}/_{2}$ cup blanched hazelnuts
45 ml/3 tbsp sugar
200 g/7 oz plain cooking chocolate
45 ml/3 tbsp milk
50 g/2 oz/$^{1}/_{4}$ cup butter
3 tbsp liqueur, such as amaretto, or brandy
30 ml/2 tbsp single cream
serves 6–8

1 ▲ Make the pastry as for the Jam Tart, beating the Marsala with the egg and lemon zest, and mixing into the dry ingredients.

2 Lightly grease a shallow 26 cm/10 inch tart or pie pan, preferably with a removable bottom. Roll out the pastry on a lightly floured surface to a thickness of about 3mm/$^{1}/_{8}$ inch. Roll the pastry around the rolling pin and transfer to the prepared pan. Trim the edges evenly with a small knife. Prick the bottom with a fork. Refrigerate for at least 30 minutes.

3 Grind the amaretti to crumbs in a food processor. Remove to a mixing bowl. Set 8 whole almonds aside, and place the rest in the food processor bowl with the hazelnuts and sugar. Grind to a medium texture. Add the nuts to the amaretti, and mix well.

4 ▲ Preheat the oven to 190°C/375°F/gas 5. In a bowl set over a pan of simmering water, melt the chocolate with the milk and butter. Stir until smooth.

5 Pour the chocolate mixture into the ground amaretti and nuts, and mix well. Add the liqueur and cream.

6 ▲ Spread the chocolate and nut filling evenly in the pastry shell. Bake for about 35 minutes, or until the crust is golden brown and the filling has puffed up and is beginning to darken. Allow to cool to room temperature. Split the remaining almonds in half, and use them to decorate the tart.

Pine Nut Tart

Pinolata

Strange though it may seem, this traditional tart is an Italian version of the homely Bakewell tart from Derbyshire in England.

Ingredients

115 g/4 oz/8 tbsp butter, softened
115 g/4 oz/generous 1/2 cup caster sugar
1 egg
2 egg yolks
150 g/5 oz/1 1/4 cups ground almonds
115 g/4 oz/1 cup pine nuts
60 ml/4 tbsp seedless raspberry jam
icing sugar, for dusting
whipped cream, to serve (optional)

For the pastry

175 g/6 oz/1 1/2 cups plain flour
65 g/2 1/2 oz/1/3 cup caster sugar
1.5 ml/1/4 tsp baking powder
pinch of salt
115 g/4 oz/8 tbsp chilled butter, diced
1 egg yolk
serves 8

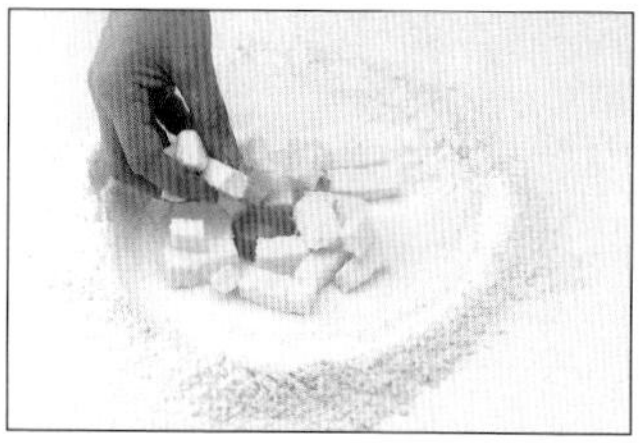

1 ▲ Make the pastry. Sift the flour, sugar, baking powder and salt on to a cold work surface. Make a well in the centre and put in the diced butter and egg yolk. Gradually work the flour into the butter and egg yolk, using your fingertips.

2 ▲ Gather the dough together, then press it into a 23 cm/9 in fluted tart tin with a removable base. Chill for 30 minutes.

3 ▲ Meanwhile, make the filling. Cream the butter and sugar together with an electric mixer until light and fluffy, then beat in the egg and egg yolks a little at a time, alternating them with the ground almonds. Beat in the pine nuts.

Cook's Tip

This pastry is too sticky to roll out, so simply mould it into the bottom and sides of the tin with your fingertips.

4 ▲ Preheat the oven to 160°C/325°F/Gas 3. Spread the jam over the pastry base, then spoon in the filling. Bake for 30–35 minutes or until a skewer inserted in the centre of the tart comes out clean.

5 Transfer to a wire rack and leave to cool, then carefully remove the side of the tin, leaving the tart on the tin base. Dust with icing sugar and serve with whipped cream, if you like.

Baked Sweet Ravioli

Ravioli dolci al forno

These delicious sweet ravioli are made with a rich pastry flavoured with lemon and filled with the traditional ingredients used in Sicilian cassata.

Ingredients
225 g/8 oz/2 cups plain flour
65 g/2½ oz/⅓ cup caster sugar
90 g/3½ oz/½ cup butter
1 egg
5 ml/1 tsp finely grated lemon rind
icing sugar and grated chocolate, for sprinkling

For the filling
175 g/6 oz/¾ cup ricotta cheese
50 g/2 oz/¼ cup caster sugar
4 ml/¾ tsp vanilla essence
1 medium egg yolk
15 ml/1 tbsp mixed candied fruits or mixed peel
25 g/1 oz dark chocolate, finely chopped or grated
1 small egg, beaten
serves 4

1 Put the flour and sugar into a food processor and, working on full speed, add the butter in pieces until fully worked into the mixture. With the food processor still running, add the egg and lemon rind. The mixture should form a dough which just holds together. Scrape the dough on to a sheet of clear film, cover with another sheet, flatten and chill until needed.

2 ▲ To make the filling, push the ricotta through a sieve into a bowl. Stir in the sugar, vanilla essence, egg yolk, peel and chocolate until combined.

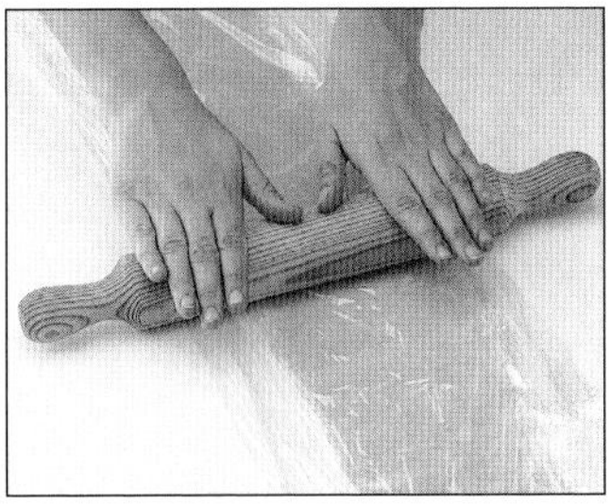

3 ▲ Remove the pastry from the fridge and allow to come to room temperature. Divide the pastry in half and roll each half between sheets of clear film to make strips, measuring 15 x 56 cm/6 x 22 in. Preheat the oven to 180°C/350°F/Gas 4.

4 Arrange heaped tablespoons of the filling in two rows along one of the pastry strips, ensuring there is at least 2.5 cm/1 in clear space around each spoonful. Brush the pastry between the dollops of filling with beaten egg. Place the second strip of pastry on top and press down between each mound of filling to seal.

5 Using a 6 cm/2½ in plain pastry cutter, cut around each mound of filling to make circular ravioli. Lift each one and, with your fingertips, seal the edges. Place the ravioli on a greased baking sheet and bake for 15 minutes until golden brown. Serve warm sprinkled with icing sugar and grated chocolate.

Chocolate Almond Biscuits

Amaretti al cioccolato

Tis delicious variation on the classic Italian biscuits includes cocoa powder, as well as the traditional almond flavouring.

Ingredients
150 g/5 oz/1 cup blanched almonds
100 g/3½ oz/½ cup caster sugar
15 ml/1 tbsp cocoa powder
30 ml/2 tbsp icing sugar
2 egg whites
pinch of cream of tartar
5 ml/1 tsp almond essence
flaked almonds, to decorate
makes about 24

1 Preheat the oven to 180°C/350°F/ Gas 4. Spread out the blanched almonds on a baking sheet and bake for 10–12 minutes, stirring occasionally until the almonds are golden brown. Remove the almonds from the oven and leave to cool.

2 Reduce the oven temperature to 160°C/325°F/Gas 3. Line one large or two small baking sheets with non-stick baking paper.

Cook's Tip
If you prefer, you can toast the blanched almonds under a hot grill. Spread them out in the grill pan and cook for a few minutes, stirring them frequently so that they brown evenly. Make sure that the almonds are completely cold before processing them with the sugar.

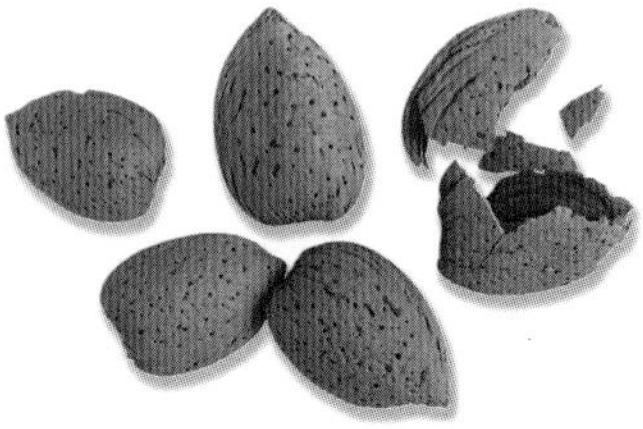

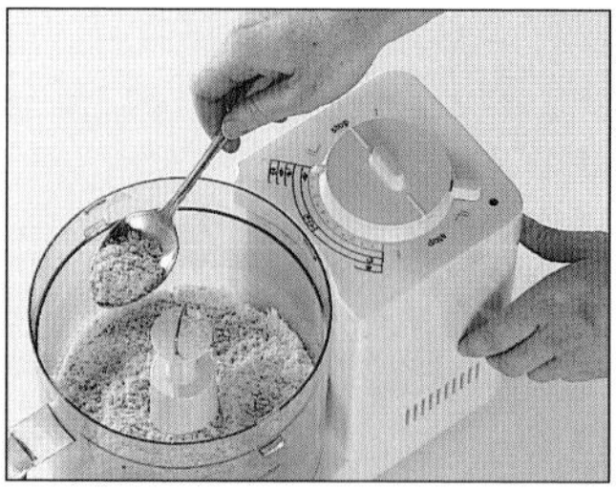

3 ▲ Process the toasted almonds in a food processor with 50 g/2 oz/¼ cup of the sugar until the almonds are finely ground, but not oily. Transfer to a mixing bowl, sift in the cocoa powder and icing sugar, stir to blend and set aside.

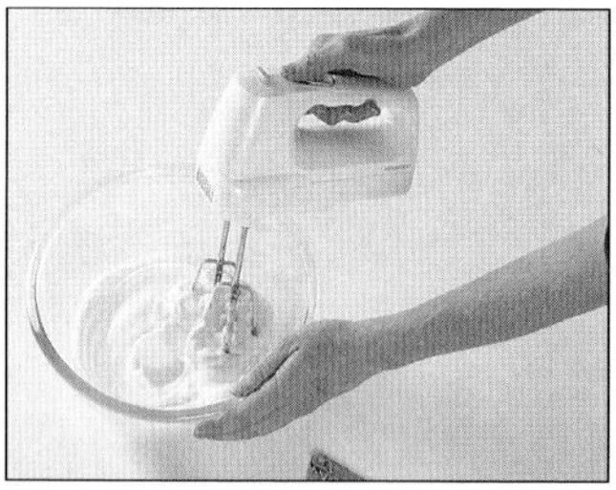

4 ▲ In a large mixing bowl, beat the egg whites and cream of tartar until stiff peaks form. Sprinkle in the remaining sugar, a tablespoon at a time, beating well after each addition. Continue beating until the whites are glossy and stiff. Beat in the almond essence.

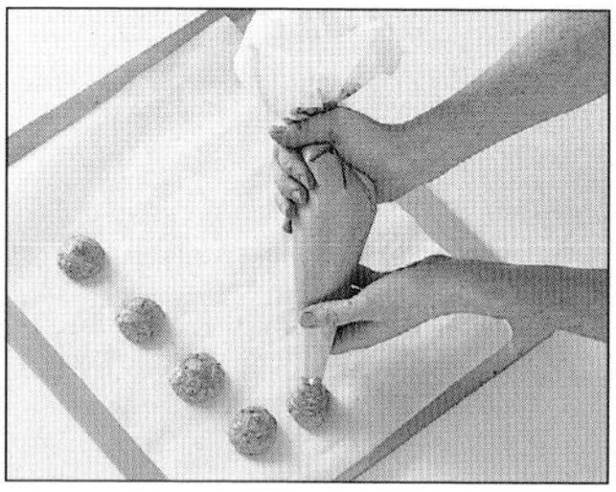

5 ▲ Sprinkle the almond sugar mixture over and gently fold into the beaten egg whites until just blended. Spoon the mixture into a large icing bag fitted with a plain 1 cm/½ in nozzle. Pipe 4 cm/1½ in rounds about 2.5 cm/1 in apart on the prepared baking sheet. Press a flaked almond into the centre of each.

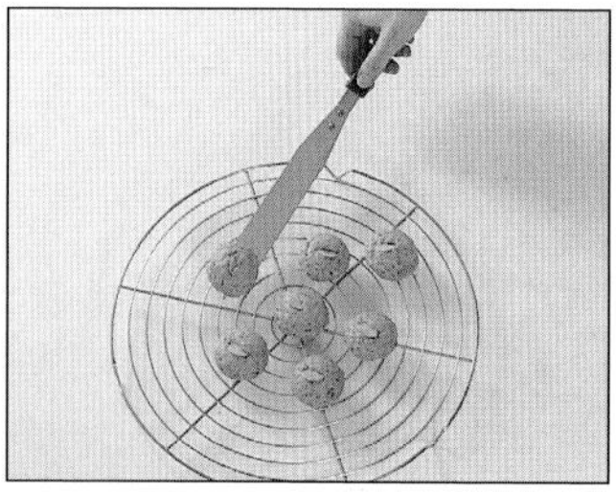

6 ▲ Bake the biscuits for about 12–15 minutes or until they appear crisp. Remove from the baking sheet using a palette knife and transfer to a wire rack to cool completely. When cold, store in an airtight container.

Choux Pastries with Two Custards

Bigné alle due creme

Italian pastry shops are filled with displays of sweetly scented pastries such as these.

Ingredients
200 ml/ 7 fl oz/scant 1 cup water
115 g/4 oz/$^1/_2$ cup butter
2 cm/1 in piece vanilla pod
pinch of salt
150 g/5 oz/1 $^1/_4$ cups flour
5 eggs

For the custard fillings
50 g/2 oz cooking chocolate
300 ml/$^1/_2$ pint/1 $^1/_4$ cups milk
4 egg yolks
65 g/2 $^1/_2$ oz/scant $^1/_3$ cup granulated sugar
40 g/ 1 $^1/_2$ oz/generous $^1/_3$ cup flour
5 ml/1 tsp pure vanilla extract
300 ml/$^1/_2$ pint/1 $^1/_4$ cups whipping cream
unsweetened cocoa powder and icing sugar, to garnish

makes about 48

1 ▲ Preheat the oven to 190°C/375°F/ gas 5. Heat the water with the butter, vanilla and salt. When the butter has melted, beat in the flour. Cook over low heat, stirring constantly, for about 8 minutes. Remove from the heat.

2 ▲ Mix in the eggs one at a time. Remove the vanilla pod.

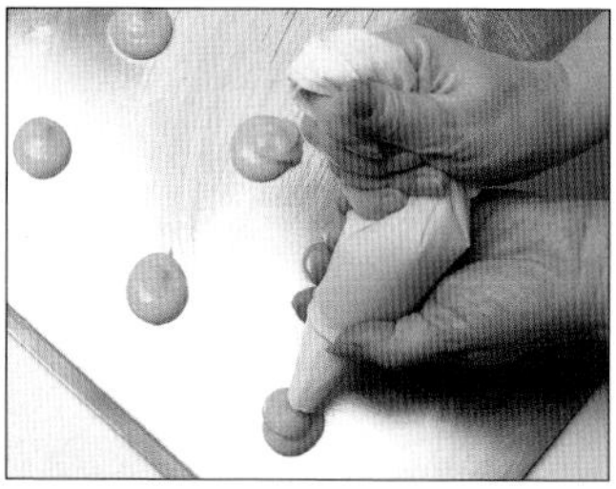

3 ▲ Butter a flat baking tray. Using a pastry bag fitted with a round nozzle, squeeze the mixture out onto the tray in balls the size of small walnuts, leaving space between the rows. Bake for 20–25 minutes, or until the pastries are golden brown. Remove from the oven and allow to cool before filling.

4 ▲ Meanwhile, prepare the custard fillings. Melt the chocolate in the top half of a double boiler, or in a bowl set over a pan of simmering water. Heat the milk in a small saucepan, taking care not to let it boil.

~ VARIATION ~

The choux pastries may be filled with fresh whipped cream flavored with 5 ml/1 tsp vanilla extract or 30–45 ml/2–3 tbsp spirit such as brandy or rum. Mix well, spoon the cream into a piping bag and proceed as in Step 6.

5 ▲ Beat the egg yolks with a wire whisk or electric beater. Gradually incorporate the sugar, and continue beating until the mixture is pale yellow. Beat in the flour. Beat in the hot milk very gradually, pouring it in through a strainer. When all the milk has been added, pour the mixture into a heavy medium pan, and bring to a boil. Simmer for 5–6 minutes, stirring constantly. Remove from the heat and divide the custard between two bowls. Add the melted chocolate to one, and stir the vanilla extract into the other. Allow to cool completely.

6 ▲ Whip the cream. Fold half of it carefully into each of the custards. Fill two pastry bags fitted with round nozzles with the custards. Fill half of the choux pastries with the chocolate custard, and the rest with the vanilla custard, making a little hole and piping the filling in through the side of each pastry. Dust the tops of the chocolate-filled pastries with cocoa powder, and the rest with confectioners' sugar. Serve immediately after filling.

Italian Almond Cookies

Biscotti

These lovely Italian biscuits are part-baked, sliced to reveal a feast of mixted nuts, then baked again until crisp and golden. Traditionally they're served dipped in vin santo, a sweet dessert wine - perfect for rounding off an Italian meal.

Ingredients
50 g/2 oz/¼ cup unsalted butter, softened
115 g/4 oz/½ cup caster sugar
175 g/6 oz/1½ cups self-raising flour
1.5 ml/¼ tsp salt
10 ml/2 tsp baking powder
5 ml/1 tsp ground coriander
finely grated rind of 1 lemon
50 g/2 oz/½ cup polenta
1 egg, lightly beaten
10 ml/2 tsp brandy or orange-flavoured liqueur
50 g/2 oz/½ cup unblanched almonds
50 g/2 oz/½ cup shelled pistachio nuts
makes 24

1 Preheat the oven to 160°C/325°F/Gas 3. Lightly grease a baking sheet. Cream together the butter and sugar using a wooden spoon until smooth.

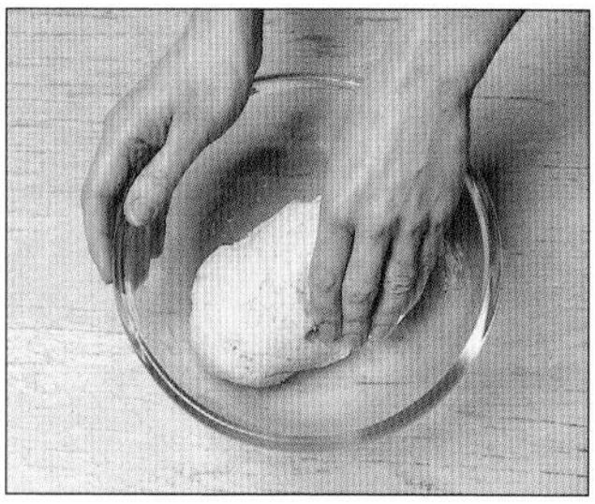

2 ▲ Sift together the flour, salt, baking powder and ground coriander into the bowl. Add the lemon rind, polenta, egg and brandy or liqueur and mix together to make a soft dough.

Cook's Tip
Use a sharp, serrated knife to slice the cooled biscuits, otherwise they will crumble.

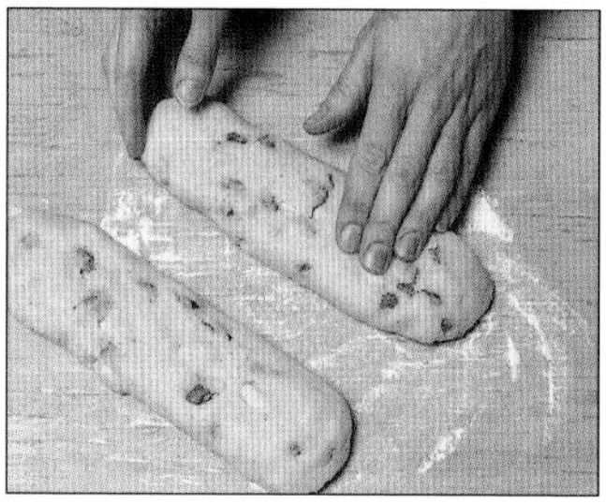

3 ▲ Stir in the nuts until evenly combined. Halve the mixture. Shape each half into a flat sausage about 23 cm/9 in long and 6 cm/2½ in wide. Bake for about 30 minutes until risen and just firm. Remove from the oven.

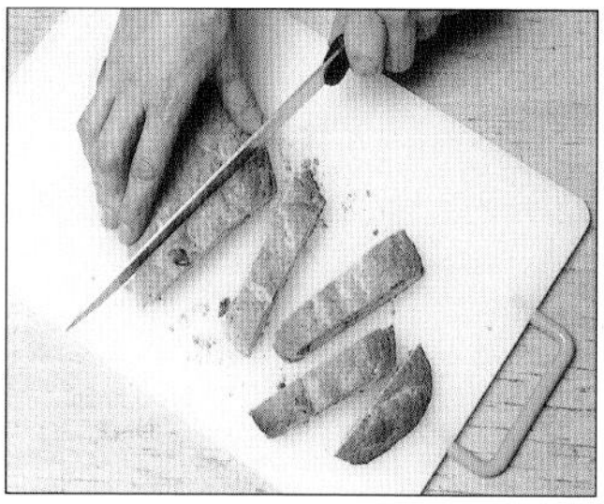

4 ▲ When cool, cut each sausage diagonally into 12 thin slices. Return to the baking sheet and cook for a further 10 minutes until crisp.

5 Transfer to a wire rack to cool completely. Store in an airtight tin for up to 1 week.

Hazelnut Bites

Nocciolini

Serve these sweet little nut cookies as petits fours with after-dinner coffee.

Ingredients
115 g/4 oz/8 tbsp butter, softened
75 g/3 oz/³/₄ cup icing sugar, sifted
115 g/4 oz/1 cup plain flour
75 g/3 oz/³/₄ cup ground hazelnuts
1 egg yolk
blanched whole hazelnuts, to decorate
icing sugar, to finish
makes about 26

1 ▲ Preheat the oven to 180°C/350°F/ Gas 4. Line 3–4 baking sheets with non-stick baking paper. Cream the butter and sugar together with an electric mixer until light and fluffy.

2 ▲ Beat in the flour, ground hazelnuts and egg yolk until they are evenly mixed.

Cook's Tip
Don't worry that the biscuits are still soft at the end of the baking time – they will harden as they cool.

3 ▲ Take a teaspoonful of the mixture at a time and shape it into a round with your fingers. Place the rounds well apart on the baking paper and press a whole hazelnut into the centre of each one.

4 ▲ Bake the biscuits, one tray at a time, for about 10 minutes or until golden brown, then transfer to a wire rack and sift over icing sugar to cover. Leave to cool.

Sultana Cornmeal Biscuits

Gialletti

These little yellow biscuits come from the Veneto region.

Ingredients
75 g/3 oz/$^1/_2$ cup sultanas
115 g/4 oz/$^3/_4$ cup finely ground yellow cornmeal
175 g/6 oz/1$^1/_2$ cups plain flour
7 ml/1$^1/_2$ tsp baking powder
$^1/_2$ tsp of salt
225 g/8 oz/1 cup butter
225 g/8 oz/1 cup granulated sugar
2 eggs
15 ml/1 tbsp marsala or 5 ml/1 tsp vanilla extract
makes about 48

1 Soak the sultanas in a small bowl of warm water for 15 minutes. Drain. Preheat the oven to 180°C/350°F/ gas 4.

2 Sift the cornmeal and flour, the baking powder and the salt together into a bowl.

3 Cream the butter and sugar together until light and fluffy. Beat in the eggs, one at a time. Beat in the marsala or vanilla extract.

4 ▲ Add the dry ingredients to the batter, beating until well blended. Stir in the sultanas.

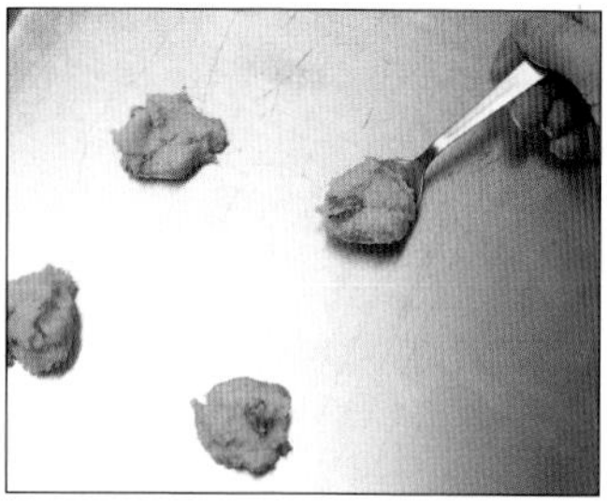

5 ▲ Drop heaped teaspoons of batter onto a greased baking sheet in rows about 5 cm/2 in apart. Bake for 7–8 minutes, or until the cookies are golden brown at the edges. Remove to a rack to cool.

Amaretti

Amaretti

If bitter almonds are not available, make up the weight with sweet almonds.

Ingredients
150 g/5 oz/1$^3/_4$ cups sweet almonds
50 g/2 oz/$^1/_2$ cup bitter almonds
225 g/8 oz/1 cup caster sugar
2 egg whites
2.5 ml/$^1/_2$ tsp almond extract or 5 ml/1 tsp vanilla extract
icing sugar, for dusting
makes about 36

1 Preheat the oven to 160°C/325°F/ gas 3. Peel the almonds by dropping them into a pan of boiling water for 1–2 minutes. Drain. Rub the almonds in a cloth to remove the skins.

2 Place the almonds on a baking tray and let them dry out in the oven for 10–15 minutes without browning. Remove from the oven and allow to cool. Turn the oven off.

3 Finely grind the almonds with half of the sugar in a food processor.

4 ▲ Use an electric beater or wire whisk to beat the egg whites until they form soft peaks. Sprinkle half of the remaining sugar over them and continue beating until stiff peaks are formed. Gently fold in the remaining sugar, the vanilla and the almonds.

5 Spoon the almond mixture into a pastry bag with a smooth nozzle. Line a flat baking sheet with baking parchment. Dust this with flour.

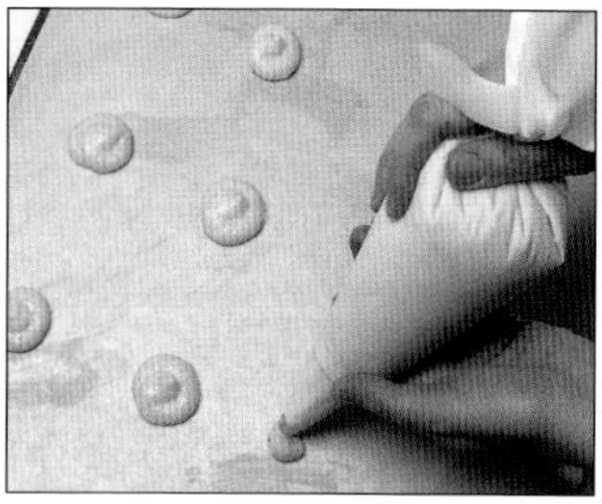

6 ▲ Pipe out the mixture in rounds the size of a walnut. Sprinkle lightly with the confectioners' sugar, and allow to stand for 2 hours. Near the end of this time, turn the oven on again and preheat to 180°C/350°F/ gas 4.

7 Bake the amaretti for 15 minutes, or until pale gold. Remove from the oven and cool on a rack. When completely cool, the biscuits may be stored in an airtight container.

Ladies' Kisses

Baci di dama

These old-fashioned Piedmontese cookies make pretty petits fours.

Ingredients
150 g/5 oz/10 tbsp butter, softened
115 g/4 oz/½ cup caster sugar
1 egg yolk
2.5 ml/½ tsp almond essence
115 g/4 oz/1 cup ground almonds
175 g/6 oz/1½ cups plain flour
50 g/2 oz plain chocolate
makes 20

1 Cream the butter and sugar together with an electric mixer until light and fluffy, then beat in the egg yolk, almond essence, ground almonds and flour until evenly mixed. Chill until firm, for about 2 hours.

2 Preheat the oven to 160°C/325°F/Gas 3. Line 3–4 baking sheets with non-stick baking paper.

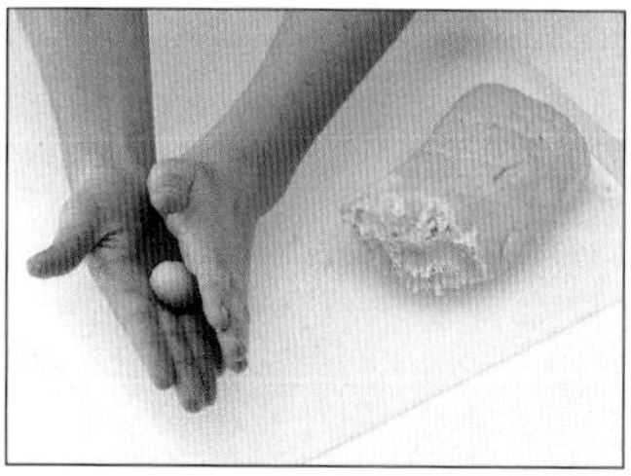

3 ▲ Break off small pieces of dough and roll into balls with your hands, making 40 altogether. Place the balls on the baking sheets, spacing them out as they will spread in the oven.

Cook's Tip
These biscuits look extra dainty served in frilly petit four cases.

4 Bake the biscuits for 20 minutes or until golden. Remove the baking sheets from the oven, lift off the paper with the biscuits on, then place on wire racks. Leave the biscuits to cool on the paper. Repeat with the remaining mixture.

5 ▲ When the biscuits are cold, lift them off the paper. Melt the chocolate in a bowl over a pan of hot water. Sandwich the biscuits in pairs, with the melted chocolate. Leave to cool and set before serving.

Tea Biscuits

Pastine da the

These biscuits are very quick and easy to make. If you don't want to pipe the mixture, simply spoon it on to the baking paper and press it down with a fork.

Ingredients
150 g/5 oz/10 tbsp butter, softened
75 g/3 oz/¾ cup icing sugar, sifted
1 egg, beaten
a few drops of almond essence
225 g/8 oz/2 cups plain flour
2–3 large pieces of candied peel
makes 20

Variation
Use 10 glacé cherries instead of the candied peel. Cut them in half and press one half, cut-side down, into the centre of each biscuit.

1 Preheat the oven to 230°C/450°F/Gas 8. Line two baking sheets with non-stick baking paper.

2 Cream the butter and sugar with an electric mixer until light and fluffy, then beat in the egg, almond essence and flour until evenly mixed.

3 ▲ Spoon the mixture into a piping bag fitted with a star nozzle and pipe 10 rosette shapes on each of the baking sheets.

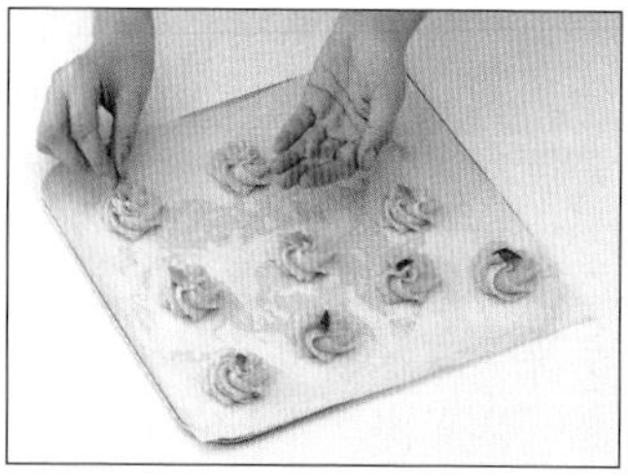

4 ▲ Cut the candied peel into small diamond shapes and press one diamond into the centre of each biscuit, to decorate. Bake for 5 minutes or until golden. Transfer the biscuits on the baking paper to a wire rack and leave to cool. Lift the biscuits off the paper when cool.

Index

Index

Index

Index

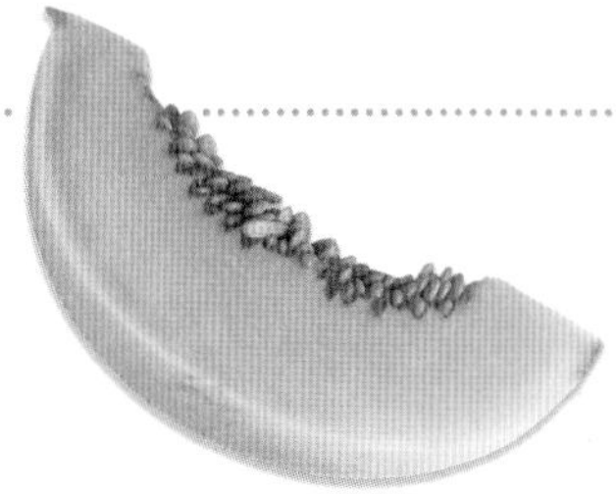

Index

Index

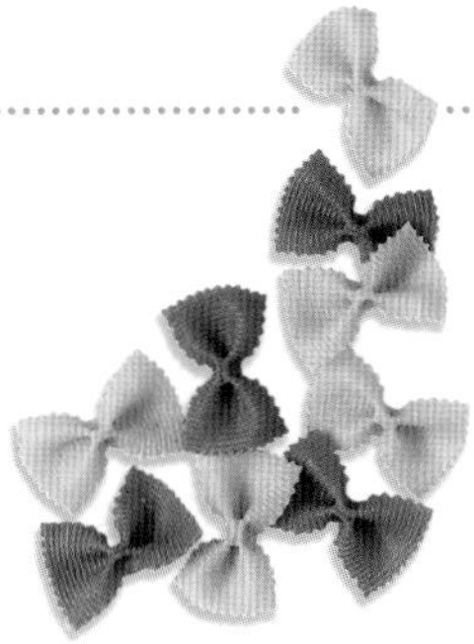

Index

Index

Index

Acknowledgements

All the photographs are by William Adams-Lingwood, Amanda Heywood and Janine Hosegood (cut-outs) except the pictures on pages 6-9, which are by John Heseltine.